A **FALCON** GUIDE®

Rock Climbing
UTAH

Stewart M. Green

FALCON GUIDES ®

GUILFORD, CONNECTICUT
HELENA, MONTANA

AN IMPRINT OF THE GLOBE PEQUOT PRESS

A FALCON GUIDE®

All black-and-white photos by Stewart M. Green unless otherwise noted.
Cover photos by Stewart M. Green.
Front cover: Ian Spencer-Green on *Scarface* in Indian Creek Canyon.
Back cover: Martha Morris liebacks a perfect crack on Blue Gramma Cliff in Indian Creek Canyon.

Library of Congress Cataloging-in-Publication Data is available

ISBN 978-1-56044-594-4

Printed in Canada
First Edition/Fourth Printing

 Text pages printed on recycled paper.

WARNING:
CLIMBING IS A SPORT WHERE YOU MAY BE SERIOUSLY INJURED OR DIE. READ THIS BEFORE YOU USE THIS BOOK.

This guidebook is a compilation of unverified information gathered from many different sources. The author cannot assure the accuracy of any of the information in this book, including the topos and route descriptions, the difficulty ratings, and the protection ratings. These may be incorrect or misleading and it is impossible for any one author to climb all the routes to confirm the information about each route. Also, ratings of climbing difficulty and danger are always subjective and depend on the physical characteristics (for example, height), experience, technical ability, confidence, and physical fitness of the climber who supplied the rating. Additionally, climbers who achieve first ascents sometimes underrate the difficulty or danger of the climbing route out of fear of being ridiculed if a climb is later down-rated by subsequent ascents. Therefore, be warned that you must exercise your own judgment on where a climbing route goes, its difficulty, and your ability to safely protect yourself from the risks of rock climbing. Examples of some of these risks are: falling due to technical difficulty or due to natural hazards such as holds breaking, falling rock, climbing equipment dropped by other climbers, hazards of weather and lightning, your own equipment failure, and failure or absence of fixed protection.

You should not depend on any information gleaned from this book for your personal safety; your safety depends on your own good judgment, based on experience and a realistic assessment of your climbing ability. If you have any doubt as to your ability to safely climb a route described in this book, do not attempt it.

The following are some ways to make your use of this book safer:

1. Consultation: You should consult with other climbers about the difficulty and danger of a particular climb prior to attempting it. Most local climbers are glad to give advice on routes in their area and we suggest that you contact locals to confirm ratings and safety of particular routes and to obtain first-hand information about a route chosen from this book.

2. Instruction: Most climbing areas have local climbing instructors and guides available. We recommend that you engage an instructor or guide to learn safety techniques and to become familiar with the routes and hazards of the areas described in this book. Even after you are proficient in climbing safely, occasional use of a guide is a safe way to raise your climbing standard and learn advanced techniques.

3. Fixed Protection: Because of variances in the manner of placement, and weathering of fixed protection, all fixed protection should be considered suspect and should always be backed up by equipment that you place yourself. Never depend for your safety on a single piece of fixed protection because you never can tell whether it will hold weight, and in some cases, fixed protection may have been removed or is now absent.

Be aware of the following specific potential hazards that could arise in using this book:

1. Misdescriptions of Routes: If you climb a route and you have a doubt as to where the route may go, you should not go on unless you are sure that you can go that way safely. Route descriptions and topos in this book may be inaccurate or misleading.

2. Incorrect Difficulty Rating: A route may, in fact, be more difficult than the rating indicates. Do not be lulled into a false sense of security by the difficulty rating.

THERE ARE NO WARRANTIES, WHETHER EXPRESS OR IMPLIED, THAT THIS GUIDEBOOK IS ACCURATE OR THAT THE INFORMATION CONTAINED IN IT IS RELIABLE. THERE ARE NO WARRANTIES OF FITNESS FOR A PARTICULAR PURPOSE OR THAT THIS GUIDE IS MERCHANTABLE. YOUR USE OF THIS BOOK INDICATES YOUR ASSUMPTION OF THE RISK THAT IT MAY CONTAIN ERRORS AND IS AN ACKNOWLEDGMENT OF YOUR OWN SOLE RESPONSIBILITY FOR YOUR CLIMBING SAFETY.

CONTENTS

Westbay, Ed Webster, Bryan Becker, Leonard Coyne, Dennis Jackson, and the rest. It was climbing with those guys and photographing them that ultimately led to this book.

Thanks goes to all those Utah and Colorado climbers who happily divulged area information and beta, proofed manuscripts, and checked topos. Special thanks and handshakes go to Ken Sims (Doctor of Geology and climber of towers); Boone Speed (freelance gear designer and hardman); John Barstow (High Exposure Calendar photog and long-time SLC climber); Bret Ruckman (desert crackmaster); Jason Stevens (Maple Canyon pioneer and guidebook author); Todd Goss (St. George guidebook author and prolific first ascensionist); John Middendorf (the Man, the Myth, the Legend of Zion climbing); Fred Knapp (fellow author and adventurer); Jim Dunn (friend and desert rock rat); Kevin Chase (Moab guide and shop owner); Lisa Hathaway (tall blonde crackmistress and Eddie McStiff's bartender); Steve "Crusher" Bartlett (Monument Basin's English connection); Ed Webster (old friend, mountaineer, and desert pioneer); Ben Folsom (SLC climber and guide); Earl Wiggins (friend, author, and the original Indian Creek crackmaster); Jeff Achey (*Climbing* magazine editor and desert pioneer); Dougald MacDonald (*Rock & Ice* editor and soft rock connoisseur); Bob Van Belle (ranger and boulderer at Capitol Reef); Dennis Jackson (climbing partner and guidebook author); Steve Petro (DMM distributor and Indian Creek crackman) and, of course, Eric Bjørnstad (friend, Moab local, guide, and old-time rock jock) who freely gave information from his reservoir of climbing lore and stacks of topos and maps.

Thanks to Falcon Publishing and its able staff who created this stunning guidebook. Thanks to publisher Bill Schneider, guidebook editor Randall Green, and the book's designers and copy editors. Special thanks goes to Martha Morris, a great climbing partner and old friend, who used her artistic sense and ability to create gorgeous topos, maps, and photo-overlays as well as proofreading the manuscript and handling other sordid details. Thanks also to those who shared my Utah trips—Ian Spencer-Green, Brett Spencer-Green, Martha Morris, Rane Morris-Dunn, Dennis Jump, Yvonne Bolton, Joel Ballasy, Fred Knapp, Heidi Benton, the Dangerous Brothers (John and Dave), Nancy Spencer-Green, and Bob D'Antonio. Also a special thanks to Nancy Spencer-Green for maintaining the homefront with good-humored aplomb, proofreading manuscripts from a lay viewpoint, and supporting these long projects.

UTAH CLIMBING AREAS

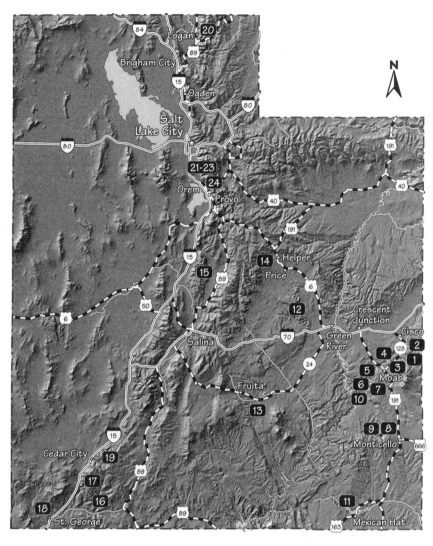

1 Castle Valley	9 Bridger Jack Spires	17 Kolob Canyons
2 Fisher Towers	10 Island in the Sky	18 St. George Crags
3 River Road	11 Mexican Hat	19 The Overlook &
4 Arches National Park	12 San Rafael Swell	Cetecean Wall
5 Wall Street	13 Capitol Reef	20 Logan Canyon
6 Long Canyon	National Park	21 Big Cottonwood Canyon
7 Kane Springs Canyon	14 Spring Canyon	22 Little Cottonwood Canyon
8 Indian Creek Canyon	15 Maple Canyon	23 Middle Bell Tower
	16 Zion National Park	24 American Fork Canyon

MAP LEGEND

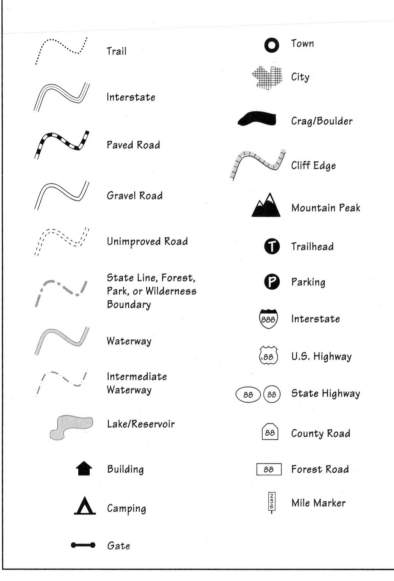

Trail

Interstate

Paved Road

Gravel Road

Unimproved Road

State Line, Forest, Park, or Wilderness Boundary

Waterway

Intermediate Waterway

Lake/Reservoir

Building

Camping

Gate

Town

City

Crag/Boulder

Cliff Edge

Mountain Peak

Trailhead

Parking

Interstate

U.S. Highway

State Highway

County Road

Forest Road

Mile Marker

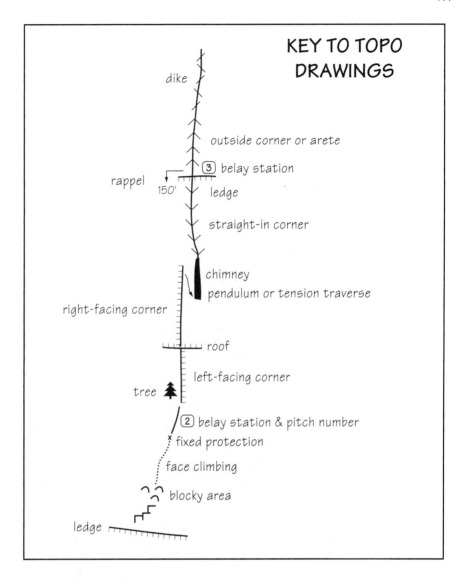

KEY TO TOPO DRAWINGS

dike

outside corner or arete

③ belay station

rappel

150'   ledge

straight-in corner

chimney

pendulum or tension traverse

right-facing corner

roof

left-facing corner

tree

② belay station & pitch number

fixed protection

face climbing

blocky area

ledge

LB	lieback	thin	thin crack(to 1 ½")
chim.	chimney	3rd	class 3
OW	off-width	4th	class 4
HB, RP	very small chocks	KB	knife blade
TCU	small camming devices	LA	lost arrow

Brett Spencer-Green on Supercrack, *Supercrack Buttress, Indian Creek.*
PHOTO BY STEWART M. GREEN

INTRODUCTION

Utah is a magnificent landscape of startling diversity and beauty, filled with extreme contrasts, immense views, and a marvelous natural and geologic diversity that is unmatched anywhere else in the world. It is a land full of hidden places and undiscovered wonders. Dominated by the red-rock Colorado Plateau, roofed by the lofty Wasatch and Uinta mountain ranges, and edged by broad sagebrush-covered basins the size of Rhode Island, Utah is a land that always amazes and astounds. Every turn of the highway, every bend in the trail, every cliff-top view offers a secret glimpse into the hidden heart of Utah's natural soul.

Numerous cliffs, crags, buttresses, and towers, composed of sandstone, limestone, granite, basalt, and metamorphic rock, scatter across the state's vastness. If all of Utah's cliff miles were added up, it could boast more exposed rock than any other state. Although much of Utah's rock is too soft and chossy to be climbable, only a step up from hard brown sugar, an abundant variety of high quality stone offers world class routes to challenge and tantalize climbers' skills and sensibilities.

This variety is part of what makes Utah a popular destination. The slickrock canyon country, with its soaring and fragile sandstone towers and endless tiers of Wingate sandstone cliffs, is a remote and inaccessible land of little rain and much beauty. It's a savage arena filled with big spaces and few people. Climbers can sample the world's best crack climbs at Indian Creek Canyon, push the envelope of security on looming sandstone walls in Zion National Park, inch up a mud-coated spire at Fisher Towers, or stand atop a pristine summit the size of a tabletop and gaze across the muddy Colorado River. Near Salt Lake City, deep canyons walled by granite slabs and colorful layers of overhanging limestone—Little Cottonwood, American Fork, and Logan canyons—provide both classic time-tested crack and face routes for the recreational climber and pumpy testpieces for the aspiring rock-jock.

Rock Climbing Utah describes 24 of Utah's best and most popular climbing areas, guiding the itinerant climber toward the quality climbing areas and routes. Hundreds of routes lace the many crags and towers in the areas that are covered here. Climbers from beginner to expert will find a superb sampling of routes. This guide will help you discover cliffs off the beaten track, long traditional-style gear routes, nervy friction slabs, or steep, bolted crimpfests and jughauls.

Venture into the desert backcountry to a reclusive tower, hike up steep talus slopes under a hot summer sun to a shadowed crag, or watch the evening sunset from a lofty bivouac ledge. It's these extraordinary moments of exploration that we climbers seek. They separate us from hikers, the recreational vehicle users, and cyclists. The stone teaches us hard lessons about our own frailness and the fragility of human life. We learn to exult in the physical, in the sheer joy of movement, in the understanding that the rock was there before us. So climb Utah's rock walls and rejoice in their beauty, appreciate their endurance, and realize that it's a rare and precious gift to stand among these towering rock gods.

CLIMBING HISTORY

Utah has long attracted climbers who come to sample the beauty and diversity of vertical adventures. The first known climbers were, of course, the ancient Anasazi and Fremont people who built small dwellings and granaries in cliff-side aeries reached only by stone axe-chopped steps and sandy friction moves.

The intimidating nature of Utah's vertical cliffs, particularly those in the canyon country, prevented many of the first American rock climbers from attempting new routes. The first real technical climbers were alpinists from the Salt Lake City area; they ventured onto the higher peaks of the Uinta and Wasatch ranges. They later brought their skills to lower elevation practice cliffs in Big and Little Cottonwood canyons. *Goodro's Wall*, one of America's first 5.10 leads, was put up in Big Cottonwood by early pioneer Harold Goodro in the late 1940s.

It wasn't until the 1960s that the first climbers ventured into the wild canyonlands of southeastern Utah. These early pioneers, including the prolific Layton Kor, had this stunning sandstone venue to themselves, and the best towers were ripe for plucking. Kor, along with various companions, was able to snag the first ascents of most of today's classic spires, including Castleton Tower, The Priest, The Titan, Standing Rock, and Monster Tower. Other desert climbers of note during the succeeding decades include Jim Dunn, Ed Webster, Earl Wiggins, Charlie Fowler, and Steve Hong.

The most recent momentous change came with the sport climbing revolution of the 1980s. A change in ethics regarding the placement of protection bolts and how routes were established opened numerous new cliffs to Utah rock climbers—including those at Logan, Big Cottonwood, American Fork, and Maple canyons, along with limestone cliffs around St. George. This new breed of climber, including Boone Speed, Jeff Pederson, and Bill Boyle, brought Utah's climbing standards up-to-date with their gymnastic, technical routes and difficult boulder problems.

Chris Cluff edges up Smiling at the Majorettes *(5.11b) at the Overlook.*
PHOTO BY TODD GROSS

GEOLOGY AND GEOGRAPHY

Utah, like every other western state, is a complicated geologic puzzle that extends far beyond the scope of a climbing guidebook. This uncompromising land of cliff, canyon, and mountain has long dictated the state's settlement patterns, placed its towns and cities in well-watered valleys, and set its highway courses. To understand this complex landscape, one has to begin with its unique geology and the main geographic provinces that comprise the state. Geographers divide Utah, the 11th largest state, into 3 distinct regions: the Colorado Plateau is a sandstone wonderland dissected by the Colorado and Green rivers that spreads across Utah's eastern half; the Rocky Mountains and other affiliated ranges twist down the state's spine from Idaho to Arizona; and the Basin and Range region stretches across Utah's western third.

The Colorado Plateau is a spectacular landscape of barebones, slickrock sandstone. The mighty Colorado and Green rivers, along with their tributaries, have excavated sharp canyons into the thick layer-cake of horizontal, sedimentary sandstone strata, creating an architectural maze of canyons, cliffs, buttes, mesas, spires, fins, castles, and basins. High volcanic mountain ranges, like the laccolithic Henry and La Sal mountains, tower above the hot desert and offer cool summer relief. The plateau's thick horizontal layers of sandstone yield some of Utah's most famous rock climbing areas, including Fisher Towers, Castleton Tower, Wall Street, and Indian Creek Canyon.

The Rocky Mountains split Utah in half, winding down its midsection like a twisted backbone. The Wasatch Range, seamed with sheer glacier- and river-carved canyons, forms a skyscraping backdrop to Salt Lake City and Provo. The range offers not only pristine alpine scenery, but some of America's finest champagne powder for downhill skiers. The Uinta Range, one of the few east-west trending range in the United States, is topped by 13,528-foot Kings Peak, Utah's highest point. The rock climbing in the state's mountain ranges is found primarily in the deep canyons, including those at Logan, Ogden, Big Cottonwood, Little Cottonwood, American Fork, and Maple canyons. Few climbing areas lie among the higher peaks, with the exception of the superb granite walls on the western flank of Lone Peak southeast of Salt Lake City.

The Basin and Range Province is exactly that—rugged fault-block mountain ranges separated by wide basins filled with alluvial deposits washed out of the mountains. Its main features include the brilliant white flats of the Great Salt Lake Desert and the Great Salt Lake, an inland sea almost 100 miles long and 50 miles wide. The lake is a small remnant of Pleistocene-age Lake Bonneville, an inland great lake that once blanketed parts of Utah, Nevada, Idaho, and Arizona. Few good cragging areas are located in Utah's Great Basin region, although some are located on limestone cliffs near Deseret Peak south of the Great Salt Lake, on the abrupt western face of Notch Peak, and on lower-lying granite domes.

CLIMBING DANGERS AND SAFETY

Rock climbing is a dangerous activity. Every climber from beginner to ace needs to recognize this fact. Every time you slip on your rock shoes and tie into your harness, you or your climbing partner might die as a direct result of your own actions or by an act of God. Rock climbing, despite all the fun and popularity, is serious business, and you need to treat it with respect. The fun quickly drains out of the vertical game when you see your buddy hauled off in a body bag. And almost everyone who has climbed for at least 10 years has had a friend or an acquaintance die in a climbing or mountaineering-related accident.

It is up to you to minimize the risks of rock climbing. Experience and physical conditioning are essential for safety and success on your climbs. If you are inexperienced or out of shape, get help. Don't jump on the sharp end and lead some horrendous runout route because you might lose face with your pals. The worst scenario sees you in that body bag, or at least hauled off to the hospital with a broken back. Safe rock climbing takes experience, and lots of it. At one time, tyros served an apprenticeship under the watchful eye and hand of a more experienced climber, but today with the burgeoning growth of rock gyms, everyone with basic climbing know-how and a handful of hard gym routes under their harness, a rope, and a dozen quickdraws thinks they're a rock-jock. It's just not true.

Many climbers are mistakenly led to believe they will be successful on any kind of natural rock. Climbers who have learned their techniques in climbing gyms should note their real limitations. Climbing inside an indoor gym is not a substitute for real-life rock climbing experience outside at the crag. Climbing in a gym is a controlled and safe activity. Climbing outside is not safe. Climbing outside requires good judgment and skills you cannot learn inside—including rope handling, placing and removing protection, setting up equalized belay anchors, rigging rappel lines and anchors, and doing all the other little things that keep both you and your partner safe on the rocks.

You can only obtain climbing experience by getting outside on the rock and doing lots of routes. If you do not have the necessary experience, it is prudent not to attempt serious or long routes especially in places like Canyonlands or Zion. Local guides and climbing schools operate in many of Utah's popular climbing areas. Their invaluable services allow you to develop the techniques and wise judgment to safely ascend many routes. Guide services and schools are listed for each area in this book (see Appendix C for a complete list of addresses and phone numbers). Before committing to a guide service, ask about their experience, their accident rates, safety procedures, and class or group sizes. If you have any question about a particular route or cliff, take the time to seek out a local and ask for his or her advice. Most local climbers and guides are happy to give updated ratings, gear lists, and topos to their area's routes.

Guidebooks: This guidebook, along with any other climbing guide or instruction book, is not a substitute for your own experience and your own sound judgment. Do not depend or rely only on the information in this book to get you safely to the top of the crag and then back down to your car. Guidebook writing is by necessity a compilation of information obtained by the author through his experience at a given crag as well as information gleaned from other experienced climbers. Errors will and do creep into route descriptions, topos, gear lists, anchor placements, fixed gear notes, and descent routes and rappels. Things change in the real world, out there on the rocks. A rockfall might obliterate that crucial set of rappel anchors, or that fixed piton at the route's 5.11 crux move might have pulled on the last leader fall. You must rely solely on your own experience and judgment to ensure your own personal safety and that of your partners.

Ratings: Rating climbing routes is a subjective process, usually arrived at by a consensus opinion. Use them with caution. Many climbing movements are subject to an individual climber's experience, technique, body type and size, and strength. Some routes may be harder for you than the grade indicated in this book. Again, use your judgment and don't let the rating fool you into thinking a route is easier than it really is. Every effort has been made to designate routes with protection ratings. If no rating is listed, then that route should be safe for anyone with experience in finding and placing protection gear. Both R and X ratings indicate more serious routes with possible serious injury, ground-fall, or even death as the result of a fall. Remember that every route, no matter what the grade, has an X rating if climbing equipment is improperly used, or placed in an unsafe manner, or if fixed protection, including bolts and anchors, fails.

Beginning climbers and gym climbers should take special note of route ratings. Gym routes rated with the Yosemite Decimal System do not accurately reflect real outdoor ratings. The fact that you are a hot 5.12 gym climber does not mean you can properly jam and safely protect a 5.9 hand crack. Consider every route seriously, no matter what the grade. Every experienced climber can relate a horror story from an "easy" route.

Climbing Safely: Keep safe on the rocks by using common sense. Most accidents and fatalities occur because of bad judgment and improper decisions. Use the following reminders to avoid accidents:

- Never hit the ground if you fall. Always protect yourself near the start of a route by placing lots of gear or stick-clipping a high bolt to avoid ground-falls.

- Always double-check your tie-in knot and harness before climbing and your harness and rappel device before rappelling.

- Do not climb beneath other parties. Rockfall can be fatal.

- Do not solo routes without a rope. Even a 30-foot fall is deadly.

- Do not climb beyond your skill level without proper safety and protection devices.

- Place protection whenever possible to safeguard yourself and your partner.

- Rope up on wet, snowy, or dark descent routes.

- Tie knots in the end of your ropes to avoid rappelling off the end of the rope.

- Tie in after completing a sport pitch and double check your knot and the rope before downclimbing or lowering.

- Remember that the belay is a crucial part of the safety link. Belayers need to be alert, competent, and anchored. Expect and remind your belayer to pay attention while you climb and not visit with the neighbors or fix lunch.

- Tie a knot in the end of the rope to avoid being dropped by inattentive belayers while they are lowering you.

- Most accidents are preventable. Rely on your own good judgment to evaluate changing conditions. Your safety depends entirely on you.

OBJECTIVE DANGERS

Accidents can happen every time you go rock climbing. Always keep that thought in mind when venturing out to the crag. Objective dangers are those that you have no control over. You will find them while walking to the cliff, climbing your route, and descending back to the car. Never consider your climbing day over until you are safely back at your car. Many accidents happen on descents due to rockfall, carelessness, loose rock, inclement weather like rain or snow, and darkness. Always rope up on any descent you have the least bit of uneasiness about—pay attention to your intuition.

Fixed Gear: Use all fixed gear with caution. Bolts can shear from the force of a fall. Fixed pitons will loosen due to rock weathering and expansion caused by repeated freezing and thawing. Metal fatigue and age also affect the useful life of gear. Always back up fixed protection whenever possible, but **always** backup belay anchors and rappel stations. **Never** rely on a single piece of gear for your personal safety. Always build redundancy into the system so the failure of one part will not affect the overall safety of the system. Never rappel or lower from a single anchor, especially in the canyon country, and don't lean straight out on a bolt. The pullout strength of bolts in sandstone is very low. Fatalities have occurred when a sandstone anchor bolt has pulled on a climber. Do not trust your life to questionable anchors or desiccated rappel slings. It's more important to leave gear to safeguard your life than to worry about the cost of the gear.

Loose Rock: The main objective danger is loose rock. You will find loose blocks and flakes on many routes, sitting on ledges or wedged in cracks and chimneys. Use extreme caution around any suspect rock. Falling rock is deadly to your belayer and friends at the cliff base; it can even chop your rope. Warn your partners if you feel a block is unstable so they can be prepared for possible rockfall. Thawing and freezing cycles can loosen flakes and boulders on rock walls. The movements of your climbing rope can also dislodge loose rock. Use care when pulling rappel ropes that you don't also pull a stone missile down as well. Wear a helmet while climbing and belaying to reduce the risk of serious head injury or death from rockfall or falling. This is especially true in the canyon country. Helmets may not be in fashion, but they're definitely in style if you want to preserve your life!

Noxious Plants and Bugs: Poison ivy and sumac, bees and wasps, and ticks inhabit many of Utah's climbing areas. Poisonous plants cause a severe itching rash that can take weeks to heal. Learn to identify their leaves. Poisonous plants grow in thickets along cliff bases. Bees and wasps live on many crags. Take note of possible hives and avoid them. Ticks are tiny blood-sucking arachnids that live in brushy and wooded areas on lower mountain slopes. They're usually active in spring and early summer. All can carry tick fever, the more serious Rocky Mountain spotted fever, and Lyme disease. Avoid tick-infested areas if possible and wear clothing that fits tightly around the ankles, wrists, waist, and neck; use lots of bug juice; and always check your clothes and pack before getting into your car. Ticks usually crawl around on you for a few hours before finally settling down for a blood-sucking party. You can usually find them before they do real damage.

Snakes: Rattlesnakes are a serious hazard in the lower-elevation climbing areas during the warmer months. They have broad, triangular heads with a depression or pit in front of each eye, hence the name pit vipers. The buzz from their tail is unmistakable and once you have heard the sound, you will never forget it. Watch for snakes along sunny access paths or hiding under boulders and dead brush on approach routes or when scrambling on easy terrain. They often climb into bushes to get off the hot ground during the day. Remember that rattlesnakes do not always warn before striking. If you do encounter a rattlesnake, don't kill it. This is their home and you are an intruder. They are simply protecting themselves. Most bites occur when people attempt to pick the snake up. A snakebite is considered a major medical emergency. If you are bitten, get to a hospital as quickly as possible. In 25 percent of bites no venom is injected, and in another 25 percent so little venom is injected that no antivenin is needed for recovery. Do not attempt first aid to a snakebite. Do not apply a tourniquet or ice and do not use a snakebite kit unless absolutely necessary. The wrong treatment can result in the loss of limb or life. Get the victim to the nearest medical help and treat for shock as needed. Keep a good eye on young children in rattlesnake country. A bite is much more serious for a small child than an adult.

Rattlesnakes inhabit almost all of Utah's crags except for the high elevation cliffs. Take particular care in the St. George area in southwestern Utah; several species of rattlesnake live here, including the dangerous and aggressive Mojave rattlesnake. This snake, *Crotalus scutulatus*, has a very potent venom making its bite potentially much more serious than the western diamondback, a species with which it is often confused. It grows to four feet long and is usually a greenish-gray color.

Weather: Keep a close eye on the weather when climbing. Summer thunderstorms can build up very rapidly, creating unpredictable weather. Torrential rain and cool temperatures can lead to potentially deadly hypothermia, the lowering of the body's core temperature. Be prepared for wet weather by carrying extra clothes and a raincoat. Heavy rain can also cause severe flash floods. When hiking through narrow canyons in the desert, keep an eye on the weather, even if the rain appears to be miles away, so you can avoid flood danger.

Also watch for lightning. Climbers and lightning are usually drawn to high points—like the summits of desert towers. Be vigilant for lightning whenever a storm is moving your way and retreat at the first sign of lightning. Avoid being on an exposed ridge or summit during a lightning storm. Climbers have been struck on top of Castleton Tower. A sign of an impending strike is St. Elmo's fire, a buzzing of static electricity and your hair standing on end. If you are trapped during a storm, flatten yourself as much as possible and move all metal gear as far away as possible. Avoid rappelling during a lightning storm. The electricity can travel down the rope and zap you. The best way to avoid lightning is to use common sense—get off the rock before the storm reaches you.

ACCESS AND ETHICAL CONSIDERATIONS

Rock climbers have long been a maverick bunch, doing their own thing at the crags like it was their God-given right. Now, however, climbers have a growing ethical responsibility to minimize their impact on the rock and the surrounding lands and realize that rock climbing is not a right, but a privilege. The world is a fragile place that is being rapidly damaged by insensitive users including loggers, miners, ranchers, mountain bikers, horseback riders, rafters, hikers, and rock climbers. Climbers should be focused on preserving and protecting their unique climbing resources rather than putting up more new routes at tired crags or debating old ethical battles.

The increasing number of climbers at crags in the United States is adding pressure that never existed 20 years ago. Many common rock climbing practices such as bolting and aid climbing are viewed as high-impact activities by management agencies such as the National Park Service and Bureau of Land Management. Land managers are often required by federal law to protect and

Craig Caviezel works up an unnamed route at the upper cave, Black and Tan Wall, *St. George area.* PHOTO BY STEWART M. GREEN

preserve the areas that they manage. They are consequently designing comprehensive management plans that regulate recreational land uses such as rock climbing in order to minimize human impact and preserve the natural resources.

Fortunately, a couple of excellent organizations, The Access Fund and The American Mountain Foundation, are working with governmental agencies and private landowners to ensure that our precious crags are kept open and generally free from bureaucratic red-tape regulations. To ensure climbing freedom, we need to adopt an environmental ethic that reflects our concern and love for the rock. We need to be more sensitive and caring toward the nation's limited rock resources, and minimize our impact at the crag. Climbers need to establish positive partnerships with landowners and management agencies as well as climbing organizations to actively preserve the rock resources. They need to be active stewards and caretakers of local areas—think globally, act locally—by investing in what Mark Hesse of The American Mountain Foundation calls "sweat equity." Devote some time to building proper trails, restoring trampled cliff-base ecosystems, picking up trash at the crag, and replacing colored slings with muted colors. Climbers must educate themselves. Many parklands are set aside to protect specific geological, ecological, or cultural resources. Preservation of these resources takes precedence over recreational uses like climbing. Our continued access to these areas depends on our sensitivity to these unique features. Climbers need to be the ones making the important decisions regarding rock climbing—not the politicians and political appointees in Washington, DC.

We can begin the process by doing all the little things that total up to a big difference. Look at the impacts climbers have had at the crags and begin mitigating them by changing your own habits. Here are a few suggestions on how you can help:

- Pick up all your trash at the crag, including cigarette butts, burned matches, tape, soda and beer cans, and candy wrappers.

- Bury human waste away from the cliff base or leave it in the open where it will rapidly deteriorate. Burn or carry out your toilet paper. Don't leave human feces on access trails or below routes (as unbelievable as it sounds, it does happen!). Use established toilets whenever possible.

- Use existing approach and descent trails. Avoid shortcutting corners and causing additional erosion. Stay off loose scree and talus slopes that easily erode. Soil erosion destroys plants and ground cover. Belay off boulders rather than the lush grass at the wall base. Don't chop down trees or tear off branches that might interfere with the first few feet of a route. Use a longer approach or descent route to protect sensitive ecological areas.

- Do not leave cheater slings on bolts or brightly colored slings on rappel anchors. Instead use colored slings that match the rock's color. Camouflage bolt hangers with matching paint.

- Respect wildlife closures. Many cliffs in places like Zion National Park are closed for nesting raptors. Climbing near active nests can cause the birds to abandon the site.

- Practice clean camping ethics, especially when primitive camping. Don't rip up trees for firewood, particularly old desert junipers. Put your fire out cold before leaving or going to sleep. Use a stove for cooking. Use only sites that show signs of   previous use.

- Follow established trails to access the cliffs. Follow the trails when descending to avoid damaging fragile plants and creating new social paths. Many trails have been constructed by the American Mountain Foundation in the canyon country to lessen climbers' impact; these include trails at Indian Creek Canyon and to Castleton Tower.

- When accessing canyon country routes, look carefully for existing climber paths or follow dry creek beds to avoid damaging vegetation and fragile cryptobiotic soil. This unique soil, a symbiosis of algae and fungi, forms a black crust on the sandy surface. It allows for the absorption of precious moisture, stabilizes the soil surface, and provides important plant nutrients. Walking on its crust severely impacts the desert ecosystem which takes as long as 100 years to recover.

- Avoid biking to reach more distant climbing sites, as mountain bikes have a greater ecological impact than hikers. An exception to this would be biking on an existing roadway.

- Do not climb near or above any Indian rock art or ruined dwellings. It's against both federal and state law to damage rock art panels or ruins. Unfortunately, climbers have damaged some by careless and thoughtless actions.

- Join and contribute money and time to worthwhile climbing organizations like The Access Fund and The American Mountain Foundation. They are working to keep our climbing areas open and free from cumbersome restrictions.

Ethics: Every climber and every area has a unique and individual ethic regarding the styles that routes are put up, ascended, and rated. Ethics are at the very heart of our sport. The style we use to climb a route means everything. We need to remember to disagree about ethics only to the point where the rock itself doesn't become an innocent victim of ethical wars and callous egos gone awry. There have been too many bolt wars; they solved nothing but left irreparable damage to the crag. A schism, although slowly healing, has existed in American climbing for the last decade between traditional climbers and sport climbers. This "us-versus-them" mentality benefits no one. It's best to remember there are only rock climbers. Enjoy the challenges of both schools and leave the petty ethical grievances behind.

The style you employ on a route is your personal choice. There is purity, beauty, and adventure in climbing a route from the ground up—placing gear, routefinding, leaving the topo behind, and accepting what the rock offers for both protection and technique. Many of Utah's classic routes were established in this traditional fashion. Modern gymnastic routes often require working, memorizing, and hang-dogging the movements before the coveted redpoint ascent from the ground to the anchors is achieved. Toproping is a legitimate tactic on some hard routes as well as airy boulder problems. It not only saves the climber from a serious fall, but also saves the rock from extra bolts.

Bolting is modern climbing's most controversial ethical dilemma. Permanent bolts on cliffs have created many of Utah's popular and newer climbing areas—Maple Canyon and American Fork Canyon—that until the last 10 years had no tradition of rock climbing. Bolts have also allowed more difficult routes to be climbed in a relatively safe manner. But bolts have also been misused. Some modern crags, the work of power drill owners gone crazy, are a gridwork of bolts. These eyesores have angered land managers as well as other users. Other crags have been subjected to bolt wars with the offended faction either chopping or placing bolts. The placement as well as the removal of bolts, however, doesn't solve the problem; instead it only damages the rock and encourages more climbing restrictions. Common sense, dialogue between climbers, and some civil decorum goes a long way toward resolving the bolting issue. Many Utah climbing areas now have severe limitations on the placement of new bolts, particularly Canyonlands National Park, which has a total ban on new bolts. Others have a bolting moratorium that allows for only the replacement of existing, unsafe anchors and bolts. Always check with land managers to learn about bolting restrictions and concerns.

The Access Fund has worked with land management agencies to resolve the use of fixed anchors, especially bolts, on public lands. Climbers should support the work they have done to establish a broad national policy for fixed anchors on our crags. The Acess Fund works to allow fixed anchors at climbing areas and urges that their use be determined on an area-by-area basis by climbers who rely on anchors for their personal safety. Climbers, not the government, should bear the responsibility for the placement and up-keep of fixed pro. The Access Fund is also working to permit the use of fixed anchors in designated wilderness areas to safeguard climbers and to minimize the impact of climbing on soils, vegetation, fragile cliff-top environments, and wildlife on public lands.

New Routes: Climbers who place new bolts and create new routes need to think long and hard about the impacts and consequences of placing new bolts.

Toprope the proposed line and see if it is indeed worthy of creating a new route. If it is, place the bolts with sensitivity to minimize rock damage. Do not place bolts next to cracks that accept gear placements. Use the natural line up the rock. Don't force it up the contrived, hardest way because everyone else will undoubtedly follow the natural weakness and line of least resistance. End the route or pitch at natural stances or ledges whenever possible. In the end, it really doesn't matter if a route is put in from the ground up or on a rappel rope. The important thing is the safety and proper placement of the fixed pro and the aesthetic qualities of the route. Don't let the ease of rap-bolting lead to over-protecting the route and don't add new bolts to existing lines—respect the style of the first ascensionists. If you don't have the skills or courage to do the route as it is, then leave it as a future challenge that you or someone else will someday meet with proper respect.

Defacement: Chipping and manufacturing holds is a growing problem on American crags. As climbers push the standards higher, they desire harder routes to test their abilities. As indoor gym climbers, usually newcomers to the climbing world, spread outward from their insulated plywood crags, they see the real rock as a malleable medium ready for their sculpting. They bring a gym ethic—viewing every hold and move as changeable—to the outside rock world. **Do not chip or chisel or glue any hold onto a route or boulder problem.** If you can't do the route with what's already there, maybe you're just not good enough to climb it or maybe that piece of rock was never meant to be climbed. Save it for the day when you are good enough, when you've worked hard enough, when you've finally earned the ascent. Chipped routes destroy the future of climbing, especially for the up-and-coming rock stars. Chipped routes reflect egotism, selfishness, and mediocrity.

In the quest for your own personal ethic, remember that neither the rock nor the route belongs to you. You're only a transient traveler across the vertical terrain. Do not allow egotism, ignorance, and arrogance to dictate your ascent style and personal climbing ethic. Be sensitive to both the cliff and the landscape, and consider each route a precious gift for everyone to open and share.

Using This Guide

A locator map at the front of the book shows the general locations of the main climbing areas.

Each area write-up includes: an **Overview,** which may include a brief summary of the climbing history and local ethics; **Trip planning information,** including condensed summaries of specific information on each area; **Directions** and **Maps** to find the areas; and specific climbing **Route descriptions,** which in many cases are accompanied by photos with overlays and topos identifying routes and showing the locations.

Overview: The Overview describes the setting, the type of rock, and climbing. Also included are recommendations for climbing equipment as well as some discussions of local climbing history and ethics.

Trip planning information: This section offers a brief synopsis of the following categories:

- **Area description:** A brief summary of the area.
- **Location:** Reference to largest nearby towns, major roads, or natural landmarks.
- **Camping:** Information on nearby developed campgrounds and suggestions for camping in undeveloped sites. When available, addresses or phone numbers are given.
- **Climbing season:** The best time of year to visit an area.
- **Restrictions and access issues:** Important issues to be aware of, such as private land, parking, safety, and land use.
- **Guidebooks:** Published sources of information for the area.
- **Nearby mountain shops, guide services, and gyms:** The names of the nearest towns with these services is given here. For a full listing of addresses and phone numbers, by town, see Appendix C.
- **Finding the crag:** Description and how-to-get-there map with directions starting at nearest major road and town.
- **The cliff name:** Detailed discussion of location, special information pertaining to equipment, approaches, and descents.

- **Route descriptions:** Routes are listed numerically, with the name and rating followed by a brief discussion of the location and nature of the climb, special equipment recommendations, length, and descent information. An overview map of each climbing area and photos—showing cliffs and route locations—accompanies the descriptions. The road map legend and key to topo map symbols are located at the front of the book on pages viii and ix.
- **Appendices:** These offer further reading (Appendix A); rating comparison charts (Appendix B); and a list of climbing equipment shops, guide services, and gyms. (Appendix C).
- **Index:** An alphabetical listing of all proper names, including people, climbs, and climbing areas.

A book of this magnitude requires a wide selection of routes of all difficulties and lengths. Errors will creep into route descriptions due simply to the sheer diversity and number of routes detailed here. A wide range of active climbers has carefully checked and double-checked the area and crag descriptions to maximize the book's accuracy. Be forewarned, however, that things on paper aren't always as they are in reality. Take every route description with a grain of salt. This book is not intended to carry you up any rock route. It will get you to the base of the cliff and point you in the right direction, but the rest is up to you and your sound decisions. This book is not a substitute for your own experience and judgment.

Almost all of the routes included in this guide are worth climbing. Routes not worth climbing have usually been omitted or described as "not recommended." If a route is especially good, words like "quality" and "excellent" may be included in the route description. Star ratings have been deliberately omitted in an effort to avoid queues and a diminished experience for everyone. These are generally subjective opinions that may or may not be true for every climber. Every climber has his or her own unique experience on every route. There are many fine routes in this guide to choose from. You are invited to decide for yourself what looks right and feels best on any given day.

RATING SYSTEM

This book uses the Yosemite Decimal System, the usual American grading scale, to identify the technical difficulty of the routes. Remember that ratings are subjective and vary from area to area. This book has tried to bring a consensus to the grades, but we have relied on previously listed grades for routes in most cases. You will find small rating variances in each area. Some climbs may seem to be more conservatively rated (read harder) than other areas. Easier sport climbs (5.8 to 5.11) seem to be harder to translate to the YDS system, although the standard of difficulty on the higher end of the scale is comparable to European grading. Older traditional routes conform to early Colorado and California ratings established at the same time. The present sticky rubber and better pro might make them slightly easier, but climbers will still find them solidly rated.

Some of the older bolted climbs have been retro-bolted, which on some level makes them seem slightly easier. 5.9 can start feeling like 5.10 when you're 40 feet out as opposed to 10 feet out! Use all ratings as a starting point in any area and expect a 1 to 2 letter grade, or even a full grade variation, from what you are accustomed to at your home area.

Many routes listed also have protection or danger ratings. These routes generally have little or no protection and a climber who falls could sustain serious injuries or death. R-rated climbs have serious injury potential. X-rated climbs have groundfall and death potential. Remember, however, that every route is a possible R- or X-rated climb.

Mountain travel is typically classified as follows:

Class 1—Trail hiking.

Class 2—Hiking over rough ground such as scree and talus; may include the use of hands for stability.

Class 3—Scrambling that requires the use of hands and careful foot placement.

Class 4—Scrambling over steep and exposed terrain; climbing difficulty is relatively easy, but a long fall could result in injury because of exposure. The lead climber trails a rope, uses natural formations for protection if available, and is on belay.

Class 5—Climbing on steep and exposed terrain where a fall would definitely result in injury or death. Hands and feet only are used for upward progress, no direct or artificial aid is employed. Ropes, belays, running belays (protection), and related techniques are used.

The Yosemite Decimal System (YDS) used to rate Class 5 climbing fails to follow mathematical logic. It is now an open-ended scale where the 5 denotes the Class and the difficulty rating is tacked on behind the decimal point, with 5.0 being the easiest and 5.15 (read five-fifteen) being the hardest (to date). When it was originally developed, 5.9 was the theoretic upper end of the scale. When routes were climbed that were obviously harder than 5.9, new "numbers" were invented to denote the difficulty. When a route has had too few ascents for a consensus or the estimated difficulty rating is unclear, a plus (+) or minus (-) subgrade may be employed (5.9+ or 5.12-, for example). Where there is a consensus of opinion, additional subgrades of a, b, c, and d are used on climbs rated 5.10 and above. Occasionally two letters may be used such as 5.12b/c. This is because the grade still requires consensus, is height dependent, or is subject to some other qualifier.

Routes are rated according to the most difficult move. Some climbs may be continuously difficult, seeming harder than other routes rated the same but with only one or two hard moves. In some instances, routes are described as "sustained" or "pumpy" to give an indication of the continuous nature of the climbing. Differences in strength, differences in reach, and distance between protection points may be factors contributing to rating variations. Where these factors seem significant, they may be pointed out in the written descriptions.

Aid climbing—using artificial means to progress up the rock—has a different set of ratings.

Class 6—Aid climbing; climbing equipment is used for progress, balance, or rest; denoted with a capital letter **A** followed by numbers progressing from 0. A capital letter **C** indicates that the aid placements are "clean aid" and pitons or hammered aid should not be used.

A0—Equipment may have been placed to rest on or to pull on for upward progress.

A1—Solid gear placements and aid slings (etriers) are used for progress because the climbing is too difficult to be free climbed.

A2—Gear placements are more difficult to install and support less weight than an A1 placement.

A3—Progressively weaker placements, more difficult to install; may not hold even a short fall.

A4—Placements can support body weight only; long falls can occur.

A5—A series of A4 placements that could result in a fall of 50 feet or longer.

A pitch or rope-length of technical climbing may have a combination Class 5 and Class 6 rating such as 5.9 A4; this means that the free climbing difficulties are up to 5.9 with an aid section of A4 difficulty. On the route "topo" drawings or marked photos in this guide, the crux (most difficult section) is often marked with the difficulty rating. Not all crux ratings are marked on routes in photo overlays or topos.

An additional grade denoted by Roman numerals I through VI is given to some longer routes. This generally refers to the commitment in terms of length and time requirements of the climb. Climbers should also consider other factors such as technical difficulties, weather, logistics, and the approach and descent. Typically a Grade I takes a few hours to complete, Grade II up to half a day, Grade III most of the day, Grade IV all day, Grade V usually requires a bivouac, and Grade VI takes two or more days.

An additional "danger" rating may be tacked on to some climbs. Where the protection may not hold and a fall could result in injury or death, an R or X may be added. A route rated 5.9 R may mean that the protection is sparse or "runout" or that some placements may not hold a fall. X-rated routes have a fall potential that can be fatal, unless one has the confidence and ability to solo a route safely with absolutely no protection and without falling.

See Appendix B for a table comparing the American rating system (Yosemite Decimal System) to the British, French, and Australian systems.

Injuries sustained from falls are always possible, even on routes that can be well protected. This guide does not give a protection rating nor does it provide detailed information on how, when, or where to place protective hardware. Suggested "standard" gear racks are described in the overview for each area, and some recommendations are made on types and sizes of protection that may be useful on some climbs.

Be advised that all rack info is the bare minimum required to safely ascend a route. It's up to you to decide if you need more or less gear than is described in the text to safely and properly climb the route. The standard desert rack mentioned in some descriptions is considered a couple sets of Friends or similar-sized camming units, a set TCUs, a selection of wired stoppers and Tricams, and some quickdraws. Ultimately, safety and the level of risk assumed are the responsibility of the climber. There's really no such thing as being "too careful."

Sport climbers should also eye their prospective route and count the number of bolts. Bolt counts are given for many routes, but things change on the real rock. Some bolts may be hidden, added, subtracted, or miscounted. Always carry extra quickdraws in case the count is wrong or you drop a quickdraw. Remember to consider what you need for the anchors and for lowering. Again, it's always up to you to provide for your own safety. Climb safe, climb smart, and have fun!

Moab Area

UTAH

Ian Spencer-Green on Scarface, *Scarface Wall, Indian Creek.* PHOTO BY STEWART M. GREEN

CASTLE VALLEY

OVERVIEW

The red-rock country east of Moab is a ragged land filled with soaring sandstone escarpments, sliced by abrupt canyons, and dominated by the mighty Colorado River. The river, its sharp erosive power periodically swollen with glacial-melt after the ice age, sculpted this landscape over the last few million years. After entering Utah from Colorado, the river dashes through remote Westwater Canyon, passes its confluence with the Dolores River, drops through a short canyon, and meanders across the broad Professor Valley. South of the valley tower the LaSal Mountains, their pointed 12,000-foot crowns often blanketed with snow. A series of canyons and valleys drains north to the river from the mountains, including Castle Valley. This wide valley, dotted with homes among pastures and pinyon pines, is flanked on the west by the lofty, unbroken Porcupine Rim. The east side of the valley is less well-defined, with a series of mesas, buttes, towers, and talus slopes forming an irregular boundary.

These buttes and towers, including Castleton Tower, The Rectory, The Priest, and Sister Superior, form one of Utah's best known climbing areas. Castleton Tower is the most well-known and popular of all Utah's desert spires. This immense block of Wingate sandstone, at the south end of Castle Ridge, is poised atop a 1000-foot-high talus cone broken by small cliff bands. It stands aloof and forbidding, separated from the surrounding cliffs and buttes. The view from Castleton's 30- by 40-foot summit is breathtaking, with mesas and canyons unfolding northward past the silty Colorado River to the distant Book Cliff Rim. Cracks and chimneys seam the 400-foot tower, offering climbers both adventure and startling beauty.

Castleton Tower deserves its excellent reputation with rock climbers. I did the sixth ascent of the tower in 1971 when it was still a little-known pinnacle. Today it has seen well over 2,000 ascents. The inclusion of Castleton in the book *Fifty Classic Climbs of North America* has doomed it to popularity, putting it on every climber's tick-list. Its classic routes are generally easier than most other desert towers, and its protection is adequate. Consequently, a queue of folks often forms at the base of the *Kor-Ingalls Route*, waiting their turn to climb to the summit. Likewise, lines form on the summit for the descent routes. To avoid the crowds, it's best to come during the week and early in the morning. Weekends in spring and fall tend to be the busiest times. On those occasions it might be better to seek out a route with less traffic.

To find something more remote, it's easy to jog north on Castle Ridge to The Rectory and The Priest. The Rectory is a 375-foot-high, narrow, blocky butte about a quarter of a mile north of Castleton Tower. Its northern end is topped by a couple of serrated, semi-detached summits called The Nuns. Some excellent crack lines ascend The Rectory, offering climbers a good alternative on busy Castleton days. The Priest is a 330-foot tower next to The Nuns. This tall pinnacle yields a classic route to its small, airy summit. From a distance, The Priest looks remarkably like a cowled priest blessing the surrounding desert.

Farther north on Castle Ridge are the Sister Superior Spires, a collection of spires sometimes called The Professor and The Students, and The Convent, another small mesa similar in size to The Rectory. Sister Superior, a 330-foot tower, is more remote than the other Castle Valley towers and offers some 3-star routes. The other spires include 150-foot North Sister, 80-foot Chimney Spire, and 60-foot Baby Sister. The Convent has seen little climbing development.

Climbing history: Much of Utah's canyon country climbing history begins with the first ascent of Castleton Tower in 1961 by geologist Huntley Ingalls and bricklayer Layton Kor. Prior to this landmark ascent, few technical rock climbs existed here. Most climbers thought the sandstone was too fragile and rotten for safe ascents and best left to the daredevils who had climbed Monument Valley's Totem Pole and Spider Rock in Arizona's Canyon de Chelly. Ingalls first discovered the tower in 1956 while working for the U.S. Geological Survey. It wasn't until five years later, however, that Ingalls was able to entice anyone to accompany him on a summit attempt. Kor, a speedy and skilled climber from Boulder, Colorado, had earlier met and climbed with Ingalls in Eldorado Canyon before accepting Ingalls's desert invitation.

The pair traveled down to this remote canyon area in mid-September and slogged up the talus cone to reconnoiter the tower. Kor scoped the obvious route up the dihedral system on Castleton's south face and set to work. The pair quickly climbed a couple of surprisingly easy pitches to a ledge halfway up the tower, but they retreated from their high point, leaving fixed ropes, as a driving rainstorm appeared to be moving toward them. The next morning they prussiked to the ledge and Kor began the crux chimney and off-width crack pitch. Kor passed a narrow constriction using some aid bolts before reaching a notch. By midday the duo had reached the summit of this lofty sky-island.

The following year a helicopter film crew and nervous model reached the summit of Castleton for a Chevrolet commercial. Until 1970, only four parties had climbed the tower on the *Kor-Ingalls Route*. In 1970 Daniel Burgette and Allen Erickson, unsure about the line of the regular route, jammed an obvious crack system up the spire's east flank and established the *North Chim-*

ney route. Castleton's next four ascents were by Jim Dunn and several partners. In 1971, Dunn climbed the *Kor-Ingalls* on a hot September day with Stewart Green for the sixth ascent. The next day he climbed the *North Chimney* with Dan Porter, an old high school pal who never climbed before or after the experience. In late November, he established the first ascent of the *West Face*, one of the hardest desert routes at that time, with Stewart Green and Billy Westbay. The following spring Dunn did the first ascent of the *North Face* with Doug Snively. Ed Webster later put up several Castleton classics, including *Black Sun* in 1977 with Leonard Coyne and Mark Hopkins, and *The Arrowhead* and *Stardust Cowboy* in 1982 with Chester Dreiman.

The Priest was the other early canyonlands spire ascent by Layton Kor in September 1961. A few days after summiting Castleton Tower, Kor linked up with Harvey, Annie Carter, and Fred Beckey to attempt The Priest. After working on the chimney route for a couple of days, Kor and Harvey Carter reached the blocky top, but a quick-moving thunderstorm denied Beckey the summit. The following day Kor climbed the route with Beckey for the spire's second ascent. The route was named *Honeymoon Chimney* in honor of the Carters' recent wedding.

The Rectory routes were climbed after most of the routes were established on Castleton and The Priest. Cleve McCarty and Harvey Carter made the first ascent of the landform via the *Empirical Route* in 1962. *Fine Jade*, the best route on the butte, was put up by Chip Chace and Pat Ellinwood in 1984. Sister Superior saw its first ascent in 1965 by Harvey Carter and David Bentley via the now-free *Savior* route. Ken Trout and Kirk Miller garnered the classic line *Jah Man* in 1984.

Climbing in the Valley: The climbing season at Castle Valley is year-round. Spring and fall are, as usual in the desert, the best times to climb. Expect warm but windy days from March to May, with occasional rain, sleet, and even snow storms moving through. Storms tend to be short-lived. Summers are hot, especially on the south-facing cliffs. Approach and climb in the early morning to avoid the debilitating heat of the day. Carry lots of water. A gallon per person per day is not too much. Watch for dangerous thunderstorms that brew over the LaSal Mountains. They can quickly move in on the towers. Lightning is a serious danger on any of these spires. Autumn brings warm days and cool nights, with lots of sunshine and low humidity. It is often too hot for comfort on south-facing walls. Winter can be snowy, but also offers many warm, sunny days for climbing.

You can easily reach the Castle Valley crags and towers by trails, although the approach hike can take over an hour to the cliff base. The trail to Castleton, The Rectory, and The Priest was constructed in 1996 by the American Mountain Foundation. Stay on the trail and don't shortcut to avoid damaging the talus slopes and the area's fragile plants. It's a good idea to always carry a flashlight or headlamp on these climbing adventures. The descents and hikes back to the car can be very dangerous in the dark, with serious drop-offs and loose rock a distinct possibility.

Dangers here include heat exhaustion and sunstroke. Always carry sufficient supplies of water and sports drinks to avoid problems. Sit in the shade during the heat of the day to conserve energy. Wear a hat in summer or on hot days here. Also use a hard hat. Loose boulders and rocks abound on ledges and are wedged in cracks. A hard hat just might save your head when the party above knocks a handful of fist-sized cobbles off their ledge.

Descents off all the towers and buttes are by rappel. Most of the rappel anchors are obvious. Use care, however, whenever rappelling. Check the existing webbing on the anchors. Double-check the safety and placement of the anchors. Tie knots in the ends of your rappel ropes, and be extremely careful not to toss or dislodge any of the loose rocks onto people below. Always carry two ropes for rappels.

Rack: You need a standard desert rack. Plan on bringing double sets of Friends and a couple of extra large pieces for off-widths including #5 Camalots or Big Bros. A set of TCUs and wired stoppers completes the rack. A bolt kit is not necessary. Remember that all rack info listed for each described route is a suggested rack only. You know best what extra gear you might need to sew up a hard crack. All the routes listed here have sufficient fixed anchors for belays and rappels.

Trip Planning Information

General description: A collection of Wingate sandstone spires and buttes that offer some of the canyon country's finest free-climbing experiences.

Location: East-central Utah. East of Moab.

Camping: Find campgrounds along River Road (Utah 128) up river from Moab. Camp only in designated campgrounds with toilet facilities. No primitive camping is allowed along River Road without camp toilets. Violators will be ticketed by BLM rangers. Primitive camping is available at the parking area below Castleton Tower. Otherwise there are lots of camping options in and around Moab, including several private campgrounds as well as BLM campgrounds at Sand Flats. Carry water whenever possible and tote out all your waste and garbage. The desert is a fragile place.

Climbing season: Year-round. Summers are almost too hot, although shade can be found. Winters can be very cold. Many routes, however, receive lots of sun and are climbable on all but the coldest days. Spring and fall are best. Spring days are generally warm, but windy. Watch for chilly storms that can bring rain, sleet, and snow. Fall is brilliant but can be too hot on the south-facing walls.

Restrictions and access issues: None currently. All the routes included here are on BLM public lands. The Castle Valley crags see a lot of usage. Do your part to minimize human impact by not leaving trash, tape, and cigarette butts. Follow existing trails and paths whenever possible to avoid damaging fragile cryptobiotic soils and creating social trails on the fragile desert landscape. Camp only in already-used areas and use clean-camping techniques.

Guidebooks: *Moab Rock East* by Eric Bjørnstad, Chockstone Press, scheduled for a 1998 release, is the comprehensive guide to Castle Valley and its environs. *Classic Desert Climbs* by Fred Knapp, Sharp End Publishing, 1996, has topos and descriptions for the area's popular routes. *500 Select Moab Classics* by Kevin Chase, 1994; available from the author at Moab Adventure Outfitters.

Nearby mountain shops, guide services, and gyms: Moab Adventure Outfitters sells gear and clothing. They also offer rock climbing classes and guided climbs. Rim Cyclery in Moab sells gear, chalk, and guidebooks.

Services: All visitor and climber services are found in Moab, including gas, food, lodging, camping, dining, and groceries. Showers are available at several locations in Moab.

Emergency services: Call 911. Allen Memorial Hospital, 719 West 400 North, Moab, UT, (801) 259-7191.

Nearby climbing areas: Wall Street, The King's Hand, Long Canyon, Day Canyon, River Road crags, The Lighthouse, Dolomite Tower, Fisher Towers, Arches National Park, The Bride, Indian Creek Canyon.

Nearby attractions: Colorado River, Fisher Towers, Deadhorse Point State Park, Arches National Park, LaSal Mountains, Manti-LaSal National Forest, Colorado River Scenic Byway (Utah 128), Slickrock Bike Trail.

Finding the crags: Drive east from Moab on Utah 128, River Road. To reach Castleton Tower, The Rectory, and The Priest, turn right or south on Castle Valley Road between mile markers 15 and 16. Follow the narrow, paved road for 4.7 miles to a parking area on the left side of the road. This is the trailhead parking for the Castleton Tower Trail. Hike up a shallow slot canyon and up a small hill. Drop right to an old road and reach the obvious trail. Follow up the steep talus slopes to the base of Castleton Tower. The trail is about 1.5 miles long and takes an hour of hiking to the tower base.

To reach Sister Superior, continue driving on Utah 128 past Castle Valley Road and Parriott Mesa, a large mesa south of the highway. After about a mile, locate a rough road that goes south up Ida Gulch just before a white bridge. This road may be gated and locked, in which case you will have to park off the highway. Walk or drive up the road for about 1.5 miles. Look for a large cairn where the road bends right into the wash. The cairn marks the start of the access trail. Follow the trail up the talus slopes to the base of the towers. If it's possible to drive as far as the first cairn, allow up to an hour for the walking approach. If the road is closed and you have to walk up the road, allow 1.5 to 2 hours to reach the base of Sister Superior.

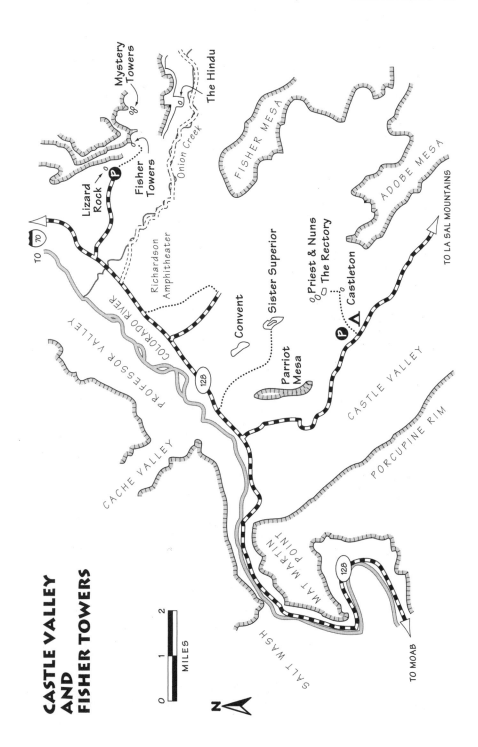

CASTLE VALLEY AND FISHER TOWERS

Mystery Towers

The Hindu

FISHER MESA

ADOBE MESA

Onion Creek

Fisher Towers

Lizard Rock

TO 70

Richardson Amphitheater

PROFESSOR VALLEY

COLORADO RIVER

Convent

Sister Superior

Parriot Mesa

Priest & Nuns
The Rectory

Castleton

TO LA SAL MOUNTAINS

128

CASTLE VALLEY

PORCUPINE RIM

CACHE VALLEY

MAT MARTIN POINT

SALT WASH

128

TO MOAB

N

MILES

0   1   2

CASTLETON TOWER

This square, 400-foot-high tower, called Castle Rock on USGS maps, is the most famous of Utah's many sandstone pinnacles. It sits atop a 1,000-foot-high cone of banded cliffs broken by steep scree- and boulder-strewn slopes. The tower is composed of Wingate sandstone coated with white deposits of calcite. The abundance of calcite on Castleton and nearby cliffs results from hydrothermal activity, which also resulted in the formation of the LaSal mountains.

To reach Castleton Tower from Moab, leave town on U.S. Highway 191 North and drive a couple of miles to its junction with Utah 128, River Road. Turn right on Utah 128 and follow it for just over 15 miles to the Castle Valley turnoff. Turn right on this route and wind up Porcupine Canyon west of Parriott Mesa. At approximately 1.5 miles enter Castle Valley, a broad valley rimmed by cliffs and mesas. A short dirt road goes left or east after 4.7 miles to a parking area and popular primitive campsite. Park here. A designated trail built by the American Mountain Foundation begins at the parking area. Hike through a small slot canyon to an old road that leads to the trail. Follow the trail upward for about an hour to the saddle north of Castleton and the base of the North Face. Access Castleton's routes by following a rocky ledge around to the south side. Access The Rectory and The Priest by hiking north on a trail along a ridge.

1. **Kor-Ingalls Route** (III 5.9) 4 pitches. Ultra-classic desert tower route first climbed by Layton Kor and Huntley Ingalls, 1961. This line probably sees more action than any other tower. Use extreme caution on the route if other parties are ahead of you or descending. As on any sandstone cliff, loose rock abounds and can severely dent your head. A hard hat is a good idea. It usually takes 4 pitches to climb this route. It follows a system of left-facing corners up Castleton's south face. Begin on the strata ledge on left side of the south face. **Pitch 1:** Climb crack (5.5) on right side of leaning pillar to squeeze chimney (5.4). Belay on a spacious ledge from a 2 bolt anchor; 140'. **Pitch 2:** Jam right-hand of 2 crack systems (in a left-facing corner) to good ledge with 2 bolts; 100'. **Pitch 3:** Work up off-width crack in large left-facing dihedral (crux 5.9) past some funky bolts to ledge by huge flake; 100'. Off-width section may also be liebacked. **Pitch 4:** Chimney behind flake before exiting left on face moves (5.7) to summit; 70'. **Descent:** Make 4 rappels down the route or preferably two 200' double-rope rappels or four 100' rappels down the north face. Because of the amount of traffic on the route, it is best to make the rappels from chained anchors down the north face to avoid congestion. The south face rappels can be busy with ascending and descending parties sharing the same sets of anchors. Have some humor and make the best of what can be an epic situation. Also take care not to dislodge rocks onto climb-

ers below. South face rappels—**Rap 1:** One 70' rappel from summit bolts to ledge. **Rap 2:** 2-rope rappel 100' down crux dihedral to ledge. **Rap 3:** 2-rope rappel 100' to first belay ledge. **Rap 4:** 2-rope rappel 140' to base of route. **Rack:** Medium and large stoppers, 2 sets of Friends to #3, some large TCUs, and runners.

2. **Black Sun** (III 5.10b) 4 pitches. A good but harder alternative to *Kor-Ingalls*. Begin at the same place as *Kor-Ingalls*. **Pitch 1:** Same first pitch as *Kor-Ingalls* to belay ledge; 140'. **Pitch 2:** Move up left into fist crack (5.8) in right-facing corner. Belay on small ledge on left; 60'. **Pitch 3:** Continue up fist crack (5.9+) to off-width (5.10) over small roof. Use off-width and fist crack to reach chockstone. Tunnel behind or turn it on left (5.10) and belay on ledge just left of last belay stance on *Kor-Ingalls*. **Pitch 4:** Jam a crack system (5.8) just left of *Kor-Ingalls* last pitch to summit anchors. **Descent:** Two 200' double-rope rappels or four 100' rappels down the north face or four 2-rope rappels down the *Kor-Ingalls Route*. **Rack:** 2 sets of Friends, a couple of #4 and #5 Camalots or #6 and #7 Tri-cams.

3. **Burning Inside** (III 5.11b) A good airy 4-pitch route that shares 2 pitches of *Black Sun*. Begin on strata ledge right of *Kor-Ingalls* and large blocky roof. **Pitch 1:** Climb small corner past a couple of horizontal cracks to left-facing, left-leaning corner. Lieback and stem up to crux moves that go left around a small roof (5.11b) and head up crack above *Kor-Ingalls* belay ledge. **Pitch 2:** Climb the first pitch of *Black Sun*, fist and off-width crack (5.8) up right-facing corner to belay stance on left. **Pitch 3:** Climb pitch 3 of *Black Sun*. Continue up increasingly difficult crack system. Fist to off-width to flare to chockstone. Belay on ledge atop the pod. **Pitch 4:** Follow thin, exposed crack system up left past several bolts (5.10). A 5.10d section is encountered before double horizontal cracks. Belay on summit. **Descent:** Two 200', 2-rope rappels or four 100' rappels down north face. **Rack:** 1 set of wired stoppers; TCUs—3 #.4, 2 #.5, and 3 #.75; Friends—3 #1, 2 #1.5, 2 #2, 1 #2.5, and 1 #3.

4. **The Arrowhead** (III 5.10+ C1) 4 pitches. First ascent by Ed Webster and Chester Dreiman, 1982. This line ascends the left side of an arrowhead-shaped flake on the right side of the south face. The first pitch makes a harder alternative start to the *Kor-Ingalls*. Begin right of the *Kor-Ingalls* on the wide ledge. **Pitch 1:** Jam short left-facing corner to roof and horizontal crack. Climb out right side of roof (5.8+) and jam up calcite-covered dihedral to off-width section (5.9). Belay above on good ledge just right of *Kor-Ingalls* belay. **Pitch 2:** Jam and stem (some 5.10d) up left side of The Arrowhead for long pitch to 2-bolt belay atop flake. **Pitch 3:** Aid up long bolt ladder (C1) on glistening white calcite wall to belay ledge. **Pitch 4:** Climb up right (5.8) and behind large detached flake to a notch. Belay here or continue another 40' to summit. You can also traverse up

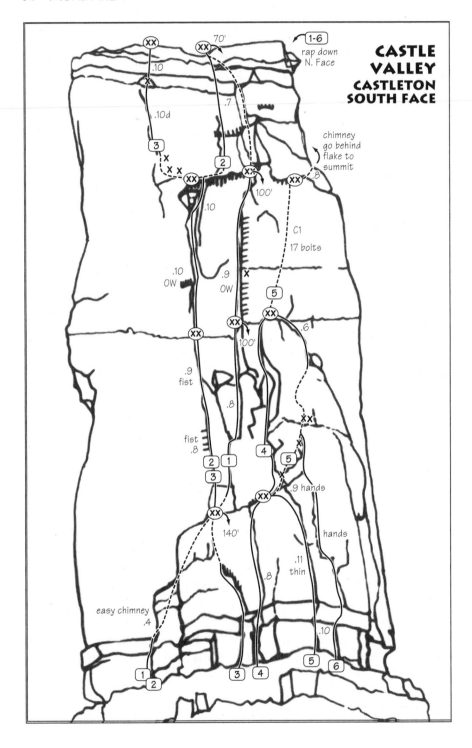

CASTLE
VALLEY
CASTLETON
SOUTH FACE

1-6
rap down
N. Face

70'

.10

.10d

.7

chimney
go behind
flake to
summit

.10

100'

C1

17 bolts

.10
OW

.9
OW

.6

.9
fist

.8

fist
.8

140'

.9 hands

hands

easy chimney
.4

.8

.11
thin

.10

left (5.8) from the belay to last pitch of *Kor-Ingalls Route*. **Descent:** Three 2-rope rappels down north face. **Rack:** A couple of sets of Friends and some wide crack gear. Some aiders are needed for bolt ladder.

5. **Stardust Cowboy** (III 5.11a C1) 4 pitches. An excellent route, put up by Ed Webster and Chester Dreiman, that joins *The Arrowhead* atop the flake. Begin right of Route 4. **Pitch 1:** Climb cracks (5.10) to small roof, pull over and jam crack (5.11a) to another roof. Jam over and continue up hand crack (5.9) to same belay stance as Route 4 on large ledge. **Pitch 2:** From far right side of ledge, face climb up right (5.8) to thin flake on *The Arrowhead*. Lieback the delicate flake (5.10) to 2-bolt belay atop *The Arrowhead*. **Pitch 3 & 4:** Same pitches as *The Arrowhead*. **Descent:** Three 2-rope rappels down north face. **Rack:** 2 sets of Friends, a set of TCUs, some medium and large stoppers, runners, and aiders.

6. **Hollow Point** (5.11c/d) A good 1-pitch route that joins the second pitch of *Stardust Cowboy*. Begin right of Route 5 on ledge. Jam a corner to small roof at first horizontal crack, pull over and continue up thin right-facing corner (5.11d) to roof. Work left and finish up hand crack to 2-bolt belay stance on sloping ledge in middle of Route 5's second pitch. Continue up *Stardust Cowboy* to summit. **Descent:** Three 2-rope rappels down the north face. **Rack:** TCUs—3 #.4, 3 #.5, 3 #.75, Friends—2 #1, 2 #1.5, 2 #2, 2 #2.5, 2 #3, and 2 #3.5, and a selection of wired stoppers. Bring aiders to continue to summit.

These routes begin on the far left or east side of the north face. Reach the start by hiking around to the north side of the tower and scrambling up from the saddle between Castleton and The Rectory to a ledge below the North Face. This ledge, traversing the entire pinnacle, offers access to all of Castleton's routes.

7. **North Chimney** (III 5.9) 4 pitches. First ascent by Daniel Burgette and Allen Erickson, 1970. An excellent, popular route that is a good alternative to the *Kor-Ingalls Route*. Start about 40' left of the *North Face* route. **Pitch 1:** Jam sustained, vertical hand cracks (5.8 & 5.9) to crux bulge; 130'. Belay 10' higher at small stance with piton. **Pitch 2:** Jam an off-width crack (5.9-) and some cracks into a moderate chimney. Continue past bolt to belay in back of chimney; 135'. **Pitch 3:** Work upward through the 5.8 chimney (hard hat is advisable for belayer because of loose rock) to notch (step across chimney into notch) between main tower and large, detached flake. Belay here. **Pitch 4:** Join *Kor-Ingalls Route* and face-climb (5.7) up left on south face for 40' to summit anchors. **Descent:** Rappel north face with three 2-rope rappels. **Rack:** 2 sets of Friends with extra #3 and #3.5, a set of TCUs, and lots of runners. #4 Camalot may be useful.

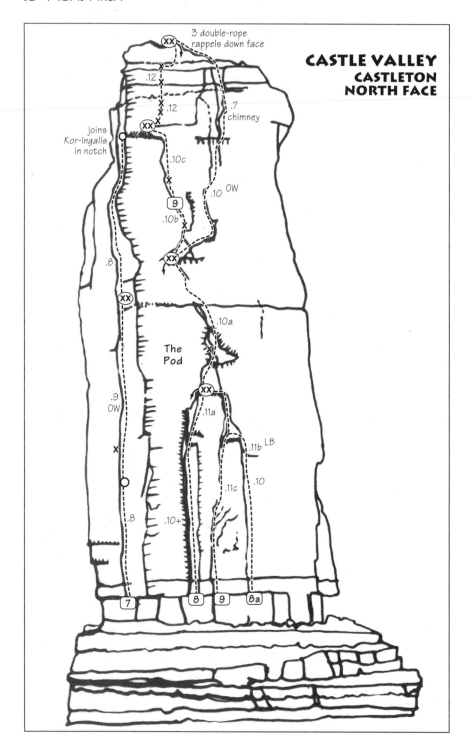

3 double-rope
rappels down face

CASTLE VALLEY
CASTLETON
NORTH FACE

.12

.12

.7
chimney

joins
Kor-Ingalls
in notch

.10c

.10 OW

9

.10b

.8

.10a

The
Pod

.9
OW

.11a

.11b LB

.11c   .10

.8   .10+

7   8   9   8a

8. **North Face** (III 5.11a) 3 pitches. First ascent by Jim Dunn and Doug Snively, 1973. A wild and exposed route up the steep north face. Scramble up the ledge at the base of the face and find a thin, right-facing corner on the left side of the face. The first pitch climbs the *Webster–Norden Variation* pitch. The original route climbed a 5.10 hand-crack to a 5.11b lieback to the right (See Route 8A on the topo). **Pitch 1:** Jam hand crack (5.10+) up corner and past small roof to the corner's end. Undercling right (5.11a) or jam finger crack straight up then left (5.11a) to belay stance with 2 bolts. **Pitch 2:** Climb crack (5.9) into The Pod and exit over roof (5.10a hands). Continue up left on flakes and ledges (5.7) to 2-bolt belay on ledge. **Pitch 3:** Move up right on flakes to off-width crack (5.10). Higher work right (5.10-) into chimney (5.7) that emerges on summit. **Descent:** Rappel the route with three 2-rope rappels. **Rack:** 2 sets of Friends with 3 #3 and 5 #3.5.

9. **Castles Burning** (III 5.12a/b) 4 pitches. First ascent by Jay Smith. This excellent, modern route shares the second pitch of the *North Face* route. Begin just right of *North Face*. **Pitch 1:** Jam and lieback thin flake-crack (5.11c) to 2-bolt belay ledge. **Pitch 2:** Climb up right (5.9) into The Pod. Exit via a roof hand crack (5.10a) and work up left to 2-bolt belay. **Pitch 3:** Short pitch. Face climb past bolt (5.10b) to gain crack in shallow right-facing corner. Jam corner past another bolt (5.10c) to shelf with a 2-bolt belay. **Pitch 4:** Another short pitch. Spectacular face climbing (two 5.12 sections) leads up calcite veneer past 5 bolts to 2 horizontal cracks. Traverse right and onto the summit. **Descent:** Three 2-rope rappels down the north face. **Rack:** Lots of thin stuff. Bring a couple of sets of TCUs and Friends to #2.5.

10. **West Face** (III 5.11b) 4 pitches. First ascent by Jim Dunn, Bill Westbay, and Stewart Green, 1971. This route ascends the only crack system on Castleton's west face. Find the start by scrambling up to the base of the north face and following a ledge system right to the west face. **Pitch 1:** Climb broken cracks left of large roof to loose, blocky section (5.9). Continue over roof (5.9+) to small belay stance with fixed anchors. **Pitch 2:** Jam dramatic V-shaped corner (5.8+) lined with calcite to belay stance atop pedestal. **Pitch 3:** Squeeze up chimney (5.9+) which becomes 5-inch crack. Lieback the crack (5.11b) to point where short face traverse heads right to very exposed hand crack. Jam to a belay ledge in cave. **Pitch 4:** Chimney up slot above which narrows to wide crack. Arm bar upward (5.10a) to roof. Work left into short right-facing corner which gains summit. **Descent:** Three 2-rope rappels down north face. **Rack:** 2 sets of Friends with extra #2.5 to #3.5 and a couple of large Camalots.

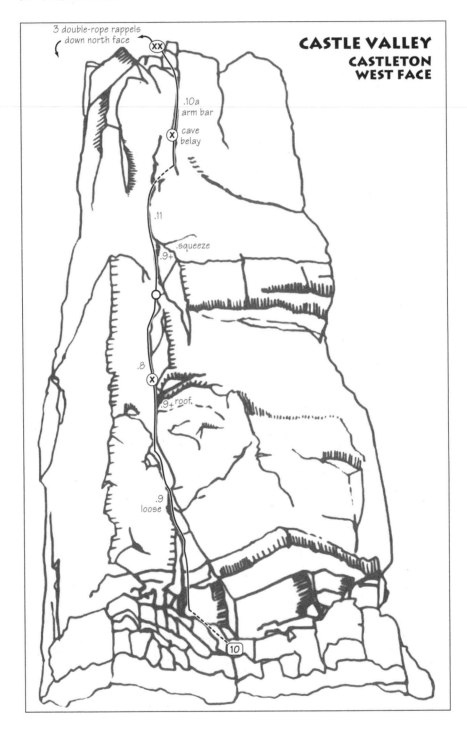

3 double-rope rappels
down north face

CASTLE VALLEY
CASTLETON
WEST FACE

.10a
arm bar

cave
belay

.11

.squeeze

.9+

.8

.9+ roof

.9
loose

Buck Norden on the first free ascent of North Face, Castleton Tower *(1979).*
ED WEBSTER, MOUNTAIN IMAGERY PHOTO

THE RECTORY

The Rectory is a long, narrow, flat-topped mesa immediately north of Castleton Tower. This sky island is walled with vertical cliffs of Wingate sandstone and capped by an erosion-resistant layer of Kayenta sandstone. This isolated landform, perched high atop talus slopes, was first climbed by Cleve McCarty and Harvey Carter in 1962 via *Empirical Route*. Later routes were put up in the 1980s and 1990s, including the crag's mega-classic line, *Fine Jade*. This superb crack route, on the narrow south face, was first climbed by Chip Chace and Pat Ellinwood in six pitches in 1984. It is the most popular route on The Rectory for good reasons. The cracks are excellent, the belays are all good, and the cruxes are short.

Fine Jade and *Empirical Route* are both equipped for descents. Make two rappels down *Empirical* or three rappels down *Fine Jade*. The Nuns are two semi-detached towers at the far north end of The Rectory. The Priest is a separate free-standing pinnacle sitting just north of The Nuns. Approach The Rectory by hiking up the Castleton Tower trail to the base of Castleton's north face. A trail follows sharp Castle Ridge north a quarter-mile to the base of *Fine Jade* on The Rectory's thin south face. The west face routes as well as The Nuns and The Priest are accessed by a trail along the base of the cliff.

11. **Fine Jade** (III 5.11a) 4 pitches. A classic and excellent route up a crack line on the south prow of The Rectory first climbed by Chip Chace and Pat Ellinwood, 1984. Approach by walking north on a trail from Castleton Tower to the south prow of the formation. Scramble atop a pedestal at the base of the route. **Pitch 1:** Jam off-width/fist crack up and over a bulge (5.10d). Continue up to small roof. Old, 2-bolt belay is off left. Pull roof and continue up hands (5.10) to fingers crack (5.10d) to bolted belay on small ledge. **Pitch 2:** Jam thin crack to horizontal break. Above is sustained finger crack (5.11a) that eases higher. Belay on good ledge from bolts. **Pitch 3:** Climb up right on sandy rock via lieback crack to loose section (5.9). Climb over small roof and belay on large ledge from bolt anchor. **Pitch 4:** 2 ways to go: (1) Traditional finish climbs short corner and makes spectacular hand traverse left (5.7) to off-width crack (5.8). Head left under roof (5.9+) and exit onto summit. Place good directional pro with long runners if you do traverse and off-width in 1 pitch to avoid rope drag. (2) Direct finish climbs the short corner and face climbs (5.11a) past 4 bolts to the summit. **Descent:** 3 rappels down route. Watch for loose rocks. **Rap 1:** 75-foot rappel to 2-bolt anchor on final belay ledge. **Rap 2:** 2-rope rappel down to first belay stance. **Rap 3:** 2-rope rappel to ground. **Rack:** 2 sets of Friends with extra #1.5, set of TCUs, medium and large wire stoppers, and a few runners.

12. **Crack Wars** (III 5.11) 4 pitches. This fine route, put up by Charlie Fowler and Glenn Randall, 1982, ascends the left side of the west face of The

CASTLE VALLEY
THE RECTORY

rap route

.11
face

.9+

.7

no anchors

.9

.11a
fingers

.10

.10d
hands

OW

11

Rectory. Approach from Castleton Tower by working north along a cliff-base footpath to a prominent crack system up the white calcite wall. Begin atop a block below the crack. **Pitch 1:** Jam thin hands crack (5.10+) that slowly widens to hands and fists. Belay on ledge to left from 2 bolts. **Pitch 2:** Continue up off-width crack (5.10) to belay stance. **Pitch 3:** Jam hand crack (5.9) to slot through roof (5.11). Climb through rotten rock to belay on left. **Pitch 4:** Jam finger crack (5.9) up obvious right-facing corner to summit. **Descent:** Two long 2-rope rappels down route or rappel *Empirical Route* or *Fine Jade*. **Rack:** 2 sets of Friends along with some wide crack pro.

13. **Empirical Route** (III 5.9) 2 pitches. This route offers one good pitch and one funky pitch. Unless you really want to mount The Rectory, it's best just to do the first pitch and rap off. The route follows a chimney system left of *Crack Wars* that separates The Rectory from The Nuns. Scramble onto a bouldery ledge to begin. **Pitch 1:** Best pitch on route. Chimney and jam up long, secure chimney (5.8) for full-rope length to 2-bolt chained anchor on ledge at notch between The Nuns and The Rectory. Cracks in chimney allow for good protection. Rap from here or continue. **Pitch 2:** Sometimes divided into 2 shorter pitches to alleviate rope drag. Jam obvious 20-foot hand crack (5.9) with calcite ribbon on its lip. Pro feels somewhat insecure in this crack. Above, climb a "muddy groove thing" (5.8R) to final chimney. 2-bolt chained anchor on top. **Descent:** Rappel route with two 2-rope rappels from chained anchors. **Rack:** 2 sets of Friends with extra hand-sizes, set of TCUs, wired stoppers, and runners.

14. **Where Have The Wild Things Gone** (II 5.11) 2 pitches. This route ascends a crack system between the 2 Nuns on the west face of The Rectory. Begin below an obvious right-facing dihedral. The left wall is coated with white calcite. **Pitch 1:** Jam crack (5.9) on right side of pillar; 25'. Lieback up steep corner (5.11) to 2-bolt hanging belay. **Pitch 2:** Jam continuous finger crack (5.11) to easier climbing that leads to notch between The Nuns. Traverse ledge system around north side of second Nun to 2-bolt chained anchor atop *Empirical Route*'s first pitch. **Descent:** One 2-rope rappel down *Empirical Route*. **Rack:** Set of TCUs, stoppers, and Friends— 2 #1, 4 #1.5 to #3, 1 #3.5, and 1 #4.

THE PRIEST

The Priest is a distinctive 330-foot-high pinnacle sitting at the north end of The Rectory and The Nuns north of Castleton Tower. From a distance, particularly the northeast, the tower looks remarkably like a cowled priest blessing this austere land of sun, rock, and wind. Approach The Priest by hiking up to Castleton Tower and following the trail northward along the narrow ridge to The Rectory and skirting it's west face.

CASTLE VALLEY
THE RECTORY

rap

85'

route hidden
on notrh face

.9
fingers

traverse ledge on
east side to rappel

.11 slot

.9
hands

65'

.11

.10+

.8
chimney

.10-
OW

The Priest

XX

.11
LB
fingers

.10+
hands

15

.9

14

13

12

15. **Honeymoon Chimney** (III 5.11b or 5.9 A0) 4 pitches. Route ascends west face of The Priest. Route can be done in 2 pitches with 200' (60-meter) rope. Begin by scrambling north along broad ledge below face to base of chimney. **Pitch 1:** Climb off-width crack with arm bars or liebacks on left side of large flake below chimney. A drilled angle and 0.25-inch bolt protect moves. Continue up unprotected off-width (5.9) 40' to wedged chockstone with slings. Enter squeeze chimney above and tunnel upwards (5.7) to flat belay ledge inside; 120'. **Pitch 2:** Follow chimney (5.7) another 70' to belay ledge with bolts on west face. A drilled angle and some pro placements protect chimney. **Pitch 3:** Work up widening chimney, eventually stemming between main tower and subsidiary summit. Clip up old bolt ladder to new bolt. From here step onto main tower and face climb (5.11b or A0) arête to narrow edge with loose blocks. Traverse up left (5.7) to good 2-bolt belay stance; 80'. **Pitch 4:** Work up left around corner before finishing up shallow left-facing corner (5.8) to summit; 70'. Direct

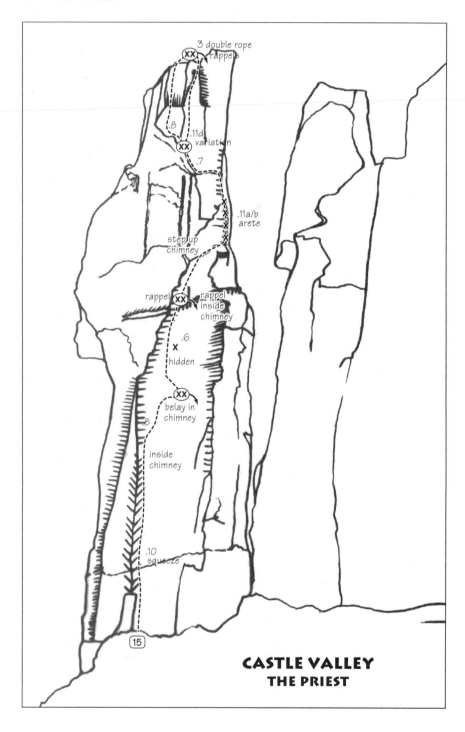

3 double rope rappels

.8

.11d variation

XX

.7

X
X
X   .11a/b
X   arete
X

step up chimney

rappel   XX   rappel inside chimney

.6
X
hidden

XX
belay in chimney

.8

inside chimney

.10 squeeze

15

CASTLE VALLEY
THE PRIEST

finish jams thin crack (5.11d) up calcite headwall above belay ledge. **Descent:** Three 2-rope rappels (with 165' ropes) to ground. **Rap 1:** 150' from summit to 2-bolt anchors atop pitch 2. **Rap 2:** 70' down chimney to ledge and anchors on pitch 1. **Rap 3:** 130' down chimney on east side of tower to ground. Make 2 rappels with 200' ropes, first to anchors atop pitch 2, and second, down east-side chimney to ground. **Rack:** A #.75 TCU, a couple of sets of Friends, wires, and a dozen quickdraws.

SISTER SUPERIOR

Sister Superior is the highest pinnacle of a group of towers on the ridge about a mile north of Castleton Tower and The Rectory. The main towers, from south to north, are Sister Superior, North Sister, Chimney Spire, and Baby Sister. All the towers have been climbed, but Sister Superior is by far the finest of the group and offers the best and longest routes. *Jah Man*, first ascended by Ken Trout and Kirk Miller in 1984, is one of the canyon country's finest tower routes, with short pitches, short cruxes, and an easy rappel descent. Moab local Lisa Hathaway calls it "one of the coolest tower routes ever!"

You can easily spot the towers from River Road on the ridge north of Castleton. The easiest approach is to drive east on Utah Highway 128 past the Castle Valley turnoff to a white highway bridge. Park here. Just west of the bridge is a rough road that heads south between Parriott Mesa, the large mesa on the right, and The Convent, the smaller mesa on the left. The road, which may or may not be open to vehicular travel, heads south up Ida Gulch. After about 1.5 miles, look for a large cairn where the road bends right into the wash. The cairn marks the start of the access trail. Follow the cairned trail up the talus slopes to the base of the towers. Stay on the trail to avoid damaging the cryptobiotic soil that covers the ground surface along the way. If it's possible to drive as far as the first cairn, allow up to an hour for the approach. If the road is closed and you have to walk up the road, allow 1.5 to 2 hours to reach the base of Sister Superior.

16. **Jah Man** (III 5.10b/c) 5 pitches. This excellent route ascends the southwest face of Sister Superior. **Pitch 1:** Face climb (a 5.9 move) up and right about 20' and traverse right to base of obvious chimney; 40'. **Pitch 2:** Squeeze (5.8) up the obvious chimney (The Sister Squeeze) in large left-facing corner to belay ledge up right; 50'. **Pitch 3:** The crux lead. Jam thin hand cracks up hollow flake in shallow left-facing corner to old bolt that protects 5.10+ move left. Above work up easier corner to good belay ledge. **Pitch 4:** Work up left into splitter small hands crack (5.10b/c) and continue to spacious belay ledge on right shoulder; 100'. **Pitch 5:** Face climb (5.9+) to the summit past drilled angles; 30'. **Descent:** Rappel the route. 5 rappels with a single 165' rope from belay ledge to belay ledge. One of the beauties of this route is that it can be climbed with a single

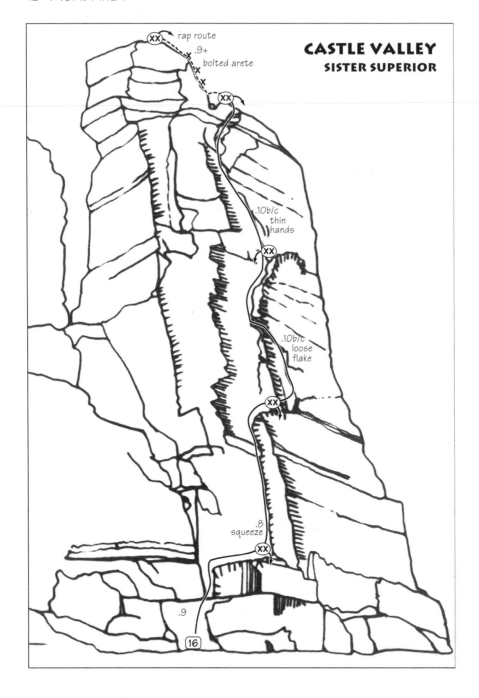

rap route

.9+
bolted arete

CASTLE VALLEY
SISTER SUPERIOR

.10b/c
thin
hands

.10b/c
loose
flake

.8
squeeze

.9

16

Carol Petrelli leads the fourth pitch of Jah Man, *Sister Superior, Castle Valley.*
PHOTO BY EARL WIGGINS

rope. **Rack:** 2 sets of Friends to #3, including at least 5 #3 Friends for pitch 4, wired stoppers, runners, and quickdraws. A #.75 TCU is handy for crux on pitch 3.

17. **Savior** (III 5.11c R) 3 pitches. No topo. This good route, free-climbed by Marco Cornacchione in 1995, ascends the opposite or northeast side of Sister Superior from *Jah Man.* It's fairly straightforward. **Pitch 1:** Arm bar up an off-width crack (5.9) before traversing way right to alcove belay. **Pitch 2:** Jam splitter finger to hand crack past some dangerous flakes and a couple of old aid bolts. Work up left to corner and belay on ledge on shoulder. **Pitch 3:** Same last pitch as *Jah Man.* Face climb (5.9+) past drilled pitons to summit. **Descent:** Rappel down *Jah Man.* **Rack:** Friends to #4 with extras in mid-sizes. Some large Camalots are useful. Set of TCUs.

FISHER TOWERS

OVERVIEW

The Fisher Towers, looming above the Colorado River east of Moab, form one of Utah's most strange and intriguing landscapes. Here, on the eastern edge of the broad Richardson Amphitheater, hides a remote maze of soaring fins, pinnacles, minarets, gargoyles, and towers—all composed of some of the most hideous sandstone imaginable. Huntley Ingalls, writing in *National Geographic* in 1962 after the first ascent of The Titan, called the Fishers "a pink, red, and orange skyscraper city in nightmare Gothic." The towers, soaring monuments to erosion, are composed of dark red Cutler sandstone topped by harder Moenkopi sandstone and draped with mud curtains.

For rock climbers, the Fisher Towers are a place of both inspiration and terror. The large spires are gigantic and intimidating. The tallest, The Titan, reaches some 900 feet from base to summit. At first glance the towers appear very climbable, with features, ledges, chimneys, and crack systems, but don't be fooled. These climbs are serious mud affairs that last for days. Expect at least 2 days of climbing on any Fisher Grade IV or V route. The sandstone, despite its nightmarish exterior, is fairly solid and dependable under the mud, but good protection is often hard to find and the cracks are generally bottoming and incipient. The exposure and fear factor on most Fisher routes is tremendous—lots of hanging belays and big air, funky belay bolts, scary rappels, and mud and dirt that manage to fill every pore, crevice, and crack in your body. Some climbers even wear safety goggles to keep the grit out of their eyes. Still, the Fisher Towers are certainly accessible to big wall climbers tired of the Yosemite scene and ready to move onto wilder terrain.

Almost all the routes in the Fishers are big aid lines that require multi-day ascents and big racks. Few of the routes are clean aid; for those that are clean, you need cunning and skill to meet their sandy challenges. This guidebook does not cover any traditional hammer-aid routes in the Fishers; it covers the best of the Fisher Towers' free climbing routes as well as a couple of big-wall aid routes that are all clean. Too much indiscriminate nailing has virtually destroyed the classic *Finger of Fate* route on The Titan and has ruined many of the placements on the King Fisher, although it goes clean now. Check Eric Bjørnstad's forthcoming comprehensive *Moab Rock East* guide for topos and info on most of the Fisher Tower aid routes. For those intrepid aiders who've exhausted the possibilities of the Fisher Towers, check out the Mystery Towers a couple of canyons to the east. These towers, including The Doric Column, The Gothic Nightmare, and The Citadel, are similar in size to the Fishers but tend to be looser, muddier, and scarier. Be prepared to excavate bolts buried by mud or replace ones almost completely eroded out. Also nearby is The Hindu, an excellent, slender spire perched above Onion Creek. While its two routes both go free at 5.12 and 5.13 respectively, they both still have piton placements so they are not included in this guide. Stevie Haston, who freed the south face route, feels continued bashing by nailers will destroy the route as a free climb.

Climbing history: The Fisher Towers were one of the canyon country's first technical climbing areas. Pioneer climbers were fascinated by these odd mud towers and their sheer size. The Titan, the largest and tallest of the towers, was the first to be climbed. Huntley Ingalls, a geologist who encountered the Fishers on a survey, scoped out the tower in 1961 and approached the National Geographic Society about supporting an expedition to climb it. On returning home to Boulder from Moab, he was surprised to find a check in the mailbox for $300 to finance the attempt. After a slide show and some cajoling, Ingalls enlisted one of the most prolific desert climbers, 6-foot, 4-inch Layton Kor and George Hurley, an English professor at the University of Colorado. In May 1962, after reconnoitering The Titan, the trio settled on a route up the east flank and north ridge of the tower. Over the course of a couple of weekends, they pushed the route up crack systems to the Finger of Fate, an obvious finger spire poised on an airy ridgeline. An exposed traverse took them under the finger to some exciting moves that led onto the upper ridges. After a chilly bivouac, Kor began drilling a tedious ladder of bolts up the ridge toward the summit and by noon the party was perched atop the tower's summit, eating lunch. After the cursory summit photos and a fly-by photo by *National Geographic* photographer Barry Bishop, they began the frightening rappels back down. Their ascent also marked the first American climb to use jumars, a European rope ascender, instead of prussik knots.

A week after the Ingalls ascent of The Titan, another Colorado team of Cleve McCarty and Harvey Carter arrived in anticipation of snagging its first ascent. After learning it was just climbed, they turned their attention to the King Fisher, the second tallest tower. Their *Northeast Ridge Route* (V 5.8 C3) is today a popular classic with lots of bolts and exposure, and minimal commitment. It also goes all clean. Echo Tower was first climbed in 1966 by the party of Fred Beckey, Eric Bjørnstad, and Carter. Immense Cottontail Tower was ascended by a Colorado Springs party that included Art Howells, Don Doucette, and Mike Dudley in 1967. Ed Webster did the solo first ascent of *Brer Rabbit* (VI 5.9 A4) up Cottontail's airy west ridge in 1978. The Boulder team of Paul Sibley and Bill Roos made the first ascent of Ancient Art's cork-

Betsi McKittrick atop Ancient Art, *Fisher Towers.* PHOTO BY JIM DUNN

screw summit in 1969, while Jim Dunn had the honors on The Cobra. On its first ascent, Dunn, in lieu of a long runner, substituted a dog leash as a tie-off around the thin spire.

After all the main summits had been reached, bold climbers turned their attention to the serious, overhanging faces on the towers. Soloist Jim Beyer stands out as the one who brought really hard aid to the Fishers with his landmark ascents of such heinous routes as *The Jagged Edge* and *Death of American Democracy* on The King Fisher, *Run Amok* and the now classic *Phantom Spirit* on Echo Tower, and *World's End* on The Titan. All except *Phantom Spirit* sport scary aid placements, minimal bolts for aid and anchors, and severe fall potential. Other modern aid routes have since been put up by Pete Takeda and Duane Raleigh, including *Dead Again* on the west side of King Fisher. The pair used some unconventional tactics on this route including an ice axe for dry-tooling up the mud curtains. The late Rob Slater was the first to reach the summits of all 23 of the Fisher Towers and the 4 adjacent Mystery Towers in 1993 after a marathon six months of commuting every weekend from Boulder to finish his mission. The first of the big towers to be climbed all-free was *Phantom Spirit* on Echo Tower by Englishman Stevie Haston in 1997. He also eliminated all but a few aid moves on The Titan in 1996; Jim Dunn previously freed most of Echo Tower in 1995.

The Fisher Towers are easy to reach from Moab via River Road and a marked dirt track that works southeast to a BLM picnic area on the north side of the tower maze. A trail works south from here, winding through sharp arroyos below the looming sandstone walls. After two miles the trail reaches a lofty viewpoint on slickrock benches above Onion Creek's tortured canyon. Climbers can reach all the towers via the trail.

Spring and fall are the best seasons for climbing in the Fishers as they are everywhere in the canyon country. Spring months, March through May, offer a variety of weather with rain, sleet, snow, and brilliant sunshine. Also expect wind. Nights can be cold here at 6,000'. October and November bring calmer conditions, but the days can still be scorching. Bring lots of water to keep hydrated. Summers are too hot to climb on the big walls. Best to stick to the small towers early in the morning when they're still shaded. Winters are cold, windy, and usually miserable, although prolonged high pressures can bring excellent weather.

Prospective climbers need to be skilled at aid climbing and prepared for any emergency. Objective dangers abound here. First and foremost are loose rock and mud. Wear a hard hat. The coarse sandstone can be very abrasive on your hands. Tape helps protect them while nailing or jumaring. Fixed anchors at belays and rappel stations may be suspect, especially on older, infrequently-climbed lines. Never rely on a single anchor here. It's wise on these older Fisher routes to carry a bolt kit and beefy bolts to reinforce belays. The rock also chews up ropes. Use heavy-duty static rope for any fixed pitches. Check

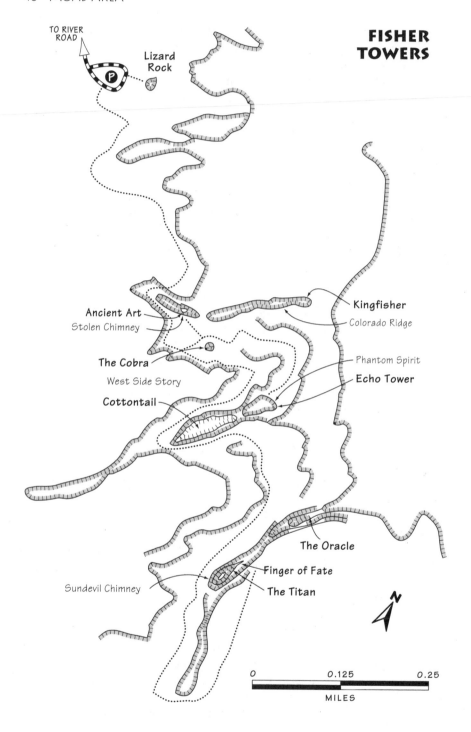

FISHER TOWERS

TO RIVER ROAD

Lizard Rock

Ancient Art
Stolen Chimney

The Cobra

West Side Story

Cottontail

Kingfisher

Colorado Ridge

Phantom Spirit

Echo Tower

The Oracle

Sundevil Chimney

Finger of Fate

The Titan

0   0.125   0.25

MILES

all fixed lines for sheath damage before jumaring or rappelling. A pair of goggles helps keep the grit out of your eyes.

Rack: For the free-climbing routes listed here, bring a small rack of Friends, hexes, and stoppers. Some big crack cams are generally useful. Most of these routes have adequate fixed gear. Aid climbers should come armed for bear. Fisher aid racks are big, with multiple sets of cams, stoppers, RPs, Tri-cams for pin scars, Big Bros or the equivalent, and an assortment of pitons from Lost Arrows and Bugaboos to Leepers and stubbie angles. Harder aid routes require trickery like rurps, Birdbeaks, hooks, Lowe Balls, and anything else. Bring at least 100 free carabiners, runners, and several ropes. Try to climb everything as clean as possible and keep the hammer holstered to avoid rock damage. If you can't climb these routes clean, best to keep off them. Indiscriminate nailing and cleaning destroys clean placements and permanently scars the rock. Take care of the stone—it won't grow back!

Trip Planning Information

General description: A group of spectacular sandstone and mudstone towers with numerous long, hard, aid routes and several good free climbs.

Location: East-central Utah. East of Moab.

Camping: The traditional Fishers' campsite is at the BLM picnic area at the Fisher Towers trailhead. Campgrounds are found along River Road (Utah 128) upriver from Moab. A river campground is just up the road, east of the Fisher Towers turn-off. Camp only in designated campgrounds with toilet facilities. No primitive camping is allowed anymore along River Road. Violators will be ticketed by BLM rangers. Primitive camping is available at the parking area below Castleton Tower. Otherwise there are lots of camping options in and around Moab—several private campgrounds as well as BLM campgrounds at Sand Flats. Carry water whenever possible and tote out all your waste and garbage. The desert is a fragile place.

Climbing season: Year-round. Spring and fall are the best seasons. Expect lots of wind in spring along with occasional rain, snow, and sleet. Summers are too hot, although early morning ascents are possible on shorter routes. Winters can be cold, but also offer a number of warm days. Snowfall tends to be light and sporadic.

Restrictions and access issues: None currently. All the routes included here are on BLM public lands. Climbers need to be aware that the rock is very soft, rotten, and fragile. Aid climbing has irreparably damaged most of the formations. All aid climbers should try to use clean gear whenever possible and should be experienced at sandstone aiding. Too many placements are blown by ignorant nailers and cleaners. If you don't know how to practice clean aid, keep off until you do!

Guidebooks: *Classic Desert Climbs* by Fred Knapp, Sharp End Publishing,

1996, has topos and descriptions for the area's popular routes. *500 Select Moab Classics* by Kevin Chase, 1994, is available from the author at Moab Adventure Outfitters. The forthcoming *Moab Rock East* by Eric Bjørnstad, Chockstone Press, 1998, has topos to most of the big routes at the Fishers.

Nearby mountain shops, guide services, and gyms: Moab Adventure Outfitters sells a great selection of gear and clothing and offers climbing classes and a guide service. Rim Cyclery also sells gear, guides, and clothing.

Services: Find all visitor and climber services in Moab, including gas, food, lodging, camping, showers, dining, and groceries.

Emergency services: Call 911. Allen Memorial Hospital, 719 West 400 North, Moab, UT, (801) 259-7191.

Nearby climbing areas: Mystery Towers, The Hindu, Castleton Tower, The Rectory, The Priest, Sister Superior, Wall Street, The King's Hand, Long Canyon, Day Canyon, River Road crags, Lighthouse, Dolomite Tower, Arches National Park, The Bride, Indian Creek Canyon.

Nearby attractions: Colorado River, Deadhorse Point State Park, Arches National Park, La SalMountains, Manti-La Sal National Forest, Colorado River Scenic Byway (Utah 128), Slickrock Bike Trail.

Finding the crags: Drive east from Moab on Utah Highway 128, the River Road, for almost 23 miles to a turnoff marked "Fisher Towers." Follow this narrow dirt road for another 2 miles to the parking area on the north side of the towers. A 2.2-mile hiking trail begins on the south side of the parking lot and winds through the towers to a viewpoint southwest of The Titan.

LIZARD ROCK

This is the 60-foot-high pinnacle sitting just east of the parking lot, picnic area, and toilet. Approach time from car to climb is a minute. Lizard Rock is a great introduction to what Fisher Towers climbing is all about. Consequently this is the only route a lot of climbers do here. The rock is surprisingly solid on the spire. These routes are not good for toproping because the summit anchors are somewhat dicey.

1. **Entry Fee** (5.9- R) Begin on southwest side. Work up past flake (sling for pro) to large horizontal flake-crack. Place a #4 Camalot behind flake to protect crux moves. Stand on flake and move up right (5.9-) to a sloping shelf and easier rock on south side. A bolt is missing here that used to protect these upper moves. Mantle onto the summit. **Descent:** Rappel from multiple anchors 65'. **Rack:** Long runner, #4 Camalot.

2. **Leaping Lizards** (5.10 R, no topo) An Ed Webster direct line up the west flank. This is a good route to climb, but it's runout. Use caution. Start left of Route 1. Follow thin crack to band of pebble knobs. Work into shallow corner and continue up rounded jugs to summit. A couple of old bolts protect route. **Descent:** Rappel 65'. **Rack:** Stoppers, TCUs, quickdraws.

FISHER TOWERS
LIZARD ROCK

Dennis Jump belays Dave Ross up Lizard Rock, *Fisher Towers.* PHOTO BY STEWART GREEN

3. **Entry Lizards** (5.9- R) A combination of the above routes and the best route on the spire. Climb first part of Route 1 to right traverse. Work straight up to summit on unprotected rock. Look for an old, hidden 1/4-inch bolt below summit for pro. Hidden summit hole provides good handhold for graceful mantle onto top. **Descent:** Rappel 65'. **Rack:** #4 Camalot or equivalent, runners.

ANCIENT ART

Ancient Art, the first major formation encountered on the trail, is a grotesquely sharper tower with 3 summits. An excellent moderate route ascends to the highest point, a balanced corkscrew that is the most unusual summit in the canyon country. Ancient Art is on the west end of a long ridge that culminates on the east with the King Fisher. Approach by following the Fisher Towers trail through a series of shallow canyons and along the base of Ancient Art's immense and intimidating southwest face. Continue past the face to a dry wash between Cottontail Tower and Ancient Art. Look left for a small path that scrambles north to the base of the prominent chimney on Ancient Art's south face.

4. **Stolen Chimney** (II 5.11a or 5.8 A0) 5 pitches. First ascent in 1969 by Paul Sibley and Bill Roos. Begin below an obvious chimney. **Pitch 1:** Climb straight up (5.7) using face holds and short hand crack to the chimney/ groove. Pinch pebbles and cobbles (5.11a or A0) past 4 drilled angles to a 2-bolt belay on ledge; 80'. **Pitch 2:** Work up the mud chimney (5.8-5.9) past a couple of drilled angles to bolted belay stance on right. **Pitch 3:** Climb onto huge block and edge up face holds on ridge (5.10+) with 3 bolts to 3-bolt belay atop it; 40'. Top 2 bolts are dubious. **Pitch 4:** A short pitch that balances across "The Sidewalk," a foot-wide ridgetop. Walk or crawl across exposed ridge to "The Diving Board," a jutting tongue of fragile sandstone. Mantle on it (5.8) and belay. **Pitch 5:** Another short pitch. Swing up on good holds (5.8) to corkscrew summit. Bolts offer good pro. Easy to set up summit toprope for the second. Last 2 pitches can be combined. Use runners to avoid rope drag on corkscrew. **Descent:** 3 rappels. Lower or rap off summit, traverse back across The Sidewalk to 3-bolt belay. **Rap 1:** Rappel to anchors at top of pitch 2. **Rap 2:** Rappel to anchors atop pitch 1. **Rap 3:** Rappel to ground. Use 2 ropes for rappels. **Rack:** Set of Friends with extra #1 and #3, quickdraws.

THE COBRA

This small, weird tower rises above the trail between Ancient Art and Cottontail Tower. In profile it resembles a reared cobra with a thin neck and bulbous head. The Cobra is very fragile-looking—be careful not to knock it over! Desert rat Jim Dunn did the first ascent.

slings

.8

x

.10⁻

xxx

FISHER TOWERS
ANCIENT ART

.8

chimney

xx

x   .11a or
AO

.7

4

approach trail

5. **The Cobra** (5.11- R) No topo. Begin on north side of pinnacle. Climb crack to ledge and find some marginal gear placements. Pinch pebbles to sloping ledge and tie off snake's neck with long sling. Crank to drilled piton, mantle onto flat summit; 60'. **Descent:** Rap from 1 drilled piton. **Rack:** Small Friends, stoppers, a long runner.

COTTONTAIL TOWER

Cottontail Tower is an immense 800-foot fin, topped by a rabbit-tail ball, between the King Fisher and The Titan. Several routes ascend the tower, including *Brer Rabbit* up the west ridge, *Road Kill* on the north face, and *West Side Story*, the original route. *West Side Story* is now a clean aid route. Dave Goldstein and Mark Hammond did the first clean ascent in 1995. The cruxes require poorly seated #0.5 Tri-cams and free climbing old aid sections. The route can be done in a day by a fast party skilled at Fisher techniques; otherwise, allow 2 to 3 days. Approach the tower by following the trail past Ancient Art to the base of the north face of Cottontail. Begin directly below the saddle between Cottontail and Echo Tower.

6. **West Side Story** (V or VI 5.9 C3) 10 pitches. First ascent, 1967 by Don Doucette, Mike Dudley, and Art Howells with help from Morgan Gadd, Herbie Hendricks, and Harvey Carter. **Pitch 1:** Climb right-facing corner to cracks (5.9) with old bolts and cams for pro; 130'. **Pitch 2:** Continue up mostly free, flared chimney/crack (5.8) with old bolts to ledge. **Pitch 3:** Climb above ledge 20' to bolt (don't go to upper drilled piton). Tension traverse left into mud groove. Use mixed free and aid (5.8 C2) up groove to junction. Keep right to belay; 100'. **Pitch 4:** Don't nail the blown-out crack above the belay. Instead use clean aid in crack to left. Follow through corner to scary face climbing (5.7) to old bolt ladder. Finish with more unprotected face climbing to saddle and bolted belay. This is a good bivy spot; 100'. **Pitch 5:** Traverse across saddle and aid up (C2+) using old bolts and Tri-cams with some free moves. Watch for rope drag on many of the bulges. **Pitch 6:** Traverse 15' right to fixed Tri-cam. Aid crack with Tri-cams (C2+) to corner (5.9) to belay atop obvious pillar on east ridge. **Pitch 7:** Make scary and exposed traverse right on the north face to fixed piton. Hard aid (C3) leads 25' straight up crack system to bolt ladder. At drilled piton, climb up and right (5.7) to belay stance; 100'. Watch for rope drag! **Pitch 8:** Continue up chimney and off-width crack system (5.9+) to belay station. This chimney slices through the tower; 60'. **Pitch 9:** Finish up chimney (5.7) to base of summit block. Missing a bolt, use small tri-cam for pro; 50'. Pitches 8 and 9 can be combined. **Pitch 10:** Traverse around south side of block to awkward hidden slot (5.9). After 20' use a bolt (C1) to reach #4 Camalot placement that protects final summit moves; 40'. **Descent:** Rappel from summit to anchors at base of summit block.

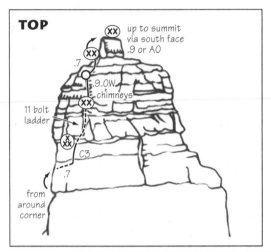

TOP

up to summit
via south face
.9 or A0

.7

.9 OW
chimneys

11 bolt
ladder

C3

.7

from
around
corner

**FISHER
TOWERS
COTTONTAIL
TOWER**

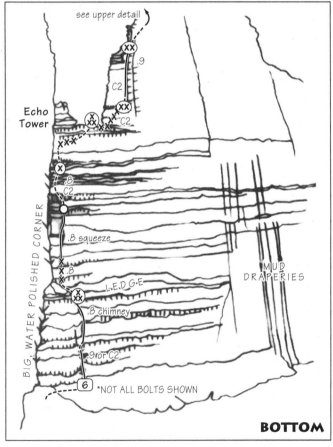

see upper detail

.9

C2

C2

Echo
Tower

.8
C2

.8 squeeze

.8

L·E·D·G·E

MUD
DRAPERIES

B·I·G. W·A·T·E·R P·O·L·I·S·H·E·D C·O·R·N·E·R

.8 chimney

.9 or C2

6   *NOT ALL BOLTS SHOWN

BOTTOM

Continue down the northwest face right of route with multiple rappels from fixed stations. Bring new webbing to reinforce old slings. Scope rappels before you leave the ground. Rappels are a major part of any big Fisher Towers climb and can be a major epic. Don't rap the route—it has bad traverses and pendulums. "It's really bad!" says Goldstein. **Rack:** No pitons. Bring a set of stoppers, 2 sets of Friends, 2 #4 Camalots, 1 #5 Camalot, a set of Lowe Tri-cams (with a filed down #.5), a set of Lowe Balls, and a couple of large hooks.

ECHO TOWER

This is the thin, soaring tower left of Cottontail Tower. Several hard routes ascend Echo Tower, including the original *North Chimney* (IV 5.8 A2) put up by Fred Beckey, Eric Bjørnstad, and Harvey Carter in 1966. Other routes are *Emotional Graffiti* (V 5.9 A4), *The Tape Worm* (V 5.8 A3), *Run Amok* (5.8 A4), and Jim Beyer's masterpiece *Deadman's Party* (VI A5+) up scary, thin cracks. The most popular route is another Jim Beyer solo line *Phantom Spirit* (IV 5.9 C3). It also goes free at scary 5.12b with two 5.11 and two 5.12 pitches. This route climbs the airy northeast ridge on mostly clean (for the Fishers) sandstone. This is a Fisher Towers Grade IV—allow 2 days up and down. The route is 7 pitches, but can be done as 5 by running pitches 1 and 2 together and 5 and 6 together. Approach from the canyon between Ancient Art and Echo Tower. Hike up the left side of the canyon to a bench that leads south to the northeast corner of the tower.

7. **Phantom Spirit** (IV 5.9 C3) 7 pitches. First ascent solo by Jim Beyer, 1986. All clean aid so you don't need a hammer! Begin below the northeast corner of the tower. **Pitch 1:** Short lead up chimney (5.6). **Pitch 2:** Some of route's harder aid with flared and awkward placements. Start with thin nailing to some mixed free (5.8) and aid (C2+) up widening crack to 2-bolt belay. **Pitch 3:** Aid zig-zag crack to clean crack (C2) to 2-bolt hanging belay. **Pitch 4:** Continue aiding up the crack (C1) to roof (C2). Traverse right under roof (C3—crux aid and free climbing) to 2-bolt sling belay. **Pitch 5:** Aid up corner (C2) past ledge to awkward off-width (5.9) to easier chimney (5.6). Belay from bolts below summit bolt ladder. **Pitch 6:** Aid up bolts (C1) and few placements to anchors. **Pitch 7:** Best pitch on route—really spectacular! Scramble across to fin and hand traverse (easy and wild) to more scrambling and actual summit. Downclimb pitch to bolt anchor atop pitch 6. **Descent:** 4 rappels down route. **Rap 1:** Top of pitch 6 to hanging belay atop pitch 4. **Rap 2:** Pitch 4 anchors to pitch 3 anchors. **Rap 3:** Pitch 3 anchors to pitch 2 anchors. **Rap 4:** Pitch 2 anchors to ground. **Rack:** Complete sets of Tri-cams, TCUs, Camalots, Friends, stoppers; some medium and large hexentrics; bring 2 or 3 sets of big cams (#3 to #4 Friend or equivalent) and a couple of bigger Camalots.

FISHER TOWERS
ECHO TOWER

4 rappels down route

.4

bolt ladder

XX

OW .9

C2 SB

XX

C3

NORTH CHIMNEY

C1 SB

XX

C2

XX

.8

C2+

.6

7

down to
main trail

TOP OF THE WORLD OVERLOOK AREA

This route, *Cooler Than Jesus*, while not in the Fisher Towers proper, lies a few miles to the east and directly below the Top of the World Overlook, a spectacular viewpoint on the lofty Wingate rimrock high above the Fisher and Mystery Towers. Steve "Crusher" Bartlett, who did the first ascent, calls it "one of the best 5.10a routes in southeastern Utah." It's an excellent crack climb on Wingate sandstone with one of the shortest approach hikes outside of Potash Road!

Finding the route: It's a somewhat tricky approach that requires a high-clearance vehicle. Turn south off Utah Highway 128 (River Road) at the Dewey Bridge and drive a good dirt road for a couple of miles. Look for signs for the Kokopelli Bike Trail and follow them south up a sloping mesa to the Top of the World Overlook, a huge vista overlooking the Fisher and Mystery towers to the west. The viewpoint is a couple of miles east of the Mystery Towers. Total driving distance is about 10 miles. Park about 20 feet from the top of the route; it follows an enormous dihedral below.

8. **Cooler Than Jesus (II 5.10a)** 3 pitches. First ascent by Steve "Crusher" Bartlett and Strappo Hughes, 1991. Locate a huge dihedral below the overlook and rappel 300' from a tree to a big loose ledge about 40' above the cliff base. It can be done in two 2-rope rappels with the first rap going 150' to the base of the chimney atop pitch 2. Next rappel is 150' to a rubble-covered ledge. Begin on the ledge below the right wall of the dihedral. **Pitch 1:** Follow crack in back of bomb bay chimney. It starts to get harder just as another finger crack to left comes into reach. Follow this crack (5.10a) up left to good belay ledge; 70'. **Pitch 2:** Thin hand cracks head up dihedral wall (5.9 and 5.10a) to loose blocks. Angle left to another ledge in dihedral below chimney; 70'. **Pitch 3:** After awkward start (5.8) chimney becomes perfect back and foot chimney (5.6). Protect chimney with gear in small cracks inside; 150'. **Rack:** Standard desert rack with sets of wires, TCUs, and Friends, runners. Emphasize #1.5 to #3 Friends.

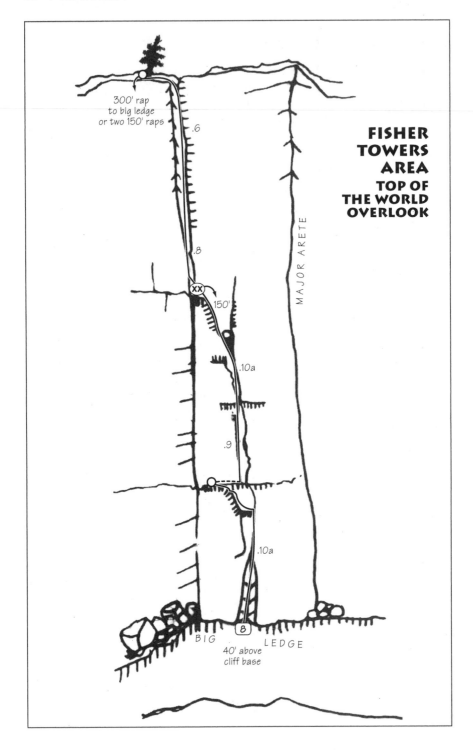

300' rap
to big ledge
or two 150' raps

.6

**FISHER
TOWERS
AREA
TOP OF
THE WORLD
OVERLOOK**

.8

XX

150'

.10a

MAJOR ARETE

.9

.10a

8

BIG   LEDGE

40' above
cliff base

River Road Crags

Overview

Utah 128, a designated state Scenic Byway, runs east from Moab along the tamarisk-lined south bank of the Colorado River in a spectacular canyon before turning north across shale badlands to Interstate 70. The highway, locally called River Road, is walled by towering Navajo and Wingate sandstone cliffs from Moab to Castle Valley. Excellent routes ascend the cliffs and several towers, including Lighthouse and Dolomite towers, above the road. The paved road offers easy access to the cliffs, making River Road crags a popular and worthwhile excursion for day climbs.

In addition to fine climbing adventures along River Road, there are numerous points of interest. These include Anasazi petroglyphs etched on the cliff faces and the intact ruins of ancient granaries tucked under overhangs. Matrimony Springs, just up the road from the junction with U.S. Highway 191, offers fresh and perennial potable water—a good place to fill your bottles. Several arches are located in the cliffs, including Updraft and Eye Socket Arches. Morning Glory Natural Bridge, a spectacular, 243-foot-long bridge in Negro Bill Canyon, lies 2.5 miles up the canyon from River Road. It's the sixth longest natural span in the United States. Past Negro Bill Canyon, abrupt walls of Wingate sandstone rise out of the river to form an unbroken escarpment along the canyon rim. Interesting points include stubby Barney Rubble Tower across the river at 4 miles, the Big Bend campgrounds and bouldering area, and White Ranch at the lower end of Castle Valley. Beyond here the road heads across broad Richardson Amphitheater and past the Fisher Towers, before re-entering the meandering river canyon. Few worthy climbing routes are located in this upper canyon. After 45 miles the highway eventually reaches Interstate 70 to the north.

Climbing history: The first route established in the River Road area was the first ascent of Castleton Tower by Layton Kor and Huntley Ingalls in 1961 when the road was just an unpaved track. At that time Kor took note of the thin shaft of Dolomite Tower and returned in 1969 with his wife, Joy, and nephew, Kordell, to make its first ascent. This was Kor's last major ascent in Utah's canyon country. The team of Gary Ziegler, Harvey Carter, and Tom Merrill climbed the adjoining Lighthouse Tower the following year via the now seldom-climbed *Northeast Route*. The intrepid team of Ed Webster and

Jeff Achey put up the three other routes on The Lighthouse in 1984 and 1985. Their *Iron Maiden* route includes a bold and dramatic stemming pitch, led by Achey, that has since repulsed many solid climbers. *Dolofright*, the other route on Dolomite Tower, is a sporty, modern route put up on lead by Tom Gilje and belayed by his wife, Julie, in 1993. This spectacular two-pitch line face climbs, a desert rarity, up an exposed arête facing the road and includes some frightening runouts.

The desert off-width master, Jim Dunn, and Chris Wood climbed The Sorcerer in 1977, and the following year Dunn and Leonard Coyne free-climbed it. Jeff Achey and Chip Chace made the first ascent of the Sorcerer's Apprentice in 1981. Dunn was also the impetus behind the ascents of the River Road Dihedrals and the intimidating aid route, *Artist's Tears*, just up-canyon on the Anasazi Wall, in the early 1970s. In 1976, Larry Bruce and Molly Higgins completed the A4 nailing route, not included in this guide.

The Bureau of Land Management manages the River Road corridor in order to protect the area's scenic attributes, fragile desert ecosystems, and recreational opportunities from overuse and abuse. Camping, once permitted almost anywhere along the road, is now restricted to existing sites and campgrounds. Three BLM fee campgrounds, Hal Canyon, Oak Grove, and Big Bend, are found along the Big Bend between mileposts 7 and 8. Primitive campsites are available along the road at areas marked by a signed tent symbol, but all campers must have a portable camp toilet to avoid polluting the area. Firewood collecting is not allowed, except for picking up driftwood along the river banks. Do not cut or damage trees for firewood. Climbers should use existing trails to the crags to avoid damaging the delicate cryptobiotic soils and creating erosion. Pick up after yourself. Don't leave tape, cigarette butts, or any trash at the base of the cliffs. Watch for loose rock on the routes, particularly on ledges and during rappels. Wear a helmet.

Rack: Bring a standard desert rack for most routes, including double sets of Friends, sets of TCUs and wires, long slings, and a couple of ropes. Remember that the suggested rack for each route described is only a recommendation. You may need more gear than is advised here. Look at the proposed route and decide for yourself.

Trip Planning Information

General description: Some crack routes on sandstone cliffs and several towers along River Road in the Colorado River's deep canyon.

Location: East-central Utah. East of Moab.

Camping: Campgrounds are located along River Road (Utah 128) up-river from Moab. Camp only in designated campgrounds with toilet facilities. No primitive camping is allowed along River Road without camp toilets. Violators will be ticketed by BLM rangers. Primitive sites are marked by tent signs.

No water is available at campgrounds on River Road. There are lots of camping options in and around Moab—several private campgrounds as well as BLM campgrounds at Sand Flats. Carry water whenever possible and tote out all your waste and garbage.

Climbing season: Year-round.

Restrictions and access issues: None currently. All the routes included here are on BLM public lands. Do your part to minimize human impact by not leaving trash, tape, and cigarette butts. Follow existing trails and paths whenever possible to avoid damaging fragile cryptobiotic soils and creating social trails on the fragile desert landscape. Camp only in established areas and using clean-camping techniques.

Guidebooks: *Classic Desert Climbs* by Fred Knapp, Sharp End Publishing, 1996, has topos and descriptions for the area's popular routes. *500 Select Moab Classics* by Kevin Chase, 1994. Available from the author at Moab Adventure Outfitters. *Moab Rock East* by Eric Bjørnstad, Chockstone Press, 1998—the complete guide.

Nearby mountain shops, guide services, and gyms: Moab Adventure Outfitters offers a selection of gear and clothing. They also teach climbing classes and guide the area towers. Rim Cyclery in Moab has gear, chalk, and biking accessories.

Services: All visitor and climber services are found in Moab, including gas, food, lodging, camping, dining, and groceries. Try Eddie McStiff's for good micro-brews. The Moab Diner has a reasonably priced breakfast. The Mondo Cafe is the best place for coffee.

Emergency services: Call 911. Allen Memorial Hospital, 719 West 400 North, Moab, UT, (801) 259-7191.

Nearby climbing areas: Wall Street, The Kings Hand, Long Canyon, Day Canyon, Castleton Tower, The Priest, The Rectory, Sister Superior, Fisher Towers, Arches National Park, Island in the Sky spires, The Bride, Indian Creek Canyon.

Nearby attractions: Colorado River, Fisher Towers, Deadhorse Point State Park, Arches National Park, La Sal Mountains, Manti-La Sal National Forest, Colorado River Scenic Byway (Utah 128), Slickrock Bike Trail, Canyonlands National Park, Negro Bill Canyon, Morning Glory Arch, Behind the Rocks, Kane Springs Canyon, Island in the Sky, Potash Road and White Rim Trail.

Finding the crags: Drive north from Moab on U.S. Highway 191 to the Colorado River. Turn east onto Utah 128, the River Road. This winding, paved road parallels the river and offers easy access to all the cliffs and towers above the highway. All the routes are on the right side of the highway. The Sorcerer and Sorcerer's Apprentice are 1 mile up the road. The River Road Dihedrals are at 2.8 miles. The Lighthouse and Dolomite Tower are above Big Bend Recreation Area at 7.5 miles. The Big Bend Bouldering Area is at 7.8 miles. Specific parking and hiking directions are given in each area's description.

RIVER ROAD

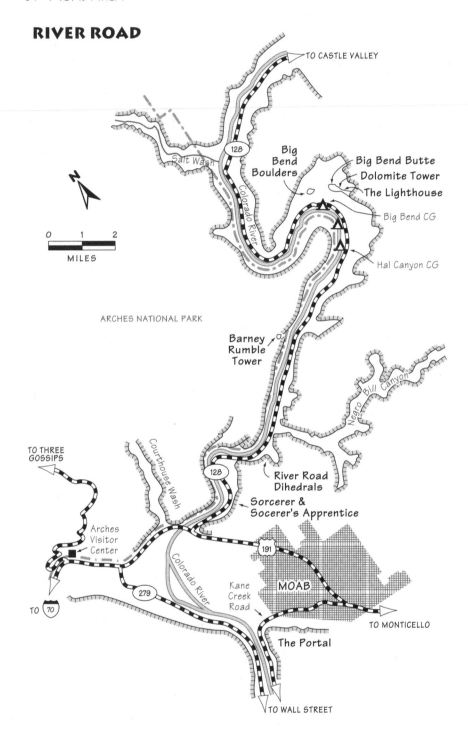

**RIVER ROAD
THE SORCERER
THE SORCERER'S
APPRENTICE**

THE SORCERER & SORCERER'S APPRENTICE

The Sorcerer and Sorcerer's Apprentice are a couple of tall pillars composed of Navajo sandstone that lean against the main cliff face above a wide highway bend a mile from the junction of U.S. Highway 191 and Utah 128. The Sorcerer is the right-hand pillar, while the Sorcerer's Apprentice is on the left. Approach by parking off the highway and scrambling up talus slopes to the base of the formations. Descent off both is by rappel.

THE SORCERER

1. **Sorcerer** (II 5.11d) 3 pitches. First ascent by Jim Dunn and Chris Wood, 1977. First free ascent by Jim Dunn and Leonard Coyne, 1978. Climbs up the left side of the pillar. **Pitch 1:** Work up off-width crack (5.10) past 3 fixed pins to 1-bolt stance. **Pitch 2:** Climb into and up chimney (5.9+) to 2-bolt belay ledge. **Pitch 3:** Continue up left side of pillar via strenuous off-width crack (5.11+) to bolted summit. **Descent:** 3 rappels down route. **Rack:** Set of Friends and extra large gear (Big Bros, #5 Camalots, whatever else will work in off-size cracks).

   Another cool 3-pitch route is **Sorcerer's Crossing** on the Sorcerer. Climb right side of formation, chimney through to left side, and finish up off-width crack. **Pitch 1:** 5.12a off-width. **Pitch 2:** (5.10) fist and off-width. **Pitch 3:** (5.11+) off-width.

THE SORCERER'S APPRENTICE

2. **Left Side** (II 5.11c) 2 pitches. First complete ascent by Jim Dunn and Maureen Gallagher, 1986. The first pitch can be broken into 2 shorter leads. To avoid the first pitch, scramble up slabs to the east and stroll across a bench to the belay ledge. Begin on the left side of the pillar. **Pitch 1:** Thin jamming and hard stemming (5.10+) up left-facing dihedral to 2-bolt belay ledge. **Pitch 2:** Awkward climbing above belay leads to sandy finger crack (5.11c) and to pillar summit. 3 fixed pitons. **Descent:** Rappel off summit with double ropes to first belay ledge. Walk-off east and scramble down slabs to base. **Rack:** Double sets of Friends with extra #.5, #1, and #1.5, wired stoppers, and RPs.

3. **Sorcerer's Apprentice Right Side** (II 5.11c) 3 pitches. First ascent by Jeff Achey and Chip Chace, 1981. This route, the best on the Apprentice, climbs 2 pitches up the right side of the formation before joining pitch 2 of the *Left Side* route or 3 pitches up the right side to the summit. **Pitch 1:** Layback and jam leftwards (5.8) up slanting corner system for 65' to stance below steep right-facing dihedral. **Pitch 2:** Muscle up strenuous off-width to steep lieback (5.10). Belay after corner kicks back; 140'. **Pitch**

3: Jam a flared finger crack up right-facing corner on right side of pillar to summit. **Descent:** Rappel down left side of pillar to ledge with 2 bolts. Third-class off via wide bench then scramble down slabs. **Rack:** 2 sets of Friends, set of stoppers.

RIVER ROAD DIHEDRALS

The dihedrals, which offer a good assortment of moderate routes including the classic *Bloody Knees*, sit just above the highway at 2.8 miles or just before the mile 3 marker. The dihedral routes ascend cracks on the lower cliff band. Above the large ledge is an obvious pillar. A couple of routes ascend this. *The Green Crack* (III 5.10 A3) is a 4-pitch outing up the obvious crack/chimney on the right side of the pillar. *The Last Supper* (III 5.10+) is a fine route that jams the obvious splitter crack on the pillar face just left of *The Green Crack*. The routes, on Navajo sandstone, are very popular due to their close proximity to Moab, short approach, scenic view of the Colorado River and its canyon, and afternoon shade on hot days. Park on a pull out on the river side of the highway and follow a climbers' path through sand to the cliff base. Approach time is a couple of minutes. Bring a tarp to keep your rope out of the sand. **Descent:** from all routes is by rappel. Avoid lowering to avoid damaging soft sandstone edges. Routes are listed right to left.

4. **Bloody Knees** (5.9+) A superb 1-pitch crack climb up the obvious dihedral on the right side of the lower cliff. Jam wide hands crack (5.8) in tight corner. Up higher it narrows into sustained hand crack (5.7). Continue

past fixed piton on right wall (use long sling for rope drag) near wide section. Jam 5.8 crack to 5.9+ crux just below 2-bolt anchor on left side of corner just below huge ledge. Belay here. **Descent:** Rappel with 2 ropes 140' to ground. Watch that your rope doesn't get stuck in crack when pulling it. **Rack:** 2 sets of Friends with extra #2, #2.5, #3, and #3.5.

5. **Oxygen Debt** (5.11+) About 20' left of *Bloody Knees* is a huge right-facing dihedral. This 1-pitch route follows an overhanging crack system up the varnished left wall of the dihedral for 70'. Jam hand crack (5.10) to fists (5.10+) to short squeeze chimney. Continue up wide fist crack (5.11+) to final off-width section and 2-bolt belay stance below obvious roof. **Descent:** Rappel 60'. **Rack:** 1 set of Friends with 2 #4, wide crack gear including 2 #1, 1 #2, and 1 #3 Big Bros or their Camalot equivalent.

6. **River Road Dihedral East** (5.9) An uninspiring name for a somewhat uninspiring 1-pitch line. Jam prominent hand crack (5.8 to 5.9) to short fist section. Belay from 2 bolts next to crack. **Descent:** Rappel 70'. **Rack:** Double sets of Friends.

7. **Little Crack** (5.9) A short pitch up the left-angling crack left of Route 6. Jam obvious flared crack for 50' to 2-bolt belay stance. Second pitch continues to large bench above. **Descent:** Rappel 50'. **Rack:** 2 sets of Friends.

THE LIGHTHOUSE

The Lighthouse is a 315-foot-high tower perched on a ridge east of the highway. Dolomite Spire and Big Bend Butte flank it on the left. The Lighthouse is a strangely shaped, blocky tower topped by a weird little ball summit that requires some unprotected climbing or trickery to stand atop. The tiny summit holds only one person at a time.

Approach the tower by driving east on River Road for 7.5 miles to Big Bend, a huge, arcing, Colorado River bend. Park at a convenient pullout across the highway from a large, calcite-covered boulder and locate the two towers to the east. The Lighthouse is the smaller one on the right, while Dolomite Spire is on the left. Follow a trail marked with cairns up the Moenkopi and Chinle formation talus slopes to the base of The Lighthouse. Approach time is 15 to 25 minutes. Stay on the existing trail to avoid damaging soils and creating erosion. Two routes ascend the river side of the tower while one is on the back side facing away from the road and river.

8. **Iron Maiden** (III 5.12a R) 3 or 4 pitches. First ascent by Jeff Achey and Ed Webster, 1985. This route ascends the crack system on the right side of the tower facing the river. The first 2 pitches can be combined. **Pitch 1:** Climb short chimney to blocky ledge. Continue up obvious right-facing dihedral (5.10d) with fixed piton to belay stance left of arête. Belay here

or work past a star-drive bolt (5.12a) to fixed pin. Above, hand traverse right (5.10) to sloping belay ledge. Earl Wiggins calls this pitch "serious, demanding, and one of the most beautiful in the desert." **Pitch 2:** Traverse left across horizontal crack (5.11) to cracks (5.9) that climb to cave feature. Straight-forward hand and fist jamming leads up clean, varnished corner (5.11) to belay ledge. **Pitch 3:** Free climb (5.12a) or aid past 3 fixed pitons (A0) to spacious ledge. Belay here or continue up. This pitch was finally freed by Jimmy Surette in 1997. **Pitch 4:** Work right to fixed anchors and climb up right on northeast face (5.9) to summit via *Lonely Vigil*'s final pitch. **Descent:** A few choices. Downclimb to anchors in notch on north side of tower and make 2 rappels down old *Northeast Face route* (1st rap to notch between The Lighthouse and Dolomite, 2nd rap from single bolt to opposite side of tower or 5.7 downclimb, scramble up to notch on south side of The Lighthouse and rap 50' to base); rappel *Lonely Vigil* on east side of tower; second short rappel to river-side base. **Rack:** Double sets of Friends including 3 #1, 3 #1.5, 2 #2, 2 #2.5, 3 #3, 2 #3.5, and 1 #4. Wired stoppers with extras in smaller sizes. Medium and large Hexentrics also work well.

9. **Poseidon Adventure** (III 5.9+) 4 or 5 pitches. First ascent by Ed Webster and Jeff Achey, 1984. This route, on river side of tower, ascends a broken crack system to an obvious notch left of the summit. **Pitch 1:** Jam crack (5.8) to broken ledge below off-width crack/chimney. **Pitch 2:** Stem up flared off-width crack (5.9+) to good belay ledge. Pro is 2 #4 Camalots and at least 1 #5 Camalot. **Pitch 3:** Jam wide crack (5.8) up fractured left-facing dihedral to chimney (5.7) that leads to belay in obvious notch. **Pitch 4:** Traverse onto northeast face (5.6) and face climb (5.9) past loose block, up to anchors just below summit; 30'. **Pitch 5:** Exciting unprotected face climbing (airy and scary!) leads to summit (5.9 R). Stand, pose, and then downclimb short pitch. Only one at a time on the summit! For those not totally solid on (5.9) it is possible to traverse around and haul a rope over summit for top-rope. **Descent:** 3 rappels down the *Northeast Face* route. **Rap 1:** From top anchors 90' to ledge with 2 bolts. **Rap 2:** 165' to notch between Lighthouse and Dolomite. **Rap 3:** Long rappel from single Kor bolt down opposite side from river or downclimb (5.7) to ground. Scramble up to notch south of The Lighthouse and make 50' rap to base. **Rack:** Double sets of Friends. Camalots, 2 #4 and at least 1 #5. Medium and large stoppers. Long runners.

10. **Lonely Vigil** (II 5.10) 4 pitches. First ascent by Ed Webster and Jeff Achey, 1985. This excellent route ascends the back or east side of The Lighthouse, opposite the road and river. Follow the access trail to the base of the river side of The Lighthouse. Rope up and do a short pitch (5.7) up to the notch on the right or south side of the tower. Belay from a 2-bolt

RIVER ROAD
LIGHTHOUSE TOWER
DOLOMITE TOWER

rap route
xx

x .10+
x
x
x

xx

x
x
x   .11r
x   face
x
x
x
x   11

approach from
other side
x

no anchors on summit

3 rappels down
east side

around corner and
up 2 pitches   to northeast face

face .12a

hand/
fist
.11

.8

.10
OW   cave

.9

.11

go behind tower
up to notch

.8   xx

.7

approach pitch
to east side
8

9

Jeff Achey on the first ascent of Iron Maiden, The Lighthouse, River Road.
PHOTO BY ED WEBSTER, MOUNTAIN IMAGERY

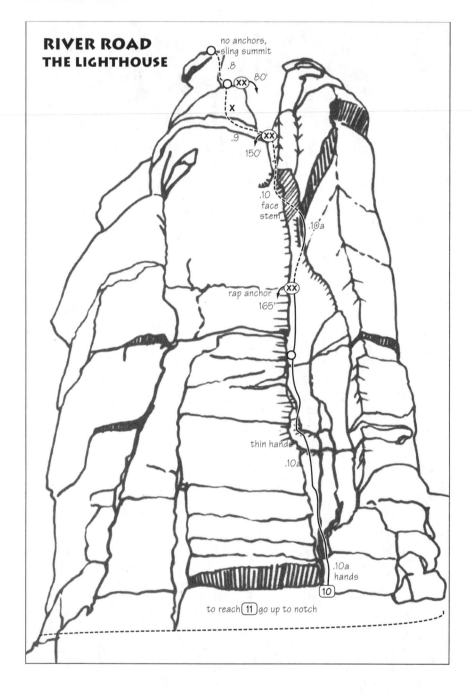

RIVER ROAD
THE LIGHTHOUSE

no anchors,
sling summit

.8

XX   80'

X

.9

150'

.10
face
stem

.10a

rap anchor

165'

thin hands

.10a

.10a
hands

10

to reach 11 go up to notch

anchor. Follow ledges around the east side of the tower to the base of a deep slot/chimney system on the right side. **Pitch 1:** Jam hands to thin hands crack (5.10a) up corners to ledge belay on left wall of slot; 140'. **Pitch 2:** Continue up corner to overhang, traverse left to ledge. Above is overhanging corner. Stem up (5.10a) past some fixed pro to traverse to anchors; 140'. **Pitch 3:** Make unprotected traverse left and continue up (5.9) past loose flake to 2-bolt anchor just below summit; 40'. **Pitch 4:** Unprotected face climbing leads to summit mantle move (5.8). Stand on the airy top then downclimb back to belay. This is the scary part. Fred Knapp says, "Most 5.9 climbers won't be comfortable climbing to the summit and reversing the moves." There are no anchors on the summit. It is possible to haul a rope over the summit to set up a top-rope. **Descent:** 3 rappels down route. **Rap 1:** From upper anchors to notch. **Rap 2:** 150' to anchors partway up pitch 2. **Rap 3:** 165' to ground. Walk back south to notch on south side and make 50' rappel to base of river side. **Rack:** 2 sets of Friends, wired stoppers, RPs for pitch 2.

DOLOMITE TOWER

Dolomite Tower is the slender finger of rock between The Lighthouse and Big Bend Butte. The 350-foot-high tower has two routes. The original *Kor Route* has little fixed gear and is ascended with some sporty hooking and aid. The other route, *Dolofright*, ascends the prominent and intimidating right-hand arête of the spire as seen from the road. This spectacular route was put up on the lead by Tom Gilje. Fred Knapp, in his book *Classic Desert Climbs*, says the route "offers the best Wingate face climbing I've ever done."

11. **Dolofright** (III 5.11 R) 3 pitches. First ascent by Tom and Julie Gilje, 1993. Approach the tower by hiking to the base of The Lighthouse. Do a short 5.7 pitch to a notch with 2 bolts south of The Lighthouse. Traverse north from here around backside of The Lighthouse and past an obvious corner between the 2 towers. Begin right of this near the right side of the spire's face. **Pitch 1:** Jam hand crack to unnerving traverse (5.5) left to old Kor star-drive bolt. Work left up chimney to belay ledge in notch between towers. **Pitch 2:** Start up crack system (*Kor Route*) with fixed pitons on face. Face climb up left to flake, continue up past bolts and arête crux (5.11d R) to 2-bolt belay stance; 120'. **Pitch 3:** Exposed and runout face climbing (5.10+ R) past 4 bolts to summit and 2-bolt anchor. **Descent:** 3 rappels with double ropes. **Rap 1:** From summit to 2-bolt anchors atop pitch 1. **Rap 2:** Rappel to notch. **Rap 3:** Rappel east to base of tower. **Rack:** Small to medium Friends, wired stoppers, RPs, quickdraws.

BIG BEND BOULDERING AREA

Just past the BLM's Big Bend Campground at 7.5 miles is the excellent Big Bend Bouldering Area on the east (right) side of the highway. Park in a designated area and walk to the nearby blocks (see map on page 64). The area offers more than 75 problems on about 15 different boulders, ranging in difficulty from V0- to *Chaos*, a V8 on the east side of the largest boulder. The problems here tend to be fairly straightforward and powerful, with slopey holds, small incuts, and sidepulls. Look for the chalk and crank. You can obtain a topo map of problems at Moab Adventure Outfitters.

Paul Preuss bouldering at Big Bend Boulders, River Road, Moab. PHOTO BY STEWART GREEN

Peter Gallagher on Mr. Sombrero, *Arches National Park.* PHOTO BY EARL WIGGINS

Arches National Park

Overview

Arches National Park, one of the National Park Service's crown jewels, is a 73,234-acre wonderland of eroded sandstone fins, towers, ribs, gargoyles, hoodoos, balanced rocks, and exquisite arches. The area, elevated from monument to park status in 1971, protects an amazing landscape that includes the largest proliferation of arches in the world. Over 2,000 arches have been catalogued by intrepid explorers, with an arch considered an opening with one side at least three feet wide. Landscape Arch, measuring 306 fragile feet, is the second longest span in the world.

Most visitors come from around the globe to view the park's stunning scenery and improbable arches—while a decided minority come to sample its rock adventures. Arches National Park, however, ranks as one of the canyon country's scariest and least user-friendly climbing areas. The Entrada sandstone that forms the park's cliffs tends to be sandy, rounded, hard-to-protect, and unforgiving. Fred Knapp, in *Classic Desert Climbs*, calls Entrada sandstone "a step down in quality from moist brown sugar. Occasionally a nice varnish makes for good rock, but more often than not the real advantage is being able to drill bolt holes with a toothbrush and a plastic hammer." Given the generally terrible rock, it's amazing that many routes were pioneered here at all. Still, the park offers some superb crack lines on decent rock and a lot of towers with unique, airy summits that are accessible by interesting climbing. Over a dozen spires up to 300 feet high lie within a 10-minute walk of the park road.

Entrada sandstone, layered on top of Navajo sandstone, forms most of Arches National Park's rock formations including the Courthouse Towers, The Windows, Devil's Garden, Delicate Arch, as well as the many other arches. The Entrada Formation, ranging in thickness from 150 to 500 feet, was deposited in arid mid-Jurassic times some 160 million years ago when large sand dunes swept across southern Utah. Over a mile of sediment was later piled atop the Entrada dunes, compressing and forming today's sandstone. Erosion, primarily by water and ice, shaped the sandstone over the last 2 million years, forming today's fins, towers, buttes, headlands, and arches. This lovely, airy region of Utah is an appropriate illustration of Thoreau's observation that "The finest workers in stone are not copper or steel tools, but the gentle touches of air and water working at their leisure with a liberal allowance of time."

Geologists divide the Entrada into three separate layers with distinctive characteristics: the Dewey Bridge Member, the Slickrock Member, and the Moab Tongue. The Dewey Bridge, the lower level, is mudstone with crinkled, contorted bedding. It forms The Windows area of the park—Owl Rock, Tonka Tower, and Turret Arch. The Slickrock Member composes the smooth, vertical walls seen throughout the park, including the Courthouse Towers and Devil's Garden formations. The Moab Tongue forms a white caprock on top of the Slickrock Member.

The sandstone here, as it does everywhere on the Colorado Plateau, defines not only the lay of the land, but also its plants and animals. Everything living here adapts for survival in a dry, unforgiving world. The scarce precipitation—8.5 inches annually—extreme temperature range, and relatively high elevation, all conspire to limit life among the rocks. Elevations at Arches range from 3,960 feet down along the Colorado River to 5,653 feet near Balanced Rock. A pygmy forest of pinyon pine and juniper covers almost 50 percent of the park; scrubby steppe and barren slickrock blanket the rest.

Climbing history: Climbing started at Arches long before it was a national park. The first scramblers were undoubtedly Fremont Indians, who scaled the high fins for a view of the surrounding landscape. The first known climbers, however, were the brother and sister team of Fred and Irene Ayres who began venturing into Arches in the early 1930s. The pair explored the area and climbed numerous arches including Double Arch, North and South Windows, and Landscape Arch via the South Chimney. The Park Service has since decided that the arches are too unique and fragile for climbing, hence all the arches are off-limits to climbers.

The first route established in Arches was Dark Angel, a sharp spire perched on the western edge of Devils Garden. The California team of Dave Rearick and Bob Kamps reached its summit in late 1962 via the west face. Old bolts from that early ascent still mark the line of this classic route.

Another early route ascended Argon Tower, a beautiful and slender spire poised above Park Avenue in the Courthouse Towers area. On a cold day in January 1964, a trio of Colorado climbers—Layton Kor, Charlie Kemp, and Bob Bradley—won permission from park officials to attempt the ascent. A *National Geographic* article that detailed Kor's earlier landmark ascent of the nearby Titan in the Fisher Towers apparently swayed the rangers that this was a seasoned and able team of climbers.

Over the next decades few new routes were put up on the soft Entrada sandstone formations. Notable exceptions were Chuck Pratt and Doug Robinson's route on Argon Tower in 1969, Allen Steck and Steve Roper's first ascent of the Three Gossips in 1970, and Michael Kennedy and Molly Higgins's excellent free route on The Three Penguins in 1976. Arches climbing finally came of age, however, in the 1980s with numerous free and aid routes going up on the many unclimbed towers and cracks. Pioneers included Todd Gordon, Ron Olevsky, Duane Raleigh, Kyle Copeland, Earl Wiggins, and the prolific Charlie Fowler. Today, most of the best lines in Arches have been climbed. Few towers remain unclimbed and those that remain virgin are rotten, crackless, and unaesthetic.

Arches National Park is easily accessed from Moab. The park entrance lies a scant 5 miles north of town on U.S. Highway 191. Arches is a fee area, with a staffed entrance station. The park's visitor center and headquarters sit just off the highway past the entrance station. Informative displays on the park's geology and natural history, a video introduction to Arches, and a bookshop with maps, postcards, and books are located in the visitor center. Water is also available year-round here. The paved park road runs north from the visitor center for 18 miles to its dead end at Devil's Garden. All of the selected routes listed in this guide lie within easy walking distance of the road and its numerous pullouts.

Climbing is possible year-round in Arches, although autumn and spring are the best seasons. Spring brings warm days, cool nights, and strong winds. Occasional rain storms, some setting in for several days, commonly occur in spring. Summer begins sometime in May as daily high temperatures begin climbing toward 100 degrees. Expect hot days in summer, with highs occasionally reaching 110 degrees. The park's relatively high elevation, however, often keeps the temperatures cooler than they are in Moab or along the Colorado River roads. Early summer mornings can be cool and delightful in Arches. May, June, and July are the driest months here, when less than 2 inches of rain falls. Expect afternoon thunderstorms in August and September, sometimes with torrential rain that quickly floods dry washes and cascades off cliffs. Autumn usually offers a succession of brilliant days with clear skies and warm temperatures. October is the wettest month with an inch of rain. The winter months can be bitterly cold and snowy; almost 11 inches of snowfall here in the average winter. But the weather can also be dry and warm, with daily highs in the 50s or even 60s when high pressure cells stall over Arizona. The climbing can, however, be pleasant in winter if you're in the sun and out of the wind.

There are few current climbing regulations at Arches National Park. Those that are in place are intended to protect the park's unique geological, ecological, and prehistoric resources. Some areas are closed because of nesting raptors. Check at the visitor center for information on current closures. Backcountry permits are required for all overnight stays outside the campground. This rule seldom applies to climbers because almost all the park's routes lie within a short distance of the road. All backcountry users must cook with a portable stove. The collection and use of firewood is prohibited. The use of white chalk is banned in the park. Climbers should use an earth-tone chalk to match the color of the sandstone. Likewise, climbers should use only rust-colored slings at belay and rappel anchors to minimize their visual impact. The use of power drills is prohibited anywhere in Arches, and the park discourages placing any new bolts or hardware except to replace unsafe existing bolts. Bicycles are allowed only on roads; no trail riding is permitted. Dogs must be on a leash at all times and are not allowed on any trail or in the backcountry. Other common sense rules to follow: pick up all your trash as well as any you encounter; do not alter the rock surface by chipping handholds or removing vegetation from cracks; follow existing trails whenever possible to the base of routes to avoid damaging the fragile cryptobiotic soil in the park. Desert soils are very sensitive to human impact and take many years to recover from damage.

Numerous objective dangers exist in the park. The hot, dry climate requires adequate water supplies. One gallon per person per day is the recommended minimum. Hot days will require more water to stay properly hydrated. Climbing at Arches is a serious matter. Its sandstone is not the best medium for rock climbing. You will often encounter bad rock, including loose blocks, sandy sections, and fragile flakes. A helmet provides important cranial protection. Buy one and use it here. Pay attention to fixed belay and rappel anchors, especially on infrequently climbed lines. Erosion can weaken the placement. Never rely on a single anchor for your safety. Always back it up. The extreme heat and dryness quickly weakens webbing and slings. Bring extras to replace worn and brittle slings.

Rack: Bring a standard desert rack that includes at least two sets of Friends or similar camming devices, a set of TCUs, and a set of wired stoppers. Tricams and hexentric nuts are also handy. The many off-width cracks encountered require large protection like Big Bros, Big Dudes, and the #5 Camalot. Bring two 165-foot (50 meter) ropes. All the gear information under each described route is a suggested rack only. It's up to you to decide if you need more or less gear on any given route.

Most of the descents require double ropes when rappelling. Bring extra runners for rope drag and extra webbing to re-thread worn rappel slings. Aid climbs require lots of nifty gadgets so they will go as clean as possible. Bring several sets of stoppers and Lowe Balls along with Birdbeaks, and ring-angle claw hooks. Some aid routes still need pitons, including Leeper Zs and stubbies. Aid routes are not listed in this guide because of the extreme damage caused to the rock by aid climbers ignorant of proper desert nailing. Try to do any aid routes in Arches as clean as possible to avoid rock damage.

Trip Planning Information

General description: Soft sandstone routes that ascend a spectacular assortment of towers and cliffs in scenic Arches National Park.

Location: East-central Utah. North of Moab.

Camping: Devils Garden Campground is at the end of the park road 18 miles north of the park entrance. The 52-site campground, open year-round, is open on a first-come, first-served basis. Fees are charged year-round. Flush toilets and water are available from mid-March through mid-October; otherwise chemical toilets are available. Water is obtained from the visitor center. Other camping areas in the Moab area include BLM sites along the River Road, Jaycee Campground on Potash Road, primitive campsites in Kane Springs Canyon and on BLM lands on Island in the Sky, and at Dead Horse Point State Park.

Climbing season: Year-round. Summers are almost too hot for comfortable climbing. Spring and fall are best, with cool nights and warm days. Spring afternoons are often windy. Winters are variable. Warm high pressure brings great climbing weather in the sun, but it can be cold, snowy, and windy. Don't climb on the sandstone after rain or snow to avoid damaging the cookie-crumble surface.

Restrictions and access issues: Arches National Park is administered by the National Park Service. Information can be obtained by writing Superintendent, Arches National Park, P.O. Box 907, Moab, UT 84532, or telephoning (801) 259-8161. A climbing permit is not necessary. A backcountry permit, however, is required for all overnight stays outside the campground. This rarely applies to climbers because almost all the routes are a short walk from the park road. No wood fires or woodgathering is permitted in the park. All backcountry users must cook with a portable stove. White chalk is prohibited. Use a red, earth-tone chalk when climbing. Likewise, use a rust or dull red sling at rappel anchors to avoid visual impacts. The use of battery-powered drills is prohibited in Arches National Park. The park recommends that no new bolts or other fixed protection be placed unless the existing hardware is unsafe. No bicycles are allowed off the park roads. Dogs must be on a leash at all times and are not allowed on trails or in the backcountry. Leave them at home so they don't get baked in the car. Do not climb on or near any archeological sites in the park, including petroglyph panels.

Guidebooks: *Desert Rock: Rock Climbs in the National Parks* by Eric Bjørnstad, Chockstone Press, 1996. A comprehensive and fairly complete guide to most of the Arches routes. *Classic Desert Climbs* by Fred Knapp, Sharp End Publishing, 1996, offers a selection of Arches classics. *500 Select Moab Classics* by Kevin Chase, 1994. Available from the author at Moab Adventure Outfitters.

Nearby mountain shops, guide services, and gyms: Moab Adventure Outfitters offers gear, clothing, climbing classes and guided climbs. Rim Cyclery also sells climbing gear.

Services: All visitor and climber services are found in Moab, including gas, lodging, camping, dining, showers, and groceries.

Emergency services: Call 911. Allen Memorial Hospital, 719 West 400 North, Moab, UT, (801) 259-7191.

Nearby climbing areas: The Marching Men, Wall Street, The King's Hand,

ARCHES NATIONAL PARK

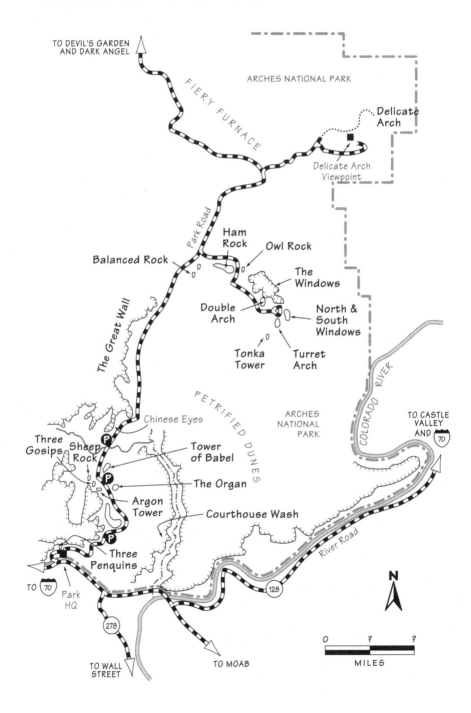

TO DEVIL'S GARDEN
AND DARK ANGEL

FIERY FURNACE

ARCHES NATIONAL PARK

Delicate
Arch

Delicate Arch
Viewpoint

Park Road

Ham
Rock

Owl Rock

Balanced Rock

The
Windows

Double
Arch

North &
South
Windows

Tonka
Tower

Turret
Arch

The Great Wall

PETRIFIED DUNES

Chinese Eyes

ARCHES
NATIONAL
PARK

COLORADO RIVER

TO CASTLE
VALLEY
AND 70

Three
Gosips

Sheep
Rock

Tower
of Babel

The Organ

Argon
Tower

Courthouse Wash

River Road

Three
Penquins

128

N

TO 70

Park
HQ

278

0 ? ?

MILES

TO WALL
STREET

TO MOAB

Long Canyon, Day Canyon, Heat Wave Wall, Moses, Washerwoman, Monster Tower, Kane Springs Canyon, River Road crags, The Lighthouse, Dolomite Tower, Castleton Tower, The Priest, The Rectory, Fisher Towers, The Bride, Indian Creek Canyon.

Nearby attractions: Delicate Arch, Fiery Furnace, Landscape Arch, Devils Garden, Klondike Bluffs, Canyonlands National Park, Island in the Sky, Dead Horse Point State Park, Corona Arch, Amasa Back, Colorado River Canyon, Fisher Towers, La Sal Mountains.

THE THREE PENGUINS

The Three Penguins, resembling a trio of perched penguins, towers above the park road as it loops up Headquarters Hill; its initial incline is just beyond the visitor center. The *Right Chimney* route, which isn't a chimney at all, is quite possibly the finest free climb in Arches National Park with good rock and superb jamming. The other two routes, both narrow squeeze chimneys, are best left for the very thin. Approach the 120-foot-high Penguins by driving up the park road to a pullout at 0.9 mile from the visitor center. Park here and scramble up a loose mudstone gully to the horizontal ledge system on which the Penguins sit. Follow the ledge to the base of the east face. You can also access the ledge via a couple of very scary direct-start pitches. Use caution. Kevin Chase notes in his local guide: "Many of the good holds are missing. Good climbers are often scared shitless on this pitch."

1. **Right Chimney** (5.10c) 2 pitches. First ascent by Michael Kennedy and Molly Higgins, 1976. This route ascends the right-hand crack system up the obvious right-facing dihedral. **Pitch 1:** Jam excellent crack that widens from hands to fists (5.10c) to 3-bolt belay on good ledge; 80'. **Pitch 2:** Continue up the steep crack—hands to fists to off-width (5.10a)—before exiting onto face climbing that leads to summit of center penguin. **Descent:** Make a double-rope, 140' rappel from 3 anchors down route to ledge walk-off. **Rack:** 2 sets of Friends with extra #2.5 to #4s, 1 #4 Camalot, and large stoppers for the start.

2. **Center Chimney** (5.9) 1 pitch. First ascent by Michael Kennedy, Larry Bruce, and Molly Higgins, 1976. This ultimate squeeze chimney gives a good dose of claustrophobia. Once you're in it you won't fall out! Follow the same approach as #1 and start about 10 feet to the left on the ledge. **Pitch 1:** Work up narrowing chimney past couple of bolts. Continue inside through very tight squeeze chimney before emerging into notch. Face climb to summit of center penguin. **Descent:** Use *Right Chimney* descent anchors. Make one 2-rope 140' rappel from 3 anchors to ledge walk-off. **Rack:** A set of Friends, some wide stuff like #5 Camalots and Big Bros.

3. **Anorexia** (5.10a) 1 pitch. First ascent by Alan Bartlett and Alan Nelson,

ARCHES
THREE PENGUINS

xxx ⌐ 2 rope rappel to ledge

140'

.10a

.9

xxx

route hidden
inside chimney

.10c

x

x

.10a

③   ②   ①

approach on ledges

1989. Another squeeze for those who enjoyed *Center Chimney*. The 8" wide crux is definitely for anorexic sport climbers making the jump to trad climbing. This route will feel lots harder than *Right Chimney*. Begin left of #2 on the ledge. **Pitch 1:** Jam overhanging fist crack (5.10a) to thin squeeze chimney that exits onto summit of left penguin. Traverse up and over middle penguin to #1's descent anchors. **Descent:** Make one 2-rope 140' rappel down to access ledge. **Rack:** Bring a selection of TCUs, Friends, lots of wide gear.

PARK AVENUE

Park Avenue, a desert wash flanked by soaring sandstone skyscrapers, begins at a roadside pull off 2.2 miles from the visitor center. A mile-long trail traverses the slickrock canyon, ending at a second parking area to the north. Some very good routes are found in and around Park Avenue, including *Tilting at Windmills* (5.8 A3), *The Carrot Cannibal* (5.12a), the first pitch of *Soft Parade* (5.10+) on Jello Tower, and the routes on The Candelabrum. The best route, however, is *Heart of the Desert* on the east side of the canyon near its north entrance. To find the route, drive 3.5 miles from the visitor center to the Courthouse Towers parking area. Park here and follow the Park Avenue Trail south up the slickrock wash past Argon Tower. The route ascends the obvious, large, left-facing dihedral on the left or east wall of Park Avenue near its north end.

4. **Heart of the Desert** (5.10c) First ascent by Jeff Widen belayed by Dawn Burke, 1985. An excellent 1-pitch route up a large left-facing dihedral on the east wall of Park Avenue. Jam the lovely hand crack for 80' to anchors. **Descent:** Rappel 80'. **Rack:** Bring Friends including 1 #2, 2 #2.5, 4 #3, 2 #3.5, and 1#4.

THREE GOSSIPS

The Three Gossips, one of the most impressive and beautiful formations in the Courthouse Towers section of the park, is a spectacular trio of blocky summits towering almost 300 feet over a rounded slickrock base above Park Avenue. The crag was first climbed by Californians Steve Roper and Allen Steck in 1970 via a mixed aid and free route up a vertical crack system on the west face. The line was free climbed by Jeff Achey and Glenn Randall in 1982.

The formation sits south of the park road and west of the Park Avenue trail. All three routes described ascend the west face of the Gossips on the side opposite the road. Reach the crag by driving about 3.5 miles from the park entrance to the Courthouse Towers/Park Avenue parking area just west of The Organ on the north side of the road. Park here and walk almost a quarter of a mile west on the road's shoulder to a dry wash on the left. Follow the wash south to the sandy slopes below the formation and continue up a climber's path to the slickrock slabs below the west flank. Avoid walking on and damaging the fragile cryptobiotic soil among the junipers by staying in the wash and walking on existing trails.

5. **West Face** (II 5.11c or 5.9 C1) 3 pitches. First ascent of the route and the Gossips by Steve Roper and Allen Steck, 1970. First free ascent was by Glenn Randall and Jeff Achey, 1982. This excellent and continuous route climbs the obvious crack system on the left side of the west face to the shoulder immediately right of the North Gossip. The hard parts can all be clean-aided. **Pitch 1:** Do awkward 5.9 mantle onto shelf. Jam beautiful flared dihedral's thin hand-to-hand crack (5.9+) until it widens. Continue over roof via off-width crack (5.10d) to good belay ledge with 2 bolts. **Pitch 2:** Continue up thin hand crack above (5.10-) and work by loose block. The crack continues as off-width (5.10) for about 50'. Stem left into parallel crack system and begin route's crux section up thin finger crack and seam in tight corner via jams and stemming (5.11). Belay from bolts on ledge below final summit block. **Pitch 3:** Work into hidden, 4' wide chimney that splits summit block and climb 50' to flat summit. **Descent:** 3 rappels down route. **Rap 1:** Summit to anchors on saddle atop pitch 2; 50'. **Rap 2:** 140' rappel (2 ropes) to pitch 1 anchors. **Rap 3:** 120' rappel to route base. **Rack:** Bring standard rack with double Friends, couple of larger pieces, lots of small wires.

6. **Lyon-Trautner Route** (III 5.11) 5 pitches. First ascent by Charles Lyon and Todd Trautner, 1981, during the second ascent of the Three Gossips formation. This 3-pitch route begins 10' right of the *West Face* route and follows the obvious right-angling crack system to the notch just north of the Middle Gossip. **Pitch 1:** Climb up left side of 30' long, semi-detached flake (5.9) and step left onto small ledge. Jam and layback up a vertical open book (5.10+). Work up right onto slanting ramp/crack (5.8) to belay ledge with 2 bolts. **Pitch 2:** Climb onto block above belay, pass a fixed piton, and continue up off-width crack on left side of pillar to belay ledge atop the pillar with 2 bolts. **Pitch 3:** Continue up the off-width crack in large, left-facing dihedral to finger crack finish (5.11). Belay at 2-bolt belay ledge at notch below Middle Gossip. **Pitch 4:** Stroll and traverse across ridge between two Gossips to belay stance below North Gossip. **Pitch 5:** 50' pitch scales easy hidden chimney (5.5) to summit of North Gossip. **Descent:** Make 3 rappels down *West Face* route. **Rap 1:** Summit to anchors on saddle; 50'. **Rap 2:** 140' rappel (2 ropes) to anchors. **Rap 3:** 120' rappel to route base. **Rack:** Bring rack of double Friends, some large pieces for off-widths, lots of small wired stoppers.

ARCHES
THREE GOSSIPS

hidden
chimney

xx
50'

xx
140'

140'

.11
fingers
OW

.11b/c
thin

xx

.10
OW

OW

.10
2"

x

.10

xx
120'

xx

4"

.10d

.9+
hands

.9

5   6

7. **Be There or Be Talked About** (III 5.11 A1) 4 pitches. This route to the summit of the South Gossip was put up by Pete Gallagher and Bego Gerhart, 1988. The route ascends the west face of the South Gossip. Access by scrambling up to the west face. The route begins on an area of sandy boulders below a broken crack system on the right side of the face. **Pitch 1:** Climb a moderate pitch through broken, slabby corners for 80' to 2-bolt anchor on ledge. **Pitch 2:** Jam obvious fist and off-width crack above belay to 2-bolt belay ledge on left side of thin pillar. Crack in narrow corner to right is 5.11d variation. **Pitch 3:** This crux lead ascends tight, flaring dihedral (hands and fingers) to bolted belay ledge on blocks up and right and below final headwall. **Pitch 4:** Aid 5-bolt ladder (A1) up overhanging block above to flat summit of South Gossip. **Descent:** Rappel route with 4 rappels. **Rack:** Double set of Friends and Camalots, wired stoppers, runners. For the pitch 2 variation bring small Friends and TCUs.

ARGON TOWER

Argon Tower is a slender, 260-foot-high spire perched atop a slickrock base on the west side of Park Avenue. The tower is obvious from the Park Avenue viewpoint. Approach Argon Tower by parking at the lot below The Organ at the north end of Park Avenue about 3.6 miles from the visitor center. Hike south up the Park Avenue trail before turning west on a climber's path that heads toward the base of the formation. Follow the rough trail up a gully below the lower walls and bend onto benches on the west side of the spire. Scramble up slabs to a horizontal pedestal ledge below the tower. Argon Tower was first climbed by Layton Kor, Charlie Kemp, and Bob Bradley on a cold January day in 1964. Four routes ascend the tower. Descriptions are included here for the two best lines.

8. **North-Northeast Arête** (III 5.11-) 4 pitches. An excellent route put up by Todd Gordon and Dave Evans in 1984 (5.9 A2) and free climbed years later in 1987 by Bret Ruckman and Tim Coats. The line ascends a crack system just left of the prow/arête on the spire's north side. Begin by scrambling onto the sloping pedestal ledge on the west side of the tower. Walk north to a crack system below the arête. A bolted belay on the sloping ledge below the crack marks the start of the route. **Pitch 1:** Climb awkward, loose rock (5.10) for 20' onto ledge below arête. **Pitch 2:** Route follows left-hand crack system. Climb flared finger/hand crack (5.10a) to thin flake flanked by cracks. Continue up right crack (5.10a off-width) to squeeze slot chimney (5.10b) protected by a couple of bolts. Pass small roof and angle left up 2" crack (5.10a) to broken ledge with 2 anchors; 130'. **Pitch 3:** Stem up thin finger crack in shallow corner (5.11) and pass broken roof to easier rock. Belay from 2 bolts on ledge atop the pillar; 50'. **Pitch 4:** Face climb past 3 bolts on the final slab (5.10c) to rounded

ARCHES
ARGON TOWER

rappel westface

xx

.10c

.11

.11b

.10

squeeze

.10
OW

8
start behind bulge
on opposite side of tower

ARCHES
ARGON TOWER

30' XXX

.10c X
X
X
XX
100'

OW
.10

XX
165'

.11a/b
fist/OW sustained

XX

.11b/c
fingers
sustained

9

summit; 30'. Last two pitches can be combined. **Descent:** 3 rappels. **Rap 1:** Drop 30' back to upper ledge. **Rap 2:** Rap with 2 ropes to second belay stance on *West Face*. **Rap 3:** Rap with 2 ropes to the base of the *West Face* route. **Rack:** Double set of Friends, a set of Camalots, a set of TCUs, runners.

9. **West Face** (III 5.11b/c) 4 pitches. Ken Sims, who did the first complete free ascent as well as the first free ascent of pitch 1 in 1996, says this route is "outstanding, hard, and continuous." Muff Cheyney and John Pease did the first ascent in 1972, with later ascents slowly pushing the line free. The route begins on the right side of the west face (opposite the road) below the obvious crack system in a right-facing dihedral. **Pitch 1:** Climb sustained finger crack with piton scars (5.11b/c) to belay ledge with 2 bolts; 50'. An easier variation pitch diagonals up broken corner to right. **Pitch 2:** Jam continuous fist to off-width crack (5.11a/b) to 2-bolt belay/ rappel station in chimney; 60'. **Pitch 3:** Continue up chimney to off-width slot (5.10) and short corner. Jam over roofs to easier rock and 2-bolt belay atop pillar (same belay as top of *North Arête's* pitch 3). **Pitch 4:** Face climb past 3 bolts to summit. 30'. **Descent:** Rappel the route. **Rap 1:** Rap 30' from summit to ledge with 2 bolts. **Rap 2:** 2 ropes to chimney belay atop pitch 2. **Rap 3:** 2 ropes to base of route. **Rack:** 3 sets of Friends #1 to #3.5, 5 #4 Friends, #7 Tri-cam, set of wired stoppers and TCUs for first pitch. Some #4 and #5 Camalots also useful.

THE GREAT WALL

10. **Chinese Eyes** (5.9+) This excellent 1-pitch line jams a left-facing corner on a huge block on the left or south end of The Great Wall, a long, unbroken wall of Entrada sandstone west of the road. Park at the Courthouse Wash pullout (4.6 miles from the visitor center) on the left side of the park road just past the Courthouse Wash Bridge. Locate the route from here and then follow a well-used trail northwest for about a quarter of a mile to the base of the obvious flake/block. The route climbs the center crack system (fingers, hands, to off-width) up a left-facing corner for 70' to a 2-bolt anchor. **Descent:** Rappel 70'. **Rack:** Bring double Friends from #1 to #3.5 and a #7 Tri-cam or #5 Camalot.

11. **Mr. Sombrero** (5.11c) No topo. Another great 1-pitch crack route. Park at the Courthouse Wash pullout (4.6 miles from the visitor center) on the left side of the road. Follow the trail to *Chinese Eyes* and then walk north along the cliff base for about 300' to a prominent left-facing dihedral. Jam and lieback up clean dihedral for 75' to 2-drilled angle anchor with rappel slings on wall. **Descent:** Rappel 75' from anchors. **Rack:** Bring a generous selection of Friends including extra #2 through #3 sizes.

OWL ROCK

Owl Rock, a classic roadside desert spire, was first climbed solo by Ron Olevsky, 1978. The 1-pitch, 100-foot-high route up this grungy-looking tower, composed of the Dewey Bridge member of the Entrada Formation, is easy and popular. The rock is much better than it looks. Owl Rock is the canyon country's easiest spire as well as Arches' most popular route. Follow the park road for 9.3 miles from the visitor center to the Garden of Eden and Windows turnoff. Turn right or east and drive 1.1 miles to the Garden of Eden parking area on the left. Owl Rock is just east of the parking area.

12. **Owl Rock** (5.8) The route, on the spire's west side, follows the most obvious of 2 crack systems. Swing up crack on big jugs, horns, and knobs to ledge with 3-bolt rappel anchor on ledge about 10' below summit. Scramble up easy rock to summit for view and downclimb back to anchors. **Descent:** Rappel 100' with 2 ropes from 3 anchors. **Rack:** A set of Friends, a #4 Camalot, lots of runners to prevent rope drag. Large hexentric nuts also work well.

TONKA TOWER

Tonka Tower is a large, blocky, 150-foot-high tower southwest of Turret Arch. The spire was first climbed by a large party that included Earl Wiggins, Katy Cassidy, and George Hurley, 1988. Drive 9.3 miles north on the park road from the visitor center and turn east or right to The Windows. Continue

ARCHES
OWL ROCK

X ← Down climb to rappel station

xxx

.8 hands

12

for 2.4 miles to the end of the road and park. Follow the trail to Turret Arch before heading southwest across slickrock and sand to the farthest south group of towers. Tonka Tower is the middle of three towers.

13. **Tonka Tower** (II 5.8 A0) No topo. 2 pitches. The fun route follows a grungy-looking crack system on the left side of the west face. **Pitch 1:** Scramble up easy rock and enter chimney/crack. Continue to ledge. Clip drilled angle on headwall above and pull (A0) up to spacious ledge with bolted belay; 120'. **Pitch 2:** This lead clips short bolt ladder (A0) to an exciting mantle (5.8) onto rounded summit. **Descent:** A 2-rope rappel descends 150' down east face from 3 drilled angles. Be careful not to get the rope stuck. **Rack:** A set of Friends, some Tri-cams, hexentrics, large stoppers, runners, 2 ropes.

DARK ANGEL

This 125-foot spire, resembling an angel with folded wings, sits amid the rugged splendor of Devils Garden in the far northern sector of Arches National Park. The *West Face* of the Dark Angel is not one of the best routes in the Park, but it sees lots of action because of its pristine wilderness setting and cool summit. The spire, one of the first technical rock routes in Arches, was first ascended on Thanksgiving Day in 1962 by Californians Dave Rearick and Bob Kamps. It was later free climbed by Tim Toula and Kathy Zaiser in 1986.

Approach Dark Angel by parking at the Devils Garden parking area at the end of the park road 18 miles north of the visitor center. Follow the Double O Arch Trail past Landscape Arch, the world's second-longest arch, and Double O Arch to Dark Angel. Double O Arch is 2 miles from the trailhead and Dark Angel towers another half a mile to the north.

14. **West Face** (5.10 or 5.9 A0) No topo. 2 pitches. The route begins on the west side of the spire on the left side of a large flake. **Pitch 1:** Chimney up soft, powdery chimney (5.7) for 40' to top of flake. Continue up good finger crack (5.9) for 15' and climb onto sloping belay ledge on northwest corner of spire. **Pitch 2:** Pull onto large block above belay (5.7) and continue up north ridge via a museum-quality bolt ladder (A0) of eroding nail drive bolts dating from first ascent. This also goes free (5.10) but be advised that only one good drilled angle will hold a fall. Kevin Chase notes in his area guidebook "...the bolts suck and probably wouldn't hold a good whipper." Last 20' is up easy but runout face climbing (5.4). **Descent:** One 2-rope rappel from fixed anchors on summit. Make sure your knot is well over edge. Stuck rappel ropes are a common problem. **Rack:** A set of Friends, medium stoppers, 2 ropes.

WALL STREET

OVERVIEW

Wall Street is an immense escarpment of 500-foot-high Navajo sandstone cliffs that towers above Utah Highway 279 and the Colorado River just southwest of Moab. The highway, also called Potash Road, is sandwiched between the cliffs and the river. Numerous pulloffs allow easy access and make Wall Street the archetypal roadside crag. In fact, the approach here is usually measured in seconds from car to cliff base. This ease of access, appealing to sportclimbers, makes Wall Street the most popular crag in the canyon country, if not in all of Utah.

Wall Street's sandstone cliffs offer a very different desert climbing experience than the usual Wingate jam cracks found at Indian Creek and Long Canyon. Most routes here are provocative face climbs with edges, flakes, in-cuts, nipples, friction smears, occasional pockets, and huecos. Over 100 routes currently line Wall Street's mile-long cliff. Most of the routes are one-pitch, bolt-protected face routes that end at rappel anchors. A selection of superb cracks also scatters above the road and gives Wall Street a startling variety of easily accessible routes. The difficulty of the routes ranges from 5.5 on some topropes to 5.12+; the majority fall in the 5.10 and 5.11 grades. Some of the routes are classic gems at a moderate standard.

Navajo sandstone, forming Wall Street's long escarpment, is a late Triassic Period formation, deposited some 200 million years ago. At that time, southern Utah was blanketed by an immense field of shifting sand dunes comparable in size and environment to the present day Sahara in North Africa. This dune field is preserved in cross-bedded strata of the Wingate and Navajo sandstone formations. The Navajo sandstone dominates the Colorado Plateau, ranging in thickness from 200 feet at sites east of Moab to 2,000 feet in the precipitous canyon walls in Zion National Park.

Before climbing here, take a minute to look at the Navajo sandstone. Notice the uniform grains of almost pure quartz sand swept into great petrified dunes by ancient winds. The sandstone tends to weather into rounded shapes where no erosion-resistant caprock tops the formation, as it does along the clifftops high above the highway. The stone is also very friable and easily crumbled. Relatively soft calcite is the main cementing agent in the sandstone, so when large flakes of Navajo sandstone fall to the ground they are quickly

Brett Spencer-Green on Lucy in the Sky with Potash, *Wall Street.*
PHOTO BY STEWART M. GREEN

reduced to sand by weathering. Wall Street's rock surface is darkly stained with desert varnish, a thin coating of iron and manganese.

Climbing history: In comparison with other Moab climbing sites, Wall Street is a relative latecomer. Climbers often bypassed the long cliff on Potash Road en route to adventures in Canyonlands National Park. It wasn't until 1987 that a group of dedicated locals began establishing routes here. Kyle Copeland, the most prolific activist, along with Charlie Fowler and others quickly put up some of today's classics including *A Fistful of Potash*, *Last Tango in Potash*, and *Walk on the Wide Side*. Once the rock rush began, others jumped in and added their own lines to the cliff face. Over the next few years numerous climbers, including the desert master Layton Kor, Jim Dunn, Jim Beyer, Alison Sheets, and Linus Platt, along with Fowler and Copeland, developed the routes with a ground-up ethic. The sheer expanse of blank walls above the road discouraged any thoughts of rap-bolting routes. All rap-bolted routes here have been chopped. Today, Wall Street is pretty much climbed out. Few, if any, opportunities remain for first ascents unless you're bold enough to continue onto the upper cliff tier.

No current restrictions on climbing are in place at Wall Street. Some com-

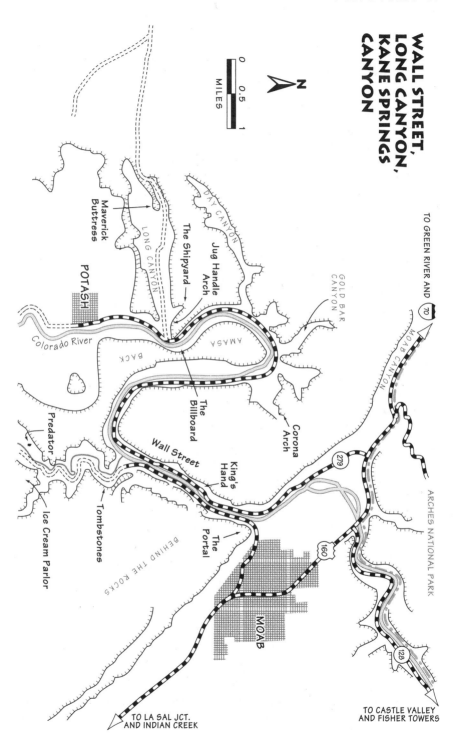

WALL STREET,
LONG CANYON,
KANE SPRINGS
CANYON

N

MILES
0   0.5   1

TO GREEN RIVER AND 70

Maverick Buttress

DAY CANYON

The Shipyard

Jug Handle Arch

LONG CANYON

POTASH

GOLD BAR CANYON

Colorado River

BACK

AMASA

MOAB CANYON

The Billboard

Corona Arch

Predator

Wall Street

King's Hand

279

ARCHES NATIONAL PARK

Ice Cream Parlor

Tombstones

The Portal

BEHIND THE ROCKS

160

MOAB

128

TO LA SAL JCT.
AND INDIAN CREEK

TO CASTLE VALLEY
AND FISHER TOWERS

mon sense rules, however, do apply. Follow them and this fine, accessible climbing area will remain free and open. Remember that Utah 279 is a highway! Lots of traffic uses the road. Park well off the pavement in the wide pullouts below the cliffs and keep your rope, equipment, dogs (many have been hit and killed), and yourself off the asphalt. Don't stop on the pavement to scope out climbs or climbers. Watch out for the Potash mine trucks that regularly use the road. They have the right-of-way and they don't like to slow down.

Keep off the rock after rain or snow. The sandstone is fragile and crumbles easily, particularly after precipitation. Allow the rock to dry thoroughly before climbing on it to avoid damaging it. Most of the routes were put up on the lead—consequently the first fixed protection is often very high. Use a clipstick and climb within your ability to avoid a ground fall. Bolts and fixed pitons can be untrustworthy in sandstone. Never rely on a single anchor to rappel or lower, and always back up anchors when toproping. Most of the routes are set up for rappelling. Rappel instead of lower whenever possible to avoid damaging the sandstone with rope grooves or wearing out fixed hardware. Toproping is not only bad for the rock, it's bad for your rope as well. Have some extra webbing or slings for rap stations. Webbing wears out quickly here in the heat and dryness. Avoid climbing on or near any Indian petroglyphs. Routes were initially established above the Indian writings at the south end of Wall Street. These are now off-limits. Watch for patches of poison ivy along the cliff base in summer. It's particularly thick near the *Flakes of Wrath* and in all the gullies. Keep yourself and your rope out of it to avoid any irritating rashes.

Rack: The usual rack at Wall Street is a dozen quickdraws and a rap device. Crack climbs usually require a double set of Friends, a set of TCUs, and a set of wired stoppers. Tri-cams are sometimes useful. A single 165-foot rope is sufficient for most routes. Two ropes, however, are sometimes needed to safely descend. A rope tarp is handy to keep your rope out of the fine sand along the cliff base.

Trip Planning Information

General description: An excellent roadside cragging area on Navajo sandstone cliffs with numerous bolted face routes and traditional crack lines.

Location: East-central Utah. Southwest of Moab.

Camping: The Jaycee Campground offers shaded sites just north of Wall Street below The King's Hand. Just downriver from the cliffs are many primitive campsites. A campground is across the Colorado River at Moonflower Canyon on the Kane Creek Road. Several campgrounds are located at Big Bend along the River Road (Utah 128) and at Arches National Park. The Sand Flat Campground has many sites near the Slickrock Bike Trail east of Moab. Several private campgrounds with showers and other amenities are located in Moab.

Climbing season: Year-round. The east-facing cliff offers sun in the morning on cool days and shade in the afternoon on hot days. Spring and fall are best. Summers can be very hot and winters cold.

Restrictions and access issues: None. Park well off the busy highway on pull-offs. Keep your rope, pack, and gear off the road. Keep dogs tied up or in your car. Watch for speeding potash-toting semi-trucks on the highway—they don't like to slow down for you!

Guidebooks: *Desert Rock: Wall Street to the San Rafael Swell* by Eric Bjørnstad, Chockstone Press, 1997, is the complete and definitive guide to Wall Street. *500 Select Moab Classics* and *Wall Street* by Kevin Chase, 1994. These are self-published and available from the author at Moab Adventure Outfitters. *Climbs to Nowhere*, the original Wall Street guide by Kyle Copeland, is available at Rim Cyclery.

Nearby mountain shops, guide services, and gyms: Moab Adventure Outfitters offers a selection of gear and clothing. They also have rock climbing classes. Rim Cyclery has a limited but high-quality selection of climbing gear.

Services: All visitor and climber services are found in Moab, including gas, food, lodging, camping, dining, showers, and groceries.

Emergency services: Call 911. Allen Memorial Hospital, 719 West 400 North, Moab, UT, (801) 259-7191.

Nearby climbing areas: Kane Springs Canyon, Tombstones, Long Canyon, Day Canyon, Ice Cream Parlor, River Road crags, The Lighthouse, Dolomite Tower, Castleton Tower, The Priest, Fisher Towers, Arches National Park, The Bride, Canyonlands National Park, Washer Woman, Monster Tower, Moses, Indian Creek Canyon.

Nearby attractions: Canyonlands National Park, Island in the Sky, Corona Arch, Colorado River, Deadhorse Point State Park, Arches National Park, La Sal Mountains, Manti-La Sal National Forest, Colorado River Scenic Byway (Utah 128), Slickrock Bike Trail.

Finding the cliffs: Wall Street is a 10-minute drive southwest of Moab in the heart of Utah's canyon country. Drive a couple of miles west from Moab on U.S. Highway 191 or 1.3 miles west of the Colorado River Bridge, to a south turn onto Utah 279, Potash Road. This turn is about a mile east of the Arches National Park entrance. Drive south on Utah 279 for 2 miles and enter The Portal where the Colorado River leaves Spanish Valley and enters a canyon. After another couple of miles the highway reaches Wall Street, a long, towering band of cliffs flanking the asphalt. The King's Hand is 3.75 miles from the junction of U.S. Highway 191 and Utah 279. The first routes at Wall Street (the *Seibernetics* area) are at 4.4 miles. The School Room is at 4.5 miles; *Bad Moki Roof/Flakes of Wrath* is at 4.6 miles; *Sedan Delivery* and a large parking area are at 4.7 miles; *Nervous in Suburbia* is at 4.8 miles; *Static Cling* and a large parking area is at 4.9 miles; *Steel Your Face* and the slabs are at 5 miles. A large Anasazi petroglyph panel marks the southern end of Wall Street.

WALL STREET

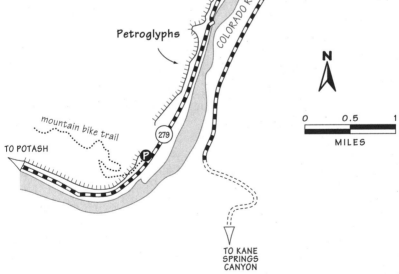

WALL STREET
THE KING'S HAND

XX
150'

hidden
chimney

XX
85'

.9

.10

XX
150'

.8R

2 1

Access Trail

THE KING'S HAND

The King's Hand is a 400-foot-high, slabby, semi-detached pinnacle that leans against the right side of an immense amphitheater. A steep, streaked wall marks the eastern edge of The Hand which lies 3.75 miles south of U.S. Highway 191 above the west edge of Utah 279. Access the pinnacle by parking at the Jaycee Campground or just down the road at the beginning of Wall Street and hiking onto a bench from the south. Follow the bench north to the base of The Hand. Use caution on the routes if you're not comfortable on runout slabs.

1. **Right Hand** (5.10a) This 4-pitch route begins below the middle of The King's Hand. **Pitch 1:** Face climb and friction straight up (5.8 R) past 1 drilled piton to 2-bolt belay stance; 150'. **Pitch 2:** Work right and up to shallow crack system with 2 angles and fixed piton (.10a). Belay on small ledge from 2 bolts; 85'. **Pitch 3:** Face climb diagonally up left into chimney/crack system (5.8) that leads to belay stance; 100'. **Pitch 4:** Traverse up along back of hand (5.8) to bolted rappel/belay stance on ledge behind fingers. **Descend:** Make 3 rappels down route. First rappel from summit anchors 150' to 2 bolts atop pitch 2. Second rappel is 85' to 2-bolt anchor atop pitch 1. Third rappel is 150' to bench. **Rack:** Bring small Friends and TCUs; a selection of wired nuts and a set of Lowe Balls are useful.

2. **Left Hand** (5.9+) Another 4-pitch climb that shares 3 pitches with the *Right Hand*. **Pitch 1:** Climb same first pitch as #1. **Pitch 2:** Traverse left into crack system and face climb 85' up past some hollows and 2 bolts to stance with 2 bolts. **Pitch 3:** Work up right and join Route 1 just below loose chimney. Continue up through fingertips to belay ledge. **Pitch 4:** The same as Route 1. Climb somewhat loose rock behind Hand to bolted belay/rappel ledge. **Descent:** Same rappels as #1. **Rack:** Bring small Friends and TCUs for first pitch.

WALL STREET

Routes are listed right to left. Use the pullouts along the highway to park. Mileages to key areas and parking spots are listed in **Finding the cliffs.**

3. **Scratch and Sniff** (5.11 TR) Thin friction climbing ascends slab right of obvious dihedral to double-bolt anchors with chains; 80'. 2 bolts. Best to toprope this one by making a delicate traverse right from anchors on *Seibernetics.*

4. **Seibernetics** (5.8) A superb pitch up the obvious right-facing corner. 2 drilled angles protect lower section. **Rack:** A set of Friends, TCUs, and wires for upper corner. **Descent:** Rap or lower 80' from double anchors.

5. **Seam As It Ever Was** (5.11b/c) Left of the gully crack about 50' south of Route 4. Crux climbing up fingertip seam leads to flare topped with a bulge; 85'. 1 bolt and 2 anchors. **Rack:** Small wired stoppers, RPs, TCUs (bring some #0s).

6. **Rude Old Men** (5.12) Sustained friction and edging past 6 fixed pitons and bolts to 2-bolt anchor in horizontal bedding seam 60' up.

7. **Faith Flake** (5.11a) A hackberry tree hides the route's start. Climb past fragile "faith flake," clipping the sling around flake. Continue up left in narrow, right-facing corner past 3 drilled angles to double anchors; 60'. **Rack:** Bring a #.75 TCU for the thin crack above the last pin.

8. **Unknown** (5.11+) Climb flakes and edges up black varnished wall past 4 bolts to Route 9's anchors.

9. **El Cracko Diablo** (5.10a) Excellent jamming up flared V-slot (finger crack) to flake with hand cracks on either side to upper crux. Step right to 2-bolt anchor. **Rack:** Friends #1-#3 and a set of TCUs. It eats #1 rigid Friends, be careful.

10. **Coup d'Etat** (5.12b) No topo. Just left of Route 9. Desperate fingertip jams and laybacks up a thin corner to a 1-bolt anchor; 35'. 1 drilled pin, 1 bolt. **Rack:** Bring some TCUs and small wires.

11. **School Room Topropes** (5.5-5.10) No topo. These topropes are above a large pullout a couple of hundred feet south of above routes. Numerous problems are found on slabs. Toprope bolts and anchors are on bench above. Back them up whenever possible. Always use more than 1 anchor when top-roping.

12. **A Fistful of Potash** (5.10a) A good, popular line up a small buttress left of the School Room. Climb up and left past 1 bolt and 2 drilled pitons to

short, flared finger crack. Pull up and over to good jams and 2-bolt anchor on ledge. Rappel the route; 45'. Do not lower or toprope off anchors—the soft sandstone edges below the ledge are being severely damaged by ropes. **Rack:** Bring small Friends and TCUs. A good TR climbs left under the bulge.

13. **Last Tango in Potash** (5.11d) An excellent and difficult route up seam on steep black slab left of Route 12. Gear protects hard moves to bolt 1 and runout to bolt 2. 5.11 cruxes at bolts 1, 2, and 3. 3 drilled angles and 2 bolts are on route. **Descent:** Rap 60' from 2-bolt anchor with slings. **Rack:** Bring small TCUs, wired stoppers.

14. **Pinhead** (5.10b) A 1- or 2-pitch line 15' left of #13. Parties often do only first 50' to anchors. Climb left-hand crack in series of broken crack systems just left of varnished slab. Set of anchors at 50', another set at 80'. **Rack:** Bring Friends, TCUs.

15. **The Potash Sanction** (5.11a) No topo. Begin in the next crack left of *Pinhead*. Lieback (5.9) up the left-facing corner to drilled piton and over roof (5.10c). Continue to rap anchors 70' up. **Rack:** Bring TCUs, Friends to #4, wired stoppers, small tri-cams.

16. **Astro Lad** (5.11a) A steep and intimidating right-facing corner up a tan wall. Climb thin crack up corner to bolt on outside edge of corner. Hard crack and face climbing leads back into corner above to 2-bolt anchor. **Descent:** Rap 60'. **Rack:** Bring Friends to #2.5 and TCUs.

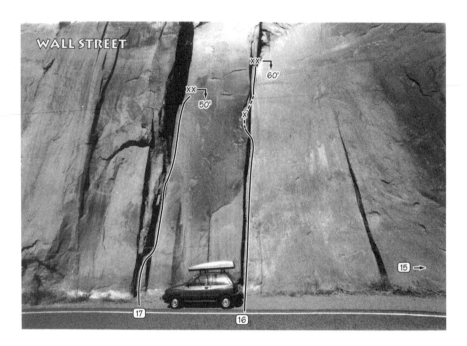

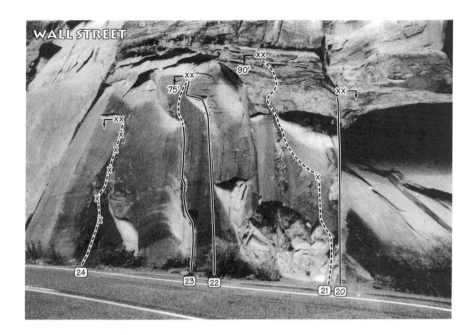

17. **Another Roadside Distraction** (5.10b) An obvious right-facing corner 20'
    left of Route 16. Climb loose, blocky crack up and right to sustained
    finger crack. Crux is thin lieback. **Descent:** Rap 50' from 2-bolt anchor.
    Rack: Friends and TCUs from #.5 to #3.5, with extra #.75.

18. **Mother Trucker** (5.11) A crack route up a 60-foot, left-facing corner. Use
    variety of layaways, jams, and stems up thin crack. Crux is at top with
    lunge left to anchors. 2-bolt anchor. **Rack:** Bring pro from TCUs to a #2.5
    Friend.

19. **Napping With The Alien** (5.11d/12a) A gymnastic, fingery, 65-foot face
    route above a parking spot. Mantle onto shelf and climb up right on good
    hands but weird feet. Crux is above bolt 4 and is grade harder for short
    folks. Also crux pulling up to anchor with a potential ankle-breaking ledge
    if you blow it. 5 drilled angles. 2-bolt anchor.

20. **Bad Moki Roof** (5.9) Climbs a large obvious roof just left of a pullout.
    Climb finger crack in right-facing dihedral for 20' to left side of large
    arch. Undercling out roof, pull the sandy crack at lip (5.8), finish up slabby
    crack to 2-bolt anchor. It's fun until the slog over the roof into the sand.
    Descent: Rap the route. Do not lower or toprope. The roof's edge is get-
    ting very grooved from irresponsible lowering and toproping. **Rack:** Bring
    TCUs, small Friends for lower crack, larger Friends for the roof.

21. **Eyes of Falina** (5.9 R) Begin on the outside edge of Route 20's large dihe-
    dral. Face climb up left on flakes to drilled angle. Continue up left past the

left edge of roof then up right on slab to 2 anchors with rappel slings. **Descent:** Rap 90' to ground.

22. **Flakes of Wrath** (5.9) A popular and classic crack line. Jam and layback hand crack to thin, reachy moves between pockets in crack (5.9). Undercling left under roof (easier than it looks) and finish at a 2-bolt anchor. Rap 75'. **Rack:** Bring double Friends from #1 to #3 and medium wired stoppers. Watch for poison ivy at the base—it's prolific from May through October. Watch pulling the ropes into it!

23. **Flakes of Wrath Direct** (5.11a/b TR) A good toprope 5' left of Route 22. Climb thin crack to flakes.

24. **Mississippi Half Step** (5.12a) An excellent, bouldery face route 20' left of Route 22. A crux, boulder-problem start leads to hard face climbing past 5 bolts/drilled angles to 2-bolt chain anchor. Watch for second crux above bolt 3. Poison ivy at base again.

25. **Frogs of a Feather** (5.10c) Begin on tan rock about 150' right of parking area. Jam thin finger crack/flake. Exit up left past bolt to left traverse (5.10c). Finish at 2-bolt anchor on ledge. **Descent:** Rap 80'. **Rack:** Bring Friends to #3 with several #1s, TCUs.

26. **Shoot Up or Shut Up** (5.11a) Same start as Route 25 but edge up left 10' off ground and pass 2 bolts to arête. Climb arête (5.11a) with 4 bolts to ledge with 2-bolt rap anchor (same as Route 25). **Rack:** Bring RPs, small wires, and #3 Friend.

27. **Wake of the Flood** (5.10c) About 25' left of Route 26. Work up widening crack past 2 bolts to small roof (5.10c). 2-bolt anchor is up left. **Descent:** Rap or lower 60'. **Rack:** Bring sets of Friends, TCUs, wires.

28. **Flash Flood** (5.11a) A white face 10' left of Route 27. Climb thin crack with 3 drilled pitons to face with 2 bolts. **Descent:** Rap 60' from a 2-bolt anchor. **Rack:** Bring Friends, TCUs, large stoppers.

29. **Visible Panty Line** (5.10a) A good but weird line up 4 thin cracks just right of parking area. Climb thin cracks past drilled angle to belay ledge/groove with 2-bolt anchor on right wall. **Rack:** Bring small Friends, TCUs, stoppers.

30. **Pounding the Frog** (5.10b) A 40' pitch on far right side of large parking area. Dicey face climbing leads to first bolt. Continue up left past another bolt to 2-bolt anchor.

31. **Bolts to Bumpy Land** (5.11c) Also called *Sedan Delivery*. Located on right side of large parking lot and slashing gully. Lots of poison ivy in gully. The 115' line ascends tan slab to varnished face above past 14 bolts to 2-bolt anchor. Crux mantle at bolt 1 or stem from right; also hard at bolts 3 and 4, and above bolt 7. **Descent:** Rappel with 2 ropes.

32. **Black Horse** aka **Wild Eyed Dear** (5.12a) Superb face route up black face about 200' left of large parking area. Delicate face climbing leads past 7 black hangers to 2-bolt anchor; 70'.

33. **Twitin Shinkies** (5.11a/b) Begin 20' left of Route 32. Climb a left-facing corner over a couple of roof-bulges past 3 fixed pitons to 2-bolt rap station. Crux above bolt 2. 55'. A grade harder for short folks. **Rack:** Bring large RPs and #1 and #2 Friends.

34. **Blowing Chunks** (5.11b/c) Spectacular line up thin left-facing corner to right side of an arch. Stem and edge up corner and its outside arête (crux between bolts 2 and 3) to 2-bolt anchor right of arch. 60'. 4 bolts. **Rack:** Bring many small wires, TCUs or small Aliens, and small cams including a #.75 TCU.

35. **30 Seconds Over Potash** (5.8) One of the area's easier classic routes. Jam and layback the large left-facing dihedral on right side of a pulloff for 80' to 2-bolt anchor. **Rack:** Bring wired stoppers, TCUs, and Friends to #3. No fixed gear.

36. **Lucy in the Sky with Potash** (5.10a) Begin 15' left of Route 35. Stem and jam crack up narrow left-facing corner for 65' to a 2-bolt anchor. Crux is reach move where crack becomes seam. Use extreme caution at the top— loose death flakes could pullout on you! **Rack:** Bring wires, TCUs, Friends to #3. No fixed gear.

37. **Nervous in Suburbia** (5.10a) Excellent face climb. Follow obvious chalked holds for 65' past 4 bolts to a 3-bolt chain anchor. It's spooky getting to first clip. Spot the leader. Technical crux is above bolt 1.

38. **Under the Boardwalk** (5.12a/b) Begin on right side of gully 40' left of Route 37. Hard face climbing leads 60' past 8 bolts/fixed pins to 2-bolt chain anchor. The finish is desperate.

39. **Something Nasty** (5.12b) No topo. On the left wall of the deep gully (watch for poison ivy). Follow right-angling crack system for 70' to anchors. **Rack:** Bring wired stoppers, many TCUs, and Friends to #3 including 3 #1s and 3 #2.5.

40. **I Love Loosey** (5.11c/d R) Sporty route 20' left of Route 39. Climb blunt arête between tan and black rock walls. Stick-clip first bolt, edge upwards past 3 more bolts to 2-bolt anchor. Watch for possible ground fall between bolts 2 and 3! 50'.

41. **Baby Blue** (5.11a) Short, sweet line 20' left of Route 40. Locate obvious, beautiful finger crack in left-facing corner. Jam and lieback for 50' to 3-bolt anchor. **Rack:** Bring wires, many TCUs, Friends to #2.5.

42. **The Slab** aka **Snake's Slab** (5.8) Popular route on left side of large gully. Follow short, bushy trail to base of obvious slabby fin. Friction upwards for 65' past 5 bolts to 2-bolt anchor.

43. **Eat the Rich** (5.10c) About 50' left of Route 42. Jam finger crack up thin, right-facing corner for 45' to 2-bolt chain anchor. Crux is last moves to anchor. **Rack:** Bring wired stoppers, TCUs, Friends to #2.5. Left of this route is another line—avoid climbing it because of petroglyphs at the start.

44. **Static Cling** (5.11a) On far right side of huge pull-off. Ascend left-facing dihedral to roof, pull over (crux), and finish at anchors. **Rack:** Wires, TCUs,

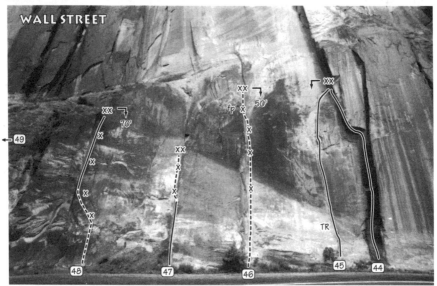

Friends to #3. Lowe Balls might provide additional pro at roof crux.

45. **Potash Bong Hit** (5.10 TR) A top rope off Route 44's anchors. Begin 10' left of Route 44. Watch for large loose flake. Good 5.11 TR link-up ascends Route 45 half-way before traversing into crux of Route 44.

46. **Unknown** (5.10) Above the pulloff. Left-facing corner with 4 fixed pitons to 2-bolt anchor.

47. **Unknown** (5.10) Left of Route 46. Right-facing corner with 2 fixed pitons to 2-bolt anchor.

48. **Skeletonic** (5.11+) Climbs a right-facing dihedral left of Route 47. Work up thin crack in dihedral past 4 bolts to 2-bolt anchor. **Descent:** Rap 70'. **Rack:** Bring medium wires, TCUs, Friends to #2.

49. **The Top Rope Area** (5.6-5.10 TR) No topo. Many toprope problems are found on this cliff behind large parking area. Some fixed anchors are found on terrace above.

50. **Slab Route** (5.7 R) No topo. Above left side of large pullout, just right of willow tree. Climb run out slab past 2 bolts. Hanger is missing on third bolt. **Descent:** Rap 90' with 2 ropes from anchors.

51. **Puppy Love** (5.9) Route begins about 140' left of large parking area, just left of trees. Line angles up right into grooved seam, frictions up 65' to 2-bolt rap anchor. 3 bolts. **Rack:** Bring Friends and TCUs from #.5 to #1.

52. **Steel Your Face** (5.10a) Brilliant friction route with great pro and dicey sequences. Begin 10' left of Route 51 and right of drain pipe. Work up steep white slab past 6 bolts to 2-bolt chain anchor. **Descent:** Rap 80'. A fun toprope, *The Flakes of Bongo* (5.10), ascends the arête to left; it's 5.11 if you stay right of the arête.

53. **Chris-Cross** (5.11a R) The prominent left-facing corner. Climb the dihedral (5.9 R) to bulge; work out left to thin face move with bolt. Go back right into crack and crux just below anchors. 1 fixed piton. **Descent:** Rap

70'. **Rack:** Bring small wires and Friends to #3.5.

54. **Just Another Pretty Face** (5.10b R) Very good line that wanders up the slab left of Route 53. Run out 5.8 climbing leads to bolt 1 about 25' up. Work up left and then back right past 5 more bolts to double-bolt anchor with chains. Crux is at bolt 4. To avoid decking below bolt 1, ascend Route 53 to a #2.5 Friend placement, traverse to bolt 1, back clean the Friend, continue. **Descent:** Rap 80'. **Rack:** #2.5 Friend.

55. **Don Smurfo** (5.10 R) Begin on far right side of black wall left of Route 54. Climb thin crack system to single drilled angle. Face climb up right and join Route 54 near its fourth bolt. **Rack:** Wires, TCUs. **Descent:** Rap 80' from Route 54's anchors.

56. **Big Sky Mud Flaps** (5.10d) Excellent and exciting pitch of continuous climbing. Begin below thin crack about 15' left of Route 55. Work up seam-crack on varnished rock to bulge and upper white headwall. **Descent:** Rap 110' with 2 ropes from 2-bolt anchor on dark rock above horizontal break.

57. **Nameless** (5.12+) Start 20' left of Route 56. Face climb discontinuous crack-seam on black rock to bolt. Work up right on steep, thin face climbing past 3 more bolts and join Route 56 on its upper slab. **Descent:** Rap 110' with 2 ropes from Route 56's anchors. **Rack:** Bring TCUs, Friends.

58. **Walk on the Wide Side** (5.10a) The perfect, off-width, practice route for those scary tower climbs! Jam and thrutch up obvious splitter off-width

crack for 80' to 2-bolt anchor just below horizontal break. Single fixed piton protects crux. **Rack:** Bring pro from 2" to 4" along with large Friends, large Camalots, and Big Bros.

59. **Armageddon** (5.12a/b) A desperate Charlie Fowler testpiece on the left side of the black wall. Begin about 20' left of Route 58. Work up and right on thin edges and smears to 2-bolt anchor. 5 bolts. 60'.

60. **Jacob's Ladder** (5.10d) A fun lead just right of a crack with 2 bushes; the holds, however, are hardly ladder-like. Face climb past 4 bolts to 2-bolt anchor. Crux is above bolt 1. 50'. A stick-clip is good for bolt 1.

61. **Shadowfax** (5.11a) Located just left of the bushy crack and right of a steep gully/pour-off. Dicey slabwork leads to bolt. Edge up right past 4 more bolts to 2-bolt anchor. Crux is at bolt 4. Stick-clip bolt 1. **Descent:** Rap 50'.

More routes are located to the left of Route 61. Do not climb these routes. They are not very good and are too close to a spectacular panel of Indian petroglyphs.

Long Canyon

Overview

Long Canyon is a spectacular and scenic 4-mile-long canyon that slices west from the Colorado River and Potash Road to the northern rim of Island in the Sky in the rugged canyon country southwest of Moab. The wide canyon is lined with immense, towering walls of Wingate sandstone. Numerous crack lines have been put up on the cliffs at a variety of areas, most reached by steep hikes up the talus slopes below the cliffs. The developed areas include Deadman's Buttress, The Shipyard, Off-Width City, Reptilian Wall, and Maverick Buttress. Jug Handle Arch, ascended via a three-pitch route, sits above the canyon entrance above Potash Road and the river. This guide covers two of the canyon's finest climbing sectors—The Shipyard and Maverick Buttress. Comprehensive local guides have information on the other areas.

The Shipyard, an area with excellent cracks along the base of an immense black wall, lies at the north end of a steep draw near the entrance to Long Canyon. Maverick Buttress, perched high above upper Long Canyon, offers a superb selection of cracks that is the best in the Moab area and comparable to those at Indian Creek. The crag's setting is simply stunning. The canyon, rimmed with ruddy Wingate sandstone walls, drops east to the Colorado River. Beyond the river stretch the pale salmon-colored fins of Behind the Rocks and beyond them the lofty, snowcapped La Sal Mountains.

Maverick Buttress, which sits at the relatively high elevation of 5,500 feet, is an excellent year-round climbing choice. The crag lies just below the rim of Island in the Sky. It is usually cooler than the river areas around Moab in summer. The buttress is sunny in the morning, making it ideal for cool weather outings, and shady in the afternoon—ideal for warmer days. The south-facing Shipyard is a great option during cold weather, but it bakes in the sun on most days.

Reach the cliffs via Long Canyon Road, a rough, narrow dirt road that climbs from Potash Road to the top of Island in the Sky north of Deadhorse Point. The road to the base of Maverick Buttress is passable to two-wheel-drive vehicles except in wet and snowy weather. Use care on the steep switchbacks on the upper road as it edges in a shelf-like fashion across steep slopes. The road past the buttress is currently closed to all but four-wheel-drive vehicles due to a large rockfall that covered the road in the winter of 1995–1996.

Climbing history: Maverick Buttress, one of the first developed crack areas around Moab, initially caught the attention of Charlie Fowler who, with Jack Roberts, did the first ascents of all the best routes in January of 1987. Mia Axon, Dougald MacDonald, and Jay Smith made other first ascents in 1989 and 1990. Jim Dunn did a couple of the more heinous off-width routes in 1991. Kevin Chase, Eric Decaria, and Cristie Waylan discovered and climbed the splitter cracks at The Shipyard in February of 1996.

Trip Planning Information

General description: Long Canyon, with miles of towering Wingate sandstone buttresses seamed with cracks, offers superb crack routes on many cliffs including the excellent Maverick Buttress.

Location: East-central Utah. Southwest of Moab. (See map page 97.)

Camping: Several primitive roadside camping areas are located in lower Long Canyon. A good spot is a quarter of a mile up-canyon at the parking area for The Shipyard. Others are located below the switchbacks farther west. Do not camp at the parking area for Maverick Buttress. The water tank below the buttress is a critical watering hole for endangered desert bighorn sheep. Other camping areas are along Potash Road beside the Colorado River just south of Wall Street, and at the Jaycee Campground above Wall Street. Many other campgrounds are located in the immediate Moab area.

Climbing season: Year-round. Spring and fall are best. Expect wind in spring. Some fall days might be too hot for climbing, except in the shade. Winters can be cold, but the south-facing climbs are usually climbable. The access road to Maverick Buttress, however, can be slick and icy. Summers can be very hot, particularly on the south-facing Shipyard. Maverick Buttress lies at a higher and usually cooler elevation, and is frequently shaded in the afternoon.

Restrictions and access issues: None currently. Do not camp at the switchback parking area below Maverick Buttress. This is an important watering area for desert bighorn sheep. Otherwise, use the usual desert etiquette by following existing trails, using campsites, and picking up all your trash including cigarette butts and tape.

Guidebooks: *Desert Rock: Wall Street to the San Rafael Swell* by Eric Bjørnstad, Chockstone Press, 1997. This book has the complete guide to Long Canyon's many crack lines. *500 Select Moab Classics* by Kevin Chase is available at Moab Adventure Outfitters on North Main Street. Kevin, one of the owners, can also provide beta and info on new routes.

Nearby mountain shops, guide services, and gyms: Moab Adventure Outfitters and Rim Cyclery in Moab.

Services: All visitor and climber services are found in Moab, including gas, food, lodging, camping, dining, groceries, film, and climbing gear. Check out Eddie McStiff's for good Utah microbrews and the Moab Diner for a cheap breakfast.

Emergency services: Call 911. Allen Memorial Hospital, 719 West 400 North, Moab, UT, (801) 259-7191.

Nearby climbing areas: Day Canyon, Potash Road, Wall Street, Deadhorse Point, Monster Tower, Washer Woman Arch, Canyonlands National Park areas, Kane Springs Canyon, River Road, Castleton Tower, the Fisher Towers, Arches National Park.

Nearby attractions: Bowtie and Corona Arches, Jug Handle Arch, Canyonlands National Park, White Rim Trail, Deadhorse Point State Park, Colorado River, Arches National Park, La Sal Mountains, Manti-La Sal National Forest, Fisher Towers, Colorado River Scenic Byway (Utah 128), Slickrock Bike Trail.

Finding the cliffs: (See map page 97.) Long Canyon, stretching west for 4 miles from Potash Road, lies 15 miles south of U.S. Highway 191 (west of Moab). Drive out of Moab on U.S. Highway 191 for a couple of miles to the Potash Road turnoff. Turn south here on Potash Road (Utah Highway 313) and follow it for 15 miles to Long Canyon. The large obvious canyon begins west of the Jug Handle Arch viewpoint. Turn west or right off the highway onto the dirt Long Canyon Road. The parking for The Shipyard lies a quarter of a mile up the canyon on the right. The Shipyard is near the head of the first draw coming in from the north. Continue up the road for 3.4 miles to the parking area for Maverick Buttress at the top of the switchbacks. A short trail heads west and up the hill to the buttress base.

THE SHIPYARD

This beautiful black-varnished cliff section currently offers 4 superb splitter crack routes similar to those at Indian Creek Canyon. The routes ascend only 70 feet of the almost 400-foot-high Wingate sandstone cliff. The wall lies at the head of the first canyon on the right or north side of Long Canyon about a quarter of a mile west of Potash Road. Drive west up the Long Canyon Road to an obvious pullout and side road on the right that leads 100 yards north to a campsite. Park and hike up the rocky draw past many cowdung patties and large boulders. A faint, cairn-marked trail winds up the canyon floor to the base of the steeper final slope. Look here for the trail to leave the draw and head northeast or to the right up a loose, rocky slope. Hike upward a couple of hundred feet to the base of the obvious black wall on the right side near the head of the box canyon. Walk north along the cliff base to find the climbs. The routes are marked with plaques and listed right to left.

1. **Shipwrecked** (5.10a) No topo. A fine 1-pitch route up a broken, open corner. Jam, stem, lieback for 70' to 2-cold shut anchor. Rappel or lower. **Rack:** Bring TCUs and Friends to #3.5.

2. **Torpedo Bay** (5.12c) An excellent 65' splitter crack up a black wall. Route, with 3 cruxes, jams thin finger to small hands crack. Caution: watch for

LONG CANYON
THE SHIPYARD APPROACH

The Shipyard

trail
cairn

LONG CANYON
THE SHIPYARD

xx
60'

hands

xx
60'

xx
65'

thin hands

hands

thin finger

4

3

2

1

dicey loose block at crux. **Rack:** Pro (in order for ascent) are 1 #1.5, 2 #.75, 3 #1, 5 #1.5 Friends, TCUs. Some small wires are also useful. **Descent:** Lower from carabiner on chained 2-bolt anchor.

3.   **Nina (5.10d)** Another great crack. Begin a few feet left of Route 2. Jam hand to fist crack for 60' to rap anchors. **Rack:** Bring a set of Friends, including extras in large sizes.

4.   **Electronic Battleship (5.10c)** The last of the splitters. Route jams obvious hand to fist to hand crack just left of long chimney system. **Descent:** Rap or lower from 2 coldshuts atop the 60' pitch. **Rack:** Bring cams to 4".

MAVERICK BUTTRESS

Reach Maverick Buttress via Long Canyon Road, a relatively rough, narrow dirt road that climbs from Potash Road and the Colorado River to the top of Island in the Sky near Deadhorse Point. The road to the base of the crag is passable to two-wheel-drive vehicles, except in wet or snowy weather. Use care on the switchbacks on the upper section—the road edges in a shelf-like manner across steep slopes. The upper section of the road past the buttress is currently impassable except for high-clearance vehicles due to a large rockfall that covered the road in the winter of 1995.

Park below the buttress on the wide corner above the switchbacks. Do not camp in the area or disturb the water tank just off the road. The area is a critical watering hole for desert bighorn sheep. A short 5-minute hike follows a trail to the buttress base. A path follows the base of the cliff, allowing access to the routes. The routes are listed from right to left or north to south beginning from the east-facing head of the buttress. Remember that the listed rack is only a suggestion. It's up to you to decide if you need more gear for a route than what's listed here. It's always nice to have extra pieces when you get gripped!

5.   **Rawhide (5.11d)** A 150' pitch up right-hand crack on east buttress face. Jam a hand crack past wide section with flake. Continue up finger crack to 2-bolt rappel anchor on small, sloping ledge. **Descent:** Rap with 2 ropes. **Rack:** 4 sets of Friends.

6.   **Miss Kitty Likes It That Way (5.11d)** Excellent 70' small hands to finger crack to 2-bolt rappel chains. Crux is at top in sequential 1" to 3/4" crack. Midway up is rattley block that flexes, but is solid to date. Don't pull out on it! **Rack:** Bring double Friends through #2.5, a set of TCUs.

7.   **Gunsmoke (5.11a)** The left-hand crack, a perfect splitter, on the left side of the buttress face. Begin atop boulder and work up left into crack. Jam finger and hand crack to rest below high, thin crux. **Descent:** A 150', 2-rope rappel from 2-bolt anchor in horizontal seam. **Rack:** Bring Friends including 2 #.75, 1 #1, 2 #1.5, 2 #2, 5 #2.5 (use a couple #3s if you don't have enough #2.5s), 1 #3, 1 #3.5, and possibly a #4.

LONG CANYON
MAVERICK BUTTRESS

8. **Boothill** (5.12b) This is the first crack around the corner and about 50' to the left or south of Route 7. Scramble through some boulders to route base. Begin just left of juniper tree. Jam thin hands-fat finger crack (2") in large right-facing dihedral into broken pod with loose blocks. Grovel to drilled piton at top of pod and over roof. Continue up sustained, steep splitter finger crack (5.12) to belay anchors. **Descent:** Rap 130' with 2

Martha Morris belays Scuter on Hot Toddy, *one of the best routes on Maverick Buttress in Long Canyon.* PHOTO BY STEWART M. GREEN

ropes. **Rack:** 2 to 3 sets of Friends with many extra #2 and #1.5 sizes.

9. **Clanton's In The Dust** (5.10d) This Jim Dunn special, a wide crack and seldom climbed line, might appeal to the grunge master. Begin just left of Route 8 below huge dihedral. Climb through wide chimney section stacked with large loose blocks. Work past flake and into off-width above. Continue over many wide sections to 2-bolt belay anchor on the left wall. **Descent:** Rappel 130' with 2 ropes. **Rack:** Lots of wide stuff—Big Bros, #5 Camalots, tube chocks, some #3 and #4 Friends.

10. **High Noon** (5.11b) A short fun route that makes a good practice toprope. Thin crack about 20' left of Route 9. Jam fingertip crack (5.11b) or lieback it (5.10d) for 35' to 2-bolt anchor. **Descent:** Lower from slings. **Rack:** Wired stoppers and TCUs.

11. **Tequila Sunrise** (5.10d) One of the finest cracks in the Moab area! The obvious splitter crack on the black-varnished, right wall of a large right-facing dihedral a couple of cracks left of *High Noon*. Start atop some broken boulders. Jam sustained finger crack (5.10d) that widens to small hands, then perfect hands. Angle left up high into large dihedral and fixed hexentric and 2-bolt anchor at off-width section. **Descent:** Rappel 80' from rappel slings. **Rack:** 2 or 3 sets of Friends from #1.5 to #4, with extra #2.5 to #3.5. A #4 Camalot is useful up high.

12. **Hot Toddy** (5.10b) Another superb but continuous crack with lots of stemming rests. Begin just left of Route 11. Awkward moves lead into black dihedral. Unrelenting perfect hand jams continue up corner to off-width move and anchors (1 bolt, 1 drilled angle, 1 fixed hex). **Descent:** Rap 80' to ground. **Rack:** Large Friends including 4 #3, 4 #3.5, and 3 #4 along with 2 #4 Camalots.

13. **Texas Two Step** (5.10) Find this and the next 2 routes by following a path west from Route 12 along the cliff base to a cul-de-sac. This route is above several large boulders. Locate beautiful crack up right-facing then left-facing corner. Jam hand to fist crack up white right-facing corner and continue up fine left-facing corner to 2-bolt anchor. **Descent:** Rap 70' to the boulders. **Rack:** 2 sets of Friends from #2 to #4 with extra #3, #3.5, and #4.

14. **Round Up** (5.11a) Scramble up through boulders left of Route 13 to base of tan face split by thin crack. Jam thin finger crack (5.11a) for 20'. Continue up wider crack above—hands and fists—to anchors. **Descent:** Rappel 80'. **Rack:** Set of TCUs for lower crack and set of Friends for upper crack. Crack continuously widens from #.75 to #4.

15. **Saddle Sores** (5.10) No topo. On the broken wall opposite #14. Climb hand crack in left-facing corner to huecoed wall and final squeeze chimney. **Descent:** Rappel 50' from 1 anchor. **Rack:** Double Friends from #3 to #4.

LONG CANYON
MAVERICK BUTTRESS

LONG CANYON
MAVERICK BUTTRESS

XX ↗ 70'

XX ↗ 80'

fist

hands

hidden

hidden

fingers

around corner to
2 bolt anchor

⇐ 15

hands

14

13

KANE SPRINGS CANYON

OVERVIEW

Kane Springs Canyon is a lovely, twisting canyon floored by Kane Creek, an intermittent stream lined with tamarisk, willow, and cottonwoods, and walled by soaring cliffs of Navajo and Wingate sandstone. Reach the canyon via Kane Creek Boulevard, which begins on the south side of Moab and travels west along the south side of Spanish Valley before reaching the Colorado River. Here it passes into the river canyon through a portal of looming cliffs. The paved road, on the opposite side of the Colorado from the popular Wall Street cragging area, hugs the east bank for 3 miles. It passes Moonflower Canyon with its petroglyphs and camping area and continues past several manmade caves that once housed an egg farm.

After the road bumps across a cattleguard and becomes dirt, it enters Kane Springs Canyon, a cliff-lined tributary of the main Colorado River canyon. The narrow, dirt road, heading southeast up the canyon, allows access to several spectacular natural areas, including Behind the Rocks, Pritchett Canyon, and Amasa Back, along with hiking and mountain bike trails and several good climbing areas. A good stop-off is Kane Springs, a roadside natural spring 2.2 miles from the cattleguard. Verdant vegetation offers welcome shade and surrounds the potable springs in summer. The road twists through the canyon for 4 miles before exiting into broad Kane Creek Valley. Past here the road rapidly deteriorates into a rough four-wheel-drive trail that edges over Hurrah Pass and then continues south another 50 or so miles to the Needles District in Canyonlands National Park.

The Tombstones are the first climbing area you will encounter in the canyon. These three immense walls, in a sweeping canyon curve called The Cirque of the Climbables, loom above the east side of the road near the canyon's entrance. Long and serious multi-pitch free and aid routes ascend these 500-foot-high monoliths. More crags, not included in this guide, are located on the cliff bands farther up-canyon, including Abraxas Wall and the roadside Hueco Wall with a couple of Jim Beyer sport routes. The Ice Cream Parlor crag, near the end of the canyon, offers a superb selection of slab and crack routes. Two towers, Space Tower and The Predator, are farther south above the road. The Tombstones are composed of Navajo sandstone, and all the other cliffs are

Brett Spencer-Green on The Possessed, *at the Ice Cream Parlor in Kane Springs Canyon.*
PHOTO BY STEWART M. GREEN

Wingate sandstone except The Predator, which is softer Cutler sandstone, the same sandstone that composes the Fisher Towers.

Climbing history: The Kane Springs Canyon area is a relative newcomer to the Moab climbing scene. Almost all of the routes and areas were developed in the 1990s. The first known route along the road was put up by the local Anasazi Indians who lived here in the 1200s. The route ascends a 5.6 chimney jammed with logs, some dating to the original climbers, at the entrance to Moonflower Canyon. Nearby are some chopped Anasazi steps that climb the cliff. Both routes are illegal to climb. A few odds and ends were put up in the 1980s, but the area's main routes were established in the 1990s. Jim Dunn and Kevin Chase did the first ascents of most of The Tombstone routes. The Ice Cream Parlor was developed by Tom and Julie Gilje with a few other partners in 1995. Space Tower saw its first ascent by Chase and Tom Gilje in 1995; Dunn, Kyle Copeland, and Eric Johnson were the first to climb Predator Tower in August of 1991.

Trip Planning Information

General description: Crack and face routes on several fine crags and cliffs in Kane Springs Canyon, including The Tombstones, The Ice Cream Parlor, and Predator Tower, a thin spire.

Location: East-central Utah. Southwest of Moab. (See map page 97.)

Camping: A campground is at Moonflower Canyon on the Kane Creek Road just south of The Portal. A large graded pull-out just south of The Tombstones is often used for primitive camping. Other primitive campsites are located along the road. Good ones are near The Ice Cream Parlor. Good drinking water flows at Kane Springs at 2.2 miles from the cattleguard near the canyon entrance. Several BLM campgrounds are located at Big Bend along River Road (Utah 128), and a fine campground at Devils Garden in Arches National Park. The Sand Flat Campground near the Slickrock Bike Trail east of Moab has many sites. Several private campgrounds with showers and other amenities are located in Moab.

Climbing season: Year-round. Summers can be hot; winters can be cold. Spring and fall are the best seasons.

Restrictions and access issues: No current access issues. All the crags are on BLM public lands. There are biological issues—this is a sensitive, desert bighorn sheep study area, and the soils are cryptobiotic and fragile—be respectful of both.

Guidebooks: *Desert Rock Climbs West* by Eric Bjørnstad, Chockstone Press, 1997, is a complete guide to all the known routes in the Kane Creek Canyon area. *500 Select Moab Classics* by Kevin Chase, 1994. Available from the author at Moab Adventure Outfitters.

Nearby mountain shops, guide services, and gyms: Moab Adventure Out-

KANE SPRING CANYON

**TOMBSTONES,
ICE CREAM PARLOR,
PREDATOR,
SPACE TOWER**

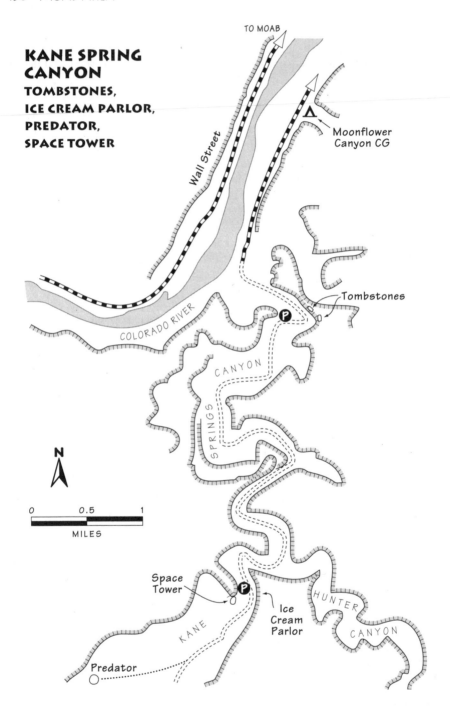

fitters offers gear and clothing. They also have rock climbing classes and a guide service. Rim Cyclery in Moab sells climbing gear and guides.

Services: All visitor and climber services are found in Moab, including gas, food, lodging, camping, dining, showers, and groceries.

Emergency services: Call 911. Allen Memorial Hospital, 719 West 400 North, Moab, UT, (801) 259-7191.

Nearby climbing areas: Wall Street, The King's Hand, Long Canyon, Day Canyon, River Road crags, The Lighthouse, Dolomite Tower, Castleton Tower, The Priest, Fisher Towers, Arches National Park, The Bride, Canyonlands National Park, Washer Woman, Monster Tower, Moses, Indian Creek Canyon.

Nearby attractions: Scott M. Matheson Wetlands Preserve, Kane Springs, Behind the Rocks, Pritchett Canyon, Funnel Arch, Canyonlands National Park, Island in the Sky, Corona Arch, Colorado River, Deadhorse Point State Park, Arches National Park, La Sal Mountains, Manti-La Sal National Forest, Colorado River Scenic Byway (Utah 128), Slickrock Bike Trail.

THE TOMBSTONES

The Tombstones are several huge Navajo sandstone faces that tower above a wide bend of meandering Kane Creek. The walls, also nicknamed The Cirque of the Climbables, lie 0.5 mile up-canyon from the cattle guard near the canyon entrance. A large flat boulder next to the road offers an excellent spot to eyeball the various routes or watch climbers on the immense faces. The best parking is located at a large lot past The Tombstones or 0.7 mile from the cattle guard. The Tombstones offer some marvelous free climbs as well as some of the canyon country's most spectacular aid routes including *Kane Cutter* (III 5.10+ A3+) and *Deep Voodoo* (III 5.7 A3+). Descriptions for these routes are not included here because they require delicate nailing and are not all-clean. Inexperienced desert aid-climbers will likely blow out many of the placements by over-sizing the placements or by cleaning them. Topos and advice for these routes are available at Moab Adventure Outfitters.

1. **Corner Route** (III 5.12-) 5 pitches. An excellent route to the notch between the first and second Tombstones that Jim Dunn and Kevin Chase free climbed in 1994. **Pitch 1:** Begin below obvious dihedral system, up and right of left-angling bolt ladder. Free climb up open corner to prominent horizontal crack. Traverse left (5.8) to ledge with 2-bolt chained anchor. **Pitch 2:** Jam wide crack (5.7) up the ramp-like corner for 75' to 2-bolt belay stance. **Pitch 3:** Jim Dunn calls this lead "a totally amazing pitch—a real beauty." Stem and jam up corner (5.10+) to 2-bolt belay ledge. **Pitch 4:** Continue up corner past a set of rappel anchors via off-width crack (5.9) to good ledge with drilled piton anchor. **Pitch 5:** Climax, crux pitch. Jam exposed splitter finger crack (5.12-) on wall left of

KANE SPRINGS
TOMBSTONES

xx → rap route
C2
xx
C2
xx
C2   .13TR
xx
.12⁻
xx
.10⁺
X
xx
.10⁺ crack
2

xx →
rap
route
.12
⇐ climb finger crack
left of corner
X
rap anchors ── xx
only   xx
.10⁺
xx
.7
xx
.8
1

X
xx
hidden
chimney .7

2

large dihedral before working up right to belay ledge with 2 bolts. Descent: Three 2-rope rappels to the base of route. Bring extra webbing to replace any dessicated and frayed slings. **Rack:** Bring 2 sets of TCUs, a set of wired stoppers, 2 sets of Friends, a couple of large pieces.

2. **Playing Hooky** (IV 5.11 C2) 6 pitches. This airy route, first climbed by Jim Dunn, Charlie Fowler, Peter Verchick, and Kevin Chase, ascends the intimidating face of the center Tombstone. Jim Dunn feels an ambitious and skilled party might be able to free most of the route. The first couple of pitches make an all-free 5.10 route. Otherwise, parties going all the way should plan on leaving fixed ropes above pitch 3 to facilitate the rappel descent. **Pitch 1:** 2 options: (1) Begin below obvious left-facing chimney. Work up through chimney (5.7) to broken ledge. Traverse right to 3-bolt belay station. (2) Free climb directly up a crack system (5.10+) below belay. Both options are 75'. **Pitch 2:** Work up right into obvious crack system. Jam (5.10+) for 60' to 2-bolt hanging belay. **Pitch 3:** Continue up steep, thin double cracks (5.12-) for 55' to another bolted hanging belay under triangular roof. This is the end of the free climbing. **Pitch 4:** Aid up thin, overhanging crack (C2) on streaked wall to bolted belay left of obvious roof; 70'. This wild, exposed crack has been toproped at 5.13. **Pitch 5:** Aid up shallow right-facing corner (C2) to 2-bolt belay stance below final headwall; 60'. **Pitch 6:** Aid up overhanging open corner to summit anchors. **Descent:** Make five 2-rope rappels down route. Leave fixed ropes above pitch 3 to ease descent. It's a good idea to bring extra webbing to replace dried and suspect rap slings. **Rack:** 2 sets of TCUs, 2 sets of Friends to #3 and single #3.5 and #4 Friends, a couple of larger cams, 2 sets of wired stoppers. Clean aid requires some trickery including Lowe Balls.

3. **For Desert Rats Only** (III 5.11) 5 pitches. A spectacular line up the third Tombstone put up by Jim Dunn and company, 1994. Begin below the obvious crack system on the right side of the wall. **Pitch 1:** Climb long and varied pitch (5.10) up cracks and corners to ledge with 2 drilled-angle belay station. This can also be broken into 2 shorter pitches. **Pitch 2:** Climb narrowing crack in perfect left-facing corner. As it becomes seam, work right and face climb up blunt, white arête with 2 bolts (5.10) to ledge with 2 bolts. **Pitch 3:** Climb cracks and corners (5.8) for about 60' to another ledge with anchors below prominent crack. **Pitch 4:** Long lead (150') up sustained 7" to 10" off-width crack to 2-bolt belay stance in upper chimney. Pro includes 5 drilled angles. **Pitch 5:** Spooky jamming up 1.5" crack left of the belay for 50' to single anchor belay/rap station. **Descent:** Rappel route with four 2-rope rappels. **Rack:** Set of TCUs, 2 sets of Friends, medium to large stoppers or Rocks, some Big Bros and other wide stuff for pitch 4.

KANE SPRINGS
TOMBSTONES

x — rap route

XX

5 bolts

7-10"
crack
OW

XX

.8

XX
x

x   .10
face

up perfect
corner-
narrowing
crack

XX

.10

1 long
pitch to
belay

.10

3

thin,
dihedral
crack 160'
5.11+

4

4. **Surface Tension** (5.11+) No topo. This excellent 1-pitch route ascends obvious clean, right-facing corner on wall right of third Tombstone. Climb up and left into corner. Jam finger and thin hand crack for 140' to 2-bolt belay/rappel station. **Descent:** Rappel with 2 ropes to ground. **Rack:** Set of Friends, several sets of TCUs.

ICE CREAM PARLOR

This very good crag sits above the east side of the road at a bend at 3.6 miles just before the canyon opens in broad Kane Valley. The routes are located on a lower tier of Wingate sandstone cliffs below a steep, somewhat fractured upper tier. There are some good slab routes on the wide, varnished slab on the left side of the cliff; the right side offers a selection of cracks and bolted routes. Most of the routes are 1-pitch long, with rappel anchors for descent. This is a good morning cliff during warmer months. It has shade until noon.

Follow the narrow, dirt Kane Canyon Road from the cattle guard at the canyon entrance for 3.6 miles to a small parking area on the right side of the road. Good primitive campsites are located off the road just before the cliff. The Ice Cream Parlor is a short hike east up a hard-to-find climber's path on steep, boulder-strewn slope. Hiking time is 5 minutes. Routes are listed from right to left.

5. **Knee Grinder** (5.9) This route begins on the right side of the cliff just right of a wide ledge. Jam wide crack system in large right-facing dihedral. 1 bolt is located on right wall up high. **Descent:** Rap 75' from anchors on ledge. **Rack:** Bring big Friends and Camalots.

6. **The Possessed** (5.11a) A very fine route up a blunt arête. A funky start moves up and left onto arête. Follow bolts, good holds to rap anchor on ledge. Make sure your carabiner doesn't lie on edge below bolt 2. 6 bolts to 2 cold-shut rappel anchor (same anchor as Route 5); 75'.

7. **The Coffin** (5.9) Begin left of *The Possessed* on wide, rocky ledge. Jam up broken cracks over roof and continue up widening crack/chimney to ledge. **Descent:** Rap 75' from 2-bolt anchor. **Rack:** Bring a set of Friends.

8. **Pulp Friction** (5.11) An excellent, sustained route up black varnished sandstone. Begin just left of base of thin, left-facing corner about 25' left of Route 7 on ledge. A thin, bouldery, face-climbing start leads up right to bolt on slab. Work right into corner. Move up a few feet before exiting onto steep arête. Continue past 2 bolts to anchor. **Descent:** Rap 70'. 5 bolts to 2-bolt anchor. **Rack:** #1 and #3 Friends are needed.

9. **Ice Cream Parlor Crack** (5.11a) The crag's classic, must-do line up a superb right-facing corner. Start a few feet left of Route 8 on wide ledge. Face climb into corner. Jam, layback, and stem up corner to 2-bolt anchor. **Descent:** Rap 70'. **Rack:** Bring a rack of thin stuff (TCUs) including 1 #.4, 2 #.5, 5 #.75, 2 #1 Friends, and 1 #5 Camalot.

10. **Good Day to Die** (5.9) A decent route up a right-angling dihedral about 25' left of *Ice Cream Parlor Crack*. Jam, layback up dihedral to couple of bolts on high slab. **Descent:** Rap 70' from 2-bolt anchor. It's easy to set up a toprope on #9 from here.

The following routes are on a dark, varnished slab 100' left or north of cracks. Follow path along cliff base to routes.

11. **RP City** (5.10) A hair-line crack up the right side of the smooth slab. Edge, smear up line using lots of RPs for pro. **Descent:** Rap 75' from anchors. **Rack:** Bring about a dozen RPs, small stoppers.

12. **Crack 1** (5.8) The right crack of a trio of cracks in the slab's center. Good climbing up the crack to anchors at the break atop the slab. **Descent:** Rap 75' from anchors. **Rack:** Bring stoppers, TCUs, small Friends. Traverse left to set up toprope on other 2 cracks.

13. **Crack 2** (5.8+) The middle crack. Lead or toprope. Rap from Route 12's anchors.

14. **Crack 3** (5.8) The left-hand crack. Lead or toprope. Rap from Route 12's anchors.

15. **Wolverine** (5.11) A 3-pitch route on the wall above the slab. **Pitch 1:** Climb *Crack 1* and belay at 2-bolt anchor. **Pitch 2:** Work up corner on steep, streaked wall (2 bolts), jam over big roof to 2-bolt belay stance. **Pitch 3:** Continue up corner above, pass another roof, end at 2-bolt belay/rappel station. **Descent:** Rappel the route. **Rack:** Bring stoppers, TCUs, Friends.

SPACE TOWER

This semi-detached tower sits a few feet away from the cliff face across the canyon from the Ice Cream Parlor. The summit appears to rest against the main cliff from a distance but is separated by a 3-inch gap. An excellent route, put up by Kevin Chase and Tom Gilje in 1995, ascends the chimney system facing the Ice Cream Parlor. Access the route by parking off the road below the Ice Cream Parlor. Cross Kane Creek and scramble up talus slopes to the east side of the tower.

16. **Hallow Souls** (5.9) No topo. Follow obvious chimney/crack system that separates tower from main cliff on right or east side of tower for 1 long pitch. Expect chimneying, jamming, and stemming. **Descent:** Rappel 165' with 2 ropes down route from anchors. **Rack:** Bring sets of TCUs and Camalots along with some Friends and many long runners.

PREDATOR TOWER

A spectacular but somewhat hidden 150-foot-high tower on the edge of wide Kane Creek Valley just up-canyon (southwest) from the Ice Cream Parlor. The free-standing tower, composed of Cutler Formation sandstone, sits at the end of a ragged ridge to the west of the road. Follow Kane Creek Road for about 4 miles from the cattleguard at the canyon entrance. After the Ice Cream Parlor the canyon opens into a broad valley. Park by some large boulders on

2 rope rappel

**KANE SPRINGS CANYON
PREDATOR TOWER**

the side of the road and hike cross-country to the base of the tower. Try to follow existing paths or drainages to avoid damaging the fragile cryptobiotic soil.

17. **Reign of Terror** (II 5.11a) This 2-pitch line, put up by Jim Dunn and Kyle Copeland on the first ascent of the tower in 1991, ascends the south side of the formation. **Pitch 1:** Work up crack (5.11a) for 60' to spacious belay ledge. **Pitch 2:** Move onto loose pillar/flake to fixed piton. Make easy traverse right to hand crack. Jam (5.9) to bulbous summit; 90'. **Descent:** One 2-rope, 150' rappel from 2 drilled angles. **Rack:** Friends, Camalots, TCUs.

Southeast

SE

UTAH

INDIAN CREEK CANYON

OVERVIEW

Indian Creek Canyon, a long rift lined with ruby-colored sandstone cliffs, is the undisputed crack climbing capital of the world. That's a bold statement to make, but once a climber jams the perfect cracks that split its soaring walls, its truth is undeniable. This stunning canyon, which lies immediately east of Canyonlands National Park, is a place renowned for parallel-sided cracks and the huge racks of cams needed to protect them. The climber who succeeds here is endowed with impeccable crack technique, endurance, a high pain threshold, and a healthy dose of bold commitment.

Variety is the key word at Indian Creek. Every imaginable type of crack is located here, ranging from fierce finger cracks to superb splitter hand cracks to strenuous off-widths that threaten to spit the climber out with every arm bar. The canyon, one of Utah's first cragging areas, is not a sport climbing area by any stretch of the imagination. Outside of a few slab routes in the upper canyon, only 1 bolted line is located here. Instead this is a place where climbers rejoice in traditional means of surmounting crack challenges.

Traditional ethics are definitely in vogue at Indian Creek. Old-style ascents are the norm. Placing bolts next to cracks is definitely a big No-No, as is hang-dogging. It takes true grit to lead a crack and place gear. The time and effort required to fiddle the right Friend in for pro exponentially increases the pump factor—the difference between lead climbing and top-roping or leading with preplaced gear varies between 1 and 4 letter grades. The size of the climber's hands also determines the grade of a route. For instance, *Supercrack* is a ladder for anyone with big hands, while those with small hands have to fist-jam or use off-width techniques. Yo-yo ascents are also accepted here, i.e., the climber leads until she/he falls off, lowers to the ground, and, leaving the rope and gear in place, jams back up past the high point until the anchors are clipped.

Indian Creek is not a beginner or even intermediate area. All of the Indian Creek routes are hard. A 5.10 here is not like a 5.10 at a sport area—a 5.10 here is tough. Everyone who climbs here comes away with a healthy respect for the grades. Few routes below 5.10 exist, so climbers should be prepared to lead solid 5.10 while placing gear or have a very limited selection of routes available.

The long escarpment that lines Indian Creek Canyon is composed of Wingate sandstone, one of the primary cliff-forming layers on the Colorado Plateau. The sandstone, averaging about 350 feet thick here, was deposited some 210 million years ago during the early Jurassic Period. During that time, steady northwest winds swept sand into immense dunes in an area similar in size to today's Sahara in northern Africa. The Wingate, named for its type-locality at Fort Wingate, Arizona, is generally buff and reddish-orange in color, streaked with dark curtains of desert varnish (iron and manganese oxide stains), and fractured by sheer, vertical cracks and fissures. The greenish-colored talus slopes below the Wingate are composed of the Chinle Formation, a layer of consolidated mud, silt, sand, and gravel deposited in lakes, swamps, and streambeds. It's also the uranium-bearing layer. Above the Wingate is the thin Kayenta Formation, an erosion-resistant sandstone that forms a caprock atop the softer Wingate. Above that lies the thick, dune-deposited Navajo sandstone.

Climbing history: The first time I saw the stunning cracks at Indian Creek was in the late autumn of 1971. Jim Dunn, Billy Westbay, and I, en route to climbing North Sixshooter Peak, stopped along the highway in the canyon and marveled at the perfect cracks splitting the sandstone cliffs. The most perfect line we dubbed The Super Crack. At that time, of course, none of those vertical cracks had been climbed and it was almost impossible to think about jamming them with only pitons and bongs for protection. The golden age of Indian Creek climbing was still years away; it awaited the invention of Friends to protect the smooth cracks. Five years later I was back at Indian Creek in early November photographing Earl Wiggins as he smoothly jammed the first ascent of *Supercrack*, methodically placing his hands in the crack and protecting its long sweep with only a handful of large Hexentric nuts.

The ascent of *Supercrack* by Wiggins, Ed Webster, and Bryan Becker swung open the door of possibilities at Indian Creek. Much of the early activity, centered in Fringe of Death Canyon, was by Colorado Springs climbers including Wiggins, Webster, and Dunn along with Utah climber Mugs Stump. The canyon received its unusual name after Wiggins led up a fingertip lieback crack in a clean corner and was unable to place any small hexentric nuts for 60 feet, putting him on the "fringe of death." This lovely box canyon was once the popular canyon camp spot with its sheltered sites and good boulders, but heavy use and abuse led to its final closure to camping and vehicles. Today it's a day-use area closed to all but foot traffic and cows; it rarely sees much climbing traffic.

Other buttresses were explored, climbed, and named during the late 1970s. Most of today's classics on Supercrack Buttress were established, including *Incredible Hand Crack* (initially called *Sedimentary Journey*) in 1978, and *Coyne Crack* in 1979. *Coyne Crack*, a.k.a. *The Left Side of Darkness*, got its name when Leonard Coyne fell on an attempt, pulling a #1 Friend which broke his glasses. The glass shards sliced and temporarily blinded his left eye.

Martha Morris leads an unnamed route, Blue Gramma Cliff, Indian Creek.
PHOTO BY STEWART M. GREEN

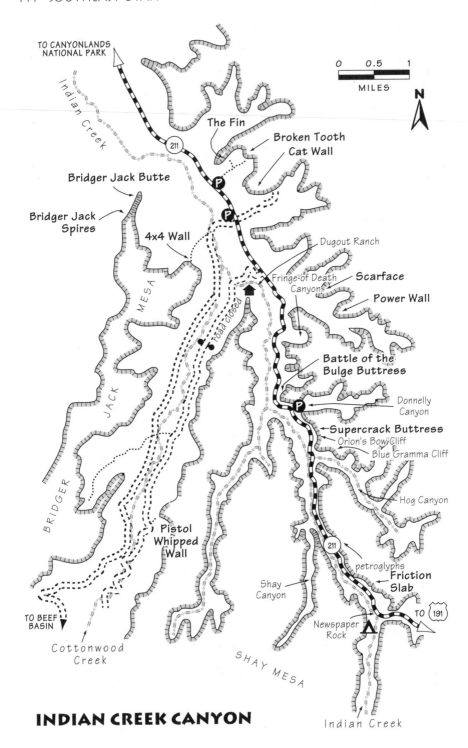

TO CANYONLANDS
NATIONAL PARK

0   0.5   1
MILES

N

Indian Creek

The Fin

Broken Tooth
Cat Wall

211

Bridger Jack Butte

Bridger Jack
Spires

4x4 Wall

Dugout Ranch

Fringe of Death
Canyon

Scarface

Power Wall

MESA

Road closed

Battle of the
Bulge Buttress

JACK

Donnelly
Canyon

Supercrack Buttress

Orion's Bow Cliff

Blue Gramma Cliff

Hog Canyon

BRIDGER

Pistol
Whipped
Wall

211

petroglyphs

Friction
Slab

Shay
Canyon

TO 191

TO BEEF
BASIN

Newspaper
Rock

Cottonwood
Creek

SHAY MESA

INDIAN CREEK CANYON

Indian Creek

While Coyne recovered, Ken Sims sent the project. Donnelly Canyon saw its first route, *Generic Crack*, jammed by Jim Dunn in 1976, while Battle of the Bulge Buttress received its name from its first route, established by Steve Hong in 1977.

By the early 1980s, when most of the early exploration was completed at Indian Creek, Steve Hong, then a medical student in Salt Lake City, set about methodically ticking all the best cracks in the canyon. Fred Knapp, a desert guidebook author, notes, "You'll be walking around and spot this awesome line. You hike up to the base and see some slings at the top and you know Steve Hong has already been there." Hong, in company with his wife, Karin Budding, and others, including the late Steve Carruthers, established over 120 first ascents in the Canyonlands. Some of his ascents include *Quarter of a Man* at Battle of the Bulge, *Dos Hermanos* in Donnelly Canyon, a lot of the routes at the stellar Cat Wall like *Johnny Cat* and *King Cat*, as well as some of the hardest Indian Creek lines. These include *Sacred Cow* (5.13a/b), *6-Star Crack* (5.13b/c), and *Tricks Are For Kids* (5.13c), a full-pitch, endurance, wide-finger testpiece.

Others have followed in Hong's hand jams, exploring new walls and putting up neo-classics along the seemingly endless escarpment of Wingate cliffs. These new pioneers include Steve Petro, Bret Ruckman, and Marco Cornacchione, who authored a select guide to Indian Creek climbs. Doug Oliver of Salt Lake City singlehandedly put up most of the routes at Pistol Whipped Wall in the mid-1990s, showing that loads of excellent potential routes still hide on the rusty canyon walls.

Until the mid-1980s, most rock climbers assumed that the Indian Creek cliffs were on public land. That situation quickly changed when the Dugout Ranch, owned by the Indian Creek Cattle Company, began closing parking areas and access trails at several cliffs as well as banning camping in the canyon. Almost all of the popular crags, including Supercrack and Battle of the Bulge buttresses, are on Dugout Ranch property, along with many canyon entrances and much of the bottomlands. For a while it appeared that the finest crack climbing area in the world might be shut down. The owner of the ranch, Heidi Redd, was justifiably concerned with the impact of so many climbers and campers on the fragile desert land including the abused campsites that dotted the canyon floors, a network of social trails that braided their way to the cliff bases, and off-road vehicle tracks that damaged grasslands. The American Mountain Foundation stepped in and began a dialogue with Redd aimed at preserving not only the climbing opportunities, but also the landscape itself. To eliminate the main causes of human impact, the canyon was designated a day-use area only. Parking areas were designated and constructed, and trails were built to the cliff bases.

At the time of this writing, the Dugout Ranch has agreed to sell 5,000 acres between Newspaper Rock and Cottonwood Creek along with its surrounding grazing allotments to the Nature Conservancy. The purchase of the property, the gateway to Canyonlands National Park, will ensure that this rare and beautiful tract of land will be preserved from development. The Conservancy aims to protect the area's ecology, as well as continue the historical recreational activities including climbing. Over the next few years climbers should look for management changes, including more parking areas, campsites, and access trails.

Climbers should abide by the following rules of conduct to avoid future regulation or possibly area closures at Indian Creek: Park only in designated parking areas or pulloffs along the highway. Follow established trails to access the cliff bases. These trails are located at Supercrack Buttress, Donnelly Canyon, and Battle of the Bulge Buttress. Follow the trails when descending to avoid damaging fragile plants and creating new social paths.

When accessing other areas, look carefully for existing climber paths or follow dry creek beds to avoid damaging vegetation and fragile cryptobiotic soil. This unique soil, a symbiosis of algae and fungi, forms a black crust on the sandy surface. It allows for the absorption of precious moisture, stabilizes the soil surface, and provides important plant nutrients. Walking on its crust severely impacts the desert ecosystem and takes as long as 100 years to recover. Avoid biking to reach more distant climbing sites, as mountain bikes have a greater ecological impact than hikers.

Do not climb near or above any Indian rock art or ruined dwellings. The ancients, enjoying this canyon as much as we do, left stunning panels of petroglyphs chipped onto varnished cliffs throughout Indian Creek Canyon and its many side canyons. It's against both federal and state law to damage this rock art legacy, and climbers have damaged some of them by their careless and thoughtless actions. There are lots of routes here that are not near rock art. No routes are listed in this guide that climb above Indian sites. Avoid the petroglyphs at Blue Gramma Cliff and Supercrack Buttress, and the ruins at Supercrack and Battle of the Bulge buttresses.

Avoid drilling new pitons or bolts except at rappel and belay stations. Camouflage any new fixed gear and leave only webbing that matches the existing rock color, i.e., red. Do not leave unsightly yellow or blue webbing. While almost all of the routes listed in this guide have good, multiple anchors, be aware that on older routes, especially on less-frequented cliffs, the anchors are often inadequate, including machine bolts pounded into smaller diameter holes. In that case it is advisable to carry a bolt kit for 3/8-inch bolts or baby angles and know how to properly use it. *Never ever* rappel or lower from a single anchor in the canyon country, and don't lean straight out on a bolt. The pullout strength of bolts in sandstone is very low. Fatalities have occurred here when an anchor bolt has pulled on a climber. Do not trust your life to questionable anchors or desiccated rappel slings.

The main objective danger here, and everywhere in the canyonlands, is loose rock. Loose blocks and flakes are located on many routes, either sitting on ledges or wedged in cracks. Use extreme caution around any suspect rock. Falling rock here is deadly to your belayer and your friends at the cliff base; it can even chop your rope. The sandstone surface is also very abrasive. Use care not to run your rope over any sharp edges. Use long runners when toproping to avoid creating grooves on edges and ledges. It's best to rappel off many routes rather than to lower off to avoid rock damage. Remember when climbing that your safety depends entirely on your actions. Make smart, prudent decisions and live to see another day. Most accidents are preventable.

Rack: Come armed for bear! Bring all your cams and then beg and borrow every one that your friends own. A triple set of Friends or other cams should be adequate for most routes. Some cracks, however, will require as many as six or seven of the same size piece. These are generally noted in the text. Most 5.10 and 5.11 routes are thin hand to hand-size cracks, requiring multiple Friends from #2 to #3.5. Unless you're planning on gunning for *The Big Baby* or some other heinous off-width, a couple #4 Friends and Camalots will work. A couple of sets of TCUs along with a selection of Hexentrics, wired stoppers, Tri-cams, and RPs complete your rack. Remember that all rack info described here is suggested only. Decide for yourself what you need, but better to bring too much than too little. Bring two 165-foot ropes for leading and rappelling. A 200-foot rope also works well on many pitches like *Supercrack*. While some routes ascend to the tops of the cliffs, most jam up for a single pitch to rappel anchors. Bring tape and lots of it. The abrasive cracks chew up unprotected hands.

Indian Creek racks are heavy for a good reason—all the pieces get used. Protection should be placed fairly close together. The standard distance is a body-length or about 6 feet between cams. Some climbers will run it out every 8 or 10 feet on wider cracks, but in thin cracks, the TCUs and small Friends should be close together. Friends can and do pull out of the parallel-sided cracks, as they did for Leonard Coyne on an early attempt on *Coyne Crack*. Some climbers leapfrog gear to avoid carrying lots of the same piece, or slide it up as they jam. This works well for solid climbers in hand, fist, and off-size cracks.

Indian Creek Canyon is a phenomenal crack climbing preserve. This is a special place, a place to be loved, protected, and tended. It's up to us to do our part, to help preserve the canyon and its adventures. When you climb here, the cracks become indelible, burning their memory into your hands and your mind. While this guide is a starting point for your climbing adventures, there are lots of ruddy Wingate walls out there, awaiting the human touch. Most of the first Indian Creek climbers left little trace of their passage, save a couple of anchors high on a wall and a plaque of sandstone at the base with the route name and grade etched into the soft rock. Come and climb, and then go, and leave no trace of your passage.

Trip Planning Information

General description: An amazing collection of crack routes on towering Wingate sandstone cliffs that line Indian Creek Canyon, including Supercrack Buttress, Donnelly Canyon, Battle of the Bulge Buttress, and Cat Wall.

Location: East-central Utah. South of Moab.

Camping: Developed sites with tables are located at the BLM's Newspaper Rock Recreation Site. Primitive camping sites are on BLM public lands. Some of the best are up Cottonwood Canyon. Bring water. The closest water tap is at the Canyonlands National Park visitor center.

Climbing season: Year-round. Spring and fall are best. Winter days can be very good on the sunny cliffs. Summers are generally too hot, although shaded routes and spells of cool weather are both possible.

Restrictions and access issues: Much of Indian Creek Canyon and its cliffs are on private ranchland and Nature Conservancy land. Know the boundaries and respect any access and use restrictions.

Guidebooks: *200 Select Classic Indian Creek Climbs* by Marco Cornacchione, Sharp End Publishing, 1995.

Nearby mountain shops, guide services, and gyms: Moab Adventure Outfitters and Rim Cyclery in Moab.

Services: All visitor and climber services are located in Moab and Monticello, including gas, food, lodging, camping, dining, and groceries.

Emergency services: Call 911. Allen Memorial Hospital, 719 West 400 North, Moab, UT, (801) 259-7191.

Nearby climbing areas: Bridger Jack Spires, North and South Sixshooter Peaks, Mexican Hat, Dreamspeaker, Texas Tower, Bluff Cliffs, Valley of the Gods, Moab area cliffs and spires, Naturita Area crags (CO).

Nearby attractions: Canyonlands National Park, Needles District, Davis Canyon, Druid Arch, Chesler Park, Abajo Mountains, Colorado River, Arches National Park, La Sal Mountains, Manti-La Sal National Forest.

Finding the cliffs: Indian Creek Canyon lies along Utah 211 between its junction with U.S. Highway 191 and the Needles section of Canyonlands National Park. Drive south from Moab or north from Monticello on U.S. 191 to the junction with Utah 211. Head west on Utah 211. After 12 miles the highway reaches the bottom of the canyon, crosses a cattleguard, and passes Newspaper Rock recreation area. All mileages begin at the Newspaper Rock sign on the north side of the highway. Friction Slab is 0.5 miles from the sign. Blue Gramma Cliff is at 3.2 miles. Supercrack Buttress is at 3.8 mile. Battle of the Bulge Buttress and Donnelly Canyon are at 4.3 miles. Fringe of Death Canyon is at 6 miles. Scarface Wall is at 6.4 miles. The Cat Wall is at 8.1 miles. The turnoff to Pistol Whipped Wall in Cottonwood Canyon is at 8.1 miles. All the walls except the ones in Cottonwood Canyon are on the north side of the highway.

Please park in designated areas, especially at Supercrack Buttress, Donnelly Canyon, and Battle of the Bulge Buttress. These are the large unmarked pull-offs on both sides of the highway adjacent to and across the road from the cliffs. Cairned trails built by the American Mountain Foundation access the cliffs. Use them and avoid creating new trails.

FRICTION SLAB

Friction Slab is a broad, white slab on the north side of the highway at 0.5 mile from the Newspaper Rock sign. A short access trail winds through sage-brush from roadside parking to the cliff base. Four bolt-protected, friction routes are located here. Routes are listed right to left.

1. **Sundance** (5.7 R) Begin about 60' left of large obvious arch. Face climbing leads up and left to bolt. Continue straight up past another bolt to sloping break and 2-bolt anchor. **Descent:** Rappel 70'.

2. **Cloud Dancer** (5.9) Start just left of a juniper. Climb straight up on thin holds past 4 fixed pitons to 3-bolt anchor at break. **Descent:** Rappel 95'.

3. **White Waltz** (5.10a) Begin downslope from Route 2. Climb past 2 fixed pins. Work left over steeper section (.10a) to another fixed piton. Climb up right onto easier rock and 3-bolt anchor at break. **Descent:** Rap 95'.

4. **Laurel** (5.11) A 2-pitch line on left side of slab. **Pitch 1:** Friction up and left past 3 drilled pitons. Crux (.10a) above 2nd pin. Long runout leads to ledge and 2-bolt anchor. **Pitch 2:** Edge up steeper headwall above past at least 6 bolts and (.11) crux to summit slabs. **Descent:** Rappel the route or walk off to the east.

Two good routes lie between the Friction Slab and Blue Gramma Cliff.

5. **Split Pinnacle** (5.9) No topo. This route jams a perfect 25-foot-long hand crack up a short pillar tucked in the trees 0.9 mile from Newspaper Rock. Park on the south side of road to access the route. **Rack:** Hand-size Friends (#3). **Descent:** Rap route from double anchors.

6. **Y-Crack Simulator** (5.9) No topo. This short 35' hand crack is on the cliff north of the highway 2 miles west of Newspaper Rock. **Rack:** Bring #3 and #3.5 Friends. **Descent:** Rap or lower from anchors.

BLUE GRAMMA CLIFF

This excellent south-facing cliff towers above the highway at the north or left entrance of Hog Canyon, a canyon that stretches east from Indian Creek Canyon. The black-varnished cliff is easily accessed from roadside parking areas. A good trail leads to the cliff base in 5 minutes. The cliff is a good cold-weather crag, receiving ample winter sunlight. All routes are 1 pitch. Routes are listed left to right.

7. **Unnamed** (5.10) Begin on left side of cliff just right of obvious gully/pour-off. More routes are farther left. Handcrack leads to large flake. Pull over awkward flake to off-width/lieback. Descend 50' from double anchors.

8. **Unnamed** (5.10) Start a few feet right of Route 7. Jam and lieback crack up left-facing flake for 50' to double anchors.

9. **Unnamed** (5.10) A thin hands to hands to off-width crack up tight left-facing corner to 2-bolt anchor. Lower 50'. **Rack:** #2.5 to #4 Friends.

10. **Dawn of an Age** (5.10b) This ascends an obvious left-facing corner just right of a rounded wall. Lieback and fist jam crack to good lieback up steep off-width section. Crux is working back left into crack above. **Descent:** Rap or lower 50' from 3-bolt anchor. **Rack:** Gear sizes are #3, #3.5, and #4 Friends, and #4 Camalot.

11. **Unnamed** (5.9+) A superb route up a large open book. Begin just right of Route 10. Lieback and jam up dihedral's hand crack for 50' to 2-bolt anchor. A second pitch continues up sandy off-width for 30' to 2-bolt anchor on slab above. **Rack:** Bring #3, #3.5, and #4 Friends. Route 10's anchors are easily reached from this route's anchors to set up a toprope.

12. **Unnamed** (5.10) An excellent, pumpy route 70' right of Route 11. Follow steep splitter finger to hand crack up thin, black-varnished, left-facing corner to 2-bolt anchor on left wall of shallow alcove. Rap or lower 80'. **Rack:** Bring TCUs for the start, and 2 #1.5, 2 #2, 3 #2.5, 2 #3, and 1 #3.5 Friends.

13. **Unnamed** (5.11) A former aid line up a steep left-facing corner 20' right of Route 12. Jam and lieback the wide finger crack for 80' to 2-bolt anchor right of crack.

14. **Unnamed** (5.11) Begin on left side of white slab below obvious flake. Easy rock leads up and right around slab to single fixed piton below left-facing

flake. Lieback up to ledge and 2-bolt anchor. Rappel 90'.

15. **Blue Gramma** (5.11) Named for the grass, not a sad grandparent. This fine route ascends the large left-facing dihedral just right of Route 14. Jam easy finger crack up right side of white slab to a vertical lieback up finger crack. Rap 90' from a 2-bolt anchor on ledge. (Same anchor as Route 14.) **Rack:** Bring TCUs, lots of small Friends.

16. **Unnamed** (5.10d) A great route up the crack in a right-facing dihedral 20' right of Route 15 and right of an overhanging prow. Jam thin hands crack for 80' to 2-bolt anchor. Crux is 2" crack. **Rack:** Bring Friends from #1 to #2.5.

17. **Petrelli Motors** (5.10b) A very different Indian Creek route with lots of different techniques. The line climbs a thin crack system up a right-facing book left of a steep white slab about 50' right of Route 16. Awkward moves lead up to finger crack. Jam and lieback to final boulder problem up short headwall. Rap or lower 55' from a 2-bolt anchor on ledge. **Rack:** Bring lots of TCUs and small Friends. A route up the dihedral to the right is off-limits and illegal because of the petroglyphs at the base. Keep off!

18. **Moon Goddess Revenge** (5.11b) A quality route. Lieback up thin, left-facing corner to good rest. The crux above jams into hand crack above corner and continues up right-facing corner to 2-bolt, 1 fixed-nut anchor. Rap or lower 60'. **Rack:** Bring 3 #1, 5 #1.5, 2 #2, 1 #2.5, and 1 #3 Friends.

ORION'S BOW

An excellent route ascends Orion's Bow, a large slab on the east side of the highway just before Supercrack Buttress. Drive to a parking area at 3.6 miles just before the beginning of Supercrack Buttress.

19. **Orion's Bow** (5.10c) 3 pitches. This Ed Webster line climbs the thin slab on the east side of the highway past Blue Gramma Cliff. The route ascends a blunt prow just left of a long, right-facing arch. Begin on the apron of the prow below an obvious juniper tree. **Pitch 1:** Climb 60' up mostly unprotected 5.6 flake to 1-bolt belay on slab. Wired nuts are useful. **Pitch 2:** Friction up slab past 3 bolts to break. Climb steeper headwall (5.10c) past a few more bolts, angle up right past 2 more bolts to crack/ramp (wired nuts) leading to 2-bolt belay; 120'. **Pitch 3:** Work up left (5.9) across water streak and past 3 bolts to slabby summit; 160'. **Descent:** 2 long rappels. First rap is from a tree. Second is from belay anchors atop pitch 2. **Rack:** Quickdraws, wired stoppers.

**INDIAN CREEK
ORION'S BOW**

XX
160'   2 raps
X
X
X
XX   rap to
165'   ledge below
X
X
X
X
X

19

SUPERCRACK BUTTRESS

Supercrack Buttress is a long, blunt buttress just right of the entrance to Donnelly Canyon. The cliff, towering above the highway, is easily reached by designated climber trails built by the American Mountain Foundation. Park below the buttress near a cattleguard at 3.9 miles from Newspaper Rock or a quarter of a mile down the highway at the entrance to Donnelly Canyon. Look for the 2 trails that ascend the talus slopes to the cliff base. The trail to *Supercrack* begins just right of the cattleguard, while another trail to the left side of the cliff begins farther up the highway and deposits you at the base of the *Incredible Hand Crack*. Follow only the existing, designated trails to avoid damaging the fragile talus slopes and creating unnecessary erosion or new trails. Routes are listed right to left. The first routes are above the highway at about 3.8 miles. Many of the routes have second and third pitches to go to the canyon rim. Descriptions for these are omitted because they are seldom climbed.

20. **Pink Flamingo** (5.13a/b) No topo, but it's an obvious thin splitter. This testpiece jams a finger crack to a 2-bolt anchor. Usually only the first 80' is climbed to anchors, otherwise it's a 140' pitch to higher anchors. **Rack:** TCUs—2 #.5 and 8 #.75; Friends—8 #1 and 8 #1.5.

21. **Nuclear Waste** (5.10) Find a large open dihedral 50' right of a large boulder against the wall and just right of a juniper tree. Jam right-hand crack (5.10) and continue to 2-bolt anchor.

Barton Moomaw on Incredible Hand Crack, *Supercrack Buttress, Indian Creek.*
Photo by Earl Wiggins

22. **Anasazi** (5.11a) A fab line. About 10' right of a large boulder/block (behind is the Anasazi Cave—look for ancient handprints high inside the cave) leaning against the wall. Lieback up obvious, dark, right-facing corner to 2-bolt chained anchor. 140'. It should have ended at 100'; be careful on last 40'. **Rack:** Lots of small Friends including 6 #1, 6 #1.5, and #2 through #3.5, and TCUs.

23. **Unnamed** (5.10) A short pitch up the right side of a small pillar left of a large boulder at the cliff base. Jam the hands crack to 2-bolt anchor atop pillar. **Rack:** Small and medium Friends.

24. **Unnamed** (5.10) No topo. Clamber over stacked boulders and enter hand crack (5.8) in tight right-facing corner. Continue up clean 12-inch-wide squeeze chimney to high anchors.

25. **Too Much Cake** (5.11c) No topo. A very good Steve Hong route. Start by liebacking or off-widthing wide crack on right side of stacked flake blocks for 15' (Big pro). Continue up black, right-facing corner crack (perfect #2s and #1.5s), turn a roof and voilà, there's a 2-bolt anchor.

26. **Unnamed** (5.10) Begin down right from small Anasazi ruin that is on ledge below large corner. This route climbs right-facing flake crack. Work up widening crack/chimney to 2-bolt belay.

27. **Painted Pony** a.k.a. **Ride the Pink Pony** (5.11b) An excellent, sustained line put up by Earl Wiggins. Jam fingers to off-width to thin hands crack in shallow offset corner. Crux is over small roof (5.11b), then thin hands up thin left-facing corner to hand crack up white rock. A 2-bolt belay is in

dark varnish above white sandstone; 160'. **Rack:** 2 sets of Friends to #3 with extra #1.5, #2, and #2.5 Friends and TCUs.

28. **Amaretto Corner** (5.11d) A great corner climb done in 2 pitches. **Pitch 1:** A short 40' lead up a right-facing corner on the right side of a pillar. Jam hands to big hands to fists to stacks crack to a ledge with 2 bolts. This pitch is a popular moderate. **Pitch 2:** The real business. Climb over loose flake into smooth, right-facing corner. Fingers and hands lead to liebacking (5.11d) and 2-bolt anchor. **Rack:** Set of Friends for pitch 1. Lots of #1.5 and 3 #2 Friends and TCUs for pitch 2. A #4 Camalot is necessary.

29. **Supercrack** (5.10) The mega-classic, splitter hand crack first led by Earl Wiggins in 1976 with a handful of large hexentric nuts. Almost all parties only climb the first pitch. It's a popular toprope for lots of folks, so take your turn and then get off so others can have a go. The hand jams are perfect (if you have big hands!); it's the feet that tire on this long splitter. Begin by liebacking 20' (5.10+) onto ledge (technical crux) left of large pillar. Jam continuous hand crack (5.10) for 80' more to shallow pod with 4-bolt belay/lowering station with chains and steel descending rings; 100'. **Rack:** Bring a small piece for the lieback (runner it well to avoid rope drag), 2 #2, 2 #2.5, 6 #3, 3 #3.5, 1 #4 Friends.

30. **Unknown** (5.9) Short and sweet crack up the left side of a blocky pillar to a ledge with 2 bolts; 25'.

31. **Fingers in a Light Socket** a.k.a. **Super Corner** (5.11d) An excellent lieback up a large right-facing dihedral to a 2-bolt anchor. Crux is last 10'. Route

is 60'. **Rack:** Lots of TCUs and #1 Friends.

32. **Coyne Crack** (5.12a) A classic and superb thin, hand crack first climbed by Ken Sims in 1979. (See **Climbing History**) The crack is a couple of grades easier if liebacked and for those blessed with small hands. Begin just right of a boulder against the wall. Jam finger to thin hands crack in shallow, offset dihedral (5.12a) over small bulge. Continue on better hand jams to 2-bolt belay at 80'. Those who haven't had enough can continue up a hand crack for another 50' to 2-bolt station. **Rack:** 1 #1, 3 #1.5, 4 or 5 #2, 2 #2.5, and 3 #3 Friends for first pitch.

33. **Keyhole Flakes** (5.10) About 40' left of *Coyne Crack* on the dark right wall of large dihedral. Jam a fine finger to hand crack for 70' to 2-bolt anchor. **Rack:** Friends #1 to #2.5.

34. **Unknown** (5.10) An excellent and fun route up a flake-crack. Start with weird step-across move from pillar to finger-lock at base of crack. Lieback up sharp edge of crack to a crux fingertip move just below 2-bolt anchor; 50'. **Rack:** Large stoppers, small Friends, TCUs.

35. **Key Flake** (5.10) A long 130' off-width pitch up right side of the Key Flake. **Descent:** Rappel from 2-bolt anchor. **Rack:** Lots of wide stuff.

36. **The Wave** (5.10d) An excellent route up the crack on the left side of the massive Key Flake. Jam and stem up long, left-facing corner to overhanging crux moves that exit to upper crack. Belay from 2 bolts. **Descent:** Rap 100'. **Rack:** At least double sets of Friends from #1.5 to #3. Nuts also useful.

37. **Unknown** (5.10) A 60' pitch up a tight black corner to a single fixed nut anchor.

38. **Three Pigs in a Slot** (5.10) Climb cracks, chimneys, and slots for 90' up tight dihedral system to anchors in a chimney-slot.

39. **Gorilla Crack** (5.10b) A great hand crack that angles up the black face on the right side of a large dihedral. Begin with hands to fists before passing some off-width sections en route to 3-bolt anchor on left side of large block; 110'. **Rack:** 1 #1.5, 2 #2, 3 #2.5, 5 #3, and 3 #3.5 Friends.

40. **Pringles** (5.12c) Just left of *Gorilla Crack*. A contrived but excellent route. A sustained lieback and stem up the large, black, open book for 110'. This route, first led by Antoine Savelli, is usually toproped from the 3-bolt anchor on Route 39. Stay off *Gorilla Crack* at the face moves crux! **Rack:** 2 #.5, 2 #1, 2 #1.5, 3 #2, 2 #3 Friends, and 3 sets of TCUs. A 200' (60-meter) rope works for slingshotting topropes on these routes.

41. **Binge and Purge** (5.11a) This route is harder than it looks. A 60' pitch to the top of a pillar. Begin below left side of pillar. A hand crack (5.9) leads to awkward and scary overhanging off-width section that is liebacked.

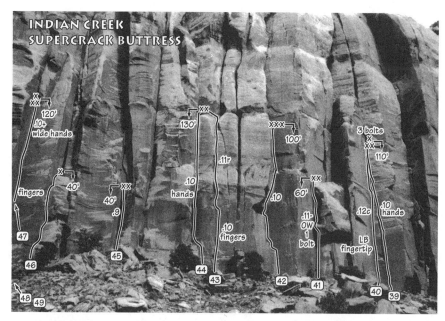

Continue up off-width crack (5.11a) to ledge with double anchors. **Rack:** Bring hand-size Friends and off-width stuff.

42. **Incredible Hand Crack** (5.10c) You will say, "That's an Incredible Hand Crack," after jamming this baby! It's more fun than *Supercrack* but much thinner and more varied in size. It's also getting wider. Repeat ascents have made it a "big" 2.5 instead of a tight 2.5! Jam and lieback up the clean, right-facing dihedral for 100' to 3-bolt belay/rappel station beneath triangular roof. Use a 200' rope or 2 ropes to get off. Look for some good rest stances before and after the crux overhanging section. **Rack:** Friends— 1 #3.5 and 7 #2.5 or 5 #2.5, 1 #2, and 1 #3.

43. **Wild Works of Fire** (5.11R) A thin finger crack (5.10) leads to thin face climbing along a seam (5.11R). Finish by working up left to *3 A.M. Crack's* anchors. Protection is hard to get on seam. Just toprope it. **Rack:** 2 sets of Friends, a set of stoppers.

44. **3 A.M. Crack** (5.10b) A great route up a dark right-facing corner. Superb hand jams up a crack in the corner to 2-bolt chained anchor; 130'. **Rack:** 2 #2, 3 #2.5, 4 #3, 2 #3.5, and 1 #4 Friends.

45. **Twin Cracks** (5.9) A short 40' pitch up double hand and finger cracks in a dihedral to 2-bolt rap anchor on ledge. **Rack:** #1 to #3 Friends.

46. **Triple Jeopardy** (5.7) Easiest route on the buttress. Up 40' crack on left side of broken pillar to single anchor on ledge.

47. **No Name Crack** (5.10b) Good hand jams lead 120' up a large right-facing corner to 3-bolt belay below V-slot. Crux is wide hands section.

Rack: Friends 3 #2.5, 3 #3, and 4 #3.5.

48. **Unknown** (5.10) No topo. 50' crack in large dihedral. Rap from 2-bolt anchor.

49. **Bad Rad Duality Crack** (5.10d) No topo. On the far left corner of the buttress. Access by walking left on a ledge to the base of a large right-facing dihedral capped by a triangular roof. Jam thin crack (5.9) to flake. Continue up 4" crack to overhanging section. Above, stem and jam (5.10+) to 2-bolt belay under roof. **Descent:** Rappel 140' from anchors. **Rack:** Friends #2 to #4 with extra #2.5.

DONNELLY CANYON

Donnelly Canyon is a mile-long canyon that reaches east from the highway and Indian Creek Canyon between Supercrack Buttress and the Battle of the Bulge Buttress. All of the climbing routes are on the left, or north, wall of the canyon and are easily accessed from the highway by designated trails. Park at a couple of roadside pullouts on the east side of the highway, 4.2 miles from Newspaper Rock. Follow the access trail up the canyon a short distance before branching left and following a trail to the base of Generic Crack Buttress. The first route listed here is about 200' left of *Generic Crack*. A climber path follows the cliff base, allowing access to all of the routes. Routes are left to right going into the canyon.

50. **Chimney** (5.10) A hand crack up a shallow left-facing corner just right of a small leaning pillar; 55'. **Descent:** Rap from 2-bolt anchor. **Rack:** Hand-size cams.

51. **Fuel Injected Hard Body** (5.12b) A few feet right of above route. Lieback the thin crack (5.12) in large varnished dihedral past single fixed piton. Rappel 60' from a 2-bolt anchor. **Rack:** Bring small Friends (extra #1.5) and TCUs from #.4 to #.75 including 6 #.75.

52. **The Naked and the Dead** (5.9) Usually done in 1 long pitch to second anchors or a short pitch to first anchors. An upper pitch is rarely done. Climb the left side of a pillar (5.8) for 40' to a ledge with a 2-bolt anchor. Continue up the large left-facing dihedral (5.9 hands to off-width) above for another 80' to a 2-bolt belay on the right wall. **Rack:** Bring a couple sets of Friends including 3 #3.5 and 4 #2 Friends. A good 5.11d toprope is the right side of the initial flake/pillar (been led on RPs).

53. **Generic Crack** (5.9+) One of Indian Creek's mega-classic cracks put up by Jim Dunn, 1976. Jam obvious splitter crack for 130' to a 2-bolt belay stance at wide spot. The sustained crack, polished white on the outside by numerous ascents, is hands to fists. 100' second pitch continues via a 5.10 off-width crack. **Descent:** Rap with 2 ropes. **Rack:** Bring lots of #2.5 to #4

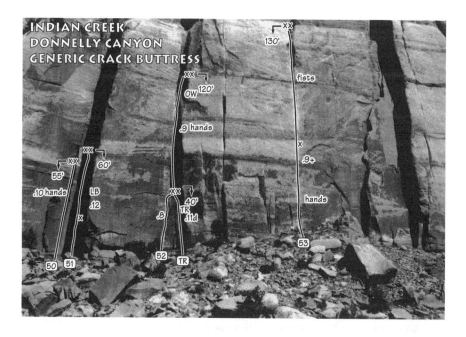

INDIAN CREEK
DONNELLY CANYON
GENERIC CRACK BUTTRESS

XX
130'

XX
OW 120'

.9 hands

fists

XX
55'
XX
60'

x
.9+

.10 hands
LB
.12

hands

XX
40'
TR
.11d

.8

x

50
51
52
TR
53

INDIAN CREEK
DONNELLY CANYON

XX
80'

11 bolts up arete →
XX

XX
50'
.9
.12b

5.10
in big
corner

54
55

Friends including 4 or 5 #2.5, 4 #3, 2 #3.5, and 2 #4.

54. **Binou's Crack** (5.9) Walk east along the cliff base from *Generic Crack* for a few hundred feet to the base of a huge, right-facing, dark-varnished dihedral. Please do not follow Binou's lead and carve your name at the base! This fun route liebacks, stems, and jams a finger crack in the dihedral for 50' to 2-bolt anchor. **Rack:** Small Friends, TCUs, wires.

55. **Let 'R Buck** (5.12b) Begin just right of Route 54. One of the few face routes here. Face climb up the beautiful arête past 11 bolts to a 2-bolt anchor. Rap 80'.

The following routes are a few hundred feet to the east from the arête. Follow a path along the cliff base to an obvious prow—The Elephant Trunk—that juts out from the cliff.

56. **Mr. Peanut** (5.11+) A 60' crack route up left side of trunk to 2-bolt anchor.

57. **Chocolate Corner** (5.10a) An excellent classic hand crack up a tight right-facing corner on the right side of the Elephant Trunk. Jam and stem for 60' to 2-bolt anchor. Often called .9+, but harder for bigger hands. **Rack:** Bring mostly #1.5, #2, and #2.5 Friends.

58. **Ocean Negro** (5.12c) A 2-pitch continuation of *Chocolate Corner* to anchors just below the rim of the canyon. **Pitch 1:** Continue stemming, jamming, face climbing up dark dihedral (5.12a) past several bolts for 140' to 2-bolt belay/rappel station. **Pitch 2:** Jam sustained, thin-hands crack up spectacular streaked, overhanging headwall (5.12c) to 2-bolt anchor. **Descent:** Rappel route. **Rack:** A couple of sets of Friends including 6 #2s (for pitch 3), a couple of sets of TCUs, and a set of stoppers.

59. **Elephant Man** (5.11c) A 3-pitch line up the right side of the Elephant Trunk to a belay just under the canyon rim. The first pitch (5.10a) is very popular. **Pitch 1:** Jam thin hand crack (5.10a) for 70' to ledge on right. Many parties toprope the route which has led to numerous grooves carved in the edge of the ledge below the anchors. Use caution on the abrasive sandstone edge. **Pitch 2:** Work up crack (5.11) using a variety of techniques for 70' to bolted belay. **Pitch 3:** Stem and chimney up right-leaning slot (5.11c) on right side of trunk to 2-bolt anchor. **Descent:** Rappel route with 3 double-rope rappels. **Rack:** A generous rack of Friends and TCUs including extra Friends from #2 to #3. Nuts also useful.

60. **Elephant Ear** (5.10d) Another fine 2-pitch line. Begin just right of *Elephant Man*. **Pitch 1:** Do short, easy lead to top of pillar. **Pitch 2:** Use stems and jams to work up and over awkward ears (5.10d) to straightforward crack finish and 2-bolt belay stance. **Descent:** Make long, 2-rope rappel to ground. **Rack:** A variety of Friends including extra #3 to #4. A #4 Camalot also useful.

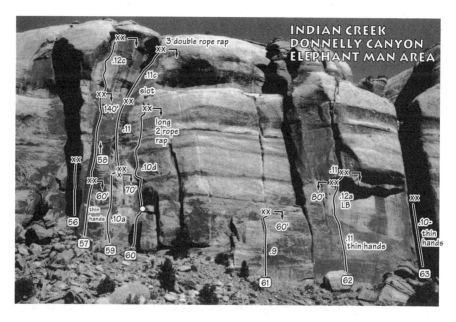

61. **Unknown** (5.9) Walk right from the Elephant Trunk to a crack that splits a broken pillar. Jam 60' to a ledge with 2 anchors.

62. **Dos Hermanos** (5.12a) A classic Steve Hong route. Find a tan streaked wall capped by a large roof. Begin by a large boulder. Jam thin, continuous cracks (5.11) to liebacking crux (5.12a). Continue up thin hand crack to 2-bolt belay under left side of roof; 80'. A short second pitch swings over roof to 2-bolt anchor. **Rack:** TCUs and Friends to #3 including 4 #1.

63. **The Drainpipe** (5.10a) Go right from *Dos Hermanos* to a deep chimney. This route jams thin hands to hands crack on right to 2-bolt anchor. **Rack:** Friends including 3 #1, 3 #2 and 3 #3.

64. **The Thang** (5.10b) No topo. Continue right from *The Drainpipe* chimney through some boulders to semi-detached tower. Scramble up gully behind tower and locate crack. Jam flared finger to tight hands crack for 70' to 2-bolt anchor.

65. **Fred's Tower Thing** (5.7) No topo. This short route climbs the short, semi-detached tower in front of *The Thang*. Scramble up to sandy saddle between tower and cliff. Climb up and right using face holds and cracks. Step right around corner and climb to summit. Rap from 2-bolt anchor.

BATTLE OF THE BULGE BUTTRESS

The Battle of the Bulge Buttress is a long southwest-facing cliff that extends from a blunt promontory at the entrance to Donnelly Canyon to another promontory where the cliff makes a sharp bend northeast. The cliff is easily ac-

INDIAN CREEK
BATTLE OF THE BULGE

cessed by designated climber trails that ascend talus slopes. Make an effort to find and use the established trails to minimize erosion caused by social trails. Park below the buttress at the entrance to Donnelly Canyon, 4.2 miles from Newspaper Rock or at another large pullout on the left another quarter of a mile down the highway. Trails built by the American Mountain Foundation begin from both of these parking areas and end at the cliff base. A good trail also follows along the base of the cliff allowing easy access to all the routes. Stay on the cairned, established trails! Routes are listed right to left from the entrance to Donnelly Canyon.

66. **Three Strikes You're Out** (5.11b) This classic lieback follows a large, right-facing dihedral at the promontory that divides Donnelly Canyon and Battle of the Bulge Buttress. Begin by climbing a short, easy crack onto a ledge atop a block below the dihedral. Lieback the 90' crack to 2-bolt anchor on right wall. Rest jams are located in "wide" sections of the crack. **Rack:** Small and medium Friends including 5 #2 and 3 #2.5.

67. **Swedin-Ringle Route** (5.12a/b) This used to be a toprope but is now a testpiece for the grade. An excellent but difficult finger crack on the dihedral wall left of *Three Strikes*. Jam the thin finger crack that slowly widens and then pinches down below the 2-bolt anchor; 60'. **Rack:** 1 or 2 of each size TCUs and Friends from #.5 to #2.

68. **The Moon Also Rises** (5.11a) Begin below a narrow right-facing corner on the right side of a prominent pillar. Work up off-width crack (5.11a) until it widens above fixed piton and becomes squeeze chimney. Belay

INDIAN CREEK
BATTLE OF THE BULGE

atop pillar and rappel to ground from bolt belay; 100'.

69. **Unknown** (5.9) Begin just left of a pillar. This 40' problem jams up hand and finger crack to ledge in chimney with 2-bolt anchor.

70. **Slim Chance** (5.11b) Start behind a large, flat boulder below a right-fac-ing corner. Jam and lieback up the corner crack (5.11 tips off the ground) to a higher 5.11 crux. Belay from 2 bolts atop flake. **Descent:** Rappel 100' with 2 ropes. **Rack:** Small and medium Friends including 3 #1.5, 6 #2, and 3 #2.5.

71. **Unknown** (5.11) Climb up and right to flake crack. Lieback and jam up-wards to drilled piton. Wild liebacking above leads to 2-bolt anchor; 80'.

72. **Unknown** (5.10) Begin just left of above route. A short thin hands to hands crack on the left wall of a short corner; 40'.

73. **Battle of the Bulge** (5.11b/c) A classic Steve Hong route up an awesome right-facing corner. This is a very sustained route. Begin atop a boulder and lieback to crux, liebacking over bulge (5.11c) to set of chained an-chors at 80'. Lower from here or if you're an animal, keep liebacking another 30' including another thin 5.11 section. Rap or lower from 2-bolt anchor; 110'. **Rack:** Small Friends including 6 #2 and some TCUs for the first 80', otherwise TCUs and Friends from #.75 to #3.5 including 8 #2.

74. **Dark Corner** a.k.a. **Black Dihedral** (5.11b) This route ascends the second black, right-facing dihedral left of #73. Lieback and jam up and over small roof. Continue to 3-bolt anchor; 90'. Several good rests are located on

route. **Rack:** Friends and TCUs, including 1 #.75, 1 #1, 2 #1.5, 3 #2, and 1 #2.5.

75. **Quarter of a Man** (5.12a) The obvious dihedral left of Route 74. Sustained liebacking and stemming (5.12a) lead to the route's only rest after 80'. Shake out and continue another 60' up crack and over bulge (5.11d) to thin hands crack that can be liebacked. Belay from 2 anchors. **Descent:** Rappel 140'. **Rack:** Lots of small to medium Friends. In order—#3, #2.5, 5 #2, 3 #1.5 (#.75 Camalots work super at crux), #2.5, and #1 to #2.5 to anchor.

76. **Cal and Andy's Route** (5.10) Jam flared cracks to 2-bolt anchor.

77. **Cave Route** (5.11a) This route is shaded in summer! Find a large pillar just left of a prominent chimney. Cool route climbs thin hands crack inside flared chimney on left side of tall pillar. Belay or lower from anchors inside pillar; 80'. **Rack:** Friends, mostly #1.5 and #2.

78. **Digital Readout** (5.12b/c) A classic splitter finger crack. Lisa Hathaway says "Tape or bleed!" Begin below obvious crack up wall just left of Route 77. Jam finger crack to 2-bolt anchor; 50'. **Rack:** TCUs to #1.5 Friends; 7 #.5 will do it or 1 #.4, 2 #.75 and 1 #1.5 if you're clever.

79. **Ruby's Cafe** (5.13a) One of Indian Creek's hardest routes and harder for small fingers. Begin below obvious roof about 200' left of Route 78. Jam thin right-facing corner before it switches (crux) to left-facing corner. Continue to roof, pull over to jug, and finish at 2-bolt anchor; 70'. **Rack:**

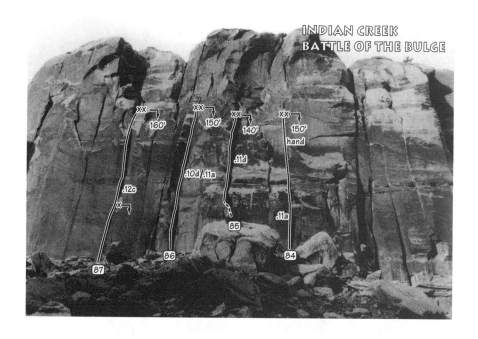

TCUs and small Friends from #.5 to #1 but mostly #.75 (6-8). Just left of *Ruby's* is *Last Battle* (5.11a), #79.1 on topo.

80. **The Warm-up** (5.8) A good, short, moderate line. Begin left of deep chimney. Climb crack on face of flake to 2-bolt anchor. 40'. **Rack:** Friends—1 #1.5, 3 #2, and 2 #2.5.

81. **Jane Fonda's Total Body Workout** (5.11b) A good workout. Begin left of an Anasazi ruin. (Another route goes above the ruin—**do not climb** to avoid damaging the ruin!) Jam off-width to hands crack up left-facing corner to 2-bolt anchor at 70'. It's possible to continue up crack above into flared chimney slot to upper anchors. **Rack:** Friends, including 5 #2, 3 #2.5, and 3 #3. A #4 Camalot helps at the start.

82. **Our Piece of Real Estate** (5.11a) The huge, right-facing dihedral. Climb onto pedestal and jam thin crack (5.10+) to upper hand crack. Belay from 2-bolt anchor. Rap 100'. **Rack:** Selection of medium to large Friends—1 #1.5, 4 #2, 5 #2.5, 3 #3, 1 #3.5.

83. **The Big Baby** (5.11+) You'll earn your off-width stripes on this baby. The obvious off-width on the left dihedral wall. Off-width up the crack to a retreat bolt. Continue up wide crack to 2-bolt anchor; 80'. **Rack:** All wide stuff like Big Bros, Big Dudes, and #5 Camalots. #4 Camalot at start.

84. **Hole in the Wall** (5.11a) Done in a single 140-foot-long pitch. Walk west from Route 83 and around an arête. This line climbs the crack just right of a right-facing corner. Jam flared hands to hands crack (5.11a) to horizontal break. Continue up sustained hand crack to 2-bolt belay. **Descent:** Rappel 150'. **Rack:** Medium to large Friends—#1.5 to #3.5, but mostly #2.5 and #3.

85. **Let's Dance** (5.11d) Walk uphill and west from Route 84 to a thin, right-facing corner system. Climb onto small pedestal below corner. Jam, lieback, stem up thin corner to very thin crack protected by fixed pitons to 2-bolt belay; 140'. **Descent:** Rappel 130'. **Rack:** Selection of Friends and TCUs.

86. **Unnamed** (5.10d/11a) Jam and stem a thin crack in narrow right-facing corner on right side of pillar. Very thin at top. 150'. **Rack:** Friends #2.5 to #3 and TCUs.

87. **Christmas Tree** (5.12c) This awesome line is on a beautiful varnished face broken only by a thin right-facing corner. Sustained liebacking and stemming lead up a tips crack in the corner for 160' to 2-bolt belay on sloping stance. Bail bolt is partway up. **Rack:** Bring TCUs and Friends, including 10 #.5, 4 #1, and 2 #1.5.

88. **Crack Attack** (5.11a) Walk a few hundred feet left from Route 87 past a large pillar and a large boulder to find this fine line. Jam thin hand crack (5.10) over small triangular roof. Continue up with fingerlocks (5.11a) to ledge with 3-bolt anchor. **Descent:** Rap 90'. **Rack:** Bring Friends—#1 to #3 with 3 #1.5, 4 #2, and 3 #2.5.

89. **Unnamed** (5.10d) This route climbs a crack on the right wall of a large open dihedral left and uphill from Route 88. Jam finger and hand crack up slabby wall for 140' to large ledge with anchors.

90. **Elbow Vices** (5.10) Jam, lieback, and stem up crack in large dihedral for 90' to 2-bolt anchor and ledge. **Rack:** A selection of medium and large Friends.

91. **Grits Grunt** (5.8) 2 pitches. Earl Wiggins calls this one of Indian Creek's "best 5.8 routes." The route chimneys up a large crack on a prominent pillar at the far left side of the Battle of the Bulge cliff. **Pitch 1:** A 5.8 squeeze chimney leads to hidden belay stance with 2 drilled angles inside chimney. **Pitch 2:** Continue squeezing up long chimney (5.8) to 2-bolt anchor at top. **Descent:** Two 2-rope rappels down route.

92. **Think Pink** (5.11a) A very good pitch up a right-facing dihedral left of *Grits Grunt.* Jam hand and fist crack up and over bulge (crux) to 2-bolt anchor. **Descent:** Rappel 100'. **Rack:** Selection of medium and large Friends from #1.5 to #3.5. A 5.11 off-width route is just left of this line.Fringe of Death Canyon

FRINGE OF DEATH CANYON

The Fringe of Death Canyon, a dead-end side draw on the east side of the highway, lies almost 2 miles down-canyon from the Battle of the Bulge Buttress and 6 miles from Newspaper Rock. The canyon was the long-time traditional campsite of early Indian Creek climbers in the 1970s until overuse by climbers who disregarded desert camping ethics led to its closure. The canyon is now open only as a day-use, walk-in area. A handful of excellent boulders laced with hard problems are on the canyon floor. Park at the entrance to the canyon at any obvious pullout and walk up the old road to access the talus slopes below the cliffs.

Because so many early desert pioneers, including Jim Dunn, Earl Wiggins, Mugs Stump, and Ed Webster, spent time here, lots of routes were put up on the canyon's cliffs. No record or bolts mark many of these routes as they were established with the clean-climbing ethic of the 1970s. The canyon itself received its unusual name after Wiggins led the first pitch of a new route and was unable to place any pro in its first 60 feet putting him on "the fringe of death." Many lines await a repeat ascent. No anchors, no bolts, the adventure awaits.

93. **Y-Crack** (5.10) No topo. This excellent route lies on the right side wall near the head of the canyon. It ascends an obvious Y-shaped crack just left of a broken left-facing dihedral. Jam the perfect hand crack to the Y. Go left. The angle lessens above and the crack flares. The right branch of the Y also goes and is a couple of grades harder. **Descent:** Rappel the route with 2 ropes. **Rack:** Hand-sized Friends.

THE FRINGE WALL

This wall faces the highway just past Fringe of Death Canyon and 6.2 miles from Newspaper Rock. Park on a pullout on the east side of the road. The excellent *Cactus Flower*, put up by Ed Webster and Mark Rolofson in 1978, climbs an obvious splitter crack system just left of a pillar and dihedral. Scramble up talus slopes to the base of the route. *Neutron Dance* is a few hundred feet to the right. Look for the obvious splitter crack above a broken ledge. A newer route (looks 5.12) jams and liebacks a thin, left-facing corner to 2 cold-shuts above ledges just right of Route 95.

94. **Neutron Dance** (5.10+) 2 pitches. Great route. Begin right of a right-facing dihedral. **Pitch 1:** Scramble across ledge and climb short, left-facing corner (5.7) to ledge. **Pitch 2:** Jam obvious steep, splitter hand crack (5.10+) to 2-bolt anchor. **Descent:** Rap 140' to ground with double ropes. **Rack:** Lots of hand-size Friends, including at least 3 #3.5 and 2 #3 and 2 #4.

An unknown 5.12 route (#94.1) climbs a thin corner crack above blocks just right of *Cactus Flower*. See photo topo for details.

95. **Cactus Flower** (5.10+) 3 pitches. Quality jamming! Begin just left of an obvious left-facing tan dihedral. **Pitch 1:** Climb broken rock section and jam fist crack (5.10) to 3-bolt belay. **Pitch 2:** Continue up crack—wide hands or fists (5.10) to some off-width moves (5.10+) below 3-bolt belay. **Pitch 3:** Jam nice hand crack to rotten (5.10) section. 2-bolt belay is at rim. **Descent:** Make three 2-rope rappels down route. **Rack:** Lots of medium and large Friends, including at least 2 #3, 3 #3.5, and 2 #4 Friends.

INDIAN CREEK
THE FRINGE WALL

SCARFACE WALL

This east-facing cliff sits on the northwest side of Fringe of Life Canyon, a side canyon north of Indian Creek Canyon. Park at 6.4 miles at a pullout on the right side of the highway. Walk north on a closed road to the bottom of the canyon before cutting northwest across gravel benches to a primitive trail up the talus slopes below the cliff. Marco Cornacchione's guide offers a selection of topos to the best routes.

CAT WALL

This excellent wall offers some of Indian Creek's best and hardest routes. Marco Cornacchione calls it, "The most stacked wall in Indian Creek." This is not a wall for the beginner or intermediate crack climber—experts only need apply. Park at 8.1 miles from Newspaper Rock at the junction of Utah 211 and County Road 104. Cross the fence at a ranch gate and walk north cross-country across short grass before dropping across the dry wash and scrambling up talus slopes to the cliff base. Total approach is about 2 miles. Some trails do exist but are hard to find. Again, use Marco Cornacchione's guide for topos.

PISTOL WHIPPED WALL

This good wall is on the east side of North Cottonwood Canyon, a long canyon lined with Wingate cliffs that runs south from Indian Creek Canyon. Doug Oliver developed most of the cliff. The west and southwest-facing Pistol Whipped Wall offers a good selection of 5.10 and 5.11 crack routes. Most lines are shorter than many other Indian Creek routes so climbers without generous racks of Friends can have some fun. Reach the cliff by driving 8.1 miles from Newspaper Rock to the junction of Utah 211 and San Juan County Road 104. Turn left on County Road 104 and follow the dirt road south into the canyon. The stream crossing a half-mile from the highway might be problematic after heavy rains. Continue south on the road to its junction with county road 104A. Turn left on this rutted dirt track. This road drops down across the creek and passes through a grove of cottonwoods that offers fine camping. Drive 0.6 mile to the road's junction with the old canyon road. Turn right on this road and drive another 1.7 miles and park on the shoulder. The black-varnished Pistol Whipped Wall is to the east and just left of the obvious blunt prow. Hike uphill for about 20 minutes to the cliff base. Routes are listed left to right, with the first route being far to the left. Reach it by following a trail along the cliff base to the route.

96. **Hijinx in the Desert** (5.11) No topo. Jam fingers to tight hands crack up right-facing corner. Pass small roof and continue up left-facing corner to 2-bolt anchor; 80'. **Rack:** Finger to hand-sized Friends.

97. **Dusty Trail to Nowhere** (5.10) No topo. Begin 30' to the right of *Hijinx*.

Fred Knapp on Coyne Crack Simulator, *Pistol Whipped Wall, Indian Creek.*
PHOTO BY STEWART M. GREEN

INDIAN CREEK
PISTOL WHIPPED WALL

Pistol Whipped Wall

approach

Jam good hands up right-facing corner that flares near top. 2-bolt anchor left of some broken rock; 60'. **Rack:** Hand-sized Friends.

98. **Rump Roast II** (5.11) No topo. About 150' right of *Dusty*. Jam crack just left of arête to stance atop flake. Continue up crack with wide fingers and tight hands to 2-bolt belay; 80'. **Rack:** Friends #1 to #3.

99. **12 Point Buck** (5.9) Just right of Route 98. Off-width up right side of flake pillar to 2-drilled angle anchor. Left side looks cool but is hollow-sounding; 40'.

100. **Coyote Essence** (5.11-) No topo. Just left of a huge detached, leaning flake. Jam great finger and hand crack up steep left-facing corner just left of right-facing dihedral; 60'. **Rack:** Friends #1 to #3.5.

101. **Unnamed** (5.11R) A long pitch up a finger crack in shallow, alternating corners to a very thin finish; 120'. **Rack:** TCUs, small Friends, Lowe Balls for the top.

102. **Coyne Crack Simulator** (5.11-) An excellent route. Jam thin hands up slight offset crack to fingery section with footholds. Finish with great hand crack up tight, left-facing corner. Anchors out right. 50'. This crack is much easier to lieback! **Rack:** Small and medium Friends.

103. **Wounded Knee** (5.11) 15' right of Route 102. Jam excellent twin finger/hand cracks for 35' to stance. Work up flake crack onto sloping ledge. Continue up into left-facing corner with some off-width to good ledge with 2-bolt anchor; 100'. **Rack:** A couple of racks of Friends.

104. **Spaghetti Western** (5.11+) Begin below an obvious and huge right-facing dihedral with a beautiful, overhanging, striped wall on the right. This sustained and spectacular line begins with thin fingers to hands jamming up and over a bulge. Continue with hands to short off-width section below ledge with 2-bolt anchor. Rappel 150'. **Rack:** Generous selection of TCUs and small to medium Friends.

105. **Revenge of the Rock Gods** (5.10+) A very good climb 40' right of Route 104. Jam finger crack for 40' up shallow right-facing corner. Continue up wide fist section in thin left-facing corner to final hand crack to ledge with 2 anchors; 80'. **Rack:** A couple of sets of Friends.

106. **Steve's Whimpout** (5.10+) A short, fun pitch that is easily toproped by reaching its anchors from the top of *Pinyon Pining's* first pitch. The route ascends a thin, left-facing corner just right of *Revenge*. Jam finger and hand crack up corner to 2-drilled angle anchor; 50'. **Rack:** Small to medium Friends.

107. **Pinyon Pining** (5.10) 3 pitches up a right-facing dihedral system. **Pitch 1:** Easy climbing up broken cracks (5.7) to 2-bolt anchor on ledge to left. **Pitch 2:** Up beautiful hand/fist crack to drilled angle that bypasses some loose blocks. Continue up broken corner 10' to 2-bolt anchor on ledge. **Pitch 3:** Jam off-width flake crack protected by drilled angle to squeeze chimney. Belay from 2 bolts in chimney. **Descent:** Rappel route. **Rack:** A couple of sets of Friends along with TCUs.

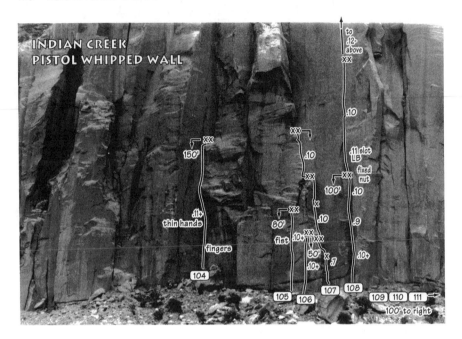

108. **Pistol Whipped** (III 5.12-) 4 pitches up a spectacular crack system put up by Bret and Stuart Ruckman. About 20' right of this route is an unclimbed killer thin fingers and tips crack that will go at 5.13. **Pitch 1:** Jam thin, broken corner (5.10+), past some loose blocks (5.9), and head up finger crack in left-facing corner (5.10) to fixed nut anchor; 100'. **Pitch 2:** Climb into slot (5.11) above belay (easier to lieback) protected by #4 Camalot. Continue up thin hands corner (5.10) and over roof to splitter hand crack. Belay from 2-bolt anchor. **Pitch 3:** Jam airy and continuous tight hands splitter up headwall (5.11+) to awkward crux (5.12-) before belay stance. **Pitch 4:** Do short chimney to 2-bolt anchor below rim. **Descent:** Rappel the route. **Rap 1:**100'. **Rap 2:**110'. **Rap 3:**100' to ground. **Rack:** TCUs, lots of Friends #1 to #4. Include extra #1 to #2.5.

109. **Skid Marks** (5.10) No topo. About 100' right of Route 108. A fingertips lieback up left-facing corner leads to thin flakes. 2-bolt anchor; 50'. **Rack:** Lots of thin stuff.

110. **Short and Stupid** (5.9) No topo. A great, short practice route on the left side of a flake. Jam thin hands crack for 25' to 2-bolt belay on shelf. **Rack:** Medium Friends.

111. **Jolly Rancher** (5.10 R) No topo. This south-facing route is a few hundred feet right of the above route. Walk along the cliff base trail until it cliffs off. Look up. Jam the long, excellent splitter hand crack past some loose blocks (scary!) to 1-bolt belay. Add a bolt and rappel 140'. **Rack:** Mostly #2.5 to #3.5 Friends.

BRIDGER JACK SPIRES & THE SIXSHOOTER PEAKS

OVERVIEW

Bridger Jack Mesa is a long, finger-like mesa that juts north into the west end of Indian Creek Canyon. North Cottonwood Creek Canyon flanks it on the east, while Lavender Canyon marks its west edge. The pointed end of the mesa that reaches into Indian Creek Canyon is a long, sawtoothed ridge of 7 spires that ends in massive Bridger Jack Butte. These serrated towers include some of Utah's finest sandstone tower routes up King of Pain, Easter Island, and Thumbelina with its classic face climbing line *Learning to Crawl*.

North and South Sixshooter Peaks loom west of Bridger Jack, perched on immense, isolated talus cones composed of shale and sandstone above the confluence of Indian and Lavender creeks just east of the Canyonlands National Park boundary. These Wingate sandstone towers are remnants of long-eroded finger mesas that once jutted south above Davis Canyon. North Sixshooter, looking remarkably like a revolver pointing skyward, boasts the *Lightning Bolt Cracks* route—one of the desert's most sought-after lines. South Sixshooter to the south is a smaller, more broken and blocky tower with twin summits. It's popular with Outward Bound and guided groups because of its moderate summit routes.

Climbing history: North Sixshooter Peak, because of its impressive location and visibility, attracted the earliest desert climbers. It was first climbed in 1962 by Huntley Ingalls, Rick Horn, and Steve Komito. The trio first attempted the route in howling winds and returned the next day to finish their effort up cracks to a notch on the south side. A bolt ladder led up crumbling rock to the peak's untrodden summit. Five years later, Californians Chuck Pratt and Doug Robinson made the second ascent of the tower, and while rappelling down spotted a possible line up the west face. The pair returned in 1969 and off-width master Pratt embarked up the smooth 8-inch crack with arm bars and heel-toe moves. This impressive lead, now a reasonable classic with Big Bros, was a landmark desert ascent. The route was utterly unprotected until Pratt reached a chockstone tie-off about 70 feet up the crack.

The Lightning Bolt Cracks, following a zig-zagging crack line up the sheer east face of North Sixshooter, was, along with *Primrose Dihedrals* on Moses, one of Ed Webster's great desert finds. Webster, along with partner Pete Will-

BRIDGER JACK SPIRES

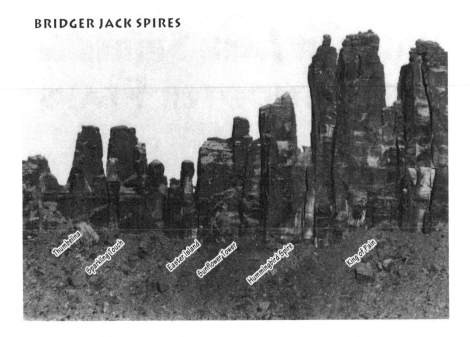

iams, drove over one Friday night in April 1979 from Colorado Springs and hiked up the ball-bearing scree slopes to the tower base. Williams, talked into the adventure by Ed, recounted later, "The roof looked huge, and I doubted that my imagination was going to get me past that section of the climb. I told Ed that the roof was his idea anyway, and demanded the first pitch which led up to it...the huge roof turned out to be the easiest part of all . . . As I watched the haul pack swing 40 feet out, Ed yelled from above the roof, 'This is the best climb I've ever done!' I had to agree."

Ed Webster was also a driving force behind the first ascents of most of the Bridger Jack spires in the early 1980s. The initial routes on this serrated ridge of towers went up in 1983. In June, Webster, Leonard Coyne, and Ellen Figi climbed *Wild Flower* (III 5.10) up Bridger Jack Butte. Later that year on the butte, Webster and Patrick Griffin ascended *The Round-Up Route* (III 5.9 A0), while Pete Gallagher and Brad Schilling did *Hydrophobic Coyote* (III 5.10). Webster and Gallagher also climbed King of Pain, the tallest tower, in 1983. Sunflower Tower via the *Original Route* (III 5.10 A1) and Hummingbird Spire fell to Webster and Alan Judish in 1984. Webster and Lauren Husted had the honors on Sparkling Touch in March 1984. The superb face climbing classic route *Learning to Crawl* on Thumbelina's southwest arête was pioneered by Webster and Jeff Achey in October 1984. Easter Island, the easiest tower and the last to be climbed, was climbed by Achey and Karen Radakovich in 1986.

The Bridger Jack Spires and The Sixshooters are easy to access from Utah Highway 211, the paved road that runs from U.S. Highway 191 into the Needles District of Canyonlands National Park. The highway passes down Indian Creek Canyon, the famed crack climbing area, en route to the park. Bridger Jack is an obvious ridge of spires to the left near the canyon's entrance, while The Sixshooter Peaks jut proudly above talus cones farther to the west. All the towers require walking approachs. Bring sturdy shoes. Camping is available on BLM lands at the parking areas for both sites. Plan on bringing water and practicing low-impact camping by using existing sites, packing out all your trash, and not building a fire or firepit.

Climbers should be competent at jamming 5.10 and 5.11 cracks, have a large assortment of gear including multiple sets of Friends, and be prepared for emergencies and self-rescue. A hard hat is a good idea on many of these routes. As is the case everywhere in the canyonlands, loose rock abounds and balances on ledges. Use extreme caution not to dislodge any rock on your belayer or others at the cliff base. Most of the anchors on these routes are good. Do not, however, trust a single anchor for a belay or a rappel. Always back it up with gear for safety. Plan on carrying sufficient water for each person. A gallon per person per day is not too much in hot weather. A raincoat and wind gear are advisable, especially in springtime.

Rack: Most routes require double sets of Friends, a set of TCUs, a set of stoppers, and at least 1 wide crack piece like a #5 Camalot or Big Bros. Some of these routes require many big crack pieces. A good assortment of runners is necessary to avoid rope drag. Plan on bringing 2 ropes for climbing and rappelling and plan on bringing your hard hat.

Trip Planning Information

General description: A collection of sandstone towers on a serrated ridge and a couple of free-standing towers atop talus cones just east of Canyonlands National Park.

Location: East-central Utah. South of Moab.

Camping: Much primitive camping is located in the area. Good campsites are just off Utah 211 on the Beef Basin Road; farther south on the road in North Cottonwood Creek Canyon; at the parking area for Bridger Jack just off the Beef Basin Road; along the Davis Canyon Road en route to The Sixshooters. The Squaw Flat Campground in Canyonlands National Park is a good developed campground with spacious sites, but it's usually filled by late morning. It's usually warmer here than up Indian Creek Canyon. Camping is also located at Newspaper Rock on Utah 211.

Climbing season: April through May and September through October are the best months. Wind, sleet, and rain occur in spring. Summers are just too hot most of the time. Winters are usually too cold, although climbing is possible during good spells. Many of the routes, however, are in the shade and may be cold.

Restrictions and access issues: None currently. Both areas are on BLM lands outside Canyonlands National Park. Use common sense here. Pack out your trash, tape, and cigarette butts; follow existing climber trails; don't walk on cryptobiotic soil; and avoid placing unnecessary bolts or scarring the rock.

Guidebooks: *Classic Desert Climbs* by Fred Knapp, Sharp End Publising, 1996. *200 Select Classic Indian Creek Climbs* by Marco Cornacchione, Sharp End Publishing, 1994. *Desert Rock* by Eric Bjørnstad, Chockstone Press, 1988, is an out-of-print classic with brief descriptions of most of the towers.

Nearby mountain shops, guide services, and gyms: Moab Adventure Outfitters offers a selection of gear and clothing. They also have rock climbing classes and a guide service. Rim Cyclery sells gear and guides.

Services: All visitor and climber services are located in Monticello and Moab. Water, maps, and a telephone are available at the visitor center at Canyonlands National Park.

Emergency services: Find a cell phone and call 911 or flag down a ranger. Allen Memorial Hospital, 719 West 400 North, Moab, UT, (801) 259-7191.

Nearby climbing areas: Wall Street, River Road crags, Indian Creek Canyon—Blue Gramma Cliff, Supercrack Buttress, Battle of the Bulge Buttress, Donnelly Canyon, Cat Wall, Reservoir Wall, The Fin, Broken Tooth.

Nearby attractions: Canyonlands National Park (Needles District), Chesler Park, Lavender Canyon, Davis Canyon, Druid Arch, Salt Creek Canyon, confluence of Green and Colorado rivers, Canyon Rims Recreation Area.

BRIDGER JACK SPIRES

Finding the towers: These spires lie along a long serrated ridge that juts into lower Indian Creek Canyon east of Canyonlands National Park. The row of towers, south of Utah 211, are easily reached from the highway. Drive 8 miles west of Newspaper Rock to the junction of Utah 211 and San Juan County Road 104. Turn left or south on County Road 104. This road is signed Beef Basin. The dirt road drops southwest and quickly reaches a crossing of Indian Creek. Drive through the creek. It's usually not too deep. Use caution after rain or in spring when it runs dangerously high. In this case, park before the crossing and begin the walking approach from here. Continue along the road as it curves southeast and look for a rough track that cuts right and heads toward the tower. Follow this road as far as is prudently possible and park. A 4-wheel-drive vehicle is helpful. Hike along existing climber trails to the base of the towers. Allow at least 45 minutes for hiking. The towers are listed left to right.

BRIDGER JACK SPIRES AND NORTH & SOUTH SIXSHOOTER PEAKS

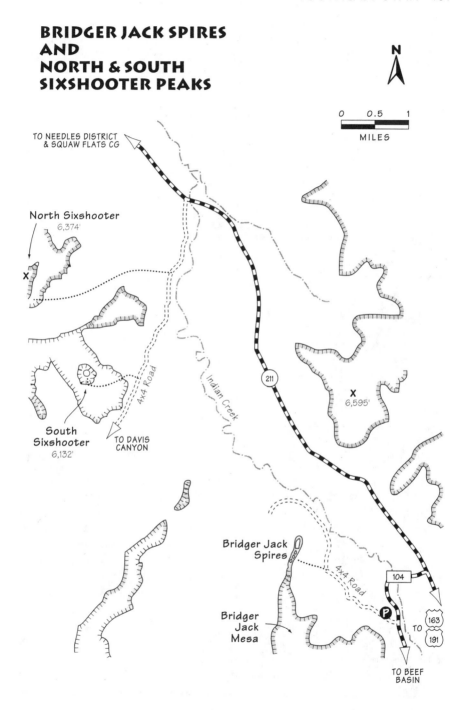

N

0   0.5   1

MILES

TO NEEDLES DISTRICT
& SQUAW FLATS CG

North Sixshooter
6,374'

X

South
Sixshooter
6,132'

TO DAVIS
CANYON

4x4 Road

Indian Creek

211

X
6,595'

Bridger Jack
Spires

Bridger
Jack
Mesa

4x4 Road

104

P

TO

163

191

TO BEEF
BASIN

Jeff Achey on the first ascent of Learning to Crawl, *Thumbelina, Bridger Jack Spires.*
PHOTO BY ED WEBSTER, MOUNTAIN IMAGERY

THUMBELINA

The farthest left of the Bridger Jack Spires when viewed from the east. This classic tower route offers a desert rarity—face climbing on quality sandstone. It's often done in 1 pitch. If so, use lots of runners to avoid rope drag at the top. Alternatively, belay at a stance below where the route joins the arête proper halfway up.

1. **Learning to Crawl** (II 5.11c) 1 or 2 pitches. First ascent by Jeff Achey and Ed Webster, 1984. The route follows the southwest arête of the tower.

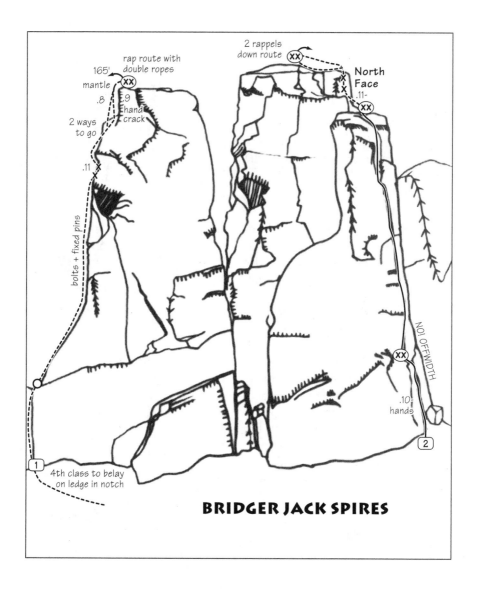

2 rappels
down route

165' rap route with double ropes

mantle

.8 .9
hand
crack

2 ways
to go

.11

bolts + fixed pins

North
Face
.11-

NO OFFWIDTH

.10
hands

4th class to belay
on ledge in notch

BRIDGER JACK SPIRES

Begin on east side of tower. Scramble up 4th class ramp/wide crack to col between Thumbelina and mesa to left. Route up arête is obvious. Face climb up steep, sharp arête and face to its right. Pro is several drilled angles and occasional nut or Friend placements. A variation near the top angles up right via a hand crack (5.9). Either way reach stance below top, and make a mantle (5.8) onto summit. The 5.11 climbing is by last 2 bolts. **Descent:** Rappel route with double ropes. **Rack:** Set of Friends with 2 #2 and 2 #2.5 if doing the hand crack variation; set of stoppers; quickdraws; 2 ropes.

SPARKLING TOUCH

The blocky tower right of Thumbelina. The route ascends a crack system on the right side of the east face and finishes up with a short stretch of face climbing.

2. **Sparkling Touch** (III 5.11) 3 pitches. First ascent by Ed Webster and Lauren Husted, 1984; first free ascent later that year by Webster and Bryan Becker. Begin left of a block at the tower base. **Pitch 1:** Jam vertical hand crack (5.10-) to 2-bolt belay ledge on left. **Pitch 2:** Continue up crack (5.10-) to corner to large ledge with 2 bolts on tower's north side. First 2 pitches can be combined. **Pitch 3:** Face climb (5.11-) past 2 bolts on short north face to flat summit. **Descent:** 2 rappels down route. **Rack:** 2 sets of Friends with extra hand-sized pieces; runners; 2 ropes.

EASTER ISLAND

The shortest and easiest of the

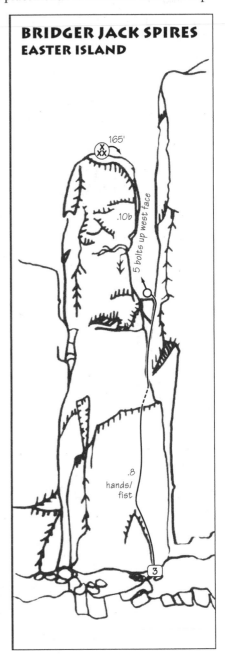

BRIDGER JACK SPIRES
EASTER ISLAND

165'

.10b

5 bolts up west face

.8
hands/
fist

3

Bridger Jack Spires. First ascensionist Jeff Achey calls the route "kinda cool." It offers enjoyable face climbing, a good summit, and relatively moderate climbing compared to the other towers. The beautiful fingertip crack right of the first pitch start still awaits an ascent. Approach from the east.

3. **Easter Island** (I 5.10b) 2 pitches. First ascent by Jeff Achey and Karen Radakovich, 1986. Begin below a crack system below a notch on the right side of the tower's east face. **Pitch 1:** Jam wide hand/fist crack (5.8) to short rightward traverse on loose flakes. Continue up moderate jam cracks to belay (no fixed anchor) by large chockstone wedged in notch. **Pitch 2:** Clamber over block, face climb onto steep west face. Exposed face climbing (5.10b) leads past 5 bolts to summit. **Descent:** One 165' rappel from summit anchors down east face to ground. **Rack:** Set of Friends; quickdraws; 2 ropes.

SUNFLOWER TOWER

This is a blocky high point on the serrated ridge. A couple of routes ascend the tower. The *East Face* route, one of the best routes on the Bridger Jack formation, follows an obvious crack system up the east face to a large ledge on the south side, before stepping around the corner and finishing up the west face.

4. **East Face** (II 5.10+) 3 pitches. First ascent by Ed Webster and Alan Judish, 1984. Begin below the obvious crack system on the east face. **Pitch 1:** Jam finger crack (5.10) past roof to stemming slot. Belay from 2 bolts on ledge. **Pitch 2:** Downclimb behind huge flake to splitter hand crack. Jam to thin left-facing corner. Head up thin hands to finger crack in corner (5.10+). Then traverse right on ledge system to west face. Belay from 2 bolts on ledge. **Pitch 3:** This pitch is a little spooky. The leader should be solid. Traverse on west face of summit block, pass a couple of bolts, and make an airy step onto a shelf. Climb short left-facing corner (5.8) to loose, crumbly rock and summit. **Descent:** Three 2-rope rappels down the route. **Rack:** Double set of Friends with extra hand-sized; set of TCUs; set of wires; runners; 2 ropes.

HUMMINGBIRD SPIRE

A tall, blocky spire with one of the canyon country's best tower pitches, as well as one of the worst pitches. Marco Cornacchione calls it "a 3-star pitch and a 1-star route." The route ascends an extremely loose pitch on the east flank to a notch between Hummingbird Spire and King of Pain. The second lead works up the overhanging north face.

5. **Hoop Dancer** (II 5.11 R) 2 pitches. First ascent by Jeff Achey and Ed Webster, 1985. Begin below an obvious notch on the right side of the east

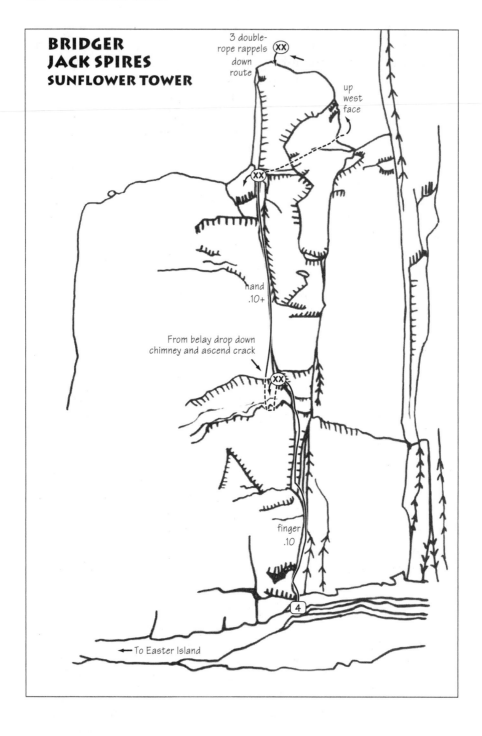

BRIDGER JACK SPIRES
SUNFLOWER TOWER

3 double-rope rappels down route

up west face

hand .10+

From belay drop down chimney and ascend crack

finger .10

← To Easter Island

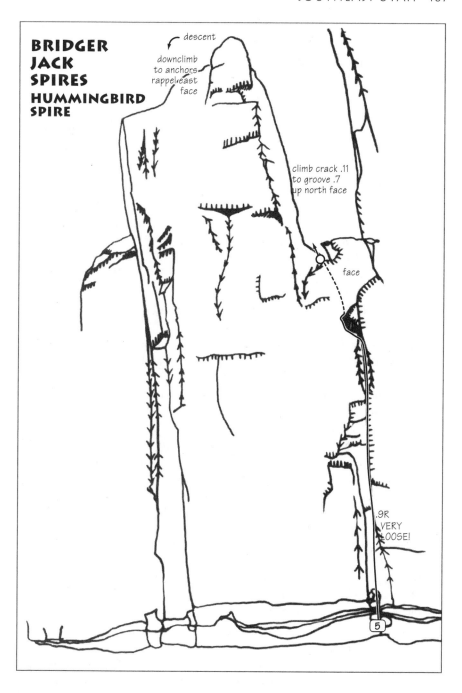

BRIDGER JACK SPIRES

HUMMINGBIRD SPIRE

descent

downclimb to anchors rappel east face

climb crack .11 to groove .7 up north face

face

.9R VERY LOOSE!

5

face. **Pitch 1:** Climb cracks and corners past many loose, wedged blocks (5.9 R) to notch. This pitch is extremely dangerous. Wear a helmet. Place gear carefully. And don't pull anything onto your belayer. **Pitch 2:** This is the business! Downclimb from belay to base of overhanging splitter hand crack. Jam spectacular, sustained thin hands to hands crack up wall (5.11) to final loose groove (5.7). **Descent:** No fixed anchors on summit. Downclimb south to lower summit and rappel down southeast flank. **Rack:** A set of Friends with 3 #2, 3-4 #2.5, 3 #3; 2 ropes.

KING OF PAIN

The twin-summited King of Pain is the tallest and largest tower on the serrated Bridger Jack ridge. Both of these routes are on the east side of the tower. A couple of other good routes are located on King of Pain. *Rites of Passage* (III 5.11+) is an awesome line up the west face with a splitter finger crack and lots of wild off-width climbing. *Sacred Space* (III 5.11 R) ascends the deadly first pitch of *Hoop Dancer* before embarking up intimidating hand, fist, and off-width cracks on the narrow, overhanging south face of King of Pain. Refer to Cornacchione's guide for topos.

6. **Vision Quest** (III 5.10+) 4 pitches. First ascent by Ed Webster and Jeff Achey, 1984. This route ascends the obvious and huge dihedral on the east face of this 2-summited tower and ends on the north summit. Begin below the dihedral on the left side of the east face in a right-facing corner with a finger crack. **Pitch 1:** Jam thin finger crack (5.10) to large semi-detached, wedge block. Work around left side of block, belay on stance with 2 bolts below off-width crack. **Pitch 2:** Thrutch up slot to fist crack to another sandy slot. Belay on ledge up right. **Pitch 3:** Climb yet another slot to fist crack (5.10+) over roof to fat hand crack. Belay on ledge below final corner. **Pitch 4:** Jam corner (5.9+) to some wildly airy face climbing above narrow notch between summits to north summit. **Descent:** Three 2-rope rappels down east face of tower. **Rap 1:** Locate anchors on north side of north summit and make 150', 2-rope rappel to notch between King of Pain and Bridger Jack Butte. **Rap 2:** Make another 150' rappel from 2 bolts to ledge with 2 bolts. **Rap 3:** Rappel 150' from 2 bolts to ground. **Rack:** Double sets of Friends; set of TCUs; set of wires. Some bigger gear like Camalots and Big Bros protect the wide stuff. 2 ropes.

7. **Ziji** (III 5.12) 4 pitches. First ascent by Chip Chace and Monika Lou, 1987. A classic hard tower route with a Tibetan name that means "monumental elegance." This sustained route ascends the smooth, varnished east face via a series of thin crack systems. Begin right of *Vision Quest* below a right-angling crack system and a streaked face. **Pitch 1:** Climb up right through some weird, shallow slots with poor pro and 2 drilled pitons to an off-width crack (5.11). A scary and runout pitch. Belay up right on a

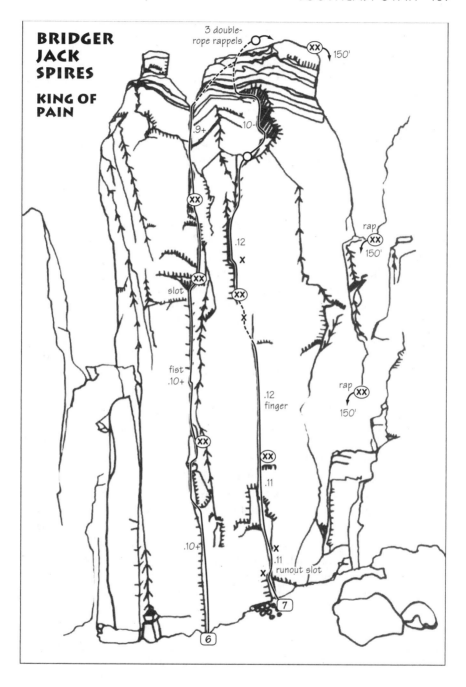

BRIDGER JACK SPIRES

KING OF PAIN

3 double-rope rappels

150'

.9+

10-

XX

.12

X

slot

XX

.12 finger

fist .10+

rap XX 150'

rap XX 150'

XX

.11

.10+

X .11 runout slot

X

7

6

ledge. **Pitch 2:** Jam a sustained and difficult finger crack (5.12) to a face climbing traverse that leads up left past a bolt to a 2-bolt belay stance. **Pitch 3:** Jam a narrow left-facing corner with tight fingers and fingertips (5.12) past a drilled pin. Continue up shallow corners in better finger cracks (1-inch) to belay stance below final dihedral. **Pitch 4:** Jam up obvious dihedral (5.10a) to large roof. Work left under roof and climb easier rock to north summit. **Descent:** Three 2-rope rappels. See Route 6 for details. **Rack:** Double set of Friends to #3, along with extra #1. A couple of sets of TCUs including extras of larger sizes. Set of wires. 2 ropes.

NORTH SIXSHOOTER PEAK

This spectacular multi-summited tower sits atop a talus cone south of Utah 211 and just east of Canyonlands National Park. The routes are classic and the summit is spacious with wide-ranging views.

Finding the tower: Drive 12 miles past Newspaper Rock on Utah 211. After crossing Indian Creek on a bridge, turn left on Davis Canyon Road. This junction is marked with a national park sign. Drive south on this rough road; 4-wheel-drive advisable. The higher the clearance of your vehicle, the closer you can get to the tower. Park after a mile or so and hike southwest up Bogus Pocket, a broad valley, toward North Sixshooter. The final section of the talus cone can be quite heinous. Try to find a climber trail to the south and approach via bouldery slopes south of the tower. The slope directly below the tower is steep, difficult, and dangerous, with ball-bearing pebbles underfoot. Use extreme caution if you get suckered into going this way!

8. **Southeast Chimney** (II 5.10 C1) 3 pitches. First ascent by Rick Horn, Steve Komito, and Huntley Ingalls, 1962. Begin on left side of east face below tapered slot-chimney. **Pitch 1:** Climb cracks on right side of slot-chimney (5.7) before stepping left and working up off-width crack (5.10) using arm bars. Belay from 2 bolts on stance above. **Pitch 2:** Do a couple of face moves (5.9) up right and enter classic, uniform, heel-toe squeeze chimney (5.8 R) that extends through tower. Exit over blocks at top to 2-bolt belay at notch. **Pitch 3:** Aid up manky bolt ladder on crumbling sandstone to some loose free climbing and flat summit. **Descent:** Two 2-rope rappels. Rappel from summit bolts back to the notch. Make 1 long 2-rope rappel from anchors in notch down west side of tower to ground. **Rack:** 2 sets of Friends; a few big pieces—large Camalots or Big Bros.

9. **Lightning Bolt Cracks** (III 5.11-) 3 pitches. First ascent by Ed Webster and Pete Williams, 1979. This superb tower route offers excellent sandstone, sustained and varied crack climbing, exposure and superb position, and good pro. The downside is its popularity—climb on weekdays to avoid traffic jams. Begin on the right side of the east face below the right-hand splitter crack. **Pitch 1:** Jam finger and thin hand crack (5.11a) that opens

Ed Webster on first ascent of Lightning Bolt Crack, *North Sixshooter Peak.*
PHOTO BY PETE WILLIAMS

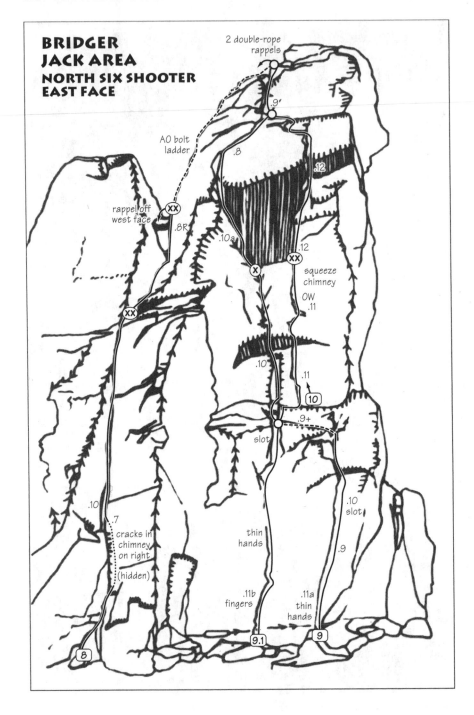

BRIDGER JACK AREA
NORTH SIX SHOOTER
EAST FACE

2 double-rope rappels

.9'

A0 bolt ladder

.8

.12

rappel off west face

XX

.8R

.10a

.12

X

XX

squeeze chimney

OW
.11

.10

.11

10

.9+

slot

.10 slot

.10

.9

.7 cracks in chimney on right

(hidden)

thin hands

.11b fingers

.11a thin hands

8

9.1

9

to hands (5.9) to awkward off-width/chimney slot section. Make short traverse (5.9) left (watch for rope drag) and belay in slot. An excellent variation first pitch climbs (Route 9.1), the crack to the left. Fingers (5.11b) to thin hands and hands over sloping ledge to belay stance. **Pitch 2:** Jam crack (off-hands and fist) over bulge (5.10) to left-angling corner crack to cramped belay under left side of huge roof. **Pitch 3:** A spectacular and airy pitch! Work out around roof—easier than it looks—and jam thin crack (5.10a) to wider but easier cracks (5.8) to squeeze chimney (5.9). Belay on summit. **Descent:** Two 2-rope rappels. **Rap 1:** South from summit anchors to notch. **Rap 2:** A long rappel down west side to ground. **Rack:** 2 sets of cams from #0.5 to #3.5, a set of stoppers. A #4 Big Bro protects the top crack/chimney. Bring long slings.

10. **Liquid Sky** (III 5.12) 4 pitches. First ascent by Jeff Achey and Chip Chace. The off-width master's dream pitch; a nightmare for the rest of us! Rumored to be impossible for large body types. **Pitch 1:** Same as first pitch of *Lightning Bolt Cracks*. **Pitch 2:** Jam thin crack (5.11) up and over bulge and continue up obvious off-width/squeeze chimney (5.11). Unprotected on first ascent but more sane now with big gear. Belay under 15-foot-wide roof. **Pitch 3:** Squeeze up off-width/chimney slot through roof (5.12), work up and left to belay stance at base of *Lightning Bolt Cracks's* final squeeze chimney. Anchor might be difficult. **Pitch 4:** Short pitch up chimney (5.9) to summit. **Descent:** Two 2-rope rappels down south and west side from anchors. **Rack:** 2 sets of Friends with 3 #3s. Off-width gear—large Camalots and Big Bros.

The following 2 routes are on the spire's west face.

11. **Shadows Route** (III 5.10+) 3 pitches. First ascent by Ken Trout and Scott Vischer, 1978. This was the first free ascent of the tower. This route climbs the analog crack on the opposite (west) side of the tower from *Lightning Bolt Cracks*. Route ascends the obvious crack system. Begin by scrambling around to the west side of the tower and onto some large boulders below an obvious slot where a large block fell out. **Pitch 1:** Jam crack (5.9) up left corner of wide slot feature capped by roof formed by keystone block. Pull over roof (5.10) and climb to second horizontal crack above roof (5.8), hand traverse left to obvious crack that leads to 2-bolt belay on ledge. **Pitch 2:** A long off-width lead nicknamed "The Sleeping Bag Simulator Pitch." Begin up off-width/squeeze (5.9) to bolt. Thrutch above (5.10d) to another fixed pin, continue up past another bolt to 5.10d section that leads right to belay ledge. **Pitch 3:** Jam obvious squeeze and off-width crack (5.9) to summit. **Descent:** Same as the others—two 2-rope rappels to notch and ground. **Rack:** Double sets of Friends and bunches of big gear to supplement the fixed pitons.

12. **Pratt's Crack** (II 5.10 A0) First ascent by Yosemite off-width master Chuck

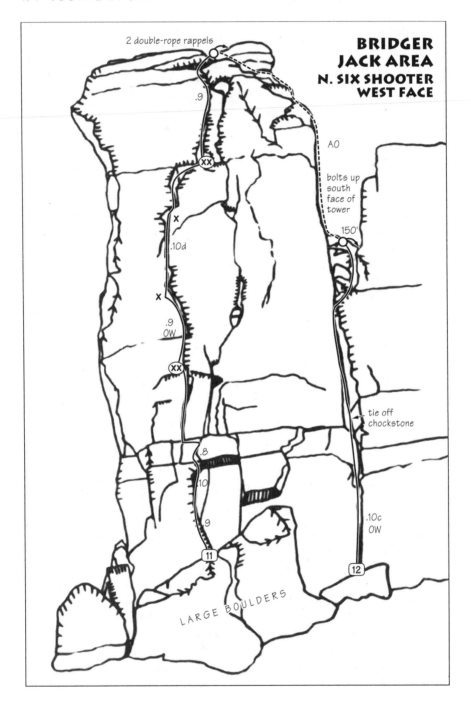

2 double-rope rappels

BRIDGER
JACK AREA
N. SIX SHOOTER
WEST FACE

.9

A0

bolts up
south
face of
tower

150'

.10d

.9
OW

tie off
chockstone

.8

.10

9

.10c
OW

11

12

LARGE BOULDERS

Pratt and Doug Robinson, 1969. A bold, unprotected lead way ahead of its time, but now reasonable with modern wide crack pro. Locate the obvious off-width crack below the notch. **Pitch 1:** Arm bar up off-width (5.10c), protected now by some Big Bros, to squeeze chimney. Tie off chockstone above, continue up squeezie to some looseness as chimney widens to belay from bolts in notch on south side of tower. **Pitch 2:** Aid up funky bolts to summit. **Descent:** Two 2-rope rappels down the route. **Rack:** Set of Friends and Big Bros.

SOUTH SIXSHOOTER PEAK

This is the smaller sister to North Sixshooter and features two distinct summits atop its talus cone. The peak's south face is very popular despite a somewhat long approach, and offers the easiest tower routes in the canyon country.

Finding the tower: Follow the directions to North Sixshooter, only continue south on the Davis Canyon Road past North Sixshooter Peak to a point below the tower and talus cone. The higher the clearance of your vehicle, the closer you can drive. Park and hike up a long scree and talus slope to the base of the south face. This road can be impassable when muddy and wet.

13. **South Face** (II 5.6) 3 pitches. First ascent by Bill Roos, Burnham Arndt, and Denver Collins, 1969. Locate an Anasazi petroglyph on the far left side of the south face. **Pitch 1:** Climb easy rock to chimney (5.6). Above

BRIDGER
JACK AREA
SOUTH SIX
SHOOTER

rap route

continue
around to
the backside

.6
mantle

150'

.4

.9

.9

.6
chimney

up from petroglyph

angle up right on easier rock to belay ledge. **Pitch 2:** Climb easy rock (5.4) to notch on summit ridge. Note the rappel anchors on face to right. **Pitch 3:** Continue through notch and traverse around north side to east side of summit block. Climb to mantle (5.6) onto summit. **Descent:** 2 rappels (see topo). **Rack:** A couple of sets of Friends.

14. **South Face Direct** (II 5.9) 2 pitches. First ascent by Kurt Rasmussen, Muff Cheyney, and John Pease, 1973. A direct line to the notch. **Pitch 1:** Jam flare with hand crack in it to ledge below notch. **Pitch 2:** Easier rock leads to face climbing (5.6) and right summit. **Descent:** Rappel the route. **Rack:** A couple of sets of Friends with extra hand-size pieces.

15. **South Face Right** (II 5.9) 2 pitches. First ascent by Frank Trummel, Mike Graber, and Hooman Aprin, 1975. Begin right of Route 14. **Pitch 1:** Jam crack to chockstone, move right with hand jams (5.9) around chock, to off-width section that leads up left to belay ledge on Route 14. **Pitch 2:** Same as Route 14. **Descent:** Rappel the route. **Rack:** A couple of sets of Friends.

ISLAND IN THE SKY

OVERVIEW

The Island in the Sky is a long, Y-shaped, 6,000-foot-high mesa that dominates the northern sector of Canyonlands National Park. A series of sharp cliffs stairsteps down over 2,000 feet from the relatively flat mesa-top to the Green and Colorado rivers on the west and east respectively. Towering cliffs of Wingate sandstone line the Island rim, while below stretches the White Rim, a wide bench floored with white Cutler sandstone. The White Rim Trail, a 100-mile-long jeep track, circumnavigates the White Rim and allows access to numerous side canyons and towers sculpted from the Island in the Sky's Wingate cliffs.

These remote towers offer a wealth of spectacular, classic routes up their soaring sandstone faces. They are generally reached via rough dirt roads, but offer some of Utah's best adventure climbing. The Wingate sandstone towers include Monster Tower and Washer Woman on the east flank of the Island; Moses, Zeus, and Aphrodite in Taylor Canyon; Charlie Horse Needle above the Green River; and The Witch in Hell Roaring Canyon north of the national park boundary. Monument Basin, cut into the soft Cutler sandstone below the White Rim, houses a wild assortment of thin pinnacles including Standing Rock.

The Island in the Sky, besides offering superb climbing opportunities, is a unique outdoor museum of natural history and geology. First and foremost the Island is a landscape dominated by rock. Here erosion has sculpted, sliced, and shaped the bedrock into cliffs, pinnacles, flying buttresses, minarets, abrupt canyons, and rounded domes. The horizontal strata of sedimentary rocks, stacked like layers on a wedding cake, yields a lesson in geological history. Each rock layer seen here—Navajo sandstone, Kayenta Formation, Wingate sandstone, the Chinle and Moenkopi Formations, White Rim sandstone, and Cutler Formation—tells a tale of the earth's varied geological history. The cliff-forming Navajo and Wingate sandstones were deposited as immense sand dune fields that blanketed most of Utah during the Mesozoic Era. Earlier formations were laid down as sand, silt, and mud on floodplains and broad river deltas during moister times. One of the Island's most unusual geologic features is Upheaval Dome. This 500-foot-deep crater excavated on the west side

ISLAND IN THE SKY

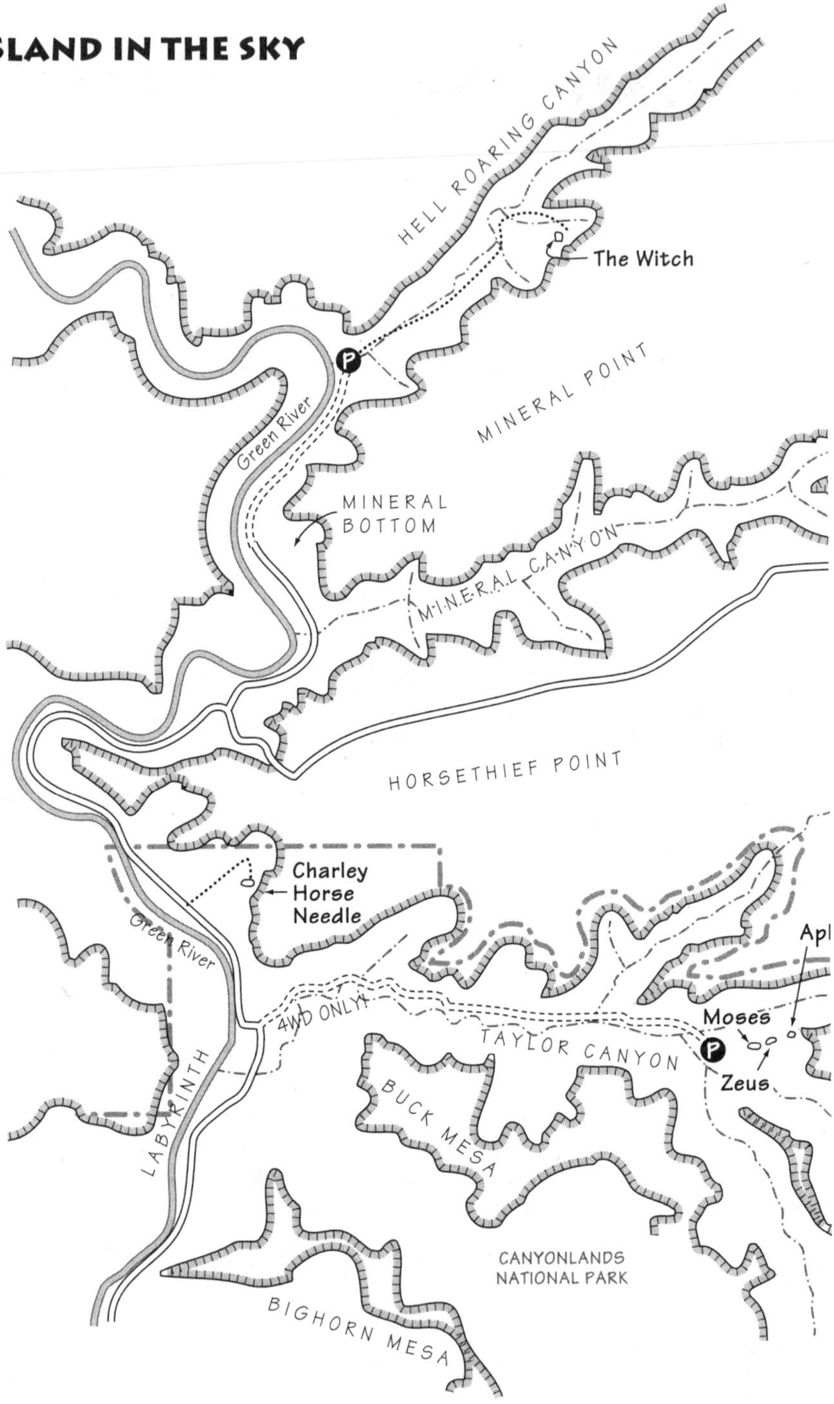

HELL ROARING CANYON

The Witch

MINERAL POINT

Green River

MINERAL BOTTOM

MINERAL CANYON

HORSETHIEF POINT

Charley Horse Needle

Green River

Apl

Moses

4WD ONLY

TAYLOR CANYON

Zeus

LABYRINTH

BUCK MESA

CANYONLANDS NATIONAL PARK

BIGHORN MESA

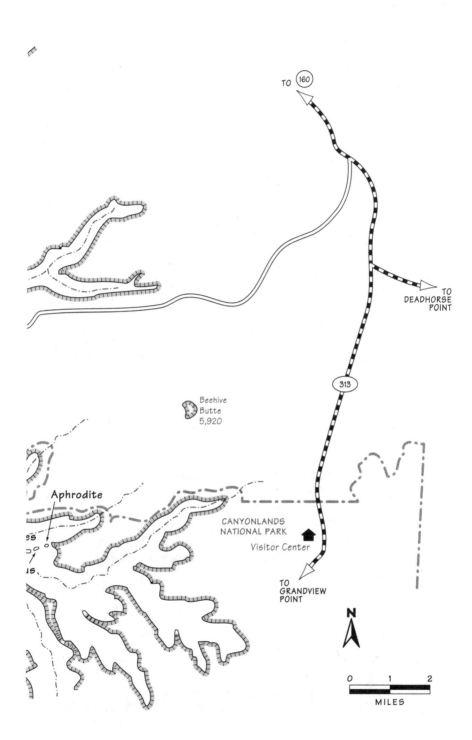

TO (160)

TO
DEADHORSE
POINT

313

Beehive
Butte
5,920

Aphrodite

CANYONLANDS
NATIONAL PARK

Visitor Center

TO
GRANDVIEW
POINT

N

0   1   2
MILES

of the mesa is a mystery to geologists. Many believe it's the impact crater of a huge asteroid that crashed here some 30 million years ago, while others contend that it's an eroded salt dome.

The area's natural history is also interesting. Life here has adapted to powerful forces. Precipitation in Canyonlands National Park averages a meager 8 inches annually, while the extreme temperature range, from 25 below zero to 115 degrees above, is one of the widest in the world. The mesa top, at a relatively high elevation, receives more moisture than surrounding canyons allowing a pygmy forest of pinyon pine and juniper to flourish. Grasses, including galleta, needle-and-thread, and blue gramma, carpet the mesa in areas where deep soil has accumulated. Other open areas are covered with cryptobiotic soil, a unique symbiotic complex of lichens, algae, moss, and fungi that forms a lumpy black crust on top of the sand. This soil crust absorbs water and decreases erosion in the harsh environment. It's also extremely fragile and sensitive to human impact. A single footstep on the cryptobiotic soil can destroy 50 years of growth in an instant. Wise desert hikers and climbers avoid stepping on the soil; they follow existing footpaths or rocky washes wherever possible.

Climbing history: The first climbers here and everywhere in the canyon country were the ancient Anasazi Indians. These incredible climbers scaled the cliffs and roamed the canyons in search of wild game and edible plants. The first technical climb on the Island in the Sky was put up on Standing Rock by desert pioneer Layton Kor with Huntley Ingalls and Steve Komito in October 1962. Their ascent of this sheer, frail spire was a wild adventure that began with the long drive out the then frightful, seldom-traveled White Rim Trail. Komito later described Standing Rock as "layers of Rye Crisp held in place by bands of moistened kitty litter." Their landmark ascent was hailed as one of the most difficult and dangerous routes on all the desert towers.

The following year, Kor, Larry Dalke, and Cub Schafer made the first ascent of Monster Tower, which didn't see a second ascent until 1982. Rick and John Horn, and Pete Carmen climbed nearby Washer Woman in the spring of 1967. The party used wooden wedges in big cracks as well as an ice piton hammered into rotten rock. This tower wasn't climbed again until Charlie Fowler and Glenn Randall put up *In Search of Suds* in 1982.

Taylor Canyon, on the opposite side of the mesa, was the focus of much activity in the 1980s. Moses, the tallest and most elegant of the canyon's towers, was first ascended in October 1972 by Fred Beckey, Eric Bjørnstad, Jim Galvin, Tom Nephew, and Gregory Markov. An aerial reconnaissance had earlier revealed this hidden spire and its slender neighbor Zeus. Beckey and Bjørnstad had first climbed Zeus, the smaller spire just east of Moses, in 1970. The pair had placed a long bolt ladder up the tower's narrow east ridge, which was unfortunately chopped by unknown climbers in the 1990s, leaving a line of scarred holes. Moses was ascended via a crack system up its abrupt north

Peter Thexton rappelling in Taylor Canyon, Canyonlands National Park.
PHOTO BY ED WEBSTER, MOUNTAIN IMAGERY

face in 6 pitches with lots of direct aid. Charlie Fowler and Chip Chace free-climbed this stunning line at 5.12 in 1981, renaming it *Pale Fire*. The second ascent of Moses came in the spring of 1973 when Bjørnstad ferried the Colorado party of Jim Dunn, Doug Snively, Stewart Green, and Kurt Rasmussen up Taylor Canyon in his old Dodge van. The quartet established a new unnamed route, now called *The Dunn Route*, over 2 days up cracks on the right side of the north face.

The Primrose Dihedrals on Moses, now considered one of the best desert tower routes, was first looked at by the Colorado party in 1973 but dismissed as unlikely with the pitons and chocks then available. In 1979 Green took Ed Webster out to Taylor Canyon to have a look at the desert prophet and pointed out the sheer crack system up the south face. Webster later recounted, "Quite simply, it was one of the most breathtaking lines I had ever seen." That April, Webster rappelled into Taylor Canyon and ascended the spectacular cracks in wilting heat using aid and placing a bolt ladder around The Ear's overhanging off-width crack. The following October, Webster recruited crackmaster Steve Hong, and the duo made a free ascent of the line. This was the first major ascent in the desert that primarily used the new-fangled Friend camming devices for protection on the characteristic parallel-sided cracks located in the soft sandstone. Webster and Chester Dreiman made the first ascent of the wafer-like spire Aphrodite in 1983.

Charlie Horse Needle, a tower sitting on a ridge above the Green River, was discovered and subsequently climbed by Ron Olevsky and Joy Ungritch in 1985. Olevsky named the tower after a horse he was riding while scouting the area bucked him to the ground. Ken Sims, Mark Hesse, and Maura Hanning free climbed the crack system in 1995. The Witch in Hell Roaring Canyon was likewise first ascended solo by Ron Olevsky in 1984 via *Midnight Rider* and also freed by Sims, Hesse, and Hanning on the same weekend as Charlie Horse Needle in 1995.

The best climbing seasons on Island in the Sky are spring and autumn. Both offer generally warm days, although wind can be an occasional bother. Summer days are hot, especially on the south-facing cliffs, although some ascents can be made during cooler periods and in shade. Winters are cold and often snowy, although occasionally warm days occur. Best to pick sunny routes in winter—start early and plan on either long drives in the dark or cold camping.

Objective dangers abound when climbing on the towers and cliffs of the Island in the Sky. Loose rock and blocks are located on many routes on ledges and wedged in chimneys and cracks. Use extreme caution and protect your belayer from falling rock. Wearing a helmet is a great idea. Carry sufficient water, especially on hot weather ascents. At least a gallon per person per day is necessary. Drink often. If you're getting thirsty you're already getting dehydrated. Approaches to the towers are time-consuming. Plan on at least an hour's walk to many of them. Tote a headlamp or flashlight in case the rappel ropes stick or other misfortunes befall your party. The descent trails are often treacherous, steep, and filled with hazardous cliffs and drop-offs.

Descents from all the towers is by rappel. Anchors are generally obvious. Double check all knots and replace frayed, worn, and desiccated webbing. Tie knots in the end of your rap ropes to avoid rappelling off the ends. Be extremely careful when tossing and pulling rappel ropes not to dislodge rocks onto those below. All descents require two 165' ropes.

Rack: A standard desert rack is required for most routes. This includes double sets of Friends and several large pieces for off-width cracks like a #5 Camalot. Sets of TCUs and wired stoppers are also necessary for many routes. Bring lots of runners to alleviate rope drag. A bolt kit is not only unnecessary but it's against the law. Placing additional bolts is prohibited in Canyonlands National Park. All the routes listed here have adequate fixed anchors for safe ascents and descents.

Several regulations pertinent to rock climbing are enforced in Canyonlands National Park. Be aware of these rules and follow them to ensure continued free access to the area's spectacular climbing opportunities. While no permit is needed to rock climb, a permit is required for all backcountry camping and bivouacking. Climbing in the park is limited to free climbing and clean-aid climbing. The park backcountry management plan, implemented in 1995, bans the placement of fixed hardware, including nuts, cams, slings, drilled pitons, and bolts. The placement of any gear with a hammer is prohibited. The only exception to this rule is replacement of unsafe existing anchors or emergency situations. These regulations limit climbers to either free ascents or hammerless aid climbing. Many routes in the area, particularly aid routes in Monument Basin, are now off-limits because of this rule.

Trip Planning Information

General description: The northern sector of Canyonlands National Park offers many excellent tower climbs in the canyons and basins between the Island in the Sky and the Colorado River.

Location: East-central Utah. Southwest of Moab.

Camping: Camping is permitted along the White Rim Trail only at designated sites, including Airport Towers and Gooseberry campgrounds. Unfortunately most of these are booked well in advance by mountain bikers. Backcountry permits, available without reservations, allow camping in or near many of the climbing sites including Monument Basin and Taylor Canyon. The permits are available at the Island in the Sky ranger station daily or by mail from the park headquarters. The permits allow backcountry camping at least a mile from the road, so walk and camp as far from the road as possible. Carry lots of water. No fires are allowed in the park. It's recommended that you obtain a backcountry permit when climbing in Monument Basin—it's just a long drive in and out. The road also is easily lost and dangerous in the dark. Primitive camping is available outside the park boundary. Good places are at Horsethief and Mineral Bottoms along the Green River.

Climbing season: April through May and September through October are the best months. Wind, sleet, and rain occur in spring. Summers are just too hot most of the time. Winters are usually too cold, although climbing is possible during good spells. Many of the routes, however, are in the shade and may be cold.

Restrictions and access issues: All Canyonlands National Park rules and regulations apply to climbers. No permits are necessary for rock climbing in the park. You will need a permit, however, for overnight backcountry stays. These are available at park headquarters or ranger stations. Climbing is limited to free climbing and clean-aid climbing. The park backcountry management plan, implemented in 1995, bans the placement of fixed hardware, including nuts, cams, slings, drilled pitons, and bolts. The placement of any gear with a hammer is prohibited. The only exception is to replace unsafe existing anchors or in emergency situations. These rules limit climbers to free ascents or hammerless aid climbing.

Guidebooks: *Classic Desert Climbs* by Fred Knapp, Sharp End Publishing, 1996. Descriptions and topos of Island classics. *500 Select Moab Classics* by Kevin Chase, 1994. Descriptions and topos. *Desert Rock: Rock Climbs in the National Parks* by Eric Bjørnstad, Chockstone Press, 1996, offers descriptions and topos of many Island in the Sky towers.

Nearby mountain shops, guide services, and gyms: Moab Adventure Outfitters offers a great selection of gear and clothing. They also have rock climbing classes and a guide service. Rim Cyclery in Moab sells gear and chalk.

Services: All visitor and climber services are located in Moab, including gas, food, lodging, camping, dining, and groceries.

Emergency services: The Island in the Sky area is a long way from anywhere. Find a cell phone and call 911 or flag down a ranger. Allen Memorial Hospital, 719 West 400 North, Moab, UT, (801) 259-7191.

Nearby climbing areas: Wall Street, The King's Hand, Long Canyon, Day Canyon, Monitor and Merrimac Buttes, Echo Pinnacle, Crow's Head Spires, Candlestick Tower, River Road crags, The Lighthouse, Dolomite Tower, Castleton Tower, The Priest, Fisher Towers, Arches National Park, The Bride, Indian Creek Canyon.

Nearby attractions: Scott M. Matheson Wetlands Preserve, Corona Arch, Colorado River, Deadhorse Point State Park, Arches National Park, La Sal Mountains, Manti-La Sal National Forest, Colorado River Scenic Byway (Utah 128), Slickrock Bike Trail.

4-5 double-rope
rappels

.11

XX

.10

XX

OW
chimney

.9

XX

squeeze

.11a
fingers

XX

squeeze
chimney

hand

.10+

XX

1

route
begins
behind
here

ISLAND IN THE SKY
MONSTER TOWER

MONSTER TOWER AND WASHER WOMAN

Monster Tower and Washer Woman are 2 large towers composed of Wingate sandstone perched on top of a talus cone on the east side of the Island in the Sky. Sandcastle, a third and smaller tower, sits on the ridge between Washer Woman and the Island rim. The location of the towers is labeled erroneously on the U.S.G.S. map of Canyonlands National Park. Their true location is on a spur two miles to the southwest. The Airport Towers are labeled incorrectly as "Washer Woman" on the U.S.G.S. map. Monster Tower is the eastern pinnacle in the group, over 600 feet tall, and offers 4 routes. It was first climbed via the *Kor-Dalke-Schafer Route* on a snowy December day in 1963 by Layton Kor, Larry Dalke, and Cub Schafer. The best route and the one covered in this guide ascends the wide north ridge, and was first climbed by Ken Trout and Kirk Miller in 1981. Washer Woman, a spectacular fin-like tower split by a huge arch, resembles a woman leaning over an old-fashioned wash tub from a distance. A good view of the formation is from the Mesa Arch viewpoint on the Island. Three routes ascend its flanks. The tower's first ascent was by Rick and John Horn and Pete Carman in 1967 up the *West Face* line. This guide includes the excellent route *In Search of Suds* put up by Charlie Fowler and Glenn Randall in 1982. Other towers on the east edge of the Island in the Sky include Blocktop, Islet-in-the-Sky, Airport Tower, Chip and Dale towers, and the Crow's Head Spires. Descriptions of these towers are located in Eric Bjørnstad's comprehensive area guidebook.

Finding the towers: Approach the twin towers via the White Rim Trail, a rough 98-mile track that follows a bench of White Rim sandstone around the Island in the Sky. The easiest approach is to drive northwest from Moab on U.S. Highway 191 for 9 miles to Utah 313. Turn left or south on Utah 313 and drive 22 miles to just before the Island in the Sky ranger station and visitor center. Turn left on the Shafer Trail, a winding dirt road that descends 1,200' and 4 miles down a series of steep switchbacks to the White Rim Trail. Do not attempt this dangerous road if it's wet, snowy, or icy. A 4-wheel-drive vehicle is advised for both the Shafer Trail and White Rim Trail roads.

The junction of the Shafer and White Rim trails is also accessible from Moab by driving north on US 191 a couple of miles to Utah 279. Turn left on Utah 279 (Potash Road) and follow the paved highway past Wall Street to the Potash Mine. Continue south on the rough dirt road for 14.5 miles to the Shafer Trail-White Rim Trail junction. This is a better and safer route during inclement weather or if Shafer Trail is wet or icy. This road can be very rough or washed out after thunderstorms. Driver beware.

From the junction of the Shafer and White Rim trails, drive the rough White Rim Trail south for about 13 miles to the head of Buck Canyon, an obvious deep draw coming in from the right. The towers are obvious. Park on slickrock and hike up the canyon, keeping left toward its head. Look for a climber path

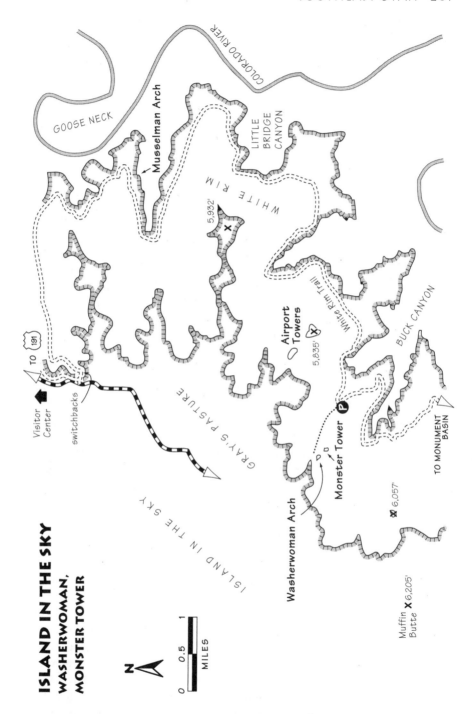

ISLAND IN THE SKY
WASHERWOMAN, MONSTER TOWER

N

0   0.5   1
MILES

COLORADO RIVER

GOOSE NECK

Musselman Arch

LITTLE BRIDGE CANYON

WHITE RIM

5,932'

X

Airport Towers

5,835' X

White Rim Trail

BUCK CANYON

TO 191

Visitor Center

switchbacks

GRAY'S PASTURE

ISLAND IN THE SKY

Monster Tower

P

Washerwoman Arch

6,057'

TO MONUMENT BASIN

Muffin Butte X 6,205'

that scrambles up steep talus slopes toward the towers. At the broken area between Monster Tower and Washer Woman, locate an obvious crack system just left of the notch left of Washer Woman. Climb a 75', 5.6 pitch up the crack. Funky old rap anchors are at its top. To reach Monster Tower's *North Ridge* scramble left across boulders to its base. *In Search of Suds* on Washer Woman is approached by following a ledge system right and around to the southwest face of the spire. This approach shortens the first pitch. Otherwise, reach Washer Woman by driving farther south on the road and scrambling up the southwest talus slopes to the base of the face.

MONSTER TOWER

1. **North Ridge** (III 5.11a) 6 pitches. First ascent by Ken Trout and Kirk Miller, 1981. This is the best of the 4 routes on this huge tower. The route begins on the northeast side of the tower, facing Washer Woman and below a hand crack. **Pitch 1:** Climb narrow, left-facing corner to some strange moves (5.9) to pedestal ledge and 2-bolt belay. **Pitch 2:** Jam hand crack (5.10+) to stance with bolt. Work up right on squeeze chimney/ramp that can be face-climbed to ledge with 3-bolt belay. **Pitch 3:** Jam finger crack (5.11a) up corner to off-width crack (can be liebacked) to squeeze to more off-width. Belay on ledge with 3 bolts. **Pitch 4:** Climb either of 2 ways: (1) Best is keep left up chimney and off-width (5.9) with 1 bolt to belay ledge with 3 bolts. (2) Climb broken, loose rock (5.9) in corner system to right. **Pitch 5:** Move up right to corner, then back left and over roof (5.10) with piton to belay ledge with 2 bolts. **Pitch 6:** Start off left side of ledge and face climb (5.11) past at least 1 bolt to summit. Alternative pitch follows A1 bolt ladder directly up summit block. **Descent:** Rappel route with four or five 2-rope rappels. **Rack:** 2 sets of Friends, including 3 #1, 3 #3, and 3 #3.5 Friends; 1 #4 Camalot; and a set of stoppers. A #3 Big Bro is nice on the top part of Pitch 2.

WASHER WOMAN

2. **In Search of Suds** (III 5.10+) 6 pitches. An excellent route up one of Canyonlands's biggest towers. The line follows a crack system up the right side of the southwest face before traversing along the ridge line to the summit. Begin on the right side of the southwest face just left of the prominent ridge if you approach from the southwest-facing talus slopes. This makes pitch 1 into a long 150' lead. Otherwise, follow a ledge system from the notch between Washer Woman and Monster Tower to a belay at the base of the crack system. This description begins there. **Pitch 1:** Jam fist crack (5.9+) in back of chimney for 80' to belay stance below small window called The Eye of the Needle that penetrates tower. Loosest pitch

ISLAND IN THE SKY
WASHER WOMAN

xx ⌐ 4 double rope
      rappels to ground

.10 face

xx
    .9
  x

.10
roof
xx

.7 chimney

arch

hidden
rap anchors
below arch
xx

.9-
hands   ← Eye of the Needle

loose

xx   .9+
2 rope   fist crack
rappel   2 ← approach from
                 other side of notch

on route—watch for rocks. **Pitch 2:** Jam hand crack (5.9-) left of Eye to chimney (5.7) to belay ledge left of roof; 80'. **Pitch 3:** Follow crack (several 5.10 moves over a bulge) to ridgeline and belay; 70'. **Pitch 4:** Traverse along easy but airy ridge to belay below headwall. **Pitch 5:** Face climb up headwall (5.9) over large arch. Pro is old pins. Belay on spacious ledge below final step. **Pitch 6:** Climb over rotten rock (5.9 R) to bolt ladder. Follow hard-to-clip bolts (5.10+ or C1) to a great summit. A short crux pitch. **Descent:** Four 2-rope rappels down the Kor route. Dangerous and loose descent. Be careful of rock fall when pulling rope! **Rap 1:** Rap back to belay atop arch. **Rap 2:** Make a scary, exposed, free rappel down arch from poorly positioned anchors to anchors on a good ledge at its base. **Rap 3:** Make a third rappel to multiple-bolt anchor on ledge. Several sets of anchors make for some confusion. **Rap 4:** Fourth rappel lands on the ground. **Rack:** 2 sets of Friends with 4 #3s; set of TCUs; set of wires, 2 ropes.

MONUMENT BASIN

Monument Basin is a remote, 2-mile-wide amphitheater that lies between The White Rim and the Colorado River southeast of Island in the Sky. The 500-foot-deep basin boasts numerous slender spires, towers, and fins chiseled from soft Cutler sandstone. Over 20 free-standing towers hide in the basin. This stark and lonely place is a stunning monument to the strangeness of erosion. Some of the formations here defy the imagination, with the tower names reflecting the bizarre and odd—The Enigmatic Syringe, The Pixie Stick, and Staggering Rock.

Climbing in Monument Basin takes a special breed of climber. All the routes here, along with the approaches and descents, are serious affairs—these ain't no sport climbs, pilgrim! Instead the climber finds strange free climbing moves over beetling overhangs and thought-provoking clean-aid up incipient crack systems. Only Fisher Towers aficionados will love this place. But those who do journey way out to the basin and manage to scratch their way up one of these wilderness towers will come back with a sense of accomplishment, a layer of gritty red dust, and the feeling that they've somehow cheated fate again.

Finding the towers: Monument Basin is in the northern sector of Canyonlands National Park below Island in the Sky and Grandview Point. Approach by driving northwest out of Moab on U.S. Highway 191 for 9 miles to Utah 313. Turn left or south here. Continue 22 miles south on Utah 313 to the ranger station at Island in the Sky. Just before the station, turn left on the Shafer Trail, a winding dirt road that descends 1,200 feet down a series of steep switchbacks to the White Rim Trail.

This point can also be reached by driving north from Moab on U.S. Highway 191 a couple of miles to Utah 279. Turn left on Utah 279 and follow it

MONUMENT BASIN

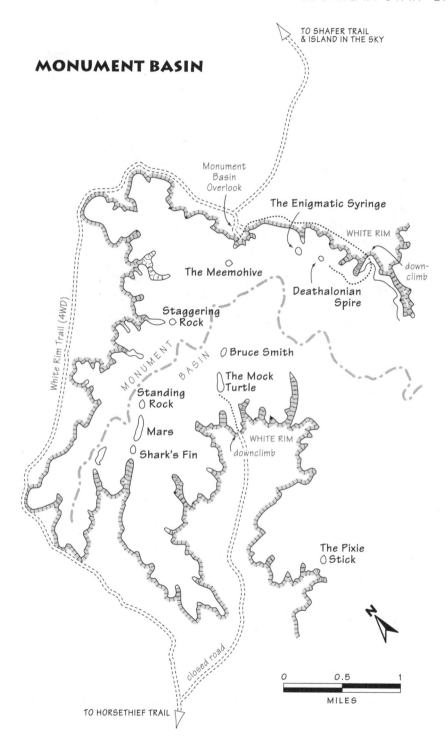

TO SHAFER TRAIL
& ISLAND IN THE SKY

Monument
Basin
Overlook

The Enigmatic Syringe

WHITE RIM

down-
climb

The Meemohive

Deathalonian
Spire

Staggering
Rock

White Rim Trail (4WD)

M O N U M E N T   B A S I N

Bruce Smith

The Mock
Turtle

Standing
Rock

WHITE RIM
downclimb

Mars

Shark's Fin

The Pixie
Stick

N

The Pixie
Stick

closed road

TO HORSETHIEF TRAIL

0   0.5   1

MILES

ISLAND IN THE SKY
MONUMENT BASIN

descent gully
white rim trail
mock turtle
shark's fin
standing rock
bruce smith
staggering rock
meemohive

looking southwest from monument basin overlook

past Wall Street and Long Canyon to the Potash Mine. Follow the dirt road south about 15 miles to the Shafer Trail-White Rim Trail junction.

The White Rim Trail is a 98-mile-long 4-wheel-drive, loop road that circumnavigates the Island in the Sky on The White Rim, a level sandstone bench. Follow the rough dirt road for 31 miles from the junction with Shafer Trail to Monument Basin and an overlook on its north rim. Allow about 3 hours driving time from the Island visitor center.

A four-wheel-drive, high-clearance vehicle is recommended for the descent and drive to Monument Basin. Make sure you have a full tank of gas—it's a long way between fill-ups. The Shafer Trail approach is dangerous when icy or slick. Use the Potash Road approach during bad or snowy weather.

From the rim of Monument Basin there are 2 approaches to the basin floor. The best approach drives 3.7 miles from the overlook to a closed road that runs northeast on a finger peninsula that juts into the basin. Walk the road for a mile to its end and find a gully that descends north to the basin floor near The Mock Turtle. Hike to the other towers from here.

STANDING ROCK

Standing Rock, also called The Totem Pole, is the sheer shaft rising above a small talus cone in the middle of the basin. It's the tallest and thinnest tower here. This is the classic Canyonlands spire with pretty good rock, decent protection, and one of the coolest summits anywhere. It's mind-blowing that it really goes free! The 300-foot finger sits in the middle of the basin.

3. **Original Route** (III 5.11c or 5.8 C2) 4 pitches. First ascent by Layton Kor, Huntley Ingalls, and Steve Komito, 1962. First free ascent by Keith Reynolds and Walt Shipley, 1993. The route begins on the north side of the round pinnacle. **Pitch 1:** Start atop large boulder below north side. Climb crack up large corner system to roof. Traverse right under roof (5.10) to airy moves up and around its right edge. Jam wide sandy crack (The Vertical Sandbox) to good ledge with fixed anchors. **Pitch 2:** Traverse right 15' on easy ledge. Climb crack in right-facing corner to steep thin crack (5.10d) to small belay stance with fixed 2-bolt belay. Watch loose block near top of crack. **Pitch 3:** The crux pitch. Climb up left from belay to fixed wire then back right to rightmost crack system. Back-clean the fixed wire to help avoid rope drag. Continue up crack to bulging smooth face (5.11c). Belay up on good ledge. **Pitch 4:** It's getting airy! Traverse up and right on easier climbing to rotten crack that leads to tiny summit platform. **Descent:** Either 2 or 3 rappels. For 2 rappels use two, 200' ropes (60 meter). **Rap 1:** Rappel 85' to the belay anchors atop Pitch 2. **Rap 2:** Rappel 180' to the ground with two, 200' ropes. For 3 rappels use double 165' ropes. **Rap 1:** Rappel 85' to anchors atop Pitch 2. **Rap 2:** Rappel 100' to anchors atop Pitch 1. **Rap 3:** Rappel 110' to ground.

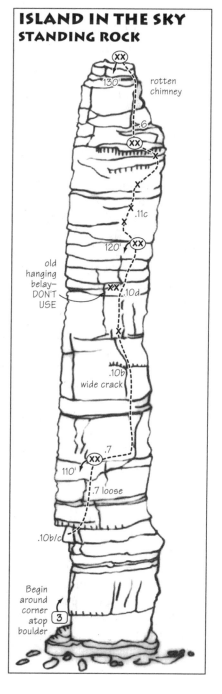

ISLAND IN THE SKY
STANDING ROCK

130'
rotten chimney
.6
.11c
120'
old hanging belay— DON'T USE
.10d
.10b wide crack
.7
110'
.7 loose
.10b/c
Begin around corner atop boulder
3

Rack: Double sets of Friends to #3.5 and 1 #4 Friend; good selection of wires; some TCUs and Tri-cams; lots of extra runners; 2 ropes.

SHARK'S FIN

A spectacular 300-foot fin southwest of Standing Rock on the south side of the basin, Shark's Fin, once connected to the rim, has eroded into a separate tower. Two routes ascend the tower. *The Wiggins Route* climbs the severely overhanging and exposed northeast arête, while the *Fetish Arête* climbs the lower-angled southwest ridge.

4. **Wiggins Route** (IV 5.8 C4) 5 pitches. First ascent by Earl Wiggins, Art Wiggins, and Katy Cassidy, 1986. This spectacular and overhanging route ascends the northeast arête of Shark's Fin, a tower southwest of Standing Rock. Dougald MacDonald, who did the first clean ascent with Dave Goldstein in 1996, calls it the "steepest multi-pitch route in the desert and an incredible clean-aid climb." The route, on mostly solid rock for Monument Basin, is fairly safe but has lots of tricky placements. Escape from the arête above the second pitch is very difficult without fixed ropes. Begin right of the obvious overhanging arête on the left side of the northwest face. **Pitch 1:** Straight-forward aid (C2) with occasional poor placements leads to belay with 1 piton on right side of ledge system. **Pitch 2:** Traverse left to arête on scary free climbing (5.8) and continue up on aid (C2+). Find dubious gear at first, then mostly excellent cams with some free moves. One hairy step is below 2-bolt belay. **Pitch 3:** Follow an easy left-facing corner to scary Tri-cam/hook traverse left (C3). Climb straight up overhanging corners on dubious gear (some good nuts) to bolted belay stance. **Pitch 4:** Aid up wild, exposed, stacked roofs. Above, aid the "Slab" to crux moves (C3+) into right-facing corner. Find good pro in pocket on left partway up corner. More tricky placements to 2 bolts. Hook move to bolted belay on sloping ledge below roof. **Pitch 5:** Bolt move off belay, then weird gear at base of roof. Fixed blade in roof leads to drilled angle at lip. Ingenuity required to pass lip! (First clean ascent placed a wire with cheater stick.) Above roof angle eases and moderate free and aid leads to top. Watch rope drag. **Descent:** Rappel the *Fetish Arête* (southwest ridge on opposite side of tower) in three 2-rope rappels from fixed anchors to ground. 2 raps down arête and last one down northwest face. **Rack:** Bring the full arsenal—you never know what will work. Double cams to 3 inches; 1 each cams to 4 inches; 1 big piece like #5 Camalot; many wires; many TCUs, sliders, Lowe Balls, Rock-n-Rollers and other trick gear; Tri-cams (vital) to #3; Pika Toucans (hand-placed camming pins); Leeper cam hooks; hooks of various sizes and shapes; 3-foot cheater stick and tape; many free carabiners and lots of extra slings; two 200' ropes.

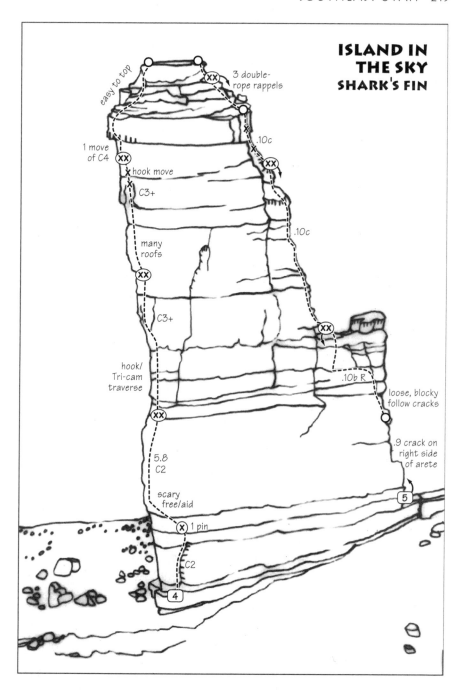

**ISLAND IN
THE SKY
SHARK'S FIN**

easy to top

3 double-
rope rappels

1 move
of C4

hook move

.10c

C3+

.10c

many
roofs

C3+

hook/
Tri-cam
traverse

.10b R

loose, blocky
follow cracks

.9 crack on
right side
of arete

5.8
C2

5

scary
free/aid

1 pin

C2

4

5. **The Fetish Arête** (III 5.10 R) 5 pitches. First ascent by Rob Slater, Bruce Hunter, Jim Bodenhamer, and Tom Cotter, 1992. First free ascent by Steve "Crusher" Bartlett, Stevie Haston, and Laurence Gouault, 1996. This route follows the lower-angled prow opposite *The Wiggins Route*. Begin below the southwest corner of the tower. **Pitch 1:** Climb short wide crack on right side of arête (5.9+) to a small ledge on southwest arête; 70'. **Pitch 2:** Traverse left on northwest face to obvious crack system. Follow this until you're forced onto face left of some loose blocks (5.10b R). Traverse left into obvious corner then climb easy rock to shoulder above. Belay from 2 bolts; 90'. **Pitch 3:** Climb arête to hard moves up vague crack through bulge (5.10c), then traverse right and up to avoid a larger, looser bulge. Belay by large block on ledge; 100'. **Pitch 4:** Mantle onto another ledge, then walk past drilled piton to thin dihedral where a long reach past a fixed pin (5.10c) gains easier climbing on large knobs. Short dihedral reaches large ledge and oddly balanced boulder belay; 70'. **Pitch 5:** Easy scrambling and one irritating mantle (5.8) gain summit. **Rack:** 2 to 3 sets of Friends, TCUs, stoppers, and RPs, and a #4 Camalot. **Descent:** Three 2-rope rappels down route. 2 raps down arête and last one down northwest face.

THE MEEMOHIVE

6. **Meemohive** (III 5.9+ C2) 4 pitches. First ascent was solo by Englishman turned Boulderite Steve "Crusher" Bartlett, 1991. This tower is on the north side of the basin near the Monument Basin Overlook. The route ascends an obvious crack system on the northwest face of the tower and is mostly 5.9 free climbing with a short aid crux that could be freed at 5.11 by a tall person. **Pitch 1:** Great stemming leads up obvious groove-crack system on right side of northwest face. Take a right where crack splits (5.9), climb to rubbly ledge/alcove with large tied-off block belay. **Pitch 2:** Climb mostly easy chimney (5.7) to 2-bolt and #3 Camalot belay stance on shoulder. **Pitch 3:** Climb left wall of chimney above belay bolts. Aid (C2) with wires and cams up 10' seam or free it with long reach (5.11) to finger slot and face climbing (5.9) that leads up left to ledge; 30'. Belay here or traverse/crawl left 25' to large alcove belay on face. **Pitch 4:** Jam crack (5.9+) through 6-foot roof, then face climb up huecos left of crack to avoid loose blocks (watch for your belayer below) and rejoin crack; 15' higher. To avoid a final overhang, traverse left on huecos to easy dihedral; 60'. **Descent:** Downclimb summit blocks to ledge. Make two long 2-rope rappels down west face. **Rap 1:** One 2-rope rappel off slings around huge boulder to 2-bolt station on face. **Rap 2:** One 2-rope rappel to the ground. **Rack:** 2 to 3 sets of Friends; a #4 Camalot; TCUs; some nuts and wires.

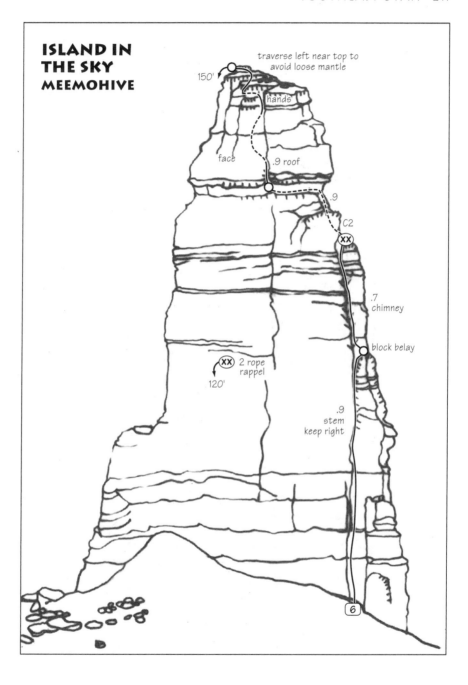

ISLAND IN THE SKY

MEEMOHIVE

traverse left near top to avoid loose mantle

150'

hands

face

.9 roof

.9

C2

.7 chimney

block belay

2 rope rappel

120'

.9 stem keep right

6

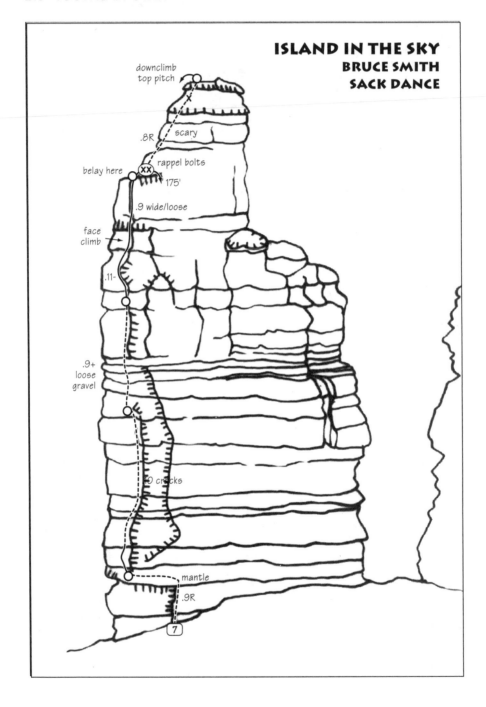

ISLAND IN THE SKY
BRUCE SMITH
SACK DANCE

downclimb
top pitch

.8R   scary

rappel bolts
belay here   XX
175'

.9 wide/loose

face
climb

.11-

.9+
loose
gravel

.10 cracks

mantle
.9R

7

BRUCE SMITH TOWER

7. **Sack Dance** (III 5.11a R) 5 pitches. First ascent by David Goldstein and Dougald MacDonald; 1995. Named for Bruce Smith, a defensive end football player for the Buffalo Bills. The northernmost of the 2 towers in the middle of Monument Basin east of Standing Rock. This all-free route climbs the obvious "leg and foot" on the northwest face of the 225-foot tower. It has a great summit and good climbing, especially on the second and fifth pitches. MacDonald warns, "Watch for dangerous garbage." Begin below a crack system on the northwest face. **Pitch 1:** Climb loose rock to first pro 12' up. Continue up right-facing corner (5.9) to unprotected mantle on right. Work back left 20' across ledge to good belay stance at the heel of the "foot." **Pitch 2:** Climb left-facing corner to some cool cracks (5.9/5.10) on left side of detached pillar ("The Bad Knee") to short lieback to "The Three-Point Stance" hanging belay. **Pitch 3:** Grovel up loose rock (5.9+) to alcove belay. **Pitch 4:** Undercling to route crux (5.11a) turning a bulge. Follow dirty crack to mantle shelf, continue up wide, loose crack (5.9) to ledge belay. The nearby bolts are for rap only— they're not in a good place for the belay. **Pitch 5:** An amazing and highly improbable pitch! Face climb (5.8 R) on pockets and edges protected with Tri-cams and TCUs in pockets to bad bolt. Above, mantle onto rounded summit. **Descent:** Downclimb top pitch to shoulder belay ledge. Make a single 175' rappel with 2 ropes (200' or 60 meter ropes) to ground from 2-bolt anchor. **Rack:** Double set of Friends; 1 wide crack piece of pro; Tri-cams; TCUs; stoppers; two 200' ropes.

THE MOCK TURTLE

8. **Mud Wrestling** (IV 5.10+) 5 pitches. First ascent by Steve "Crusher" Bartlett and Strappo Hughes, 1990. Does the name say it all? You decide! This is the largest free-standing tower in Monument Basin and the only one with a White Rim sandstone cap. It was the first tower here to be free climbed and offers a superb last pitch on good sandstone. The route ascends the northeast side of the formation. **Pitch 1:** Climb with jams and stems up prominent dihedral on northeast corner of tower and pass wide section (5.10+) before moving left to ledge with bolts; 125'. **Pitch 2:** Step right and climb up continuation of lower crack (5.10 and 4" to 5" wide) until face moves gain ledge on left under chimney system; 70'. **Pitch 3:** Work up obvious chimney above to large ledge with 2 bolts; 80'. **Pitch 4:** Move out right up loose gully (4th or low 5th class) to mantle (5.9) onto shoulder of formation and 2-bolt belay anchor; 90'. **Pitch 5:** Excellent face climbing (5.9+) protected by RPs brings one to 3-foot roof crack in white summit block; 40'. Summit belay bolts may be very poor due to very soft rock! **Descent:** 4 rappels to the ground with double ropes from bolt anchors.

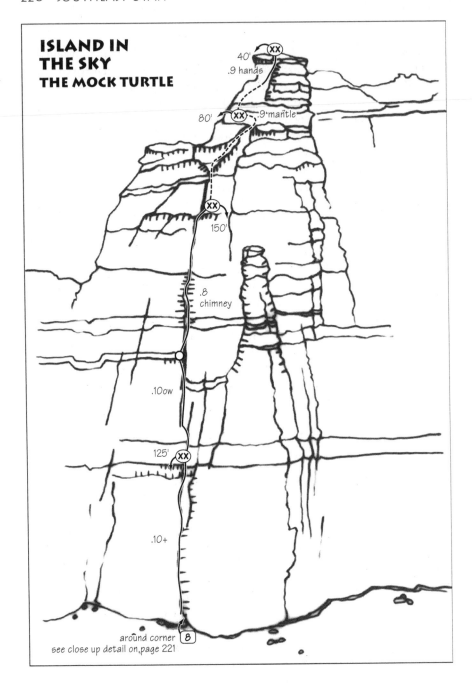

ISLAND IN
THE SKY
THE MOCK TURTLE

40'
.9 hands

80' .9 mantle

150'

.8
chimney

.10ow

125'

.10+

around corner 8
see close up detail on page 221

ISLAND IN THE SKY
MOCK TURTLE
MUDWRESTLING

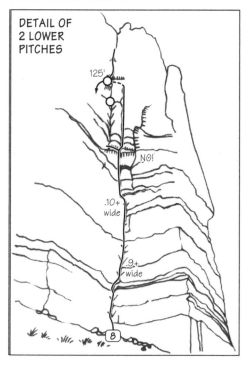

DETAIL OF 2 LOWER PITCHES

125'

NO!

.10+ wide

.9+ wide

8

Rap 1: Summit to shoulder anchors; 40'. **Rap 2:** Shoulder to pitch 3 anchors; 80'. **Rap 3:** Pitch 3 anchors to pitch 1 anchors; 150'. **Rap 4:** Pitch 1 anchors to ground; 125'. **Rack:** 2 sets of Friends with 4 #3 and 4 #4; 3 or 4 #4 Camalots and 2 #5 Camalots or big Tri-cams. The top pitch uses wide crack gear and RPs. Two 200-foot ropes.

TAYLOR CANYON
AREA (SEE MAP PAGE 199.)

Taylor Canyon, lying on the northern boundary of Canyonlands National Park, is a sharp canyon lined with towering Wingate sandstone walls. The canyon fingers east from the Green River to The Neck, a narrow rocky divide atop the Island in the Sky. The upper part of the canyon houses a stunning selection of towers perched atop a ridge—Moses, Zeus, and Aphrodite. Moses is, of course, one of the most famous and popular of all of Utah's sandstone skyscrapers.

Finding the towers: Drive northwest from Moab on U.S. Highway 191 for 9 miles to the left turnoff for Utah 313 to Dead Horse Point and Island in the Sky. Drive approximately 12 miles to a right turnoff signed Horsethief Trail. Follow this dirt road across the mesatop to the edge of the canyon rim. Descend the Horsethief Trail—steep switchbacks, rough and narrow. A high-clearance vehicle is advised. It's dangerous and slick when wet or icy. Use caution. At Horsethief Bottom on the canyon floor turn left or south and follow the White Rim Trail for 0.8 mile to the national park boundary. Continue south a couple of miles to the well-marked left turn up Taylor Canyon. Follow the rough road (four-wheel-drive, high-clearance, tire pump, and shovel recommended) for almost 5 miles to the base of Moses. The track is alternately sandy and rocky. It is impassable after rain. Road conditions vary from year to year. It may be passable all or partway with a two-wheel-drive. Check at the Island in the Sky ranger station for conditions and details.

MOSES

9. **Pale Fire** (IV 5.12c) 4 pitches. First ascent of the route and tower (5.8 A3) by Fred Beckey, Eric Bjørnstad, Jim Galvin, Tom Nephew, and Gregory Markov, 1972. First free ascent by Chip Chace and Charlie Fowler in 1981. The original route up Moses. Once an aid climb, now it's a sustained and exposed free route up the spire's dead-vertical, 600-foot-high north face. The route is usually climbed in 4 pitches with a 200-foot (60-meter) rope or 6 pitches with a 165-foot cord. Begin by scrambling up talus slopes to the base of the obvious crack system on the left side of the north face. **Pitch 1:** Jam a thin, flaring finger crack (5.12c with sustained .11d jamming) past a 3-bolt sling belay to hand cracks (5.10) to 3-bolt belay; 180'. This lead can also be done in 2 pitches. **Pitch 2:** Follow up the right-angling hand crack (5.10) for 100' to a hanging belay from 3 bolts. Belay here or continue jamming crack to face (5.11-) with old bolts to crack to belay from 3 bolts; 160'. **Pitch 3:** Follow line of old bolts up face (5.11) and onto slab ridge to belay ledge on the prophet's shoulder; 80'. **Pitch 4:** Short face climbing (5.8) pitch past a couple of old bolts to the summit; 80'. **Descent:** Four 2-rope rappels down route with 2 hanging, stanceless stations (kinda scary but chained anchors) or five 2-rope rappels down the *South Face Directissima Route* left of *Primrose Dihedrals* on the south face. The rappels down *Pale Fire*: **Rap 1:** Summit anchors to 3-bolt anchors on shoulder; 80'. **Rap 2:** Shoulder anchors to 3-bolt anchor. **Rap 3:** 160' rappel to 3-bolt anchor. **Rap 4:** 165' rappel to ground. **Rack:** Lots of Friends—2 #1, 3 #1.5, 2 #2, 2 #2.5, 3 #3, 3 #3.5, 3 sets of TCUs, set of wires, quickdraws and runners, two 200' ropes.

10. **Dunn Route** (IV 5.11) 5 pitches. First ascent and second overall of the tower by Jim Dunn, Stewart Green, Doug Snively, and Kurt Rasmusson, 1973. First free ascent by Jeff Achey and Glenn Randall, 1982. This route climbs corners on the right side of the north face. Begin right of *Pale Fire* below some broken bands and a large dihedral. **Pitch 1:** Face climb over broken rock and bulge (5.9+) to right-facing corner. Off-width up corner (5.9-) to 2-bolt hanging belay; 80'. A 7-inch piece will protect the OW. **Pitch 2:** Continue up dihedral stemming and jamming (5.10-). Just past fixed pin, route divides. Continue up right crack to squeeze chimney (5.10). Belay on good ledge with 2 bolts at notch; 165'. If you go up the left system, follow crack (5.9 R) past a possible belay stance and continue to large ledge. This requires a 200' rope. Watch for loose rock on this pitch. **Pitch 3:** Face climb left across slab (5.8) to crack. Jam up and left (5.9+) to spacious ledge. **Pitch 4:** Undercling and fist jam obvious overhanging crack (5.11) past some fixed pitons until it's a bomb bay chimney big enough to squeeze into (5.11). Small folks can tunnel through (5.8). Belay from bolts on ledge on Moses's shoulders; 130'. **Pitch 5:** Face climb (5.8) past a couple

ISLAND IN
THE SKY
MOSES
NORTH FACE

.8-face
80'
.11
squeeze
chimney
.11
fists
.11
undercling
.9+
160'
.11-
165'
SB
.10
squeeze
.10+
hands
.9R
SB
.9 165'
.10
hands
stem
.10-
80'
.12c/.11d
fingers
.9+
10
9

of pins to summit. **Descent:** Rappel *Pale Fire* or the *South Face Directissima*. Either way it's multiple raps with double ropes. **Rack:** 2 sets of Friends with 4 #3.5 and 3 #4. A couple of #4 Camalots are useful, as is a 7-inch piece. 2 ropes.

11. **Primrose Dihedrals** (IV 5.11d) 7 pitches. First ascent solo by Ed Webster, 1979. First free ascent by Webster and Steve Hong, 1979. This is the most famous Canyonlands tower route and one of the most popular hard desert lines. Plan on a full day of climbing to do this classic. Most of the cruxes are boulder problems. The route ascends the steep southeast face of the tower. Begin below the obvious crack system on the right side of the face. **Pitch 1:** One of the crux leads. Climb broken rock bands to inverted chimney slot (5.11d). Continue up broken rock to good ledge with 2 bolts; 80'. This pitch can be avoided by approaching route from north to notch east of Moses. Step down (5.8) and traverse left to belay ledge. **Pitch 2:** Jam obvious corner above. Fingers (5.10-) to hands (5.10) over roof, pass fixed pin to lieback (5.10-). Belay from bolts on crowded stance in alcove. **Pitch 3:** Clip fixed piton and move down and left (5.8) to leftward traverse. Climb cracks and stacked flakes (5.10-) to sloping belay ledge with 2 bolts. **Pitch 4:** Jam crack up large right-facing dihedral. Climb large spike into corner. Jam and lieback (5.10) to pin, turn a roof, and continue up fist and off-width crack to semi-hanging belay stance from bolt and gear. **Pitch 5:** Short pitch up dihedral past loose, stacked blocks (5.9) to belay below The Ear, an overhanging flake. **Pitch 6:** The real crux with scary, airy climbing. Lieback or off-width up 8-inch overhanging crack (5.11b) using bolt ladder for great pro. Higher, squeeze into crack and end on good ledge with belay bolts. **Pitch 7:** Work up chimney (5.8) to left to Moses's shoulder, face climb (5.8) to summit. **Descent:** Rappel down *Pale Fire* (North Face) via four 2-rope rappels. Some are scary because they have hanging stanceless stations. Or rappel the *South Directissema Route* left of *Primrose* via four or five 2-rope rappels. **Rack:** 2 sets of Friends, with 3 #1.5, 3 #3, and 3 #3.5. Extra #1-#2 Friends and 5-inch piece also useful. Sets of TCUs and wires, quickdraws, and extra runners. 2 ropes.

ZEUS

12. **Sisyphus** (III 5.11 R) 3 pitches. First ascent by Jim Dunn and Doug Snively in 1973 after the second ascent of Moses. First free ascent by Jeff Achey and Chip Chace. This is a spectacular route up the dihedral system on the left side of the south face. Begin below broken rock and a right-facing corner. **Pitch 1:** Climb up corner to better rock. Stem up The Pod, an obvious right-facing corner (5.11a), to mantle (5.10). Continue up finger crack above (5.10) to good belay ledge with no anchors. **Pitch 2:** Jam and fingertip-lieback (5.11) strenuous crack up large left-facing dihedral to

ISLAND IN
THE SKY
MOSES

5 rappels down face

.8

.8 hidden
chimney

EAR

.11b
LB

.9
loose

.10
scary

sloping ledge

.10-

.10b

.10 roof

step down
approach
notch from
north side

fingers

.11d
slot

11

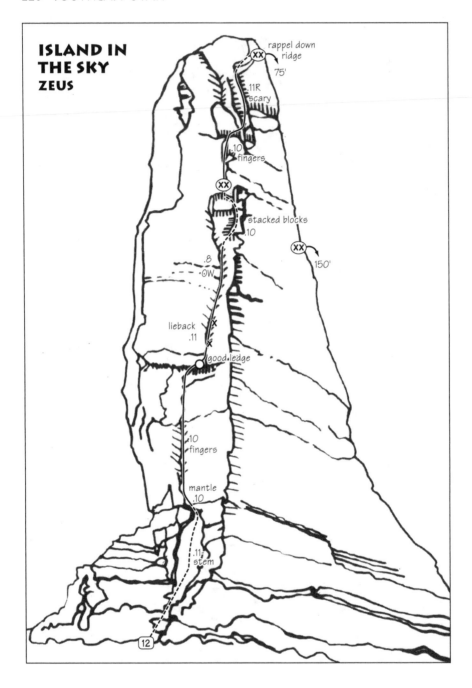

**ISLAND IN
THE SKY
ZEUS**

rappel down
ridge
75'

.11R
scary

.10
fingers

stacked blocks
.10

150'

.8
OW

lieback
.11

good ledge

.10
fingers

mantle
.10

.11
stem

12

short off-width section (5.8). Finish by angling up right over loose blocks (5.10) to 2-bolt belay ledge. **Pitch 3:** Jam corners above (5.10 fingers) and work right across ledge to final sloping move (5.11 R crux) over bulge in corner (poor pro). Easy climbing (5.7) leads up summit cap. **Descent:** 2 rappels. Rappel from anchors 75' to bolted stance on northeast ridge. Rappel 150' over an arch to the ground. **Rack:** Lots of Friends—3 #1, 2 #1.5, 2 #2, 2 #2.5, 2 #3, 1 #3.5, 1 #4. 2 sets of TCUs including 4 #.5. Set of wires. Runners. 2 Ropes.

APHRODITE

13. **East Ridge** (III 5.10c) 4 pitches. First ascent by Ed Webster and Chester Dreiman, 1983. This route, following the east ridge of this thin, blocky tower, offers some good climbing interspersed with some crumbling and poorly protected sections. Begin on the far right side of the tower below an obvious notch that separates it from the rimrock. **Pitch 1:** Climb up to left-facing dihedral that faces rimrock. Jam off-width crack past bolt to

ISLAND IN THE SKY
APHRODITE

down climb from summit

95'

.7

.10c

100'

.9

155'

.9
OW

13

belay ledge; 150'. **Pitch 2:** Face climb up ridge on sometimes crumbling rock (5.9) past a couple of fixed pins to belay ledge with bolts; 100'. **Pitch 3:** Face climb (5.10c) the scary unprotected step above to ledge. Continue up rotten slab (5.7) past pin to belay on The Plank ledge; 95'. **Pitch 4:** Follow ridge (5.6) to summit. **Descent:** Downclimb upper pitch to The Plank. Make three 2-rope rappels down the route. **Rack:** A set of Friends, with 1 large piece; TCUs; wires; and 2 ropes.

CHARLIE HORSE NEEDLE

Charlie Horse Needle is a somewhat remote 250-foot spire on a sawtooth ridge that overlooks the Green River. Ken Sims, who did the first free ascent of the tower, notes that it has a "great summit, sustained and difficult climbing, is well-protected, seldom climbed, and has good quality rock." The spire sits just south of the park boundary below the rimrock east of the Green River.

Finding the tower: Drive northwest from Moab on U.S. Highway 191 for about 10 miles to the left turnoff for Utah 313 to Dead Horse Point and Island in the Sky. Drive approximately 12 miles to a right turnoff signed Horsethief Trail. Follow this dirt road across the mesatop to the edge of the canyon rim. Descend the Horsethief Trail—rough and narrow. A high-clearance vehicle is advised. It's dangerous and slick when wet or icy. Use caution. At Horsethief Bottom on the canyon floor turn left or south and follow the White Rim Trail for 0.8 mile to the national park boundary. Park about a mile south of the boundary when the spire is visible to the east in the rimrock. Hike east up a prominent wash in a wide canyon. Toward the end of the wash bear right up a subsidiary drainage and climb steep, bouldery, scree slopes to the northeast side of the needle. Access it by walking out a broad terrace to the base of the tower. Allow about an hour to hike to the base.

14. **Sims-Hesse-Hanning Route** (III 5.11a/b or 5.12a) 3 pitches. First ascent of the tower by Ron Olevsky and Joy Ungritch (5.7 A2). Ken Sims, Mark Hesse, and Maura Hanning made the first free ascent of the route in 1995, although the first ascent of the first pitch variation described below was done later by Sims and Paul Drakos. This is a remote desert tower with a great view of the Green River and its canyons. The route begins on the northeast (shady) side of the tower. **Pitch 1:** 2 ways to go: (1) Standard route climbs broken rock for 35' to large ledge below main crack system. Jam twin cracks—an off-width crack on the right and a fist crack on the left—up obvious right-facing dihedral (5.9+) to chimney (5.7) with loose blocks. Belay from gear at Shangri-la ledge at base of obvious airy window; 80'. The *Sims Crack* variation climbs broken rock up and right to thin, striking, 40-foot finger to thin hands crack (5.12a) that leads to 5.7 chimney. **Pitch 2:** Reach curving hand crack on right wall of chimney/slot. Jam and stem finger to hand crack (5.10c) to off-width to narrow ledge

ISLAND IN THE SKY
CHARLIE HORSE NEEDLE

xx
80'

.11b
thin
hands

.11c fingers

xxx
160'

OW

.10b hands

"Shangri-la" belay

9+
OW

.12 fingers

14

approach

and 3-bolt belay; 70'. **Pitch 3:** Step right from ledge to gain short, difficult fingery section (5.11a/b) of sustained thin hands crack to short off-width section. Belay from 2 bolts in notch between two summits; 80'. Face climb (5.6) 10' to summit and downclimb back to lower summit. **Descent:** Two 2-rope rappels down route to ground. **Rack:** 2 sets of Friends; a couple of large pieces like #7 Tri-cam or #5 Camalot; large wires; 2 ropes.

THE WITCH

The Witch, lying on the south edge of Hell Roaring Canyon just north of Canyonlands National Park, is a remote 350-foot Wingate sandstone tower. The Warlock is adjacent to The Witch. The described route up the tower is a difficult crack climb with a spectacular second pitch up a stemming corner. The first ascent of The Witch was solo by Ron Olevsky on Halloween, 1984.

Finding the tower: Drive northwest from Moab on U.S. Highway 191 for about 10 miles to the left turnoff for Utah 313 to Dead Horse Point and Island in the Sky. Drive approximately 12 miles to a right turnoff signed Horsethief Trail. Follow this dirt road across the mesatop to the edge of the canyon rim. Descend the Horsethief Trail—rough and narrow. A high-clearance vehicle is advised. It's dangerous and slick when wet or icy. Use caution. At Horsethief Bottom on the canyon floor turn right on a rough road and drive north along the river for a few miles past Mineral Canyon to Hell Roaring Canyon. With a four-wheel-drive, follow a uranium prospector's track up Hell Roaring Canyon for a couple of miles to a landslide that blocks the road. Park here and walk up the canyon another mile. The Witch and The Warlock are obvious towers in a cirque to the south. Scramble up talus slopes to the base.

15. **Sims-Hesse-Hanning Route** (III 5.11+ R) 4 pitches. First ascent by Ron Olevsky solo, 1984. The route, named *Midnight Rider*, was rated 5.7 A3. Ken Sims, Mark Hesse, and Maura Hanning free climbed the line in 1995. A spectacular route up a remote tower. The route climbs the southwest side of the tower. Begin just right of a huge block below an obvious corner system. **Pitch 1:** Climb thin right-facing corner (5.10a/b) past horizontal limestone band. Belay on ledge up left from 2 bolts. **Pitch 2:** Sustained and spectacular but spooky pitch. Jam and stem finger crack (5.11+) up obvious corner to 2-bolt belay. Ken recommends a bolt be placed at no-hands rest half-way up. Bring lots of #0 and #1 TCUs. **Pitch 3:** Continue up corners (5.9) past 3 bolts to a 5.10b/c section. Above here traverse left (5.9 face climbing) to right-angling crack (5.7) that leads to 2-bolt belay on ridge. Don't go directly up crack system above first corner. A large and dangerous flake is poised on the ridge above and would be fatal for anyone below. **Pitch 4:** Face climb (5.9+) past 3 bolts to ledge, continue up easier rock (5.6) to the summit. **Descent:** Four 2-rope rappels down route. **Rack:** Double sets of Friends; lots of TCUs including at least 6 each of #0 and #1; set of wires; runners; 2 ropes.

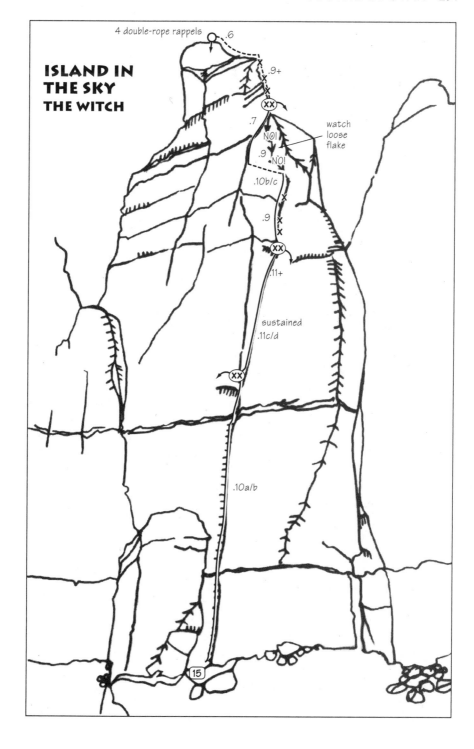

4 double-rope rappels

.6

**ISLAND IN THE SKY
THE WITCH**

.9+

.7

watch
loose
flake

NO!

.9

NO!

.10b/c

.9

.11+

sustained
.11c/d

.10a/b

15

Mexican Hat

Overview

Mexican Hat, one of Utah's strangest rock formations, balances a flattened pancake disk atop a banded, 300-foot-high talus cone. It's really not a hat at all, but a sombrero with a wide brim jutting above a narrow head. The rock, a famed landmark along U.S. Highway 163, sits east of the highway above the tamarisk-lined, west bank of the meandering San Juan River. The river, beginning far to the east in Colorado's San Juan Mountains, cuts through the Raplee Anticline and makes a bowknot bend just north of Mexican Hat. Below the hat, the river enters a spectacular, sinuous gorge aptly called The Goosenecks where it twists back on itself in a series of entrenched meanders before emptying into the placid waters of Lake Powell.

Mexican Hat, a geological oddity, is a caprock of Cedar Mesa sandstone that sits on top of a pedestal and talus cone of the Halgaito Formation, a bed of red shale and siltstone that also comprises the surrounding valley floor. Both formations, part of the Cutler Group, date from the Permian Period, over 250 million years ago. The Halgaito shales were deposited by sluggish streams that wandered across a humid, heavily vegetated lowland along the coastline of a shallow sea. Early ancestors of the dinosaurs populated the ancient landscape, leaving fossilized skeletons and bones as a record of their ancient passage. Recent erosion dissected the Halgaito shale, leaving this spectacular remnant capped by a summit of hard, erosion-resistant sandstone.

Climbing history: Mexican Hat, because of its proximity to southeastern Utah's major highway and its formidable appearance, begged to be climbed. Its first recorded ascent came in May 1962 by Royal Robbins and Jack Turner, although a pole on top indicated that locals had somehow attained the summit previously. The duo nailed out the wild roof via an A4 crack on the river side of the rock. *The Robbins–Turner Route* is rated A2 today. *The Bandito Route*, the best route to the summit, was ascended by Banditos Stan Mish and Dan Langmade in 1981. The pair placed five bolts and a fixed piton to surmount the immense roof. The hat is somewhat notorious since it appeared in a fake ad for "clear lycra" in a spoof section of *Rock & Ice*; it had as many as 7 climbers on the summit at once.

Mexican Hat offers a novel route and airy summit for desert climbers. The standard route is a bolted, clip-up aid route that is a piece of cake for anyone with aid experience. **Rack** is a dozen free carabiners and a couple of sets of aiders. Some of the bolts may be missing on the route. Bring replacements, extra hangers, or a clip-stick to bypass those sections.

Trip Planning Information

General description: An easy aid route up the balanced sandstone disk of Mexican Hat, one of Utah's strangest rock formations.

Location: Southeast Utah. North of the town of Mexican Hat near the Arizona border.

Camping: Primitive camping along the San Juan River on the east side of Mexican Hat. Primitive camping also at the Valley of the Gods just north of the formation and U.S. Highway 163. Sand Island BLM Campground is at Bluff.

Climbing season: Year-round. Summers can be hot. Winters can be cold. Expect wind in spring.

Restrictions and access issues: None. Mexican Hat is on BLM public lands.

Guidebooks: *Classic Desert Climbs* by Fred Knapp, Sharp End Publishing, 1996, includes a brief description of Mexican Hat. The now out-of-print *Desert Rock* guide by Eric Bjørnstad covers Mexican Hat and surrounding areas including Valley of the Gods.

Nearby mountain shops, guide services, and gyms: None in the immediate area. The nearest climbing shops are Moab Adventure Outfitters and Rim Cyclery, in Moab, 175 miles to the north.

Services: All services are found in Bluff, including gas, food, lodging, and camping. Limited services in Mexican Hat.

Emergency services: Call 911.

Nearby climbing areas: Fry Canyon, Texas Tower, Dream Speaker, Bluff Cliffs, Valley of the Gods (Petard Tower, North Tower, Eagle Plume Tower, Tom-Tom Tower, Angel's Fear, and Hidden Pinnacle), Goosenecks Bouldering Area—a scenic bouldering area on a cliff-band below the Goosenecks Overlook 8 miles north of Mexican Hat. Monument Valley (AZ) offers many spectacular spires for climbing. Unfortunately they are on the Navajo Indian Reservation and off-limits to climbing unless permission is obtained from grazing land permitholders. Ask around if you want to climb King on a Throne, The Rabbit, The Bear, or Shangri-la.

Nearby attractions: Goosenecks Overlook, Valley of the Gods, Grand Gulch, Muley Point Overlook, Natural Bridges National Monument, Glen Canyon National Recreation Area, Hovenweep National Monument, Monument Valley Tribal Park (UT-AZ), Navajo National Monument (AZ).

Finding the tower: Mexican Hat lies just east of U.S. Highway 163 about 2.5 miles north of the town of Mexican Hat. Find a rough dirt road between highway mile markers 23 and 24 and turn east. Follow the road, keeping right. Go a mile or so to the back or east side of the formation and park. Primitive camping is also possible here. Scramble up talus slopes and short cliff bands on Mexican Hat's northeast side to the cliff base.

1. **Bandito Route** (I C1) At the base of the formation, find the easiest-looking path and scramble up 4th class rock ledges and short cliffs to the base of the sombrero. The route ascends the southwest or highway side of the final brim. Straight-forward aid (C1) leads out the huge roof via 5 bolts and a fixed piton to the huge slickrock summit. Don't stand too close to the edges—you might tip the balanced block over! Some of the bolts and hangers might be missing or stolen. Bring extra hangers and a clip-stick to pass possible reachy sections. **Descent:** Make an 80' rappel back to the base of the formation. **Rack:** Free carabiners and aiders.

Central

UTAH

SAN RAFAEL SWELL

OVERVIEW

The 900-square-mile San Rafael Swell, an immense domelike uplift, is one of Utah's little-known scenic wonders. It's a place of sheer cliffs, abrupt canyons, wide basins, lofty mesas and buttes, shale badlands, and towering sandstone escarpments chiseled by the San Rafael River and its dry tributaries. It's a superlative desert landscape that should have been preserved and protected as a national park years ago. The Swell, in fact, was one of 3 Utah canyon areas recommended by early 20th century conservationists to be designated as a national parkland. The other two, Arches and Natural Bridges, acquired federal protection, but the San Rafael Swell was left open to economic development and multiple use.

The Swell, a place once inhabited by ancient Indians as long as 5,000 years ago and later by desperadoes like Butch Cassidy and his gang, is still haunted by those spirits. Today it is a special place without much protection. Its delicate landscapes, except for some wilderness study areas, are managed for multiple use by the BLM and are open to use and abuse by a host of recreationists as well as miners and ranchers. Continuing threats to the area include uranium and petroleum claims, cattle grazing on sensitive lands, and off-road vehicles. Unfortunately the ORVs and motorcycles have ventured far beyond established roads and common sense, criss-crossing some areas of the Swell with tire tracks and tearing up the fragile cryptobiotic soils.

Lying on the northern edge of the Colorado Plateau, the San Rafael Swell is an anticline, an elevated area of uplifted layers of sandstone. The strata located here, including ruddy Wingate sandstone, the principal cliff-forming and rock-climbing layer, occurs elsewhere in Utah's canyon country. Wingate is a hard sandstone that was primarily deposited as desert sand dunes. The Chinle Formation, with alternating layers of sandstone and shale, lies below the Wingate cliffs as steep talus slopes broken by cliff bands, while the thin Kayenta Formation and the buff-colored Navajo sandstone, another dune formation, crown the Wingate.

The stunning San Rafael Swell is fringed by an almost impassable perimeter of tilted strata. Numerous abrupt canyons lined with sheer walls break through the outer wall on the east, emptying onto shale badlands. The San

Rafael River, originating high on the snowy Aquarius Plateau to the west, slices through the northern swell in a deep, cliff-lined gorge. Its lower canyons, the Upper and Lower Black Boxes, are watery slots well known to intrepid canyon explorers. The Swell, with a wide range of elevations, includes numerous ecosystems. A riparian zone lines the river; saltbush scatters across sere shale badlands; pinyon pine and juniper woodlands cloak the higher slopes; and occasional ponderosa pines stud high, north-facing slopes.

The San Rafael Swell boasts a long and varied human history that began with early Paleo-Indian hunters who crossed its rugged vastness. A few spear points located on the west side of the region mark their tenuous passage. Later the Desert Culture flourished here until 500 A.D. These hunters and gatherers migrated seasonally through shelters in the cliffs and left extensive pictograph panels as their legacy. The pictographs, painted in what archeologists call the Barrier Canyon style, have a ghostlike human form with long, tapered bodies and strange headdresses. One of the best and most accessible art panels stretches for 100 feet along a sheltered cliff face along the Buckhorn Wash road a few miles north of the San Rafael River. Later the Fremont Indians, who had a culture similar to the Anasazi farther south, lived here. They built small granaries to store harvests, grew corn and beans on the canyon floors, and left petroglyphs on the varnished sandstone walls.

The Spanish Trail, pioneered by Spanish priests Escalante and Dominguez, crosses the northern part of the Swell on its 1,200-mile journey from Santa Fe to San Francisco. The San Rafael Swell also boasts a colorful outlaw history. Numerous desperadoes eluded sheriffs' posses in the maze of canyons, escaping south to Robber's Roost east of Hanksville. Butch Cassidy and his Wild Bunch often passed through the area, and staged a daring train robbery at nearby Castle Gate in 1897. Matt Warner, a wealthy rancher turned bank robber, left an inscription in Buckhorn Wash in 1920.

Climbing history: The Swell's climbing history isn't nearly as exciting as its human history. The area was so remote that it was inaccessible to most people until Interstate 70 pushed through in 1970. It was seldom visited by rock climbers until the early 1990s. Some of the first recorded routes here were by Jim Langdon and several partners beginning in 1973. Langdon snagged the first ascents of spectacular Bottleneck Peak and Window Blind Butte. George Hurley and Bill Forrest climbed The White Knight, a pinnacle north of I-70, in 1977.

The early 1990s saw the first major development in the Swell. Salt Lake City climbers, tired of the long commute to Indian Creek, began exploring the area and located some great cliffs. The Dylan Wall, the most developed crag in the Swell, had its first route *One More Cup of Coffee* established by Mike Friedrichs and Mary Ellen Gage in 1991. Friedrichs was the main motivator behind the further development of the wall as well as other area cliffs. Now there are hundreds of established routes in the Swell, and the potential exists for many more routes as well as first ascents of unclimbed backcountry towers.

Most of the route information in the Swell has traveled by word of mouth and been kept secret. This helps lessen climbing impacts and protects some of the area's remote atmosphere. This guide purposefully includes only a small selection of routes to help preserve the quality of the area's climbing adventures. These routes are a good starting point for further explorations into this magnificent desert land. Be aware that most of the established cliffs are spread over a huge area and long approaches are the norm.

Spring and autumn are the best seasons for climbing. Expect hot temperatures at the south-facing Dylan Wall on warm days. This cliff definitely bakes all day in the sun. Shaded routes are located along the Buckhorn Wash road. Late spring can also be very buggy. Summer temperatures often exceed 100 degrees. Climbing is out of the question on most days. Better to find a shaded, wet slot-canyon to explore. Winter often offers climbable days on the sunny cliffs. The big problem is access. All the dirt roads are dangerous when wet or snow-covered and even four-wheel-drive vehicles will have problems navigating the slick clay surfaces when wet.

Many dangers are located here. Carry lots of water, at least a gallon per person per day on hot days, to avoid dehydration and sunstroke. Plan on chemically treating, boiling, or filtering all water to avoid *Giardia*. Wear a hat when it's hot. The approaches are long and steep. A headlamp is a good idea if you're coming down late. Practice clean camping by staying in existing sites, burying all human waste and burning toilet paper, using existing fire rings or, better yet, dispersing the rings and having no fire at all. Do not destroy or damage trees for firewood. Pack out all your trash as well as any that others have left behind. When hiking to cliffs, follow existing trails whenever possible. Otherwise follow washes to avoid damaging fragile cryptobiotic soils. Rappel whenever possible instead of lowering from anchors to avoid damaging the sandstone.

Rack: A day's climbing requires triple sets of Friends or other camming devices, several large Camalots or Big Bros, a set of stoppers, quickdraws, and a couple of 165-foot ropes.

Trip Planning Information

General description: Numerous routes ascend the Wingate sandstone cliffs and towers in the northern sector of the remote San Rafael Swell.

Location: East-central Utah. West of Green River and north of Interstate 70.

Camping: The San Rafael Campground, BLM fee area, sits alongside the San Rafael River and offers easy access to the area cliffs. The campground has toilets, tables, fire grills, and raised tent pads, but no water. There is no trash pick-up. Pack out all your rubbish. Numerous primitive camping options exist along the area roads. There are many existing sites. The best ones for climbers are in Buckhorn Wash and at the pullout off the Mexican Mountain Road below the Dylan Wall. Practice clean camping by using existing sites, dispersing any fire rings, not tearing down trees for firewood, using only deadwood from flash floods for firewood, and properly disposing of human waste.

Climbing season: Spring and fall are the best seasons. Sunny days can be very hot on the south-facing Dylan Wall. Carry lots of water and find shade during midday. Winter days can be excellent; roads, however, may be impassable due to snowmelt. Summers are prohibitively hot.

Restrictions and access issues: None currently. The cliffs are on BLM public lands. The ORVs and motorcycles do far more environmental damage in the area than the climbing impact in all of Utah. Practice clean camping ethics by using existing sites and fire rings, by collecting only deadfall for firewood along the river, and by packing out all your trash. Smart desert campers/climbers forego the fire and only use a stove for cooking to preserve the delicate environment.

Guidebooks: *Moab Rock: Wall Street to the San Rafael Swell* by Eric Bjørnstad, Chockstone Press, 1997, offers photos and descriptions of many routes and crags in the Swell. *Classic Desert Climbs* by Fred Knapp, Sharp End Publishing, 1996, has a topo to the Dylan Wall.

Nearby mountain shops, guide services, and gyms: None nearby. Closest shops are in Moab and the Salt Lake area.

Services: None in the immediate area. Closest services are about 50 miles away in Green River, Price, or Castle Dale. Come prepared by bringing adequate food, water, and a full tank of gasoline.

Emergency services: Call 911. Castleview Hospital, 300 N. Hospital Drive, Price, (801) 637-4800. Emergency numbers are: Castle Dale/Emery County Sheriff (801) 381-2404. Carbon County Sheriff (801) 637-1622.

Nearby climbing areas: Bottleneck Peak, Buckhorn Wash crags, numerous unexplored canyons, cliffs, and towers in the Swell, Spring Canyon, Moab area crags.

Nearby attractions: San Rafael Swell canyons, San Rafael Reef, Eagle Canyon, Upper and Lower Black Boxes, Black Dragon Wash, The Wedge Overlook, Buckhorn Wash, Cleveland Lloyd Dinosaur Quarry, Swasey's Cabin, Temple Mountain, Goblin Valley State Park, Hondoo Arch, hiking, backpacking, canyoneering, mountain biking.

Finding the crags: The easiest approach to the Dylan Wall and San Rafael River area is via Interstate 70. From the west or east, leave I-70 at Exit 129 on top of the Swell. This exit is 29 miles west of Green River. Follow the Cottonwood Wash Road for 3 miles alongside the Interstate 70 before turning north and dropping down the wash. Follow this road for 20 miles from I-70 to the heart of the Swell at the San Rafael River and the BLM campground.

To reach the Dylan Wall: Cross the river on a new bridge next to an historic

SAN RAFAEL SWELL

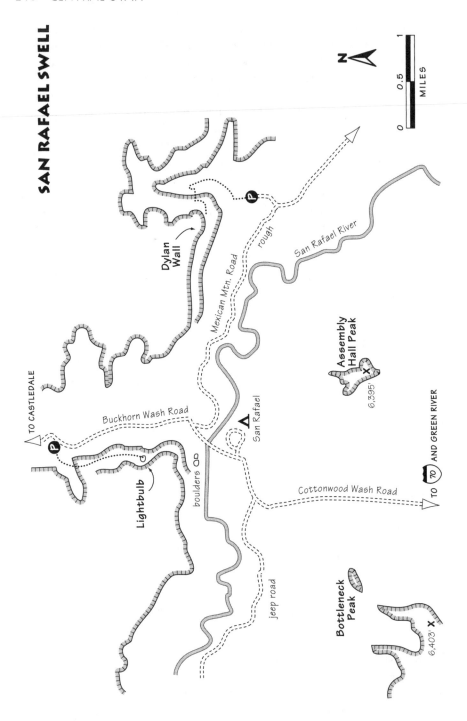

N

0   0.5   1

MILES

TO CASTLEDALE

Buckhorn Wash Road

Lightbulb

boulders

Dylan Wall

Mexican Mtn. Road

rough

San Rafael River

San Rafael

jeep road

Cottonwood Wash Road

TO 70 AND GREEN RIVER

Assembly Hall Peak

6,395' X

Bottleneck Peak

6,403' X

swinging bridge and drive a couple of hundred yards to a road junction at the head of Buckhorn Wash. Turn east on the Mexican Mountain Road and follow this track along the river's north bank for 1.8 miles to the top of a steep hill. Turn left or north here on a dirt track and drive 0.1 mile to a parking area and turnaround. This is also a good campsite. The Dylan Wall is the obvious varnished buttress immediately northwest.

The cliff approach is hard to describe and hard to follow. Use your best judgment to find the way. After parking, hike north up the obvious gravel wash or up a lefthand wash that parallels the main one for about a half of a mile. Two ways scale the broken cliff bands to your left. The most direct follows a faint trail up through talus and boulders to easy scrambling. Keep left up high, go behind a large block, and climb 15 feet of 5.5 to a bench, or continue up the main wash another quarter of a mile to a more broken cliff band. Scramble through boulders to the bench. Either way, walk along the bench to several large boulders split by cracks. A cairned trail winds up the final talus slope to the base of the wall. A trail follows the cliff base for route access. Allow about 45 minutes for the approach.

To reach The Lightbulb, continue up Buckhorn Wash Road from the bridge for 0.8 mile. Look up left or west and spot the obvious thin tower below the rim. Continue up the road to an obvious parking area on the left. Hike up slopes and contour right into a deep side-canyon. Look for a break in the cliff band marked with a cairn and scramble onto a bench. Follow the bench south a half-mile to the final talus slopes below the tower. Allow up to 45 minutes for the hike.

Both areas can also be reached from Utah 10 and Castle Dale to the northwest. Turn east 1.6 miles north of downtown Castle Dale and follow a dirt road for 12.1 miles to Buckhorn Well. Continue 5.6 miles to a road junction and turn south or right onto the Buckhorn Wash Road and drive about 10 miles down the spectacular canyon to the river.

DYLAN WALL

This south-facing, Wingate sandstone cliff perches high above the San Rafael River a couple of miles east of the BLM campground and the swinging bridge. Routes are listed right to left (east to west) from the top of the approach trail.

1. **Bob Can't Climb** (5.10b) Locate this crack system about 75' left of a large roof split by an off-width crack. Jam fingers to hands to off-width to chimney crack up shallow right-facing corner to 2-bolt anchor; 155' long. **Rack:** Friends with extra #1s, TCUs, and Camalots to #4 or #5.

2. **Watching the River Flow** (5.11c) 40' left of Route 1. Hard face climbing up thin right-facing corner leads 20' to horizontal break. Continue up thin crack with finger jams and stems to 2-bolt anchor right of obvious triangular block; 110'. **Rack:** Friends #2 to #3.5, TCUs, and wires.

Bob D'Antonio edges up a bolted face route at The Dylan Wall in the heart of the San Rafael Swell. PHOTO BY STEWART M. GREEN

SAN RAFAEL SWELL
DYLAN WALL

155'

125'

110'

4

3
hidden in corner

2

1

SAN RAFAEL SWELL
DYLAN WALL

135'

165'

155'

130'

115'

5

4

3

base trail

9

8

7

6

3. **Isis** (5.12b/c) A superb, aesthetic line up a prominent left-facing dihedral right of a black wall. About 100' left of #2. Lieback and jam up large dihedral (5.10) to overhanging crack that angles out left under roof. Thin underclings and strenuous liebacks with foot smears head out past bolt to finish at 2-bolt anchor on left face; 130'. **Rack:** Bring a selection of Friends with extra #1 to #2 and lots of TCUs.

4. **Simple Twist of Fate** (5.11b) A quality route on the black wall 30' left of *Isis*. Jam thin, flared crack up black and tan face with occasional rest pod jams past lone bolt to 3-cold shut anchor; 125'. **Rack:** A selection of mostly small Friends and TCUs including 3 #0s.

5. **Obviously Five Believers** (5.10c) Begin around the arête 30' left of Route 4 and just right of large cliff-base boulder. Jam obvious left-facing corner past several ledges and broken sections to 2-bolt rappel anchor; 135'. **Rack:** Friends and TCUs.

6. **One More Cup of Coffee** (5.10d) The first route established on the cliff. Classic jamming. Locate a large left-facing dihedral 50' left of Route 5 and just right of jumble of boulders. Jam and stem up corner to some liebacking that leads to final face move and 3-bolt/cold shut anchor on small ledge out left; 165'. **Rack:** A large selection of gear—TCUs, large stoppers, and Friends including extra #1 and #1.5 sizes.

7. **Unknown** (5.11) Begin just left of some boulders. This excellent, sustained line follows a row of 10 bolts up a seam to a 2-cold-shut anchor; 115'. **Rack:** Quickdraws and Friends.

8. **Positively 4th Street** (5.11a) A long pitch up a crack system with finger to hand jamming and face climbing. 3 bolts at thin moves to 2-cold-shut anchor; 155'. **Rack:** Lots of Friends with many #1 to #2s, TCUs, and stoppers.

9. **Like a Rolling Stone** (5.11b) Just left of Route 8 and 4 cracks left of Route 6's dihedral. Jam obvious crack system through pod to strenuous flared finger crack over bulge to bolt. Continue up flared finger crack to a 2-bolt rap anchor; 165'. **Rack:** Many Friends with extra #1, #2.5, and #4, and medium stoppers.

10. **Blood on the Tracks** (5.12a) A gorgeous tips route up a stunning red corner about 50' left of Route 9 and around an arête. Lieback and stem up thin crack in open corner to 2-bolt anchor; 80'. **Rack:** Lots of TCUs including 3 #0 and 7 #1, and Friends from #1 to #2.5.

11. **Blowin' in the Wind** (5.10b) The huge left-facing dihedral 20' left of Route 10. Begin on boulder at dihedral base. Jam, stem, and lieback up dihedral; where main crack pinches near top, use double cracks on the right wall. Finish at a 2-bolt anchor on left; 130'. **Rack:** Double set of Friends.

12. **Idiot Wind** (5.11c) An excellent route up the black face left of Route 11. Jam splitter finger crack with rest pods to 3-cold shut anchor; 80'. **Rack:** Lots of TCUs and Friends to #3.

13. **Million Dollar Bash** (5.10c) About 40' left and around an arête from Route 12. Fun climbing up the obvious open book. Jam and stem the obvious black dihedral (hands, small hands, and fingers) to a 3-cold shut anchor; 150'. **Rack:** A couple of sets of Friends, TCUs, and medium to large stoppers.

14. **The Mighty Quinn** (5.12a) 2 pitches. Begin 10' left of Route 13. **Pitch 1:** Thrutch up off-width (5.9) on right side of a 50' block to belay. **Pitch 2:** The business pitch. Jam thin crack (.12a) with rest pods up thin left-facing corner to 2-bolt rap anchor; 140'. **Rack:** Lots of thin stuff—TCUs, Aliens, Friends, and wires.

15. **Along the Watchtower** (5.11) 2 pitches. This spectacular route ascends the left side of The Watchtower, a slender, detached, pointed pillar 45' left of Route 14. **Pitch 1:** The best lead. Wild, sustained climbing up left-facing dihedral to 2-bolt rap anchor; use all techniques—hands, small hands, offwidth, and liebacking; 155'. **Pitch 2:** Up overhanging corner to crux 6-inch crack. Easier climbing and chimneying leads to 3-bolt anchor below summit; 100'. **Rack:** A couple of sets of Friends, TCUs, and a couple of big pieces.

16. **Don't Think Twice It's All Right** (5.11b) Crack/seam up the black and tan face 20' left of *Watchtower*. Edge past bolt to start then up flared finger

crack to 5 more bolts up a seam to a 1-bolt, 2-cold shut anchor; 80'. **Rack:** Small to medium Friends.

17. **Knockin' On Heaven's Door** (5.10b) Around the corner and 50' from Route 16. Start by some boulders. Climb onto pedestal, clip a bolt and face climb to a left-facing flake/crack. Jamming and liebacking up the flake leads to a 2-bolt anchor; 75'. **Rack:** Medium and large Friends.

18. **Planet Waves** (5.11b) No topo. Quality route. The obvious corner just left of *Knockin'*. Climb thin cracks for 20' to bolt, then jam and lieback up crack in beautiful, red, left-facing corner above to 3-cold-shut anchor; 100'. **Rack:** TCUs, small to medium Friends, and stoppers.

19. **Changing of the Guard** (5.8+) No topo. Hike left about 400' to an immense fallen block. This unusual Wingate face route ascends a blunt arête on west side of block. Edge up past 7 bolts to a 2-bolt anchor on a bouldery ledge; 110'.

20. **Buckhorn Skyline Rag** (5.11c) No topo. A cool short route just left of Route 19. Climb thin crack to weird, off-balance crux to perfect lieback up right-facing corner. Clip 2-bolt anchor on a ledge up left; 40'. **Rack:** Friends to #2.5, TCUs, and stoppers.

21. **Every Grain of Sand** (5.11d) No topo. About 80' left of Route 20. Jam the crack in a left-angling, tight, left-facing corner (flared fingers and thin hands) to a 2-bolt anchor; 110'. **Rack:** Lots of small Friends.

THE LIGHTBULB

22. **The Lightbulb** (II 5.10 C1) This awesome, 185-foot lightbulb-shaped tower sits below the rimrock near the south entrance of Buckhorn Wash. It was first ascended solo by James Garrett in 1990. The route was first done in 2 pitches, but is better done in 3 to alleviate rope drag. Drive up the road from the river bridge about 0.8 mile and spot the tower to the west high above the lower cliff band. Continue up the road a short distance to an obvious parking area on the left. Hike onto a rocky ridge and contour right into a deep side-canyon; continue up and left to an unobvious break in the lower cliff band that leads to a flat bench. Walk south on the bench and scramble up bouldery talus slopes below the tower to its base. Approach time is 30 to 45 minutes. Begin the route on the right side of the east face. **Pitch 1:** Climb loose corner for 20' to ledge. Jam beautiful thin hands to hands crack (crux 5.10) up northeast side for 30'. Make awkward moves left along wide crack and onto rotten ledge on east face. Climb up to bolt above and downclimb back to ledge and set belay. This stance could use some belay bolts to back funky gear! 60'. **Pitch 2:** Climb rotten off-width past fixed pin to good, steep hand crack (5.10-). Belay on

SAN RAFAEL SWELL
THE LIGHTBULB

XXX
200'

10-bolt ladder upface

.10

X

.10

22

good ledge on south side of summit block from 2 bolts; 75'. **Pitch 3:** Aid up 10-bolt ladder (C1) on steep south face of bulb to 3-bolt anchor on narrow, exposed summit; 50'. **Rack:** A couple of sets of Friends including extra #3 to #4. A #4 Camalot is useful. Free carabiners and a couple of sets of aiders. Two 200-foot ropes for the rappel. **Descent:** Make a single 2-rope rappel with two 200-foot ropes (185' to the ground) down south-east side of the spire. Make sure to get the knot over the edge—it's hard pulling the ropes.

CAPITOL REEF NATIONAL PARK

OVERVIEW

Capitol Reef National Park, Utah's least-visited national park, protects the Waterpocket Fold, a spectacular fold that stretches over 100 miles across south-central Utah. The Fold, one of the state's major geologic features, is an immense wave of sandstone layers draped against higher plateaus to the west. The Fold, a formidable barrier cleanly split by only 5 canyons, reminded early travelers of an ocean reef. They gave the name Capitol Reef to the northern section of the Fold around today's visitor center area after noting one looming dome traced an outline like the U.S. Capitol.

Capitol Reef, more than any other area of Utah, is dominated by rock. Each rock layer here tells a distinct story about different environments, climates, and ecosystems that spread across ancient lands. Here are the stone remnants of winding Permian-age rivers, the mud flats and swamps of the Triassic, the vast sandy deserts of the Jurassic, and the landlocked seas of the Cretaceous Period. Most of these rock formations in the park date from the Mesozoic Era, the Age of Dinosaurs, from 230 to 65 million years ago. The dominant formations are the Jurassic-age Wingate and Navajo sandstones, which form steep cliffs and towering rounded domes. The Wingate, a widespread formation on the Plateau, also offers most of the park's rock climbing adventures.

Almost all of Capitol Reef's rock routes are found along the park's Scenic Drive, a paved, 8-mile road that runs south from the visitor center and Utah 24 on the west side of the Reef. Not a lot of climbing has been done at Capitol Reef. The vast park does, however, offer numerous opportunities for new routes. Although much of the rock here is soft, sugary, and loose, the rock quality varies tremendously throughout the park. The Wingate formation, with its fractured surface of cracks and flakes, is the most popular and firmest of the park's sandstone for climbers. The park also offers some moderate slab climbing. Bob Van Belle, a park ranger and climber, calls it "really sandy, poorly consolidated stone. Sort of a cross between a schoolyard sandbox and the Glacier Point Apron. Very sporty. Ice tools or rock shoes? It's a toss-up."

Capitol Reef is the kind of place where climbing is almost an afterthought. It's a great place to do a few routes and then put the gear away and go exploring. The scenery here is simply stunning and the hiking and canyoneering opportunites are superb. Many of the higher domes like Ferns Nipple are scaled via semi-technical ascents that involve complex route-finding and 4th and low 5th class climbing and scrambling; they also offer exciting downclimbing descents. Other adventures include exploring the great slot canyons sliced through the Reef. Some of the better known slots include Sulphur Creek Narrows west of the visitor center, Burro and Sheets Washes off the Notom Road, and the remote Muley Twist Canyon and Halls Creek Narrows in the far southern end of the park. Ask at the visitor center for information on these and other park activities.

Climbing history: The first recorded technical rock climbs in Capitol Reef went up along the beautiful Wingate cliff north of Utah 24 just east of the visitor center. All of these routes are now closed to climbing due to their proximity to prehistoric rock art and historic sites and orchards. The Golden Throne, a looming landmark above Capitol Gorge, saw its first ascent via a 3-pitch, 5.8 route up the southwest corner of the summit block by George and Jean Hurley, and Dave Rearick in 1974. In the mid-1980s Mark Bennett and several partners including Seth Shaw and Bill Simmons made ascents around Chimney Rock as well as of the classic *Capitol Roof.* Many of the 3-star splitter cracks in Grand Wash and on the Basketball Wall were first jammed by the team of Marco Cornacchione and Bret Ruckman in 1993. The Fracture Zone above Slickrock Divide saw its first routes established in the spring of 1997 by Bob D'Antonio, Martha Morris, and Stewart Green.

Capitol Reef National Park is a clean climbing area. Visiting climbers should try to minimize their impact as much as possible. This means leaving only webbing on retreat or rappel slings that match the color of the surrounding rock. Follow existing climber trails whenever possible. The use of white chalk is prohibited. Only use a colored chalk that matches the rock. Power drills are also prohibited and new bolts may only be used to replace existing unsafe bolts and anchors. Ropes may not be fixed for more than 24 hours and they should be out of reach from the ground and accessible only by technical climbing. Permits are not needed for climbing. Backcountry camping, however, requires a free permit available at the visitor center.

Several areas in Capitol Reef are closed to rock climbing. Please abide by these few restrictions. The cliff section north of Utah 24 between the Fruita Schoolhouse (Mile 80.6) and the east end of the Krueger Orchard (Mile 81.4) is closed because of many rock art panels and historic sites. Additionally, no climbing is allowed above or within 100 feet of any rock art panel or prehistoric structure in the park. Other closed areas are Hickman Natural Bridge, all other natural bridges and arches in the park, Chimney Rock, and the Temple of the Sun and Temple of the Moon in Cathedral Valley.

Rockfall is the greatest objective danger here, as it is everywhere on the Colorado Plateau. Loose boulders and flakes abound, particularly at areas that have not seen a lot of traffic. Pull down and not out on flakes whenever possible. A helmet is a good idea on many routes, even for the belayer. Sew up the routes with pro. Friends can and do pull out of the soft parallel-sided cracks. Summer temperatures are hot, usually between 90 and 100 degrees. Seek out shaded routes and carry lots of water. A gallon per person per day is a good rule of thumb, but you'll probably need more! Water is available at the visitor center and the campground. Wear a hat to keep your head cool. Afternoon thunderstorms accompanied by lightning occur regularly on July and August days. Keep off high places. The sandstone is also weakened when it is wet after heavy rain or snow. Avoid climbing then so the fragile rock is not damaged.

Rack: A standard free climbing rack at Capitol Reef includes two sets of Friends, sets of TCUs and stoppers, some extra runners, and two 165-foot ropes. It's a good idea to have some extra earth-tone webbing and rap rings to replace worn gear at rap stations.

Trip Planning Information

General description: Crack routes on Wingate sandstone cliffs along the Scenic Drive in Capitol Reef National Park.

Location: Central Utah. Southwest of Interstate 70.

Camping: The best camping area that is close to climbing and hiking is at the national park's Fruita Campground a mile south of the visitor center and Utah Highway 24. The 3-loop, fee campground has 71 sites available on a first-come, first-served basis. The area is popular with RVs, trailers, and tents. Plan on arriving in the morning to obtain a site. All of the sites are shaded and grassy with tables and fire grills, water and restrooms. Primitive campsites and forest campgrounds are west of the park on Boulder Mountain.

Climbing season: Year-round. The park is relatively high—5,000 feet—compared to other desert climbing sites. Spring and autumn are the best seasons. Winters can be cold and snowy. Summers are hot, but not unbearable. Daily highs are usually in the 90s and shaded routes can be found. Severe thunderstorms occur on July and August afternoons. Watch for lightning.

Restrictions and access issues: Capitol Reef is a clean climbing area. Use of white chalk is prohibited. Use an earth-colored chalk. Power drills are prohibited. Bolts may be placed only when replacing existing unsafe bolts. Leave only webbing on rappel anchors that matches the surrounding rock color. Fixed ropes may not be left for more than 24 hours and the end of the rope should be out of reach from the ground to prevent tourists from using them. The cliff north of Utah Highway 24 between the Fruita Schoolhouse (mile 80.6) and the east end of the Krueger Orchard (mile 81.4) is closed to climbing because of many rock art panels. Other closed areas are Hickman Natural Bridge, other arches and bridges, Chimney Rock, and the Temple of the Moon

CAPITOL REEF
NATIONAL PARK

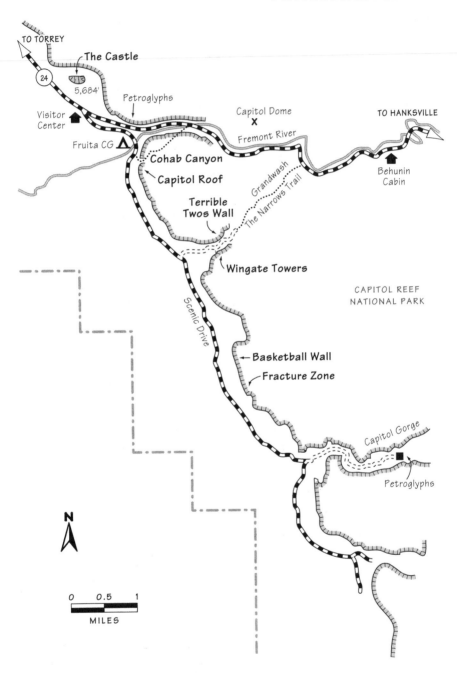

TO TORREY

The Castle

24

5,684'

Petroglyphs

Capitol Dome
X

TO HANKSVILLE

Visitor
Center

Fremont River

Fruita CG

Cohab Canyon

Capitol Roof

Grandwash
The Narrows Trail

Behunin
Cabin

Terrible
Twos Wall

Wingate Towers

CAPITOL REEF
NATIONAL PARK

Scenic Drive

Basketball Wall

Fracture Zone

Capitol Gorge

Petroglyphs

N

0   0.5   1

MILES

and Temple of the Sun in Cathedral Valley. Avoid climbing on the sandstone when it's wet or damp to avoid damaging the fragile surface.

Guidebooks: *Desert Rock: Rock Climbs in the National Parks* by Eric Bjørnstad, Chockstone Press, 1996, offers photos and descriptions of routes and crags in the park. Ask in the visitor center for any new route info.

Nearby mountain shops, guide services, and gyms: None nearby. Closest shops would be in Moab and the Salt Lake area.

Services: The closest services are in Torrey, west of the park on Utah 24. Gas, lodging, and groceries are available. Otherwise go about 50 miles east to Hanksville. Best to come self-contained and equipped.

Emergency services: Call 911 or notify a park ranger. Report all accidents and injuries at the visitor center.

Nearby climbing areas: San Rafael Swell cliffs and towers, The Horn in the Henry Mountains.

Nearby attractions: Cathedral Valley, Chimney Rock, Sulpher Creek Narrows, Grand Wash, Capitol Gorge, Hickman Bridge, Fruita historic sites, Waterpocket Fold, Burr Trail, Halls Creek Narrows, San Rafael Swell areas, San Rafael Reef, Goblin Valley State Park, Henry Mountains, Bull Creek Pass Back Country Byway, hiking, backpacking, canyoneering, mountain biking, fruit orchards.

Finding the crags: All of the routes are along the 8-mile-long Scenic Drive south of the visitor center and Utah 24. *Capitol Roof* is above the campground at 1.2 miles from the visitor center. The marked Grand Wash turnoff is at 3.4 miles. The Basketball Wall is at 5.1 miles. Slickrock Divide and the Fracture Zone are at 5.9 miles. Capitol Gorge is at the end of the paved road at 8 miles.

COHAB CANYON

1. **Capitol Roof** (5.11) No topo. A superb route. Access by hiking up the Cohab Canyon Trail which begins opposite the first campground loop a mile south of the visitor center on the Scenic Drive. Hike up the trail about a half-mile to the entrance to Cohab Canyon. The route ascends an obvious splitter over a roof just right of the canyon entrance. Jam the hands and thin hands crack for 80' to a bolted rappel station. **Rack:** Friends from #1 to #3 including extra #2.5.

GRAND WASH

Grand Wash is a deep, narrow canyon that slices through the upturned layers of Capitol Reef. It's a popular and excellent hike. Some easily accessible routes ascend the Wingate cliffs, including the Terrible Twos Wall and the Wingate Tower, above the road to the wash parking area. Drive south for 3.4

miles from the visitor center on the paved Scenic Drive to the Grand Wash turn. The dirt road twists for 1.2 miles to the parking area at road's end.

TERRIBLE TWOS WALL

This south-facing wall sits above the north side of the road 0.7 mile from the Scenic Drive. Find a wide place to park by the wash and scramble up talus slopes to the cliff base. Routes are left to right.

2. **Unknown** (5.13) No topo. On the left side of the wall. An awesome splitter finger crack up a streaked wall to a 2-bolt anchor; 140'.

3. **Soapstone Dihedral** (5.11c) An obvious right-facing dihedral. Jam and stem the corner to a 1-bolt anchor; 40'.

4. **Terrible Twos** (5.11d) An excellent thin hands and finger crack to a 2-bolt anchor; 80'. **Rack:** Small to medium Friends including 3 #2.5, and some TCUs.

5. **Thinner** (5.12a) About 15' right of Route 4. Jam strenuous splitter finger crack to 2-bolt anchor; 60'. **Rack:** Small Friends and TCUs.

6. **Left Practice Crack** (5.10) 50' right of Route 5. Jam splitter hand crack to 2-bolt belay atop a pillar; 40'. **Rack:** Medium-sized Friends.

7. **Right Practice Crack** (5.11c) Just right of Route 6. A finger/hand/off-width crack to the 2-bolt belay atop pillar; 40'. **Rack:** TCUs and Friends.

CAPITOL REEF
WINGATE TOWER
ROUTES 8-10

WINGATE TOWER

This short flake/pillar sits on the south side of the road opposite the Terrible Twos Wall. Park at 0.7 mile and scramble up talus to the cliff base. Three short practice routes ascend the pillar. *Sandy Dihedral* is on the left at 1.2 miles.

8. **Pussy Bolt** (5.8) Layback left side of pillar past lone bolt to 2-bolt anchor on ledge; 60'. Rap from anchors to base. **Rack:** Friends and TCUs.

CAPITOL REEF
BASKETBALL WALL

9. **Wingate Arête** (5.12a) A toprope route up obvious blunt arête to 2-bolt anchor; 60'.

10. **Sharon's Crack** (5.10a) Jam left-angling finger and thin hand crack to bolted belay ledge; 60'. **Rack:** TCUs, Friends, and stoppers.

Drive 1.2 miles down the Grand Wash Road and locate an obvious left-angling corner system on left or north side of canyon.

11. **Sandy Dihedral** (5.10b) No topo. Layback and jam the tight corner to 2-bolt belay; 80'. **Rack:** TCUs, stoppers, and small Friends.

BASKETBALL WALL

The Basketball Wall is a west-facing Wingate cliff on the high escarpment east of the Scenic Drive. All these routes were put up in 1993 by Bret Ruckman and Marco Cornacchione. Drive south from the visitor center on the Scenic Drive for 5.1 miles to a parking spot on the left side of the road. Locate the crag on the left side of the high cliff to the east. Hike east up washes, through cliff bands, and up talus slopes to the base of the wall. The approach is not easy to find or follow. Look for existing climber trails. Allow about a half-hour to approach the cliff. Routes listed left to right.

12. **Bench Warmer** (5.10a) Locate a splitter hand crack right of a chimney and corner. Jam excellent crack to 2-bolt rap anchor. **Rack:** Friends.

13. **White Boys Can't Jam** (5.10a) Jam hand crack 20' right of Route 12 to 2-bolt rap anchor. **Rack:** Friends.

14. **Foul Line** (5.11c) 20' right of Route 13. Another splitter crack to 2-bolt

rap anchor. **Rack:** Medium to large Friends.

15. **Phi Slamma Jamma (5.11d)** Walk right for a few hundred feet past a bunch of splitters to splitter finger to hand crack with 2-bolt anchor. **Rack:** Friends.

THE FRACTURE ZONE

This excellent 60-foot-high, west-facing cliff forms a long wall below the towering Wingate escarpment directly east of Slickrock Divide. The top of the cliff is a wide, broken terrace accessed by scrambling up ledges on the south. There are numerous splitter cracks on this little crag, most still awaiting first ascents. The 3 described routes were put up in 1997 by Bob D'Antonio, Martha Morris, and Stewart Green.

Reach the area by driving 5.9 miles south on the Scenic Drive from the Visitor Center to Slickrock Divide. Park in the lot on the west side of the road. There is really only one good way to reach the cliff from the road. Follow the divide east up shale ridges to a break in the lower cliff band. Scramble up ledges and then up left over loose talus and boulders to the base of the cliff. Approach time is about half an hour by car to cliff.

The routes offer good jamming, but are a little sandy and loose in places, particularly the top 5 feet of the cliff. There are no anchors as new bolts are not permitted in the park, so either top out and belay from gear and trees or tie off a rope and drop it over the cliff top for a lowering anchor. Either way, be careful not to dislodge any loose rock onto your partners below. The cliff is called The Fracture Zone for good reason—there are lots of loose blocks on routes and along the cliff base that have fallen from this actively forming crag! Routes are listed right to left.

16. **Stick Fracture** (5.12a/b) On the right side of the cliff locate a splitter finger crack up a salmon-colored wall right of a large right-facing dihedral. Scramble onto ledge and belay. Jam and face climb thin double cracks to awkward stance (5.11-) then up wide finger crack to pod to more wide fingers (5.12a) to hand jam. Exit into weird chimney and belay from trees atop cliff. Soft rock at top; 45'. **Rack:** Stoppers, Aliens, TCUs, and small Friends.

17. **Fractured Fairy Tale** (5.12b/c) An awesome corner route. An obvious, varnished, open corner left of Route 16. Scramble onto ledge and belay. Lieback, stem, and finger jam up thin crack in corner. Soft rock at top; 50'. **Rack:** Aliens (2 blues at crux), TCUs, stoppers, #1, #1.5, #2 Friends.

18. **Pink Pillar** (5.10d) Walk left of Route 17 to an obvious pink pillar in the cliff's mid-section. This fine route jams the right side of the pillar via a hand crack to a thin hand crux to fists. Very loose and blocky up top. Drop an anchor rope down to the top of fist section or use extreme caution finishing up crack; 55'. **Rack:** Friends #2-#4 and #4 Camalot.

Bob D'Antonio leads the Pink Pillar *at The Fracture Zone, Capitol Reef National Park.* PHOTO BY STEWART M. GREEN

Martha Morris seconds The Price is Right, *an excellent lieback crack in Spring Canyon.*
PHOTO BY STEWART M. GREEN

Spring Canyon Crag

Overview

Spring Canyon Crag, also called Indian Rock, lies on a sandstone cliff band in scenic Spring Canyon west of the old railroad town of Helper. Numerous cliffs interrupted by talus slopes line the canyon's steep sides. The developed climbing area, however, sits just above the road at its junction with Boulder Canyon. A selection of bolted sport routes and a few crack climbs ranging from 5.7 to 5.12 are located on the 50-foot-high cliff. This is a good cliff for a quick stop when traveling between Salt Lake City and the canyon country. Most climbers will do all the routes they want in a 3 to 4 hour stopover. Some good boulder problems are located on the numerous large blocks below the cliff and on the north side of the canyon.

The sandstone, part of the Mesa Verde Formation, is a compact layer that erodes into slabs and vertical faces broken by cracks and corners. Expect smears, edges, occasional pockets, and jams. The thick formation, divided into Castle Gate and Starpoint sandstones, is seamed with layers of shale and coal that form the talus slopes between the harder sandstone strata. A large coal mine once operated here, the relics of which are in an old railroad bed and bridge beneath the wall and a still-standing flagpole perched atop a craggy prow. A rough road shelves up above the north cliff to the pole, passing an old bed of blooming yellow roses.

Climbing history: The cliff has long been used by central Utah climbers for climbing programs run through the Carbon County Parks and Recreation Department. In the early 1990s local climber Cory Pincock bolted and ascended almost all the sport routes here. But unrelated vandalism to historic mining structures in the area almost closed the canyon to climbing and other recreational uses in 1993. In 1995 the cliff and surrounding property were sold to Colorado-based Cyprus-Plateau Mining Company, who promptly closed the area because of the vandalism and the liability issues. An adjoining landowner "policed" the area with a gun, chasing away all visitors. The mining company, however, negotiated a change of ownership of the land, deeding it to Carbon County to avoid liability and to keep it open for rock climbing.

Trip Planning Information

General description: A small selection of bolted routes and cracks on a sandstone cliff in Spring Canyon.

Location: Central Utah. Four miles west of Helper.

Camping: None in the canyon. Price Canyon Recreation Area, a BLM campground, is off U.S. Highway 6 north of Helper.

Climbing season: Best seasons are spring and fall. Winter days are possible when it's warm, but it can be cold and snowy. Summer is often hot, but the north side of the cliff band gets lots of shade.

Restrictions and access issues: Climbers should keep a low profile and minimize their impact. Pick up after yourself and others. Park well off the road.

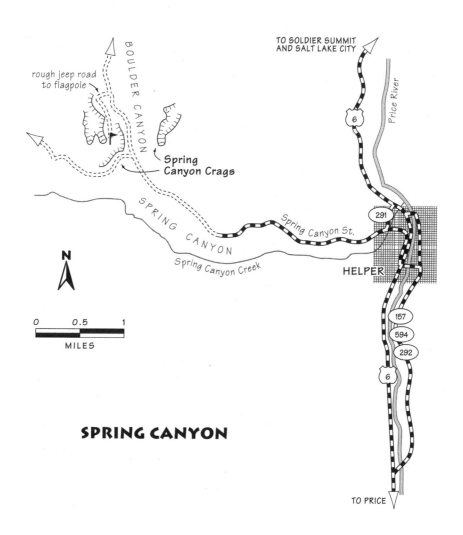

SPRING CANYON

Guidebooks: *Spring Canyon Crag: A Guide to Climbing in Carbon County* by Cory Pincock and Aimee Faucheux. A small, locally available guide to the cliff.

Nearby mountain shops, guide services, and gyms: None locally. Nearest stores include Black Diamond, IME, and REI in Salt Lake City. Mountainworks (Provo), and Hansen Mountaineering (Orem). Gyms are Wasatch Front Climbing Gym and Rockreation in Salt Lake, and Rock Garden in Provo. Guides include Wasatch Touring, Exum Mountain Guides, and Mastodon Mountaineering (Ben Folsom).

Services: All services are in Helper and Price. Price is the larger town and has more complete services including a large selection of restaurants and motels.

Emergency services: Call 911 for all emergencies. Castleview Hospital, 300 North Hospital Drive, Price, (801) 637-4800. Carbon County Sheriff, (801) 637-1622 or 637-0893 (weekends and holidays). Helper Police Dispatch, (801) 637-0890.

Nearby climbing areas: Indian Canyon offers some great bouldering. Access by driving north from Helper and turning east on U.S. Highway 191 into the canyon. Some climbing and bouldering is also located on the sandstone cliffs along U.S. Highway 6 north of Helper. Other nearby areas are San Rafael Swell and Joe's Valley.

Nearby attractions: College of Eastern Utah Prehistoric Museum (Price), Helper Mining and Railroad Museum, Cleveland-Lloyd Dinosaur Quarry, Museum of the San Rafael (Castle Dale), Nine Mile Canyon Back Country Byway, Manti-La Sal National Forest.

Finding the crag: The crag is west of Helper. From Interstate 15, take the U.S. Highway 6 exit in Spanish Fork and drive over Soldier Summit to Helper. From Price, drive north on U.S. Highway 6 to Helper. Turn onto Carbon County Road 291 (jogs through the town on a couple of streets) and follow it for 4 miles from U.S. Highway 6 to the crag. The crag sits where the canyon splits into 2 obvious forks. Park alongside the road. Approaches are 30 seconds at the most. The cliff on the left fork is the Volkswagen Wall; the one on the right fork is the Boulder Canyon Wall.

VOLKSWAGEN WALL

This is the cliff band on the left or main canyon fork. An old mining road skirts the base of the talus below the cliff above the main road. Routes are listed left to right. Routes 1 to 4 have no topos, but are easy to find.

1. **Midnight** (5.10c) No topo. This route lies on the left side of the wall left of an obvious deep chimney and under the power lines. Face climb past 5 bolts to 2-bolt anchor; 60'.

2. **Blister in the Sun** (5.9) No topo. About 300' right of Route 1 and left of a left-facing corner. Climb over series of broken ledge-overlaps to a horizontal break.

Continue straight up to chains. 4 bolts to 2-bolt chain anchor; 50'.

3. **Happy Days** (5.10) No topo A harder variation to Route 2. Veer right at the horizontal break and second bolt. 4 bolts to 2-bolt chain anchor (same as Route 2); 50'.

4. **The Secret** (5.11b) No topo Climb left edge of huge, left-facing flake. 4 bolts to 2-bolt chain anchor.

5. **The Lieback** (5.7) Good and fun. A cool lieback up large left-facing corner to 2-bolt chain anchor; 45'. **Rack:** Small to medium Friends.

6. **Over the Top** (5.9) A variation to Route 5. Lieback up to slab flake, thin liebacking leads back to upper crack.

7. **Project** (5.11+) This jams a prominent overhanging, left-angling, finger and thin hand crack (sometimes sandy) to a 2-bolt chain anchor; 50'. **Rack:** Small to medium Friends.

8. **Headliner** (5.10a) Face climb up tan rock left of black streak on wall below flagpole. 5 bolts to 2-bolt chain anchor; 45'.

9. **Scarecrow** (5.11a/b) The twin to Route 8. Face climb up steep pocketed slab right of the black streak, joining Route 8 at bolt 3. 5 bolts to 2-bolt chain anchor; 45'.

10. **No Mo' Money Project** (5.12?) Ran out of cash before all the bolts were in? Face climb the steep face creased with horizontal breaks below the flagpole. Look for large Friend placements in first 40' to 2-bolt upper slab. End at a 2-bolt chain anchor; 75'.

BOULDER CANYON WALL

This is the shady cliff band on the right or north side of the cliff band. Routes are listed left to right from the prow below the flagpole. There are no topos, but the routes are obvious.

11. **Unknown** (5.8) Scramble up to ledge left of big corner and belay. Move out left on ledge above roof and work up discontinuous cracks to 2-bolt chain anchor.

12. **Head With a Hole** (5.10a/b) Begin in trees right of ledge and below corner. Pull up around flake to bolt then run it out to another bolt. Continue over striped, inverted black tongue. 3 bolts to 2-bolt anchor.

13. **Backslider** (5.11b) On slab right of large, broken, open book. Thin edging up smooth, black-streaked slab to anchors just below top. 3 bolts to 2 cold-shut anchor; 45'.

14. **Unknown** (5.11) Begin right of huge roof and left of deep corner. Climb steep crack past bolt to block with bolt above it. Move up right into shallow right-facing corner to anchors on ledge. 3 bolts to 2-bolt anchor. **Rack:** Small gear and medium Friends.

15. **Bolting Sucks** (5.9) The slab right of Route 14. Climb a dark tongue of rock to a couple of potholes and bolt 1. Continue to horizontal break, pull a roof, and cruise to 1-bolt anchor; 45'. **Descent:** Walk off. Don't rappel, lower, or toprope off the single bolt. Better yet—add another one.

16. **The Price is Right** (5.11a) Quality. An excellent crack with a rating dependent on finger size. Easier for small fingers. Walk right of Route 15 past steep wall to obvious lieback crack in corner right of striped wall. Thin hand jams and fingertip liebacks lead to top. No anchor. Belay off trees. **Rack:** Small Friends, TCUs, and stoppers.

17. **Broken** (5.12a) On the far right side of the cliff. Climb black and tan streaked wall right of overhanging prow. 4 bolts to 2-bolt chain anchor; 35'.

Mia Axon on Kiss the Cobble, *Maple Canyon.* PHOTO BY STEWART M. GREEN

Maple Canyon

Overview

Maple Canyon slices into the eastern flank of the San Pitch Mountains, a long narrow mountain range bordered on the west by the broad Juab Valley and on the east by the fertile Sanpete Valley. The spectacular canyon, floored by a trickling creek and a dusty road, is an abrupt defile lined with soaring ramparts, fins, buttresses, minarets, and castles composed of a very coarse conglomerate rock. The area lies at the southern tip of Uinta National Forest.

The rock is a strange medium for a climbing surface. The concrete-hard matrix cements a bizarre assortment of pebbles, cobbles, and boulders into the high cliffs. At first glance the canyon walls appear to be a dry vertical streambed. But the rock is surprisingly solid and made for rock climbing with lots of positive edges, rounded potato-shaped holds, sinker in-cut scoops, and shallow dishes that formed where cobbles have fallen out. The climbing seems odd at first, but after learning to trust and pull on the embedded cobblestones, it's great fun. The routes, however, are all pretty much the same without a lot of distinctive characteristics or variety—just plain and simple cobble-pulling!

The canyon lies well off the beaten track and has kept a low profile since its first routes went up in the early 1990s. The cobbled walls allow for a diversity of climbing experiences that range from slabby affairs to overhanging jughauls and crimpfests. All the routes here are bolted, with lowering or rappel anchors. Most of the routes can be done with a single 165-foot rope, although several require a 200-foot rope. Most of the routes were put up on lead and consequently are well-protected with closely-spaced bolts. The quartz in the rock's matrix tends to quickly dull drill bits.

Four main areas in Maple Canyon offer rock climbing opportunities—the Left Hand Fork, the Campground Area, the Bridge Area, and Box Canyon. The Campground, Left Hand Fork, and Bridge areas lie on Uinta National Forest land, while Box Canyon is on private property. The Campground Area, with Black Magic Rock, Toilet Buttress, Schoolroom, Road Kill Wall, and Engagement Alcove, offers the greatest assortment of easier routes from 5.7 to 5.10 as well as some harder lines on the Petroglyph Wall. The Hot Zone, an area on a south-facing cliff west of the campground, has 5 routes including a 5.13a. The Bridge Area, centered around a bridge over the creek midway up

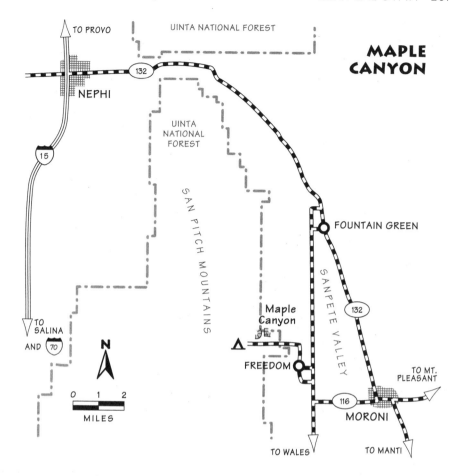

Maple Canyon, has many 5.11 routes along with a few easier offerings on shaded walls. Many other areas are under development, including the Zen Garden, Melon Wall, The Pipeline, The Rostrum (a smaller lookalike to its famous Yosemite counterpart), Low Standard Cave, along with some other top-secret areas. Check forthcoming editions of Jason Stevens' comprehensive guide for details.

Box Canyon is a spectacular slice carved by flash floods draining from the higher mountains. The canyon, its narrow entrance just north of the road, is a twisting 250-foot-deep slot with a 20- to 30-foot-wide floor covered by broken boulders and cobbles. The overhanging walls of the slot yield some amazingly steep and difficult rock climbs. Most of the routes lie within the first few hundred yards of the sinuous canyon, although a few have gone up farther up-canyon.

Climbers should be aware that Box Canyon is private property. All climbing and access here is contingent on cordial relations with the landowner. Climbing in the Box Canyon is a privilege, not your right. Climb, as always, at your own risk and take responsibility for your actions. Demonstrate to other local users, including hikers and sightseers, that rock climbers are a polite, friendly, and caring user-group. Pack out all your trash, cigarette butts, and tape, as well as that left by others. Box Canyon can be very busy, especially on weekends. During those times, consider heading up the main canyon and finding less crowded venues. Otherwise, don't hog routes. Let others have a turn on your draws. It is very important that all climbers use the restrooms at the campground all the time. Don't even consider relieving yourself anywhere around Box Canyon.

Maple also offers some excellent ice climbs. Jason Stevens authored the area's ice guide, with over 60 established routes. Stevens, Doug Heinrich, Seth Shaw, and a few others spent considerable time and money developing good rappel and belay stations and well-protected mixed routes. The season, however, can be short and fickle. Check with locals beforehand for current ice conditions.

Climbing history: Maple Canyon is a relative newcomer to the Utah climbing scene. Prior to the early 1990s, rock climbing did not exist as a sport here. Its subsequent discovery led to an explosion of routes. Local Jason Stevens, who authored the area's comprehensive guidebook, did many of the moderate lines in the canyon, while Salt Lake activists, including American Fork pioneers Bill Boyle and Jeff Pederson, bolted and ascended many of the harder routes in Box Canyon. Two more prolific Maple climbers are Bill Ohran and Tim Hannig, who did the first ascents of many of The Cobble Roof routes.

Trip Planning Information

General description: Superb sport climbing on cobblestone walls over 200' high in Maple Canyon and Box Canyon.

Location: Central Utah. Southeast of Nephi and Interstate 15.

Camping: A Uinta National Forest campground, open spring through fall, is located at the end of the road in Maple Canyon. The area has restrooms, but no water. (Water is available in nearby Fountain Green). Sites have tables and firepits. This is a fee area. Primitive camping areas are also available in the national forest.

Climbing season: Spring through fall. Watch in spring for cobbles loosened by winter's freeze and thaw. It's a good idea to wear a helmet while belaying! Summers can be hot, although Box Canyon offers cool shade. Fall days are excellent. Mornings might be too cold for comfort in the Box Canyon. Winter is usually cold and snowy. Ice climbs form on some of the walls.

Restrictions and access issues: No current restrictions are in effect, nor are there any current access issues. That situation could change with increased use by climbers. Remember that Box Canyon and the land east (down-canyon) of the Uinta National Forest sign is private property. Keep a low profile, be a responsible land user and guest, and respect the wishes of the landowner. Box Canyon is often crowded, particularly on weekends. Keep toproping of routes to a minimum during busy times to allow others to enjoy the routes. Moderate climbers would be better served by concentrating their efforts on the routes on national forest land around the campground. Always use the restroom at the campground—no exceptions. It's not that far to walk or drive. Areas of the canyon around the climbing areas are often filled with tissue flowers from inconsiderate users. Parking is a real problem on busy days, particularly at Box Canyon. Carpool when possible. If you're camping in the campground, walk the mile down to the canyon. Otherwise park in the many wide pulloffs well off the road.

Guidebooks: *Maple Canyon Rock Climbing* by Jason Stevens, 1997, offers a complete guide to Maple Canyon, and nearby New Canyon and Round Valley.

Nearby mountain shops, guide services, and gyms: Maple Leaf in Ephraim has a small assortment of gear and is a good source for area info and updates. Otherwise the nearest shops are Mountainworks in Provo and Hansen Mountaineering in Orem about 60 miles to the north.

Services: All services are located in Nephi, Mount Pleasant, Ephraim, and Manti. Limited services are located at Moroni and Fountain Green.

Emergency services: Call 911. The closest hospital is Sanpete Valley Hospital, 1100 S. Medical Dr., Mt. Pleasant, (800) 870-0346. Ephraim Medical Clinic, 525 N. Main, Ephraim, (801) 283-4076. Gunnison Valley Hospital, 64 East 100 North, Gunnison, (801) 528-7246.

Nearby climbing areas: New Canyon, east of Ephraim, offers bouldering and a few bolted routes. Round Valley, southeast of Manti, has bolted routes and topropes. Choke Cherry Dike, just northeast of Utah 132 on the Nebo Loop Road, has some easy bolted lines. Dry, Axhandle, and Coal canyons, west of Ephraim, have top-ropes and lots of undeveloped rock. Dry Canyon is lined with a band of limestone. Consult Jason Stevens's Maple Canyon guidebook for more info, topos, and directions. A new area is a limestone canyon on the north side of the San Pitch Mountains. The mountains and the surrounding canyons have lots of undeveloped rock. Check at the Ephraim shop for updates on new areas.

Nearby attractions: San Pitch Mountains, Mt. Nebo Wilderness Area, Nebo Loop Scenic Byway, Uinta National Forest, Yuba State Park, Manti LDS Temple, fishing, hiking, backpacking, and excellent mountain biking in the area around Maple Canyon.

Finding the crags: Maple Canyon is easily reached from Nephi and Interstate 15 south of Salt Lake City and Provo. It's just over 100 miles from Salt

Lake City and about 65 from Provo. Take Exit 225 at Nephi and drive east on Utah Highway 132 for 14 miles to the town of Fountain Green. At the south end of town turn right or west at the Maple Canyon sign. The road heads west and shortly turns south as Freedom Road. Follow the paved road for just over 7 miles past many turkey farms to an unmarked turn in the old townsite of Freedom. Turn right or west on a narrow road with an abandoned house on the southwest corner. A half-mile up is a marked right turn to Maple Canyon. Follow the rough dirt road another mile into lower Maple Canyon. The parking area for Box Canyon is 9 miles from Fountain Green. The final dirt road into the canyon may be impassable in winter and early spring. It's usually possible to drive to the campground until about Thanksgiving. The canyon is reached from Salina and Interstate 70 to the south by driving north on U.S. highway 89 and Utah 132 to Moroni. Turn west on the far side of town on a road that heads straight to the mountains. Make a right turn on Freedom Road after a few miles and follow it north to the abandoned house turn.

BOX CANYON

This is the most popular sport climbing area in Maple Canyon. Box Canyon, also called The Corridor, is an abrupt, narrow abyss that runs north from the road. The slot lies a mile from Maple Canyon's entrance. Park at pulloffs near the entrance to the obvious slot and walk north into the canyon. Parking may be limited with lots of cars along the road. Box Canyon can also be very busy. Be considerate of other climbers and hikers. Don't bring dogs into the canyon. There is no place for them to roam without bothering others. Also, there are no sanitary facilities for dogs here, let alone humans! Always use the toilets at the campground—no excuses! Walk or drive up canyon, it's not that far. Routes are listed beginning at the entrance to the canyon and right to left on the east wall before coming back to the entrance on the west wall.

ENTRANCE OR EFS WALL

The first 7 routes are on the right wall in the corridor at the canyon entrance. The first 3 routes have open cold-shut anchors—use extreme caution if you top-rope these routes. Leave the last bolt clipped for safety. This type of anchor has a very low loading capacity and can open further under stress.

1. **Spray** (5.10a) First route on the right side of the corridor. A good introduction to Maple. Short but pumpy for the grade. 3 bolts to 2 open cold-shut anchors. 25'.

2. **Dixon Butz** (5.11a) 4 bolts to 2 open cold-shut anchors (same anchors as Route 3). 30'.

3. **Skeet Shoot** (5.10d) 4 bolts to 2 open cold shuts. Shares anchors with Route 2. 30'.

MAPLE CANYON
BOX CANYON

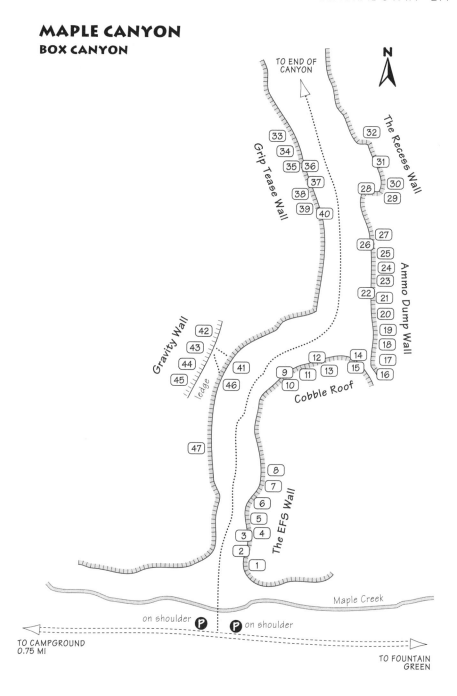

TO END OF
CANYON

N

The Recess Wall

32

31

28   30

29

33

34

35 36

37

38

39 40

Grip Tease Wall

27

26   25

24

23

22   21

20

19

18

17

16

Ammo Dump Wall

42

43

44

45

Gravity Wall

ledge

41

46

12   14

9   15

11 13

10

Cobble Roof

47

8

7

6

5

3   4

2

1

The EFS Wall

Maple Creek

on shoulder P P on shoulder

TO CAMPGROUND
0.75 MI

TO FOUNTAIN
GREEN

4. **EFS** (5.11d) Start on Route 3 but swing up left over overhang to break and wide brown hole. 5 bolts to 2-bolt chain anchor. 40'.

5. **Meathook Sodomy** (5.12d) Steep and thin. Shares anchors with Route 4. 5 bolts to 2-bolt chains. 40'.

6. **Dancing with Rednecks** (5.12b) Climb an overhang to smooth rock band. Work through hole (kneebar) to final headwall. 4 bolts to 2-bolt anchor.

7. **Brown Hole** (5.12b) Long, sustained, and fun. Up left-leaning arch and past large brown hole. 9 bolts to 2-bolt chain anchor. 85'.

8. **Unknown** (5.11) 7 bolts to 2-bolt chain anchor. 70'.

COBBLE ROOF

This wall ain't no slab! This is the steep overhanging roof/wall on the right as the canyon bends right. Expect hard cobble pulling and some weird moves.

9. **Kiss The Cobble** (5.13b) On the far right side of the Cobble Roof is this Jeff Pederson masterpiece. Climb past cave-like hole to hard pebble and pocket pulling over steep roof. 7 bolts to 2-bolt anchor. 50'.

10. **The Stoning** (5.13b) A "girdle" traverse that begins on Route 9 and ends on Route 11.

11. **Cobble Killer** (5.13b/c) This Tim Hannig route will slay you with its devious cruxes. 9 bolts to 2-bolt anchor. 65'.

12. **Meat Eater** (5.13a/b) 9 bolts to a 2-bolt anchor. 70'.

13. **Body Dump** (5.13c) A classic Maple hard route with a drop-knee crux move, good foot cams, and technical moves. 9 bolts to 2-bolt anchor. 65'.

14. **Gong Show** (5.12c) Begin on *Loser*, go right at horizontal break and finish on *Body Dump*. 70'.

15. **Loser** (5.13a) A Maple classic. On the left side of the roof and just right of the obvious deep chimney/slot. A long, pumpy, and excellent route (first ascent by Bill Ohran) that fries you on the technical final headwall. Look for a good kneebar rest. 10 bolts to 2-bolt chains. 70'.

AMMO DUMP WALL

The right side of this popular wall is a deep chimney/slot and its left edge is a blunt arête. Lots of good routes lace this wall, offering popular warm-ups for the harder lines. Most of these routes can be stick-clipped.

16. **Man Muncher** (5.8) Jam and stem up the obvious chimney and end at *Watermelon Sugar's* anchors. Some large cams are useful. 8 bolts to 2-bolt anchor. 85'.

17. **Devil's Plaything** (5.11a) Popular and fun. Great warm-up in cave-like

sanctuary left of chimney. Sometimes dark and musty—locally called "Swamp Cooler." 5 bolts to 2-bolt anchor. 50'.

18. **Downloader** (5.11a) Another quality warm-up. 5 bolts to 2-bolt anchor. 50'.

19. **Watermelon Sugar** (5.11c) A popular Bill Boyle classic. Wanders up and over to fun headwall. Following the bolt line all the way is .12a—most step right at that technical crux. 9 bolts to 2-bolt anchor. 70'.

20. **In The Meantime** (5.12b) The right side of the bulging wall. 8 bolts to 2-bolt anchor. 60'.

21. **Sluggo** (5.13b) Very hard and bouldery with 2 distinct cruxes. Doesn't see lots of ascents. 8 bolts to 2-bolt anchor. 50'.

22. **Bazooka** (5.13b/c) A right to left traversing route. Begin on *Sluggo* and finish on *Bomb Squad*.

23. **Ammo Dump** (5.12d) Finishes at Route 21 anchors. 8 bolts to 2-bolt anchor above lip. 50'.

24. **Shoot 'Em Up** (5.13a) Excellent and pumpy route with cool finishing moves. Up the slab to 30-foot overhang. 6 bolts to 2-bolt anchor. 50'.

25. **Bomb Squad** (5.12d) A little easier than *Shoot 'Em Up*, but not much. Slab to roof. 6 bolts to 2-bolt anchor above lip. 50'.

26. **Point Blank** (5.12b) The popular hard route on this wall. Sees lots of action. Good power moves up overhanging wall. 6 bolts to 2-bolt anchor. 50'.

27. **Football** (5.12b/c) On the left side of the wall. 5 bolts to 2-bolt anchor (same as Route 26). 50'.

THE RECESS WALL

On the right (east) side of the canyon just past the Ammo Dump Wall is a deep recess followed by a steep wall broken by a large arch.

28. **Maple Pickles** (5.11a) Good route next to the arête and right of a deep chimney slot. 7 bolts to 2-bolt anchor.

29. **Melon Head** (5.11b) Left of the crack/chimney system. A fun, long pitch with an airy traverse above a bulge. 11 bolts to 2-bolt anchor on a ledge.

30. **Stalker** (5.13) Out the right side of the deep cave to a black trough. 11 bolts to a 2-bolt anchor.

31. **Project** (5.12?) Out the left side of the cave to a headwall.

32. **Cobble in the Sky** (5.12c) Begin left of the obvious cave. Climb over several steep bulges to an airy upper headwall. 19 bolts to 2-bolt anchor. 100'. Use a 200-foot rope. Don't get lost on this long route.

THE GRIP TEASE WALL

This wall is directly across the canyon (west side) from The Recess Wall and The Ammo Dump Wall. Several excellent routes (put up by Bill Ohran and Bill Boyle) ascend the overhanging wall. Routes are right to left. Lots more fine routes are farther up-canyon. Consult *Maple Canyon Rock Climbing* for directions, names, and ratings of these routes.

33. **The Hammer** (5.13a/b) On the far right side. Ascends steeply overhanging wall from a ledge. Kinda funky. No anchors. Down-aid from last bolt. Desperately seeking anchors.

34. **Busload of Faith** (5.13a) Out left side of cave formation to a roof from a ledge. 5 bolts to a 2-bolt anchor (shared with Route 35 and Route 36).

35. **Straw Man** (5.12c) Run up an easy slab to the overhanging wall and pinch cobbles upward. 7 bolts to a 2-bolt anchor (shared with Route 34 and Route 36).

36. **Lucky Boy** (5.12a/b) Really good and popular. Ditto as above routes— slab to pumpy wall. Same start as *Straw Man*, but head left at bolt 1. 8 bolts to 2-bolt anchor (shared with Route 34 and Route 35).

37. **Bolts Not Bitches** (5.12c) Good, long, classic. 7 bolts to 2-bolt anchor. 70'.

38. **Breaking the Eye** (5.12d) A good one to try for the elusive hard Maple on-sight. Pumpy and sustained. 8 bolts to 2-bolt anchor (shared with Route 37).

39. **Grip Tease** (5.12a) Excellent for a first .12 to work on. 8 bolts to 2-bolt anchor. 70'.

40. **Pasties and a G-String** (5.11d) Fun climbing up a vertical streambed with a slopey crux. 5 bolts to 2-bolt anchor. 60'.

GRAVITY WALL

This wall is down-canyon (toward the canyon mouth) from The Ammo Dump Wall on the upper wall on the canyon's west side. This is a good private place to escape the weekend hordes. The routes begin from a spacious ledge 80' up and accessed by the easy *Tennis Shoe Approach* route. Routes are right to left.

41. **Tennis Shoe Approach** (5.0) This easy route accesses the upper ledge by swinging up jugs on a slab. 3 bolts. 80'.

42. **Against a Dark Background** (5.11c/d) Right-hand route on the upper wall. 8 bolts to 2-bolt anchor.

43. **The Gravity Well** (5.12a) 9 bolts to 2-bolt anchor (same as Route 42).

44. **Prosthetic Conscience** (5.11c) 8 bolts to 2-bolt anchor.

45. **Beyond Neon** (5.11b/c) 9 bolts to 2-bolt anchor (same as Route 44).

46. **Clean Air Turbulence** (5.11a) A long bolted route up west wall of canyon that begins from the streambed left of Route 41. Ends at a 2-bolt anchor.

2-rope rappel.

47. **Shootin' Blanks** (5.12b) On the short, overhanging wall just left (west) of the Box Canyon entrance. Fun, pumpy climbing up short, leaning cliff. 4 bolts to 2-bolt anchor. To the left are a couple of projects.

THE BRIDGE AREA

This excellent area in the main canyon offers plenty of fine routes, many shaded in summer, as well as easy access from the road and great scenery. Continue driving west up the canyon road from the Box Canyon to the bridge across the creek. Park at a pullout just west of the bridge. The first routes are on the steep walls directly south of the parking area and bridge. They are all well-protected. Routes are listed right to left.

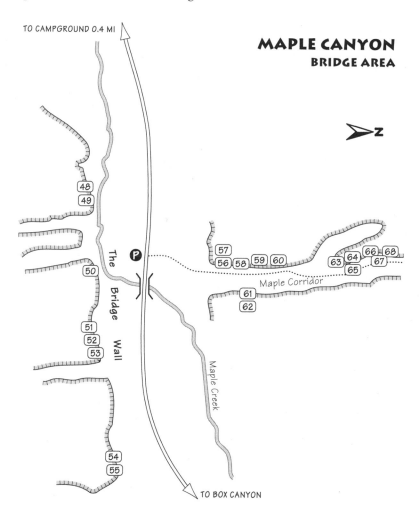

THE BRIDGE WALL

48. **Crime Scene** (5.11a) Walk right from the bridge past the overhang over the creek to 2 routes. 8 bolts to 2-bolt anchor. 70'.

49. **Hit Man** (5.11b) Left of Route 48. 7 bolts to 2-bolt anchor. 70'.

50. **Taking The Bullet** (5.10d) A long, good route opposite the bridge. 10 bolts to 2-bolt anchor. 80'.

51. **The Dark Along The Way** (5.11d) Walk down the road and scramble through grass to the cliff base. Watch for rattlesnakes. 7 bolts to 2-bolt anchor. 50'.

52. **New Fandango** (5.11b) 9 bolts to 2-bolt anchor. 50'.

53. **The Arraignment** (5.11b) 9 bolts to 2-bolt anchor. 50'.

54. **Criminal Ballastics** (5.10c) Farther east on the left side of a buttress. 3 bolts to 2-bolt chains. 30'.

55. **Vehicular Manslaughter** (5.11b) A lot of bolts on this one—definitely not under-protected! 7 bolts to 2-bolt chains. 35'.

MAPLE CORRIDOR

These 2 east-facing walls are hidden in a brushy canyon north of the bridge. Park by the bridge and follow a path north across the creek and up to the cliff base. Continue north to the second wall. Watch for rattlesnakes in the brush.

56. **Environmental Impact Statement** (5.10b/c) A popular line visible from the road. Shaded by trees. 5 bolts to 2-bolt anchor.

57. **Raindrops on Lichen** (5.9) Another popular classic. Start up Route 56 but step right from bolt 1. 5 bolts to 2-bolt anchor.

58. **Your Little Sister** (5.9+) Stick-clip bolt 1. 4 bolts to 2-bolt anchor.

59. **Spoils of War** a.k.a. **Crocodile Nasties** (5.11d) Keep left of the bolt line. 5 bolts to 2-bolt anchor.

60. **Unknown** (5.11c) Steep and fun. 5 bolts to 2-bolt anchor.

61. **Monkey Nuts** (5.8) This route is on the opposite (east) side of the canyon from Route 58. Veer right at bolt 3. 6 bolts to 2-bolt anchor.

62. **Loogie** (5.8) Twin route to *Monkey Nuts*. Start up Route 60 but step left at bolt 3. 6 bolts to 2-bolt anchor.

63. **Turning Formosa** (5.8) 7 bolts to 2-bolt chain anchor.

64. **Meconium 23** (5.9-) 5 bolts to 2-bolt anchor (open cold shuts).

65. **Beer Quester** (5.11a) 4 bolts to 2-bolt chain anchor.

66. **Fear Fester** (5.11c) 7 bolts to 2-bolt anchor.

67. **The Lost Letter** (5.11b) 7 bolts to 2-bolt anchor.

68. **Rainmaker** (5.11a) On the far right side of the cliff. Joins *Lost Letter* at its last bolt. 7 bolts to 2-bolt anchor.

THE CAMPGROUND AREA

Many cliffs and canyons surround the campground near the end of the gravel road. A wide selection of moderate routes are here along with some bouldering areas. Access the area by continuing west up the canyon road from the bridge for about half a mile to the campground. A large parking area is on the right, otherwise park in your campsite if you are camping. A good bouldering traverse, *Manburner Traverse* (5.12c) is behind the toilets and on the north side of Black Magic Rock opposite the toilets. *Cobblestone Cacamaimie* (5.9+) ascends the east corner of Black Magic Rock past 4 bolts to anchors.

THE SCHOOLROOM

This popular area is directly east of Toilet Buttress. Access it by following a trail east from the toilets or a trail north from the large parking lot. You can easily set topropes on many routes. Routes are listed left to right.

69. **The Redemption of Madonna** (5.8+) Short, steep, and fun. The first route encountered. Just right of a tree. 4 bolts to 2-bolt chain anchors. 25'.

70. **The Big Kahuna** (5.10b) Just right of Route 69. This is named for the giant boulder embedded in the route. 4 bolts to 2-bolt chain anchors. 30'.

71. **Hi-C & Crackers** (5.9) Top-rope. Scramble up to anchors just below the summit. Climbers can wander all over this wall left of the chimney. 70'.

72. **Humpty Dumpty's Chimney Sweep Service** (5.5) Works up obvious chimney in open corner. Bring a variety of gear or toprope it. End at Route 71 anchors.

73. **Chocolate Doobie** (5.7) Good fun route immediately right of chimney. 6 bolts to 2-bolt anchor.

74. **Drowning Baby Fish** (5.7) Just right of moss streak. 5 bolts to 2-bolt chain anchors. 35'.

75. **Extra Credit** (5.7) Left of tree. 4 bolts to 2-bolt chain anchors. 30'.

76. **Moss Pocket** (5.6) Slab right of tree. 4 bolts to 2-bolt anchor. 40'.

77. **Bob's Bolts** (5.4) On left side of narrow corridor opening. 4 bolts to 2-bolt anchor. 40'.

78. **Marble Slate** (5.7) Top-rope on slab right of corridor.

79. **Fruit Jets** (5.9-) 3 bolts to 2-bolt chain anchors.

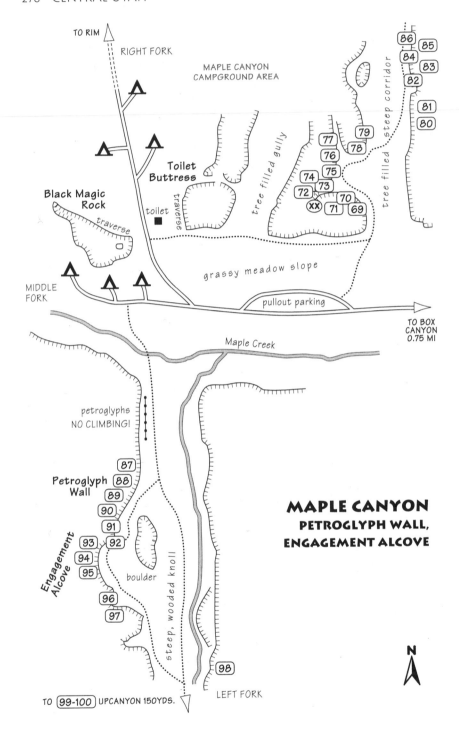

TO RIM

RIGHT FORK

MAPLE CANYON
CAMPGROUND AREA

tree filled steep corridor

86
85
84
83
82
81
80

Toilet
Buttress

79
78
77
76
75
74
73
72
XX
71
70
69

tree filled gully

Black Magic
Rock

traverse

toilet

traverse

MIDDLE
FORK

grassy meadow slope

pullout parking

TO BOX
CANYON
0.75 MI

Maple Creek

petroglyphs
NO CLIMBING!

Petroglyph
Wall

87
88
89
90
91
93   92
94
95
96
97

Engagement
Alcove

boulder

steep, wooded knoll

MAPLE CANYON
PETROGLYPH WALL,
ENGAGEMENT ALCOVE

98

TO   99-100   UPCANYON 150YDS.

LEFT FORK

N

ROAD KILL WALL

This west-facing wall hides in the trees northeast of The Schoolroom. Reach it by following a trail for 100' east from Route 79 through the forest to the cliff base on the opposite side of this wide corridor-canyon. Follow the existing trail—no extra trails in this sensitive area please! Routes are right to left.

80. **Massengile the Moose** (5.8) On the wall right of a groove. 4 bolts to 2-bolt anchor. 35'.

81. **Grease Bunny** (5.7) Next to Route 80. 4 bolts to 2-bolt anchor. 35'.

82. **Armadillo Waffles** (5.8+) Just left of the groove. 3 bolts to 2-bolt chain anchors. 35'.

83. **Canned Beaver** (5.7) 3 bolts to 2-bolt chain anchors. 35'.

84. **Porcupine Mush** (5.6) Solo up or step left from Route 83's anchors to set a top-rope. 2-bolt chain anchor. 30'.

85. **Flea Market** (5.6) Good beginner route. 6 bolts to 2-bolt chain anchors. 50'.

86. **Worm Hole Boodie** (5.10c) A steep start to a slab. 4 bolts to 2-bolt chain anchors. 30'.

THE PETROGLYPH WALL & ENGAGEMENT ALCOVE

These 2 walls lie on the west side of the Left Hand Fork, a side-canyon that branches south from the main canyon on the south side of the campground. A trail that climbs to the range crest begins from the road and heads south through this canyon, allowing access to the climbing routes. A panel of Indian pictographs and petroglyphs, protected by a fence, is near the canyon mouth. At the south end of an eroded pit, find a climber's path that works right up a scree slope 50' to the cliff base. The first route is about 100' left of the petroglyph fence. Some of the routes are very long here. Use 2 ropes or a 200-foot cord. Routes are listed right to left from here.

87. **The Streak** (5.11c) Begin just left of a large maple tree. A long, excellent route up a black water streak on the cobbled headwall. Can be hot in summer. 10 bolts to 2-bolt chain anchors. Anchors on the left side of an indented ledge. 100+'.

88. **Unknown** (5.11b) Long and good route up the wall left of a black streak. Same start as *The Streak* then up left. 12 bolts to 2-bolt chain anchors. 100+'.

89. **The Beekeeper** (5.10d) Fun, continuous climbing up the vertical wall. 11 bolts to 2-bolt chains. 85'. If possible use a 200-foot rope to lower/rappel.

90. **The Emancipation of Dissonance** (5.11c) Scramble 20' onto a large flake with a bolt-chain belay anchor. Climb right past 3 bolts then up through

a black streak. 6 bolts to 2-bolt chain anchors.

91. **Unknown** (5.9+) This and the following routes are in the Engagement Alcove. 7 bolts to 2-bolt chain anchors.

92. **Unknown** (5.10a) Just left of large flake/boulder. An excellent route up an arête that marks the left edge of the Petroglyph Wall. 7 bolts to 2-bolt anchor.

93. **Mylanta** (5.11) Work straight up the vertical wall above a large flake. 7 bolts to 2-bolt chain anchors.

94. **An 80/20 Ratio** (5.10b) 6 bolts to 2-bolt chain anchors.

95. **Choose Your Weapon** (5.9-) Classic line. Great cobbling up the wall right of a water streak. 6 bolts to 2-bolt anchor.

96. **Wet Itchies** (5.8) Left side of obvious trough feature. 6 bolts to 2-bolt anchor. An excellent ice climb forms up this route in winter.

97. **Penal Atrophy** (5.7) A juggy line left of a corner on the left side of the alcove. 7 bolts to 2-bolt anchor.

The Pipeline, looming over the dry streambed, is a new area immediately east of the Engagement Alcove. One route exists on the wall, the rest are projects.

98. **Poop Chute** (5.10c) Steep and juggy climbing on the far right (south) side. 4 bolts to 2-bolt anchor.

A couple of excellent routes are located on the *Orangutan Wall*; 150 yards up the canyon from the Engagement Alcove. The routes are on the west wall.

99. **Monkey Duodenum** (5.9+) Long and fun. 10 bolts to 2-bolt chain anchor. 105'. Use 200-foot rope.

100. **Full Moon Monkey** (5.8) Another 3-star moderate classic! 9 bolts to 2-bolt chain anchor. 85'.

Southwest

UTAH

ZION NATIONAL PARK

OVERVIEW

The Virgin River, springing from melting snowdrifts atop the lofty 9,000-foot-high Markagunt Plateau, created dramatic and steep-walled Zion Canyon after slicing through thousands of feet of colorful, layered strata in southwestern Utah. This breathtaking canyon is the centerpiece of Zion National Park, a 147,000-acre parkland that protects a spectacular landscape of high plateaus, sheer canyons, and abrupt monolithic cliffs. Climbers know Zion for the immense rock walls, ranging from 600 to 2,200 feet high, that line Zion Canyon in the park's scenic heart. These towering sandstone cliffs offer a variety of climbing challenges, most of them long, serious, and potentially dangerous. Shorter routes, mostly following cracks, are located on smaller cliff bands and along the base of some of the big walls.

Zion National Park is preserved for its superb natural beauty as well as for its diverse ecosystems. Geologist Clarence Dutton, after visiting Zion Canyon in 1880, wrote, "There is an eloquence to their forms which stirs the imagination with singular power and kindles in the mind a glowing response. Nothing can exceed the wondrous beauty of Zion." It's still that way. Zion's canyons and mesas boast an exquisite beauty in a state filled with mysterious and beautiful places. Zion Canyon itself is like a desert oasis. The Virgin River riffles across the canyon floor below towering cliffs. Its cobbled banks are lined with groves of box elder, willow, cottonwood, and ash. Wide alcoves in the cliff faces hide dripping springs that nourish ferns and wildflowers in lush hanging gardens. The park hosts 4 major life zones that lie between its lowest elevation of 3,666 feet and its 8,740-foot high point. Over 70 mammal species and 272 bird species live in this immense swath of rugged canyon country.

Navajo sandstone, the main type of climbing rock, dominates Zion's 8 major rock formations. The sandstone, stretching across the entire Colorado Plateau, reaches its maximum thickness of 2,200 feet at Zion. The thick strata, ranging in color from ruddy red to alabaster white, was deposited some 200 million years ago as a giant dune field similar in shape and size to the modern-day Sahara. Over the ensuing millions of years, heat and pressure cemented the dunefield and preserved the cross-bedding seen in the sandstone today. Later, the Virgin River and its tributaries went to work on the sandstone,

West Guardian Temple, Zion National Park. PHOTO BY STEWART GREEN

excavating and sculpting the park's sharp, sheer canyons and lining them with high cliffs. In its upper canyon, an abrupt defile called The Narrows, the river dashes through a deep, narrow, slot canyon with a gradient as steep as 80 feet in a mile.

Most of Zion's climbing is on the lower, dark red part of the Navajo sandstone. This medium breaks into sharp dihedrals, cracks, and chimneys, and is generally solid and clean. Ledges and chimneys are, however, often cluttered with loose debris and blocks. The white upper half of the formation generally forms steep aprons above the red half, and sweeps upward to the flat summits of lofty rock islands. This sandstone tends to be very sandy, friable, and extremely scary to climb. Ron Olevsky, one of Zion's big-wall pioneers, notes, "To find the best rock, avoid confusing an aesthetic summit with an aesthetic climb."

Zion's stunning beauty and relative accessibility makes it justifiably popular with both tourists and climbers. The park's burgeoning number of visitors, now millions each year, stay mainly in easily accessible Zion Canyon. In summer, a daily string of buses and countless autos disgorge tourists and travelers at every scenic overlook where they click photos and gape at the soaring cliffs. The sheer volume of visitors, particularly in summer, has overloaded the park's human carrying capacity. This is a place being literally loved to death. Shuttles through Zion Canyon are planned for the near future to help alleviate vehicle congestion during peak visitation times, which fortunately don't coincide with the best climbing weather.

Climbing history: Zion has a long and colorful rock climbing history that began in 1927 with the first ascent of the Great White Throne, a prominent canyon landmark, by William H. Evans, a daring young climber described in a park memo as a "daredevil type and a mountaineer." On June 27, Evans, armed with 15 feet of rope and water, scrambled up what is now considered to be a 5th class slab on the south side to the Throne's summit. He lit a signal fire that night to prove his ascent to onlookers below. On his descent the next day, Evans took a 200-foot sliding plunge and ended up with bruises and a cracked skull on a ledge above the south saddle. He endured a couple of painful days of delirium before being rescued. Four years later, Donald Orcutt, an unemployed Californian, walked to Zion from Los Angeles, repeated the Throne, but later fell and was killed during a solo ascent of The Cathedral. The Cathedral, the first 5th class climb in the park, was first ascended by Rudolph Weidner and Walter and Fritz Becker in 1931. Through the 1930s other peaks were climbed including East Temple, West Temple, and The Sentinel.

The serious nature of Zion's cliffs and the lack of climbing equipment and advanced crack techniques prevented anything but brushy, mountaineering ascents over the next several decades. Many well-known climbers including Fritz Wiessner, Fred Ayres (who climbed many of the arches in Arches National Park), and Herb and Jan Conn enjoyed the canyon and summited the park's major summits. By the 1960s, Layton Kor brought the big-wall techniques developed in Yosemite National Park to Zion's walls. He attempted one of the major faces in Kolob Canyon. In 1967, however, the park's first major route was put up the Northwest Face of the Great White Throne by Fred Beckey, Galen Rowell, and Pat Callis. The late 1960s also saw the first ascents of Mt. Spry, The Twin Brothers, the west face of Bridge Mountain, and the east face of The Sentinel.

By the early 1970s Zion was primed to enter its golden age of big-wall climbing. Jeff Lowe was the motivating force behind these efforts, doing some serious first ascents including *The Toad* on The Sentinel, *Southeast Buttress* on Jacob, the *East Face* and *Lowe Route* on Angels Landing, and the megaclassic *Moonlight Buttress*. These Lowe routes were also instrumental in the development of the first camming devices for parallel-sided cracks. Another superlative effort was the first ascent of *Angel Hair* on Angels Landing by Jim Dunn and Dean Tschappat in 1974. The pair, encountering hard nailing and off-width cracks, placed no bolts on the route.

By the late 1970s many of the obvious lines had been climbed. A couple of new pioneers, Ron Olevsky and Dave Jones, arrived on the scene to push more difficult and exposed lines up Zion's walls using Friends, a new camming device that protected previously unprotectable cracks. Olevsky used the new technology to allow for environmentally friendly routes that required no pitons or the hammer nailing that ultimately destroys aid placements and the sandstone. He created placements that would take clean gear on many of his routes or left fixed pitons and bolts to bypass those sections. Olevsky called this technique HAFWEN for "Hammered Anchors Fixed Where Necessary." Many of his classic routes, including *Touchstone Wall*, *Prodigal Sun*, and *Space Shot*, were put up in this style and are featured in this guide. At the same time Dave Jones began exploring new walls and pushing free climbing standards. Some of Jones's best finds were *Shune's Buttress* on Red Arch Mountain, *Empty Pages* on Angels Landing, and almost all of the superb routes on the south face of East Temple.

The 1980s and 1990s saw an increase in aid skills as well as technological advances that allowed harder and more serious routes to be ascended than ever before. Some of these routes include *The Radiator*, a 15-pitch Grade VI on Abraham that was put up by John Middendorf and Walt Shipley in 1990; the *Swiss-American Route* on the north wall of Angels Landing by Middendorf and Xaver Bongard in 1991; and 2 very difficult lines up the drastically overhanging Streaked Wall—*Rodeo Queen* by Conrad Anker and Mugs Stump in 1990 and *Latitudes* by Paul Gagner and Eric Brand in 1994. The thin nailing on *Latitudes* requires a rack with 35 Beaks and Peckers along with 30 assorted knifeblades.

These decades also saw free-climbing limits pushed upward on both old and new lines. The classic *Monkeyfinger* was freed by Mike O'Donnel and Craig Kenyon in 1989. *Moonlight Buttress*, Zion's classic hard route, was free climbed by Johnny Woodward and Peter Croft in 1992. *Tricks of the Trade*, first ascent by Middendorf, Brad Quinn, and Bill Hatcher in 1993, boasts only 2 pin placements and 60 feet of aid in 19 pitches and an aesthetic 500-foot-long hand crack. Another notable 1993 achievement was Doug Byerly and Doug Hall's free ascent of *Gettin' Western*, a 2,000-foot 5.11+ climb up the huge East Face of West Temple that is probably the longest all-free sandstone route in the United States. In 1997 Alan Lester free-climbed the first 5 pitches of *Prodigal Sun* on Angels Landing and freed much of *Space Shot*.

Zion Canyon is a true adventure climbing arena. This, Utah's sandstone version of Yosemite Valley, is the place for intrepid desert climbers to come and test all their skills. It's not a place for the beginner or novice, nor the sport climber that likes a bolt every 6 feet. In contrast, this is a serious area with serious routes and a host of potential disasters just waiting to happen. Numerous myths have arisen about Zion climbing and most of them are true, including tales of crumbling, rotten rock; vertical bushwhacking through inhospitable plants; dangerous and epic descents; unprotected off-widths and insecure aiding—all taking place in an extreme climate.

Believe the stories—they're all true. But it's also true that the competent party will have a most excellent adventure finding classic cracks, stunning beauty, and few other climbers. Zion routes, however, require a high level of commitment and experience. Most of the wall routes are long and sometimes complicated. The quality of sandstone varies dramatically from excellent to terrifyingly loose. Approaches and descents are time-consuming and dangerous, with some descents taking as much time as the routes themselves. Many lines require good routefinding skills to navigate upward through a maze of cracks, corners, roofs, ramps, and ledges.

Every climber thinking of Zion needs to be highly competent. The canyon's relative remoteness and lack of rescue facilities prevent any possibility of being plucked off some wall or isolated summit, requiring climbers to be competent at self-rescue. Climbers need to be competent at leading cracks of all sizes and placing adequate protection. Most routes require solid 5.10 crack climbing skills. The "easier" pitches tend to be rubble-filled chimneys. Climbers should also be competent at setting up safe, equalized belay anchors and organizing hanging belays, competent at evaluating objective and subjective dangers, of knowing when to bail and when to be bold, and competent at setting up rappels and able to endure a chilly forced bivouac.

Inexperienced sandstone climbers should approach Zion's walls with some wariness and respect. This is not the place to venture immediately onto a wall without experience on the medium. John Middendorf, one of Zion's most prolific 1990s climbers, notes in *Rock & Ice*, "Many climbers come to Zion under the misconception that it's possible to learn sandstone climbing on shorter crags in the area. There are no 'trainer routes' in Zion." Climb some of the shorter crack routes like those at the base of Cerberus Gendarme and perhaps a hammerless classic like *Organasm* to understand the fragility of the Navajo sandstone. Don't underestimate the length and difficulty of any route. Remember, too, that Zion is not a sport area. Those who want a sport climbing or cragging experience should drive over to the excellent sport crags around St. George rather than linger at Zion.

Routes ascend almost every major face in Zion Canyon. The more popular walls and trade routes are on Angels Landing and Cerberus Gendarme. Other less-frequented venues include The East Temple, Mount Spry, Isaac in the Court of the Patriarchs, The Spearhead, Red Arch Mountain, and the walls in the Temple of Sinawava. This guide describes and topos many of the best routes in the canyon, along with approach and descent directions, and necessary gear. The decision to list only free climbs and clean, hammerless aid routes in this guide is an attempt to help prevent zealous neophytes from over-nailing the canyon's sandstone.

No complete guide to all of Zion's big walls is available, and most Zion climbers want it that way to retain some of the adventure, boldness, and ingenuity required for a successful ascent. For information and topos for big walls not listed here, check out the three notebook volumes at the backcountry desk in the visitor center. These are a loose collection of notes, topos, and route descriptions left by other climbers and first ascensionists. Take this unedited information with a grain of salt. Many of the descriptions are ambiguous and even misleading. User beware. Topos can be sketched from the books. Use them but don't always believe them. Be aware that glaring inaccuracies often occur in these logs. Some climbers have also penciled in their own erroneous "corrections," giving the books the nickname "Zion's Fiction."

The weather in Zion Canyon can be characterized in a word—extreme. Hot summer temperatures, usually over 100 degrees daily, allow almost no climbing unless it's in the early morning. Spring and fall are the best times. The weather in April and May, and September and October is usually warm and sunny with highs between 60 and 90 degrees. Expect occasional cool and even rainy spells during these months. Autumn is probably the best time for a Zion visit, with clear days and mild nights. Winter is generally not good for climbing in the north-south trending canyon. Few walls face south so the main cliffs almost never warm up for the whole day. The best cold-weather route is the south-facing *Touchstone Wall* on Cerberus Gendarme. In warm weather, an early start on routes, especially those on the east side of the canyon, allows much climbing in cool temperatures and shade before the sun swings onto the walls. Angels Landing's northeast face gets morning sun and a lot of afternoon shade.

Don't climb on the sandstone after rain and thunderstorms. Sandstone loses over half its strength when wet and the cementing agents between sand grains dissolve, making its surface crumbly and unstable. Bring plenty of water, especially during warm weather. A gallon per climber per day is not too much. It gets very hot on the sun-baked walls, even in the cooler spring and autumn months. Also watch for lightning from quick-moving summer thunderstorms.

Zion National Park is a fragile area. A few park regulations help preserve this fabulous environment and climbing area. The cliff closures that protect nesting sites for endangered peregrine falcons and other raptors is the regulation that most impacts climbers. Several pairs of falcons nest on a variety of Zion cliffs, which has led to the closure of many popular walls (about 80 percent of the climbing areas) until the end of nesting season. The usual closures are in effect from February 1 until August 1, or until park biologists have determined that the young birds have fledged. Once park biologists have determined the nesting sites, unaffected cliffs are reopened to rock climbing. Check at the visitor center for exact dates and what areas are closed. Cliff closures in the past have included the Great White Throne, Cathedral Mountain, Angels Landing, Mt. Spry, The East Temple, Court of the Patriarchs, Mount Moroni, and The Watchman. The Temple of Sinawava is usually open. Park regulations require you to obtain a backcountry permit for climbs that last more than one day.

Climbers need to remember that Zion is a fragile area that is easily damaged by thoughtless actions. For climbers to continue enjoying the vertical challenges here, they need to mitigate their impact as much as possible. The sandy slopes below the cliffs are easily eroded. Follow existing trails whenever possible to access the route base. Carry out all your trash on the walls. Don't pitch it off and hope to find it later. Likewise, don't toss bags of human waste off the cliffs. Pack it out instead with a kitty litter-filled toilet tube. The several cragging areas in the park have the highest climber impact with their easy access and variety of short routes. An Anasazi ruin atop the Practice Cliffs is being trampled by climbers setting up topropes and hiking down. To alleviate damage, the park service is discouraging climbing in some of the areas and prohibiting it in others; it has been prohibited on the popular Practice Cliffs.

Practice clean climbing and aiding techniques to avoid damaging the sandstone. All of the routes listed in this guide are clean. Hammers and pitons are not needed, and don't even think about carrying one. Anyone caught hammering on any of these routes just might be lynched by locals—at the very least their car might get hammered on! In the spring of 1997, an unknown and uncaring party used hammer aid on *Space Shot*, destroying several clean-aid placements. Poor piton craft on nailing routes irreparably damages the rock. Also be sensitive and alert to damage caused by careless cleaning. Learn proper clean aid and piton nailing techniques for sandstone before venturing onto any of Zion's walls.

Rack information is given for all the long Zion routes included here. Use them only as a suggested rack; some items you may need might not be listed. Scope your route and use your own judgment for what else you'll need. A standard rack for the routes listed here usually includes two to three sets of Friends or Camalots, sets of hexentrics and wired stoppers, quickdraws and free carabiners, and a bunch of 24-inch slings. Wide crack pro is usually desired, like Big Bros or large Camalots. Aid routes require ascenders and multiple sets of aiders. Two ropes are necessary. Consider using 200-foot ropes. Bring extra webbing for rappel anchors.

Trip Planning Information

General description: Numerous multi-pitch climbing routes up to 2,500 feet long ascend the big sandstone walls of Zion above the Virgin River in Zion National Park.

Location: Southwest Utah. The park is easy to reach from Interstate 15 via Utah 9. It's 4 hours from Las Vegas and 5 hours from Salt Lake City.

Camping: Two campgrounds are in Zion and both lie near the southern park boundary along the Virgin River in Zion Canyon. Watchman Campground is on the right just after entering the park. South Campground, with 140 sites, is a mile up the road on the right. Both campgrounds offer restrooms, plentiful shade trees, water, telephones, an amphitheater with summer programs, and a dump station. Both campgrounds can be very busy, especially on weekends, holidays, and during the summer. Private campgrounds are along UT 9 southwest of the park. Showers are available at the campground in Springdale.

Restrictions and access issues: Zion National Park is a federal park area run by the National Park Service. The main restriction is the closure of certain areas for nesting raptors from spring until late summer. Check at the visitor center for the closure locations and dates. Climbers do not need to register for day climbs. All overnight climbers must register at the visitor center and obtain a backcountry permit. Fires are permitted only in designated campgrounds. Keep off the sandstone cliffs after heavy rain or snow to avoid damaging the friable, wet rock. Zion is a fragile natural area. Climbing here is a privilege. Practice minimum impact by using existing climber trails to the cliff base, avoid stepping on and damaging the vegetation, pack all your trash off the route, use a closed container to tote human waste (do not toss shit-bags off the cliffs!). Practice clean climbing whenever possible by not using a hammer and pitons. Poor use of pitons scars the rock forever. If you don't have the skill to aid and clean a route without scarring it—keep off it and learn the proper techniques first. This guide does not include any routes with hammer aid. All routes are clean and hammerless. For info on Zion National Park and climbing regulations contact: Zion National Park, Springdale, UT 84767-1099 or call (801) 772-3256.

Guidebooks: *Desert Rock: Rock Climbs in the National Parks* by Eric Bjørnstad, Chockstone Press, 1996. *Classic Desert Climbs* by Fred Knapp, Sharp End Press, 1996 has a selection of Zion routes. *Rock & Ice* #77 has a good section on Zion by pioneer John Middendorf. Several climbing route books are kept in the visitor center. Ask at the backcountry desk to look at them—but don't believe everything you read there! Some locals call them "Zion's Fiction."

Nearby mountain shops, guide services, and gyms: Outdoor Outlet in St. George is the nearest climbing shop. Todd Goss with Paragon Climbing Instruction (801) 673-1709 offers basic and intermediate climbing courses as well as guiding services and area tours.

Services: All visitor services are in Springdale, including gas, groceries, restaurants, lodging, film processing, and basic supplies.

Emergency services: Call 911. Nearest hospital is Dixie Regional Medical Center, 544 South 400 East, St. George, UT 84770, (800) 326-4022.

Nearby climbing areas: Virgin River Gorge (AZ), Kolob Canyons, The Overlook, Cetecan Wall, Cedar City crags, St. George crags, Chuckawalla Wall, Black and Tan, Sumo Wall, Snow Canyon State Park, Crawdad Canyon Climbers Park, Prophecy Wall, Black Rocks.

Nearby attractions: Virgin River Narrows, East Rim Trail, West Rim Trail,

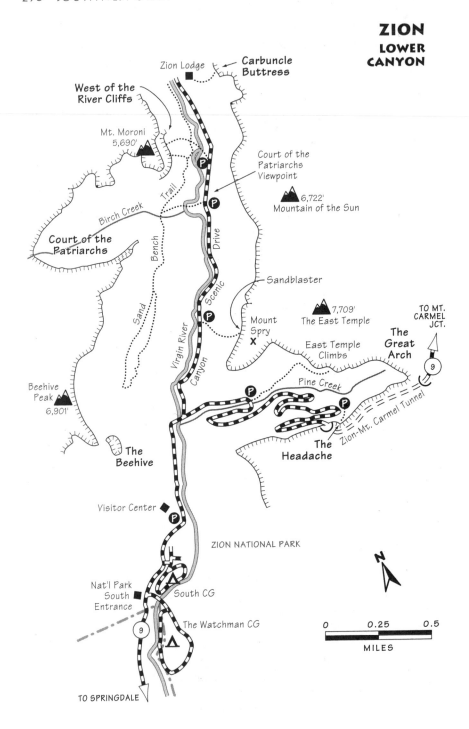

ZION
LOWER
CANYON

Zion Lodge
Carbuncle Buttress

West of the River Cliffs

Mt. Moroni 5,690'

Court of the Patriarchs Viewpoint

6,722'
Mountain of the Sun

Birch Creek

Trail

Bench

Court of the Patriarchs

Scenic

Drive

Sand

Sandblaster

7,709'
The East Temple

Mount Spry
X

East Temple Climbs

The Great Arch

TO MT. CARMEL JCT.

9

Virgin River

Canyon

Beehive Peak 6,901'

Pine Creek

The Beehive

The Headache

Zion-Mt. Carmel Tunnel

Visitor Center

ZION NATIONAL PARK

N

Nat'l Park South Entrance

South CG

9

The Watchman CG

0   0.25   0.5
MILES

TO SPRINGDALE

Angels Landing Trail, Orderville Canyon, Kolob Finger Canyons, Kolob Arch, Virgin River Gorge, Smithsonian Butte Back Country Byway, Coral Pink Sand Dunes State Park, Cedar Breaks National Monument, Pine Valley Mountain Wilderness Area, Snow Canyon State Park, Pipe Springs National Monument (AZ).

Finding the cliffs: Zion National Park is easy to access from Interstate 15 between Salt Lake City and Las Vegas via Utah Highway 9. Route 9 begins at I-15's Exit 16 10 miles northeast of St. George. The park entrance is about 45 miles east from here. Alternatively, east-bound Utah 9 heads west from Mount Carmel Junction from its junction with U.S. Highway 89 17 miles north of Kanab. All the routes and cliffs described here are located in Zion Canyon along with a few in Pine Creek Canyon. To reach the cliffs, enter the park and drive to the bridge northeast of the visitor center. All mileages begin here. Specific distances and trail directions are included under each cliff description.

MT. SPRY

1. **Sandblaster** (IV 5.11) 8 pitches. First ascent by Jeff Lowe and Mark Wilford, 1987. Mt. Spry is a spur peak of The East Temple that looms over the confluence of the Virgin River and Pine Creek. This excellent all-free wall route ascends the central pillar of the northwest face of the peak. It gets lots of shade in the morn-

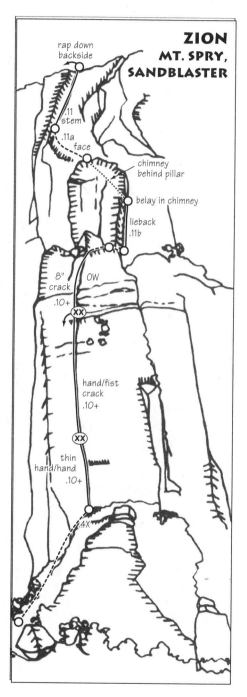

ZION
MT. SPRY

rap down side

ing; with an early start it makes a good summer climb if it's not too hot. A couple of other more moderate routes put up by Jim Beyer in 1979 ascend the broken face right of *Sandblaster*, including *Moria* (III 5.8) and *Black Crack* (III 5.9). *Dancing with Zully* (5.10+), put up by John Middendorf and Dave Jones in 1996, is a superb 5-pitch route 500 yards right of *Sandblaster*. Topos are available in the climber's book in the visitor center. The Mt. Spry routes may be closed due to raptor nesting in the spring and summer. Check at the visitor center for possible closures.

Approach by parking at a pullout on the right (east) side of the road 0.7 mile up the canyon from the bridge. The route is obvious on the wall overhead. It ascends the left-hand of 3 obvious crack systems on the lower wall's buttress/pillar. Scramble up steep talus slopes to the base of the wall (about 45 minutes).

Begin down left from the crack system. Rope up and scramble up a 3rd and 4th class ramp system to a 5.4 X move up a rock step. Belay above on a spacious terrace on top of a pillar below the left-hand crack on the buttress face. **Pitch 1:** Jam steep thin hand and hand crack (5.10+) past roof on right to semi-hanging belay from 2-bolt anchor in pothole on left. **Pitch 2:** Continue jamming long hand and fist crack (5.10+) past some pods to 2-bolt belay in large scoop. **Pitch 3:** Work up flaring 8-inch crack (5.10+) in roof to more off-width arm bars and narrow chimney. Belay on large ledge. **Pitch 4:** Move belay to right side of ledge below large right-facing dihedral. Jam and lieback up leaning dihedral (5.11b lieback) to chimney belay. **Pitch 5:** Continue up moderate chimney to belay ledge atop pillar. **Pitch 6:** Move out right and face climb (5.11a/b) to right-angling corner that leads to belay stance below obvious tight corner. **Pitch 7:** Wild stemming up exposed right-facing corner above (5.11) leads to right-leaning corner and to cliff top. **Descent:** It's possible to just climb the first 3 pitches and then rap back to the ground. For the summiters the descent is somewhat complicated and requires route-finding skills. Descend into the canyon behind the route with rappels and downclimbing; continue by rappelling down the gully between Mt. Spry and The East Temple. **Rack:** Bring 3 sets of Friends, 1 set of TCUs, 1 set of stoppers, a #4 Big Bro, other optional big crack pro like large Camalots, runners, 2 ropes.

WEST OF THE RIVER CLIFF

This Wingate sandstone cliff band lies directly opposite or west of the scenic drive. The cliff, below Mt. Moroni, offers some good crack climbs. They are, unfortunately, often sandy. Water drains off the talus slopes above, depositing sand, silt, and mud in the cracks. They are often filled with impacted debris near the top. Use caution when pulling onto the talus above the cliff so you do not dislodge any boulders onto your belayer. Cliff-top belays are set up from trees. Do not damage any of the junipers. Opposite this crag on the east side of the canyon are the Practice Cliffs. This overused area is now off-limits to climbing because an Indian ruin on top of the cliff is being damaged. Do not climb at this area. **Descent** from all routes is via rappel from trees. **Rack:** A generous selection of Friends, Camalots, and TCUs.

Finding the cliff: Park at a pullout on the west side of the road at 1.9 miles or 0.3 mile past the Court of the Patriarchs viewpoint. Walk west, wade the river, and scramble up steep slopes to the cliff base. Try to find a climber's trail to access the area. It can also be reached via the Sand Bench Trail by parking at the Court of the Patriarchs viewpoint, walking west to a river bridge, and following the trail (watch for horse poop) around and north to a spot below the cliffs. The slopes below the cliff are dense with prickly pear cacti. Routes are listed right to left.

2. **Left Book** (5.8) An okay route up the obvious huge left-facing dihedral on the right side of the cliff. Squeeze up an off-width crack to some hand jams to a pod. Above climb a shallow flared crack to the top.

3. **If the Shoe Fits** (5.9) Best line on the cliff. Jam excellent and continuous thin hand/hand crack to tree belay. 50'.

4. **Chocolate Donuts** (5.10) Next crack left of #3. Climb up through weird slot to ledge at obvious break. Hard off-width moves lead up crack to pod. Continue up off-width and wide fist crack to top. 70'.

5. **Roof Crack** (5.10+) Start behind a large holly bush. Climb a chimney past wedged chockstone, swing out on hand jams across big roof to a hand/fist/off-width crack above. 70'.

6. **Aton's Chimney** (5.10) A wild route! Climb a flared chimney—watch for loose blocks in the back—into a steep slot. Find pro in double cracks. Work past a chockstone at the roof lip, and finish up a squeeze chimney. Belay from trees. 80'.

7. **Jericho** (5.10-) Next crack left of *Aton's Chimney*. Locate obvious deep slot between 2 large roofs. Jam sandy thin hand crack (left-hand crack) for 25' to roof and rest pod. Overhanging hand jams lead to short off-width section below top. 80'.

8. **Off-Width Delight** (5.9+) Begin about 100' left of *Jericho*. Climb a sandy chimney to the break. Stem into off-width crack and arm bar to top. 80'.

9. **Sandbag** (5.9) Pretty fair route. The straightforward line ascends the large, leaning, left-facing dihedral. Climb broken rock to ledge. Lieback up sandy corner to top. A variation steps 5' left near top to thin right-facing corner. Belay from trees. 80'.

ZION
CARBUNCLE BUTTRESS

2 rope
rappel

.7

to gully

around
corner

.9

.7

fingers

14

.9

.8

12   13

10   11

CARBUNCLE BUTTRESS

This is a short, fat buttress directly behind the Zion Lodge. Locate a large buttress/pedestal. Down and to the right is the Carbuncle Buttress. Several 1-pitch routes ascend cracks up its face. Approach by parking at the lot across the road (west) from Zion Lodge at 3 miles and hiking east up brushy talus slopes to the cliff base. Allow for 20 minutes of approach hiking time. Routes are listed left to right.

10. **Just Another Jam** (5.8) A good warm-up route. The far left-hand crack on the face. Jam thinning hand crack to tree belay. Scramble off and downclimb the bushy gully to the north.

11. **Handy Route** (5.9) The obvious crack up the left-facing dihedral just right of Route 10.

12. **Deadend** (5.7) Jam and stem up the flared chimney-corner and exit up right with cool moves. Belay on the ledge. **Descent:** Rap off a tree with 2 165-foot ropes.

13. **Lizardosis** (5.9) A good finger crack with stemming up top.

14. **Carol's Crack** (5.7) A big crack up the slabby face to an arching left-facing corner. Bring big pro.

rap route

**ZION
THE SPEARHEAD**

15

THE SPEARHEAD

15. **Iron Messiah** (III 5.10) 10 pitches. First ascent by Ron Olevsky, 1988. First free ascent by Darren Cope and Jeff Rickerl, 1988. This excellent and classic free route ascends a prominent left-facing dihedral system up to the shoulder left of The Spearhead, a southern spur of Cathedral Mountain that towers over the Grotto Picnic Area. The route may be closed in spring for nesting raptors. The route gets lots of morning and midday sun, but shade in the later afternoon.

Approach the southeast-facing route from the parking area at the picnic area (3.3 miles from the bridge). The approach is not obvious. Begin by crossing the bridge over the Virgin River and turning left on the West Rim Trail along the river's west bank. Hike south on the trail to the second or third drainage that crosses the path and hike up either drainage to the base of the wall. Locate the route start by finding the long upper corner system and aiming for a line drawn down from it to the cliff base.

Begin by climbing a bushy 3rd Class groove/ramp that angles up right for about 150' to a ledge down and left of an obvious large roof arch. **Pitch 1:** Face climb short black wall (5.9) with 5 bolts right of right-facing dihedral. Belay on bushy ledge. **Pitch 2:** Continue up large right-facing corner (5.8) to groove (5.7) that leads up left to good belay on bushy ledge below prominent dihedral. **Pitch 3:** The crux lead. Climb thin crack (5.10c) into large, black, left-facing dihedral. Continue (5.7) to 2-bolt belay stance on left wall where dark rock below meets a band of white sandstone. Avoid a strange 3-pitch aid variation done on the first ascent that climbs corners up left and pendulums back right to dihedral. **Pitch 4:** Jam and stem long, beautiful dihedral (5.9) to 2-bolt belay in shallow hollow to left and below thin arch. **Pitch 5:** Climb chimney in dihedral (5.8/9) to 2-bolt belay atop a pedestal out to right. **Pitch 6:** Continue up chimney (5.8) into band of white rock. Belay up left on large bushy, white ledge with 2 bolts. **Pitch 7:** Climb short pitch up a large, black, left-facing dihedral (5.8) to bolt belay on small stance to left. **Pitch 8:** Continue up black corner (5.10b) to 2-bolt belay on bushy ledge. **Pitch 9:** Work right up groove (5.7) to sandy crack (5.10-) to belay by large pine tree. **Pitch 10:** Face climb up left (5.4 X) on unprotected slab to ridge left of summit. Scramble up right to summit. **Descent:** Rappel the route with 2 ropes. Look for 1 set of anchors out left partway down the dihedral. **Rack:** 2 to 3 sets of Friends, TCUs, and stoppers, with an optional #5 Camalot; runners; 2 ropes.

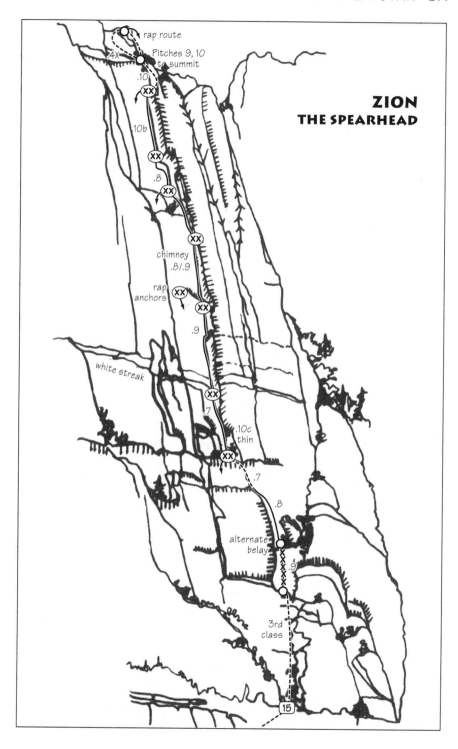

rap route

Pitches 9, 10
to summit

.10

XX

.10b

XX

.8

XX

XX

chimney
.8/.9

rap
anchors   XX

XX

.9

white streak

XX

.7

.10c
thin

XX

.7

.8

alternate
belay

.9

3rd
class

15

**ZION
THE SPEARHEAD**

RED ARCH MOUNTAIN

16. **Shune's Buttress** (IV 5.11c) 6-8 pitches. First ascent by Steve Chardon and Dave Jones, 1980. Route done all free by Conrad Anker and Dave Jones, 1992 (Anker freed the aid sections as a second), while Chip Chace did the first all-free ascent. This excellent route ascends Shune's Buttress, the northeast buttress on the north face of Red Arch Mountain. The route is left of the huge arch and right of an obvious gully between Red Arch Mountain and Great White Throne. The line climbs the left side of an obvious pillar to a steep crack system between a blunt arête/prow on the right and a steep headwall to the left. The route is very hard to see from the road. Some of the pitches can be shortened from the following description.

Park at the Grotto Picnic Area at 3.3 miles and hike southeast from the parking area to an inconspicuous path that ascends brushy slopes to the base of the buttress left of the huge arch. Allow about 30 minutes of approach hiking. **Pitch 1:** Jam an awesome right-facing corner (5.11). Don't be led astray by extra bolts out left. Belay on ledge. An alternative start variation jams a crack in an arête (5.11-) to the right. **Pitch 2:** Move up right and do face moves into crack (5.10b) to ledge with tree. Step left into chimney with bolt. Above lieback (5.10) left-facing corner to 2-bolt belay/rappel station. This lead can be broken into 2 shorter pitches. **Pitch 3:** Continue up corner (5.9 fists) into chimney and belay from 2-bolts on back side of prominent pillar. **Pitch 4:** Face climb out left (5.11a) past several bolts and move straight up past a couple of corners to 2-bolt belay ledge. **Pitch 5:** Work left around arête and into 1"-crack. Jam over roof (5.11) and follow strenuous, widening crack (5.10+) to belay with bolt. **Pitch 6:** Good jamming (5.9) leads up left past possible cave belay to face and crack (5.8) and the top of the route. Another 700' of scrambling leads to the summit of Red Arch Mountain. **Descent:** Rappel the route in 5 rappels. The first 2 rappels descend the face right of the arête and route to the notch behind the pillar. Make 3 more rappels down the route to the ground. **Rack:** Bring a couple of sets of Friends, with extra hand-sized pieces, sets of TCUs and stoppers, extra runners, and 2 ropes.

GREAT WHITE THRONE BASE

The Great White Throne, one of Zion's tallest cliffs, is an immense 2,500-foot-high wall that looms over the scenic drive and the upper canyon. The wall, one of Zion's chief landmarks, is a masterpiece of erosion. Some long routes have gone up on the Throne's north face, some over 25 pitches long. The wall, the first of Zion's big walls to be climbed, was first ascended by Fred Beckey, Galen Rowell, and Pat Callis in 1967. The upper face of white sandstone is reputedly of very poor quality, similar in texture and hardness to dry

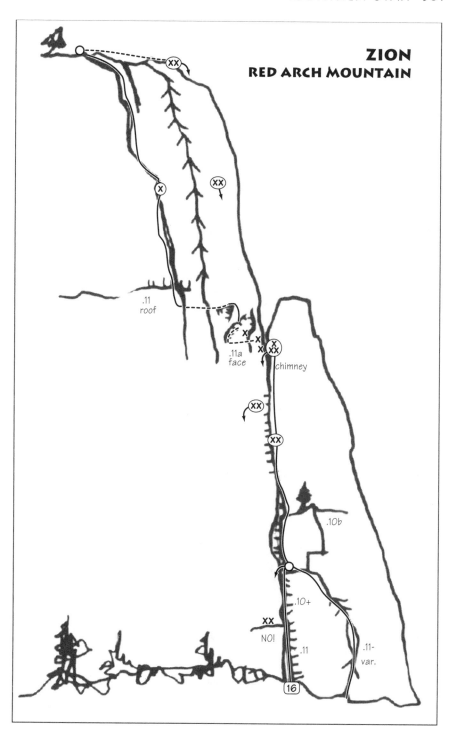

ZION
RED ARCH MOUNTAIN

.11
roof

.11a
face

chimney

.10b

.10+

xx
NO!

.11

.11-
var.

16

ZION
UPPER CANYON

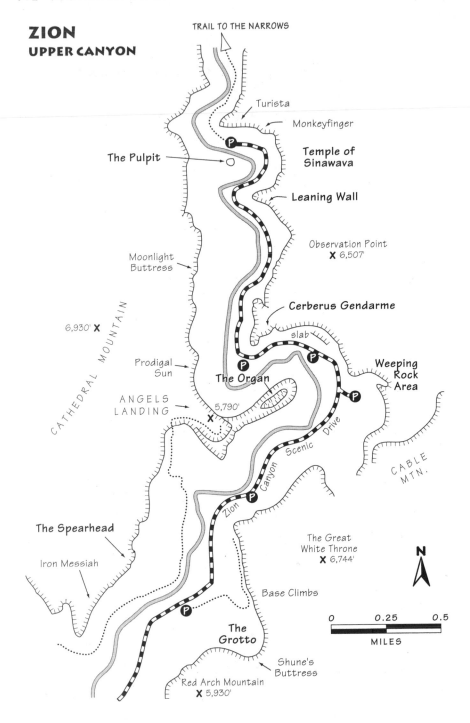

TRAIL TO THE NARROWS

Turista

Monkeyfinger

Temple of Sinawava

The Pulpit

Leaning Wall

Observation Point
X 6,507'

Moonlight Buttress

Cerberus Gendarme

slab

6,930' X

CATHEDRAL MOUNTAIN

Prodigal Sun

The Organ

Weeping Rock Area

ANGELS LANDING

5,790'
X

Zion Canyon Scenic Drive

CABLE MTN.

The Spearhead

Iron Messiah

The Great White Throne
X 6,744'

N

Base Climbs

0   0.25   0.5

MILES

The Grotto

Shune's Buttress

Red Arch Mountain
X 5,930'

brown sugar. Hence the wall sees little climbing action.

A selection of one- and two-pitch free climbs, however, ascends the base of the Throne on its north and west flanks, offering climbers a good afternoon pump. Many of the routes were put up by Jim Beyer and Bob Sullivan in the late 1970s. The west face lines above the Grotto Picnic Area were put up in 1994 by Dave Jones and company. All the routes jam or lieback up cracks to ledges. Descents are tricky as some of the routes do not have anchors. Look instead for slings around sturdy trees for rappel and belay anchors. Routes are listed right to left beginning on the west flank and moving around to the wall's north side. The Great White Throne is often closed in spring and early summer for raptor nesting. Check at the visitor center for closures.

The first 4 routes are located on the southwest flank of the Great White Throne, above the Grotto Picnic Area. Drive to the picnic area (3.3 miles from the bridge) and park. Walk east on an old road past a stone house and angle up past bushes to the cliff base. Allow about 15 minutes to approach. The routes lie above several large boulders and are listed right to left.

17. **Edge of Delight** (5.10) 2 pitches. This route ascends a beautiful left-facing flake corner. **Pitch 1:** Begin just right of obvious, thin, left-facing corner. Lieback and undercling (5.10) past small roof to belay from gear. **Pitch 2:** Lieback up gorgeous flake (5.8) to 2-bolt belay/rap anchor. **Descent:** Rappel 150' to the ground. **Rack:** Bring 3 each Friends from #2 to #3.5 and 3 #4 Camalots.

18. **Scotch on the Rocks** (5.8) Begin above house-sized boulder with lightning bolt crack on its left side and left of obvious right-facing corner. Climb broken cracks with bushes to 2-bolt belay stance. **Descent:** Rappel 120'.

**ZION
BASE OF GWT**

Rack: Bring a set of Friends with extra #3 to #4.

19. **Fourplay** (5.11) 2 pitches. Start north of the large boulder and right of a left-angling ramp. **Pitch 1:** Climb beautiful right-facing corner for 80' to 2-bolt belay on varnished rock. **Pitch 2:** Sustained liebacking and jamming (5.11) up great sandstone past roof and through wide section to 2-bolt belay on left. 130'. **Descent:** 2 rappels to the ground. **Rack:** Medium and large Friends.

20. **One for the Road** (5.10-) Jam and lieback up an open book to anchors. 80'. **Descent:** Rappel the route. **Rack:** TCUs and Friends, including 2 each #1 to #2.5.

The following routes are on the northwest corner of the Throne. Access them by driving north from the Grotto Picnic Area for 0.4 mile (3.7 from the bridge) and park in a large pull-out on the west side of the road. A short trail climbs through scrub to the cliff base. The routes are listed right to left. The first ones are right of a huge blocky roof.

21. **Rookie Crack** a.k.a. **Deception** (5.9) Begin about 150' right of large roof below obvious beautiful open corner. Climb flared crack to open corner. Lieback thin hand crack and find gear and tree anchors on bushy ledge above. **Descent:** Scramble left 20' to *Grasshopper's* 2-bolt rappel anchor and rap 80' to the ground. **Rack:** Lots of thin stuff—TCUs and wires— and some small to medium Friends.

22. **Grasshopper** (5.9+) Climb hand and fist crack up gorgeous right-facing dihedral to 2-bolt belay/rappel anchor on bushy ledge. 80'. **Descent:** Rappel 80' to ground.

23. **Psychobolt** (5.10) Start just left of *Grasshopper*. Scramble onto broken ledge with junipers about 70' right of huge roof. Jam flared crack in right-facing corner to chockstone thread in wide section. Stem left onto ledge and continue up thin finger crack to ledge to poor bolt. Belay on wide ledge above. **Descent:** Scramble right a few feet to Route 22's anchors.

24. **Illusion** (5.9) Find 2 cracks that split a vertical wall left of huge roof. Jam right-hand, thin hand crack past slot and stacked blocks. Keep left at top to terrace. Watch for loose stuff up high. Find a convenient tree from which to belay and rap.

25. **Twin Crack** (5.9) Climb left-hand crack to mid-height crux with double cracks. Continue to terrace ledge above. Belay and rap off a tree.

The next 2 routes are around the corner of the Throne buttress to the left. Both face north and are easily seen from a pullout at 3.8 miles from the bridge. Access them from the climber trail that begins at the 3.7-mile pullout.

26. **Nemesis** (5.11-) This route, ascended by Jim Beyer and Bob Sullivan in 1979, is Zion's first recorded 5.11. Despite this claim to fame, it's seldom climbed. Locate an obvious off-width crack over 4-foot roof. Thrash up 6-inch crack over roof (5.11) and continue up off-width crack (5.10) to tree anchors; 50'. **Descent:** Rappel from slings around the anchor juniper. **Rack:** Lots of big stuff for a 6-inch crack.

27. **Crack of REM** (5.10) For sleepwalkers only. Jam a hand crack over a 4-foot roof (5.10) and continue up large right-facing corner to the same tree belay as *Nemesis*. 40'. **Descent:** Rap from slings around the tree.

The following 3 routes ascend the base of the Great White Throne's immense north wall. Park at a pullout on the right (south) side of the road 3.9 miles from the bridge and hike up a short climber's path to the cliff base.

28. **Box Elder Jam** (5.8+) Good and popular. Climb blocky rock to crack with several pods, pass large box elder tree at roof and jam a great left-facing corner (fist and hand—5.8+) to 2-bolt rap anchor. 65'.

29. **Free Bird** a.k.a. **Merced Red** (5.9) Begin 10' left of Route 29. Face climb through loose blocky roofs to a thin finger crack (5.9). Can belay off gear here. Face moves lead up left along seam to roof and flared corner. Jam finger and thin hand crack up left (5.9 and licheny) to ledge. Locate anchors and rappel to ground with 2 ropes.

30. **Rain** (5.9+) Quality sustained line. Climb a blocky left-facing corner (5.8+) to a box elder tree on a slab. Pull over roof in flared finger/hand crack and continue up steep fingers and hands (5.9+) to ledge with boulder. Locate anchors and rappel off with 2 ropes.

ZION
BASE OF GWT

THE ORGAN

The Organ, lined with vertical crack systems resembling organ pipes, is a massive 400-foot-high fin that juts east from Angels Landing above a bow-knot bend of the Virgin River. Many of the crack systems—mostly chimneys and off-width cracks on the south side—were climbed in the late 1970s by Jim Beyer and others. The 2 best routes on the formation, however, lie on the prow that faces Weeping Rock and the north wall that faces Cerberus Gendarme. Check at the visitor center in spring and summer for possible raptor nesting closures on The Organ. Park for these routes at a pullout on the left (south) side of the road 4.7 miles from the bridge. Follow a short trail down to the canyon floor, cross the river, and scramble up short, bushy talus slopes to base of the routes.

31. **Organasm** (III 5.8 C2) 4 pitches. First ascent by Ron Olevsky and Mike Strassman, 1983. This is a very good clean aid route and a warm-up for the big walls. Also a good warm weather route with lots of shade. It's located on the Northeast Buttress of The Organ. **Pitch 1:** Climb crack (5.8) up left side of pillar for 25' to bolt, continue up the open book to hanging belay on right from 2 fixed anchors. 2 rap anchors farther right. **Pitch 2:** Aid or free up hand-size crack to huge roof, climb roof (5.11d or C1) and belay 20' above roof at a 2-bolt belay with rap chains in flared left-facing corner. This is an exposed spot above the roof! Rappel 145' to the ground or continue up. **Pitch 3:** Aid clean crack (C2) in flared corner to big ledge. **Pitch 4:** Climb short right-facing corner (5.7) to ledges. **Descent:** Rappel from top of pitch 2 or walk off right across ledges and downclimb brushy 3rd class cliffs on north side. **Rack:** A couple of sets of Friends with extras from #2 to #3, set of stoppers and TCUs. Leave your hammer behind!

32. **Organ Grinder** (II 5.9+) 2 pitches. First ascent by Bill Westbay, Larry Derby, and Mike Weiss, 1975. This route is located on the left side of the north face of The Organ. The line ascends a crack system to a bushy terrace halfway up the face. Park at the Angels Landing viewpoint parking area, wade across the river and scramble up to the base of the wall. **Pitch 1:** Use variety of techniques to stem, jam, and chimney up crack (5.9+) to belay on ledge to left. **Pitch 2:** Continue jamming crack (5.9+) to terrace. **Descent:** Work left across ledge system and then down broken and bushy rock to base. **Rack:** Bring a rack of Friends, mostly large sizes, as well as some big crack pro.

ZION
THE ORGAN

to walkoff descent

.9+

.9+

32

ZION
CERBERUS GENDARME

to rap gully

33   33   46

CERBERUS GENDARME

33. Touchstone Wall (III 5.11 C1 or 5.9 C2) 8 pitches (Begin 100' right of Route 45 **Flip the Coin**). First ascent by Ron Olevsky, 1977. An excellent Zion classic. Leave your hammer behind, this one is all clean. The route ascends the Cerberus Gendarme, a south-facing buttress that looms over the road between the Weeping Rock and Angels Landing parking areas. The route lies opposite *Organ Grinder*. Park at the Angels Landing lot (5.0 miles from the bridge) or at the Photo Point parking area (4.7 miles from the bridge) to the east. Either way, walk along the road and locate a short path to the route base. Find the start by locating a long bolt ladder next to a large juniper tree. **Pitch 1:** 2 ways to go: (1) Do a 14-bolt ladder to C1 crack to 3-bolt chained belay stance. (2) Begin to the right in juniper tree and aid mostly fixed C1 crack over roof to mantle (5.6) onto ledge. **Pitch 2:** Outstanding airy pitch! Climb crack with some fixed pro to roof with fixed rurp (C2). Continue up thin crack above (C1, many stoppers) to 2-bolt hanging belay below small roof. Ignore anchors out right. **Pitch 3:** Jam finger crack (5.11- or C1) to superb splitter (5.10). Belay out left from 2 bolts. **Pitch 4:** Continue up thin hand

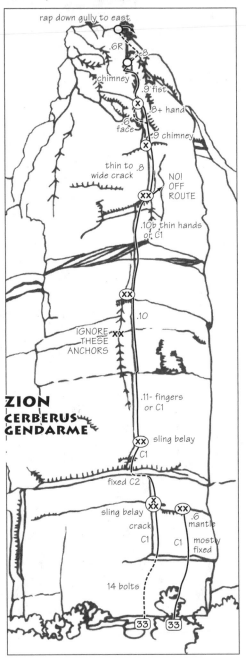

rap down gully to east

.6R
.8
chimney
.9 fist
X
.8+ hand
.6
face
.9 chimney
X

thin to .8
wide crack
NO!
OFF
ROUTE
XX

.10b thin hands
or C1

XX

.10

IGNORE
THESE XX
ANCHORS

**ZION
CERBERUS
GENDARME**

.11- fingers
or C1

XX sling belay
C1

fixed C2

sling belay
crack
C1

X
XX
XX
.6
mantle
C1
mostly
fixed

14 bolts

33   33

crack (5.10b) to pedestal 2-bolt belay ledge. **Pitch 5:** Work up thin crack to wide crack (5.8). Belay on ledge with 1 bolt. Keep in left-hand crack at start of pitch. **Pitch 6:** Move up chimney (5.9) to hand crack in left-facing corner (5.8+) or traverse left at top of chimney and finish up right-facing corner (5.6). Belay on ledge from bolt. **Pitch 7:** Climb up right to fist crack (5.9) in left-facing corner, continue up right to chimney and belay on ledge with tree. **Pitch 8:** Move right on ledge and face climb (5.8) up left past 7 bolts to runout face (5.6 R) to top. **Descent:** Descend north into a notch just right of Cerberus Gendarme's summit. Make several 2-rope rappels down a steep gully to the base of the wall. **Rack:** Bring double sets of Friends, TCUs, and stoppers; free carabiners (40 or so); 2 ropes. Leave your hammer in the car.

CERBERUS GENDARME BASE

The canyon's best selection of 1-pitch free climbs ascends the base of the Cerberus Gendarme, a towering buttress that sits north of the scenic road between the Weeping Rock and Angels Landing parking areas. Drive 5.0 miles from the bridge turnoff to the Angels Landing turnout (it's necessary to drive to the road's end and double back to park here), park and walk east alongside the road about 150' to a couple boulders next to the road. A climber's trail begins here and works up talus to the cliff base. Partway up it divides. The left branch goes to the left-side routes, while the right branch leads to the *Cherry Crack* area. Routes are listed left to right from the parking area.

34. **Cave Route** (5.7) One of the first short climbs established in the canyon; done by Jim Dunn, 1973. This fun route ascends the obvious right-facing corner on left side of cliff. Climb off-width to hand and fist crack to cave. Belay from a bolt. A #4 Camalot is useful on the first section. **Descent:** Walk off through the cave.

35. **No Holds Barred** (5.8) 40' right of Route 34. Climb the right-hand crack in shallow slot to ledge with bolt. Continue up loose chimney above to belay ledge. Walk-off.

36. **Squeeze Play** (5.10a) 60' right of Route 35. Jam thin hand crack 20' into left-facing corner. Lieback and jam up double cracks to 2-bolt anchor on ledge. 85'.

37. **The Fat'hedral** (5.10d) 150' right of Route 36. A good line up large right-facing dihedral. Climb a finger-hand crack (couple off-width sections) up dihedral to 2-bolt chain anchor under large roof. 85'.

38. **Fails of Power** (5.11b/c) 25' right of Route 37. Ascends a right-facing corner. Lieback and jam finger and thin hand crack up and over striped bulge to 2-bolt chain anchor; 70'. If you're tough, continue another 30' up the thinning crack (5.11+) over a roof to a 2-bolt anchor.

39. **Scarlet Begonias** (5.11a) 10' right of Route 38. Lieback up clean, right-facing flake-corner to 2-bolt chain anchor. 65'.

40. **Tails of Flails** (5.9) 20' right of Route 39. Jam thin hand and finger crack up tight, black dihedral. Where it widens work up left in flake crack past 3 bolts to 2-bolt anchor on lip of small roof. 130'.

41. **Electrica** (5.11c/d) 20' right of Route 40. An excellent bolted sport route. Steep face climbing edges up bullet-proof sandstone past 9 bolts to 2-bolt rap/belay anchor on ledge. 120'. First ascent by Drew Bedford and Conrad Anker.

42. **Dire Wolf** (5.12a A0) 5' right of Route 41. Lieback and stem up a steep open book with thin crack to loose ledge with 2-bolt anchor.

43. **Cherry Crack** (5.9 or 5.10c) 20' right of Route 42. Sometimes it's called *Watt's Crack* because an anti-Watt billboard was hung from the anchors before James Watt's (former Secretary of the Interior) Zion visit in the early1980s. Begin behind obvious oak tree. Jam splitter crack (thin hands, hands, fist, and some off-width pods) up vertical wall to 2-bolt belay anchor on small broken stance; 140'. If you don't want to do the full pitch, opt for the weenie-way—jam the thin hands crack (5.9) for 35' and step left to a ledge with a 2-bolt chain anchor.

44. **Intruder** (5.11c) 100' right of Route 43. A Randy Leavitt line. Jam clean finger crack up tan wall to 2-bolt anchor below a wide pod. 65'.

ZION
CERBERUS BASE

slings
XX
130'

slings
XX

behind
boulder

140'
XX

XX

85'
XX

XX
chains

chains
XX
65'

9
bolts

rap
XX

37
38
39
40
41
42
43

ZION
CERBERUS BASE

XX
80'

XX
65'

44
45

45. **Flip of the Coin** (5.10d) 80' right of Route 44. Thrutch up tight left-facing corner with finger and hand crack in its back to bolt below large roof. Move up right around airy corner to 2-bolt belay anchor. 80'. Watch for rope drag at the top.

46. **Coconut Corner** (5.10 or III 5.11a) 1 to 4 pitches. 20' right of *Touchstone's* right-hand start and just left of obvious gully. This old route works up an off-width and squeeze chimney crack in a large right-facing dihedral on the right side of Cerberus Gendarme. The first pitch is usually climbed unless you're an off-width masochist. **Pitch 1:** Climb chimney and off-width over bulge, pass bolt, and continue up flared off-width/fist crack to 3-bolt belay; 80'. If you haven't had enough, continue up for 3 more pitches to an obvious stance where the dihedral becomes a gully. Rap the route.

47. **Face-tastic** (5.11) No topo. This slab route is to the east or right of the Cerberus base. Park at the Photo Point turnout (4.7 miles) on the south side of the road. The route is 100' to the east and ascends a white slab between 2 obvious arching caves. Begin just left of a small juniper tree and smear up past 9 bolts to a 2-bolt belay and rap anchor; 100'. Two 5.11 cruxes are encountered: first one is between bolts 3 and 4, and second is between bolts 7 and 8.

48. **Cynthia's Handjob** (5.9) No topo. This excellent route is on the northwest face of Cerberus Gendarme. Park at the Angels Landing lot and walk up the road (north). Look for a beautiful, dark, right-facing corner about 100' left of a huge flake. Jam fingers and thin hands crack to 2-bolt belay/rappel anchor on right wall.

ANGELS LANDING

Angels Landing is a huge buttress looming above the west side of the canyon. The Virgin River makes an immense loop around the formation and the neighboring Organ. Most of the climbing here has focused on Angels Landing's 1,400-foot northeast face. The face offers 9 big-wall routes, including the all-free *Northeast Buttress* on its far left side as well as some hard nailing lines. The only all-clean aid route is *Prodigal Sun*. It's a good idea to scope the routes out from the parking lot below with binoculars. Park at the Angels Landing viewpoint parking area at 5.0 miles from the bridge. The short hiking approach crosses the river from the parking area and scrambles up to the cliff base. The descent, unlike most Zion walls, is an easy walk down the paved 2.5-mile Angels Landing/West Rim Trail. Angels Landing is often closed in spring and summer because of raptor nesting. Check at the visitor center for possible closure areas.

49. **Northeast Buttress** (IV 5.11a) 9 pitches plus 200' of 3rd class to top. First ascent by Randy Aton, Mark Austin, and Phil Haney, 1981. First all-free

ZION
ANGELS LANDING

to trail

one pitch to ridge
from south side → 49

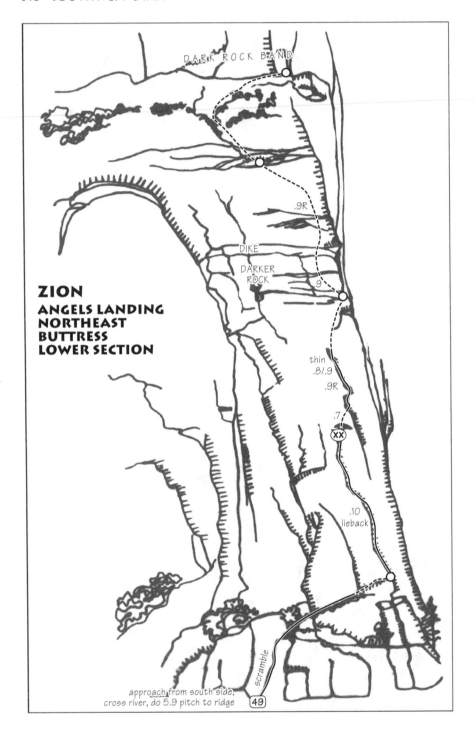

DARK ROCK BAND

.9R

DIKE

DARKER
ROCK

.9

ZION
ANGELS LANDING
NORTHEAST
BUTTRESS
LOWER SECTION

thin
.8/.9
.9R

.7

XX

.10
lieback

scramble

approach from south side,
cross river, do 5.9 pitch to ridge
49

ZION
ANGELS LANDING
NORTHEAST BUTTRESS
TOP SECTION

Angels Landing summit

walk off ➡

3rd class scramble to summit

.6

.8

hands
.8

.8

LIGHT ROCK

DARK ROCK

thin
.11a

.9 roof

DARK BAND OF ROCK

pitch 4

ascent was by Conrad Anker et al, 1991. This excellent free route ascends the obvious blunt arête/prow that separates the northeast and south faces of Angels Landing. Approach the route by climbing a pitch up a wide crack (5.9) on the south side of the ridge between Angels Landing and The Organ. Scramble 300' along the ridge to the base of the arête and solo 3rd class rock 40' to a ledge atop a pillar where the actual route begins.

Pitch 1: Follow left-facing corner system—chimney to lieback flake (5.10+) to 2-bolt belay stance below shallow arch; 100'. **Pitch 2:** Face climb right on loose flakes (5.7) to lieback (5.9 R) up thin, left-facing corner that is hard to protect. Continue up thin flake (5.8/9) to some face climbing and belay stance after 130'. Belay here if you don't have a 200-foot (60-meter) rope. Continue up right to belay stance at 185'. **Pitch 3:** Move left and up mossy slab/groove (5.9), cross onto thick band of white rock and face climb just left of arête (5.9 R) that separates buttress from northeast face. Move left to belay ledge; 160'. **Pitch 4:** Short, moderate pitch wanders up left and back right to ledge at obvious break where white rock meets major dark band; 80'. **Pitch 5:** The crux lead. Climb over small roof (5.9) and work into steep, thin, right-facing dihedral with bolt (5.11a). Exit left at top and traverse around arête (5.8) left of mossy corner and belay on broken ledge; 140'. **Pitch 6:** Angle up left on jugs to hand crack in right-facing corner (5.8), step left into another crack in left-facing corner (5.8) and belay above on small ledge; 120'. **Pitch 7:** Climb up right-facing corner (5.6) to groove with bushes and looseness. Belay where comfortable or continue to bushes below large pine if you have a 200-foot rope; 175'. From here climb 200' of 3rd class rock up a bushy open book to the summit. **Descent:** Walk down the Angels Landing Trail. The lower part is paved. **Rack:** A couple of sets of Friends, a couple wide pieces, set of TCUs, set of stoppers, runners. A 200-foot (60-meter) rope is useful.

50. **Prodigal Sun** (IV 5.5 or 5.8 C2) 9 pitches. First ascent was solo by Ron Olevsky, 1981. Excellent steep route for the first-time big wall climber, with good gear, minimum difficulty, and generally fast climbing. A fast party can do it in a day, otherwise fix the first few pitches. A 200-foot rope and extra gear and biners allow some of the pitches to run together. The route is all-clean and is done hammerless. Do not carry a hammer— it's not needed! A bomber aid placement or fixed piece is located every 6', and the C2 placements are found only on pitches 4, 5, and 7. The first 5 pitches, freed by Alan Lester in 1997, make an excellent 5.12 free climb. The route, a brilliant piece of route-finding by the first ascensionist, follows a series of incipient cracks linked by bolt ladders up the wall's right side.

Approach from the Angels Landing viewpoint parking area by crossing the river and scrambling up slopes right of the route to avoid a cliffband. Hike south to the base of the route. **Pitch 1:** Use a Black Diamond hook

walk off

ZION
ANGELS LANDING

50

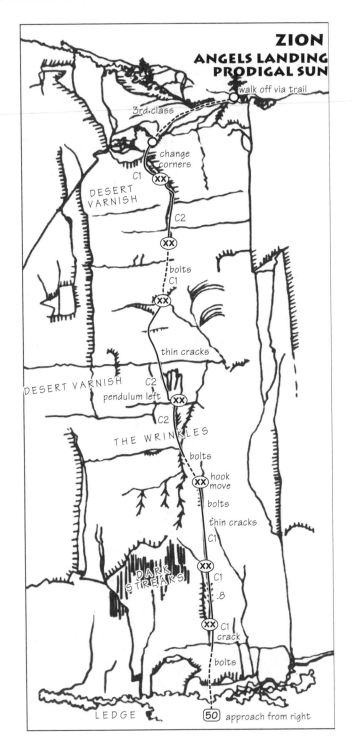

ZION
ANGELS LANDING
PRODIGAL SUN

walk off via trail

3rd class

change corners

C1

DESERT VARNISH

C2

bolts
C1

thin cracks

DESERT VARNISH

C2
pendulum left

C2

THE WRINKLES

bolts

hook move

bolts

thin cracks

C1

DARK STREAKS

C1
.8

C1
crack

bolts

50 approach from right

LEDGE

on a cheater stick to clip first bolt over roof and follow bolt ladder to C1 crack. Belay on left from 2 bolts where crack widens. **Pitch 2:** Free climb (5.8) up right-facing open book to C1 aid to 2-bolt belay. **Pitch 3:** Aid thin cracks (C1) to bolt ladder in right-facing corner. Belay from 2 bolts. **Pitch 4:** A hook move leads to left-angling bolt ladder. Above follow thin cracks in shallow corners (C2) through The Wrinkles to bolted belay. **Pitch 5:** Do short pendulum left into corner and aid up thin airy cracks (C2) to bolt ladder and 2-bolt belay. **Pitch 6:** Aid (C1) up the Arch Crack to short bolt ladder that leads right to 2-bolt belay below arching crack right of gray slab. **Pitch 7:** Aid (C2) up arching corner past some bolts to 2-bolt belay. **Pitch 8:** Continue aiding (C1) via placements and bolts up arch, changing corners with a short leftward pendulum. Aid to large ledge with 2 bolts. Use runners on some of the bolts on this pitch to alleviate rope drag. **Pitch 9:** Climb the 3rd class ramp up right in 1 or 2 pitches to north ridge of Angels Landing. Be careful not to dislodge rocks onto anyone below. **Descent:** Walk off via Angels Landing Trail. **Rack:** 1 set of Friends, set of TCUs, many small stoppers and RPs (smallest placement is #3 RP), Tricams #1 to #6, several small wires with sliding nuts for use on hangerless bolts, a hook, some keyhole bolt hangers, at least 50 free carabiners. Leave your hammer behind.

MOONLIGHT BUTTRESS AREA

The Moonlight Buttress is a jutting prow on the west side of the canyon just north of the long sweep of Angels Landing's northeast wall. The famed *Moonlight Buttress* route, a stunning free climb up sheer corners, ascends the prow itself. To the left are a couple of good aid routes—*Lunar Ecstasy* (V 5.10 A3+) and *Sheer Lunacy* (V 5.9 C2). The 9-pitch *Lunar Ecstasy* works up the obvious crack system just left of *Moonlight Buttress*. This good line is not included in this guide because it requires nailing. *Sheer Lunacy* ascends the wall left of *Lunar Ecstasy*.

51. **Moonlight Buttress** (IV 5.13a or 5.9 C1) 10 to 12 pitches. First ascent by Jeff Lowe and Mike Weiss, 1971. First free ascent by Johnny Woodward and Peter Croft, 1992. This is Zion's classic free route. It's a stunning line with high exposure and position, hard jamming and liebacking, an easy approach and paved descent trail. The first 4 pitches, however, detract from the overall quality.

Moonlight Buttress ascends the prominent buttress on the west side of the canyon, across from the Temple of Sinawava. Begin from the road by crossing the river and scrambling to the cliff base. The route starts left of the buttress below a right-angling ramp and crack system. The first 4 pitches work up right to the Rocker Block at the base of the buttress itself. Crux here is a bolt-protected traverse (5.11c) to the right that avoids a C1

ZION
MOONLIGHT BUTTRESS

walk off

51

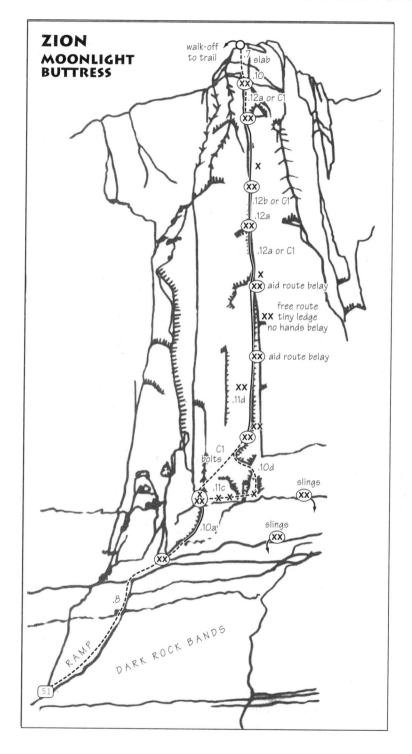

ZION
MOONLIGHT
BUTTRESS

walk-off
to trail
.7 slab
.10
.12a or C1
X
.12b or C1
.12a
.12a or C1
X
aid route belay
free route
XX tiny ledge
no hands belay
aid route belay
XX
.11d
XX
C1
bolts
.10d
.11c slings
.10a slings
XX
.8
RAMP
DARK ROCK BANDS
51

bolt ladder. Pitches 5 and 6 have 2-bolt hanging belay anchors for aid ascents. All the belays except for the top of pitch 1 have at least a 1-bolt anchor. Crux climbing is a thin crack in a corner on pitch 6. The 5.13a rating is for the on-sight; 5.12d if worked. The pitches above all have 5.12 sections. Watch for rope drag on the slab (5.7) on the last pitch. Best bivy ledge is atop pitch 7. **Descent:** Walk down the paved Angels Landing/West Rim Trail. **Rack:** A couple of sets of Friends, lots of TCUs, wired stoppers, runners. More if aid climbing. A 200-foot (60-meter) rope is useful. This route goes hammerless.

LEANING WALL

The Leaning Wall is on the east side of the canyon 0.6 mile up-canyon (toward the road's end) from the Angels Landing parking area. Park at a pull-out on the west side of the road below the wall 5.6 miles from the bridge turnoff. *Space Shot* ascends the outside edge of a huge incut arch. Farther left are 3 other good lines: *Cosmic Trauma* (V 5.10 A3+), *Moon Patrol* (V5.10 A2), and *Equinox* (IV 5.10+), which lies on the left side of the buttress. A couple of good short routes are on the face below *Space Shot*.

52. **The Alpine Start** (5.9) 1 pitch. A short lieback route up right side of small obvious pillar above parking area. Descend from 2-bolt chain anchor. 45'.

53. **Karmic Edges** (5.12b) 1 pitch. Scramble up the brushy 5.5 first pitch of *Space Shot* to the base of a steep buttress face. Face climb up past 5 bolts (5.12b) to crack (#2 Friend). Exit the crack (5.12a) and climb up right past 3 more bolts (5.11+) to thin crack. Continue (5.10) to a 2-bolt stance. **Descent:** Rap route with 2 ropes.

54. **Space Shot** (IV 5.10 C2) 8 pitches. First ascent by Ron Olevsky and Dave Jones, 1978. Much of the route was freed by Alan Lester in 1997. This is a spectacular, exposed, and classic aid route up the left outside edge of an immense arch that looms over the drive. Competent parties can easily do it in a day. The descent is also fairly easy by Zion standards. This is an all-clean, hammerless route. Do not bring a hammer or attempt to nail any of the route with pitons. Otherwise your head needs to be hammered on! In April, 1997 someone wielded a hammer and destroyed clean placements on the first and second pitches. Park at 5.6 miles and scramble up talus slopes to the base of the wall. **Pitch 1:** Angle up left (5.5) on brushy terrain to ledge. **Pitch 2:** Climb right-angling crack system (5.6) to another ledge. **Pitch 3:** Move out right on easy but bushy terrain (5.4). Watch for loose rock, sandy ledges, and a fixed pin. Move back left and belay on ledge below bolt ladder on the headwall and the finger-like Reboze Pinnacle. **Pitch 4:** Aid up long bolt ladder to easy aid crack (C1) and 2-bolt belay. **Pitch 5:** Climb crack (C1) to short bolt ladder to another crack (C2) and 2-bolt hanging belay. Above the bolts retreat is almost impossible. **Pitch**

ZION
LEANING WALL

to rappels

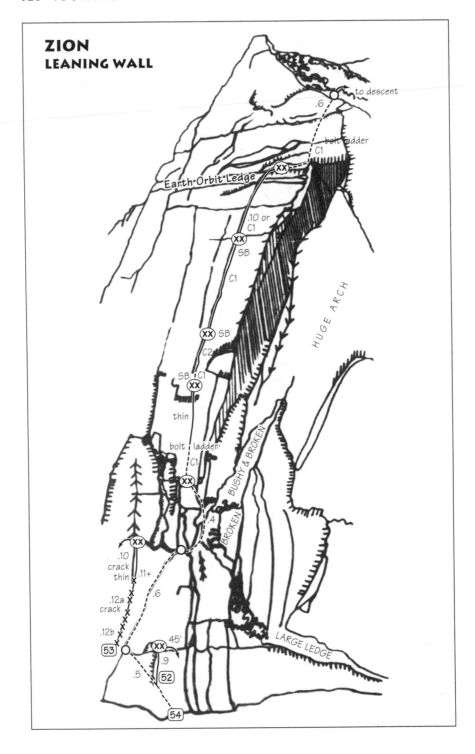

ZION
LEANING WALL

to descent

.6

bolt ladder

C1

XX

Earth Orbit Ledge

.10 or
C1

XX
SB

C1

HUGE ARCH

XX SB

C2

SB   C1

XX

thin

bolt ladder

C1

XX

.4

BUSHY & BROKEN

BROKEN

XX

.10
crack
thin   .11+

.6

.12a
crack

.12b

53

45'

XX

.9

.5   52

LARGE LEDGE

54

6: Follow widening crack (C1) to 2-bolt hanging belay. **Pitch 7:** Continue up steep, exposed crack (5.10 or C1) to 2-bolt belay on spacious Earth Orbit Ledge. **Pitch 8:** Walk to right side of ledge and aid up bolt ladder to free climbing (5.6) and route summit. **Descent:** Hike east to obvious drainage and rappel off a large tree. Below, scramble about 80' down slabs and sandy ledge to bolted rap anchor. Make several rappels off good gear and ledges to the ground and walk 5 minutes to the road. **Rack:** 2 sets of Friends, with extras from #2 to #3 (if aiding pitch 7 bring extra #3 to #4 Friends; 2 sets of stoppers; a set of TCUs; at least 50 free carabiners; and 2 ropes. No hammers or pitons.

TEMPLE OF SINAWAVA

The Temple of Sinawava, lying at the end of the scenic drive (6 miles from the bridge), is where the Navajo sandstone reaches its greatest thickness—2,400 feet. This area, the gateway to The Narrows of the Virgin River, is very popular with steering wheel recreationists. The Narrows, up-river from the parking area, is a spectacular slot canyon that is as narrow as 20 feet with sandstone walls that soar overhead and leave the sky as a thin blue slit. Waterfalls as tall as 1,000 feet pour off the Temple's cliffs after summer thunderstorms. There are several good routes in the Temple, including the superlative *Monkeyfinger*. A popular 1-pitch line is *Turista*. Pulpit Rock, a small pinnacle along the river, sees occasional action on its runout free route; it has a good, clean aid line (5.5 C2) up a thin overhanging crack on its parking lot side.

Reach the Temple of Sinawava by driving up the scenic drive to its very end and finding a parking space—the first crux of any climb here. Parking is a serious problem at the Temple, especially on weekends or in the summer. Come early to get a parking spot, otherwise plan on parking down-canyon and walking the road. Since *Monkeyfinger* gets a lot of morning shade, it's a good warmer weather route. Plan on starting early to avoid the mid-afternoon heat.

55. **Monkeyfinger** (III 5.12) 9 pitches. First ascent by Ron Olevsky and Rob Schnelker in 1978, with the first free ascent by Drew Bedford and Pokey Amory in 1984. Later Jonny Woodward made the first complete redpoint ascent. Zion pioneer Jeff Lowe calls this the "*Astroman* of Zion, a little shorter than its Yosemite brother, but with a more difficult crux." The route ascends a spectacular right-facing dihedral on the east side of the road about 0.1 mile before the Temple of Sinawava parking area and the road's end. Begin right of the corner at the cliff base. **Pitch 1:** Climb up left through bushes and trees on ramp (5.6) to belay ledge below dihedral system or climb directly up slab (5.9 R) to ledge. **Pitch 2:** The real work begins here. Face climb left (5.11a) across base of Pillar of Faith, a flake pillar wedged in the corner, to crack on pillar's left side. Move up crack and then back right to crack up its right edge (5.10). Belay on top of pillar

ZION
TEMPLE OF SINAWAVA

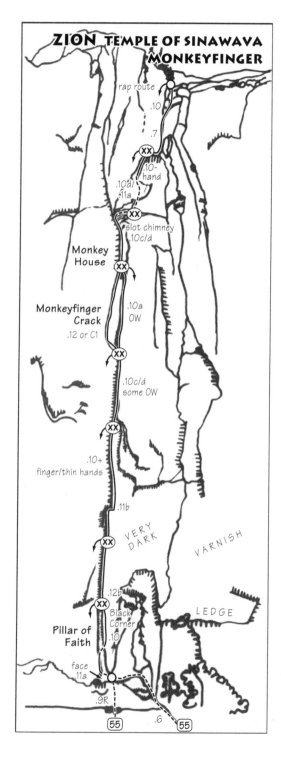

at 2 bolts. It's 160' to the ground from here. **Pitch 3:** The crux lead up the beautiful Black Corner. Jam, lieback, and stem up corner (5.11c to 5.12c depending on finger size but usually rated .12b). Finish up chimney (5.9) to 2-bolt belay on The Butt Ledge (butt on a ledge, feet in slings). **Pitch 4:** Work up broken right-facing corner and undercling out roof (5.11b). Continue up steep, finger and thin hands crack (5.10+) to 2-bolt hanging belay. **Pitch 5:** Jam long, strenuous, hand and fist (some offwidth pods) crack (5.10c/d) up the open book to 2-bolt semi-hanging belay in wide pod. **Pitch 6:** Climb one of 2 double cracks. The Monkeyfinger Crack on the left is a wild 5.12 finger crack (or C1) up the black face. The right-hand crack is an off-width (5.10a). Either way end at The Monkey House Ledge and 2-bolt belay below a wide slot. **Pitch 7:** Jam crack (5.10c/d) up slot chimney to 2-bolt belay and bivy ledge up right. **Pitch 8:** Face climb up right on steep tan slab (5.10d/ .11a) to hand crack (5.10-) that leads to spacious belay ledge (another good bivouac) below final corner. Watch for rope drag! **Pitch 9:** Climb into obvious left-facing corner (5.7) and up chimney to some wedged blocks (5.10) to belay on rim. **Descent:** Fastest way down is to rappel the route. Make 5 to 7 double-rope rappels from anchors to the ground. Be careful not to knock any rocks off and tie knots in the end of your ropes. Or walk off to the south by continuing up to Observation Point (4th class to 5.5 climbing). Follow the trail from Observation Point to the East Rim Trail which switchbacks down to the Weeping Rock trailhead. Total trail distance is 4 miles. **Rack:** Bring double sets of Friends and TCUs; 2-3 sets of wired stoppers, and 2 ropes.

56. **Turista** a.k.a. **Tourist Crack** (5.9+) 1 pitch. An excellent free route near the Temple of Sinawava parking area at the end of the scenic drive. Climb it and you're guaranteed a crowd! Begin at the cliff base up and right from the restrooms. Locate a beautiful left-facing corner with slings near its top. Jam and lieback the crack (5.9+) to 2-bolt anchor. **Descent:** Rappel the route. **Rack:** A couple of sets of Friends and TCUs.

PINE CREEK CANYON

Pine Creek Canyon is a deep drainage that runs east from the main Zion Canyon northeast of the visitor center. Mount Spry and 7,709-foot East Temple flank the canyon's north side, while the northern cliffs of 6,803-foot Bridge Mountain lie on the shady south side. Utah Highway 9 climbs the south side of the canyon before entering the long Zion-Mt. Carmel Tunnel. Many routes have been climbed in the Pine Creek drainage, notably some excellent long free routes on the East Temple and an assortment of shorter lines near the tunnel. To reach the cliffs, drive east from the visitor center and cross the bridge and the Zion Canyon Scenic Drive turn-off.

57. **The Headache** (II 5.10) 3 pitches. First ascent by Brian Smith and Dana Geary, 1975. This excellent route, one of the best in the park, ascends a crack system up the left side of a pillar east of the tunnel entrance. Drive up the road for 2.5 miles from the river bridge to the easternmost upper switchback, park at a pullout on the right just before the switchback or on the wide outside shoulder of the switchback. The route is obvious above. Follow a sandy path up the edge of a roadcut to the cliff base. The route begins just left of a blunt prow on the pillar and follows an obvious crack system for 3 sustained pitches. Expect lots of 5.9 jamming in finger, hand, and fist cracks, with the 5.10 crux on the third pitch. All belays are bolted. **Descent:** Make 2 rappels alongside a wide crack system left of the route from bolted anchors, or rappel the gully farther left. **Rack:** Sets of stoppers and TCUs, double sets of Friends, 2 ropes.

58. **Migraine** (5.12a) 1 pitch. Around the prow and 25' right of *The Headache.* Jam finger and thin hand crack to 2-bolt anchor. **Rack:** TCUs, small Friends, and stoppers.

ZION
PINE CREEK CANYON

rappels down gully

XX

2 rappels
to ground

.10

XX

rappel
anchors

.9

XX

.9

.12a

57

58

59. **Masterblaster** (II 5.5 C1) 2 pitches. No topo. A good practice clean aid route for aspiring big-wall climbers. Locate an overhanging crack that splits twin roofs about 150' left of Route 57. **Pitch 1:** Climb low 5th class rock up right to ledge left of left-facing corner. Belay here or continue up overhanging crack, aid over double roofs and belay in slings from 2-bolt anchor. **Pitch 2:** Continue up steep crack above to 2-bolt anchor. **Descent:** Rappel 160' to the ground from the upper anchors. **Rack:** 2 sets of TCUs, a few large wires, Friends—3 #1, 5 #1.5, 5 #2, 1 each #2.5 to #4.

EAST TEMPLE

The 7,709-foot East Temple, a huge sandstone peak that looms over Pine Creek Canyon, offers a spectacular array of mostly free lines on its sheer south face. A false-rim cliff line separates the lower wall from the slabs that lead to the Temple's summit. All of the routes end on top of this cliff line. Some of the routes here include *Lovelace* (V 5.10 C2+), *The Fang* (V 5.10 A3+), *Cowboy Bob Goes to Zion* (IV 5.10 C2+), *Uncertain Fates* (IV 5.11a C1), and *Freezer Burn* (IV 5.11+). Descriptions for a couple are included here. Otherwise check the visitor center books or John Middendorf's *Rock & Ice* guide for topos. The wall is often closed for raptor nesting. Check at the visitor center for possible closures. The cliff receives lots of sun. Carry plenty of water in warm weather.

Approach the East Temple by driving east from the visitor center on Utah 9, cross the Virgin River bridge at 0.5 mile, pass the turn to the scenic drive, and continue another 0.5 mile to a stone bridge. Park at a designated area here below the tunnel switchbacks. Follow a trail east up Pine Creek and head up talus slopes below The Fang to access the described routes. Allow about 45 minutes of hiking time.

60. **Lovelace** a.k.a. **The Fang Wall** (V 5.10 C2+) 8 pitches. First ascent by Dave Jones and Gary Grey, 1983. Locate The Fang Spire, a prominent 650-foot-high, semi-detached spire on the left side of the East Temple south face. This route ascends a crack system on a wall directly behind Fang Spire. From base of wall left of the spire do 200' of scrambling/climbing to start of pitch 1 on a bushy ledge. Pitch 3 (160') is C2+ up triple crack system—don't use pitons! Lots of TCUs and Rock 'n Rollers on this pitch. Continue up the crack and chimney system to the false rim. Look for some occasional A0 moves on the upper pitches. **Descent:** Rappel route from top of Pitch 9. **Rack:** Bring a couple of sets of Friends and stoppers, with extra sizes of small wires and Rock 'n Rollers; off-width pro; and 2 ropes. A 200-foot lead rope is useful.

61. **Cowboy Bob Goes to Zion** (V 5.10+ C2+ R) 9 pitches. First ascent by Hugh O'Neall and Dave Jones, 1986. This route climbs the left-hand of the three Towers of Fate on the south face of East Temple. It's mostly free,

rap route

ZION
EAST TEMPLE

60

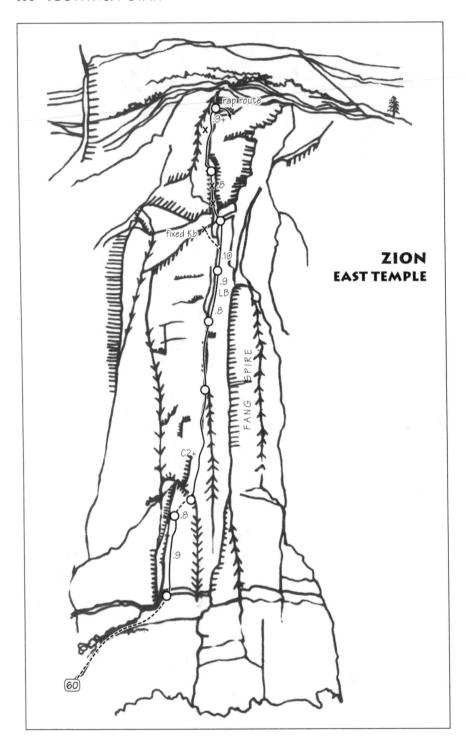

rap route

.9+

.8

fixed Kb

.10

.9
LB

.8

C2+

.8

.9

ZION
EAST TEMPLE

FANG SPIRE

60

rap down gully

natural pro

ZION
EAST TEMPLE

61

61

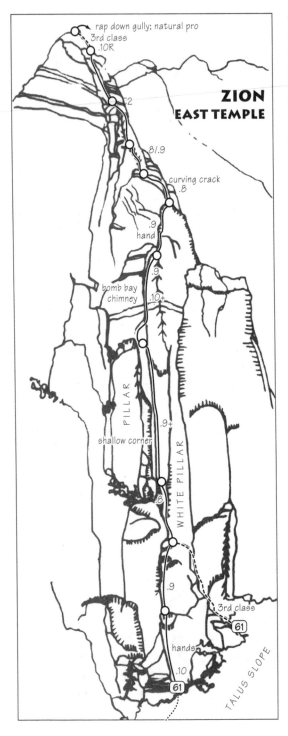

rap down gully; natural pro
3rd class
.10R

ZION
EAST TEMPLE

.8/.9

curving crack
.8

.9
hand

.9

bomb bay
chimney   .10+

PILLAR

.9+

shallow corner

WHITE PILLAR

.8

.9

3rd class

61

hands

.10

61

TALUS SLOPE

with only 5 aid moves on the last pitch. Don't count on finding fixed anchors on this route. Approach up the highest scree slope below the face. The route begins about 100' left and down from the top of the scree. Locate a white finger-shaped pillar halfway up the wall, the line climbs cracks right of this pillar. **Pitches 1 & 2:** Two possible starts: (1) Climb 2 pitches up vertical hand crack (5.10+ and 5.9) to bushy ledge. (2) Begin 50' from top of scree slope and angle left up 3rd class gully to bushy ledge (30' of low 5th class at top of gully). **Pitch 3:** Angle up left; don't climb the obvious off-width, but keep left to a belay ledge below right side of white pillar. **Pitch 4:** Climb (5.9+) shallow eroding white corner (left of an obvious off-width) before exiting left at roof up high. Face climb left and belay on top of pillar. **Pitch 5:** Climb up right along flake to main crack. Do wild but safe bomb bay chimney (5.10+) with good pro in back. Belay above chimney or follow crack (5.9) above in right-facing corner that eases back to good belay. **Pitch 6:** Climb hand crack (5.9) up left side of pillar to belay ledge atop it. **Pitch 7:** Jam excellent left-curving crack (5.8) up tight corner to bushy ledge. **Pitch 8:** Climb cracks (5.8/.9) up outside face of another flake pillar to belay atop pillar. **Pitch 9:** Climb crack (5.10) up white rock that leads to 5 aid moves (C2+). **Pitch 10:** Edge up run-out slab above (5.10 R) to belay by small tree. **Pitch 11:** A short 3rd class scramble to summit on left Tower of Fate. **Descent:** Make multiple rappels down big slot gully that angles southeast from summit. No fixed rap anchors—all natural. Make 2 rappels down ridge right of route, with first rap off tree atop pitch 9. Make 4 more rappels down steep gully to top of scree slope right of route's start. Bring extra webbing to reinforce dried rap slings. Be careful of loose rock. **Rack:** A couple of sets of Friends, TCUs, and stoppers, with extra off-width gear; runners; extra rappel slings; 2 ropes.

KOLOB CANYONS

OVERVIEW

The Kolob Canyons, lying in the far northwest corner of Zion National Park, are a series of deep, west-draining, finger canyons sliced into the lofty Kolob Terrace behind the escarpment of the Hurricane Cliffs. The canyons, hidden from Interstate 15's view, lie a few minutes east of this major highway. Three of the canyons are carved by the North, Middle, and South forks of Taylor Creek. Massive Navajo sandstone cliffs line the canyon walls, while forests of scrub oak, ponderosa pine, and Douglas fir in the higher and moister elevations scatter across the hillsides. Almost all the climbing routes in this area of Zion are in the South Fork Canyon, except for some big-wall routes including a few Grade VIs that are to the south on Timbertop Mesa's north flank.

The canyons, at an altitude above 6,000 feet, were part of the ancestral homeland of the Paiute Indians who hunted game in the canyons and on the mesas above. Part of their heritage lives on in area place-names, including Tucupit Point, a long mesa that divides the North and Middle Fork canyons. *Tucupit* is a Paiute word that means mountain lion. Paiute myth tells of *Kinasava*, a small, furry, human-like creature that lives in the canyons and utters unearthly screams at night—perhaps a reference to the area's many lions. The Virgin River band that inhabited the Zion region numbered about 1,000 in the mid-1800s but were wiped out by disease and starvation, with the last member dying in 1945. Later, the Mormons settled the valleys below the Kolob Canyons and established Fort Harmony near the base of the Hurricane Cliffs in the 1850s. The name Kolob itself comes from the Mormons who believe Kolob is the nearest star to God's home, where a day equals 1,000 earth years. The Kolob section of the national park was originally protected as Zion National Monument in 1937 and then incorporated into the park in 1956.

Navajo sandstone is the dominant rock layer at Kolob Canyons, forming immense salmon-colored walls. The formation, as thick as 2,200 feet at some places in the park, preserves the graceful curves of an ancient sand dune field that spread from Arizona to Wyoming over 150 million years ago. Water erosion and frost wedging later contoured the sandstone, weathering it into slot canyons, towering palisades, sharp buttes, rounded domes, and huge alcoves. The color of the Navajo sandstone ranges from deep red to bright white,

KOLOB CANYONS

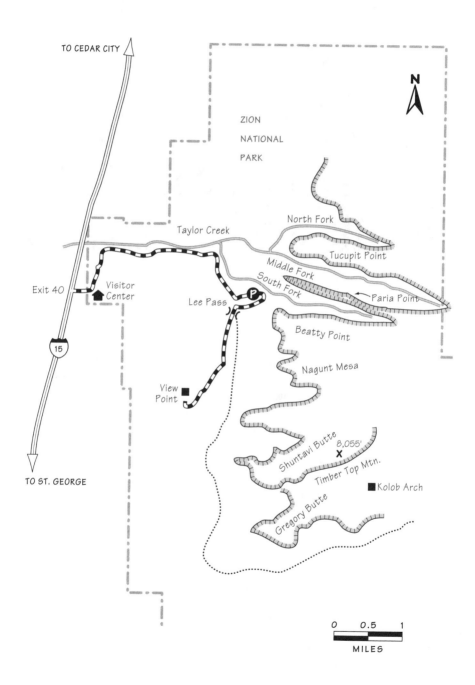

TO CEDAR CITY

N

ZION

NATIONAL

PARK

Taylor Creek

North Fork

Tucupit Point

Middle Fork

South Fork

Paria Point

Exit 40

Visitor
Center

Lee Pass

Beatty Point

15

Nagunt Mesa

View
Point

Shuntavi Butte

8,055'
X

Timber Top Mtn.

Kolob Arch

Gregory Butte

TO ST. GEORGE

0   0.5   1

MILES

A winter storm sweeps through the Middle Fork of Taylor Creek in the Kolob Canyons, Zion National Park. PHOTO BY STEWART M. GREEN

depending on how much iron oxide is in the rock. Climbers prefer the harder red cliffs of the sandstone. The upper white section tends to be very crumbly and soft, more akin to brown sugar than sandstone. The Hurricane Cliffs, the escarpment just east of I-15, separates the western boundary of the Colorado Plateau geographic province from the Basin and Range province with a major fault below the mountain front.

Climbing history: Compared to the more famous Zion Canyon on the other side of the national park, the Kolob Canyons are relatively route-poor and virtually ignored by climbers. Early Zion pioneer Jeff Lowe provided much of the impetus for route development in Kolob Canyons with the publicity surrounding the first ascent of *Wind, Sand, and Stars* with French rock star Catherine Destivelle in 1991. Lowe said that the route as a free climb "would be among the very finest long routes in North America." The prophecy was fulfilled the following year when Lowe, Steve Petro, and Lisa Gnade freed the line. Previous long Kolob routes were done by Bill Forrest and Bill March, as well as Ron Olevsky. Olevsky's many Kolob big-wall first ascents include *The Thunderbird Wall* (VI 5.9 A3), a 16-pitch line up the north wall of Timbertop Mesa. Many of the slab routes in this guide were put up in the 1980s and 1990s by Washington climber David Thomas and friends. The two most popular bolted routes at Kolob, *Huecos Rancheros* and *Namaste*, were bolted and ascended on the lead by Conrad Anker and friends in 1990 and 1991.

The Kolob Canyons, lying within Zion National Park, are subject to all the park's climbing rules and regulations. The use of power drills is discouraged as this is a proposed wilderness area. Hangers and bolts on routes should be camouflaged whenever possible. Red-tinted chalk is recommended. Permits are required only for overnight bivys. Several areas of the park are closed to climbing during falcon nesting season from February 1 to July 31. These closures include the Middle Fork of Taylor Creek. The South Fork, with most of Kolob's climbing, is unaffected by raptor closures. After rain and snow the sandstone is particularly fragile and crumbly; climbers should avoid the sandstone after precipitation to avoid damaging it. Climbers are also advised to wear helmets, particularly on the big walls, because there are loose rocks and boulders on many routes.

Trip Planning Information

General description: Slab, crack, and big wall routes in the Kolob Canyons section of Zion National Park.

Location: Southwestern Utah. Off Interstate 15 between Cedar City and St. George.

Camping: None in the park here. Campgrounds are found in Dixie National Forest, and the St. George and Cedar City areas.

Climbing season: Spring, summer, and fall. Winters are generally snowy, although climbing is possible on good days on south-facing walls.

Restrictions and access issues: Zion National Park regulations apply. Most cliffs in the Middle Fork of Taylor Creek are closed seasonally for raptor nesting; the described routes here, however, are in the South Fork. The use of battery-powered drills is discouraged as this is a proposed wilderness area. Permits are required for overnight bivouacs. Avoid climbing after rain or snow when the sandstone is friable and crumbly.

Guidebooks: None to Kolob Canyons. A looseleaf notebook is available at the ranger station off I-15 with many of the routes. *Desert Rock: Rock Climbs in the National Parks* by Eric Bjørnstad, Chockstone Press, 1996, has a Zion section with mention of Kolob.

Nearby mountain shops, guide services, and gyms: Outdoor Outlet in St. George and Cedar Mountain Sports in Cedar City. Todd Goss at Paragon Climbing Instruction (801) 673-1709 offers basic and intermediate climbing courses as well as guiding services and area climbing tours.

Services: All visitor and climber services in Cedar City and St. George, including restaurants, motels, groceries, and gas.

Emergency services: Call 911. Valley View Medical Center, 595 South 75 East, Cedar City, (801) 586-6587. Dixie Regional Medical Center, 544 South 400 East, St. George, (801) 634-4000, (800) 326-4022. Also contact a ranger in any emergency.

Nearby climbing areas: Black Rocks, Cougar Cliffs, Turtle Wall, The Green Valley Gap, Gorilla Cliffs and Simeon Complex, The Diamond, Black and

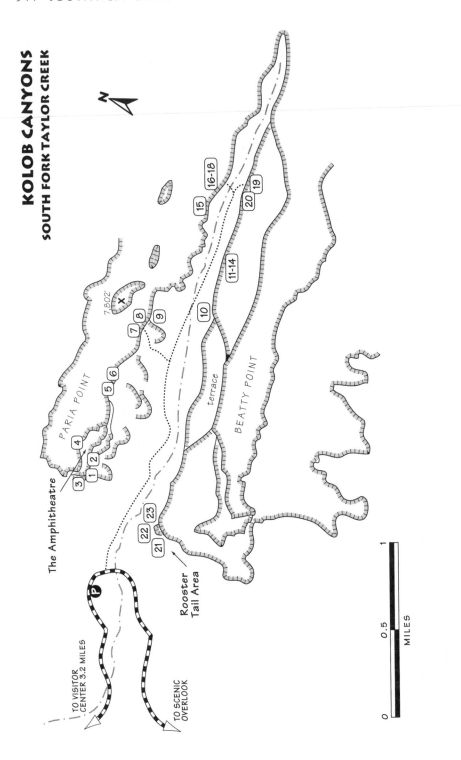

KOLOB CANYONS
SOUTH FORK TAYLOR CREEK

N

The Amphitheatre

PARIA POINT

7,802'

The Amphitheatre

Rooster
Tail Area

terrace

BEATTY POINT

TO VISITOR
CENTER 3.2 MILES

TO SCENIC
OVERLOOK

0   0.5   1

MILES

Tan, Welcome Springs crags, Crawdad Canyon Climbers Park, Prophecy Wall, Snow Canyon State Park, Virgin River Gorge (AZ), Zion National Park, The Overlook, Cetacean Wall, Cedar City areas.

Nearby attractions: Pine Valley Mountain Wilderness Area, Zion National Park, Smithsonian Butte Back Country Byway, Virgin River Narrows, Kolob Canyons, Kolob Arch (largest in world), Cedar Breaks National Monument, Joshua Tree Natural Area (farthest north Joshua tree area), Virgin River Gorge (AZ), Beaver Dam Wilderness Area (AZ), Paiute Wilderness Area (AZ), Gold Butte Back Country Byway (NV).

Finding the cliffs: The Kolob Canyons section of Zion National Park is accessed via Exit 40 on Interstate 15 between Cedar City and St. George. Turn east at Exit 40, pass the ranger station, and drive up the paved, scenic park road for 3.2 miles to a large parking lot on the right at the entrance to the South Fork Canyon. Park here and follow a trail east up the canyon to the routes. Bouldering areas are: Concrete Jungle at 1.7 miles; Hamburger Bluffs at 3.8 miles; and Kolob Roadside Boulder at 4.4 miles. A handout on the bouldering is available at the Kolob Visitor Center.

Routes are listed from left to right beginning with Paria Point to the north.

1. **Spiderfingers** (5.12a) Walk up the trail to the second gully, which drops south from the obvious towering buttress to the north. Follow a sandy trail up the gully to slopes on the right to a cave-like amphitheater. Continue north to a small buttress behind some ponderosa pines. This obvious route jams a zig-zagging splitter finger crack up a gorgeous black-varnished wall to a 2-bolt rap anchor at a horizontal crack. 50'. **Rack:** Lots of small gear—TCUs and small Friends.

2. **Unknown** (5.9) Just right of Route 1 is this line. Follow right-angling crack to single bolt. Do the crux move and clip 2-bolt chain anchor. 40'. **Rack:** Small to medium Friends.

3. **Peristalsis** (5.10-) Around the arête to the left of Route 1. Jam, stem, and off-width up long, obvious crack in large, left-facing dihedral for 100'. **Descent:** Walk off. **Rack:** #2.5 to #4 Friends, #4 and #5 Camalots, and Big Bros.

4. **Wind, Sand, and Stars** (IV 5.12) 11 pitches. First ascent by Jeff Lowe and French climber Catherine Destivelle, 1991. First free ascent by Jeff Lowe, Steve Petro, and Lisa Gnade in May, 1992. This route, one of America's best long free-climbs, was put up in the classic mixed free and aid style. Lowe later returned with crackmasters Petro and Gnade and freed the whole route establishing an audacious modern testpiece. The first 4 pitches climb corners, mantles, jamcracks, and a chimney. Pitches 4 and 6 are the crux. The remaining pitches are cracks, corners, traverses, and face climbing to the top of Paria Point. Find the route by scrambling up the second

KOLOB CANYONS

KOLOB CANYONS

5 raps down west face

4

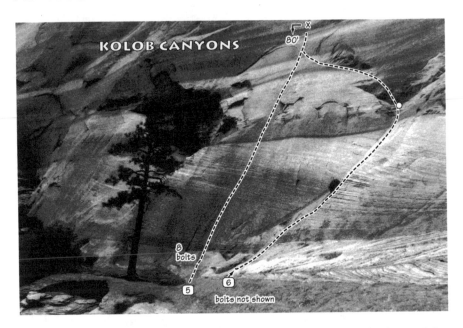

gully (same approach as route Route 1), but continue to the base of the obvious corner system. **Pitch 1:** Corners (5.10a) with 1 bolt to 2-bolt anchor; 80'. **Pitch 2:** Work up slot to mantle (5.11-) to corner crack (5.10). End at 2-bolt belay on ledge. **Pitch 3:** Climb an enjoyable chimney (5.9) and offwidth. No pro on this pitch; 150'. **Pitch 4:** Hand crack (5.9) to traverse (5.7). **Pitch 5:** Stem and jam steep 120' corner (5.12b/c) past crux with 2 bolts to 3-bolt anchor. A fixed birdbeak also offers pro on this pitch—do not remove! 6 bolts. **Pitch 6:** Another corner system with hard jamming and stemming (5.12b/c) past 9 bolts to a 2-bolt anchor; 120'. **Pitch 7:** Cracks (5.10a) to 5.9 face; 140'. **Pitch 8:** Corner (5.9 to 5.7) to 2-bolt anchor; 80'. **Pitch 9:** Continue up crack system (5.9) to belay stance with bolt and fixed nut. **Pitch 10:** Runout face climbing (5.10a) to 1-bolt ledge belay; 150'. **Pitch 11:** The route steps left here. Face climb (5.11) up crack system past bush to 8 bolts and pitons to 2-bolt belay ledge; 155'. **Pitch 12:** Face climb up and left (5.9). No pro here, needs a couple of bolts. Belay up top. **Descent:** 5 rappels down West Face from fixed anchors, then 1 to 1.5 hours of 3rd and 4th class down-climbing to base of Paria Point. Avoid a rappel by going through a tunnel part-way down. **Rack:** 2 sets of Friends, 2 sets of TCUs with 4 #.5 TCUs, 2 sets of wires, and a dozen quickdraws.

5. **High Noon** (5.11a/b) A quality slab line. Hike to the 5th drainage on the left about a half of a mile up the canyon. This is just past a small cave along the trail and before the log steps. Follow this wide wash north over slickrock and through ponderosa pines to an apron below the towering wall.

Begin right of a tall pine. Sustained face and friction climbing leads 80' to a ledge. 8 bolts to 1-bolt anchor.

6. **Compulsive Obsessive** (5.10c) A shorter, easier route just right of Route 5. Climb up and right to ramp, trend up left past bolts to join #5 at its last bolt. 4 bolts to 1-bolt anchor. 80'. **Rack:** Bring small and medium wires.

7. **Without A Doubt** (5.9) 2 pitches. Aesthetic slab climbing but some runouts. Hike to Route 5 but head right at the base of the wall and hike east to the top of a piney ridge. Begin by twin pines. **Pitch 1:** Straight up to #2 Friend placement in flake then up left past 3 bolts to 2-bolt anchor. **Pitch 2:** Up left to bolt then crux friction (5.9). Head past 3 more bolts to 2-bolt anchor. **Descent:** Rap route.

8. **Unknown** (5.10) Start just right of Route 7. Angle up and right on excellent slab for 150' to belay ledge at break. Some 25-foot runouts. Put a medium Friend placement in flake between bolts 6 and 7. 7 bolts to 2-bolt anchor.

9. **Protect the Dream** (5.12a/b) Unfinished. 2 pitches. Hike to Route 7 and drop east down ledges to the base of an awesome flake or hike up the trail to a point where the canyon begins to narrow. Bushwhack through scrub oak to the base of the immense wall. The route begins at a tall pine tree. **Pitch 1:** Delicate face climbing (5.12) leads past 2 bolts and fixed pin to layback flake. Belay on ledge from 2 bolts; 50'. **Pitch 2:** Jam, layback, and aid (5.11 A1)

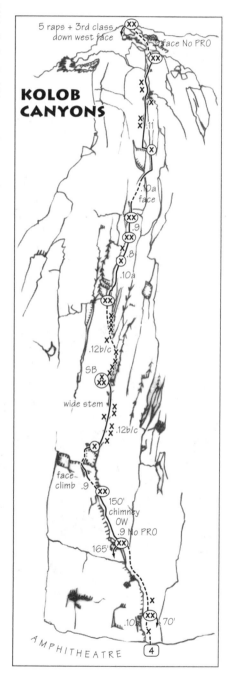

KOLOB CANYONS

KOLOB CANYONS

160' XX

7 bolts

8 bolts not shown

7

2 pitches up left

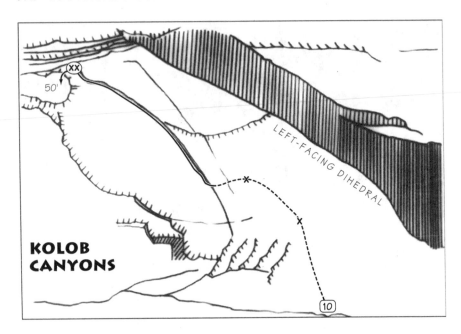

**KOLOB
CANYONS**

up thin fingers and tips crack in narrow, left-facing corner above for 70' to a 1-bolt anchor on left wall. This exposed and wild pitch would go free. Needs another anchor up there. **Rack:** TCUs, small Friends, and wires.

10. **Last Rites** (5.10d) Quality crack climb. Hike a mile up Taylor Creek to a large, overhanging, left-facing dihedral above the creekbed. This route ascends an obvious left-angling crack. Face climb past 2 bolts (5.8) and edge left across flakes to the crack. Jam this superb thin hands crack to a 2-bolt anchor. **Descent:** Rap 80'. **Rack:** At least 10 cams (TCUs, Tech Friends, Aliens, and Friends) from .25-inch to 2-inch with extra #1.5.

Hike east up the trail along the canyon floor for just over a mile to a narrow part of the canyon with a huge ampitheater on the north. The following routes ascend a licheny slab capped by a steep wall on the right.

11. **Hall of Smears** (5.11c/d) A large alcove, the Frosted Flakes Alcove, is 50' up the slab. This super slab route begins left of the alcove and right of a wide water streak. Begin in the dry streambed. A hard mantle leads to thin, delicate friction climbing with 2 distinct cruxes. 9 bolts to 2-bolt chains. 90'. **Descent:** Double rope rappel to the ground.

12. **Frosted Flakes** (5.7) Right of Route 11. Moderate climbing past 1 bolt to 2-bolt anchor on right side of the alcove. 50'. **Descent:** Rap from 2-bolt anchor.

13. **Static Cling** (5.10 TR) A fun face and friction top-rope off Route 11's anchors.

14. **Life of Brian** (5.9) Right of Route 12. Face climb left of thin corner past 1 fixed piton to a 2-bolt anchor in a pod. 40'.

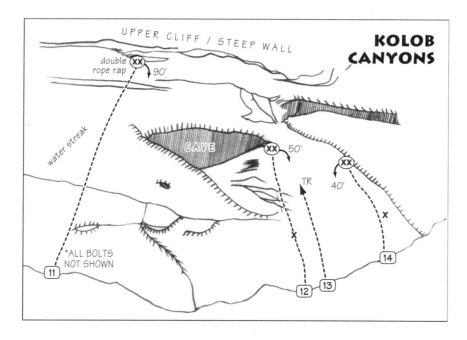

Continue hiking up Taylor Creek to a severely overhanging, huecoed, striped wall on the right near the end of the canyon. Routes 15 to 18 ascend a gray slab below a terrace and opposite this wall.

15. **Pins and Needles** (5.11a/b) This is the farthest west route on the slab. Follow a well-protected line of 9 bolts to a 2-bolt anchor. **Descent:** Rap 120'.

16. **Pulp Friction** (5.10c) Right of Route 15 and just left of a small flake. Fun, well-protected friction up the slab past 8 bolts to 2-bolt anchor. 85'.

17. **Sand Surfin'** (5.10b) Begin left of a small corner system. Face climb and friction straight up to a couple of 5.10 spots near the top. 7 bolts to 2-bolt anchor. 130'.

18. **Self Abuse** (5.9) Basically an easier variation of Route 17. Follow Route 17 to bolt 3 (5.9), trend left onto an easy ramp/flake and romp straight up past 2 more bolts to ledge. **Descent:** Rap from Route 17s anchors.

19. **Huecos Rancheros** (5.12c) No topo. A totally rad sport route up the striped, overhanging, huecoed wall near the end of the canyon. Cool and shaded in summer. This is the left-hand route up a line of huecos and potholes left of a wide black streak. Chase the pump up the wall past 15 bolts to 2-bolt chain anchor. 150'. **Descent:** Rappel with 2 ropes.

20. **Namaste** (5.12a) No topo. Another superb line put up on lead by Conrad Anker and friends. Begin in the streambed right of Route 19. Another long jug-haul—no move is harder than 5.10. Be prepared to get pumped! 14 bolts to 2-bolt chain anchor. 150'. Watch the king swing if you try to toprope

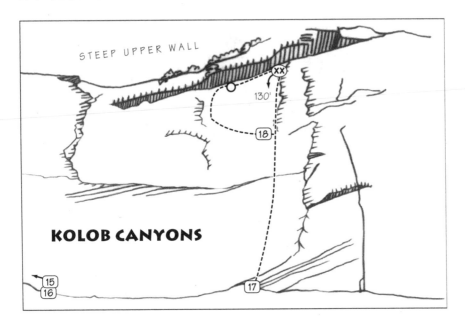

STEEP UPPER WALL

130'

18

KOLOB CANYONS

15
16

17

this route; keep some of the draws clipped to avoid crashing into trees. Descent: Rappel with 2 ropes.

ROOSTER PINNACLE

This is a flake pinnacle on the right (south) wall near the entrance to South Fork Canyon and is visible from the parking area. Hike up steep slopes through trees to the base of the pinnacle. Routes are right to left.

21. **Southern Comfort** (5.11 or 5.8 A1) 1 pitch. Follows the dihedral system on the right side of the Rooster. Climb past a 1/4-inch stud to a thin tips crack (5.11) with a bolt and fixed piton. Continue above on 5.9 and 5.10 climbing to another bolt. Here the angle eases. Follow hand/fist crack (5.7) past bolt to ledge. Step left onto face and climb easy rock (5.4) up left to summit. 140'. **Descent:** Rappel with 2 ropes. **Rack:** Gear to 3" including TCUs to #3 Friends.

22. **Center Route** (5.10b/c) The center crack system. Begin with hard-to-protect flare to long hands and fist crack (5.10b/c) to cave hole. Finish up easy rock to the top. 140'. **Descent:** Rappel with 2 ropes. **Rack:** Medium and large Friends including 2 #4s.

23. **Tail of the Cock** (5.10a/b) 2 pitches. A beautiful route up the left side. **Pitch 1:** Face climb a slab to left-facing corner. Jam corner crack (spot of 5.10a) to belay in notch. **Pitch 2:** Jam left-facing dihedral (5.10a/b) to the top. A little loose rock near the summit. 140'. **Descent:** Rappel with 2 ropes from 2-bolt anchor on back wall. **Rack:** Set of wires and Friends to #3. Small cams useful.

KOLOB CANYONS

St. George Area Crags

Overview

St. George, the capital of Utah's Dixie and the largest town in the state's southern half, is surrounded by a wild and rugged landscape. Thick layers of ruddy sandstone are smoothed by water into abrupt canyons, sharp buttresses, and soaring walls. The area is dotted with dark volcanic cinder cones and dense layers of lava that poured atop the upper sandstone layers, forming lofty, erosion-resistant rims of chocolate-colored basalt. Soaring escarpments of Navajo sandstone loom to the east above the swift Virgin River in Zion National Park. Ragged mountain ranges tower south and west of town, their steep, arid flanks raked by deep limestone canyons and interrupted by broad basins. Long bajadas, or outwash plains, slope away from the mountains into the basins.

The abundance of diverse rock, including basalt, sandstone, and limestone in the St. George area offers climbers a special user-friendly and scenic environment in which to pursue their vertical craft. Within a half-hour drive from town are over 20 separate areas with several hundred bolted routes of varying grades. New cliffs are being developed at a rampant pace, with projects outnumbering finished routes at several crags. Developed cliffs here include the Virgin River Gorge just over the border in Arizona (not included in this guide), Welcome Springs, Black and Tan, Gorilla Cliff, Snow Canyon State Park, Chuckawalla Wall, The Black Rocks, Prophecy Wall, and Crawdad Canyon Climbing Park. Farther afield are Kolob Canyons and the big walls in Zion National Park.

The dominant sedimentary rock found in the area is Navajo sandstone, a thick layer of pink, red, and white rock deposited in a huge sand dune field that covered a Sahara-sized region of North America from Wyoming to Arizona during Triassic and Jurassic times in the Mesozoic Era. The stone is essentially petrified sand dunes, a form revealed in the extensive cross-bedding characteristic of shifting dunes. The color of the quartz sand ranges from dark red to pure white, depending on the amount of iron oxide present. The Navajo sandstone is best seen in the sweeping cliffs at Snow Canyon State Park.

The basalt along the canyon rims formed from volcanic activity, mostly over the last half-million years. Magma rose through faults in the crust to the earth's surface. The resulting vents spewed cinders and lava across the wide

A Swiss climber on High Fidelity, *The Integrity Wall, Crawdad Canyon, St. George area.*
PHOTO BY STEWART M. GREEN

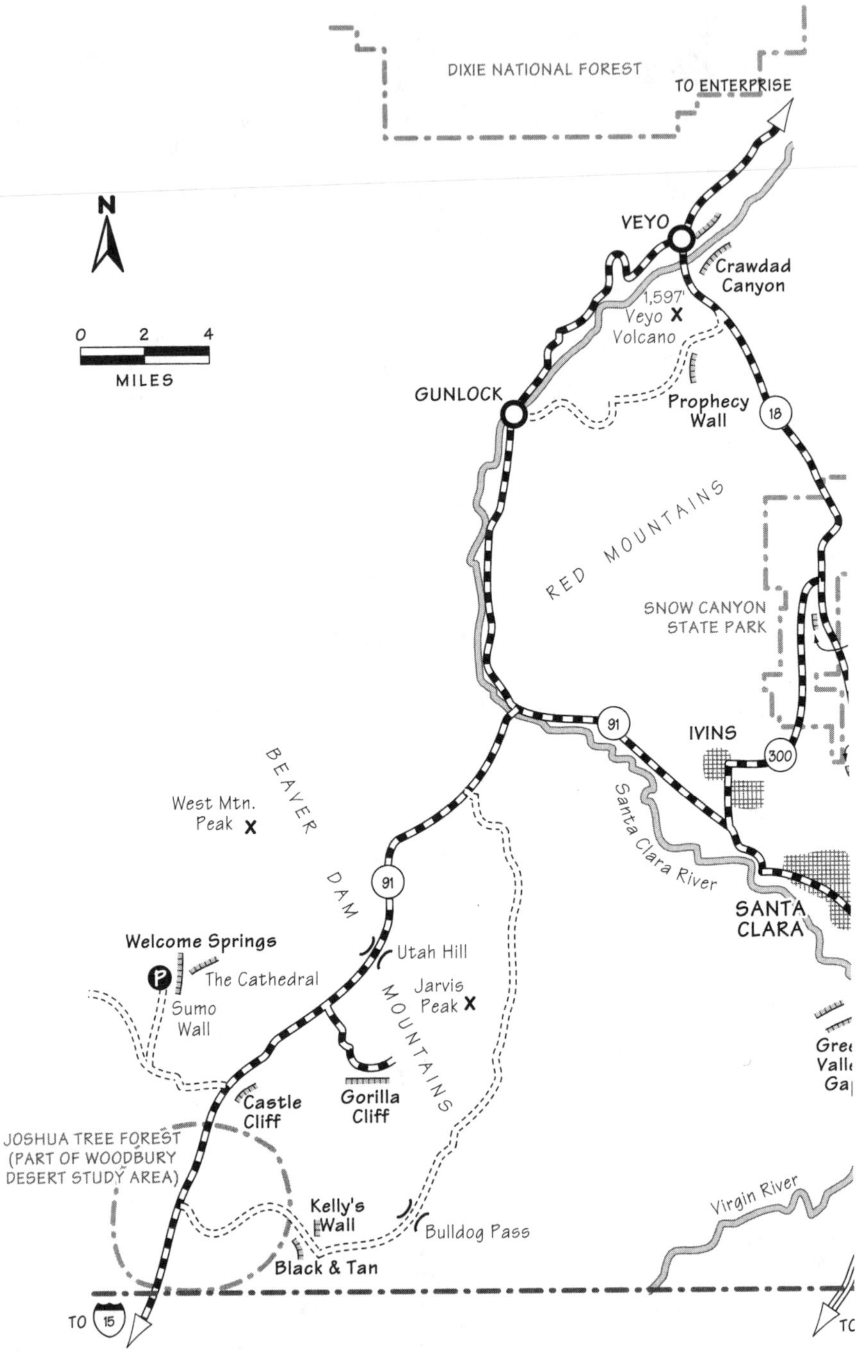

DIXIE NATIONAL FOREST

TO ENTERPRISE

N

0 2 4
MILES

VEYO

Crawdad Canyon

1,597' Veyo **X** Volcano

GUNLOCK

Prophecy Wall

18

RED MOUNTAINS

SNOW CANYON STATE PARK

IVINS

300

Santa Clara River

91

BEAVER DAM

West Mtn. Peak **X**

91

SANTA CLARA

Welcome Springs

P

The Cathedral

Utah Hill

Jarvis Peak **X**

Sumo Wall

MOUNTAINS

Gre
Val
Ga

Castle Cliff

Gorilla Cliff

JOSHUA TREE FOREST (PART OF WOODBURY DESERT STUDY AREA)

Kelly's Wall

Bulldog Pass

Virgin River

Black & Tan

TO 15

TO

ST. GEORGE CRAGS

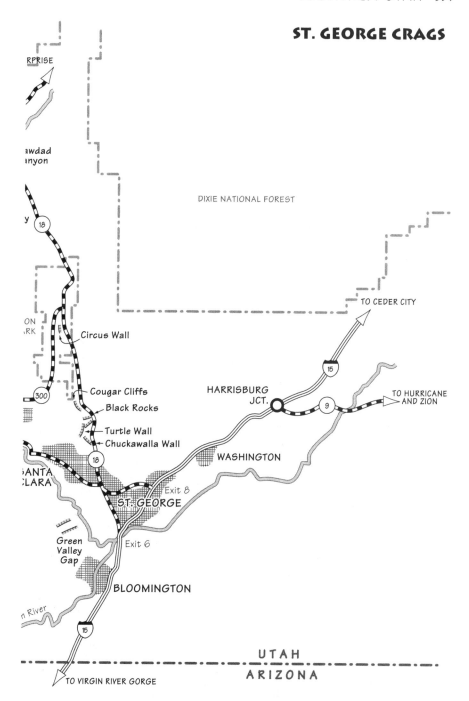

RPRISE

awdad
anyon

DIXIE NATIONAL FOREST

18

y

TO CEDER CITY

ON
RK

Circus Wall

15

300

Cougar Cliffs

HARRISBURG
JCT.

TO HURRICANE
AND ZION

Black Rocks

9

Turtle Wall

Chuckawalla Wall

WASHINGTON

18

SANTA
CLARA

Exit 8

ST. GEORGE

Green
Valley
Gap

Exit 6

BLOOMINGTON

n River

15

UTAH

TO VIRGIN RIVER GORGE

ARIZONA

mesas north of St. George, forming an erosion-resistant cap on top of the soft sandstone. The cliffs at Black Rocks and Crawdad Canyon include some of the finest basalt exposures in the area.

Besides its superb climbing opportunities and interesting geology, the St. George area is fascinating for the naturalist. The area boasts a wide range of elevations from 2,000 feet near the Virgin River Gorge to 10,500 feet atop Pine Valley Mountain. The area is an ecological melting pot, for between the two heights exists an amazing diversity of climates, ecosystems, plant communities, and animals. Journeying between the two is like taking a telescoped trip from Mexico to Canada. Here, where Utah, Arizona, and Nevada meet, lies the juncture of three of North America's 5 great deserts. The Colorado Plateau Desert, reaching west from the slickrock canyon country, encompasses the higher elevations with its characteristic pinyon pine and juniper forest. The Great Basin Desert, the cold, sagebrush desert of Nevada and Oregon, fingers into the mid-elevations, while the Mojave Desert and its dominant plants, the Joshua tree and creosote bush, lies in the hot, lowland areas.

Lots of animals live in the area too, including deer, mountain lions, desert bighorn sheep, lots of rattlesnakes, gila monsters, chuckwallas, scorpions, and desert tortoises. The tortoise, *Goperus agassizi*, is one of the most interesting and most rare of Utah's inhabitants. This endangered species, reaching lengths of fourteen inches, roams the arid and dusty desert. It derives moisture, unlike most other reptiles, from a vegetarian diet of leaves, grass, and cacti but is also able to withstand long drought periods and dehydration without ill effect. These slow, ungainly animals inhabit the drier regions of the St. George area—in Snow Canyon State Park, on the sandstone bench near Chuckawalla and Turtle walls, and in the Joshua tree forests around Welcome Springs and Black and Tan. A Tortoise Habitat Conservation Area is currently proposed for the area between Utah Highway 18 and Snow Canyon. Climber access and use of this area will change when the plan is implemented. Do not pick up or bother the tortoises you may encounter. Like any wildlife, they are sensitive to human contact and intrusion into their specialized habitat. Climbers should also be aware of scorpions in pockets, chuckwallas wedged into cracks, and rattlesnakes lurking among boulders and in underbrush.

The St. George crags are best during cooler weather. Southwestern Utah's mild winter weather and lack of measurable snowfall makes it an excellent winter destination. Winter daytime highs often reach into the 50s with warmer temperatures during periods of high pressure. February is usually a great climbing month. Spring, March through April, also offers excellent climbing weather. Days can sometimes be hot and afternoons windy. Autumn is also good, although October days are often too warm. The summer months from May through September are hot, with daily high temps regularly topping out above 100 degrees. The lowland climbing areas are generally too hot for comfort, although early mornings in the shade can be good. Crawdad Canyon is the best bet for summer climbing, with its shade trees and north-facing exposures, as well as the Kolob Canyons and areas around Cedar City.

Climbing history: The St. George crags are part of Utah's emerging wealth of sport crags. The first developed climbing here, outside of Zion National Park, was on the sandstone walls of Snow Canyon State Park north of town. Zion big-wall pioneer Ron Olevsky put up many of the first routes here on the Circus Wall beginning in 1988. The nearby Virgin River Gorge on Interstate 15 just over the border in Arizona was initially developed in the early 1990s by a strong contingent of Salt Lake City and Southern California climbers who quickly began eyeing the area's other limestone possibilities. They, along with some motivated locals, began bolting new cliffs.

Jorge Visser put up the first routes on Chuckawalla Wall in 1993. The following year Mike and Elizabeth Tupper and Todd Goss developed The Black Rocks, today the area's most popular crag. The limestone cliffs were bolted by numerous climbers including Shane Willet, Boone Speed, Tim Wagner, Jeff Pederson, Mike Tupper, Todd Goss, and Michael Nad. Crawdad Canyon, one of the newest areas, was bolted by St. George climbers Goss, Nad, the Tuppers, T. Broderick, and Ian Horn in 1996 and 1997. New crags are being discovered annually and the pace of development continues rapidly. At Crawdad, a climbing area on private property, new routers were on a deadline in early 1997. "The landowner says he wants 100 routes up and ready by May 1," notes Todd Goss, the area's rock climbing advisor. "I think we're going to make it, although 26 of our routes right now are still projects."

Few restrictions occur on the St. George area crags. Most lie on BLM public lands. Climbers, however, need to keep a low profile and use common sense at the cliffs. Follow access paths whenever possible and camp in existing sites. Pick up all your trash as well as any you find on the trail or at the cliff-base. Don't leave the impression that we're all slobs. Leave the wildlife, including the tortoises, alone. Don't make fires in the Black and Tan area as this is a sensitive ecological site. Snow Canyon is a Utah State Park. Pay the daily admission fee and keep the paid sticker on your windshield. Keep off the friable sandstone after rain or snow to avoid rock damage.

Crawdad Canyon Climbing Park is on private property and climbing is allowed only through the good graces of the landowner, who welcomes climbers to play on his cliffs. It, along with the Veyo Pool and Resort, is operated as a for-profit area. At the office, sign a liability release, log sheet, and pay the daily $2.00 entrance fee. If the park is closed during the colder months, ask at the Outdoor Outlet store in St. George for access information. No traditional climbing is allowed here; all routes are bolted. No free soloing or high bouldering is allowed. A clip-stick is necessary for the first bolt on many routes. A rental stick is available in the office. Keep profanity to a minimum as this is a popular summer swimming area for locals.

Dangers at the St. George crags include loose rock, rotten rappel slings, and missing gear at rap/belay stations. A real problem here is gear stolen or messed with by rappellers. As Todd Goss notes, "They'll steal anything not epoxied to the rock." Double check any station that has access from above to make sure everything is in order. Many of the routes are also set up for a rappel descent rather than lowering. Watch for scorpions and rattlesnakes in the warmer months, including the large, aggressive, and dangerous Mojave rattlesnake. This species has a potentially deadly venom for which no specific antivenin has been developed. They reach 4' in length with distinctive diamond and hexagonal patterns on their backs and a green color. Watch your kids. Keep an eye for snakes when scrambling over talus and rocky cliffs, or among scrubby growth. Carry a snake stick to probe interesting areas and remember they don't always sound a warning rattle.

Trip Planning Information

General description: Many excellent sport crags on a wide variety of rock, including sandstone, limestone, and basalt, surround the city of St. George.

Location: Southwestern Utah around St. George.

Camping: Snow Canyon State Park has an excellent fee 36-unit campground with showers 8 miles north of St. George off UT 18. Crawdad Canyon Climbing Park at Veyo offers a selection of walk-in campsites in the trees below the cliffs. Quail Creek State Park, 14 miles northeast of St. George off I-15, has 23 sites. Gunlock State Park, a popular reservoir area 16 miles northwest of St. George on UT 9, has a campground. The BLM maintains a good, but sometimes noisy campground at a rest area in the Virgin River Gorge just south of St. George. There are many places for primitive camping in the surrounding desert. Some of the better ones include along the roadside at Black and Tan Crag, in the canyon beyond the Sumo Wall and Welcome Springs (4-wheel-drive only), in the canyon near Gorilla Cliff, as well as off other remote public roads in the area. Keep a low profile and pick up after yourself.

Climbing season: Fall, winter, spring. The St. George area has very mild weather and is Utah's best winter climbing destination. Winters in this area have climbable temperatures almost every day, with highs regularly in the 50s. Low temps rarely dip below freezing. It's easy to find sunny routes on the lower elevation cliffs. Fall and spring are also excellent, although it can be hot. Shaded climbs are common. Summers are hot. Daily highs usually exceed 100 degrees. Climbing at the lower elevation crags is almost impossible. The higher elevation crags like Crawdad Canyon are a better bet in summer, with temps as much as 20 degrees cooler than the lowland inferno.

Restrictions and access issues: Most of the crags are on BLM lands and currently have no restrictions. Use common sense, however, by keeping all impact to a minimum. Park in designated areas. Camp only in existing primitive sites. Use climber trails to the cliff base whenever possible. Pick up all your trash and any that was left previously, including cigarette butts and tape.

Leave all wildlife alone. It is illegal to pick up and traumatize desert tortoises. Also watch for chuckwallas in cracks and scorpions in pockets.

Snow Canyon State Park has a moratorium on new route development and the placement of new bolts while the park management creates a comprehensive resource management plan. Parking and access to several areas outside the park is regulated by the Habitat Conservation Plan which expands Snow Canyon's current boundaries to the east. The affected areas include Chuckawalla Wall, Turtle Wall, Cougar Cliffs, and Black Rocks. The plan manages the area for the endangered desert tortoise and other animal species. Some cliffs are occasionally closed in Snow Canyon for raptor nesting. Check with the ranger for any closures in spring and summer. Access points to the area are at Chuckawalla Wall, the Black Cliffs, and Cougar Cliffs. A trail leads to Turtle Wall from Chuckawalla Wall.

Crawdad Canyon Climbing Park is private property. All climbing here is subject to the landowner's approval. For continued access to this fabulous area, follow all the park rules and keep your impact to a minimum. Park in the lot outside the canyon and walk down to the cliffs. Pay the $2.00 entrance fee per person at the office and sign a liability release. No traditional climbing is allowed; all routes are bolted for safety reasons. No free soloing or high bouldering. Also, watch the profanity as families use the pool and canyon in summer.

Guidebooks: *Too Much Rock Not Enough Life: A Sport Climbing Guide to St. George and Southwestern Utah* by Todd Goss, Paragon Climbing Guides, 1996. A good topo guide to all the major sport crags in the St. George area as well as the nearby Virgin River Gorge. *Snow Canyon Select* by Todd Goss, Paragon Climbing Guides, 1995. This is a select guide to all the routes worth doing at Snow Canyon State Park. *A Climber's Guide to Crawdad Canyon* by Todd Goss (1997), available at the park and the Outdoor Outlet in St. George, is a complete topo guide to the area.

Nearby mountain shops, guide services, and gyms: Outdoor Outlet, in St. George, sells climbing gear, chalk, and guidebooks. Todd Goss with Paragon Climbing Instruction (801) 673-1709 offers basic and intermediate climbing courses as well as guiding services and area climbing tours.

Services: All visitor and climber services in St. George, including restaurants, motels, groceries, and gas. Winter motel rates can be darn cheap. Check around for deals.

Emergency services: Call 911. Dixie Regional Medical Center, 544 South 400 East, St. George, (801) 634-4000, (800) 326-4022.

Nearby climbing areas: Pioneer Park Bouldering Area, Black Rocks, Cougar Cliffs, Turtle Wall, The Green Valley Gap, Gorilla Cliffs and Simeon Complex, The Diamond, The Wailing Wall, The Cathedral, Virgin River Gorge (AZ), Zion National Park, Kolob Canyons, The Overlook, Cetacean Wall, Cedar City areas.

Nearby attractions: Pine Valley Mountain Wilderness Area, Zion National

Park, Smithsonian Butte Back Country Byway, Virgin River Narrows, Kolob Canyons, Kolob Arch (largest in the world), Cedar Breaks National Monument, Joshua Tree Natural Area (farthest north Joshua tree area), Virgin River Gorge (AZ), Beaver Dam Wilderness Area (AZ), Paiute Wilderness Area (AZ), Gold Butte Back Country Byway (NV).

Finding the cliffs: All of the crags are west and north of St. George, the largest town in southwestern Utah. St. George is easily accessible by Interstate 15 from Las Vegas, Nevada and Salt Lake City. Take Exit 8 (St. George Blvd.) or Exit 6 (Bluff Street). The Welcome Springs and Black and Tan crags can also be accessed from Interstate 15 in Littlefield, Arizona, below the Virgin River Gorge. Directions for getting to each crag are listed under its specific section below.

CHUCKAWALLA WALL

The 60-foot Chuckawalla Wall is a superb training cliff just north of St. George off Utah 18. This is probably the most popular crag in the area with its easy access and wide selection of good routes from 5.10 to 5.13. The southwest-facing sandstone wall, at an elevation of 2,900', gets lots of sun which makes it a great cool weather crag. On hot days, however, it is best to get here early in the morning before the sun hits the rock face. Most of the routes were put up by Jorge Visser, Todd Goss, and Todd Perkins. Mike Tupper did the cliff testpiece *Three Bars Black* in early 1997. All routes are bolted.

ST. GEORGE CRAGS

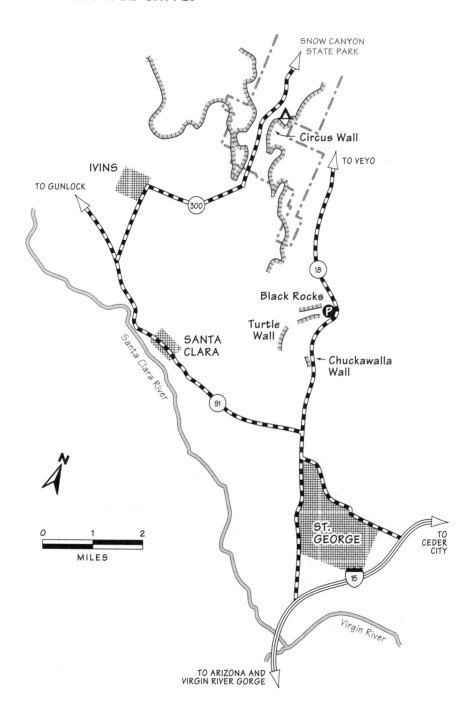

Rack: A dozen quickdraws is adequate.

Finding the cliff: Reach Chuckawalla Wall by driving north from St. George on Utah 18. Bluff Street turns into Utah 18. Go 1 mile north on the highway from Sunset Boulevard to an obvious left turn on a rough dirt road. Park at the Snow Canyon boundary fence, cross the fence, and follow a closed road about 0.2 mile downhill to the cliff. Turtle Wall lies about another mile up the closed road. Or park at Black Rocks parking area, cross the fence, and angle southwest across the mesa. At its edge, descend to a wash and the crag. Turtle Wall, an east-facing cliff, is another great sandstone crag with an assortment of 18 routes from 5.8 to 5.12. It's similar to Chuckawalla Wall, only steeper.

Chuckawalla Wall routes are listed right to left.

1. **Apostasy** (5.10a) A fun, pocketed route up right side of crag. 4 bolts to 2-bolt chains. 45'.

2. **Dirtbag** (5.10a) A clone of Route 1. 4 bolts to 2-bolt chains. 45'.

3. **Tombstone Bullets** (5.10b) Huecos, crimps, and potholes. 5 bolts to 2-bolt chains. 45'.

4. **Sand Witch** (5.11b) Similar to the first three—only harder. 4 bolts to 2-bolt chain anchor. 45'.

5. **Second Coming** (5.12a) One of the crag's finest! Climb steep edges to final overhanging prow. End on a ledge above. 7 bolts to 2-bolt chains. 60'.

6. **Still Waiting** (5.12a) Just left of #5. Crimps and edges up leaning wall. 6 bolts to 2-bolt anchor with rap rings. 60'.

7. **Say Your Prayers** (5.11d) You won't need a long prayer to send this one. 5

ST. GEORGE
CHUCKAWALLA WALL

bolts to 2-bolt anchor with slings next to thin pothole. 60'.

8. **As The Jerks Fly** (5.12a) Shares the start with Route 9. Edge past 2 bolts before embarking up right. Hard with slopey holds. 7 bolts to 2-bolt chain anchor on cliff-top. 60'.

9. **Pilgrimage** (5.12a) Keep left at bolt 2. Seems easier than Route 8 with more positive holds. 6 bolts to 2-bolt chains. 60'.

10. **Mecca** (5.11c) Climb up discontinuous seams left of brown streak. Go left at top past double bolt anchor to chains of Route 11. 6 bolts to 2-bolt anchor to 2-bolt chains. 55'.

11. **As The Crows Fly** (5.11b) Steep and excellent. 5 bolts to 2-bolt chains. 55'.

12. **The Cross** (5.12b) Edges and pockets in a brown streak. 6 bolts to 2-bolt chains in groove. 50'.

13. **The Garden of Eden** (5.10d) On the edge of the corridor. Use belay bolt on ledge. Pull an overhang to steep wall. 7 bolts to 2-bolt chain anchor. 45'.

14. **Three Bars Black** (5.13b/c) A difficult route that wanders up and left in the shaded corridor. Crimps lead up and left to pockets and tough left-angling traverse across top of streaked wall. Pull huecos to the top. 6 bolts to 2 open cold-shut anchor. 45'.

SNOW CANYON STATE PARK

This parkland encompasses a beautiful canyon flanked by soaring sandstone cliffs. It's a wonderful maze of buttresses, ledges, walls, and fins. Almost 200 routes have been put up here, but a lot are hardly worth climbing with poor sandstone, loose rock hazards, and inadequate protection. This guide concentrates on the popular roadside Circus Wall and the adjoining Aftershock Wall. This immense sweep of sandstone, rising some 400' east of the road, is easily accessible by a short 2-minute trail. The cliff offers great cool weather climbing with its west-facing exposure, as well as good summer climbing in early morning when the cliff is still in the shade. All of the routes on The Circus Wall were put up by Ron Olevsky, a prolific sandstone pioneer both here and at nearby Zion National Park.

Almost all of the routes on the cliff are bolt-protected with good, chained rappel anchors. The Circus Wall, the left side of the cliff, is a confusing array of drilled angles and routes. Some of the routes have color-coded protection, although the colors are not always obvious due to weathering. Lots of variations and link-ups are possible. The routes presented here are the best and most obvious lines. **Rack:** A dozen quickdraws for most routes, although a small rack of camming devices is occasionally necessary on the longer routes. Two ropes are necessary for rappelling off the routes.

Finding the cliffs: Reach Snow Canyon by driving north from St. George

ST. GEORGE CRAGS
SNOW CANYON STATE PARK

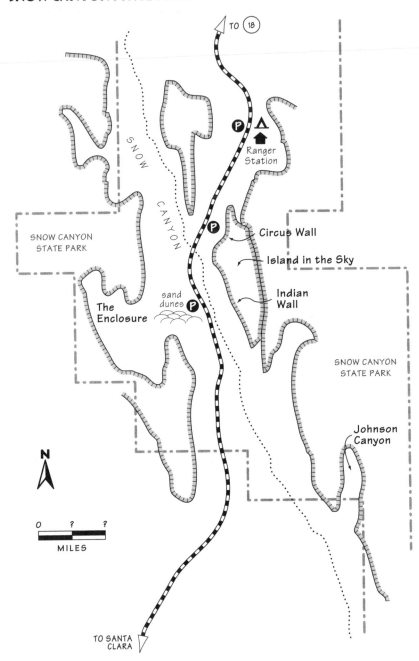

TO (18)

Ⓟ ▲
Ranger
Station

Ⓟ

Circus Wall

Island in the Sky

S
N
O
W

C
A
N
Y
O
N

SNOW CANYON
STATE PARK

sand
dunes Ⓟ

Indian
Wall

The
Enclosure

SNOW CANYON
STATE PARK

Johnson
Canyon

N

0   ?   ?
MILES

TO SANTA
CLARA

on Utah 18 for about 8 miles to a left turn onto Utah 8 that leads down into the state park. Drive down the park road (Utah 8) and reach the ranger station and campground at 2.3 miles. Pay the park entrance fee here ($4.00 in 1997). The Circus Wall is 0.4 mile south from here. Park at a large area on the east side of the road. Follow a marked path to the cliff base. Approach time is about 2 minutes. The Sand Dunes and Indian walls are 0.6 mile down-canyon opposite the sand dunes. An alternative drive accesses the park by driving through Santa Clara to Ivins on Utah 91. Turn north at the designated right turn and drive 4 miles to the park boundary. The Circus Wall is at 4.9 miles. Routes are listed from left to right.

THE CIRCUS WALL

1. **The Barbarian** (5.6) Climbs atop flake on prow on left side of the wall. 2-bolt rap anchor. 2 fixed pegs.

2. **Jimmy the Geek** (5.9) The leftmost route on the main wall. Belay on the sloping ledge below a slab. Move up fun chickenheads and edges to a bolted rap ledge. Continue up and right past 2 bolts to large pothole—The Pygmy Pit. The drilled angles are blue. Rap from several chained anchors 165' with 2 ropes. An alternative finish goes out left to an angle then up the outside of a large flake before working back right to the pothole belay. 13 or so fixed pitons.

3. **Freak Show** (5.9) Friction up easy slab and face climb up varnished wall above, crossing a couple of flake-corners. Work left to intermediate rap

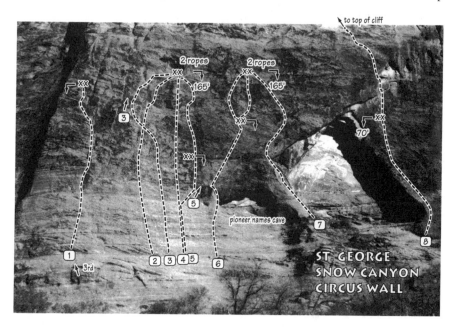

anchor then up final 2-bolt headwall to The Pygmy Pit. **Descent:** Rap with 2 ropes 165' to the base. 8 drilled pins.

4. **Pygmy Alien** (5.7) The easier twin of Route 5. Follows a long line of 12 drilled angles to The Pygmy Pit. **Descent:** Rap with 2 ropes. 165'.

5. **Illegal Alien** (5.10b) Clip the first bolt of Route 4 then up right to a bolt at the break above the slab. Continue straight up past an intermediate rap anchor to (5.10b) crux. Finish by working up left to The Pygmy Pit pothole. The drilled pins are painted red. **Descent:** Rappel 165' with 2 ropes from multiple chained anchors. 13 drilled angles.

6. **Roar of the Greasepaint** (5.10a) A fun route that works above the pioneer names carved in a cave. Begin on the slab. Climb past bolt to a bolt on left side of cave. Step up left and follow line of bolts up and right (5.10a) to intermediate anchor. Two variations are possible here. Go mostly straight up (5.9) or traverse right and then up varnished rock (5.10b). Either way reach a bolted anchor with rappel chains. **Descent:** Rap 165' down with 2 ropes. 16 drilled angles.

7. **Trapeze** (5.10) You'll need to be a trapeze artist to keep the rope drag in control on this one. Scale a prow right of the small cave to a drilled angle. Work out left then back right past many fixed pitons. Don't clip the 3rd one to ease rope drag! Continue up fun rock past large black varnished area before moving up left to anchors of Route 6. **Descent:** Rap with 2 ropes from chains. 9 drilled pitons.

THE AFTERSHOCK WALL

8. **Living on the Edge** (5.10c) 4 pitches. Usually only the first 2 or 3 pitches are climbed. This is the area mega-classic. Don't miss it. **Pitch 1:** Follow right edge of arch with exposed but fun face climbing (5.10a). 7 bolts to 2-bolt chained anchor; 70'. **Pitch 2:** Wild and airy. Climb directly up past some loose rock to break in headwall above. Work back left (5.10c) onto steep, sustained slab (5.10a) and belay from 2 bolts on ledge; 80'. **Pitch 3:** Move out right to loose flake mantle (scary) and angle up on friction (5.10c) to 2-bolt belay stance below overhang. Rap from here or do **Pitch 4:** Jam and stem up crack and corner (5.9) to summit. It's hardest right over belay. **Rack:** Bring quickdraws and some cams for the last pitch. Begin right of the triangular-shaped arch. **Descent:** Rap from tops of Pitches 1, 2, and 3 with double ropes. Otherwise walk off and down climb the north ridge of the formation (5.2) to the ground. (45-minute descent).

9. **Circus Maximus** (5.11?) Looks good, but lots of bail slings on it. Maybe just put an anchor at the top and call it quits? 6 bolts.

10. **Aftershock** (5.11b) 4 pitches. Another great classic. **Pitch 1:** Climb a slab, angling up right (5.10a) to left side of flake. Jam corner crack (#1 Camalot)

walk off

walk off
45 min.

ST. GEORGE
SNOW CANYON
AFTERSHOCK WALL

.9

.11b
fingers

xx

.10c

.8

xx
165'

.10a

.11b

xx

.10c
loose

rap
anchor

xx

.10c

xx
70'

xx
50'

xx chains

.10a

xx
50'

.11

.10a

8

9

10

to 2-bolt chained belay stance atop flake. **Pitch 2:** Face climb up and right (5.10c) past bolts to 2-bolt belay in large exposed hole. **Pitch 3:** Move left out of hole past a couple of bolts (5.11a) then straight up slab above past more bolts to 2-bolt belay ledge. **Pitch 4:** Follow obvious crack system (5.11b) to summit. **Rack:** Bring an assortment of medium and large cams for pro. **Descent:** Rap the route or down climb the north ridge (5.2).

CRAWDAD CANYON CLIMBING PARK

Crawdad Canyon is a sharp little canyon chiseled by the Santa Clara River into a basalt layer 18 miles north of St. George. The 70-foot-deep canyon, at 4,000', lies east of the highway bridge immediately south of the small town of Veyo, and is filled with trees, birdsong, and the trickling river. The river, beginning high in the Pine Valley Mountains, is also fed by thermal springs that keep its temperature in the canyon at about 70 degrees—too warm for trout but not too warm for crawdads.

The canyon is a unique climbing area as it, along with the adjoining pool, is privately owned and operated as a for-profit operation. The landowner here welcomes climbers to enjoy the cliffs on his property. The area was developed by St. George climbers, including climbing advisor Todd Goss, Mike and Eliza-

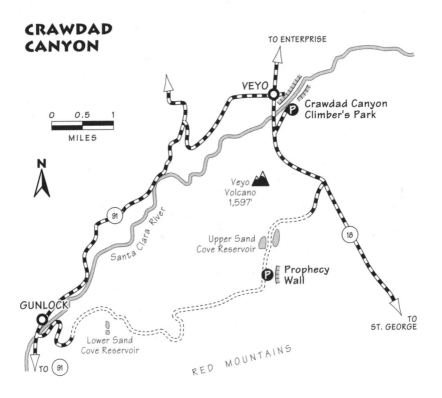

beth Tupper, Michael Nad, and Ian Horn. After acquiring the property in 1996, the owner saw lots of climbers at The Black Rocks one day when driving north to Veyo. He thought his cliffs looked a lot better than those and asked locals to assess their potential. They were astonished by the possibilities and catalyzed the development of this great climbing resource.

When you visit Crawdad Canyon, walk down the hill from the parking area to the park office next to the pool. Register here by signing a liability release and check-in form and paying the small fee of $2.00 (as of 1997) per person. Those who don't pay will be banned from climbing here for a year. Leave your rack in your trunk; no trad climbing is allowed here for liability reasons. There is no free soloing or high bouldering and no profanity because families also use the area facilities.

There are lots of cliff sections being developed in the canyon. This guide covers two of the more easily accessible and popular sectors—The Rubicon Wall and The Integrity Wall. Brass plaques at the base of each route give its name, rating, and first ascensionist. Ask at the park office or the Outdoor Outlet in St. George for topos to new areas. **Rack:** A dozen quickdraws, a 165-foot rope, and a clip-stick. A clip-stick is also for rent in the office. Lots of routes have high first bolts to keep inexperienced climbers off.

Finding the cliffs: Drive north from St. George on Utah 18 for about 18 miles. As the highway drops down a long hill to the village of Veyo, look for a right turn on Veyo Resort Road. Follow this paved road for 0.5 mile to a large parking area on the canyon rim. Walk through the gate and down the steep hill into the canyon. The office is on the left at the bottom of the hill. To find

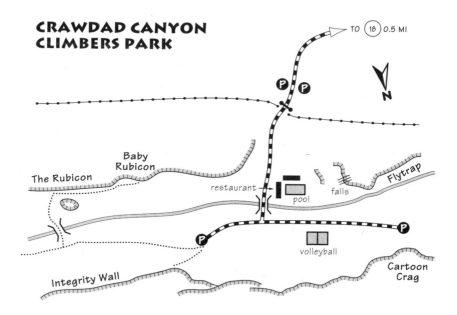

**CRAWDAD CANYON
CLIMBERS PARK**

TO (18) 0.5 MI

N

Baby
Rubicon

The Rubicon

restaurant

pool

falls

Flytrap

Integrity Wall

volleyball

Cartoon
Crag

the cliffs, cross the river via a bridge and turn right. The Integrity Wall is on the left after about 50 yards. The Rubicon Wall is another 100 yards up canyon. Cross the river on a small footbridge.

THE RUBICON WALL

The north-facing Rubicon Wall is the most developed crag in Crawdad Canyon. All routes are 60' unless otherwise noted. A stick clip is necessary on many of the routes. Routes are left to right from the bridge over the creek and the large boulder at the cliff base. Distances between routes are approximate.

1. **Aerial Dentistry** (5.13a) Begin opposite large boulder at cliff base. Pull up slightly overhanging tan wall with crimps and edges. A technical face to a black slab. 5 bolts to 2-bolt anchor. 4' to next climb.

2. **Victim of Circumstance** (5.11b) Crack to large right-facing flake to streaked slab. 6 bolts to 2-bolt anchor. 10' to next.

3. **Burning Bridges** (5.12a) One of the crag's very best lines. Sustained and steep with lots of incut holds. Up cracks and flakes to blunt prow. 6 bolts to 2-bolt anchor. 2' to next.

4. **Project** (5.13+) An impossible-looking Michael Nad route. He says there are holds up there. . . . A steep tan face left of large open book. 6 bolts to 2-bolt anchor. 2' to next.

5. **I Climb Therefore I Sweat** (5.11d) A stemming problem up the obvious tan dihedral. Go left at top up left-facing corner. 6 bolts to 2-bolt anchor. 5' to next.

6. **I Stink Therefore I Am** (5.11b/c) Pockets up the black streak. 7 bolts to 2-bolt anchor. 2' to next.

7. **Narcolepsy** (5.8) One of the crag's easier offerings. Swing up a pillar to broken crack system to ledge. 5 bolts to 2-bolt anchor. 45'. 6' to next.

8. **Unnamed Project** (5.11d) A steep, tan, right-facing corner to Route 7 anchors.

9. **Leap of Faith** (5.13a) Superb climbing, but hard. Overhanging pockets lead to blind dyno and technical crux. 7 bolts to 2-bolt anchor. 8' to next.

10. **Rubicon** (5.12b) Steep and powerful face left of left-facing corner to triangular roof. Committing move at crux bulge. 7 bolts to 2-bolt anchor. 4' to next.

11. **Irreconcilable Differences** (5.13b) Up tan wall right of shallow, left-facing corner and right at top of prow. 6 bolts to 2-bolt anchor. 5' to next.

12. **Kissing Chi Chi's Ass** (5.12a) Climb face right of strange, black, right-angling crack. Above work back up face left of crack in left-facing corner. 7 bolts to 2-bolt anchor. 5' to next.

13. **Pushing Sport Climbing** (5.11a/b) Same start as Route 12. Split right at bolt 5 and finish up right. 8 bolts to 2-bolt anchor.

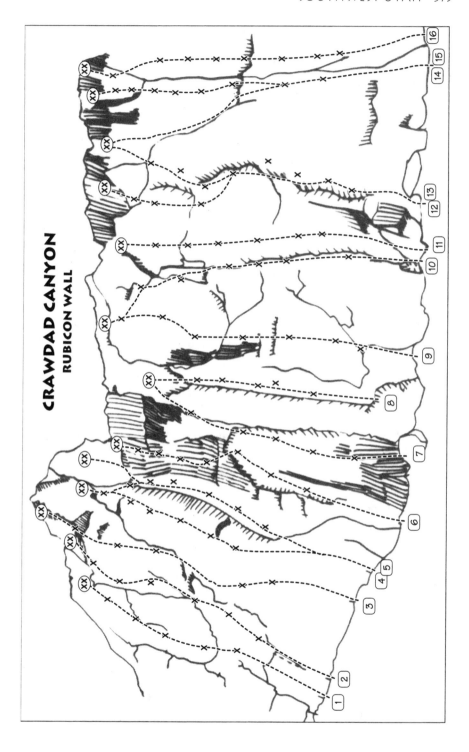

CRAWDAD CANYON
RUBICON WALL

14. **Gypsy Dance** (5.12d) Climb assorted cracks to bolt 2. Move up left along thin crack and finish up Route 13. Some bolts are hard to clip. 5 bolts to 2-bolt anchor.

15. **The Reckoning** (5.12b) Start on Route 14 but head straight up over bulges with black streaks. 8 bolts to 2-bolt anchor. 15' to next line.

16. **Rude Awakening** (5.12c) Up left of blunt arête. 8 bolts to 2-bolt anchor.

17. **Just Say No To Posing** (5.12d) Posers need not apply. A stellar route up blunt arête left of obvious right-facing dihedral. Look for kneebar in horizontal crack. 6 bolts to 2-bolt anchor. 10' to next.

18. **Return of the Jedi** (5.11b) Jams and stems up right-facing dihedral. 6 bolts to 2-bolt anchor. 6' to next.

19. **Where's Your Messiah Now** (5.11d) Over bulging roof feature to tan and black wall. 4 bolts to 2-bolt anchor. 6' to next.

20. **Toxic Emotions** (5.11b) A beautiful tan face route between crack systems. 6 bolts to 2-bolt anchor. 10' to next.

21. **Sparkle and Fade** (5.11a) 5 bolts up hand crack to 2-bolt anchor. 10' to next.

22. **Manifest Destiny** (5.12a) Some of the coolest rock in the canyon on this great route. Swing up edges of sculptured black rock to crimp crux below obvious break, then up black streak. 7 bolts to 2-bolt anchor.

23. **The Talisman** (5.12c/d) Start up Route 22 but keep right to tan face. A double undercling crux in big roof leads to final pumpy prow. 7 bolts to Route 22's 2-bolt anchor. 6' to next.

24. **Hard Cranking Dude** (5.11d) Up right then left side of deep crack. 4 bolts to 2-bolt anchor.

25. **Monkey Business** (5.11b) Right of deep crack. Same start as Route 24 but veer right at bolt 2. Up tan face with black streak to dark headwall. 6 bolts to 2-bolt anchor. 10' to next.

26. **Veyo Quickie** (5.12b) Short and steep to ledge. 4 bolts to 2-bolt anchor. 45'. 10' to next route.

27. **Slash and Burn** (5.11a) First ascensionist Todd Goss calls this "the worst route on Rubicon." Climb up and right past weird moves at bolt 4. 6 bolts to 2-bolt anchor. 12' to next.

28. **Calypso** (5.9) Fun route up thin black corner. 5 bolts to 2-bolt anchor. 20' to next. A project with only anchors is just to the right of *Calypso*.

29. **Morning Sickness** (5.11c) 4 bolts to 2-bolt anchor.

30. **Project** (5.12?) 30' to next.

31. **Spit Shine** (5.7+) Easy but good line up left side of dark slab. 4 bolts to 2-bolt anchor. 45'. 5' to next.

32. **Subject to Change** (5.6) The crag's beginner lead. 4 bolts to 2-bolt anchor. 45'.

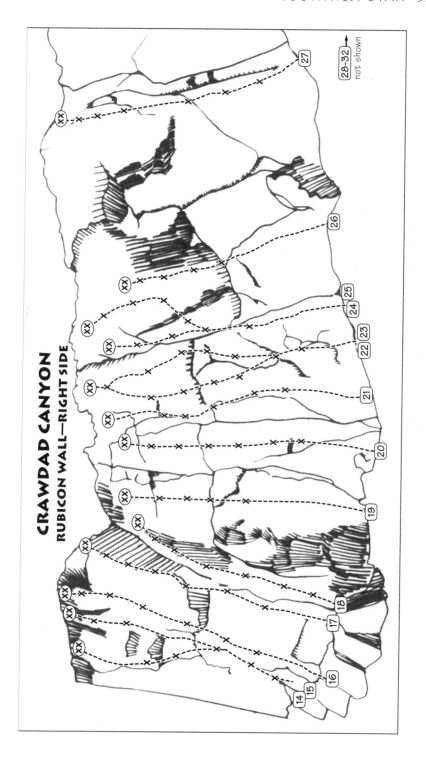

CRAWDAD CANYON
RUBICON WALL—RIGHT SIDE

28-32
not shown

INTEGRITY WALL

This south-facing wall sits on the north side of the canyon. A stick clip is needed on all these routes to protect the first moves. All routes are 50' long. Routes listed left to right.

33. **Talk The Talk** (5.10c) A tight right-facing corner. 4 bolts to 2-bolt anchor.

34. **Walk The Walk** (5.10a) Good face climbing left of left-facing corner. 5 bolts to 2-bolt anchor.

35. **No Holds Barred** (5.11d) Face climbing up thin crack. 5 bolts to 2-bolt anchor.

36. **High Fidelity** (5.11d) Gorgeous arête route with final slopey hold to clip anchors. 4 bolts to 2-bolt anchor.

37. **Honor Amongst Trees** (5.11a) Pockets up a vertical face. 4 bolts to 2-bolt anchor.

38. **Truthful Consequence** (5.11a) Another fun arête route. 4 bolts to 2-bolt anchor.

39. **Round Two** (5.10d) Layaways up left side of sharp arête. 3 bolts to 2-bolt anchor.

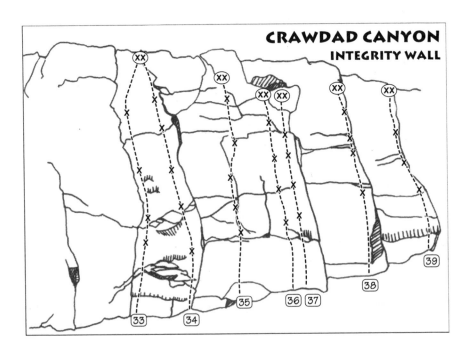

CRAWDAD CANYON
INTEGRITY WALL

WELCOME SPRINGS

Welcome Springs sits on the southwest side of the rugged Beaver Dam Mountains in the far southwestern corner of Utah. The springs themselves seep out of the hills above a cattle corral tucked at the head of a shallow canyon. A series of abrupt limestone cliffs, accessible by walking or driving up a rough four-wheel-drive track on the canyon floor, rim the canyon edge. The first crag is The Sumo Wall, an east-facing crag lying on the west side of the canyon at almost 5,000'. There is some fine bouldering on huge blocks scattered on the dry streambed below, including a 4-bolt project on the largest. Farther up-canyon sit The Wailing Wall and The Cathedral. Both north-facing crags perch on the south rim, high above the canyon floor. A steep approach trail limits activity at both walls, making them an ideal getaway for solitude, views, and great climbing. Local guidebook author Todd Goss says The Cathedral is perhaps "the single finest crag in the St. George area." His comprehensive regional guide includes a topo. His guide also includes the routes on the more easily accessible Sumo Wall.

The Sumo Wall receives morning sun and afternoon shade. Time your visit accordingly. Winter afternoons might be too cold for comfort, while mornings during warmer months will definitely be too hot. All the routes are bolted with either chain lowering anchors or large rap hangers. Use the hangers to rap, not lower. **Rack:** A dozen quickdraws is adequate along with a 165-foot rope.

Finding the crag: Reach Welcome Springs and the Sumo Wall via Utah 91 (old U.S. Highway 91) between Shivwits west of Santa Clara and Littlefield, Arizona, off Interstate 15. To reach the Welcome Springs turnoff from St. George, turn west on Sunset Boulevard on the northwest side of town. Follow Sunset, which turns into Utah 91, through Santa Clara for about 12 miles to a junction at the old site of Shivwits. Keep left at the highway junction here and proceed another 11.7 miles over the mountain range to a sign marked "L & R Bird Ranch 10 miles" just past roadside Castle Cliff, a limestone escarpment on the left side of the highway.

This junction is also accessible from Interstate 15 below the Virgin River Gorge. Leave the interstate at Exit 8, the Littlefield exit. This exit is 28 miles southwest of St. George. Drive north from Littlefield on old U.S. Highway 91 for 12.5 miles to the Welcome Springs turn at Castle Cliff.

Turn right or west on this good gravel road and follow it for 2 miles to a side road. Turn right on this gravel road marked "Welcome Springs" and continue north another 2 miles through a Joshua tree forest to a parking area at a cattle corral. Park here if you have a two-wheel-drive or follow a rough wash east with a four-wheel-drive. Either way, head up the wash for almost a mile, keeping left at the big cottonwood trees at an obvious canyon fork. There is space for a couple of vehicles in the wash below The Sumo Wall. Otherwise park just up the canyon where it widens. There are also good primitive campsites here. An access path begins up-canyon from the cliff and contours south to the base. Total walking time from the corral to cliff is 15 to 20 minutes. The Cathedral and Wailing Wall are another mile east up the canyon. Continue up the wash to the cairned trail.

THE SUMO WALL

Routes are listed from left to right.

1. **Project** (5.13?) The direct start off a cornchip edge is probably 5.14. Most tries come in from the first bolt of Route 2 to traverse bolt to the second bolt of this one. 7 bolts to 2 bolts with rap hangers.

2. **Dragonseed** (5.13b) On far left side of overhanging wall. Thin technical climbing up slightly overhanging tan rock. 7 bolts to 2-cold shut anchor. 60'.

3. **Project** (5.14?) Desperate-looking route! Up first 2 bolts of Route 2 then up and right past some holes to chain anchors right of large hole. 5 bolts to 2 cold-shut anchors.

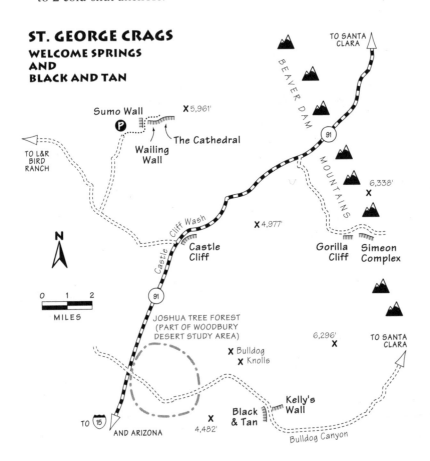

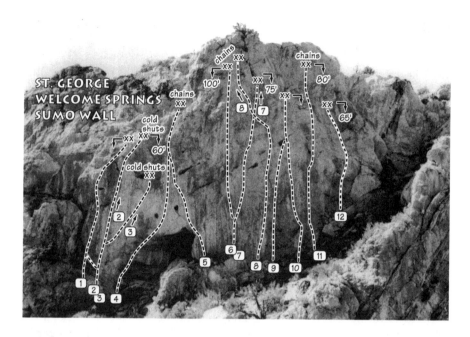

4. **Project** (5.13d) Another heinous cling. Begins just left of deep cave. Up and out the bulging wall. 7 bolts to 2-bolt chains.

5. **Picking Sumo's Nose** (5.12b) Right of the cave. Swing up and left on nose feature on good holds. Pull through above on thin holds to huge pocket and continue up headwall. 6 bolts to 2-bolt chains. 60'.

6. **Falling Bats** (5.11c) First route on the crag. Begin right of Sumo's Nose atop some flake boulders. Climb seam to slab to final headwall. 11 bolts to 2-bolt chains. 100'.

7. **Too Fat for a Sleeping Bag** (5.11d) Gotta be lean for this one. Same start as Route 6 but angle up right at bolt 1. Continue up gorgeous tan to gray limestone to anchors. 12 bolts to 2-bolt chains. 100'.

8. **Love Handles** (5.11d) Start off the right side of flakes. Climb steep tan rock to gray super slab. Finish at anchors by crack. 10 bolts to 2-bolt anchor with rap hangers. 75'.

9. **Geisha Knife Fight** (5.10d) Local guide Todd Goss calls this "the best route on the crag." Begin just right of some flake boulders. Climb stellar limestone on pockets and edges to final slab. 7 bolts to 2-bolt rap anchors. 70'.

10. **Nipple Extractor** (5.11a) A slightly harder twin to Route 9. Pull up and over a bulge between bolts 3 and 5 to a slab. Finish up Route 9. 9 bolts to 2-bolt rap anchor. 70'.

11. **The Wasteland** (5.8) Superb route for the grade on immaculate stone. Follow grooved corner to anchors on upper headwall above ledge. 10 bolts to 2-bolt chains. 80'.

12. **Cheeks of Chong** (5.9) Another fun one. Start off blocks on far right side. Up headwall to slab and anchors below roof. 6 bolts to 2-bolt rap hangers. 65'.

BLACK AND TAN & KELLY'S WALL

The Black and Tan Wall and Kelly's Wall, lying at 3,600 feet, are two brilliant limestone crags hidden in the remote southern reaches of the Beaver Dam Mountains just a mile north of the Arizona border. The cliffs offer not only excellent sport routes, but sit in a spectacular desert setting among steep peaks, sharp canyons, and a unique Joshua tree forest. This area is protected as the Joshua Tree National Landmark, a sensitive ecological site that includes the farthest north grove of Joshua trees as well as the Woodbury Desert Study Area. The 3,040-acre study area was the site of primary research on the rare and endangered desert tortoise conducted by Drs. Woodbury and Hardy from 1936 to 1948. Besides the tortoise, other wildlife here includes chuckwallas, gila monsters, and various rattlesnakes, including the dangerous Mojave rattlesnake. Climbers should treat this unique area and its inhabitants with utmost care to preserve its wild attributes. The road to the cliffs is also a designated Utah Scenic Backway that travels 16 miles through Bulldog Canyon past Jarvis Peak to Wittwer Canyon and the Shivwits Indian Reservation.

The east-facing Black and Tan is a true hardman's wall with half a dozen 5.13s and several 5.14 projects in its double caves. It also hosts several very technical vertical routes. Kelly's Wall, a north-facing cliff tucked into a nearby scenic side canyon, yields some very good 5.9 to 5.12 routes with rock that is, unfortunately, extremely sharp on the fingers. More traffic should comfortize the edges on its great routes. Black and Tan was developed by Salt Lake City climbers including Boone Speed, Jeff Pederson, Geoff Wigand, along with locals Todd Goss and Michael Nad. The lines on Kelly's Wall, all unnamed, were put up by Kelly Oldrid and Brian Meacham. All routes on both crags are bolted. **Rack:** A dozen quickdraws and a 165-foot rope.

Finding the crags: The cliffs are southwest of St. George. They can be accessed from St. George to the northeast or from Interstate 15 in Arizona to the south. To reach them from St. George, turn west on Sunset Boulevard on the north side of town and drive 12 miles on Utah 91 (old U.S. Highway 91) through Santa Clara to the junction at Shivwits. Keep left on Utah 91 here and follow it over Utah Hill and past the Welcome Springs turn-off for 14.5 miles to a small sign on the left that says "Woodbury Desert Study Area." This same turn is reached from Interstate 15 at Littlefield, Arizona, below the Virgin River Gorge by driving north on old U.S. Highway 91 for 9.6 miles. Turn east

onto gravel Bulldog Canyon Road and drive through the Woodbury Desert Study Area for 3.8 miles, crossing 3 cattleguards. Past the third cattleguard, look for a pullout on the right just below Black and Tan. A 2-minute, uphill approach leads to the cliff base. To find Kelly's Wall, park at the pullout, walk down the road for 50 yards and find a faint trail across a creosote-covered bajada to a dry wash in a canyon. Hike up the wash for about 100 yards to the obvious cleft and cliff.

BLACK AND TAN

Routes are listed left to right from the lower cave.

1. **Campus Boy** (5.13c) Follow a white streak over the roofs. Powerful, devious, and sharp on upper runout. 4 bolts to 2-bolt chains. 55'.

2. **Dickheads** (5.13a) Work up left on steep black rock. 4 bolts to 2-bolt chains on a ledge. 60'.

3. **Da Riddler** (5.12c) Steep and powerful with underclings and layaways. Run it out up top on easy rock to anchor. 4 bolts to 2-bolt anchor with fixed biners. 60'.

4. **Dull Boy** (5.11d) Up and left over shallow right-facing corner to same anchor as Route 3 below break. 5 bolts to 2-bolt anchor. 60'.

5. **Bed Head** (5.11c) Good fun on the right side of the cave. 4 bolts to 2-bolt anchor in horizontal break. 60'.

6. **Smoking Drum** (5.13c) A cool Jeff Pederson route on the far left edge of the upper cave. Pull across big roof then up right to double bolt anchor. 6 bolts to 2-bolt anchor. 60'.

7. **Talking Smack** (5.13c) Another powerful roof route. Climb tan rock to roof, swing across and finish up a groove. 7 bolts to 2-bolt anchor with fixed carabiners. 60'.

8. **Project** (5.13+?) A roof leads to steep, technical, black slab. 7 bolts to 2-bolt anchor. 85'.

9. **Open Project** (5.14?) Serious crimps and sidepulls on this project right of Route 8. Pulling the roof is only the first problem. The techno-slab above leads to bolt 7 on Route 8. 9 bolts to 2-bolt anchor.

10. **Sniffing Glue** (5.13a) A good cave route. Pull tan rock to a black streak then up left to a tan streak and elongated hole. Difficulty eases above bolt 3 but it's runout to bolt 4 by hole. Finish up excellent stone. 5 bolts to 2-bolt anchor. 60'.

11. **Project** (5.14?) A Geoff Wiegand project that angles left from bolt 3 on Route 10. Has some serious, somewhat runout, technical climbing on the black vertical wall above. 6 bolts to 2-bolt anchor with fixed biners. 65'.

12. **Project** (5.13?) Same start as #10 but up right on tan rock to small overhang to black streak. 4 bolts to 2-bolt anchor on ledge. 55'.

13. **Unnamed** (5.14a) A Wiegand 1-bolt, left-angling link-up between Routes 12 and 10.

14. **Unnamed** (5.13a) Destined to be a B&T classic. Begin on right side of cave. Climb steep tan rock to black streak. End on ledge. 3 bolts to 2-bolt chains. 50'.

15. **Unnamed** (5.11b) A good line on the vertical wall right of the fence. Climb pockets and edges up black and white streaks. 5 bolts to 2-bolt anchor. 55'.

16. **Unnamed** (5.12a) A thin, sharp, technical gray streak left of small alcove.

4 bolts to 2-bolt anchor. 50'.

17. **Unnamed** (5.12d) Start just left of the big boulder at the base. Very thin, sequential face climbing up beautiful black limestone. 5 bolts to 2-bolt anchor (same as Route 16). 50'.

18. **Unnamed** (5.11d) Short, fun route with some sharp holds that angles up left. 4 bolts to 2-bolt anchor. 40'.

19. **Drunken Speed Fisherman** (5.10b) Easiest route up here but quality. 5 bolts to 2-bolt chains. 80'.

20. **Tickman** (5.11b) Walk right around a sloping buttress and past some caves to a short wall. This is the left-hand route. Good cranking past 4 bolts to 2-bolt anchor on a ledge. 50'.

21. **Pangs of Ignorance** (5.11a) Just right of *Tickman*. Good rock, good route. 4 bolts to same 2-bolt anchor. 50'.

More routes are up right on a steep wall, unfortunately many of the hangers were stolen. A small wall, The Annex, is 100' left of the lower cave. Three routes ascend this wall. From left to right: *Clean Sweep* (5.11b—4 bolts to 2-bolt anchor), *The Prying Game* (5.10b—3 bolts to 2-bolt anchor), and *Block Party* (5.10a—4 bolts to 2-bolt anchor).

KELLY'S WALL

A beautiful wall in the side canyon opposite Black and Tan. Belay in the bouldery dry streambed. Routes listed right to left.

22. **Kelly One** (5.12b) The rightmost route. Up good tan rock to angling cracks. Sharp up high. 6 bolts to 2-bolt anchor. 80'.

23. **Kelly Two** (5.11b) One of the best limestone routes in the area. Start off the boulder at the base and climb tan rock up and over a couple of roofs. 7 bolts to 2-bolt anchor. 75'.

24. **Kelly Three** (5.12c/d) Left of the water groove and black streak. An easy slab to steep, technical wall to final slab. Finish just left of large hole. 7 bolts to 2-bolt chains. 75'.

25. **Kelly Four** (5.11b) Another quality line. Move up slab to scoop and pull thin headwall above to gray slab. 6 bolts to 2-bolt anchor. 70'.

26. **Kelly Five** (5.10b) Slab to steep face. Cool climbing but sharp edges. 4 bolts to 2-bolt chains. 65'.

27. **Kelly Six** (5.11b) Thin slab with smears and edges. Go left for 5.9 variation. 5 bolts to 2-bolt chains. 60'.

28. **Kelly Seven** (5.9) Fun short route but scary for 5.9 leaders. 2 bolts to 2-bolt chains. 35'.

29. **Kelly Eight** (5.10a) On the left side. Scramble up eroded flutes to a scoop and pull up steep rib. 2 bolts to 1-bolt anchor or continue to ledge up high. Good and easy slabs to left for beginners but could use a couple of bolts.

THE OVERLOOK & CETACEAN WALL

OVERVIEW

Cedar City, lying along Interstate-15, sits at the western foot of the abrupt escarpment of the Markagunt Plateau. This lofty plateau, capped by erosion-resistant layers of volcanic rock, reaches heights above 11,000 feet. Sharp canyons and desiccated badlands, carved by dashing torrents of winter snowmelt and summer thunderstorms, are chiseled into the plateau's lofty edges. Best known of these is Cedar Breaks National Monument, a huge amphitheater of colorful sandstone fancifully sculpted into a fairyland of gargoyles, minarets, pinnacles, and stair-stepped ridges. Several developed climbing crags hide on the plateau near Cedar Breaks, the best of which are The Cetacean Wall and The Overlook. Both are good summer alternatives to the hot, lower elevation crags west of Cedar City and around St. George.

The Cetacean Wall, sitting just above Utah Highway 14, is on a band of soft limestone that lines Cedar Canyon. Only this small section of the canyon's many cliffs has been developed. The southeast-facing, 50-foot wall, reached by a 5-minute trail from a highway pullout, offers a selection of bolted sport routes that range from 5.10 to 5.12. The mostly vertical routes offer bouldery, technical moves on crisp edges, crimps, and pockets. The area is a good stop-off when en route to The Overlook. Most climbers will tick the best routes in an afternoon. The wall, sitting at about 8,500 feet, is climbable from May through October.

The Overlook is an excellent area perched on the northwest edge of the lofty Markagunt Plateau. The view from atop the tier of cliffs is stunning. Below spreads a green carpet of spruce, fir, and aspen on rolling ridges that break abruptly into sharp, cliffed canyons. Beyond stretches the broad Parowan Valley with the Red Hills on its far margin; distant, desert mountain ranges rim the western horizon. Climbers, mostly locals, come here for the marvelous views, the cool summer weather, and a choice of great short routes.

The Overlook, sitting at 10,400 feet, is a band of cliffs composed of welded volcanic tuff. The routes climb pockets and edges on mostly vertical, lichen-covered faces. Almost all of the routes, ranging in height from 30 to 70 feet, are bolted with lowering anchors. This is still a developing climbing area so there are several projects and unclimbed faces. Primitive camping is available at the circular parking area just above the cliffs. Practice no-trace, clean camping techniques to preserve the area's beauty. Be prepared in summer for severe thunderstorms and lightning. Also use caution on the cliff top—the lichens on the rock surface are often slick when wet. There is loose rock on steep slopes below the cliffs. The area around The Overlook is also excellent mountain biking terrain with rolling countryside laced with trails and backroads. The cliff is generally climbable from mid-June until October. Otherwise it's buried under deep snow.

Climbing history: Both of these areas were developed in the mid-1990s by climbers from Cedar City and St. George. Bob Draney, author of the Cedar City area guidebook, established many of the routes at The Cetacean Wall, as well as some of the classics at The Overlook including *Blue Suede Shoes* and *Smiling at the Majorettes*. Draney named many of The Overlook's routes after a couple of lines in the Genesis song "Broadway Melody of 1974." Most of The Overlook routes were put up by prolific Todd Goss from St. George.

Trip Planning Information

General description: A couple of limestone and volcanic sport crags in the mountains above Cedar City.

Location: Southwestern Utah. East of Cedar City.

Camping: Great free primitive camping is found at the turnaround above The Overlook. Plan on cool nights. Bring water and practice no-trace camping techniques. Otherwise there is a good campground at Cedar Breaks National Monument and a Dixie National Forest campground off Utah 14 between The Cetacean Wall and Zion Overlook.

Climbing season: Summer and fall. The snow doesn't melt away from the cliff base at The Overlook until late June, while the Cetacean Wall is snow-free by early May. Expect cool temperatures and possible heavy thunderstorms at The Overlook in summer.

Restrictions and access issues: None currently. Both areas lie in Dixie National Forest.

Guidebooks: *Pumping Iron* by Robert Draney, 1995. A good guide to both crags and others in the Cedar City area. *Too Much Rock, Not Enough Life* by Todd Goss, 1997. This St. George area guide includes topos to The Overlook and other Iron County sport routes around Cedar City.

Nearby mountain shops, guide services, and gyms: Cedar Mountain Sports in Cedar City and the Outdoor Outlet in St. George. Todd Goss with Paragon Climbing Instruction (801) 673-1709 offers basic and intermediate climbing courses as well as guiding services and area climbing tours.

Services: All visitor and climber services in Cedar City. Escobar's is a popular Mexican restaurant. Showers can be had at the local KOA campground and at the Southern Utah University PE Building. Limited services near The

Overlook are in the small ski resort of Brian Head.

Emergency services: Call 911.

Nearby climbing areas: Cedar City crags—Iron Mine Rocks, Pocket Rocks, Public Lands Cracks, Bubble Rock, Parowan Gap (excellent conglomerate); St. George area crags—Black Rocks, Cougar Cliffs, Turtle Wall, The Green Valley Gap, Gorilla Cliffs and Simeon Complex, The Diamond, The Wailing Wall, The Cathedral, Virgin River Gorge (AZ); Zion National Park and the Kolob Canyons.

Nearby attractions: Pine Valley Mountain Wilderness Area, Zion National Park, Smithsonian Butte Back Country Byway, Virgin River Narrows, Kolob Canyons, Kolob Arch (largest in world), Cedar Breaks National Monument, Bryce Canyon National Park, Dixie National Forest.

THE CETACEAN WALL

This 50-foot-high wall, the lower of two cliff tiers, offers a selection of bolted sport routes on a very soft limestone that resembles sandstone. The routes, mostly in the 5.11 and 5.12 range, begin with vertical rock, have slabby mid-sections, and end with a final steep headwall. Be prepared for thin bouldery moves, steep edging, positive crimps, sequential cruxes, and some desperate mantles. **Rack:** Bring 10 quickdraws and a 165-foot rope. **Descent** on all routes is by lower-off from chained and bolted anchors.

Finding the cliff: The southeast-facing cliff, which receives morning sun, is accessible via a short trail from Utah 14. Reach the cliff by driving 9.3 miles up route Utah 14 from the junction of Center and Main streets in downtown Cedar City. Park in a large pullout on the left (east) side of the highway as it runs south up cliff-lined Cedar Canyon. The Cetacean Wall is seen to the west as a cliff band below a prominent overhanging prow. Walk up the highway about 150' and cross Crow Creek on large flat stones. Follow a path up through the forest to the cliff base. Approach time from the highway is about 5 minutes. Routes are described left to right.

1. **Fragment "G"** (5.12a) Line goes up left of a large roof and begins between 2 trees on the left side of the crag. Climb steep rock past dike, edge up steep slab, and finish up right on headwall. 5 bolts to 2-bolt chain anchor.

2. **Booga Beluga** (5.11a/b) One of the easier offerings here. Route follows a blunt arête right of the big roof and a huge drapery of bat guano. Climb short crack (medium pro) and then up right edge of the prow. 5 bolts to 2-bolt chain anchor.

3. **Sound Image** (5.11c) Begin right of Route 2 and a juniper tree. Face climb beautiful stone up left to a crimpy crux. Finish at anchors left of overhanging block boulder. 5 bolts to 2-bolt chain anchor. An intermediate anchor is half-way up.

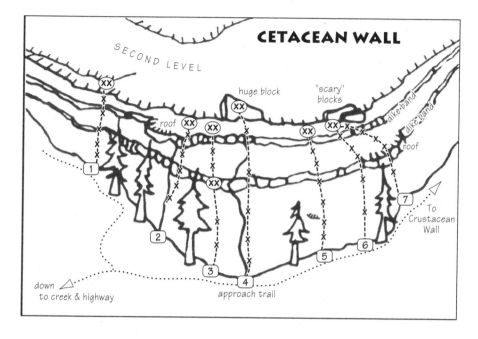

4. **Tursiops Leap** (5.12b) Quality moves. Start directly below huge block perched on cliff top. Follow tan seam left of black streak up steep rock to final crux mantle. Anchors are on overhanging block face. 5 bolts to 2-bolt anchor.

5. **Wailing** (5.12a/b) Just right of a towering spruce tree. Edge up steep gray rock to a 3rd bolt crux. Continue up tan slab. 6 bolts to 2-bolt chain anchor.

6. **Sailing** (5.11d) On the right side of the southeast face. Begin behind tall spruce right of Route 5. Work up left to high, thin crux and anchors below some dangerous stacked boulders on cliff top. Avoid these blocks! 5 bolts to 2-bolt chain anchor.

7. **Bailing** (5.12a) Begin on the right side of the buttress prow behind a spruce. Climb up left over roof to crimp crux below blocks. Move left and clip Route 6's anchors. 5 bolts to 2-bolt chain anchors.

Farther right from Route 7 is a short line with botched bolts. Continue on a path along the cliff base northwest from here for about 10 minutes to reach The Crustacean Wall. Two good routes are located here. *Rock Lobster* (5.11a) is a worthy 5-bolt line on the left side. *Smoking Crawdads* (5.10c), the area's easiest route, begins up *Rock Lobster* before moving right and then finishing at the same anchors. A slab with some bolted routes is found farther up Cedar Canyon from the parking area. Look for a large pullout on the right and the slab in the trees above to the west.

THE OVERLOOK

The Overlook is an excellent north and northwest-facing 50-foot-high crag composed of welded tuff at the high elevation of 10,500 feet. The area, over-looking the Parowan Valley, offers an excellent assortment of bolted sport routes up to 80 feet long. Most routes ascend pockets and edges, along with an occasional crack move. **Rack:** 12 quickdraws and a 165-foot rope is ad-equate for a day's fun. **Descent** from all routes is by lower-off from anchors. Some might require leaving quickdraws on the anchors that are easily retrieved from the cliff top.

Finding the cliff: The driving approach from Cedar City takes about an hour. The walking approach from the parking area is about 2 minutes to the cliff top. From the intersection of Center and Main Streets in Cedar City, drive east on Center which becomes Utah 14. Follow the scenic highway for 20 miles to Utah 148. Turn left (north) on route 148 and drive north through Cedar Breaks National Monument (great overlooks) for 7.7 miles to Utah 143 on the monument's north edge. Turn right (east) on Utah 143 and drive 4.7 miles across rolling countryside to Forest Road 048, signed Sidney Valley Road. Turn left (north) on this good gravel road and drive through meadows and aspen groves for 4.4 miles to an obvious circular parking area to the left. Park here. The Overlook's cliffs are only minutes from the parking.

Walk right along a trail to access most of the routes. The path drops down through breaks in the cliff on both the left and right sides. The first 9 routes described begin on the far left side of the cliff band. Reach them by turning left (southwest) on a mountain bike trail and hiking about 5 minutes to a break left of the obvious cliffs.

THE SLIDE AREA

1. **Stolen Thunder** (5.10d) First route on the far left side. Left of blocky rock peninsula. 3 bolts to 2-bolt anchor. 30'.

2. **Crime Doesn't Pay** (5.11a) 3 bolts to 2-bolt anchor. 30'.

3. **Trads Make Me Laugh** (5.10a) Left of Route 2 on the side of the penin-sula. 4 bolts to a 2-bolt anchor. 40'.

THE ZOO

4. **Midget Marathon** (5.10a) First route on the right side of the rock penin-sula. Approach right down short gully to west-facing wall. A short line up licheny face left of overhanging boulder. 3 bolts to 2-bolt anchor. 30'.

5. **It's No Secret** (5.11b) Just left of Route 4. Follow right edge of overhang-ing prow up good pockets. 4 bolts to 2-bolt chain anchor. 35'.

6. **Orange Krush** (5.12b) Swing up the overhanging tan face left of prow to

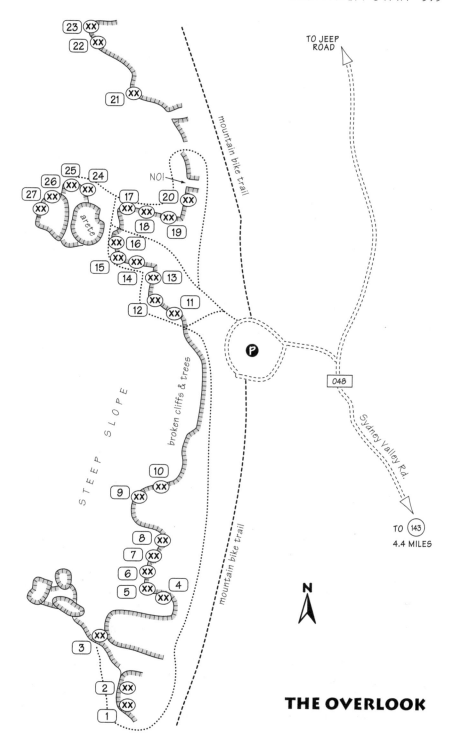

THE OVERLOOK

anchors on narrow ledge. 4 bolts to 2-bolt anchor. 40'.

7. **Dwarf Tossing** (5.12d) 2 bolts to 2-bolt anchor on ledge. 30'.

8. **Oxygen Deficit** (5.12c) Just right of large corner and left side of overhanging wall. 4 bolts to 2-bolt anchor above roof.

9. **Fits of Rage** (5.12d) Go left from Route 8 around prow to licheny face left of dead tree. Climb steep, overhanging face. 6 bolts to 2-bolt anchor. 55'.

10. **Angst** (5.12a) Left of Route 8. Climb up a path through the lichen. 6 bolts to 2-bolt anchor. Left of *Angst* is a 4-bolt route called *How Ya Lichen It* (5.11c).

THE STARTING BLOCK

The following routes are directly west from the parking area. Hike to the cliff top and move left and down broken boulders to the face base.

11. **Willie The Pimp** (5.10a) A fun jug haul on the right side of the cliff. Climb up blocks and ledges to roof. Swing over and finish up slab. 5 bolts to 2-bolt anchor. The anchors are easily clipped from the top for a toprope.

12. **Suck It Up Crybaby** (5.12b) An excellent area testpiece. Scramble up left from Route 11 to base of leaning wall on right side of big dihedral. A steep jugfest leads to technical headwall finish. 6 bolts to 2-bolt anchor on the top of the cliff. 55'.

13. **Must Suck Being You** (5.12c) A hard, crimpy line left of Route 12. 6 bolts to 2-bolt anchor.

14. **Pumping Out of Gas** (5.11a) Route 14 and Route 15 are on the southwest-facing wall left of Route 13. Pull over roof to short wall to ledge. Fun climbing heads up thin left-facing corner to top. 4 bolts to 2-bolt anchor. This is a good toprope (clip the 2-bolt chained anchors from above).

15. **Funky Boss** (5.10c) Just left of Route 14. Best 5.10 here. Grip pockets to big ledge. Continue up bulging wall to top. 4 bolts to 2-bolt anchor. Anchors can be reached from above for top-roping.

16. **No Rhyme or Reason** (5.10a) On the broken prow of the cliff band. Scramble left from Route 15 into notch between main rim and rock island. Climb obvious broken dihedral to anchors up left. 3 bolts to 2-bolt anchor. Bring some medium Friends.

Easiest way to reach the following routes is by walking along a cliff-top trail to the right of the cliff prow and rock island to a steep gully in a slot. The routes are to the left on a beautiful, smooth, northeast-facing wall.

17. **Blue Suede Shoes** (5.12a) A 3-star route! Begin left of arête and climb up past jug pocket onto gorgeous yellow-lichened rock. Crux is at the last bolt. 5 bolts to 2-bolt anchor.

18. **Howard Hughes** (5.11c) Another super line. Pull cool pockets up blue-gray lichen streak. 4 bolts to 2-bolt anchor. *Heimie the Mexican Gynecologist* (5.11d) is just left of this route.

19. **Dr. Diaper** (5.9) On the short wall left of Route 18. Jam quality thin crack past a couple of horizontal breaks to 2-bolt anchor. 30'.

20. **Wind Screen Wiper** (5.11c TR) Climb Route 19 and set a toprope on anchors. Face climb lichen-covered face right of the crack.

HIGH RISE AREA

21. **The Song and Dance Begins** (5.9 TR) Walk right along the cliff-top from the descent gully and spot a couple anchors atop a gray wall. Reach down and clip them for this toprope face route. *Angering the Cheese Gods* (5.10b) is just left of this route.

22. **Virtual Ecstasy** (5.11c) Right of Route 21. Up an excellent sharp arête. 6 bolts to 2-bolt anchor. 50'.

23. **The Crucible** (5.13a) On wall left of arête. Farther right is *Birth Canal* (5.11d).

THE SLUMS

Routes 24 to 27 are on the north side of the rock island below the main cliff band. Access by descending steep slopes along the cliff face below Route 17 to the northern base of the island.

24. **Smiling at the Majorettes** (5.11b) This excellent route ascends left side of obvious arête. A low crux leads to superb face moves. 6 bolts to 2-bolt chain anchor. 70'.

25. **Smoking Winston Cigarettes** (5.11d) The harder twin of Route 24. Step around arête and face climb to top. 7 bolts to 2-bolt chain anchor up left (same anchor as Route 24).

26. **Mercy Street** (5.12a) Right of Route 25. 7 bolts to a 2-bolt anchor.

27. **Angle of Repose** (5.12a) The longest route at the crag on the outside edge of the rock island. 11 bolts to rap anchors. *Slum Lords* (5.11a) is on the southwest corner of The Slums island.

Wasatch Front

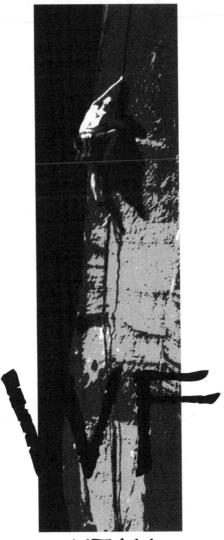

UTAH

LOGAN CANYON

OVERVIEW

Logan Canyon, a sheer-walled canyon lined with limestone and quartzite cliffs, runs northeast from Logan and the fertile Cache Valley. This sharp canyon, excavated by the Logan River, is a sport climber's paradise with its diverse assortment of bolted routes. Over 300 mostly bolted routes, ranging in difficulty from 5.5 to 5.14, ascend the canyon's steep walls. Logan is best known for its hard routes at the China Wall Cave. Here, on this unassuming, radically overhanging, smoke-stained cave, hides a selection of America's hardest lines including *Super Tweek* (5.14b) and *Whiteout* (5.14a). Most of the canyon's climbs, however, lie in the 5.10 to 5.12 range which makes it a great area for aspiring hardmen and women.

The canyon is traversed by U.S. Highway 89, a designated national forest scenic byway, as it meanders along the river. Most of the climbing is located in the first 15 highway miles out of Logan. The scenic river canyon, lying above 4,500 feet, is floored by a lush riparian zone with dense groves of willows. The higher canyon slopes are blanketed with Douglas-fir and ponderosa pine. The cliffs in the lower canyon are composed of quartzite and black dolomite. Farther along above the road and river stretch the long bands of limestone and dolomite that offer most of the canyon's routes.

Logan Canyon is a 3-season area. Summer temperatures range from the 50s at night to the 80s in the daytime. It's easy, however, to find shaded, cooler routes. The China Cave receives little direct sun and is in full shade through the whole afternoon in summer. Spring and autumn offer great climbing weather, with highs usually between 50 and 70 degrees. Winters are just too darn cold for visitors to think about climbing here. Peter Sinks, near the head of the canyon, boasts the dubious distinction of being Utah's coldest recorded place with an unofficial 1888 record of 65 degrees below zero and an official 1979 low of 49 degrees below zero. There are some good icefalls in the canyon. Info on them is located in the area's comprehensive guidebook.

The canyon's climbing crags are intensively managed and monitored by Wasatch National Forest. The local ranger district has worked closely with local climbers, conservationists, and botanists to protect the area's unique scenic qualities and the rare and endangered plant species that inhabit the cliffs. A positive and proactive stance by climbers allowed an equitable man-

Mia Axon on Secret Sharer, *China Cave, Logan Canyon.* PHOTO BY STEWART M. GREEN

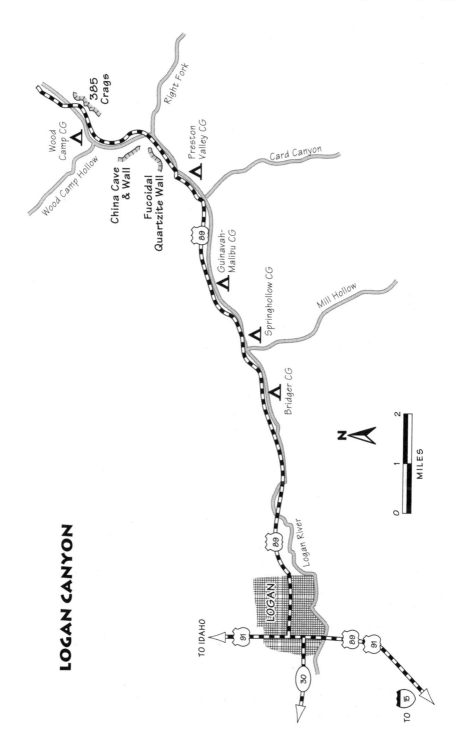

LOGAN CANYON

385 Crags

Wood Camp CG

Wood Camp Hollow

China Cave & Wall

Fucoidal Quartzite Wall

Right Fork

Preston Valley CG

Card Canyon

89

Guinavah-Malibu CG

Springhollow CG

Mill Hollow

Bridger CG

N

0   1   2

MILES

89

Logan River

LOGAN

TO IDAHO

91

30

89

91

15

TO

agement policy to evolve that allowed cliffs to remain open. The policy also stressed the impacts that climbers had on this fragile area. The climbing and rappelling policy protects both climbers' rights as well as the rights of the area's plants and their habitats.

The rare Maguire primrose is endemic to Logan Canyon. The primrose and four other sensitive species live on wetter sections of the limestone cliffs, coming in direct conflict with climbers. Under the Endangered Species Act, the Forest Service must take steps to protect the plants, therefore no climbing or rappelling is allowed within 50 feet of any threatened or endangered plant species. This rule has closed about 10 percent of the canyon routes. Other provisions of the policy include no rock alteration, chipping, chiseling, or gluing; no removal of vegetation from the cliffs; fixed gear should be camouflaged; climbing and rappelling is not allowed in Logan Cave; and no rappelling is allowed from the top of China Wall or Greenhouse Wall. Follow these guidelines to avoid damaging the good relations that now exist between area climbers and the Forest Service.

Climbing history: Because of the outdoor-oriented student population at Utah State University in Logan, Logan Canyon has a long and varied climbing history. Many of the area's first routes were put up on the quartzite in the lower canyon including topropes and gear routes on the First and Second Practice walls. It was the sport climbing revolution of the late 1980s, however, that brought the canyon into the climbing mainstream with its hard bolted routes. Boone Speed, with his ascents of *Tweek* (5.13d) and then *Super Tweek* (5.14b) in the early 1990s, solidified the upper grades at the China Cave. In 1996, teenager Chris Sharma went on a tear here, repeating Speed's hard routes and then making his own link-up of *Whiteout-Super Tweek* and calling it 5.14b. In 1997 Australian Garth Miller upped the ante with another link-up called *Super Geek*, also 5.14b.

Logan Canyon's crags and climbs are mainly located within a 10-minute hike from the highway, although a number of higher, more remote cliffs give more solitude to those willing to walk farther. Plentiful parking is found in pullouts along the highway; well-trodden access trails reach all of the cliffs listed here. **Rack:** The standard rack for all Logan sport routes is a 165-foot rope and 10 quickdraws. A larger rack with cams and stoppers is required for traditional-style routes. **Descent:** Get off most routes by lowering or rappelling from anchors. If you toprope off anchors, use quickdraws to run the rope through rather than the anchors.

Trip Planning Information

General description: Numerous routes, mostly bolt-protected sport climbs, ascend limestone and quartzite crags in scenic Logan Canyon.

Location: North-central Utah. East of Logan along U.S. Highway 89.

Camping: Numerous Wasatch National Forest campgrounds, usually open from May to October, lie along U.S. Highway 89 in Logan Canyon. Primitive campsites are found in Right Hand Fork and Temple Fork canyons. Call the Wasatch National Forest office in Logan at (801) 753-2772.

Climbing season: Spring, summer, and fall. Summer days can be hot, but shaded walls, notably China Cave, are climbable. Spring is variable, but most crags are sunny. Fall is perfect, with warm, sunny weather. Winters are cold and snowy, with ice climbs found on the walls.

Restrictions and access issues: The canyon, in Wasatch National Forest, is home to several rare plant species including the endemic Maguire primrose, a flower protected under the Endangered Species Act. A number of routes and walls are closed to climbing to preserve this cliff-dwelling plant. Climbing and rappelling within 50' of the plants is prohibited, a rule which closes about 10 percent of the canyon's routes. Some of these closures are on the China Wall. Obey any signage marking climbing closures. The Forest Service allows bolting but asks climbers to exercise restraint when creating new routes and not to crowd routes to avoid damaging fragile plants. A climbing and rappelling policy also prohibits rock alteration including chipping, gluing, or drilling holds; it also prohibits the removal of vegetation from cliff faces, bases, and tops. There is no climbing or rappelling at Logan Cave and no sport rappelling at China Wall or the Greenhouse Wall. Power drilling is prohibited in designated wilderness areas.

Guidebooks: *Logan Canyon Climbs* by Tim Monsell. A comprehensive guide to about 300 routes in Logan Canyon.

Nearby mountain shops, guide services, and gyms: The Trailhead (Logan), Adventure Sports (Logan), Outdoor Pursuits—USU Outdoor Recreation Center Climbing Gym (Logan), Hansen Mountaineering (Provo), IME (Salt Lake City), Black Diamond (Salt Lake City), REI (Salt Lake City).

Services: All services are found in Logan. You can get a shower at the HPER Building on the Utah State University campus.

Emergency services: Call 911.

Nearby climbing areas: Hyrum Canyon, Ogden Canyon, Salt Lake areas. City of Rocks (ID) is about 2 hours away.

Nearby attractions: Logan Canyon Scenic Byway, Mount Naomi Wilderness Area, Bear Lake, Beaver Mountain Ski Area, Wellsville Mountain Wilderness Area, Cache Valley, Minnetonka Cave, Great Salt Lake.

Finding the crags: The cliffs lie along U.S. Highway 89 just east of Logan in north-central Utah. To reach Logan from Salt Lake City, drive north on Interstate 15 for 50 miles to Brigham City and exit east on U.S. Highways 89/91. Follow this highway for 24 miles to Logan. Salt Lake City to Logan is 81 miles. Drive into downtown Logan and turn east on U.S. highway 89. Drive east past Utah State University and drop down to the canyon entrance. Mileages begin from the junction of U.S. Highway 89 and Canyon Road at the entrance to Logan Canyon. All of the crags are along the first 15 miles in the canyon. Fucoidal Quartzite Crags are at 8.8 miles. The China Wall is at 9 miles. Crag 385 is at 11 miles.

FUCOIDAL QUARTZITE CRAGS

This collection of crags offers some of Logan Canyon's best rock and largest selection of easier routes. The cliffs scatter across the north side of the canyon above mile marker 383.20, or 8.8 miles from the mouth of the canyon. Park at a large pullout on the north side of the highway at the Fucoidal Quartzite interpretative sign. Check out the slab by the sign. It's 400-million-year-old cemented beach sand covered with fossilized castings, filled burrows, and trails of marine worms. The crags and routes are listed from left to right when you face them.

MIDDLE TOWER

1. **Limestone Cowboy** (5.11d) A good sport route up steep white rock on the left side. It's a grade harder for short folks. 6 bolts to 2-bolt anchor.

2. **Blood and Guts** (5.7) Climb right-angling crack to set of anchors and top-rope face below. The route does continue up obvious crack above (5.10a) but isn't climbed because a tree is now growing out of it. Double bolt anchor at 30'. Bring a selection of gear.

3. **Tiny Toons** (5.8 TR) Set a toprope from the mid-anchors on a small ledge for a short middle grade toprope adventure. A variety of ways to go from 5.5 to 5.8.

4. **Adios Amigos** (5.12a) Long route with pumpy climbing to steep finish. 11 bolts to 2-bolt anchor.

5. **Mission** (5.10c/d) Jam and edge up left-facing corner before working right to 2-bolt anchor above ledge. 7 bolts.

6. **Community Effort** (5.9) Quality fun route for the grade. Follow line of bolts right of slabby arête to 2-bolt anchor above ledge (same anchor as Route 5).

7. **Gully Route** (5.7) Work up obvious gully between 2 towers to cliff-top belay. Walk off.

EAST TOWER

8. **Jam Crack** (5.5) A hand crack to a ledge. Move left and finish up Route 7. Bring hand-sized cams.

9. **Begging For Bolts** (5.11a) You won't be begging on this one. Face climb up steep wall past a couple of crux roofs to a 2-bolt chain anchor. 13 bolts. 100'. Double ropes are needed to rappel off this route.

10. **Terminalogical Inexactitude** (5.11b/c) Can be done in 2 pitches. First pitch to chains is 5.10b and very popular. Above, climb the south wall to roof. Finish up right at 2-bolt chain anchor. 12 bolts. 100'. Use a 200-foot rope or two 165-foot ropes to get off.

11. **Gill's Grace** (5.10c) An obvious left-facing dihedral just right of Route 10. Lieback and jam up crack to belay stance. Walk off. **Rack:** Set of Friends and stoppers.

12. **Unknown** (5.10) No topo. Climb the blunt prow right of large left-facing corner just right of Route 11. Face climb past several ledges to 2-bolt chain anchor on ledge. 5 bolts.

THE AMPHITHEATER

The Amphitheater is a small horseshoe-shaped cirque right of the East Tower. A few good routes are located here. Access via a short trail that climbs a steep slope to the base.

13. **Tonic Sphincter Syndrome** (5.11a/b) Follow crack system on steep east-facing wall on upper left side of The Amphitheater. Climb up shallow corner and move left to small stance, continue past juggy roof and crux finger crack to 2-bolt anchor. 4 bolts and a fixed pin. **Rack:** Bring some small cams and stoppers. 50'. *Relaxed Bowl* (5.10c) is an easier variation to the crux. Work up left near top to avoid roof and finish at anchors.

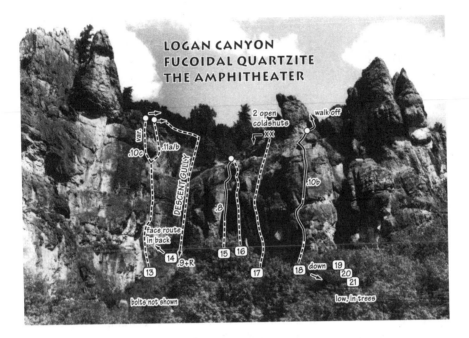

LOGAN CANYON
FUCOIDAL QUARTZITE
THE AMPHITHEATER

14. **Cranial Compromise (5.9+ R)** A short face route up black wall at the head of the cirque.

15. **Lieback Crack (5.8)** Lieback an obvious crack on right wall of Amphitheater. Rap off a tree—anchors are stolen. **Rack:** Bring Friends and stoppers.

16. **Black Knight (5.12a/b)** Just right of *Lieback Crack*. Thin climbing up leaning black streak to top of *Lieback Crack*. 3 bolts.

17. **Kings Gambit (5.12c/d)** Right and downhill from *Black Knight*. Steep face climbing up white to black wall to 2-bolt anchor. 6 bolts to 2-open cold shut anchor.

18. **Cushions (5.10b)** Climbs a prow on the right side of The Amphitheater. Face climb past 2 bolts to double cracks, work up past 2 more bolts and finish atop a buttress. Walk off. **Rack:** Bring a small rack of Friends and stoppers.

The next 3 routes are on the far downhill/right side of The Amphitheater. Access via a short trail. All the routes are in a shallow alcove.

19. **Tennis Ball (5.8)** A steep, fun black slab on the left side of the alcove. Face climb to 2-bolt anchor; 30'. 3 bolts. Just right of this is an unknown route (5.11) that climbs steep white limestone past 5 bolts to a 2-open cold shut anchor.

20. **Cannonball (5.10c)** A steep left-facing corner on right side of alcove.

Lieback, stem, and face climb to a 2-bolt anchor. 1 bolt. **Rack:** small gear.

21. **Man and Woman** (5.12b) On the right-hand wall of the alcove. Thin face climbing up slightly overhanging black rock. 6 bolts to 3-bolt chain anchor.

CHINA WALL & CHINA CAVE

The east-facing China Wall, towering above the rushing Logan River, yields some of Utah's hardest rock routes on the severely overhung China Cave. The wall lies on the west side of the river and the highway. Drive 9.0 miles from the canyon entrance to a large parking area on the left just before a highway bridge. The crag is located at the 383.40 mile marker. Park and follow a trail through dense woods along the river's west bank for a quarter of a mile to the cliff base. There are a number of routes on the black wall above the access trail. Many of these lines are closed to climbing because of their proximity to the endangered Maguire primrose. Do not climb here. Two short, steep sport routes—*Luna Land* (5.12a/b) and *Groping for Luna* (5.12a)—that are legal are found just before the path drops down to China Cave.

China Cave is very popular with the hard crowd, with lots of folks milling about and watching the activities on busy days. Unfortunately the routes get crowded and backed up because there are basically 2 starts to most of the routes. Don't "work" on the long routes like *Coast to Coast* or *Crimpfest* when others are waiting to climb. There are many tough variations and link-ups on the cliff. Routes are listed left to right.

CHINA CAVE

22. **Trench Warfare** (5.13c) The leftmost line. Begin on horizontal sooty rock and follow the upside-down trench/crack out long roof to pumpy rock above. 11 bolts to 2-bolt anchor.

23. **Big Brawl** (5.13c) A traversing route that works up left to 2-bolt anchor in left-facing corner. A strange sequence of moves off pockets above roof's lip includes an off-balance cross-through. 10 bolts to 2-bolt anchor.

24. **Slugfest** (5.13d) A variation to *Big Brawl* that features a direct finish to *Tweek's* anchors. 9 bolts to 2-bolt anchor.

25. **Tweek** (5.13d) A classic hard route put up by Boone Speed. Winch up to the end of the horizontal roof or start off the wooden table if available. Powerful climbing to left-angling traverse and final overhanging headwall finish. 9 bolts to 2-bolt anchor. The V9 boulder problem start in the back of the cave increases the difficulty by a letter grade to 5.14a.

26. **Super Tweek** (5.14b) Do the V9 boulder problem start at the back of the roof and climb *Tweek*. Finish with direct V9 finish. 8 bolts to 2-bolt anchor.

27. **Blackout** (5.13d/14a) Use the winch or table start to *Tweek*. Climb up

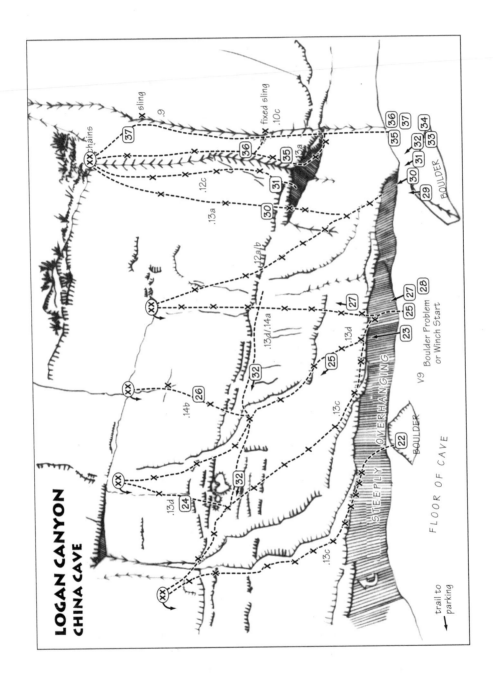

**LOGAN CANYON
CHINA CAVE**

right on powerful and difficult moves to *Oboe's* anchors. 7 bolts to 2-bolt anchor.

28. **Whiteout** (5.14b) Do the V9 boulder problem start and follow *Blackout* up right.

29. **The Oboe** (5.12a/b) The most popular route at China Cave. Begin atop a large boulder on the right side of the cave. Clip first bolt and A0 up to second bolt. Work up and out left side of roof and climb pockets up left on steep face. 7 bolts to 2-bolt anchor. The direct start off the boulder is V5; unfortunately shorter people can't reach the starting holds from the boulder.

30. **Secret Sharer** (5.13a) Use the same start as *The Oboe* by winching up to bolt 2. Steep, powerful climbing leads up right above roof past widely spaced bolts on upper wall. 7 bolts to 2-bolt chain anchor.

31. **Cunning Runt** (5.12c) Another popular line. Same start as Route 30 to bolt 2. Follow *Secret Sharer* to above roof then diverge right to blunt arête. 8 bolts to 2-bolt chain anchor.

32. **Sportfest** (5.12d) A grand traverse of the cave. Begin with *The Oboe* and swing up left across long line of holds and past 10 bolts to *Trench Warfare's* anchors.

33. **Crimpfest** (5.13b) A superb and pumpy traversing line. Begin with *The Oboe* and finish 13 bolts later at *Tweek's* anchors.

LOGAN CANYON
CHINA WALL CAVE

34. **Coast to Coast** (5.12c) Another traverse. Begin with *The Oboe* and climb as far left as possible to large pocket. 14 bolts to 2-bolt anchor.

35. **Vulcan Crawl** (5.13a) Kind of a cool route up and over the horizontal roof on the right side of China Cave. Traverse left under roof to powerful pocket pulls that lead onto technical headwall above. 5 bolts to 2-bolt chain anchor.

36. **Gang of Four** (5.10c) Begin below obvious right-facing dihedral on right side of China Cave. Climb up dihedral to fixed sling above prominent roof. Work out left past 3 bolts to run-out climbing and a 2-bolt chain anchor.

CHINA WALL

The following routes are on the right side of the China Wall, a more vertical and technical cliff right of the cave.

37. **Dihedral Route** (5.9) One of those "why bother" routes. Climb obvious right-facing dihedral past fixed pin to point just above where it's possible to traverse left to Route 36's anchors.

38. **Minnowmaker** (5.12b) A technical masterpiece right of the dihedral. Use layaways and some high-steps to work up good rock. 10 bolts to 2-bolt anchor. A 200' rope is needed on this route to lower off!

39. **Praise the Lowered** (5.12c/d) Thin, tricky face climbing up obvious black streak. 6 bolts to 2-bolt anchor.

40. **Beijing** (5.12c) Dicey but well-protected face climbing past 12 bolts to 2-bolt anchor.

41. **Bolt Ladder** (5.12b) Face route up steep black wall. Climb 50' to first set of anchors. 5 bolts to 2-bolt anchor. Above is an old bolt ladder that isn't usually climbed.

42. **Crotch Shot** (5.11a) This face line ascends the right side of the wall inside a wide, flaring chimney. Stem and edge for 75' up wall. 8 bolts to 2-bolt anchor.

43. **Viable Option** (5.11b) Climb south-side, blunt arête of a semi-detached pinnacle. Work up 40' past 3 bolts to 2-bolt anchor.

44. **Doogie Doo** (5.11c/d) A long face route up the riverside of the semi-detached pinnacle. 13 bolts to 2-bolt anchor. Bring 200' rope for the descent.

45. **Orcstone** (5.9) Done in 1 or 2 pitches. Face climb the obvious crack above the river to Route 44's anchors. Rap with 2 ropes or a 200' rope. Bring small and medium gear.

46. **Dog Food** (5.12b) Begin on the river's edge during low water. Climb up and right (5.12b) to bolt belay/lowering anchor or continue (5.11) to higher anchors and rap or lower with 200' rope. 10 bolts to 2-bolt anchor.

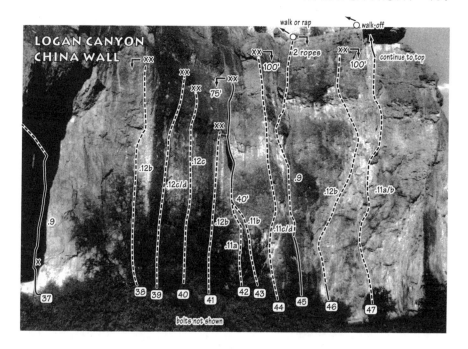

47. **Illusion Dog** (5.11a/b) Start where the cliff meets the river. This route might not be accessible until late summer and autumn because of high water. Climb crack system up steep rock to belay stance under bulging roof. Pull the roof (5.11) or climb easier rock out left. Bring an assortment of gear with an emphasis on small and medium pieces.

CRAG 385

A very good cliff on the south side of the highway above mile post 385 about 11 miles up the canyon. Park at a small pullout on the north side of the highway. Space is limited here on busy days. The cliff is accessed by a short trail through woods to the base of the lower wall. The upper left wall is reached by scrambling over boulders and up steep slopes to its base. Routes are listed left to right beginning with the left or east flank of the upper left wall.

UPPER WALL

48. **Oh No Mr. Bill** (5.12c/d) Begin on far left side of upper wall atop large boulder. Face climb up black streak to bush, step left and continue straight up to anchors. 8 bolts to 2-bolt anchor.

49. **Being the Glue** (5.12a) Start on large boulder just right of Route 48. Climb light rock to shallow crack, keep right of bush, and pull the bulge above to anchors. 7 bolts to 2-bolt anchor.

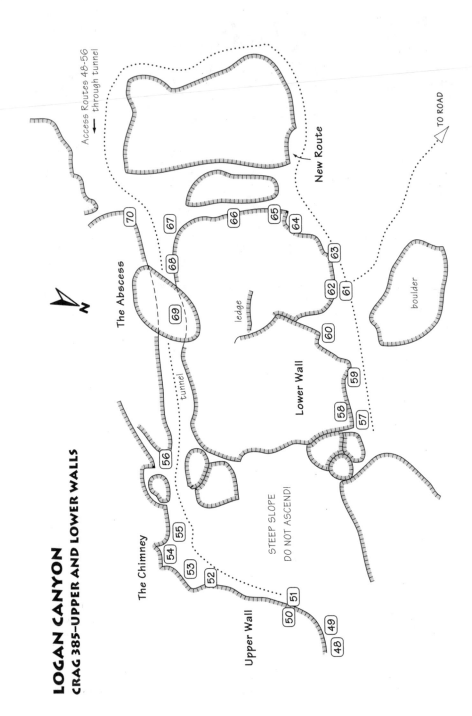

LOGAN CANYON
CRAG 385–UPPER AND LOWER WALLS

50. **Heat Miser** (5.11d) Climb excellent crack/flake to black streak. Continue up and left on steep rock to thin leftward traverse. 7 bolts to 2-bolt anchor. 70'.

51. **Heat Seeker** (5.12b) A superb line. Clip the first 3 bolts of Route 50, then work up right with pebbled edges and sidepulls over small roof and onto dark gray face. 8 bolts to 2-bolt anchor. 70'.

52. **Goat Debris** (5.11a) One of the canyon's best routes—do this before it gets polished. Begin below a dark streaked face. Do a boulder problem start or traverse left to a ramp. Climb up vertical and gently overhanging rock. Finish up right to anchors. 10 bolts to 2-bolt anchor. 70'.

53. **Talk of the Town** (5.10d) Don't talk about it, just climb it. Swing up right side of huge flake to narrow stance. Pull through crux and head up steep but juggy gray/tan streak. 6 bolts to 2-bolt anchor (same as Route 52). 65'.

54. **Grunt Crack** (5.8) A grungy chimney and off-width crack for the masochist sport climber.

55. **Nuclear Fallout** (5.11c/d) The steep bulging arête right of *Grunt Crack*. Climb right side of arête to stem onto left wall at the top (without the crucial stem the face climbing is 5.12a). 6 bolts to 2-bolt chain anchor. 55'.

56. **Finger Fire** (5.11c/d) Right of Route 55 and near the tunnel. It's harder than it looks. Stick-clip bolt 1 to avoid decking and jam finger crack up arête to slabby face. 5 bolts to 2-bolt anchor.

LOWER WALL

These climbs sit on the Lower Wall behind a large boulder. Routes are listed from left to right.

57. **Pigs in a Python** (5.11c) This 80-foot line climbs the obvious arête on left edge of wall. Work up left after 3 bolts then straight up. A right variation, *Python*, goes right at bolt 3 and up .12b/c rock to rejoin *Pigs*. 10 bolts to 2-bolt anchor.

58. **Unknown** (5.11) Climb steep left wall of right-facing corner just right of Route 57 to anchors on slabby rock. 7 bolts to 2-bolt anchor. 70'.

59. **Unknown** (5.10) Work up rock right of right-facing corner using sidepulls and edges. 5 bolts to 2-bolt anchor. 50'.

60. **Dream Fire** (5.12a) Up tan rock on left side of prominent chimney about 40' right of Route 57. Edge up black slab (runout above bolt 1), step left onto narrow ledge, and pull up overhanging black streak to final roof problem. 9 bolts to 2-bolt anchor. 80'.

61. **Zion Pickles** (5.11c) Climb crack up gray face for 30' to small ledge. Move up and then right to anchors just below top. 10 bolts to 2-bolt anchor. 90'. Use a 200' rope or 2 ropes to get off.

62. **Brigham Pickles** (5.12c/d) A difficult variation finish to Route 61. Go up left onto a black arête above bolt 7; 90'. Use a 200' or 2 ropes to rap or lower.

63. **Pale Face** (5.12d) A super line with great rock and sustained, hard movements. Follow thin edges and pockets up long, overhanging gray wall to crux moves over small black roof below anchors. 11 bolts to 2-bolt chained anchor; 90'. Use a 200' rope or 2 ropes to get down.

64. **Nuclear Fingers** (5.11d/12a) Right of Route 63 near far right edge of wall. Climb vertical face up right to stance. Step left and up overhanging rock past 4 bolts to 2-bolt anchor under obvious roof. 9 bolts to 2-bolt anchor; 80'. A 5.12a finish pulls the roof above the anchors and ends at Route 63's anchors.

65. **Conventional Arms** (5.11a) An excellent outing at this grade. Begin just around corner arête from Route 64 at base of broken chimney. Work up black wall to stance. Hard climbing above leads onto arête. Anchors are in a break below the roof. 7 bolts to 2-bolt anchor. 80'.

66. **Stormin' Norman** (5.11b/c) On west side of buttress above chimney. Follow left-angling seam, pull a roof, and face climb to anchors. 8 bolts to 2-bolt anchor. 70'.

67. **Friendly Fire** (5.11b) Right of Route 66 on the outside edge of the tunnel wall (southeast corner of buttress). Scramble onto boulders above chim-

LOGAN CANYON
CRAG 385
LOWER WALL

upper wall

80'

80'

90'

90'

62

90'

1 open coldshut
XX chains

var.

61

80'

chains
XX

XX

64

57   58   59   60   61   63
62

trail from road

bolts not shown

ney to begin. Thin climbing up left-leaning arch (4 bolts) leads to crack. Bring small Friends, TCUs, and stoppers. Or move left at break above bolt 4 and clip the top 2 bolts of Route 66. 4 bolts to 2-bolt anchor. 60'.

68. **The Abscess** (5.11c) This and the next 2 routes are back in The Abscess, an alcove roofed by a large boulder. A tunnel leads through the back of the recess to the Upper Wall routes. Climb dicey black slab up left to roof. Pull over and continue to anchors. 5 bolts to 2-bolt chain anchor. 50'.

69. **Burning from the Inside** (5.11b) Begin farther back in the dark recess. Friction and edge up slippery black slab to black roof. 5 bolts to 2-bolt chain anchor (same as Route 68).

70. **Order and Chaos** (5.11a) On the right side of The Abscess. A short overhanging wall with 4 bolts and a 2-bolt anchor.

BIG COTTONWOOD CANYON

OVERVIEW

The Wasatch Range forms a towering and ragged backdrop to Salt Lake City. Deep canyons, carved by cascading creeks swollen with snowmelt, slice into the mountain front. Big Cottonwood Canyon, flanked by towering alpine ridges, is one of the longest and most scenic of these canyons. The canyon begins above timberline in wildflower-strewn glacial cirques nestled against the range's lofty crest. Brighton and Solitude ski areas lie near the canyon's head. The upper canyon is a broad, glaciated valley, while the lower canyon, below the glacier's farthest west reach, is steep and V-shaped, chiseled by Big Cottonwood Creek. Here stretches a rough landscape defined by sharply upturned and gnarled crags of variously-colored metamorphic quartzite that stud steep ridges and slopes above the canyon's twisting floor.

Big Cottonwood Canyon's lower crags are justifiably popular. They're close to Salt Lake City, most of the cliffs are easy to access, and they have a wide variety of grades. The routes climb up the rugged, soaring buttresses, walls, arêtes, slabs, and cliffs. *Wasatch Climbing North*, by Bret and Stuart Ruckman, lists almost 50 separate climbing areas in Big Cottonwood with literally hundreds of routes. This plentiful assortment of lines, ranging from 1 to 4 pitches in length, is mostly bolt-protected sport routes with an occasional classic crack. Many of the routes are steep and overhanging, with hard, continuous climbing on incut edges and sidepulls.

The canyon is part of the Wasatch National Forest and has no current climbing restrictions or access problems. The one prohibition that applies to all visitors is that dogs and horses are not allowed in the canyon because it is part of Salt Lake City's drinking watershed. Few ethics debates have arisen over Big Cottonwood Canyon climbing. Other than some early, bold routes put up in a ground-up traditional manner, most of the lines are bolted from the top down on rappel. This is partly because the canyon quartzite is just too hard to hand drill a bolt hole. The placement of additional bolts on existing routes and the chipping and manufacturing of holds is, of course, seriously frowned upon.

When visiting the canyon, use some common sense to avoid making an unnecessary environmental impact. The canyon is not only heavily used by rock climbers, but also by all the urban refugees from Salt Lake City. Follow existing trails to the cliffs whenever possible. Use the national forest restrooms at the various recreation areas throughout the canyon, including Dogwood, Ledgemere, and Storm Mountain picnic areas, as well as the trailhead to Lake Blanche below the S-Curve. Pick up all your litter plus any that other thoughtless climbers have left at the cliff base.

Climbing history: Rock climbing in Big Cottonwood Canyon evolved hand-in-hand with Little Cottonwood Canyon, its more popular neighbor to the south. The first routes done in the canyon were by the prolific early pioneer Harold Goodro, including the classic *Steorts' Ridge* at Dead Snag Crag in the late 1940s and *Goodro's Wall* on Storm Mountain Island in 1949. This excellent, overhanging crack, now rated 5.10c, was probably Utah's first 5.10 and certainly one of the country's hardest routes at that time. Goodro later wrote *Wasatch Quartzite*, the canyon's first guidebook.

It wasn't until the sport climbing, rap-bolting revolution came to Utah in the 1980s that Big Cottonwood Canyon began fulfilling its rock climbing potential. Beginning in the mid-1980s, a host of local hardmen began exploring and naming Big Cottonwood Canyon's numerous crags and putting up new routes. These Bosch pioneers, reading like a Who's Who of Salt Lake City climbing, include brothers Stuart and Bret Ruckman, Gordon Douglass, Drew Bedford, Merrill Bitter, Conrad Anker, John Storm, and Brian and Jonathan Smoot. Most of the plums were picked in the 1980s boom which left only scattered harder problems for 1990s climbers to clean up.

Trip Planning Information

General description: Numerous quartzite crags, laced with a few hundred sport and trad routes that ascend cracks, slabs, and steep faces, line a deep canyon in the Wasatch Range.

Location: North-central Utah. East of Salt Lake City.

Camping: The best campgrounds for climbers are the two national forest areas in upper Big Cottonwood Canyon. Spruces Campground, with 121 sites, is at 9.8 miles, and Redman Campground, with 50 sites, is at 13.2 miles. Little Cottonwood Canyon to the south also has a couple of good forest campgrounds—Tanners Flat Campground, with 38 sites, is at 4.1 miles, and Albion Basin Campground, with 26 sites, is at the road's end near Alta Ski Resort. All are fee areas, with water, restrooms, and tables. Pets are not allowed because the canyons are part of Salt Lake City's watershed.

Climbing season: Year-round. It's almost too hot in summer on the south-facing cliffs. Pick a shady wall on the south side or go in the early morning. Spring offers variable weather, but good days are not uncommon. The creek crossing can be very dangerous during snowmelt runoff. Autumn has the best climbing weather, with clear, warm days. Winter days are often warm enough to climb in the sun, and snow quickly melts off the sunny slopes. When a cloudy, cold temperature inversion blankets Salt Lake City, it is often sunny and mild above the lower air layer up in the canyon.

Restrictions and access issues: The canyon is in Wasatch National Forest. There are currently no restrictions on climbing and no access problems. Dogs are, however, prohibited in the canyon and on the trails because the canyon is part of the Salt Lake City watershed. This canyon is heavily used by Salt Lake City residents; climbers should maintain a conservationist attitude. Follow existing trails to the cliffs. Don't make fires outside of designated areas. Pick up after yourself, including mylar energy bar wrappers, cigarette butts, and tape.

Guidebooks: *Rock Climbing the Wasatch Range* by Bret and Stuart Ruckman, Chockstone Press, 1998; a comprehensive guide. *Wasatch Range* by Bret and Stuart Ruckman, Chockstone Press, 1997; a select guide to over 200 routes in Big and Little Cottonwood canyons and American Fork Canyon.

Nearby mountain shops, guide services, and gyms: Stores include Black Diamond, IME, REI, Mountainworks (Provo), and Hansen Mountaineering (Orem). Gyms are Wasatch Front Climbing Gym and Rockreation in Salt Lake, and Rock Garden in Provo. Guides include Wasatch Touring and Exum Mountain Guides.

Services: Salt Lake City and its suburbs offer everything the traveling climber desires.

Emergency services: Call 911 for all emergencies. Alta View Hospital, 9660 South 1300 East, Salt Lake City, (801) 567-2600. Cottonwood Hospital, 5770 South 300 East, Salt Lake City, (801) 262-3461. St. Mark's Hospital, 1200 East 3900 South, Salt Lake City, (801) 268-7129.

Nearby climbing areas: Little Cottonwood Canyon, Parley's Canyon, Millcreek Canyon, Pete's Rock, Ferguson Canyon, Bell's Canyon, Big Willow Canyon, Lone Pine Cirque, American Fork Canyon.

Nearby attractions: Alta, Snowbird, Big Cottonwood Canyon, Salt Lake City attractions (Temple Square, Brigham Young Monument, Beehive House, Utah State Capitol, Utah Museum of Natural History, Utah Museum of Fine Arts, This is the Place State Park, Hogle Zoo), Great Salt Lake, Bingham Canyon Mine (largest pit mine in world).

Finding the crags: Big Cottonwood Canyon is best accessed from I-215 on the east side of Salt Lake City. From Interstate 15, follow Interstate-215 to Exit 6 (6200 South). Signs are marked for the ski areas. Drive east up a hill and join Wasatch Blvd. Follow it to its junction with Ft. Union Blvd. (7200 South) at 1.7 miles from I-215. A 7-11 is on the southwest corner. Turn east at this traffic light. All mileages are taken from this road junction at the mouth of the canyon.

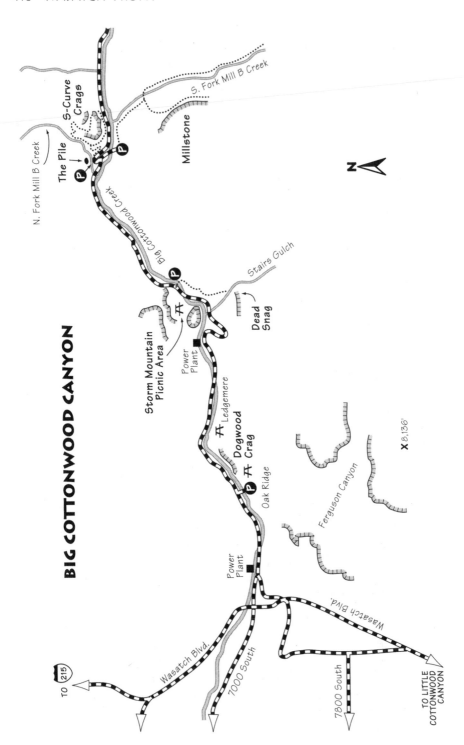

BIG COTTONWOOD CANYON

DOGWOOD CRAG

This slabby, north-facing, quartzite crag rises out of the creek on the right side of the road, 1.3 miles from the canyon mouth. A selection of decent routes, mostly bolted, ascend the crag. This is a good summer cliff in the morning when it's shaded. Approach by parking at a large pullout on the right side of the road and following a trail to the creek. Wade or stone-hop across to the base of the wall. If the creek is too full, park just down the canyon at the Dogwood Picnic Area and hike upstream on a climber's path to the cliff. Scramble up a tree-filled gully on the right side to access the cliff top for setting top-ropes or for a walk-off descent. Routes are listed right to left.

1. **Unknown** (5.7 TR) Find TR chains on the right side of the wall.

2. **Take Me to the River** (5.7) Best to toprope this one. Face climb up slab's right side to 2-bolt chain anchor. Bring a selection of small stuff for fiddling in pro.

3. **On the Skids** (5.8) A good line. Start where creek and cliff meet. Angle up left on polished slab to anchors. 6 bolts to 2-bolt anchor. Again, use biners for toproping.

4. **Unknown** (5.8) Begin just left of Route 3. Climb smooth slab to ledges at bolt 2, then up fun face to 2-bolt anchor. 4 bolts.

5. **Unknown** (5.8) Begin on creekside boulders, angle left above creek, then straight up and over right side of roof. Continue up great rock to top. 5 bolts to 2-bolt chain anchor.

BIG COTTONWOOD
DOGWOOD CRAG
ROUTES 10-13

65'

xx

belay above rock

.11c

finger/
hand

through hole

.11c

.11d

.13a/b

.11c

13

12

11

10

6. **I Think I'm Going Bald** (5.9-) Start same as Route 5, but angle up left side of slab to left side of roof. Pull over to beautiful polished face to anchors. 6 bolts to 2-bolt chained anchor (same as Route 5). 75'.

7. **The Lion of Zion** (5.6) Begin at creek. Follow roof system right to flake, undercling up right to trough/groove. Face climb to top. Belay from trees. **Rack:** Friends and stoppers. Direct start to right side of roof/flake is 5.6 R.

8. **A Modest Man from Mandrake** (5.9) No topo. Begin on left side of cliff, left of some broken cracks and corners. Scramble up short corner to bushy ledge. Cool climbing leads up polished slab to anchors. 6 bolts to 2-bolt anchor. 85'.

9. **Hyper-Gamma Spaces** (5.9 R) No topo. Move up left from broken corner to thin, right-angling crack. Belay from 2 bolts (same anchors as Route 8). Rap 85'. This is a good top-rope after doing Route 8. **Rack:** Thin stuff—RPs and small wires. Some decent moderates ascend broken face left from here.

The following routes are located on the far left side of the cliff on a large pillar.

10. **Little Creatures** (5.11c) A wild route in back of huge chimney formed by main face and broken pillar. Jam and lieback steep, pumpy flake up chimney's left side, through slot to belay ledge. 70'. **Rack:** Bring lots of cams—TCUs to #3 Friends.

11. **Cross-Eyed and Painless** (5.13a/b) One of Big Cottonwood's testpieces put up by Stuart Ruckman and Gordon Douglass in 1989. A stunning line up leaning edge of giant pillar. Face climb arête, finding jams and dynos, to anchors. 8 bolts to 2-bolt anchor. 65'.

12. **This Ain't No Party, This Ain't No Disco** (5.11d) The easier twin of Route 11. Start on west edge of pillar. Face climb past 2 bolts (5.11d) to ledge. Continue up strenuous, leaning finger/hand crack (5.11c) to 2-bolt anchor. **Rack:** A #2 Friend is handy up high.

13. **Life During Wartime** (5.9- R) Just left of Route 12. Climb black slabs up small overlaps and corners to ledge belay. **Rack:** Small pro—wires, RPs, and TCUs.

THE DEAD SNAG CRAG

The Dead Snag Crag is an east-facing wall that flanks the uptilted west side of Stairs Gulch, a steep side-canyon that climbs south from the main canyon. This superb quartzite cliff offers a trio of excellent moderate routes with great rock, fun climbing, and a short approach. Numerous other outcrops, including Challenge Buttress, Glass Ocean, and Vector Madness Wall, line the west side of the gulch and form a maze of cliffs and crags. There are many excellent and harder routes on these cliffs; they are thoroughly covered in the Ruckmans'

walk to rappel anchors

XX
80'

XX
80'

.4

.6

.6

XX
75'

.6

corner   .6

.6
roof

BIG COTTONWOOD   16   14   15
DEAD SNAG AREA

comprehensive *Rock Climbing the Wasatch Range* guidebook.

Finding the crag: Drive 2.8 miles up the canyon to a large parking area on the right or east side of the highway just past the turnoff to the Storm Mountain Picnic Area. Locate the start of the Storm Mountain Trail on the right side of the parking area. Follow the trail, an old rocky road, southward. It skirts beneath a large talus slope and then steeply ascends through trees and past some large pipes. After about a third of a mile the trail reaches an obvious clearing on the slope with a clear view west to the Dead Snag Crag. Follow a climber's path to the right that begins here, drops down into brush, crosses the creek, and wanders through evergreens to the cliff base. Allow about 15 minutes of approach time. Routes are listed right to left from the obvious arête that forms the right margin of the face.

14. **Steorts' Ridge** (5.6) 3 pitches. One of the area's oldest routes, this was first done by Harold Goodro and Lee Steorts in the 1940s. Locate the obvious arête that divides the north and east faces of the cliff. Begin left of the arête. **Pitch 1:** Face and crack climb up and over roof (5.6). Continue up easier, broken rock to belay on good ledge atop pillar below slanted roof. **Pitch 2:** Climb up right and follow wide crack left of arête to small belay stance on arête. **Pitch 3:** Face climb up steep, exposed arête to belay from trees on terrace atop wall. **Descent:** 3 single-rope rappels from bolted anchors down left (south) side of cliff. Consult topo for details. **Rack:** Sets of Friends and stoppers.

15. **Jig's Up** (5.6) 3 pitches. Another fun moderate. **Pitch 1:** Climb same first pitch as Route 14 to ledge belay. **Pitch 2:** Angle up right, pass right edge of small arch (5.6) and work directly up good double crack system to sloping belay ledge. **Pitch 3:** Continue up double cracks to a tree belay on ledge atop cliff. **Descent:** 3 single-rope, 80-foot rappels from bolted anchors down left (south) side of cliff. Consult topo for details. **Rack:** Sets of Friends and stoppers.

16. **East Dihedrals** (5.6) 3 pitches. Another good one. Begin left of Route 14 below right-facing corner and roof. **Pitch 1:** Ascend to corner and pass roof (5.6). When corner ends, exit left and climb headwall to small shady ledge below obvious right-facing dihedral. **Pitch 2:** Jam crack and corner (5.6) out small roof. Continue up excellent dihedral (5.4) to sloping belay stance. **Pitch 3:** Work up broken corners to 2-bolt belay on large ledge. **Descent:** 3 single-rope, 80-foot rappels from bolted anchors down left (south) side of cliff. The first rap is from belay anchors. Consult topo for details. **Rack:** Set of Friends and stoppers.

STORM MOUNTAIN ISLAND

This complicated area, not covered in detail in this book, offers a multitude of fine routes on several crags surrounding the Wasatch National Forest's Storm

Mountain Picnic Area. Users are subject to a daily use fee. The climbing is, however, excellent, varied, and of all grades. Drive 2.8 miles up the canyon and turn left into the picnic area, pay your use fee, and park. The main climbing is on Storm Mountain Island, a blocky island of rock on the west side of the creek and area, and on the Bubble Bee, Psychobabble, and Static walls on the north side. Psychobabble Wall has some of the canyon's best sport routes. The cliffs are well documented in the Ruckmans' comprehensive Wasatch climbing guide; consult it for directions and route specifics. Recommended routes include:

STORM MOUNTAIN ISLAND

Le Creme de Shorts (5.9) Good finger to hand crack.

Layback Crack (5.5) 2 pitches up a corner.

Goodro's Wall (5.10c) An excellent overhanging finger and thin hand crack that was first climbed by Harold Goodro in 1949. It's possibly Utah's first 5.10.

Six Appeal (5.6) A 6-bolt sport route next to *Goodro's Wall*.

Padded Cell (5.12a/.12c) A 5-bolt line up a steep smooth wall.

Big in Japan (5.12b) A really good 4-bolt route over 2 roofs to anchors.

PSYCHOBABBLE WALL

The Enemy Within (5.12a) A pumpy endurance line up an arête.

Eye in the Sky (5.12a/b) A very 1980s-style sport route with RP placements between bolts.

Psychobabble (5.10b/c) A great diagonaling crack line.

Psychostematic (5.10a) A stemming problem.

Rebel Yell (5.11c) Another fine arête line.

Rock Capades (5.10d) A thin left-facing corner.

Eyes Without a Face (5.11a) Thin crack, great climbing.

S-CURVE CRAGS

The S-Curve area, lying north above the switchbacking S-shaped curve in the upper canyon, is one of Big Cottonwood's most popular climbing locales. The approach is short and easy, and the routes are bolted, clean, and fun. Drive 4.5 miles up the canyon and park at the large parking lot on the inside of the upper switchback. If this is full, try the lower parking areas along the road. Hike up the trail to the left side of the Lower S-Curve Wall. Locate a climber's path and follow it along the lower wall's base. The trail to the upper wall ascends a gully right of the lower wall. The Pile is reached via a 1-minute walk up a short trail to Hidden Falls, while New Cliche Crag is about 10 minutes up the trail past the S-Curve Wall.

THE PILE & NEW CLICHE

The Pile is a small east-facing cliff on the west side of Hidden Falls Trail just before the falls. It's a popular crag with bolted lines and cool temperatures moderated by the creek. It got its name when the late Mugs Stump first saw the cliff and said, "What a pile! You oughta call these routes Right Pile and Left Pile." Routes are listed left to right.

17. **Gomer Pile** (5.10a) Jugs along the left margin of crag. 5 bolts to 2-bolt anchor.

18. **Left Pile** (5.12b) Steep, pumpy, and overhanging line up left side. 4th clip below crux is tough. 5 bolts to 2-bolt lower-off anchor.

19. **Right Pile** (5.11d) Pumpy jugs up the middle of the face. 5 bolts to 2-bolt lower-off anchor. A link-up between *Left* and *Right Pile* is *Pile Surgery* (5.12a). Climb right from bolt 3 on *Left Pile* past a bolt.

20. **Dog Pile** (5.10b) Short, sweet, and jugs, but still a pumper. 4 bolts to 2-bolt anchor.

New Cliche Crag, a south-facing cliff, is above the creek and north of the falls. Hike up the trail for 10 minutes to the top of the switchbacks; scramble across the creek and up to the base of a short south-facing crag.

21. **New Cliche** (5.12c/d) No topo. Swing up and over the big roof to a dyno (5.12c). 5 bolts to 2-bolt anchor. *Kiss it Goodbye* (5.12d) is just left of this route.

LOWER S-CURVE WALL

This is the broken wall directly above the S-Curve. Many of the routes are similar in quality and movement, with edges and pulls up sharp quartzite holds. But it is a good and popular spot for a quick afternoon pump. Almost all of the routes are bolted and have lowering or rappel anchors. Standard gear is a 165-foot rope and a dozen quickdraws. The crag gets lots of sun, making it a great cool weather area. Summer days can be hot here. Try early morning then. Routes are listed left to right.

22. **Dog Eat Dog** (5.13d) On left side of big roof. Scramble up to 2-bolt anchor under roof. Follow line of bolts via strenuous slopers and edges to ramp/crack. Lower from fixed pro. 5 bolts.

23. **S-Curve Overhang** (5.11c) 2 pitches. Classic, weird, and well worth the effort. **Pitch 1:** Climb broken corner (5.4) to 2-bolt belay under immense roof. **Pitch 2:** Climb up right (5.11c) and swing across strange ramp/

BIG COTTONWOOD
THE PILE

crack that angles left to final pull (5.10) over lip. 9 bolts and fixed pitons to 2-bolt anchor. 75'. **Descent:** Rappel 70' from 2 bolts back to belay stance, then rappel 80' to the ground.

24. **High Life** (5.11c) A great pumpfest! Climb Route 23 to 2-bolt belay. Angle up right (5.11c) then over huge roof. 5 bolts to 2-bolt anchor.

25. **Melting Point** (5.10b) Climb edge of slabby prow right of big roof. 9 bolts and fixed pins to 2-bolt anchor.

26. **Clastic Cling** (5.10d) 1 or 2 pitches. **Pitch 1:** Pull over small roof (5.10d) then work up right to 2-bolt anchor. 4 bolts; 50'. Many lower here. **Pitch 2:** Move up left over overhanging stair-stepped rock (5.10a) to Route 25's anchors. 5 bolts and fixed pins to 2-bolt anchor.

27. **Ionic Bonding** (5.11a) 2 pitches. First pitch is really popular. **Pitch 1:** Pull over multiple roofs (5.9+) then up broken slab to Route 26's anchors. 5 bolts to 2-bolt chain anchor. **Pitch 2:** Swing up incuts on overhanging wall to anchors. 4 bolts to 2-bolt chain anchor.

28. **Alpenbock Route** (5.9) 2 pitches. One of the first routes here. **Pitch 1:** Climb groove up ramp to belay stance on left side of roof. **Pitch 2:** Move up broken corner to airy hand traverse under roof. 3 fixed pitons to cliff-top belay. **Descent:** Walk off to east. **Rack:** Bring an assortment of wires, TCUs, and small to medium Friends.

29. **Mass Wasting** (5.11c) 2 pitches. Airy and pumpy. **Pitch 1:** Up ramp below big roof to belay stance. **Pitch 2:** Follow bolts and jugs up right over obvious roof. 6 bolts to 2-bolt anchor. 80'.

30. **Red Light District** (5.9+) Climb steep wall right of ramp to anchors right of roof. 6 bolts to 2-bolt anchor. 70'.

31. **Madison Avenue** (5.10d) An ad-man's dream route! Work up steep wall left of some roofs to anchors in groove. 5 bolts to 2-bolt anchor. 60'.

32. **City Slave** (5.10d) Begin 10' right of Route 31. Pump over 3' roof on jugs, continue up steep rock to Route 31's anchors. 4 bolts to 2-bolt anchor. 60'.

33. **Times Square** (5.11a) Scramble onto big sloping ledge in middle of wall. Climb overhanging left-facing corner over big angling roof to lip crux. 6 bolts to 2-bolt anchor.

34. **Black Monday** (5.11a) Quality climbing. Begin down right of Route 33. Follow line of big jugs up overhanging wall. 8 bolts to 2-bolt anchor (same as Route 33).

35. **Think Tank** (5.12b/c) Climb broken easy groove up right then up and over big roof. Follow left-hand line of bolts with a dyno crux. 5 bolts to 2-bolt anchor. 80'.

36. **Gas Chamber** (5.11b/c) The right-hand, easier-but-still-steep brother to Route 35. 5 bolts to 2-bolt anchor. 80'.

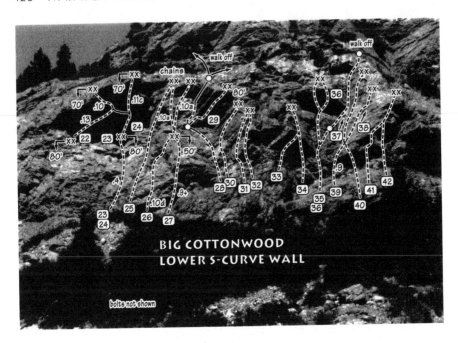

BIG COTTONWOOD
LOWER S-CURVE WALL

bolts not shown

37. **Tres Facile (5.6)** 2 pitches. Easiest offering at the crag. **Pitch 1:** Up big grooved, right-angling dihedral to good ledge. **Pitch 2:** Continue up groove corner to cliff top. Belay and walk off.

38. **Chorus Line (5.9)** Great fun. Begin right of gully on left side of row of roofs on far right side of cliff. Pull the cruxy roof (5.9) then cruise. 6 bolts to 2-bolt anchor. 70'.

39. **Choir Boy (5.9)** A left-hand variation to *Chorus Line*. Veer left above bolt 3. 6 bolts to 2-bolt anchor. 80'.

40. **Skid Row (5.11a)** A harder but cool variation start to *Chorus Line*. Start 15' right of Route 38 and crank over roof on jugs. 2 bolts.

41. **Cross Town (5.11c)** Takes the steepest line up row of roofs on far right margin of cliff. 8 bolts to 2-bolt anchor. 60'.

42. **Bourbon Street (5.10d)** The direct start to *Cross Town*. Steep climbing past 3 bolts then up Route 41.

THE MILLSTONE

The Millstone is an excellent cliff band that sits high above Mill B Stream southeast of the S-Curve. The steeply angled band of quartzite, facing east and southeast, yields a brilliant selection of mostly vertical sport routes up to 80' long as well as spectacular views of the surrounding canyons and peaks. The hiking approach to the crag is fairly steep and rigorous, keeping the traffic to

BIG COTTONWOOD CANYON
THE MILLSTONE

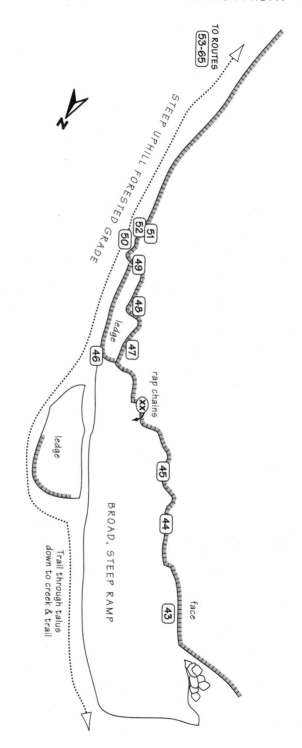

TO ROUTES
53-65

STEEP UPHILL FORESTED GRADE

52
51
50
49
48
47
46
ledge

rap chains
xx

45

44

43
face

ledge

Trail through talus
down to creek & trail

BROAD, STEEP RAMP

N

a minimum. Don't expect crowds up here! Keep your pack light for the approach with only a dozen quickdraws, a rope, and water. The cliff gets morning sun and afternoon shade. Be prepared for the weird, somewhat disorienting angle of this cliff.

Finding the crag: The approach trails, while seemingly complicated, are fairly straightforward. Begin by driving up the canyon and parking in the Lake Blanche Trailhead at 4.4 miles. The paved parking area is on a short spur road that ends just east of the highway at the lower S-curve. The trail begins here at the restrooms alongside the creek.

Walk east up the trail (here an old road) on the south bank of the creek. After about a quarter of a mile, Mill B Creek tumbles in from the south. The marked Lake Blanche Trail begins here. Follow it by turning right, or south, and following this good path along the west bank of Mill B Creek for another quarter of a mile to a bridge crossing. Don't cross the bridge; instead, turn right off the main trail here and follow a subsidiary climber's path south along the west bank of the creek through dense foliage. The trail finally climbs out of the creek bed and follows a bench above it. Continue south until thickets block the path. An obvious rocky drainage and trail heads west here. Turn right and follow this path through trees and then left onto the bottom of a huge talus field. The cliff is obvious at the top of the talus.

Make your way up the laborious talus field. A rough, cairned trail follows the right-hand talus branch. Eventually the trail ends at a huge polished slab at the lower end of the cliff band. Allow 30 to 40 minutes of hiking time to reach the cliff from the parking area. Routes are listed right to left beginning with those above the steep smooth slab. All distances between routes are approximate.

43. **Intelligent Life Form** (5.8) Good position at lower end of cliff. Carefully scramble across slab to route base. Fun moves up short pretty slab. 4 bolts to 2-bolt chain anchor. 40'.

44. **Tie Die** (5.10c) 40' left of Route 43. A cool face right of right-facing, leaning corner. 5 bolts to 2-bolt chain anchor.

45. **Private Hell** (5.10a) 20' left of Route 44. Feels weird with the sloping ramp beneath. Up right wall of leaning dihedral. 4 bolts to 2-bolt chain anchor.

The following routes are on the main southeast-facing cliff. Follow a steep trail along the cliff base to access all routes. Routes are listed right to left.

46. **Calling All Karmas** (5.12b) 75' left of Route 45. This is on the left side above the sloped ramp. A few thin moves down low on sharp arête then onto ledge. Step left and finish up 3-bolt headwall. 7 bolts to 2-bolt anchor.

47. **Angle of Repose** (5.10a) 4' left of Route 46. Up slab to big ledge up another slab. 6 bolts to 2-bolt anchor.

48. **Personal Jesus** (5.10d) 20' left of Route 47. Right of a big corner on the

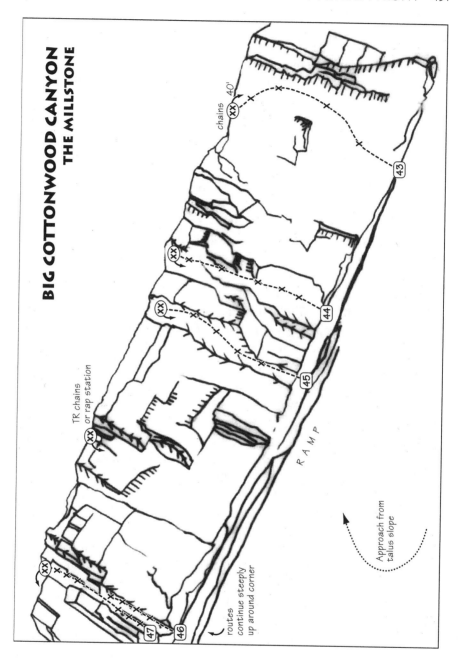

BIG COTTONWOOD CANYON
THE MILLSTONE

chains 40'

43

44

45

TR chains
or rap station

RAMP

Approach from
talus slope

routes
continue steeply
up around corner

46
47

left side of arête. 4 bolts to 2-bolt chains. 40'.

49. **Milling About** (5.11b) 20' left of Route 48 at the top of a ramp. Good jamming route but not climbed often. Begin on a ramp. Lieback and jam thin hands up double right-facing corners. Belay up top. **Descent:** Scramble up left to Route 50's anchors and rap 60'. **Rack:** Bring small and medium Friends.

50. **Eraserhead** (5.11a) Starts almost directly below Route 49 on the ground. An excellent tan face left of a sharp arête with flat edges and sustained edging. Bring some small gear for cracks between bolts 1 and 2 and bolts 4 and 5. 4 bolts to 2-bolt anchor. 60'.

51. **Pencilneck** (5.10c) 20' left of Route 50. Begin below left-facing flake. Edge out right and follow steep thin crack that diagonals up right. Decent gear for the leader, but makes a good top-rope off Route 50's anchors.

52. **Hollow Excuses** (5.9 R) Same start as Route 51. Fun liebacking up the big, hollow, left-facing flake, but may be better to top-rope off Route 53's anchors.

53. **Against the Establishment** (5.11b) 10' left of Route 52. A beautiful lichen-covered face with thin edgy pulls. 5 bolts to 2-bolt chain anchors.

54. **Bush Doctor** (5.7) 20' left of Route 53. A right-angling ramp with a bush. Belay up top and scramble left to Route 55's anchors.

55. **Miller Time** (5.10c) Good climb—pop the tops! Start up big flake, crank over small roof on jugs, then finish up steep slab. 4-bolt to tree anchor.

56. **Earthling** (5.11a) 10' left of Route 55. Steep with blocky sidepulls. 6 bolts to tree belay.

57. **Moonwalk** (5.11d) 30' left of Route 56. Start on boulders by a white pine. Climb up and left of hanging flake with steep, pumpy finish up headwall. 8 bolts to 2-bolt belay up top.

58. **Strong Arm With the Lads** (5.11a) 20' left of Route 57. Tough guys only need apply. Roof to slab to roof crux. Pumpy jugs. 8 bolts to 2-bolt anchor (same as Route 57).

59. **Stone Ground** (5.11b) 15' left of Route 58. Quality line. Start right of left-facing corner and roof. Up thin angling crack with everything—blocky jugs, sidepulls, edges, and underclings. 6 bolts to 2-bolt anchor.

60. **The Maize** (5.12a) Same start as Route 59. Go left at bolt 2 and up thin, steep overlaps. 6 bolts to 2-bolt anchor (same as Route 59).

61. **The Odd Get Even** (5.11b) 15' left of Route 60. Start just left of left-angling roof and bush. Over top edge of roof then steep technical headwall. 5 bolts to 2-bolt anchor.

62. **Stick Figure Stays Home** (5.11a) Same start as Route 61. Up left on a smooth slab keeping left of thin corners to a final roof. End on slab with slings under small roof. 5 bolts to 2-bolt anchor.

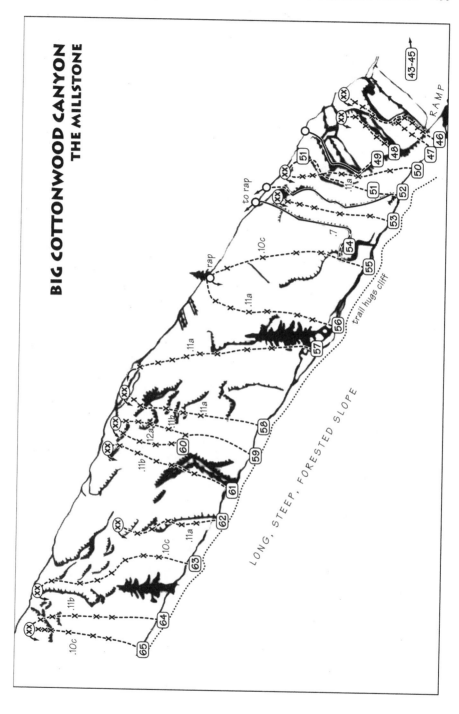

BIG COTTONWOOD CANYON
THE MILLSTONE

63. **Cat Juggling** (5.10c) 40' left of Route 62. A long route that angles left. Climb a lichen-covered slab to tan face with liebacks and sidepulls. 7 bolts to 2-bolt anchor right of broken corner. Some longer runouts on this one—don't blow the 3rd clip. You'll deck!

64. **Lead Balloon** (5.11b) 35' left of Route 63. Start by some big fir trees and left of a broken corner. Move up slab to headwall. Pump crux over roof—undercling to sidepulls. 5 bolts to 2-bolt anchor.

65. **Yuppie Love** (5.10c) 10' left of Route 64. Good climbing through overlaps. 6 bolts to 2-bolt anchor (same as Route 64).

LITTLE COTTONWOOD CANYON

OVERVIEW

Little Cottonwood Canyon slices west through the Wasatch Range southeast of Salt Lake City. This grand, U-shaped gorge, excavated long ago by a huge valley glacier, offers a spectacular selection of climbing adventures on its white granite walls. These popular and accessible cliffs, laced with hundreds of climbing routes, yield excellent jam cracks from fingertips and perfect hands, to dark off-widths and dank chimneys; thuggish face lines that swing up incut edges, and white slabs requiring delicate smears and exquisite gracefulness.

This is a place to grow as a climber. Unlike neighboring American Fork Canyon with its juggy limestone sport routes, Little Cottonwood only allows passage to those who earn their stripes. Brute strength won't get you up a Little Cottonwood Canyon jam crack or friction slab. These climbs require techniques you learn in the open air, on the rock, away from the indoor gym. You also must be competent at placing gear, wedging stoppers into thin seams, cramming opposed TCUs in a spartan crack under an overlap, and setting up a proper trad belay.

Almost all the routes here are located on the south-facing slopes in the lower third of the canyon. There are lesser lines on broken slabs on the shady north-facing side to the south; Hellgate, with its loose limestone pillars and faces, lies in the upper canyon between the ski resorts of Snowbird and Alta. The most popular cliffs are within 15 hiking minutes from the highway and the canyon floor, while some of the longer and better routes scale more lofty formations reached by 20 to 30 minute approaches. The canyon also offers a wealth of superb ice climbs, including the classic *Great White Icicle*, that forms on the south slopes during the winter.

Little Cottonwood Canyon is composed primarily of quartz monzonite, an igneous rock similar in quality and hardness to granite. The formation, locally called Wasatch granite, was originally formed in a huge batholith of molten magma beneath the earth's surface. Slowly the magma cooled and hardened, forming crystals and harder inclusions nicknamed "chickenheads" that now poke through the granite matrix. In other places, fissures developed in the cooling rock and the green mineral epidote was deposited in these weaknesses. It's easiest to see epidote on the fracture planes in Green Adjective Gully. The canyon itself was shaped and sculpted by a huge glacier that spilled west from the range crest. The glacier left behind the classic U-shape characteristic of glacier-carved valleys, as well as some hanging valleys perched high above the canyon floor, and large polished boulders deposited near the canyon's mouth.

The canyon is a mixture of both private and public land, including Wasatch National Forest. Most of the climbing crags, however, sit on private land owned by the LDS Church. This property stretches from west of the Church Buttress and the church's underground archive vault to east of the Gate Buttress. In 1989 "No Trespassing" signs were erected along the highway boundary, but local activists, including Ted Wilson, an early first ascensionist and mayor of Salt Lake City, negotiated continued access to these excellent and historic crags. Climbers should remember that climbing here is a privilege, not a right. Respect this private land by obeying all laws, not parking on church roads to the archives, not walking on church roads when accessing cliffs, not making fires, and picking up after yourself. One other regulation to remember is that dogs are not allowed in the canyon because it's part of Salt Lake City's watershed.

The canyon offers year-round climbing adventures. Autumn is probably the best time to climb, with warm but not hot days on the south-facing cliffs. Many summer days are almost too hot to climb comfortably, especially in July and August. Try to come early in the morning or in the evening. Good afternoon crags include the west side of Green Adjective Gully and The Dihedrals. Winters can be iffy. The ski areas at Alta and Snowbird get hammered with snow all winter, although the lower canyon has a much more moderate climate. Best bets include Crescent Crack Buttress, The Coffin, and The Gate Buttress. Approaches may be snowy and muddy. Spring brings a mixed bag of weather, with snow, sleet, rain, sun, and wind, sometimes all in the same day.

Climbing history: Little Cottonwood Canyon and environs is one of Utah's first technical rock climbing areas. Local alpinists in the Wasatch Mountain Club made the first climbs on the lofty granite face of nearby Lone Peak in the late 1950s. The Alpenbock Climbing Club made the earliest forays into Little Cottonwood Canyon, putting up several routes on Gate Buttress. In 1961 Layton Kor and Fred Beckey visited and did the first ascents of the now-classic routes *The Hook* and *Beckey's Wall*. In 1962 more plums were knocked off including *Tingey's Terror* and *Standard Thumb* on The Thumb. In 1964, Ted Wilson and Californian Royal Robbins free climbed the *Robbins Route* on The Thumb with the canyon's first two 5.10 pitches. Later that summer Wilson teamed up with Mark McQuarrie and Steve Ellsworth to boldly jam up *S-Crack*.

McQuarrie teamed up with Ogden climber George Lowe in 1964. Together the pair began free climbing numerous canyon cracks, including most of today's classic jams, like *The Coffin* and, in 1965, *The Dorsal Fin*, a serious crack and face climb on The Fin. This route, now rated 5.10d, featured difficult face climbing and dangerous runouts—serious stuff for guys clad in leather hiking boots. Later that year, however, tragedy struck when McQuarrie and Lowe were attempting a new route on Church Buttress. McQuarrie took a leader fall, severed the rope over a sharp flake, and fell to his death in the church archives parking lot before a busload of shocked visitors. Afterward the alarmed LDS church banned climbing on that cliff. In spite of the tragedy, Lowe continued climbing and added numerous more bold first ascents to the granite walls.

The mid-1970s brought new blood and new activity to the local scene after the first area guidebook was published. Climbers began repeating the tried and true classic lines and then turned their attention to unclimbed cracks and slabs. In 1977, Kim Miller and Jim Knight put up *Intensive Care*, the canyon's first 5.11, after several tries. The name came after Mark Ward skated off its smooth slab on an earlier attempt and ended up in the hospital. Numerous climbers, including brothers Jonathon and Brian Smoot, Mugs Stump, and Les Ellison put their mark on the canyon crags; Ellison did more first ascents than almost anyone else before or since. Crackmaster Steve Hong, then in medical school in Salt Lake City, also was active. His 1980 ascent of the much-tried *Coffin Roof* established Little Cottonwood Canyon's first 5.12 route. Hong's later ascent of *Fallen Arches* was the canyon's first 5.13. Rap-bolting came into vogue in the 1980s with Stuart Ruckman's controversial *All Chalk & No Action* in the Green Adjective Gully. The ethical debate has now passed and the route is deemed a neo-classic. Other modern activists include Drew Bedford, John Storm, Bret Ruckman, Merrill Bitter, and the late Steve Carruthers.

Rack: Use the specific rack information listed for some of the routes here as a guideline only. Scope every route and decide for yourself what you need for protection. Everyone protects routes differently. The sin is usually not taking too much gear, but too little gear. An average Little Cottonwood Canyon rack includes sets of stoppers, TCUs, and cams, along with hexes or wide crack gear.

Little Cottonwood Canyon—it's a place to entertain your climbing soul. Come and climb here if you like brilliant white slabs that glimmer in the sun or perfect jam cracks that encase your hand like a crystal glove. For the real Little Cottonwood experience, leave the busy Gate Buttress below and venture up onto The Fin, a lofty backbone poised high above the busy canyon floor. Here the climber, poised on thin holds, feels the wind rippling across the granite slab, hears the distant growl of highway traffic, and makes another movement up the perfect prow toward a shocking vault of azure sky overhead. That's what it's all about.

Trip Planning Information

General description: Over 500 slab and crack routes ascend numerous granite cliffs in glacier-carved Little Cottonwood Canyon.

Location: North-central Utah. Southeast of Salt Lake City.

Camping: The nearest and best campgrounds are 2 national forest areas in upper Little Cottonwood Canyon. Tanners Flat Campground, with 38 sites, is

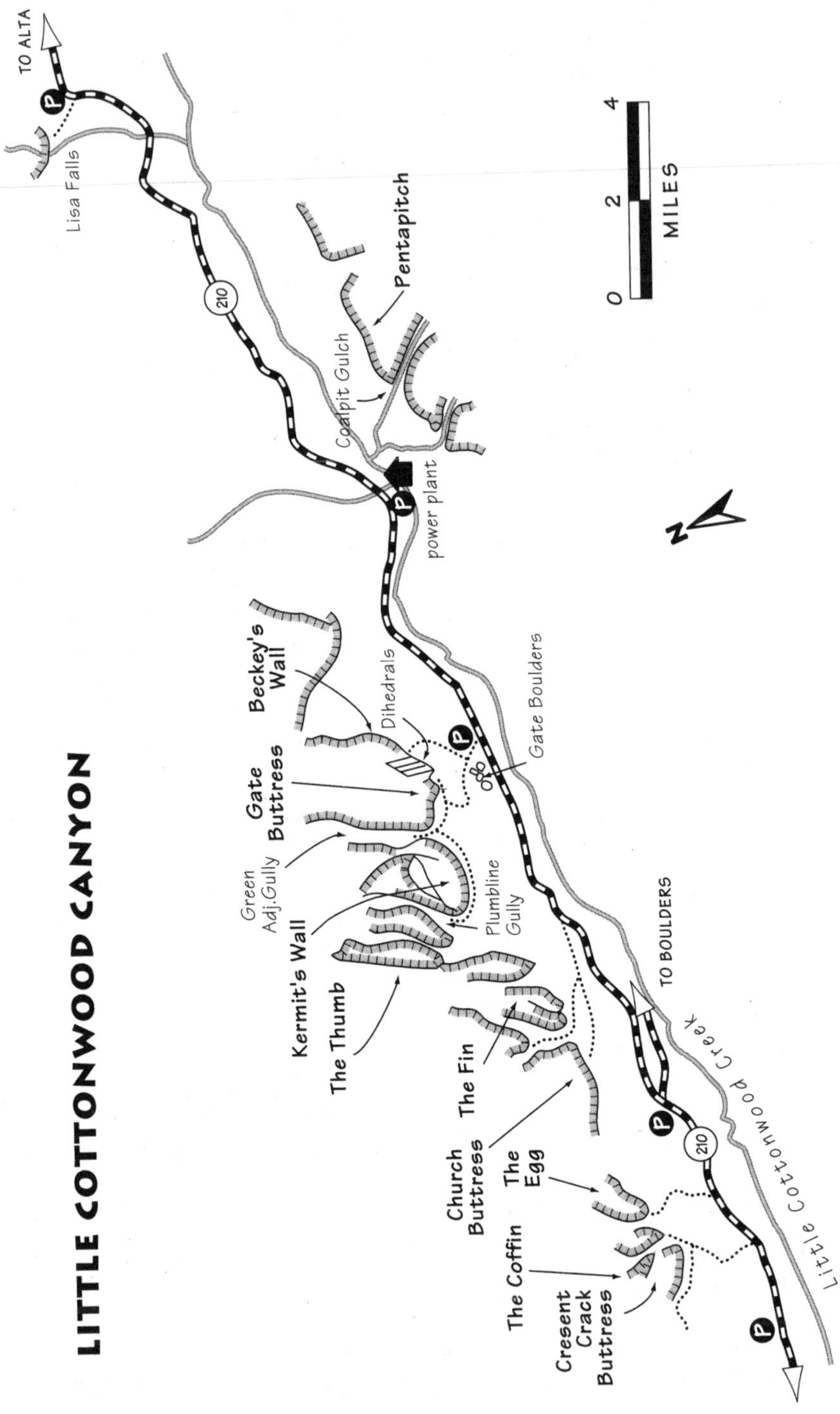

LITTLE COTTONWOOD CANYON

TO ALTA

Lisa Falls

210

Coalpit Gulch

Pentapitch

power plant

Beckey's Wall

Gate Buttress

Dihedrals

Green Adj. Gully

Gate Boulders

Kermit's Wall

Plumbline Gully

The Thumb

The Fin

Church Buttress

The Egg

The Coffin

Cresent Crack Buttress

TO BOULDERS

Little Cottonwood Creek

210

N

0   2   4
MILES

at 4.1 miles. Albion Basin Campground, with 26 sites, is at the road's end near Alta Ski Resort. Neighboring Big Cottonwood Canyon to the north has Spruces Campground, with 121 sites, at 9.8 miles, and Redman Campground, with 50 sites, at 13.2 miles. All are fee areas, with water, restrooms, and tables. Pets are not allowed because the canyons are part of Salt Lake City's watershed.

Climbing season: Year-round. Summer days are often too hot on the sun-baked slabs, but shady north-facing routes are common. Climb in the morning and evening for the best summer temperatures. The Green Adjective Gully routes are good in summer. The east side is shaded in the morning, while the west side receives afternoon shade. Autumn offers excellent conditions with generally dry, warm days. Spring offers variable weather. Expect some of everything—sun, wind, rain, and snow. April is usually rainy. Winter days are great when the sun warms the south-facing cliffs. Approach trails are often muddy or snowy. Bring boots for hiking to the crags.

Restrictions and access issues: Much of the canyon and cliffs are on private property owned by the LDS Church. The church's property is from just west of the archive vaults under Church Buttress to past the Gate Buttress. Although there are signs along the road saying "No Trespassing," climbers have had continued access to all the crags except Church Buttress. Do not climb on that buttress and do not use or park on or near the church roads that lead to the vaults. Don't use the roads to access areas including The Thumb; instead follow bushwhacking approaches. Most of the other canyon crags are on Forest Service land. Climbers should minimize their impact on the canyon cliffs and ecosystems. Follow existing trails whenever possible and try to avoid the straight-uphill approaches that erode the slopes. Pick up after yourself; this means cigarette butts, tape, and energy bar wrappers.

Guidebooks: *Rock Climbing the Wasatch Range* by Bret and Stuart Ruckman, Chockstone Press, 1998. The updated and complete guide to almost every route you would ever want to climb in Little Cottonwood and the rest of the Wasatch. *Wasatch Range* by the Ruckmans, Chockstone Press, 1997. A select guide to 200 routes in the Salt Lake area.

Nearby mountain shops, guide services, and gyms: Stores include Black Diamond, IME, REI (Salt Lake City), Mountainworks (Provo), and Hansen Mountaineering (Orem). Gyms are Wasatch Front Climbing Gym and Rockreation in Salt Lake, and Rock Garden in Provo. Guides include Wasatch Touring, Exum Mountain Utah, and Mastodon Mountaineering (Ben Folsom).

Services: All services are found in Salt Lake City and its suburbs. Supermarkets and gas stations are just below the canyon in Sandy.

Emergency services: Call 911 for all emergencies. Alta View Hospital, 9660 South 1300 East, Salt Lake City, (801) 567-2600. Cottonwood Hospital, 5770 South 300 East, Salt Lake City, (801) 262-3461. St. Mark's Hospital, 1200 East 3900 South, Salt Lake City, (801) 268-7129.

Nearby climbing areas: Hellgate Cliffs, Big Cottonwood Canyon, The Millstone, Ferguson Canyon, Pete's Rock, Parley's Canyon, Bell's Canyon, Lone Peak, American Fork Canyon.

Nearby attractions: Alta, Snowbird, Big Cottonwood Canyon, Salt Lake City attractions (Temple Square, Brigham Young Monument, Beehive House, Utah State Capitol, Utah Museum of Natural History, Utah Museum of Fine Arts, This is the Place State Park, Hogle Zoo), Great Salt Lake, Bingham Canyon Mine (largest pit mine in world), Timpanogos Cave National Monument.

Finding the area: Little Cottonwood Canyon lies about 15 miles southeast of downtown Salt Lake City. It's easy to find from Interstate 15, the main north-south highway through town. From the south, leave Interstate 15 at Exit 298 (90th Street) and follow Alta Ski signs to the canyon's mouth. From the north, exit onto Interstate 215, the east beltway, and drive south to Exit 7 (6200 South). Again, follow signs south to the canyon. All mileages to the crags are taken from the road junction at the canyon mouth.

CRESCENT CRACK BUTTRESS

This sprawling buttress, the first main crag in the canyon, is named for the obvious crescent-shaped crack on its main wall. The buttress is divided into 3 sectors: the left side with mostly short crack climbs; the 350-foot center wall with some great multi-pitch slab and crack routes; and The Coffin, a stellar slab topped by a coffin-shaped block. The crag is deservedly popular, with a short approach, sunny cliffs, and some of the canyon's best routes.

Finding the crag: Drive up the highway 0.3 mile from the highway junction at the canyon mouth and park on the right shoulder. A well-worn trail begins on the north side of the asphalt and threads through oak thickets to the cliff base. Keep left at the trail junction.

LEFT SIDE

1. **Spanish Fly** (5.11c) A pretty good friction route. Begin on far left side of buttress. Climb over small roof and traverse right to bolt on face. Smear up and left onto ridge and follow to anchors. 6 bolts to 2-bolt anchor. 80 feet.

2. **Mexican Crack** (5.10a) A mega-classic crack climb. Start 40' right of Route 1 in a small, shady alcove. Climb corner crack (5.9+) and step left onto slab. Move up thin cracks to stunning left-angling finger and hand crack. Good jams lead to a 2-bolt anchor. 80'. **Descent:** An 80-foot rappel. **Rack:** Wires, TCUs, a good assortment of small to medium Friends.

3. **Less Than Zero** (5.12a) Meanders up arete; step left at bolt 6 to thin crack. 6 bolts to 2-bolt rap anchor. 60'. **Rack:** Quickdraws and stoppers.

4. **C.P.O.S.** (5.11b) Name is short for "Classic Piece of Shit." A tough crack climb with 1 bolt. Finish at Route 3's anchors. 60'.

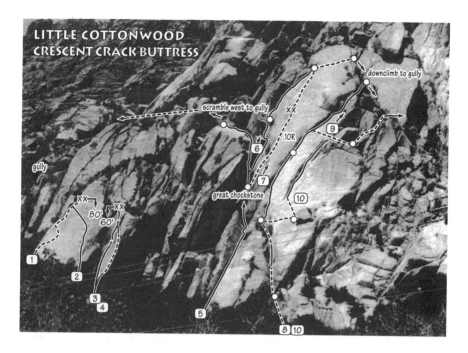

LITTLE COTTONWOOD
CRESCENT CRACK BUTTRESS

downclimb to gully

scramble west to gully

xx

.10R

9

6

gully

7

xx
80'
60'
xx

great chockstone

10

1

2

3
4

5

8 10

CRESCENT CRACK AREA

5. **The Great Chockstone** (5.7) 2 pitches. Not climbed as much as it once was, but offers lots of fun chimneying. Begin left of a slab below an obvious chimney system. **Pitch 1:** Ease up chimney on left side of slab (some 5.6). Above work up corner under Great Chockstone and set belay behind it. **Pitch 2:** Climb overhanging right-facing corner on left (5.7) and continue to large sloped platform belay. **Descent:** Scramble west behind buttress to base of left side. **Rack:** Set of stoppers, set of Friends to #3, and long slings.

6. **Lazarus** (5.8) 4 pitches. Same start as Route 5. **Pitch 1:** Chimney up the first pitch of Route 5 to chockstone belay. **Pitch 2:** Climb steep corner (5.7) on Route 5. Exit right under small roof and follow wide crack to sloping ledge. Climb crack on left side of ledge to belay stance. Directly up from ledge right side is alternative pitch 3 up 5.10 hand crack. **Pitch 3:** Angle up right-facing corner (5.7) to belay up left. **Pitch 4:** A runout crack (5.7 R) traverses summit slab. **Descent:** Downclimb gully between buttress and The Coffin to the east.

7. **Missing Link** (5.10 R) 4 pitches. Good smearing up the steep central slab. Start at the same place as Route 5. **Pitch 1:** Climb pitch 1 of Route 5 up chimney to chockstone belay. **Pitch 2:** Begin atop Great Chockstone and work up grooves (5.9) to arch roof. Follow roof right and up shallow

corner to 2-bolt slab. Belay higher from 2 bolts. **Pitch 3:** Traverse right to bolt (5.9) and continue up past 2 horizontal cracks to belay up left (same as Route 6). **Pitch 4:** Follow runout crack (5.7 R) across summit slab. **Descent:** Downclimb gully to the east between buttress and The Coffin. **Rack:** Set of stoppers and Friends to #2.5.

8. **Crescent Crack** (5.7) 2 or 3 pitches. Pitches 2 and 3 can be combined. A great moderate route (one of the best 5.7s here) that follows the crescent-shaped crack. Begin near the toe of the buttress below an angling groove gully. **Pitch 1:** Climb left up chimney in gully (spot of 5.7) to ledge belay with trees. **Pitch 2:** Move up right-facing blocky corner (5.7) into main crack system. Continue up chimney (5.7) to small belay stance. **Pitch 3:** Continue up easier chimney to down-sloping ramp that drops right to belay ledge. Put pro in for second above ramp. **Descent:** Scramble up right and down the gully between the buttress and The Coffin. **Rack:** Sets of stoppers and Friends to #4.

9. **Crescent Crack Direct** (5.9-) Direct last pitch finish. Instead of traversing right on the ramp, continue up crack system (5.9-) to higher belay near *Coffin Crack's* start.

10. **Ross Route** (5.11a) 3 pitches. Begin at the same spot as Route 8. **Pitch 1:** Ascend *Crescent Crack's* first pitch. **Pitch 2:** Face climb up right from belay to thin crack (5.10). Belay left of huge boulder on ledge. **Pitch 3:** Thin face climbing (5.11a) leads up left past bolt to right-angling crack. Jam crack to ramp belay on #8. **Descent:** Scramble up right and into the gully between the buttress and The Coffin.

THE COFFIN

The Coffin is a small, semi-detached buttress that sits on the right shoulder of Crescent Crack Buttress. The crag is a brown and white mottled slab topped by a huge coffin-shaped, overhanging block. All the routes are excellent—some of the canyon's best offerings.

Finding the crag: Drive up the highway 0.3 mile from the highway junction at the canyon mouth and park on the right shoulder. A trail begins on the north side of the asphalt and threads through oak thickets to a junction. Keep right and head up a gully right of The Coffin. Near the east corner, scramble west up slopes, ramps, and ledges to the face. Routes are listed left to right.

11. **Exsqueeze Me** (5.11d) Sustained face climbing on the left side of the face leads to a final crux. 5 bolts to 3-bolt anchor. **Descent:** 75-foot rap from 3 bolts.

12. **The Coffin** (5.9 R) This 5-star crack, first freed by Little Cottonwood Canyon pioneers Mark McQuarrie and George Lowe in 1964, jams the rattley wide-finger to hand crack that splits the face. The usual start is to angle up right on runout face holds and a seam (5.8 R) to the crack. Or

climb one of 2 cracks to the right (5.9 R). Continue up the perfect crack to the big roof, traverse left (5.8) under the roof and belay from 3 bolts. Or belay out right at top of crack if you want to continue up *Coffin Right*. **Descent:** Rap 80' from 3-bolts. **Rack:** Sets of stoppers and TCUs, and Friends to Route 2.

Ed Webster attempts a free ascent of Coffin Roof, Little Cottonwood Canyon (1979). ED WEBSTER, MOUNTAIN IMAGERY PHOTO

13. **Coffin Roof** (5.12a) The roof, the canyon's first 5.12, was free climbed by Steve Hong in 1980. Climb *The Coffin* to the 3-bolt belay. The difficulties are obvious. Jam a finger crack in the 10-foot roof. Above the lip it slabs out and becomes 5.6. **Descent:** Down-aid the roof to the belay and make an 80-foot rappel to the ground or go to the top of the block. **Rack:** TCUs.

14. **Coffin Right** (5.9) A variation pitch 2 to Route 12. After jamming *The Coffin*, step right to a 2-bolt chain belay. Jam crack up dihedral right of The Coffin block and belay up top. Be ready for a surprising finish!

15. **The Viewing** (5.10a) Excellent but runout face climbing on the right side of The Coffin. Climb start to *The Coffin* crack, above inverted Y-cracks traverse out right past black knob and up to bolt. Continue up the awesome face to a 2-bolt chain anchor. 4 bolts. **Descent:** Rap 85' from 2-bolt chain anchor.

THE EGG

The Egg presents a prominent, brown and tan mottled face to the highway parking area below Crescent Crack Buttress. This excellent, south-facing crag is studded with knobs and edges and seamed by grooves and cracks. Most of The Egg's routes are excellent 1-pitch face climbs, with rappel descents from established anchors.

Finding the crag: Park at a wide spot at 0.4 mile on the highway's right shoulder. Follow a trail that leads into the gully immediately east of The Egg.

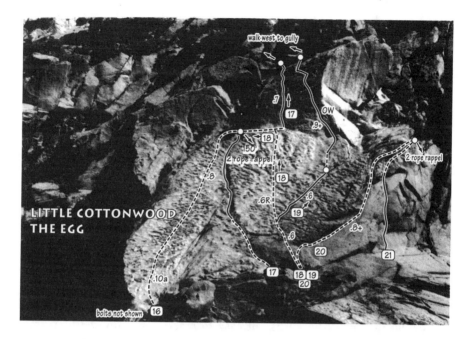

Near the base of the west face, angle up right to a ledge below the crag's south face. Routes are listed left to right.

16. **Leggo My Eggo** (5.10a) This bolted route ascends the left side of the face. Stiff face climbing (5.10a) on smooth rock starts the route. Fun climbing up knobby rock leads to final 5.8 crux. Belay out right by a tree. 8 bolts. **Descent:** A 2-rope rappel from anchors. **Rack:** Quickdraws and a long runner to tie off a tree for the final traverse.

17. **Variety Delight** (5.7) 2 pitches. A delightful variety of face and crack moves. Begin on the ledge below an obvious left-slanting groove. **Pitch 1:** Climb groove and crack to tree belay. **Pitch 2:** Move right on ledge and climb wide groove (5.7) to top. **Descent:** Walk off west into the gully.

18. **Huevos Rancheros** (5.7 R) 3 bolts. Fun but runout. Begin on the ledge just right of Route 17. Climb unprotected face to bolt (5.6 R). Continue up past 2 more bolts to ledge, step left and belay in trees. Bolt 2 is hidden in a pocket. **Descent:** A 2-rope rappel from anchors.

19. **Lowe Blowe** (5.9+) 2 pitches. This route, put up by George Lowe and Eric Eliason in 1968, was one of Little Cottonwood Canyon's first hard crack routes. Same start as Route 18. **Pitch 1:** Climb unprotected face to right-angling groove/crack (5.6). Belay near its end. **Pitch 2:** Face climb to another groove to left-leaning off-width crack. Grunt up this hard, awkward crack (hardest where it dog-legs—5.9+). It protects well with big Friends and Camalots. Belay on sloping summit slab. **Descent:** Walk off to west.

Rack: A selection of stoppers and Friends and a bunch of wide crack gear.

20. **Groovin'** (5.8+) Same start as *Lowe Blowe*, but move right to a right-angling corner system. Follow system past some fixed gear to crux (5.8+) where corner steepens. Belay up right from tree. **Descent:** Rappel 75' to the ground.

21. **Go Van Gogh** (5.9+) Begin on the slabs right of the mottled face. Climb short corner to fixed piton out left. Jam steep crack (5.9+) to slab, pull a small roof and belay up right at a tree. **Descent:** Rappel 75' to the ground.

THE FIN

The Fin, perched high above the canyon floor, is one of Little Cottonwood Canyon's most aesthetic formations. In profile from up-canyon, the crag's blunt western prow resembles a huge fin on the back of some titanic granite beast. The Fin, reached by a stiff uphill hike, offers some of Little Cottonwood Canyon's finest routes on impeccable white granite. Despite the superb rock and routes, The Fin is never crowded—this is the place to get away from the mobs at Gate Buttress.

Finding the crag: The Fin is not easy to reach, especially the first time. Allow at least a half a day to approach, climb, and descend. The crag is above and right of the LDS archives vault and access road. Drive up the highway and park at about 0.9 mile on the wide right shoulder just past the archives road. There are no easy ways to reach the cliff base. Use your own common sense and judgment to find the best way. The traditional approach bushwhacks west through dense oak thickets above the church road and into the gully west of The Fin. Hike up the gully and then climb ramps up right to the base of the cliff. The other approach is to hike up the gully on the right side of The Fin. Look for a way up the maze of slabs and cracks on the southeast apron of the formation. Some 3rd and 4th class climbing may be encountered. Expect at least 45 minutes of hiking time.

22. **The Fin Arete** (II 5.10b) 3 pitches. This classic route, put up by brothers Jonathan and Brian Smoot in 1978, ascends the prominent prow. Expect spectacular and exposed climbing on knobs, edges, and smears. There are also some runouts, especially on pitch 3. Begin on left side of a smooth slab below a large roof. **Pitch 1:** Move up left to bolt, face climb above (5.9) to easier prow. Edge past dike to bolt and traverse left (crux 5.10b) then straight up past left side of roof to 2-bolt belay. 4 bolts. 150'. **Pitch 2:** Face climb (5.9) up right to roof. Pull its left side to crack. Above angle right on steep knobs (1 bolt) to 2-bolt belay on ridgeline. **Pitch 3:** Superb climbing leads up airy prow (5.7) to bolt. Don't be lulled—this is sustained climbing. Continue up runout ridge (5.5 R) to 2-bolt belay on summit slabs. **Descent:** Make one 80-foot rappel west into gully and downclimb to base of route. **Rack:** Quickdraws, a few wires, TCUs, and small cams.

LITTLE COTTONWOOD
THE FIN

80' rap to gully

.5r

.7

.8

.9

.9

descent gully

.9

.11

.11

.10b

.10b

.10d

23

.9

22

24

approach slabs

23. **Dark Horse** (II 5.11 R) 3 pitches. First and last pitches are on *The Fin Arête*. First ascent by Mark Ward and Kim Miller, 1979. A superb, 3-star face route right of the arête. Expect some serious runouts. **Pitch 1:** Same start as *The Fin*. Edge up slab to dike, but instead of traversing left, climb straight up and over large roof (5.11) to 2-bolt belay below shallow arch. 3 bolts. **Pitch 2:** Move up slab (5.11 above belay) to bolt at 25', climb past another bolt to second roof. Traverse right under roof to bolt above its right side, then up past dike to possible bolt belay or continue up prow (5.9) to 2-bolt belay (same as *Fin Arête*). This is a serious lead with injury potential. It can be broken into 2 pitches. **Pitch 3:** Follow the arête (5.7)

to a bolt, then runout slabbing (5.5 R) to summit bolts. **Descent:** Rappel 80' to west into gully, downclimb to base of route. **Rack:** Quickdraws, wires, and TCUs.

24. **The Dorsal Fin** (II 5.10d) 4 pitches. First ascent by George Lowe and Mark McQuarrie, 1965. This is the all-time Little Cottonwood Canyon classic slab testpiece. Imagine edging up it like the bold first party in the mid-1960s with leather hiking boots! Begin down right from *The Fin Arête* below the right side of the obvious roof. **Pitch 1:** The crux climbing. Work past right-facing flake to bolt. Edge up right to thin crack to far right edge of roof. Climb past bolt (5.10d) to belay from 2 bolts atop large chickenhead. **Pitch 2:** Move right past knob to bolt then straight up slab (5.10b) to groove and right-facing corner. Belay from gear and fixed pin. **Pitch 3:** Climb corner to dike and traverse left to prominent arching crack/ corner. Lieback up crack (5.9) to 1-bolt/gear belay stance. **Pitch 4:** Continue up crack. It's awkward to protect. Exit at its top on face climbing (5.8) to runout slab (5.6). Belay at bolted belay. **Descent:** Make an 80-foot rappel west into gully, and downclimb to base of route. **Rack:** Quickdraws, sets of TCUs and stoppers, and Friends to #2.5.

THE THUMB

The Thumb, topped by a thumb-like pinnacle, is the largest cliff in the canyon. This complex, south-facing crag is broken by 2 large angling fractures that divide the wall into 3 distinct slabs with the Thumb itself poised atop the right side of the highest edge. Several excellent long routes ascend the slabby wall, offering brilliant crack climbing as well as some excellent friction pitches on the upper wall. Some of the routes when combined together yield the canyon's longest route—an all-day 9-pitch Grade IV adventure that ends atop The Thumb's summit block.

Finding the cliff: The hiking approach to The Thumb takes about 30 minutes. The best approach begins from the Gate Buttress parking area 1.3 miles up the highway. Hike up the trail to the Gate Boulders; at the first boulder, follow a trail west through oaks to a boulder field. Don't go too high. Cross the boulders and continue up left to the base of The Waterfront, a tall cliff lined with black streaks. Follow the cliff base west to the base of the Plumb Line Wall, a short knobby cliff split by a perfect crack. This is a good place to rack up and stash your packs so you don't have to retrieve them later from the route base after descending from the summit. Continue west along the cliff-base trail to the toe of the buttress. This involves some scrambling on a bushy ledge system above lower slabs.

Descent: Descent off all the routes that don't go to the summit slabs is by rappel. Fixed rappel anchors are found on *S-Direct*, *Nob Job*, and right of *S-Crack*. Two 165-foot ropes are needed for all rappels. If you go to the summit slabs or the top of The Thumb it's a walk-off/rappel descent. The descent goes east and south from the summit block. It requires some careful routefinding. Rappel 100' off the east side of The Thumb pinnacle and descend a gully to a bushy ledge. Work left around a corner to a 2-piton anchor and rappel 65'. Keep left down a gully and work down broken slabs to a drop-off. Rappel 85' from 2 bolts and drop down and right. Be careful not to get hosed by going onto slabs to the east above the Plumb Line Gully. Keep right down slabs and descend the gully to the packs at Plumb Line Wall.

25. **Standard Thumb/Indecent Exposure** (III 5.7) 9 pitches. The classic long, easy route here. The *Indecent Exposure* variation (pitches 2 and 3) avoids some groveling gully pitches. Begin by scrambling up left along ledges to the base of the obvious gully that marks the western edge of the buttress. Belay on a ledge below a right-facing corner. **Pitch 1:** Climb corner, step left into chimney and belay above from bolts. **Pitch 2:** Start up loose gully, then move right to steep crack (5.6). Continue through trees to belay. **Pitch 3:** Jam hand crack to big roof, undercling right (5.7) and belay up right on spacious Lunch Ledge. **Pitch 4:** Walk right along ledge (4th class) to obvious belay stance near its end. **Pitch 5:** The exciting Trough Pitch. Climb up right in 4-inch crack to overhang. Bridge up The Trough (5.7), a deep awkward groove, to belay stance below chimney. **Pitch 6:** Squeeze up chimney (5.6) and belay below The Ear. **Pitch 7:** The tough guy way is up the bomb bay chimney around The Ear (5.7+ and no pro) or traverse right around bulge (5.5) and follow ramp to convenient belay in bushes. **Pitch 8:** A long easy slab lead (5.2) to north side base of The Thumb's summit block. **Pitch 9:** Stand on edge of big defile and fall or reach across to big handholds. Face climb (5.5) to bolt and mantle onto summit platform. There are no anchors on top. To descend from summit, reverse this pitch which is airy and kinda spooky. An alternative last pitch is the *Robbins Crack* (5.10), an off-width crack on the west face of the summit block. **Descent:** See instructions above. It's a walk-off/rappel descent to the east and south. **Rack:** A set of stoppers and a set of Friends.

26. **S-Crack** (III 5.8 C1, 5.11d A0, 5.12a) 4 pitches. An excellent classic crack route to Lunch Ledge. Aid is minimal on it and the hard cruxes are well-protected. Begin near the toe of the buttress and right of a huge pillar. **Pitch 1:** Climb easy cracks into large right-facing dihedral (5.6). Belay in upper trees. **Pitch 2:** Work up classic squeeze chimney (5.8) and exit onto ledge atop pillar. Good gear is found in back of chimney. Many protect this by climbing crack to right, placing gear high, then downclimbing and doing the chimney. **Pitch 3:** 3 ways to do the start. Traditional way is to climb corner to right and pendulum into S-Crack. Most climbers now tackle it directly. Clip a bolt with long sling on it and make long dyno/ jump (5.12a) to narrow ledge or pull through (A0) on sling. Either way get onto ledge and move off left, reach right to put pro in crack, and step

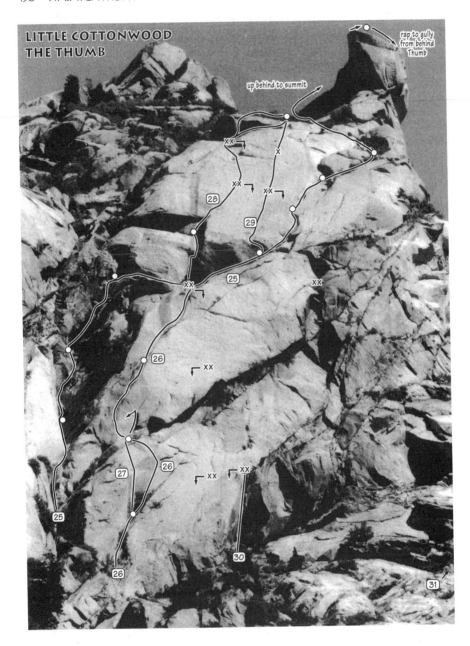

LITTLE COTTONWOOD
THE THUMB

rap to gully
from behind
Thumb

up behind to summit

right into crack. Jam and lieback up wide fingers/thin hands crack to gear belay in some blocks. **Pitch 4:** Continue liebacking and jamming up lower-angle hand crack (5.7 and awkward to protect) to off-width groove (5.8) that ends on Lunch Ledge. 150'. Continue up *Nob Job* or *S-Direct* to summit slabs or descend from here. **Descent:** Make 3 double-rope rappels back to base. **Rack:** Set of stoppers, 2 sets of TCUs, Friends to #3, and a #3 Camalot.

27. **Coyne Crack** (5.11d) First ascent by Coloradan Leonard Coyne, 1978. An excellent variation second pitch for *S-Crack*. Climb first pitch of *S-Crack* to tree belay in dihedral. Jam perfect finger crack (5.11d) up steep wall on left. Higher it widens to off-fingers but angle decreases. Belay at base of *S-Crack*'s pitch 3. **Rack:** 2 to 3 sets of TCUs.

28. **S-Direct** (II 5.9+ R) 4 pitches. First ascent by George and Jeff Lowe, 1967. This superlative slab route ascends upper slab above Lunch Ledge. Most parties climb first 3 pitches and rappel from last set of bolt anchors. Above that, you're committed to downclimb descent. On the slab, look for next bolt before setting off. Do either *S-Crack* or *Indecent Exposure* to Lunch Ledge. Begin at widest part of ledge below left-facing corner. **Pitch 1:** Fun face climbing up corner using huge chickenheads (5.6) to 1-bolt/1-piton belay on sloping ledge right of huge roof. Tie off the knobs for pro. **Pitch 2:** Move right up crack past roof edge and onto upper slab. Wander from chickenhead to chickenhead (5.9) and 3 bolts to 2-bolt belay. **Pitch 3:** Friction up to bolt, traverse right to another bolt, then straight up (5.9) to third bolt. Angle up left (5.8 R) to flake overlap. Find some pro under it and continue to 2-bolt belay above another overlap. A 5.9 variation climbs directly up from first bolt to second before running it out to belay. **Pitch 4:** Do this and you're guaranteed a walk-off. Climb directly up (5.7) to large roof. Jam wide crack/chimney (5.8) or undercling (5.4) right under roof. Either way finish up long easy slab above to tree belay. **Descent:** Walk off using the above description. Most parties simply rappel from bolted stance above pitch 3. Make 2 double-rope rappels back to Lunch Ledge and then 3 more to cliff base. **Rack:** Quickdraws, TCUs, small to medium stoppers, and several 24-inch runners to tie off chickenheads.

29. **Nob Job** (5.10d R) 3 pitches. First ascent by Mugs Stump and Jack Roberts, 1977. A serious slab line right of *S-Direct*. Watch for long runouts and 0.25-inch bolts. Begin on the right side of Lunch Ledge below an obvious, slanting, left-facing flake-corner. **Pitch 1:** Undercling left up crack (5.10d) to mantle and slab above. Continue up runout rock on chickenheads, divots, and smears past 3 bolts to 2-bolt belay. **Pitch 2:** Edge up slab (5.10d) past a couple of bolts. Most parties traverse left at bolt 2 onto *S-Direct*. Otherwise climb unprotected slab to 1-bolt belay anchor (0.25-inch buttonhead). **Pitch 3:** Head up easier but unprotected slab past right side of big overlap to belay. **Descent:** If you complete pitch 2 you're committed to the walk-off descent. If you finish at the 3rd belay of *S-Direct*, make 2 double rope rappels back to Lunch Ledge and 3 more to the ground. **Rack:** Quickdraws, TCUs for the first crack, and several 24-inch runners to tie off chickenheads.

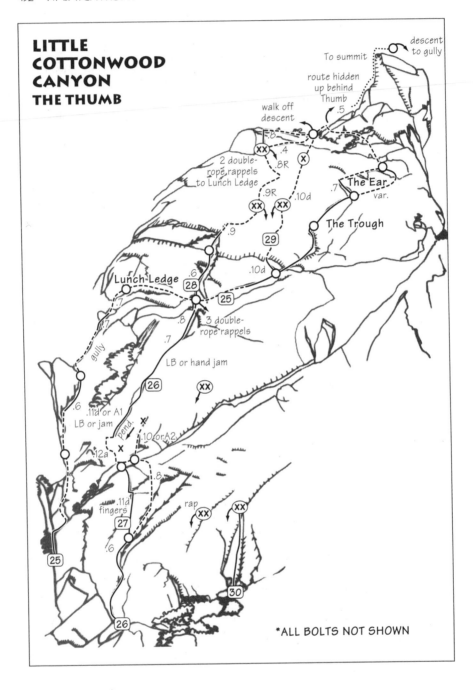

LITTLE COTTONWOOD CANYON
THE THUMB

descent to gully

To summit

route hidden up behind Thumb

walk off descent

.5

.8

2 double-rope rappels to Lunch Ledge

.4

.8R

X

XX

The Ear

.7

var.

.9R

.10d

XX

XX

.9

29

The Trough

Lunch Ledge

.6

.10d

28

.7

.10d

25

.7

.8

3 double-rope rappels

.7

LB or hand jam

26

XX

.6

.11d or A1

LB or jam

pend.

.10 or A2

.12a

X

.8

.11d

fingers

rap

XX

XX

27

.6

25

30

26

*ALL BOLTS NOT SHOWN

30. **Monkey Lip** (5.13a/b) 1 pitch. A tough sport route. Climb easy slabs and bushes left of Plumb Line Wall to the base of an overhanging southeast-facing wall split by a crack. Lieback and undercling up steep, strenuous crack to 2-bolt anchor. 6 bolts.

31. **Plumb Line** (5.10a) No topo. Great crack route up the short Plumb Line Wall down and right of The Thumb buttress. Locate obvious splitter thin crack on south-facing wall. Jam fingers to thin hands crack for 50'. **Rack:** Wires, TCUs, and small Friends.

KERMIT'S WALL

Kermit's Wall, a large slabby buttress, forms the left outside wall of the Green Adjective Gully. This popular south-facing cliff is good on cool days. Most of the routes are slab/face and thin crack climbs.

Finding the wall: Approach the wall by hiking up the westernmost trail from the Gate Buttress parking area, generally keeping left at trail junctions. Eventually the path meanders into a huge boulder field below the Green Adjective Gully. Boulder-hop and scramble upwards, keeping either left or right around the largest blocks, to the base of the wall on the left side of the gully's entrance.

32. **Paranoia Streak** (5.10c R) No topo. You will be paranoid of falling on long runouts on this Bill Cramer and Hank Armantrout slab testpiece. Some groundfalls have occurred on the first slab—only the competent and cool-headed need apply. Begin on the left side of the cliff just right of

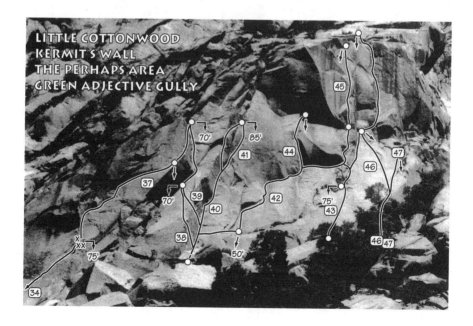

LITTLE COTTONWOOD
KERMIT'S WALL
THE PERHAPS AREA
GREEN ADJECTIVE GULLY

LITTLE COTTONWOOD
KERMIT'S WALL

a broken corner system. Move right up a ramp before frictioning up a
black streak on a steep slab past a single bolt; run it out 25' to 2 side-by-
side bolts on an overlap. Pull through the overlaps (5.10c) to a bolt above
the crux. Move up left over 2 overlaps and into a flared corner with a
hand crack. Belay from 2 bolts above corner. **Descent:** 120' rappel with 2
ropes. **Rack:** Some thin gear for overlaps and cams to 2-inches.

33. **Koyaanisqaatsi** (5.12c) No topo. Hopi for "Life out of balance." A thin-edge, balancey finish to *Paranoia Streak*. Climb Route 32 to final overlap. Move straight up black streak on steep headwall to 2-bolt anchor. 4 bolts. Watch for rope drag. **Descent:** 165' rappel with 2 ropes.

34. **Kermit's Wad** (5.10a) No topo. A great slab route with thoughtful moves. Begin on left side of wall, right of broken right-facing corner. Angle up right via a crack/ramp. Fiddle in some small gear and then make commit-ting moves right onto knobby face. Edge to a dike, some hard moves on smooth rock head out right to headwall finish. Belay from 3 bolts on a small ledge. 5 bolts. **Descent:** Rappel 75'.

35. **Smitty's Wet Dream** (5.9) No topo. Start left of short, right-facing corner. Climb finger crack onto right edge of smooth slab to 1 bolt. Move right (5.9) and follow thin crack to 3-bolt belay. The direct corner start is 5.10d. **Descent:** Rappel 75'. **Rack:** Wires and TCUs.

36. **Cranial Prophylactic** (5.8) No topo. Begin up right from *Smitty's* by scrub oak tree. Jam thin crack to bolt (15'); continue up crack system to 3-bolt belay ledge. **Descent:** Rappel 75'. **Rack:** Wires, TCUs, small cams.

37. **Lend Me A Dime** (5.12a) 2 pitches. Airy, exposed, and brilliant face climb-ing on Kermit's upper headwall. Do 1 of the 3 lower routes to the 3-bolt belay. **Pitch 1:** Head up right-facing corner (5.7) to exposed right-angling crack. Face climb (5.11c near the anchors) right along crack past 5 bolts to 2-bolt hanging belay on prow. Many parties rap from here. **Pitch 2:** Face climb up right to prow's edge and step right around corner to airy finish and 2-bolt belay. 4 bolts. A Drew Bedford bolted project is on the overhanging wall below the final pitch. **Descent:** Rappel 165' with 2 ropes.

GREEN ADJECTIVE GULLY

This deep gully divides Kermit's Wall on the west from Gate Buttress on the east. The excellent granite walls on either side of the gully offer some of Little Cottonwood's hardest and best routes. The area is very popular, with easy access and summer shade. The area is named for green epidote, a crystalline mineral veneer found on many of the granite's cleavage planes in the gully.

The West Face on the right or east side of the gully is shaded through much of the day in summer, but sunny on cooler autumn and winter days. The East Face on the left or west side gives afternoon shade in summer and warm sun during the cooler months.

Finding the cliffs: Approach the gully by walking up the westernmost trail from the Gate Buttress parking area, generally keeping left at trail junctions. Eventually the path meanders into a huge boulder field below the gully. Boul-der-hop and scramble upwards, keeping either left or right around the largest blocks, into the gully itself.

Kimber Almond belays Tony Calvert up Gordon's Hangover, *Green Adjective Gully, Little Cottonwood Canyon.* PHOTO BY STEWART M. GREEN

LITTLE COTTONWOOD
GREEN ADJECTIVE GULLY
2 rappels

EAST FACE

The East Face flanks the west side of the Green Adjective Gully. The face is separated from Kermit's Wall by a blunt prow. Routes are listed left to right, or from downhill to uphill.

38. **All Chalk and No Action** (5.12a) A controversial Stuart Ruckman sport route put down on rappel in 1987, but now a tested classic line. Begin around corner right from Kermit's Wall below a large right-facing dihedral. Route moves up vertical left wall of dihedral on edges, sidepulls, and crimps. Look for no-hands rest near slabby top. 5 bolts to 2-bolt chain anchor. 70'. **Descent:** Rap or lower 70'.

39. **Touch Up** (5.9+) 2 pitches. Classic traverse on the first lead. **Pitch 1:** Climb easy crack for 40' up large dihedral to broken area. Swing out left on thin flake (5.9) past a couple of fixed pins to 2-bolt belay. Many rap 70' from here. **Pitch 2:** Angle left into right-facing book. Stem up (some 5.9) corner into another corner. Climb airy flake (5.8) to belay up top. **Descent:** 2 rappels down route.

40. **Gordon's Hangover** (5.10a) Great jamming for the sober. A couple of starts gets you to the good climbing. Do it in either 1 or 2 pitches. **In 1 pitch:** Climb big dihedral (5.7) to obvious "hangover" crack on left. Undercling left and around big flake (5.10a) to good hand crack (5.9+). Belay on stance with 2 bolts up right. **In 2 pitches: Pitch 1:** Climb big dihedral for 50'. Make rightward traverse to shallow right-facing corner. Belay below it from 2 bolts. **Pitch 2:** Lieback up corner, step left on flakes to overhanging flake and follow above description. **Descent:** 2 rappels down route with 1 rope. **Rack:** Sets of Friends and wires.

41. **Gordon's Direct** (5.11b R) A worthwhile but runout variation. Climb *Gordon's Hangover* to the flake overhang. Instead of underclinging left, climb straight up thin, airy crack (5.9 R); pro is RPs. Crux is reaching up left to another crack (5.11c). Easier for tall folks. Belay from 2 bolts above. **Descent:** 2 rappels down route.

42. **Perhaps** (5.7) 2 or 3 pitches. Good and fun liebacking. *Perhaps* ascends the obvious right-facing slab dihedral that angles across face. Begin below large dihedral. **Pitch 1:** Climb dihedral for 50' before angling right across slabs and corners (5.7) to 2-bolt belay on ledge. Protect second on traverse so they avoid a pendulum fall. **Pitch 2:** Climb shallow right-facing corner that leads to arching dihedral. Continue liebacking (5.7) up dihedral to undercling under big roof to groove. Downclimb 25' to 2-bolt belay atop *Green Adjective*. Again, protect the second on upper traverse. This pitch is 160'. Use lots of runners to avoid rope drag or break it into 2 shorter leads. **Descent:** 1 75-foot rappel from anchors. **Rack:** Sets of stoppers and Friends.

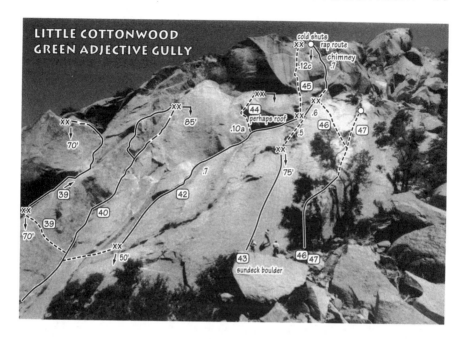

LITTLE COTTONWOOD
GREEN ADJECTIVE GULLY

43. **The Green Adjective** (5.9) 3 pitches but most do only the first. A Little Cottonwood mega-classic, must-do route. Begin up right from the start of *Perhaps* on a big ledge (The Sundeck Boulder) below the white slab. **Pitch 1:** Climb pin scars up thin splitter crack (5.9) to 2-bolt chained belay stance; 75'. Find good pro. **Pitch 2:** Climb groove to right-facing corner (5.5). Where it steepens, move right into 5.6 green corner. Belay above on spacious ledge from bolts. 150'. **Pitch 3:** Squeeze up chimney (5.7) to top. **Descent:** Rappel the route. **Rack:** Friends, TCUs, stoppers, and RPs.

44. **MA #1** (5.10a) 2 pitches, but usually only the first is done. Climb *Green Adjective* to its first belay. Ascend groove to *Perhaps* roof, undercling left to slanting corner on its left side. Stem up corner (5.10a); good feet on left wall. Continue up corner above (5.9+) to chain belay by pointed flake. **Descent:** Rappel the route.

45. **Meat Puppets** (5.12c) This good face route, climbed by Drew Bedford in 1988, ascends the leaning, streaked headwall above the *Green Adjective* slab. To reach the route's start, climb *Green Adjective* to its belay. Don't belay here but continue another 30' to a 2-bolt chain belay under a small overlap in the right-facing corner above. Move over the overlap to a slab with 1 bolt to the headwall base. The line continues on edges up the steep wall to a 2-cold shut anchor just below the upper lip. 85'. 10 bolts. A couple of projects are on the wall to the left, and another is up the seamed corner to the right.

46. **Prepositional Phrase** (5.11a) Begin just right of The Sundeck. Climb short crack onto slab, clip a bolt and edge through crux. Continue up and left on slab to 2-bolt anchor below corners. 7 bolts. **Descent:** Rappel the route with 2 ropes.

47. **Dangling Participle** (5.11a R) Good slabbing but not often climbed. Same start as #46, but angle up right at bolt 2 to thin grassy crack. Belay at small tree anchor (use caution) or continue higher to bolts. The second should be competent as a fall might result in falling over the edge to the right.

WEST FACE

The West Face is the right-hand wall flanking Green Adjective Gully. Routes are listed from top to bottom, or left to right when facing the cliff. The routes begin where some immense boulders block the gully. The routes on the lower section of the wall are severely overhanging crack testpieces. Bring tape and huevos to jam these ones!

48. **Wheels on Fire** (5.8+) No topo. A superb and very popular route that is old-style 5.8—hard and continuous. Read that as 5.9. Scramble up the gully to the base of the East Wall (right-hand wall) below some immense boulders in the narrowest part of the gully. Do some slick 3rd class moves around boulders to base of good-looking crack system. Begin atop boulders. Step right into flared crack on right side of steep slab. Jam finger and hand crack to blocky left-facing corner (5.8+). Undercling left on large flake, then lieback and jam to 2-bolt anchor on ledge. **Descent:** Rappel 130' with double ropes. **Rack:** A good selection of Friends and large stoppers.

49. **Wheels on Fire Direct** (5.10a) No topo. A good direct finish to *Wheels*. Instead of underclinging left, continue liebacking and jamming the thin crack above to ledge belay.

50. **St. Alphonso's Pancake Breakfast** (5.9+) No topo. Begin on right side of steep slab downhill from *Wheels*. Work up easy, broken crack to undercling left under shallow arch. Climb left 20', pull roof, and continue up bushy crack to ledge belay. **Decent:** Rap from tree anchor.

51. **Fallen Arches** (5.13a/b) No topo. 2 pitches but often only the first is done. This Little Cottonwood classic testpiece was first freed by Steve Hong and Steve Carruthers in 2 pitches in 1985. Sustained and excellent. The route ascends the obvious arch above *Wheels of Fire*. Easiest access is to scramble up a 4th class ramp/ledge system right of Route 50 to a large ledge below the arch. The route is often done in only 1 pitch but described here in 2. **Pitch 1:** Jam and lieback quality crack up arch (5.10 to 5.12a) to crux (5.12d) at double cracks. Continue up left (.12a) to belay stance on ramp at far left end of arch. **Pitch 2:** Finish up short, thin crack (5.9) to

top. **Descent:** Rappel the route. **Rack:** Stoppers, TCUs, and Friends to #3.

52. **Trinity Left** (5.12d) The left crack of the classic *Trinity* routes. All 3 routes share a common start. Begin near the bottom of a slabby, left-angling ramp downhill from *Fallen Arches*. Start below obvious V-shaped roof. Work up right under roof's point and jam up its right side to second V. Thin jamming leads up left-leaning crack and over roof to 2-piton belay/rap station above. Crux is changing from thin right-facing corner into left-facing corner at roof. A bolt with link is under roof. **Descent:** Rap or lower 80' to the ground. **Rack:** Lots of thin gear—wires, Aliens, and TCUs.

53. **Trinity Center** (5.13a) Powerful, pumpy, devious, but quality. Same *Trinity* start, but keep right at second V up flake crack to big roof. Strenuous moves over (5.13a) lead to 2-bolt station on small stance above roof. There may or may not be fixed gear. **Descent:** Rap or lower 85' to the ground. **Rack:** Thin crack gear.

54. **Trinity Right** (5.12a) 2 pitches, but usually only the first is done. The easiest of the *Trinity* trio, but still a stiff workout. Brachiate up *Trinity Center* to final roof. Keep right here by underclinging under roof to 1-piton/1-bolt semi-hanging belay station. Most dyno to anchors. Lower here (might be hard to clean!) or climb **Pitch 2:** Climb up right to bolt. Thin face climbing (5.11c) leads to easier thin cracks to final overlap. Belay from 2 bolts and 2 cold-shuts on ledge. **Descent:** Rappel 140' with 2 ropes. **Rack:** Lots of thin gear and selection of small and medium Friends.

55. **Mother of Pearl** (5.11c R/x) Superb and sustained, but sometimes wet. Done in 1 to 3 pitches. The more pitches, the easier the route. Begin 75' downhill from the *Trinitys* just right of a large, ground-level roof and behind a boulder. **Pitch 1:** Definitely the psychological crux! A serious lead with serious deck potential. Face climb (5.11b) up shallow, right-facing corner with black streak to narrow roof. Continue up groove-crack over another small roof to 1-bolt chain belay stance up left in crack. Find a #3.5 Friend placement at bottom, above is shallow crack for TCUs below first roof. The start is often wet with seeping water and bat guano. **Pitch 2:** Follow crack up left over streak to bolt. Barndoor liebacking (5.11c) up shallow corner leads to belay below left-angling dihedral. **Pitch 3:** Jam and lieback dihedral to final roof problem and 2-bolt belay. **Descent:** Rappel with 2 ropes; 140'. **Rack:** A selection of Friends, TCUs, wires, and RPs.

56. **Looney Tunes** (5.11b R) 2 pitches. **Pitch 1:** The same serious start as Route 55, but veer right to 2-bolt belay stance at 65'. **Pitch 2:** Step right into large left-facing dihedral. Jam good cracks (5.8) to 2-bolt belay ledge up right with boulder on it. **Descent:** Rappel the route. 2 raps—60 and 65'. Or one 2-rope rappel to the ground. **Rack:** Friends, TCUs, and wires.

57. **Badlands** (5.12a) A tough second pitch for *Looney Tunes*. **Pitch 1:** Climb *Looney Tunes* to 2-bolt stance. **Pitch 2:** Lieback thin, strenuous crack in arching, left-facing corner above past fixed gear to spread-eagle stem to steep roof, finger crack finish. Belay from 2 bolts on ledge. **Descent:** 2 rappels down the route. **Rack:** Friends, TCUs, wires, and RPs.

58. **Catalyst** (5.10c) One of the easier cliff offerings, but still a pump. A long pitch. Begin down right from *Looney Tunes*. Undercling right along arching roof (5.10c); good feet. Protect it from a shoulder stand to get started. Pull around on good holds onto rest. Continue up corner cracks to large roof. Lieback and jam out left side and continue up easier crack (5.8) to 2-bolt anchor on ledge. It's possible to break this into 2 pitches by belaying from the *Looney Tunes* belay, or even rapping from there. Otherwise, carry runners for rope drag. **Descent:** 1 double-rope rappel; 140'. **Rack:** Sets of stoppers, TCUs, and Friends.

59. **Nip and Tuck** (5.12b/c R) Expect hard face climbing and poor gear. Begin downhill from *Catalyst*. Climb fractured rock (5.7) to left-angling crack. Move up and pull roof with bolt (5.12c). Steep face climbing leads to 2-bolt belay ledge. **Descent:** A double-rope rappel.

60. **Old Reliable** (5.10b R) Bold, kind of scary, and some hard-to-find pro, but a real classic. Begin downhill from *Catalyst*. Loose face climbing (5.7) leads to roof with bolt. Pull over and continue up thin lieback cracks to final roof (5.10a) Belay on 2-bolt ledge. **Descent:** Rappel route with double ropes. **Rack:** Sets of stoppers, TCUs, and Friends.

THE GATE BUTTRESS

The Gate Buttress, a large south-facing wall, sits above the Gate Boulder parking area. The buttress is complex at first glance, but easy to figure out. The Green Adjective Gully flanks the west side of the wall. The popular School-room Wall, topped by a large roof, lies on the west side of the buttress. The Dihedrals are an obvious collection of southeast-facing corners north of the parking lot. The cliff, with over 90 routes, offers some of Little Cottonwood's best beginner and moderate routes as well as a selection of classic, must-do crack climbs. Lots of good boulder problems are found on the boulders along the access trail above the parking area.

THE SCHOOLROOM WALL

The Schoolroom Wall lies on the left side of the Gate Buttress. *Hatchet Crack*, a prominent curving crack, marks its left edge, while some broken crack systems lie between the Schoolroom Wall and The Dihedrals on the east. Descent off all the routes here is by rappel. Many finish by downclimbing and scrambling west to *The Schoolroom* rappel station. Others finish at the *Callitwhatyouplease* rappel station on the right. Either way, locate both the rappel stations before leaving the ground.

Finding the wall: Park at 1.3 miles in a large parking area on the north side of the highway. The cliff trail begins on the west side of the lot. Follow the path through trees and past numerous boulders. Keep left along the well-

downclimb to rappel

easy up to descent

.6

.8

XX

66

xx

80'

schoolroom rappel

.5

.7

.11b

.10

.6

chimney

68

65

67

.7

.6

61

XX

.12

.7

.6

63

62

65

.6

.5

.5

.9

.7

65 62 63 64

66

LITTLE COTTONWOOD
GATE BUTTRESS
SCHOOLROOM WALL

bolts not shown

trodden trail to a slippery slab beneath a large overhang. Scale this and follow the trail straight up to the west side of the wall below *Hatchet Crack* and *The Schoolroom*. A cliff-base trail heads east to other routes. Allow about 10 minutes to reach the cliff base from the parking area.

61. **Hatchet Crack** (5.7) Start off sloped ledge below obvious right-facing corner on southwest side of wall. Work up chimney in corner to arching crack, continue up crack (bit of 5.7) to anchors. **Descent:** Rappel the route. **Rack:** Stoppers and Friends to #3.

62. **Schoolroom West** (5.7) 5 short pitches. Some of the pitches can be combined. A fun line up a series of cracks and corners on the west edge of the Schoolroom Wall. Begin below an obvious ledge with several trees. **Pitch 1:** Angle left up blocky corner then back right (5.5) to ledge with several trees. **Pitch 2:** Go left up corner to bulge (5.7). Belay on small ledge. **Pitch 3:** Lieback up right (5.7) then back to belay below overlap. **Pitch 4:** Pull over some airy, awkward roofs (5.7) and belay at a tree left of large roof (Schoolroom Roof). **Pitch 5:** Jam hand crack (5.6) in tight corner up left to ledge belay. **Descent:** Scramble left on ledge system and downclimb chimney to Schoolroom Rappel 2-bolt anchors. Rap 80' to the base. **Rack:** Sets of Friends, TCUs, and stoppers.

63. **Unknown** (5.12) A technical and difficult slab. Begin same place as Route 62 and climb its pitch 1 to the tree belay next to a rock spike. Face climb directly up black streak on smooth, technical face using knobs, edges, and smears. End at 2-bolt anchor in left-angling seam. 6 bolts.

64. **Mantle Route** (5.9) Begin just right of Route 62 below a ledge and rock spike. Clip a bolt, do a cool mantle onto narrow shelf, and continue up dark streak past 2 more bolts to spike and tree. **Descent:** Rap route.

65. **Schoolroom** (5.6) 5 pitches. Super classic and very popular moderate route that wanders up the wall below the big roof. Same starting point as Route 62. **Pitch 1:** Climb broken corner up left then angle back right (5.5), move across ledge system and belay below curving crack. **Pitch 2:** Jam hand/fist crack up right (5.6); near its top step right onto chickenhead and edge up slab to good belay ledge. **Pitch 3:** Jam middle of 3 cracks (5.6) to belay stance in trees below left-facing dihedral. **Pitch 4:** Squeeze up awkward chimney (5.6) in dihedral to base of Schoolroom Roof. Traverse left (5.5) on slabs below roof to belay at tree just left of roof. Protect this traverse for seconds! **Pitch 5:** Move up left into steep hand crack (5.6) and belay on terrace above. **Descent:** Walk left on terrace and downclimb chimney to 2-bolt rappel station (Schoolroom Rappel). Rappel 80' to base left of *Hatchet Crack*. **Rack:** Sets of Friends, TCUs, and stoppers.

66. **Schoolroom Direct** (5.7) Most climb only the first pitch of this route and finish up *Schoolroom*. Begin 40' right of Route 65. Jam excellent finger to

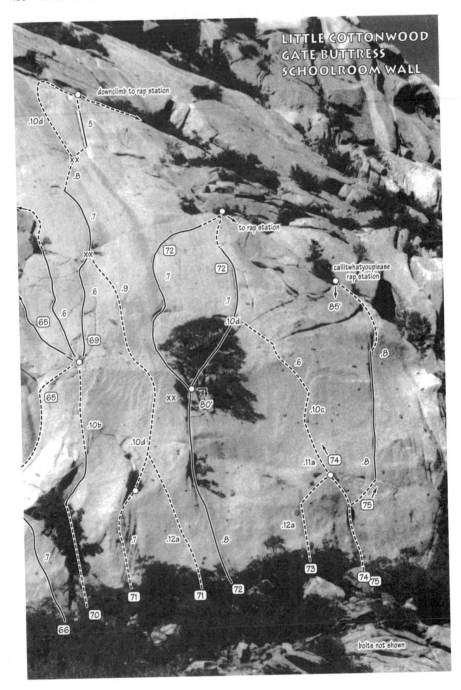

LITTLE COTTONWOOD
GATE BUTTRESS
SCHOOLROOM WALL

downclimb to rap station

.10d

.5

XX

.8

.7

72

to rap station

72

callitwhatyouplease
rap station

XX

.6

.9

.7

.7

85'

65

.6

.10d

.6

69

.8

65

XX

80'

.10c

.10b

.10d

.11a

74

.8

75

.7

.12a

.12a

73

74 75

.7

.12a

.8

71

71

72

70

66

bolts not shown

thin hand crack. Exit left to a few slab moves that lead to belay below curving crack. The route's next 3 pitches continue up crack to School-room Roof, finishing up 5.8 squeeze chimney right of roof. Most parties continue up *Schoolroom*.

67. **Knobs to Gumbyland** (5.10c) 1 pitch on the upper wall. Quality route. Access it by climbing *Schoolroom* to belay stance below big roof. Step right and edge and smear up black streak on left margin of slab and right of Schoolroom Roof. 5 bolts to tree belay. **Descent:** Angle up left to top of *Schoolroom* and follow its descent.

68. **State of Confusion** (5.11b) 1 pitch on the upper wall. Access it by climbing Route 65 to the belay stance below the roof. Move the belay right atop a large flake. Friction up the slab past 7 bolts to a belay under an overlap. **Descent:** Traverse easy 5th up left to ledge atop *Schoolroom*. Follow *Schoolroom* descent/rappel description.

69. **The Hook** (5.8 R) 3 pitches on the upper wall (5 pitches total). First ascent by Fred Beckey and Layton Kor, 1961. Quality, classic line. To begin, climb the first 2 pitches of *Schoolroom* to a ledge belay. **Pitch 1:** Angle right up crack (5.6) to 2-bolt belay stance at base of hook-shaped crack. **Pitch 2:** Lieback The Hook crack and exit right at its top. Traverse on knobs to bolt then straight up (5.8) to 2-bolt belay beneath flake. **Pitch 3:** Move right and jam wide groove-crack (5.5) to belay under overlap. For more excitement, climb *The Hook Direct* (5.10c R) by smearing up streak above belay past 2 bolts and a .75 TCU placement to same belay. **Descent:** Traverse right onto broken ledges and downclimb through trees and grooves to *Callitwhatyouplease* rappel station. Rappel with double ropes from 2-bolt anchor to ground. **Rack:** Friends to #3, TCUs, and stoppers.

70. **The Great Ripoff** (5.10b) 1 pitch to top of Route 65s second pitch. Begin just right of *Schoolroom Direct* below clump of trees. Bushwhack up through trees and follow the right-angling flake. Step left onto slab and climb direct past 2 bolts to belay ledge (*Schoolroom* pitch 2). Continue up any of the above routes.

71. **Mind Blow** (5.10d) 2 pitches to *The Hook*. Begin 10' right of Route 70. **Pitch 1:** Short lead up broken crack to belay stance by small tree. **Pitch 2:** Move right and up steep slab (5.10d) past 4 bolts to lower-angle rock. Continue up left past 3 more bolts to 2-bolt belay at base of *The Hook* crack. Continue up *The Hook*. 7 bolts. A direct start, called *Talus Food*, begins right of pitch 1 and moves up difficult wall (5.12a) and joins route at its first bolt.

72. **Bushwhack Crack** (5.8) 2 pitches. Super jamming! Many just climb pitch 1 and rap. Begin on boulder below perfect splitter crack. **Pitch 1:** Jam thin hands crack to scrub oak (5.8). Follow easier crack to hanging oak grove and shaded 2-bolt chain belay. Rappel 80'. **Pitch 2:** Climb either right-

arching crack above (5.7) or groove-crack (5.7) to right. Belay on ledge. **Descent:** Downclimb to *Callitwhatyouplease* rappel station. **Rack:** Friends to #2.5, small to medium stoppers, TCUs.

73. **Chicken Little** (5.12a) A short, hard, height-dependent variation start to *The Bungle*. Begin 20' right of Route 72. Thin face climbing past 2 bolts with crux move to knob. Belay up right at flake anchor. 35'.

74. **The Bungle** (5.11a) 1 pitch. Good route. Climb broken right-facing corner to flake. Edge and reach up left (5.11a) to left-facing flake. Swing up flake to hard mantle and bolt; traverse up left (5.10c) onto runout slab (5.6). Belay in angling crack. Finish by continuing up the crack to ledge belay. **Descent:** Downclimb to *Callitwhatyouplease*'s rappel anchors. **Rack:** Set of stoppers and TCUs, and small Friends.

75. **Callitwhatyouplease** (5.8) 1 pitch. Another George Lowe classic crack. Begin by climbing a broken corner (same as Route 74). At flake, traverse right 10' on narrow ledge to right-angling crack system. Jam awkward but fun hands to off-width crack. Above step right, pull over roof and climb slab to belay at tree. **Descent:** Rappel the route from anchors. **Rack:** Friends to #3.

THE DIHEDRALS AND BECKEY'S WALL

The Dihedrals area and Beckey's Wall, sitting directly north of the parking area at 1.3 miles, is one of Little Cottonwood Canyon's most popular cragging areas. All of the routes are stellar. Most are exposed 1-pitch crack routes up steep dihedrals or longer slab routes on Beckey's Wall. The Dihedrals get afternoon shade which makes them a popular summer evening destination.

Finding the cliffs: Park at the Gate Boulder parking area at 1.3 miles. Follow the path through the boulders before switchbacking back right and up to the base of the cliff. Scramble up and left on 3rd class rock to a sloping ramp below The Dihedrals. To reach Beckey's Wall, scramble up 3rd class rock to the base of its large dihedral. The routes begin on the lower left side of the wall.

76. **Incubator** (5.12c) 3 bolts. A short sport line with two 5.12 cruxes on the far left side of The Dihedrals wall. Swing up powerful liebacks to ending dyno to good jug. Finish at 2-bolt anchor on boulder atop good ledge.

77. **Half A Finger** (5.9+) Pumpy, sustained movements. Climb right-facing corner past several roofs to cool cut-loose moves off "hanging finger" at top. Belay and rappel from 2-bolt chain anchor. **Rack:** Set of stoppers, set of TCUs, and Friends to #3.

78. **Black and White John and Mary** (5.10c) Climb blocky corner for 15' and step right into main dihedral. Wild stemming and liebacking leads to strenuous but delicate exit moves. Belay and rappel from 2-bolt chain anchor (same as Route 77). Optional direct start is 5.11a R. **Descent:** Rappel 85'.

Rack: Set of stoppers, set of TCUs, and Friends to #3.

79. **Equipment Overhang** (5.11a) Great route but hard every time you do it! Jam and stem crack up steep corner to bolt. Tricky face moves (5.11a) lead to another bolt and overhang. Finish up short, slabby crack to 2-bolt chain anchors. **Descent:** Rappel 85'. **Rack:** Medium Friends, TCUs, and stoppers. **Rack:** Set of stoppers, set of TCUs, and Friends to #3.

80. **Equipment Overhang Right** (5.10b) Another classic crack. Lieback up right-facing corner, jam thin crack to high crux, finish up corner at Route 79's anchors. Avoid crux by stepping left out of crack and face climbing to roof. **Descent:** Rappel 85'. **Rack:** Set of stoppers, set of TCUs, and Friends to #3.

81. **Lisa's Shoulder** (5.9 R) Ascends the left wall of the 5th dihedral from the left. Begin atop boulders. Climb obvious dihedral to thin face holds (5.9) on left wall. Finish up right at anchors. Protection is tricky, but there. **Descent:** Rappel 80' from 2-bolt chain anchor. **Rack:** Small to medium stoppers and TCUs.

82. **Stem the Tide** (5.10d R) A tough finish to *Lisa's Shoulder*. Climb Route 81 to a ledge. Head up right wall via thin, stemming crack with 3 bolts. There is serious fall potential below bolt 3. Belay at 2 bolts. **Descent:** 80-foot rappel from 2-bolt chain anchor. **Rack:** Stoppers, TCUs, and a few Friends to #2.5.

83. **Satan's Corner** (5.8) 1 or 2 pitches. Mega-classic, must-do George Lowe crack route—one of Utah's very best 5.8s. This is real-life jamming—the

LITTLE COTTONWOOD
BECKEY'S WALL

saying here is: "Crack climbing skills or pay the coroner's bills!" Start below obvious corner just left of *Beckey's Wall* dihedral. Jam superb wide hand crack (5.8) for 50' to small ledge with tied-off horn. A possible belay here. Continue up beautiful corner above, stemming and liebacking, to airy exit move left to belay ledge. Leaders should have good pro skills; people have taken long falls and died on this route. **Descent:** Rappel 80' from 2-bolt chain anchor. **Rack:** Set of Friends to #3 and a set of stoppers.

84. **Beckey's Wall** (5.7) 3 pitches. Classic Fred Beckey and Layton Kor line up the obvious huge open book. **Pitch 1:** Climb obvious open book (spot of 5.7) to 2-bolt chain belay on right wall. **Pitch 2:** Continue up dihedral. Keep left up steep lieback-jam crack (5.7) where corner forms Y. Finish up slabby corner to good ledge with 2 bolts. Rappel with 2 ropes to ground or 2 rappels down route. **Pitch 3:** A quick lead up corner (5.4) to tree belay. **Descent:** From top of pitch 2 make 2-rope rappel to ground. From top of pitch 3, downclimb left down bushy ledges and cracks to Five Fingers Rappel west of *Satan's Corner*. Rap 80' to the ground. **Rack:** Sets of stoppers, TCUs, and Friends.

85. **Fingertip Variation** (5.8+ R) Pretty hard and runout 5.8. The right crack variation to *Beckey's Wall* pitch 2. Climb *Beckey's Wall* to the obvious Y. Continue up right to lieback (5.8) and belay on ledge above. **Descent:** 2 single-rope or 1 double-rope rappels down the route. **Rack:** RPs, stoppers, and TCUs.

86. **Unknown** (5.9) An alternative last pitch to *Beckey's Wall*. Climb first 2 pitches of Route 84 to ledge belay. Friction up right on white slab past 4 bolts to 2-bolt chain belay. **Descent:** Rappel route.

87. **Date With Fate** (5.9) Another last pitch to *Beckey's Wall*. From top of pitch 2, traverse right on slab above headwall then up shallow corner. Follow 2 bolts up slab's right side to a 2-bolt chain anchor. **Descent:** Rappel route.

88. **Split Fingers to Split Pants** (5.11c) 2 pitches. Hard undercling and lieback. Hard to protect. **Pitch 1:** (*Split Fingers*) Climb *Beckey's Wall* to the Y. Lieback up right crack (5.11c) then undercling out big roof to gully belay. **Pitch 2:** (*Split Pants*) Bushwhack up gully to large roof. Traverse right under roof (5.6) to gully belay. Best to continue up *Tingey's Terror* from here (description below) or scramble down gully just east of *Tarzan*. **Rack:** RPs, TCUs, and stoppers.

89. **Cheetah** (5.11b R) 4 pitches. Great slab climb. Usually only first 2 pitches are done. Start on a ledge/ramp right of *Beckey's Wall*. **Pitch 1:** Edge up left past 3 bolts to left side of the slab, clip double bolts and face climb (5.11b) up right to 2-bolt belay stance. (60'). **Pitch 2:** Angle up right past 3 bolts (5.9) on slightly runout smears to 2-bolt chain belay under overlap. Most rappel to ground from here with 2 ropes. **Pitch 3:** Exciting

climbing! Climb onto sloping ledge and step up left to bolt. Exposed climbing leads up left above roof (5.10) to bolt right of overlap, continue up and right on slab past 4 bolts to gully belay right of the *Split Pants* roof. **Pitch 4:** Face climb up right edge of roof (5.9 R) and work onto slab above. Continue to belay in trees. **Descent:** Traverse west and down to Five Fingers rappel station above Route 83. **Rack:** TCUs, stoppers, Friends, and quickdraws.

90. **Tarzan** (5.10a) 2 pitches. Classic crack. Begin just right of *Cheetah*. **Pitch 1:** Cruxy slab moves (5.10a) past 2 bolts to right-angling crack. Belay from 2 bolts on good stance. **Pitch 2:** Angle right up thin crack to well-protected cracks. Belay at 2-bolt chain anchor below overlap. (Same as *Cheetah*). **Descent:** One 2-rope rappel to the ground. **Rack:** Small to medium Friends.

91. **Sweet Jane** (5.7) A variation start to *Tarzan* that keeps whole route at 5.7. Begin just right of Route 90. Climb shallow left-facing corner (5.7) to slab to *Tarzan's* crack and belay. Continue up another pitch to chain anchors.

92. **Tingey's Terror** (5.7) No topo. 6 or 7 pitches. Excellent, long, and easy. Descent is a bit of a bushwhack. Some pitches can be combined. Watch the rockfall—others are below. **Pitches 1 & 2:** Climb first 2 pitches of *Sweet Jane* to bolt anchors. **Pitch 3:** Make short traverse right into gully and scramble up right to tree belay beneath long slab. **Pitch 4:** Angle up left in right-facing flake corner (spot of 5.7) to flat belay by trees. **Pitch 5:** Traverse right on gorgeous white slab (5.5 R) then straight up past 3 bolts (5.7) to spacious 2-bolt belay on Fudd Ledge. **Pitch 6:** From left side of ledge, up flake then right up groove to ledge belay with trees. **Pitch 7:** Climb flake-crack up left to large bushy terrace. **Descent:** 3rd class west across and down ledges, slabs, grooves, and cracks to *Schoolroom* rappel station on far left side of Gate Buttress.

LISA FALLS

Lisa Falls, a good beginner's area on the north side of the canyon farther east from Gate Buttress, is a south-facing slab divided by a pretty waterfall. This is a popular and busy area, especially on weekends. Most routes are done as topropes. Descent is by rappel from bolt anchors on a ledge near the summit or by walking off.

Finding the crag: Park at a large parking area on the north side of the road at 2.8 miles and follow a 5-minute trail up and left to the base of Lisa Falls, a small waterfall on the left side of the buttress. Routes are listed left to right.

93. **Lisa Falls Left** (5.8+ R) No topo. Climb thin, shallow corner to 2-bolt chain anchor. This route is best as a top-rope. Scramble up from left to anchors.

LITTLE COTTONWOOD
LISA FALLS

94. **Unknown** (5.9) No topo. A good thin slab route just left of the falls. 4 bolts to 2-bolt chain anchor.

95. **Flee Flicker** (5.7+) Begin right of falls by large boulder. Climb up past 3 bolts to ledge. Step right to 2-bolt anchor.

96. **Fleeting Glimpse** (5.9+) 1 short pitch. Begin just right of Route 94. Thin slabbing and slippery friction past bolt (5.9+), continue over overlap with awkward mantle and past 2 more bolts to 2-bolt anchor on ledge.

97. **Lisa Falls Right** (5.5) 2 pitches. Great beginner's route. **Pitch 1:** Same starting place as Route 95. Work right up crack in shallow corner before moving back left (5.5) over small ledges to 2-bolt belay ledge. **Pitch 2:** Work out right on slab into shallow corner. Climb up left (5.4) to 2-bolt belay/rappel anchor. **Descent:** 2 rappels or walk off back.

98. **Lefty** (5.4) Climb any of above routes to 2-bolt ledge. Climb up left to left-facing corner. Angle left to tree and climb back right on easy slab (5.4) to 2-bolt anchor on ledge. **Descent:** Rappel 85'.

99. **Safety Blitz** (5.8+) 1 pitch. No topo. On right side of cliff. Jam crack to overlap. Move up right into right-facing, leaning corner. Work up corner (5.8+) to upwards traverse left to 2-bolt belay ledge. **Descent:** Rap 85'.

MIDDLE BELL TOWER

OVERVIEW

Bells Canyon, parallel to and immediately south of Little Cottonwood Canyon, is a beautiful, glacier-carved valley that slowly rises to a lofty cirque perched high on the northwest flank of Lone Peak. Numerous cliffs dot the canyon's sides, particularly on its south-facing north slope, where three granite walls called the East, Middle, and West Bell Towers overlook the canyon floor. This trio of cliffs yields some of the finest granite climbs in the Wasatch Range. Most of the rock, a quartz monzonite like that in neighboring Little Cottonwood, is fairly sound, although the upper third of almost all the routes tends to be rotten and loose due to weathering.

Climbers will find great rock adventures and solitude in Bells Canyon on the long, multi-pitch lines on the Bell Towers. These are not sport-climbing routes, but crack climbs and slab routes put up in traditional style in the days before Fires and Friends. The best of the canyon's routes are found on a sweep of immaculate granite on the Middle Bell Tower, the biggest and best of the three Bells. Three of the lines on this central slab—*Cymbals of the Sun, Arm and Hammer*, and *Butcher Knife*—would rate three stars on anyone's scale with their superb and sustained edging, their runouts on some of the Wasatch's best rock, their excellent position and views, and their call for commitment.

Numerous other lines ascend the Middle Bell Tower. Info and topos on these routes as well as those on the other Bell Towers are found in Bret and Stuart Ruckman's comprehensive *Wasatch Climbing North* guidebook. The *Ellsworth-McQuarrie Route* (III 5.7) up the great dihedral on the right side of the Middle Bell is classic, but marred by loose rock on the upper pitches. West Bell Tower, the left-hand wall, offers *The Nerve* (II 5.11a) with a great first pitch up a thin corner and *Crown of Creation* (IV 5.10 A3), a dramatic nailing route that finishes up an airy arête. East Bell Tower is more broken and vegetated than its sheer neighbors. Best of its routes is the popular *Route of All Evil* (II 5.6), a four-pitch crack line up a right-facing dihedral.

Climbing history: The Bell Towers, with their height and mountain atmosphere, had some of the Wasatch Range's first technical routes put up on their granite flanks. In 1963, the prolific Fred Beckey, on one of his trips through Salt Lake City, teamed up with Larry Evans, Rich Ream, and Dick Ream and climbed the *Beckey Route*, a four-pitch 5.9 on the West Bell. Later that year Rich Ream and Ted Wilson did the difficult *Wilson-Ream* (III 5.8) up grooves and cracks on the west side of the Middle Bell in committing circumstances. After these initial routes, many of the obvious crack systems on the Bells were ascended by parties that included Mark McQuarrie, and George and Jeff Lowe. The next two decades saw some bold vertical journeys by area climbers, notably Brian Smoot and Les Ellison. Their nervy creations include the excellent classics *Arm and Hammer* in 1979 (first free in 1985) and *Cymbals of the Sun* by Smoot and Ellison in 1990. *Butcher Knife*, another Middle Bell classic, went to Ellison and Rick Wyatt in 1982, with Merrill Bitter and Bret Ruckman getting the first free ascent in 1984.

Middle Bell Tower is readily accessible from the Salt Lake City metroplex. The climber can pick up bagels and coffee, hike in and do a multi-pitch route in a remote mountain setting, and still have time in the evening to stop off for dinner. The canyon is adjacent to and parallel with Little Cottonwood Canyon. The trail ascends about a mile and a half up the canyon from its suburban trailhead to the base of the Middle Bell. Allow one to two hours for the approach march. **Descent:** Most parties rappel the routes rather than do the last groveling pitch to the summit and walk-off. Two ropes are needed for the rappel descent. **Rack:** A basic rack for these routes would include sets of Friends, TCUs, and stoppers, along with a big crack piece like a #4 or #5 Camalot. Bring a dozen quickdraws, extra runners, and two ropes.

Trip Planning Information

General description: A selection of excellent, multi-pitch crack and slab routes up the south-facing center wall of Middle Bell Tower in Bells Canyon.

Location: North-central Utah. Southeast of Salt Lake City.

Camping: The nearest and best campgrounds are 2 national forest areas in upper Little Cottonwood Canyon. Tanners Flat Campground, with 38 sites, is at 4.1 miles. Albion Basin Campground, with 26 sites, is at the road's end near Alta Ski Resort. Neighboring Big Cottonwood Canyon to the north has Spruces Campground, with 121 sites, at 9.8 miles, and Redman Campground, with 50 sites, at 13.2 miles. All are fee areas, with water, restrooms, and tables.

Climbing season: Spring, summer, and fall. Spring and fall are best. Sunny days, particularly in summer, can be very hot on this south-facing crag. Summer mornings are best when much of the cliff is still in the shade. Winter offers some warm days, but the approach can be snowy, mucky, and slow-going.

Restrictions and access issues: None currently, except dogs and horses are not allowed in the canyon because it is the SLC watershed. The canyon lies in Wasatch National Forest. The access, however, is through a subdivision. Best to be unobstrusive and respectful of private property.

Guidebooks: *Rock Climbing the Wasatch Front* by Bret and Stuart Ruckman, Chockstone Press, 1998. A comprehensive guide to Bells Canyon and environs.

Nearby mountain shops, guide services, and gyms: Stores include Black Diamond, IME, REI (Salt Lake), Mountainworks (Provo), and Hansen Mountaineering (Orem). Gyms are Wasatch Front Climbing Gym and Rockreation in Salt Lake, and Rock Garden in Provo. Guides include Wasatch Touring, Exum Mountain Utah, and Mastodon Mountaineering (Ben Folsom).

Services: All services are located in Salt Lake City and its suburbs. Supermarkets and gas stations are just below the canyon in Sandy.

Emergency services: Call 911 for all emergencies. Alta View Hospital, 9660 South 1300 East, Salt Lake City, (801) 567-2600. Cottonwood Hospital, 5770 South 300 East, Salt Lake City, (801) 262-3461. St. Mark's Hospital, 1200 East 3900 South, Salt Lake City, (801) 268-7129.

Nearby climbing areas: Little Cottonwood Canyon, Hellgate Cliffs, Big Cottonwood Canyon, The Millstone, Ferguson Canyon, Pete's Rock, Parley's Canyon, Lone Peak, American Fork Canyon.

Nearby attractions: Alta, Snowbird, Big Cottonwood Canyon, Salt Lake City attractions (Temple Square, Brigham Young Monument, Beehive House, Utah State Capitol, Utah Museum of Natural History, Utah Museum of Fine Arts, This is the Place State Park, Hogle Zoo), Great Salt Lake, Bingham Canyon Mine (largest pit mine in world).

Finding the area: The best approach is from Stone Ridge Estates, a housing subdivision below Lower Bells Reservoir off Wasatch Boulevard. Drive 0.3 mile south on Wasatch Blvd. from its junction with 9800 South. Turn left on Bell Canyon Road (10025 South) then immediately left onto Stone Mountain Lane. Continue uphill for 0.3 mile to a dead-end parking area. Walk up a dirt road (closed to traffic) to Lower Bells Reservoir. At the east end of the reservoir, pick up a trail that climbs over a ridge shoulder and into Bells Canyon. Hike up the trail on the south side of the creek until you are opposite the obvious Middle Bell Tower (the third large buttress) to the north. Cross the creek and hike up through a boulder field to the base of the face.

1. **Cymbals of the Sun** (III 5.11d) 6 or 7 pitches. First ascent by Brian Smoot and Les Ellison, 1990. Begin by scrambling up 3rd class rock below the smooth center slab to a belay ledge below a huge roof and a right-angling dihedral. This dihedral is the *Ellsworth-McQuarrie Route*. **Pitch 1:** Lieback and jam obvious dihedral (5.7) up to and out big roof to belay atop large wedged chockstone. **Pitch 2:** *Cymbals* officially begins here. Face climb (5.11d) out left to thin, left-facing corner. Climb up it and then left to 2-bolt belay. 7 bolts. **Pitch 3:** Edge up left (5.9) to left side of The Crescent (a pointed flake). Pass some fixed pins, continue above flake (5.9) to 2-bolt belay on The Pedestal Ledge. This upper section is also part of *Arm and Hammer*. 3 bolts and 2 fixed pins. **Pitch 4:** Climb the impeccable slab

MIDDLE BELL TOWER

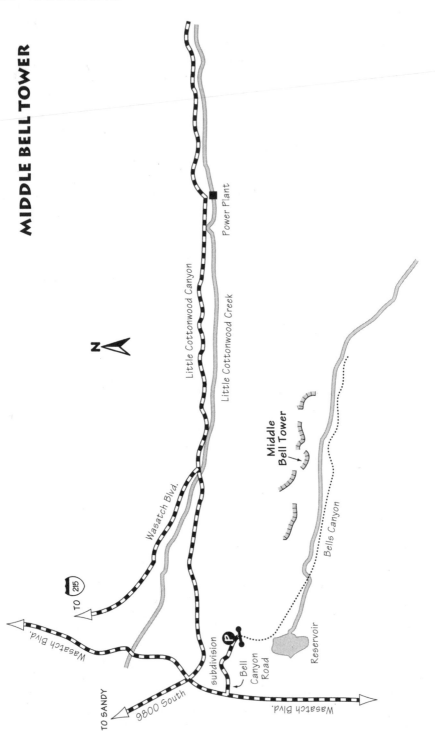

N

Little Cottonwood Canyon

Little Cottonwood Creek

Power Plant

Wasatch Blvd.

TO 215

TO SANDY

Wasatch Blvd.

9800 South

Wasatch Blvd.

subdivision

Bell Canyon Road

P

Middle Bell Tower

Bells Canyon

Reservoir

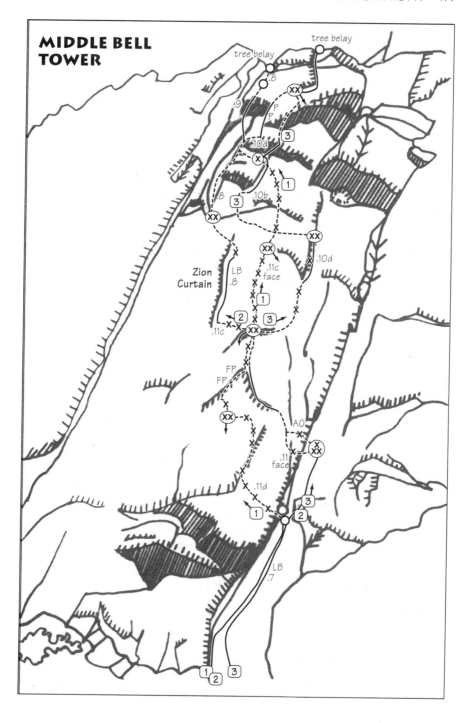

MIDDLE BELL
TOWER

tree belay

tree belay

.8

.9

P
P

XX

3

.10d

X

.8

3

.10b

1

XX

XX

XX

.10d

X

Zion
Curtain

LB
.8

.11c
face

X

1

2

3

.11c

XX

FP
FP

XX

AO

XX

.11
face

.11d

1

3

2

LB
.7

1
2

3

above (5.11c) past some thin corners to 2-bolt belay stance. **Pitch 5:** Up right (5.9) and then back left to 1-bolt belay under thin roof. 4 bolts. **Pitch 6:** Out left edge of roof (5.10d) then up shallow corner to 2-piton belay. 3 bolts and 3 fixed pitons. Many parties rap from here rather than do last loose pitch. **Pitch 7:** Move up obvious right-facing dihedral to a tree belay. 1 bolt. **Descent:** 5 double-rope rappels down route from the top. From the top of the buttress, the first rap goes 90' off a tree. Otherwise 4 rappels from bolt anchors. **Rack:** A mixed rack of cams, TCUs, and stoppers. Quickdraws and two 165-foot ropes.

2. **Arm and Hammer** (III 5.11c or 5.10a A0) 6 pitches. First ascent by Les Ellison and Russ Jacobs, 1979. First free ascent by Drew Bedford, David Casey, Ron George, and Karen Kelley, 1985. This is it—the mega-classic, must-do long route in the Salt Lake area! Begin with the same start as Route 1—scramble up to the base of the dihedral below the big roof. Pitches 1 and 2 can be combined into a long pitch. **Pitch 1:** Climb first pitch of *Ellsworth-McQuarrie Route* up obvious dihedral and past big roof (5.7) to belay atop chockstone. **Pitch 2:** Continue up dihedral (5.7) to 3-bolt belay. **Pitch 3:** Start of route. Two ways to go. First angle out left to high bolt and tension traverse (A0) off bolt to thin face climbing (5.10) to left-angling ramp on right side of The Crescent, a large pointed flake. Or face climb left from lower bolt (hard 5.11) to ramp. Above flake continue straight up face (5.9) past 2 bolts to 2-bolt belay on The Pedestal Ledge. **Pitch 4:** A spectacular lead! Traverse left from ledge past 2 bolts. Continue edging left (5.11c) or pendulum left (A0) off second bolt to Zion Curtain, an 80-foot-high expanding flake that is less than an inch thick in places. The curtain's edge, while not as sharp as it once was, is still thin and unsettling. Lieback the flake (5.8) then move up left to 2-bolt ledge belay. **Pitch 5:** Climb left-facing corner (5.8) to right-facing corner. Jam hand crack over roof (5.9) or move left around it (5.8) and belay above by a tree. **Pitch 6:** Move up moderate rock (5.8) to tree belay. **Descent:** 5 double-rope rappels down the face. **Rack:** Sets of Friends, TCUs, and stoppers, quickdraws, runners, and 2 ropes. Bring a #4 Camalot.

3. **Butcher Knife** (III 5.11c or 5.10d A0) 6 pitches. First ascent by Les Ellison and Rick Wyatt, 1982. First free ascent by Merrill Bitter and Bret Ruckman, 1984. Another superb but tough classic face route. The only 5.11 section is the tension traverse section on *Arm and Hammer's* first pitch, otherwise the hardest climbing is 5.10d. **Pitches 1, 2 & 3:** Follow the first 3 pitches of Route 2 to The Pedestal Ledge 2-bolt belay. **Pitch 4:** Move to right end of the ledge and face climb (5.9) 40' straight up past 2 bolts to small roof. Step right from roof into shallow right-facing corner (5.10). Above, face climb left and follow thin left-facing corner (5.10d) to 2-bolt belay stance. 3 bolts. **Pitch 5:** Traverse straight left about 35' above *Cym-*

bals belay to bolt. Continue traversing (5.9) to ledge. Jam hand and off-width crack to chimney (5.10b) and belay from 1 bolt below narrow roof (same as *Cymbals* pitch 6 belay). Swing up and over roof above (5.10c) to crack to another pumpy roof (5.10d) Belay up left from 2-piton belay stance. Rap from here or do last loose pitch. **Pitch 6:** Climb obvious right-facing corner (5.8) above to a tree belay. **Descent:** 5 double-rope rappels down the center of the slab. **Rack:** A selection of Friends, TCUs, and stoppers, quickdraws, runners, and two 165' ropes.

Boone Speed on Malvado, *El Diablo Wall, American Fork.* PHOTO BY STEWART M. GREEN

AMERICAN FORK CANYON

OVERVIEW

American Fork Canyon is an abrupt abyss deeply sliced into the Wasatch Range east of the town of American Fork. The canyon, excavated by rushing American Fork Creek, is flanked by the ragged peaks of the Lone Pine Wilderness Area on the north and the long, lofty ridge of 11,749-foot Mt. Timpanogos and its surrounding wilderness area on the south. Long bands of limestone, broken by sharp gullies, talus fields, and hanging forests, loom above the highway and the canyon floor.

These cliffs of Mississippian-age limestone and dolomite were deposited some 350 million years ago on an ancient sea floor. Later, during the uplift of the Wasatch Range, the limestone was tilted, twisted, faulted, and then eroded and shaped by the snowmelt-laden river and water trickling through the permeable rock.

The diverse layers of limestone, at first glance, appear chossy and devoid of good holds. Closer inspection of the abrupt cliffs, however, reveals in-cut edges, pockets that range from mono-doigts to full-hand jugs, sharp sidepulls, and finger crimps. Almost all of the canyon's routes overhang. Slabs are seldom seen and dime-sized edges are never used. The cliffs offer hundreds of routes that range in difficulty from 5.7 to 5.14 and range in length from 30 to 100 feet. The area is a traditionalist's nightmare—all of the routes are bolted, clip-and-go climbs. The cliff tops are generally loose and blocky; consequently all the routes end at lowering stations on the faces below. American Fork is not a beginner's area. There are few routes below 5.10, with most lines in the 5.11 and 5.12 grades. The Hell Wall itself offers over 20 5.13 routes and variations. All of the routes are one pitch long with lowering or rappel anchors.

The loose and broken rock surface required extensive cleaning and prying by first ascensionists to get down to the good stuff underneath the choss. Area pioneer Boone Speed says, "When Bill Boyle and I put up the first route on the Division Wall, we levered at least a ton of rock off the cliff." Most of the canyon routes now, especially the well-traveled ones, are generally clean and stable. Some, however, still change from season to season as flakes and key holds break off; a good example of this is *Malvado* on the El Diablo Wall. Other hard routes feature glue-reinforced holds to keep the same experience and grade for succeeding climbers. This philosophy is a totally accepted ethic, given the often dubious nature of the limestone. The ethic does not, however, allow for the chipping or manufacturing of holds, especially on established routes. Chipping holds to bring a climb down to your low standard is unethical. Raise your abilities to equal the route. Chipping also destroys the future of climbing by taking away hard routes from up-and-coming climbers.

The climbing here is conveniently concentrated, with over 35 bolted crags crammed into the two-mile highway stretch from Timpanogos Cave National Monument (where no climbing is allowed) and the exit road from Little Mill Campground. Most of the cliffs lie within a 5-minute walk of the highway, although a couple of crags, including the excellent Hideaway and The Billboard, are accessible only by steep uphill hikes.

American Fork Canyon is a year-round cragging area. The best conditions are between April and the end of October. Spring brings warm days but wet conditions as the limestone and its pockets seep water. Rockfall is also a danger; limestone chunks, loosened by winter's freezing and thawing, pry loose from the cliff faces. Summer is a surprisingly good time to visit American Fork, although hot temperatures are not uncommon. The summer crags along the south flank of the shaded canyon floor are generally cool, with temperatures moderated by the roaring creek, low humidity, and dense vegetation. Autumn is the best time to climb at American Fork—warm days, cool nights, colorful changing trees, and few tourists on the highway. Winter offers iffy conditions, depending on snowfall amounts and cold temperatures. The Billboard and Hideaway crags, perched high on the northern side, are often flooded with sunlight and warmth while the canyon floor is locked in snow and cold. The highway through the canyon is occasionally closed due to avalanche danger.

Convenient camping is located at Little Mill Campground. Climbers bivouacking here often leave their cars and walk to nearby crags including the Division Wall, Gray Cliffs, and Hard Rock crags. The fee area is open from May through October. Summer nights, particularly on weekends, can be hectic with lots of RVs, screaming children, and other noise. Fortunately the sites are spread out along the road so it is possible to find some privacy and quiet. Another campground is up the North Fork Road, and free camping is located on a dirt road just past Tibble Reservoir off the North Fork Road. The best sites are often taken by long-term campers and climbers. Otherwise several RV-style campgrounds are located in the American Fork/Provo area, along with the usual city amenities like fast food, grocery stores, and a couple climbing shops. The Lehi Swimming Pool, just off Interstate 15, is a good place for showers and a swim in summer.

Climbing history: American Fork Canyon was, like so many of today's popular sport climbing areas, an undeveloped pile of suspect rock until the late 1980s when it's potential was first discovered. Although a few routes were done previously in a ground-up, traditional style, no bolted routes existed here until 1988 when Bill Boyle, Jeff Pederson, and Boone Speed found, toproped, cleaned, and bolted the first lines. Over the next few years this trio, along with other inspired locals and travelers, put up hundreds of routes and firmly established these backwater cliffs as an international rock-jock destination.

Bill Boyle did more to develop the canyon than any other climber, bolting and ascending over 100 first ascents. Boyle, with a severe case of American Fork fever, even headed up the canyon during lunch breaks from his job to drill bolts and clean loose rock. Boone Speed, with over 40 first ascents, created most of the canyon's 5.13s and classics like *Hell*, *Shining*, and *Black Magic*, the canyon's first sport climb. Some notable ascents include J.B. Tribout's first ascent of *Cannibals* and Scott Franklin's testpiece *Blow of Death*. Other activists were Jeff Baldwin who almost single-handedly developed The Hideaway, Drew Bedford at Hard Rock, and Brian Smoot at Hard Rock and Escape Buttress.

Rack: A rack of 15 quickdraws and a 165-foot rope is sufficient gear for most routes. A 200' (60-meter) rope is necessary to lower off a few routes.

Trip Planning Information

General description: Numerous bolted sport routes, ranging from 5.8 to 5.14, ascend the many limestone crags along a three-mile section of deep American Fork Canyon.

Location: North-central Utah. Northeast of Provo.

Camping: Little Mill Campground, operated by the Forest Service, offers 79 campsites along the creek in American Fork Canyon. The fee campground, open May through October, has restrooms, water, tables, and tent sites. Granite Flat, a 32-site forest campground, is about 4 miles up the North Fork Road (FR 085) above the canyon. Take a left turn at the road fork just past Little Mill Campground to reach the area. Free primitive camping is located just past Tibble Reservoir on a rough dirt road that turns right at the first switchback above the lake. Drive about half a mile to a sign where camping begins. Sites are along the creek.

Restrictions and access issues: Uinta National Forest administers American Fork Canyon and its climbing areas. A use pass is required to climb, camp, hike, and fish in American Fork Canyon. Both daily and annual passes can be purchased at a toll booth near the canyon mouth.

Local climbers and the Forest Service have adopted several important regulations, most of which pertain to climbing at the Little Mill Campground area:

1. Climbers should park outside the campground on pull-offs on the main highway and walk in to access the routes on the Division Wall and other crags. Do not park on the busy, narrow campground road.

2. Do not climb on the cliff behind campsite Route 33 if it is occupied. If someone moves into the site while you are climbing, pack up and leave for another area. Do not climb here even if you are granted permission.

3. Do not walk through campsite Route 64 to reach the Division Wall. Follow the short path just east of the site by the restroom to access the cliff.

4. Do not leave quickdraws hanging overnight on routes in the campground.

5. No new routes in Mill Creek Campground.

6. No camping except in designated campgrounds.

7. No climbing in Timpanogos Cave National Monument or at the Hanging Rock area.

Other common sense rules include: Follow established trails to the cliff bases. Pick up litter and garbage on the trails and at the cliff base. Always use the restrooms whenever possible.

Guidebooks: *Climber's Guide to American Fork and Canyon Rock Canyon* by Stuart Ruckman and Bret Ruckman, Chockstone Press, 1995. A very complete topo guide to the Provo area crags including American Fork Canyon, Rock Canyon, and Hobble Creek Canyon. *Wasatch Range* by the Ruckmans, Chockstone Press, 1997, is a select guide to American Fork and Little and Big Cottonwood Canyons.

Nearby mountain shops, guide services, and gyms: Mountainworks (Provo), Hansen Mountaineering (Provo), IME (Salt Lake City), Black Diamond (Salt Lake City), REI (Salt Lake City), Rock Garden gym (Provo), Wasatch Front Climbing Gym (Sandy), and Rockreation gym (Salt Lake City).

Services: All services are located in Lehi, American Fork, Lindon, Pleasant Grove, Orem, and Provo. Nearest stores and restaurants are in American Fork. You can get a shower in the summer at the Lehi Swimming Pool at 400 East near Exit 281 off Interstate 15.

Emergency services: Call 911. American Fork Hospital, 170 North & 1100 East, American Fork, UT, (801) 763-3300.

Nearby climbing areas: Rock Canyon, Lone Peak Cirque, Big Willow Canyon, Bells Canyon, Little Cottonwood Canyon, Ferguson Canyon, Big Cottonwood Canyon, Mill Creek Canyon, Parley's Canyon.

Nearby attractions: Timpanogos Cave National Monument, a trio of small caves reached by a 1.5-mile hike, is well worth a visit. Other points of interest include Alpine Scenic Highway, Mt. Timpanogos Wilderness Area, Lone Peak Wilderness Area, Wasatch Mountain State Park, Bridal Veil Falls, Provo Canyon, Uinta National Forest, Utah Lake State Park, Salt Lake City attractions.

Finding the crags: American Fork Canyon lies northeast of Provo and southeast of Salt Lake City. It is easily accessible from Interstate 15, Utah's main north-south thoroughfare. Take Exit 287 just north of Lehi and drive east on Utah 92. After a few miles, the highway passes through the suburb of Highland and shortly afterwards reaches the V-shaped mouth of the canyon. The

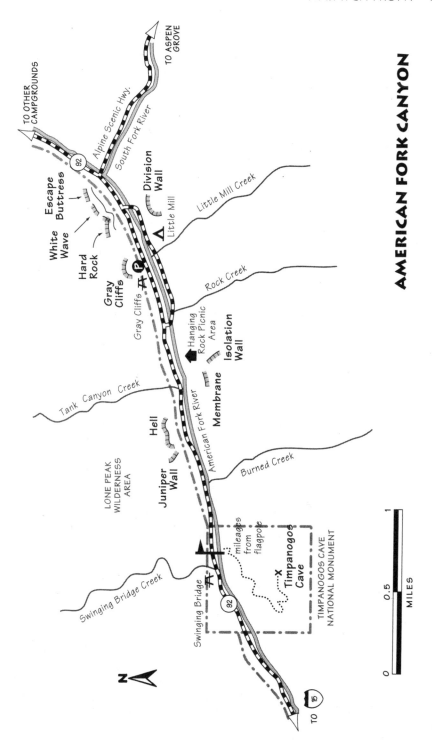

AMERICAN FORK CANYON

road winds up the canyon and reaches Timpanogos Cave National Monument after a couple of miles. No rock climbing is allowed in the monument. Almost all of the canyon's climbing lies along the 2-mile highway stretch east of the monument. The traditional reference point for mileage to the various crags is from the flagpole on the south side of the highway opposite the national monument visitor center. The cliffs are obscured by vegetation or hidden from highway view. Most, however, you can reach with a short walk from the highway pullouts.

JUNIPER WALL

This fine west-facing wall offers sunshine and warmth on cool days or morning shade in summer. Juniper and Hard walls are easily accessible from the Hell area. Park at the large parking lot on the south side of the highway 0.65 mile past the national monument flagpole. From the west end of the parking lot, cross the highway and follow the short uphill trail to Hell. From the El Diablo Wall, the right-hand side of Hell, follow a contouring trail west across talus and down and around a protruding buttress on the west side of Hell. Continue a couple of hundred feet west to a large fir tree in a talus field. Hard Wall, a short overhanging cliff, is directly north and uphill from here. Continue west on the trail around another buttress to Juniper Wall. An alternative trail, not recommended, climbs directly uphill from the highway just down-canyon from Hell parking. Routes are right to left going uphill.

1. **Cranial Bypass** (5.11a) A direct line up the steep wall. Move up right and then left to break above bolt 6 (5.11a). 7 bolts to 2-bolt anchor. 70'.

2. **Cranial Impact** (5.11c) A fine line that works up and left onto a beautiful upper wall of excellent rock. Go left above bolt 4 to crux at last bolt. 7 bolts to 2-bolt anchor. 65'.

3. **Blood on the Rocks** (5.10b) Climbs the blocky, loose face right of large crack/corner. 3 bolts to 2-bolt anchor (same anchor as Route 2). 60'.

4. **Child's Play** (5.9) Just right of the obvious pine beside the wall. 4 bolts to 2-bolt anchor.

5. **Time Crunch** (5.8) A slabby 45-foot line behind a large pine tree. 4 bolts to 2-bolt anchor (same anchor as *Child's Play*).

HARD WALL

Three short, power routes swing up this small, overhanging wall on the east end of the buttress. It is located east of and around the corner from the Juniper Wall. Easily accessed from Hell by walking on a trail that contours west from below Hell to Juniper Wall. At a large fir tree, scramble up scree to obvious small cave. Routes are right to left. No topos for these routes.

AMERICAN FORK
JUNIPER WALL

6. **Empiricist** (5.12a) 5 bolts to 2-bolt anchor. 30'.

7. **The Nihilist** (5.12d) A superb power route for hardmen. 4 bolts to 2-bolt anchor. 30'. Stick-clip the first bolt.

8. **Dogma** (5.12a) 6 bolts to 2-bolt anchor above lip. 35'. Stick-clip bolt 1.

THE HELL AREA

Hell, a horseshoe-shaped, south-facing cirque of cliffs, is the American Fork destination spot for top elite climbers as well as wannabe posers. Hell Wall is a steep cliff on the left side of the cirque and offers some classic lines including *Hell* itself. Hell Cave is a dark, radically overhanging cave blackened by count-

Boone Speed on Burning, *Hell Cave, American Fork.* PHOTO BY STEWART M. GREEN

less fires and crisscrossed by powerful, gymnastic routes that make even the strongest climber chase the pump to the anchor. A cone of scree, washed down the pour-off above the cave, hides the front of Hell Cave and makes a convenient perch to watch struggling climbers and to stick-clip the upper bolts. Jim Karn, in an old issue of *Climbing*, said about Hell, "It's sick when you climb a 65-foot route and can still stick-clip the anchors." The El Diablo Wall, enclosing the east side of the cirque, houses some of Hell's best and most difficult routes including *El Diablo* and *Blow of Death*.

Reach Hell by a short, uphill approach. Drive 0.65 miles east from the national monument flagpole to a huge gravel parking area on the right or south side of the highway. Park here, walk to the west end of the parking lot, cross the highway, and find a short access trail that winds uphill around the prow of a prominent buttress. The first cliff encountered is El Diablo Wall. A short contouring trail crosses a scree slope west of El Diablo Wall to Hell Wall and Hell Cave. Total approach time is about 5 minutes from car to cave. Routes are listed left to right beginning with Hell Wall.

HELL WALL

9. **Church of Skatin'** (5.12c) A good warm-up line for the hardman. The anchors, however, need to be moved down to avoid a funky clip. 6 bolts to 2-bolt anchor.

10. **Romeo's Bleeding** (5.11b) Climb obvious corner above broken alcove. 7 bolts to 2-bolt anchor.

11. **Guillotine** (5.12d) An excellent, easier version of *Hell* with hard sequences. Crux is below upper roof. 5 bolts to 2-bolt anchor.

12. **Hell** (5.13a) A classic hard route put up by Boone Speed. Expect bouldery moves, no rests, and lots of polish. 6 bolts to 2-bolt anchor.

13. **High Water** (5.13c) Pumpy climbing swings up left to join upper third of *Hell*. 7 bolts to Route 12's 2-bolt anchor.

14. **The Blight** (5.12a) One of the slabbier routes here, but thin edges make for tough, technical climbing. 5 bolts to 2-bolt anchor.

15. **Reanimator** (5.12d) Steep climbing leads to crimpy crux over and above roof. 5 bolts to 2-bolt anchor. A good variation, *Brimstone* (5.13d), follows bouldering traverse from Route 12 right to first 2 bolts of Route 14, works up right past another bolt, and joins Route 15 at its 3rd bolt.

16. **Reaching for Razors** (5.11d) The usual Hell warm-up. This popular Bill Boyle slab route is technical and harder than it looks. 4 bolts to 2-bolt anchor (same as Route 15).

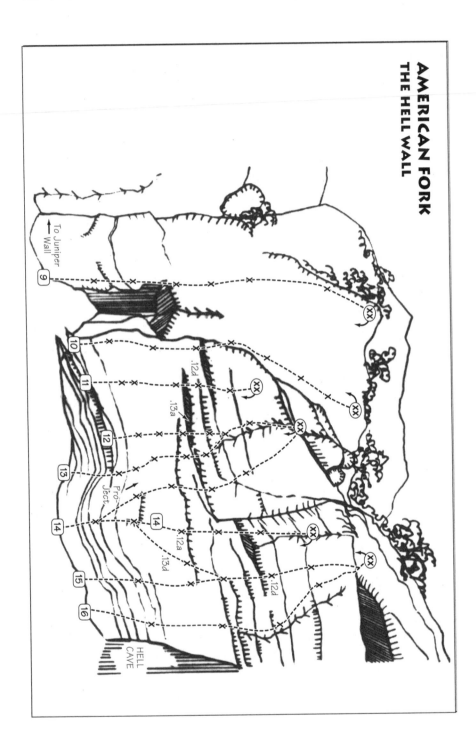

AMERICAN FORK
THE HELL WALL

HELL CAVE

Hell Cave is the deep, smoke-darkened recess at the back of the limestone amphitheater. A large scree cone hides the cave from casual observers. All of the routes are steep and powerful. Many variations are possible. Most end at a set of anchors at the far right side of the large roof that tops the cave. These can be stick-clipped from the talus cone. Draws are often left on routes here—respect their owners by leaving them in place. Hell Cave is, at first sight, a complex and bewildering maze of routes and bolts. Sit down and scope the routes out to familiarize yourself with the lines. Routes are left to right.

17. **Jitterbug Boy** (5.12a) A good but strange route up the left side of Hell Cave. Follow left edge of cave to roof, above step right onto ledge, and continue up right past right side of large roof to anchors. 6 bolts to 2-bolt anchor.

18. **Wasatch Reality** (5.12a) The easiest route in Hell Cave. A long line that begins on far left margin of cave and follows broken crack system up and right under large roof to anchors. 7 bolts to 2-bolt anchor.

19. **Burning** (5.13b) An excellent route. Begin at the same place as Route 18 only climb up right to the first bolt. Chase the pump up and right on good but widely spaced holds to bolt under large roof. Undercling right past bolt to anchors. 11 bolts to 2-bolt anchor.

20. **Linus** (5.13d) A powerful mega-pump. Begin just right of *Burning*. Difficult moves lead up and over bulge past 4 bolts to bolt 5 on Route 19. Continue straight up (5.13c) past 2 more bolts to bolt 4 on Route 18. Do the rest of *Wasatch Reality* to anchors. 11 bolts to 2-bolt anchor.

21. **Fryeing** (5.13c) A tough link-up put up by Scott Frye that is essentially a variation of *Burning*. Swing up *Burning's* crux to bolt 6, work up right to *Cannibals'* bolt 7, continue through *Wizard's* crux to the 2-bolt anchor. Don't stop here. Pull the roof (*Bats Out of Hell* 5.12d) past bolt to anchor. 11 bolts to 1-bolt anchor.

22. **Cannibals** (5.13d/.14a) Powerful climbing with few rests on this long route first ascended by French climber J.B. Tribout. Begin on right side of cave to right of deeply recessed alcove. Climb up left (5.13d) past 7 bolts. Angle right to *Wizards'* 5.13b crux and finish with the *Bats Out of Hell* roof. 11 bolts to 1-bolt anchor.

23. **Melting** (5.12d/.13a) This popular, traversing Boone Speed line is also one of the cave's 3-star routes. Begin just right of Route 22 on *Wizards*. Work up to large hole (5.12c) and 3rd bolt. Angle up left past bolt to *Burning's* bolt 8. Continue up *Burning* to the 2-bolt anchor. 8 bolts to 2-bolt anchor.

24. **Wizards** (5.13b) A great route up the right side of the cave. Climb up left to large hole below 3rd bolt. Pull straight up on pockets (5.13b) to anchor. Tape for pocket handjams! 6 bolts to 2-bolt anchor. *I Scream,* a

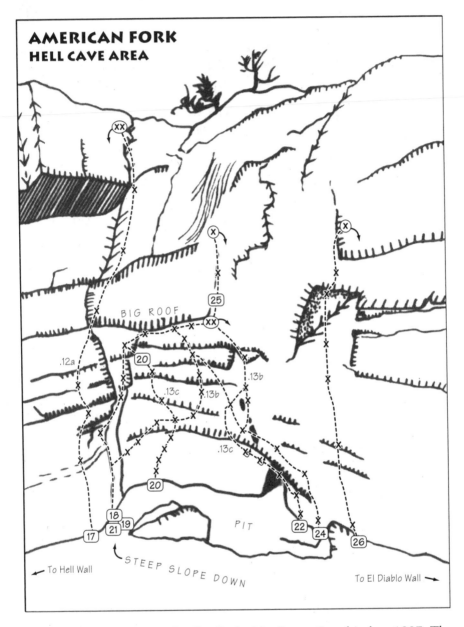

AMERICAN FORK
HELL CAVE AREA

BIG ROOF

.12a

20

.13c   .13b

.13b

.13c

20

18
21 19
17

PIT

22
24

26

To Hell Wall

STEEP SLOPE DOWN

To El Diablo Wall →

longtime project, was finally climbed by Boone Speed in late 1997. The route, with a current rating of 5.14c, is one of the hardest in the U.S. Climb thin holds up right from bolt 1.

25. **Bats out of Hell** (5.12d) A final roof/headwall for those who want the maximum pump. Climb any route to 2-bolt anchor on right side of the cave. Pull upper roof (5.12d) to slab above and anchor.

26. **Side Show Bob's** (5.13c/d) The farthest right route in Hell Cave. Stick-clip bolt 2 at start and crank over roof. 5 bolts to 1-bolt anchor.

EL DIABLO WALL

This wall sits on the east side of the Hell Cave cirque and is the first one you reach on the access trail. The routes are powerful and crimpy. Routes are listed uphill from right to left.

27. **Half Acre** (5.12a) No topo. The easiest route on the wall. Lies on the far right or south side of the cliff and is the first one reached by the trail. Climb up and over a couple of small roofs. 5 bolts to 2-bolt anchor.

28. **Soul Fission** (5.13c) A bouldery Boone Speed testpiece. Work over a couple of roofs with few holds and powerful sidepulls. 7 bolts to 2-bolt anchor.

29. **White Noise** (5.13b) Difficult and continuous climbing that joins Route 28's upper section. Stick-clip bolt 2 to avoid decking. There is a kneebar rest above bolt 3. 7 bolts to 2-bolt anchor. A project is between Route 29 and Route 30.

30. **I'll Take Black** (5.12c) A short, popular, 35-foot line. 4 bolts to 2-bolt chained anchor.

31. **Body Count** (5.13d) Powerful moves up a leaning wall. 5 bolts to 2-bolt anchor.

32. **Cop Killer** (5.13d/.14a) Out the right side of the low roof. Extreme crimping, sidepulls, and underclings on severe wall. Crux is above roof. 5 bolts to 1 open cold-shut anchor.

33. **Blow of Death (Dead Souls)** (5.13d/.14a) The Scott Franklin masterpiece and one of the canyon's best hard routes. Technical pulling and crimping up overhanging wall. 6 bolts to 1 open cold-shut anchor.

34. **El Diablo** (5.12d) A superb route. Work over several small roofs and crank up right from the 3rd bolt. 6 bolts to 2-bolt anchor with an open cold shut. Skip bolt 2 on redpoint. 50'.

35. **Malvado** (5.13a) One of the canyon's best 5.13s. Use the same start as Route 34 only continue straight up on pumpy climbing to final technical slab move. Skip bolt 2 on redpoint. 6 bolts to 2-bolt anchor with an open cold shut. 50'.

36. **Inferno** (5.13b) Powerful climbing up overhanging wall to crux above 5th bolt. 6 bolts to 2-bolt chained anchor.

37. **Satanism and Sports** (5.13d) Over right side of huge, obvious roof. 6 bolts to 2-bolt anchor.

38. **Power Junkie** (5.13d) An excellent Boone Speed crimpfest over large roof. 5 bolts to 2-bolt anchor.

THE MEMBRANE

A popular crag with easy access, a fun assortment of routes, and a cool summer micro-climate beside the river. Park a mile up-canyon from the national monument flagpole at a large pullout on the right or south side of the highway. Follow a trail down right to the creek and cross a large log to the base of The Membrane. Early season crossings might be impossible and dangerous during high water. Routes for the Membrane are listed right to left.

39. **Riptide** (5.11a) A popular line up the right side that ends with crux moves up the overhanging prow. 7 bolts to 2-bolt anchor. 70'.

40. **Mandela** (5.12a) Begin just left of Route 39. Angle up left with stems to roof crux. 8 bolts to 2-bolt anchor. 65'.

41. **Flight Fright** (5.12c) Steep continuous climbing on route that is basically a harder variation of Route 42. 9 bolts to 2-bolt anchor. 60'.

42. **License to Thrill** (5.11c) One of American Fork's finest routes. This steller line, overhanging 15' in 60', follows good but often wet pockets to roof finish. 7 bolts to 2-bolt anchor.

43. **Route 66** (5.12a) Pumpy pockets to a strange roof sequence. 8 bolts to 2-bolt anchor. 60'.

44. **Steel Monkey** (5.10d) Another fine line with good pockets and crux at third bolt. 5 bolts to 2-bolt anchor.

45. **Caress of Steel** (5.10a) A must-do, 5.10 classic route, but getting polished. Beautiful jugs up slightly overhanging wall. 5 bolts to 2-bolt anchor.

chains
xx
70'

xx chains

chains
xx
60'

chains
xx

chains
xx

41

45

44

43

42 41

40 39

AMERICAN FORK
THE MEMBRANE

46. **Bad Faith** (5.9) No topo. This lies about 50' left of Route 45 and a large mossy wall. Begin left of left-facing corner. Work up left past low crux. 6 bolts to 2-bolt anchor.

47. **Little Big Wall** (5.11d) No topo. Walk farther left past a project to a short route over an obvious bulge. 4 bolts to 2-bolt anchor.

ISOLATION WALL

A short black wall in a shallow alcove around the corner to the east and uphill from The Membrane. Follow the cliff base east to the wall. All 3 routes are short and bouldery. No topos.

48. **Siberia** (5.12c/d) Swing up left side of wall past 4 bolts to 2-bolt anchor. 35'.

49. **Isolation** (5.12b/c) Excellent but pumpy climbing up steep cliff. 4 bolts to 2-bolt anchor (same as Route 48). 35'.

50. **Wilderness** (5.12a/b) The right-hand route. A boulder problem route on small crimps and edges. 3 bolts to 2-bolt anchor. 35'.

THE GRAY CLIFFS

A south-facing wall that overhangs above the Gray Cliffs Picnic Area. Park at the main lot at the Gray Cliffs Picnic Area 1.7 miles east of the national monument flagpole and just east of the entrance to Little Mill Campground. The picnic area is a national forest fee area. From the first picnic site west of the parking lot, scramble about 100' north up broken, bushy slopes to the cliff base. A short ramp leads up right to a narrow ledge below the routes.

51. **Snaked from New York** (5.13b) Start on far left side of broken ledge. Desperate climbing leads up left onto right edge of overhanging blunt arete. 7 bolts to 2-bolt anchor.

52. **Forty Something** (5.12d) The same start as Route 51 but continue up over left side of prominent roof to another roof. Above waits bouldery headwall. 5 bolts to 2-bolt anchor.

53. **Syllogism** (5.12c/d) Begin on ledge and climb up and left over strenuous 3-foot roof (5.12c/d). Continue up powerful wall. 7 bolts to 2-bolt anchor.

54. **Too Young to be Human** (5.12a/b) An excellent route. Begin on ledge. Work up and over right side of long roof to strenuous pocket-pulling on leaning headwall above. 6 bolts to 2-bolt anchor.

55. **Slimabeing** (5.11c) Begin up Route 54 and head right from its second bolt into crack system. The top is hand crack in tight corner. 7 bolts to 2-bolt anchor.

56. **The Argument** (5.12a) Begin on right side of ledge system above brushy slopes. The route ascends steep white rock broken by a couple of roofs and ledges with reachy crux bulge at top. 7 bolts to 2-bolt anchor.

AMERICAN FORK
GRAY CLIFFS

XX

.12a
reach

XX

hands

XX

.11c/d

XX

XX

.12a/b

.12d

up arete

55

.12c/d

56

54

53

51

52

x   belay bolt

up from picnic area

HARD ROCK

Hard Rock, White Wave Wall, and Escape Buttress are buttresses that sit high on the north flank of the canyon above a tier of lower cliffs and the road. Many excellent routes are located here on the vertical-to-overhanging, pocketed limestone. The cliffs get good sun in the cooler months, offering warm climbing sites, as well as morning and afternoon shade in summer. Hard Rock is the farthest west of this group of crags.

Access the cliffs by driving 1.7 miles east from the national monument flagpole to the paved parking area at the Gray Cliffs Picnic Area on the north side of the highway. Park here (remember it's a fee area). Or park just east on the highway shoulder on some narrow pullouts on the south side of the asphalt. Follow a short, paved trail east from the parking area to the last picnic site or find a tree-lined trail from the highway that climbs north into a stream drainage west of the cliffs and through an avalanche swath of broken trees to the base of Hard Rock. The approach takes about 5 minutes.

Hard Rock faces southwest and south. The routes begin on a steep wall just right of a dry, slabby waterfall. Routes are listed left to right along the cliff-base trail.

57. **Suicide Blonde** (5.11b) Fun, steep climbing with pockets and incuts to slab conclusion. 5 bolts to 2-bolt anchor. 50'.

58. **Beehive** (5.12b) A long line up steep prow, climbed in 1 or 2 pitches. Swing up steep rock (5.12b) to double-chained anchors on ledge. Belay or

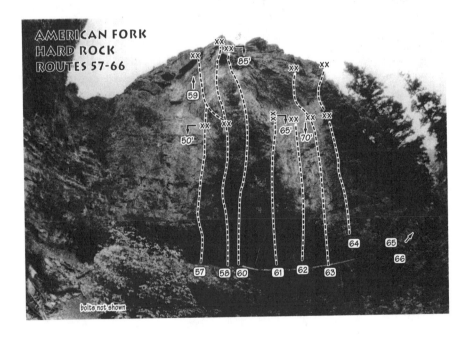

to
2 bolt
anchors

xx
100'

xx
65'

xx
70'

xx
55'

70 belay high

67

68

69

bolts not shown

AMERICAN FORK
HARD ROCK SOUTH

lower here, or continue climbing up long prow to 5.12a crux left of roof. **Pitch 1:** 6 bolts to 2-bolt anchor. **Pitch 2:** 6 bolts to 2-bolt anchor. Stick-clip bolt 1 for extra safety. 85'.

59. **Dreadlocks** (5.12b) Climb Route 58 to the first set of anchors. Diverge left onto steep upper wall left of prow by following crack to bulge to final roof pull. 7 bolts to 2-bolt anchor or 14 bolts if done in 1 pitch.

60. **Teeanova** (5.11d/12a) An excellent, powerful, endurance route. Began right of Route 58 behind trees. Pull up on great pockets and incuts, passing 3 bulges separated by rest stances to a roof at the top. 11 bolts to 2-bolt anchor. 85'.

61. **Cyberlag** (5.11d) Another fun pocket-pulling climb. Follow bolts up steep rock to lowering stance in obvious alcove below large roof bulge. 7 bolts to 2-bolt anchor. 65'.

62. **Primal Magic** (5.11b) This line starts right of a small maple tree. Use sidepulls and edges to surmount the wall—it's steeper than it looks. 6 bolts to 2-bolt anchor in alcove.

63. **Juggernaut** and **Juggernaut Roof** (5.11b & 5.12b) A great route with a stiff finish for the way-honed. **Pitch 1:** Classic. Work up and right on excellent rock to alcove belay stance at 70'. 6 bolts to 2-bolt anchor. Rap, lower, or belay here. **Pitch 2:** Brachiate up and over huge roof above the alcove to anchors above the lip. 5 bolts to 2-bolt anchor.

64. **Punch the Clock** and **Punch the Clock Roof** (5.10a & 5.12a/b) Another 2-pitch line with a tough top roof. Begin behind the large trees and climb upwards via good pockets and mailbox slots to alcove belay ledge. 5 bolts to 2-bolt anchor. Rap, lower, or belay. Pitch 2 uses pockets and strength to surmount roof. 5 bolts to 2-bolt anchor.

65. **Vaporous Apparition** (5.9) Locate this by walking around the blunt corner of the buttress to a broken slab. Pull juggy roof to lower angle rock. 5 bolts to 2-bolt anchor. 50'.

66. **Gas Boost** (5.8) Just right of Route 65. Handle big pockets on the steep up to a dark striped slab. 4 bolts to 2-bolt anchor. 60'.

This and the following routes are farther east from Route 66 on Hard Rock's south face. Continue walking along the cliff base to a large dihedral right of a prow.

67. **Eight to Eleven** (5.11b/c) This route is done in 1 or 2 pitches. Pitch 1 (5.6) is the usual climb. Work up moderate rock just right of low angle prow past 3 bolts to 2-bolt anchor below roof. Rap or lower 55'. The route continues up and over couple of roofs to upper crux on white rock. 9 bolts to 2-bolt anchor.

AMERICAN FORK
WHITE WAVE WALL

68. **Stoic Calculus** (5.8) Good climbing just right of Route 67 up dark striped slab. 4 bolts to 2-bolt anchor. 65'.

69. **Rockapella** (5.7) A popular outing, one of American Fork's easiest routes, ascends the right side of the big dihedral. Climb the fine south-facing slab past roof crux to anchors under large roof. 5 bolts to 2-bolt anchor. 70'.

70. **Platinum Blonde** (5.10a) Begin right of Route 69 below a crack/left-facing corner. Belay on a high stance with a 165-foot rope, otherwise on the ground with a 200-foot (60-meter) rope. Sustained face climbing heads up and right on long, narrow face to anchors on high ledge in white rock. 6 bolts to 2-bolt anchor.

WHITE WAVE WALL

This steep, excellent buttress, an eastern continuation of the Hard Rock cliff band, sits high above the canyon floor. Access by continuing on the climber's path along the cliff base from Hard Rock for a few hundred feet. Be careful on the path. Precipitous dropoffs are a stumble away below the trail!

71. **Naked Nebula** (5.12a) The left-hand route. Climb striped slab and keep left above bolt 2. Work up around roof (5.12a) and finish at anchors just below top. 10 bolts to 2-bolt anchor. 75'.

72. **Knuckle Up** (5.12d) A quality, airy line. Begin the same as Route 71 only trend right above bolt 2. Continue up striped slab to overhanging, pocketed white wall to final bulge. 9 bolts to 2-bolt anchor. A project squeezes between Route 71 and Route 72.

73. **The Edge of Chaos** (5.11b/c) Exposed pocket climbing up good rock on the prow of the buttress. Work up right over some arching roofs and head straight up on fine holds to slabby top. 9 bolts to 2-bolt anchor.

74. **Sans Nom** (5.11b/c) No topo. Around the corner from Route 73 on the steep, flattish south face of the wall. Pull over left side of long roof and stray up right on exposed rock. 5 bolts to 2-bolt anchor.

75. **Virtual Reality** (5.11d) No topo. Chase good pockets up and over roof to steep, pumpy climbing. 5 bolts to 2-bolt anchor.

ESCAPE BUTTRESS

The Escape Buttress is an excellent cliff laced with fun, moderate routes. It perches high on the north side of the canyon, opposite Little Mill Campground. It is approached by hiking up the trail through the avalanche debris from the Gray Cliffs Picnic Area to Hard Rock. Continue east along the climber's trail past Hard Rock and White Wave Wall for about quarter of a mile to this south-facing cliff. Use extreme caution on this exposed, traversing trail as it

AMERICAN FORK
ESCAPE BUTTRESS

wends along abrupt 100-foot dropoffs. The cliff is about 200' east of White Wave Wall and on the same cliff band. Routes are listed left to right.

76-78 **Unknown.** These 3 bolted routes ascend the far left side of Escape Buttress. Consider them adventure climbs!

79. **Jug for Joy** (5.10b) Just right of a large broken corner. Fun climbing past 6 bolts to a 2-bolt chain anchor. 55'.

80. **Monkey Meet** (5.10d) Quality pocket climbing. 9 bolts to 2-bolt chained anchor. 70'.

81. **Inside Information** (5.10d) Pockets over the crux bulge. 7 bolts to 2-bolt chain anchor. 55'.

82. **Twist and Shout** (5.10a) Classic pocket pulling. 7 bolts to 2-bolt cold-shut anchor. 50'.

83. **Steel Graffiti** (5.10b) A long, moderate line with the hard climbing up to bolt 3. 8 bolts to 2-bolt anchor. 85'. A 200-' line allows a little extra rope on this long route.

84. **Awakening** (5.10a) Left of the crack/corner. Another long, mostly moderate line. 9 bolts to 2-bolt chain anchor. 80'.

85. **Denied** (5.10c) On a buttress between crack systems. Steep climbing up and right on jugs to upper slab. 5 bolts to 2-bolt chain anchor. 55'.

86. **Motherload** (5.10b/c) A short route up a small buttress. 5 bolts to 2-bolt anchor. 45'.

87. **Body Bag** (5.11a) Steep, sustained climbing on face right of crack system. 5 bolts to 2-bolt chain anchor. 60'.

88. **Dead on Arrival** (5.11b) Far right side of wall. Hard, continuous face climbing. 5 bolts to 2-bolt chain anchor (same as Route 87).

DIVISION WALL

The north-facing Division Wall lies on the south canyon wall just above Little Mill Campground. The crag is justifiably popular because of its easy access and quality routes. It's best to visit it on weekdays. Summer weekends are mad, with ropes on many routes and campers and RVs filling the campground. Unless you're staying in the campground (a good place to camp for climbing convenience) it's necessary to park at several pullouts on the south side of the highway near the campground exit about 2.3 miles east of the national monument flagpole. Park here or near the Gray Cliffs Picnic Area and walk through the campground exit (do not attempt to drive in or your tires will be shredded) and down the road 0.3 mile to a short trail beside a pit toilet and just east of campsite 64 that leads to the base of the cliff. Do not walk through site 64 to reach the cliff. The Division Wall has two faces divided by a bulging prow. The Northwest Face lies on the right, while the Northeast Face is on the left.

NORTHWEST FACE

Routes are left to right.

89. **Isotoner Moaner** (5.12a/b) Belay on the large ledge or at a smaller stance with a bolt. This long, excellent route works up face just right of prow and pulls a couple of small roofs to anchors. 11 bolts to 2-bolt anchor. A 200"-rope (60-meter) is needed to get back to the big ledge when lowering.

90. **Rush Hour** (5.11b) The route just right of a grungy, right-angling crack. Begin on flat ledge. Climb beautiful rock to thin crux and then up pockets. 7 bolts to 2-bolt anchor.

91. **Remote Control** (5.11a) Great pockets head up the steep wall to a final pumpy crux. 6 bolts to 2-bolt anchor.

92. **The Atheist** (5.11b) This line and Route 93 start on right side of flat ledge. Go up and left past 10 bolts to 2-bolt anchor.

93. **39** (5.11b) First climbed on Bill Boyles' 39th birthday. Clip first 3 bolts of Route 92 before venturing out right on steep, continuous climbing. 7 bolts to 2-bolt anchor.

The following 3 routes ascend the leaning, striped wall right of a flat ledge.

94. **Running Woman** (5.11a) Keep left all the way up. 5 bolts to 2-bolt anchor.

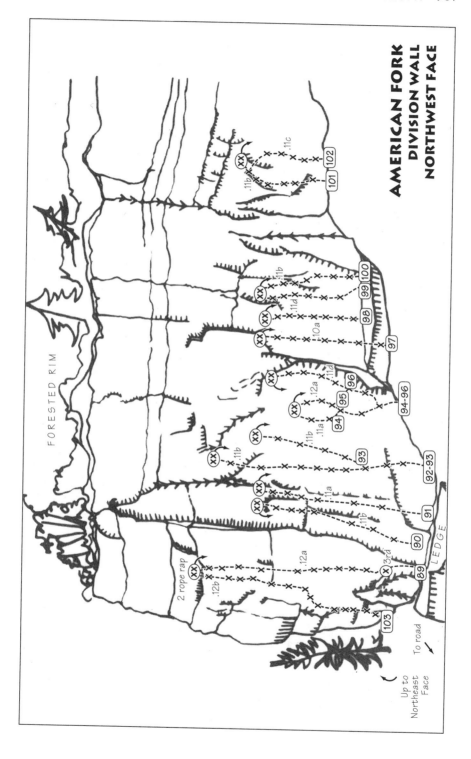

AMERICAN FORK
DIVISION WALL
NORTHWEST FACE

95. **Struggling Man** (5.12a) Follow Route 94 but go right at bolt 3 up overhanging pocketed wall. An upper crux and clip will make you struggle. 6 bolts to 2-bolt anchor.

96. **Division** (5.11d) The crag's classic line. Work up and right on steep rock with slightly polished holds. 7 bolts to 2-bolt anchor.

97. **Les is More** (5.10a) The first route right of dirty, right-facing corner system. A good outing for the grade. Pockets lead up dark gray and white slab. 7 bolts to 2-bolt anchor.

98. **Pocket Change** (5.11a) Fun climbing to tricky crux below anchors. 7 bolts to 2-bolt anchor.

99. **Total Recall** (5.11d) A good, steep line on fine limestone. 6 bolts to 2-bolt anchor.

100. **Blurred Vision** (5.11b) Bring your glasses on this one to see all the holds. Crux is over small roof above bolt 3. 7 bolts to 2-bolt anchor (same anchor as Route 99).

101. **Baghdad** (5.11b) A steep face with bulges to slabby finish. 6 bolts to 2-bolt anchor.

102. **Nowhere to Go** (5.11c) The uppermost route on the Northwest Face. A short boulder-problem crux to bolt 3 and then easy finishing moves to chains. 6 bolts to 2-bolt anchor (same anchor as Route 101).

NORTHEAST FACE

The Northeast Face is the wall left of the prow that divides the buttress. Routes are listed right to left, or uphill from the prow and access trail.

103. **Secret Weapon** (5.12b) The first route left of the prow but below the right corner of a large roof. A long line with lots of bolts. Climb up right below arching right-facing corner. Step right onto stance after 4 bolts. Move up steep headwall above using slopers and edges, and work right around prow to some bulging roofs to finish. 14 bolts to 2-bolt anchor. A 200'-rope is needed to lower off.

104. **Shark Club** (5.11b) Climb to right side of big roof. Pull and stem groove to anchors. 9 bolts to 2-bolt anchor.

105. **Litmus Test** (5.11c) Start behind a large tree. Good pockets lead to crux left side of large roof. 7 bolts to 2-bolt anchor.

106. **Teenagers in Heat** (5.10) Begin just left of the tree. A steep wall punctured by pockets and technical slab ending. 9 bolts to 2-bolt anchor.

107. **Physical Therapy** (5.9+) You'll queue up for this one on weekends. Fun climbing on pockets to right side of blunt arete. Slab finish up top. 6 bolts to 2-bolt anchor.

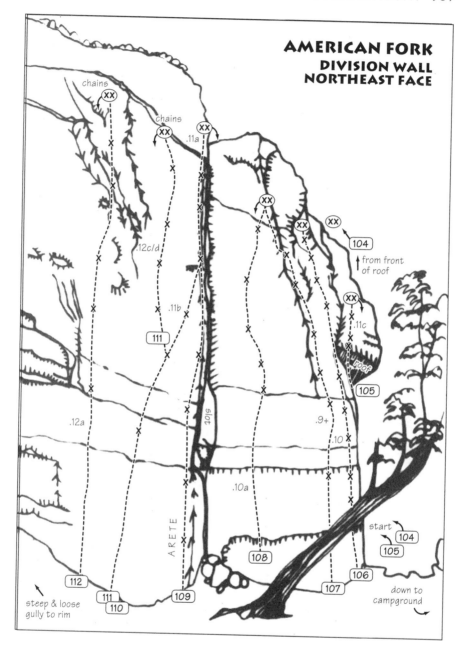

AMERICAN FORK
DIVISION WALL
NORTHEAST FACE

chains

chains

.11a

.12c/d

104

from front
of roof

.11b

111

.11c

roof

105

.12a

.9+

.10

slot

.10a

108

ARETE

start

104

105

106

112

111

109

107

110

steep & loose
gully to rim

down to
campground

108. **Black Hole** (5.10a) Another popular and easier offering up the wall right of the large, off-width dihedral. Pockets and edges lead you up right to Route 107's anchors. Thin crux at bolt 2 features a reachy move to a mailbox jug. 5 bolts to 2-bolt anchor.

The following routes are on the steep wall left of the large corner:

109. **Deep End** (5.11a) Flake out the rope a few feet left of the corner. Pumpy pulling up the leaning wall to crux moves below anchors. 7 bolts to 2-bolt anchor.

110. **Shallow Beginning** (5.11b) An excellent link-up of Routes 109 and 111. Climb 2 bolts up on *The Abyss* before working up right (5.11b) to small roof on Route 109. Waltz upward to its upper crux. 6 bolts to 2-bolt anchor.

111. **The Abyss** (5.12c/d) One of American Fork's most popular and polished hard routes. It's seen a lot of doggin'. Swim up steep rock to strenuous bulge. Anchors on slab above. 6 bolts to 2-bolt anchor.

112. **Liquid Oxygen** (5.12a) Another fine classic line that sees lots of action. Chase the pump up steep pocket climbing on far left margin of face. 5 bolts to 2-bolt anchor.

Other Areas

UTAH

OTHER UTAH CLIMBING AREAS

Utah is littered with rock and rock climbing areas. Most of these are not covered in this volume due to space and ethical considerations. Utah climbers have their own private areas that they do not want located and described in a guidebook. To find and climb at these areas, it's best to stop at the local shops and talk to local climbers and area activists. Most are more than happy to give you a topo and directions to their favorite crags. It goes without saying, of course, that you should leave your drill at home unless you're invited to contribute a new line by the folks that regularly climb there. The following is a partial list of other Utah rock climbing areas along with resource information. Lots of "secret" areas are not included or mentioned here. To find them—you're on your own.

MOAB AREA

ISLAND IN THE SKY AREA

Some excellent tower routes and free-climbing cliffs are located in the northern Island in the Sky area between U.S. Highway 191 and Canyonlands National Park. Recommended routes include Echo Pinnacle, Aeolian Tower, and some crack routes up Merrimac Butte. One of the best lines is *The Window Route* (II 5.10d) on Echo Pinnacle. This great three-pitch route offers a funky first pitch below the obvious window, a superb second pitch up a thin hand crack (5.10d) to a hanging belay, and a third lead up an airy off-width and squeeze chimney to "interesting" exit moves and the summit.

The Heat Wave Wall, 1.4 miles east of Utah 313, has some fine crack climbs similar to Indian Creek. The cliff has the advantage of winter warmth making it a good off-season crag.

A fun roadside slab with several bolted routes from 5.8 to 5.11 lies a couple of miles south of U.S. Highway 191 on the west side of Utah 313. Some hard hueco routes put up by Jim Beyer ascend the steeper wall to the right.

The Bride is a spectacular, thin Wingate sandstone spire tucked into a hidden canyon between Moab and Utah 313. The spire, reached via a rough four-wheel-drive road, is ascended by several mixed free and aid routes.

The southern Island in the Sky area offers many additional spire routes besides the classics described in this guide. The Crow's Head Spires sit near the head of a steep drainage between Dead Horse Point and the Island in the Sky. Several good routes ascend these 250-foot-high towers.

Farther south on the east side of the Island are some obvious towers, all of which have been climbed. These include the twin Chip and Dale Towers, blocky Airport Tower and the adjoining thin Tiki Tower, Sandcastle just west of Washer Woman, and slender Islet in the Sky and Blocktop spires. Candlestick Tower, a large butte, lies southwest of the Island in the Sky above The White Rim and Green River.

Information, topos, and directions to all these areas and towers are in Eric Bjørnstad's *Moab Climbs West* guidebook.

OTHER CANYONLANDS AREAS

Canyonlands National Park and the remote lands adjoining it in Glen Canyon Recreation Area offer many rock climbing adventures for the intrepid explorer. Not a lot of documented routes have been done in this vast area, allowing for a true wilderness climbing experience. One of the best established routes ascends 6,520-foot Cleopatra's Chair. This excellent 5.6 route climbs the west face and south shoulder of this formation on North Point in Glen Canyon Recreation Area just west of Canyonlands National Park. The relatively easy route gives stunning views of the surrounding canyon country. The Buttes of the Cross are twin buttes overlooking the Green River in the northern part of the recreation area. A couple of routes ascend the buttes.

Other routes are found on Ekker Butte, Bagpipe Butte, and Bathtub Butte. Standing Rock-in-the-Maze, the other Standing Rock in Canyonlands National Park, is located in the Land of the Standing Rocks in the park's Maze District. Mark Hesse did an all-free 5.11 ascent of the slender Cutler sandstone tower. Farther south hide The Pinnacles, a series of small towers in Happy Canyon just west of Glen Canyon National Recreation Area. These remote spires, reached by what Eric Bjørnstad calls "an epic desert approach," yield some fine free climbs. Farther south, in the rugged wilderness north of the Dirty Devil River, are Sewing Machine Needle and Middle Finger Tower.

Information, topos, and directions to all these areas are in Eric Bjørnstad's *Desert Rock: Rock Climbs of the National Parks* guidebook.

THE POTASH ROAD

In addition to the numerous sport and crack routes at Wall Street, the Potash Road area offers several other cragging sites. One of the best is Day Canyon, a west-trending canyon a few miles west of Wall Street. Numerous crack climbs have been done here. Some of the best lines are *Kiss of the Spider*

Woman (5.12), *Android's Waffle Hot Line* (5.10+), *Brush Painted Datsun* (5.10), and *Acromaniac* (5.10). Two towers—Raptor and Bootleg Towers—are found in the canyon. Good routes are *Moonshine* (5.10c) and *Buzz Lust* (5.12) on Bootleg Tower. *Buzz Lust* is a unique, 9-bolt sport route that features excellent face climbing.

SOUTHEAST UTAH

VALLEY OF THE GODS

The Valley of the Gods sprawls across an arid, empty basin north of Mexican Hat and U.S. Highway 163 in far southeastern Utah. Numerous towers, up to 400 feet high and composed of Cedar Mesa sandstone, perch atop broken talus cones. This is a place only extreme sandstone connoisseurs could love. Wear a helmet and expect loose rock, rubble-filled chimneys, scary protection, and bad bolts. Be aware that portions of formations as well as whole towers have collapsed within recent memory! Routes ascend all the major towers, including Petard Tower, North Tower, Tom-Tom Tower, Eagle Plume Tower, Angel's Fear, and Hidden Pinnacle. Some of the best routes are found on North Tower. Eric Bjørnstad's old *Desert Rock* guide has topos and descriptions.

TEXAS TOWER & DREAMSPEAKER

Texas Tower and Dreamspeaker are a couple of remote spires hidden in lovely Arch and Texas canyons north of Utah 95 between Blanding and Natural Bridges National Monument. Texas Tower (IV 5.11d or 5.10d A1) is an intimidating 600-foot-high pinnacle that offers a seven-to nine-pitch route with off-width crack climbing on all but two pitches. The tower, reached via a difficult four-wheel-drive trail, is a hard tick. The crux on pitch 5 is an overhanging 5- to 7-inch crack that is usually aided by sliding big gear up. It also goes at 5.11+. Dreamspeaker (II 5.11) has a two-pitch line up its south face. The 5.11 crux is a thin hands crack on the first pitch. Directions and descriptions for both towers are in Fred Knapp's *Classic Desert Climbs* and Eric Bjørnstad's out-of-print *Desert Rock* guidebook.

OTHER SOUTHEAST UTAH AREAS

Southeastern Utah is the state's empty quarter. Out here is an amazing wonderland of canyons, mesas, buttes, spires, basins, valleys, and mountains.

There's a lot of climbing here, but most of it is either unrecorded or hasn't been done yet. It's probably best to keep this as an adventure climbing arena. Some of the rock that's been climbed includes Jacob's Chair (II 5.10) and The

Needle (II 5.11 A0), a couple of isolated towers in the Fry Canyon area west of Natural Bridges National Monument. Grand Gulch Spire, also called Shima Sani, is a semi-detached pinnacle in lower Grand Gulch. The spire, reached via a 42-mile float down the San Juan River, is half a mile up Grand Gulch from the river canyon. The 5-pitch *Corso de Gallo Route* (III 5.11) ascends the tower's west flank. The Bear's Ears, a couple of Wingate sandstone buttes north of Utah 95, offer some crack routes at about 9,000 feet.

Glen Canyon National Recreation Area, which includes Lake Powell and its 1,800 miles of shoreline, is a climber's dream waiting to happen. Much has been done here, but even more awaits the adventure climber. Some routes and bouldering have been done in the Hite Crossing area. Otherwise, you're on your own.

MONUMENT VALLEY

Monument Valley, one of the most famous and scenic areas on the entire Colorado Plateau, has a startling selection of sheer spires, buttes, and mesas composed of DeChelly sandstone. The area, a Navajo Tribal Park sprawling along the Utah and Arizona border, is also one of the plateau's oldest climbing areas. This region saw many early ascents of its stunning spires, including The Three Sisters and The Totem Pole, by desert pioneers like Layton Kor and Fred Beckey. Most of the spires are definitely off-limits to rock climbers. Some of the towers in Utah have been climbed in recent years. It's best to ask permission from the local grazing permit holder before climbing any of the towers, otherwise it's climb at your own risk. Possible penalties including confiscation of equipment, fines, and jail sentences.

Excellent routes are found on Stagecoach, King on a Throne, The Rabbit and The Bear, and Shangri-la. Shangri-la, a large blocky tower, offers a great route (IV 5.10a A0) that begins on the north side and ends up chimneying through to finish up the south face. Nearby are Jacob's Ladder, a 300-foot spire resembling Standing Rock, and Eagle Rock Spire (III 5.9 A3+) on the north side of Eagle Mesa. Info on all these routes is found in Eric Bjørnstad's out-of-print *Desert Rock* book.

CENTRAL UTAH AREAS

Lots of rock scatters across central Utah, most of it unclimbed. A few areas are being developed. It's best to ask around for more info and directions. The Henry Mountains south of Hanksville have some good crags including The Horn, a volcanic cliff with cracks and face climbs. Bob Van Belle, a ranger at Capitol Reef National Park, reports an excellent bouldering area twenty minutes west of the park in Rabbit Valley. It has "really good andesite, lots of extremely high, steep, technical pocket pulling and edging problems in a wild, beautiful setting." Another great bouldering area is Joe's Valley. Stacks of problems on hundreds of sandstone boulders lie in the valley off Utah 29 west of Castle Dale. In the Ephraim area are numerous small crags with cracks and bolted sport routes. One of the best is the short, sandstone cliffs in Round Valley, 3 miles south of Manti. *Maple Canyon Rock Climbing* by Jason Stevens has a topo and route descriptions to Round Valley. Other crags are at New Canyon, along the Nebo Loop road, Dry Canyon, Axhandle Canyon, and Coal Canyon. Ask at the climbing shop in Ephraim for info and directions.

NORTHEAST UTAH AREAS

Most of northeast Utah's climbing centers around Vernal and Dinosaur National Monument. One of the more popular areas is the White Wall at the base of Cliff Ridge. The area, with bolted sandstone face routes up to three pitches long, is along the mountain base northeast of Jensen. Lots of sandstone—but few routes—is found at Dinosaur National Monument. Near the Quarry area north of Jensen is the Prophecy in Stone formation with several crack routes, including 300'-long *Emily's Crack* (5.7) and the 2-pitch *Doc's Crack* (5.10) as well as some bouldering areas. Northwest of Vernal in Dry Fork Canyon are some spectacular, soft sandstone spires, including Tyrolean Tower, the thin, 150-foot-high Red Twister, and Vulture's Roost across from Remember the Maine County Park.

WASATCH FRONT

HYRUM CANYON

A good selection of sport routes on limestone cliffs is located in Hyrum Canyon southeast of Logan in northern Utah. This area makes a good alternative to Logan Canyon, especially on weekends when Logan is crowded. Ask at the climbing shops in Logan for more info.

OGDEN

Ogden, lying north of Salt Lake City at the base of the Wasatch Front, offers a generous assortment of sport and traditional routes on quartzite, gneiss, and limestone as well as lots of excellent bouldering. Some of the good crags in Ogden Canyon include Nuts and Bolts, 5.8 Wall, Utah Walls, Roadside Attraction, and The Blob. Other crags include the Schoolroom Wall, a large quartzite cliff with numerous adventure routes, and the popular 9th Street Crag. Many climbers consider Ogden's strength to be its fine boulder fields. Area guidebook writer Brian Mechem says, "It is the best climbing to be had in Ogden." The quartzite boulders have numerous holds including sidepulls, edges, pockets, and slopers. The best bouldering is located at the 26th Street Boulder Field with over 30 named blocks. Area info, descriptions, and topos are found in Brian Mecham's *Ogden Rock Climbs*.

PARLEY'S CANYON

Parley's Canyon, just east of Salt Lake City along the Interstate 80 corridor, has several small, bolted cliffs near the canyon's mouth that are literally road cuts. All the climbing is on two steep, north-facing, quartzite slabs, Riptide Wall and the Iron Curtain Wall. Both are easily accessible from downtown Salt Lake City. There are cliff topos and route descriptions in the Ruckmans' *Wasatch Climbing North* guidebook.

MOUNT OLYMPUS

This towering peak, looming over Salt Lake City, yields some great moderate routes up immense slabs on its northern flanks. The Ruckmans' *Wasatch Climbing North* details 3 routes on the slabs, the best of which is *The West Slabs*. This long 5.5 route, one of the Wasatch's classic, easy mountaineering-type routes, offers over 10 pitches of roped climbing up the gentle slab overlooking the city.

FERGUSON CANYON

Ferguson Canyon is a steep, shallow canyon that is parallel to and south of Big Cottonwood Canyon. Numerous north-facing crags stud the canyon's south slopes, offering a cool, shaded getaway for climbers on hot days. The generally short routes, both trad and sport, ascend steep granite cliffs. Most of the crags lie in Twin Peaks Wilderness Area. The Watchtower, one of the first cliffs encountered, is justifiably popular with over 30 routes. The Tower of Babel, uphill from The Watchtower, will leave you tongue-tied after climbing the superb arête on *Fuego* (5.12a). The Cathedral is also popular and laced with fine routes. Topos and descriptions are in the Ruckmans' *Wasatch Climbing North* guidebook.

LONE PEAK

Lone Peak, towering southeast of Salt Lake City, lifts its craggy summit to 11,253 feet in the Lone Peak Wilderness Area. This high, glaciated mountain, flanked by 3 major cirques, is the Wasatch Range's main alpine climbing area. The west cirque is walled by immense granite cliffs up to 600 feet high that are split by long, vertical crack systems. The cirque, a summer-only climbing area, is popular with locals who trek up the lengthy approach to climb in relative coolness while urban Salt Lake City below swelters under the hot sun. Drawbacks to climbing at this superb area are the almost day-long forced marches up hard-to-follow trails and the lack of water once the cirque's snowfields are melted in mid-summer. Most climbers hike up the day before, bivouac at the base of the cliff, climb the next day and then descend back to their car.

Numerous classic crack and knobby face routes are located on the cirque's walls. A glance through the area guidebook reveals many 3-star classic routes up to 5 pitches long. The Summit Wall, a slabby buttress directly below Lone Peak's summit, yields some excellent lines. Not to be missed adventures include *Triple Overhangs* (III 5.10a), *Vertical Smile* (III 5.10a), *Undone Book* (III 5.9+), and the classic moderate *Open Book* (III 5.7). The Question Mark Wall on the southeast side of the cirque is undeniably Lone Peak's best cliff. The wall, named for a question mark-shaped feature on its face, is ascended by two of Utah's best granite routes. *The Lowe Route* (II 5.8), put up by George and Jeff Lowe in 1970, follows exposed cracks up the left margin of the wall. The *Question Mark Wall Route* (III 5.12b or 5.7 C1) is a three-pitch directissima up the center of the face. This mega-classic contains thin crack climbing or clean aid-nutting with RPs on the first two pitches, and a superb and airy 5.8 last pitch with knobby face climbing to the ridge summit. *Wasatch Climbing North* by Bret and Stuart Ruckman gives all the details, directions, and topos to Lone Peak's classic climbs.

ROCK CANYON

This deep canyon slices into the mountain front immediately east of Provo. The canyon offers both quartzite and limestone cliffs, with mostly bolted sport routes. The area is very popular with locals, crazy rappellers, and students from nearby Brigham Young University. Good quartzite crags near the mouth of the canyon include the juggy Superbowl Wall, the mostly moderate lines on The Red Slab and The Ed and Terry Wall, and the popular Kitchen. Farther up-canyon are some excellent limestone cliffs that offer powerful and technical routes. Good climbs are found on Bug Barn Dance Wall and The Projects. The west-facing Projects, reached via an uphill hike, offer numerous hard routes including *Junkie Pride* (5.13b) and *Valhalla* (5.13b/c). There are detailed topos and access information in the Ruckmans' *Climber's Guide to American Fork Canyon and Rock Canyon.*

APPENDIX A

FURTHER READING

A Climber's Guide to Crawdad Canyon, Todd Goss, Paragon Climbing Guides, 1996.

Canyon Country Climbs (out of print), Earl Wiggins & Katy Cassidy, Pruett Publishing, 1989.

Canyoneering: The San Rafael Swell, Steve Allen, University of Utah Press, 1992.

Classic Desert Climbs, Fred Knapp & Michael Stevens, Sharp End Publishing, 1996.

Climber's Guide to American Fork Canyon and Rock Canyon, Bret Ruckman & Stuart Ruckman, Chockstone Press, 1995.

Desert Rock (out of print), Eric Bjørnstad, Chockstone Press, 1988.

Desert Rock: Rock Climbs in the National Park, Eric Bjørnstad, Chockstone Press, 1996.

Desert Rock: Moab West, Eric Bjørnstad, Chockstone Press, 1997.

Desert Rock: Moab East, Eric Bjørnstad, Chockstone Press, 1998.

Exploring Canyonlands & Arches National Parks, Bill Schneider, Falcon Publishing, 1997.

Hiking Zion & Bryce Canyon National Parks, Erik Molvar & Tamara Martin, Falcon Publishing, 1997.

Logan Canyon Climbs, Tim Monsell.

Maple Canyon Rock Climbing, Jason Stevens, 1996.

Ogden Rock Climbs, Brian Mecham.

Pumping Iron: A Guide to Mostly Sport Climbs in Iron County, Robert Draney, DIY Press, 1995.

Roadside Geology of Utah, Halka Chronic, Mountain Press Publishing, 1990.

Rock 'N Road: Rock Climbing Areas of North America, Tim Toula, Chockstone Press, 1995.

Snow Canyon Select, Todd Goss, Paragon Climbing Guides, 1995.

Too Much Rock, Not Enough Life: A Sport Climbing Guide to St. George and Southwestern Utah, Todd Goss, Paragon Climbing Guides, 1996.

Spring Canyon Crag: A Guide to Climbing in Carbon County, Cory Pincock & Aimee Faucheux.

Wasatch Climbing North, Bret Ruckman & Stuart Ruckman, Chockstone Press, 1998.

Wasatch Range, Bret Ruckman & Stuart Ruckman, Chockstone Press, 1997.

200 Select Classic Indian Creek Climbs, Marco Cornacchione, Sharp End Publishing, 1995.

500 Select Moab Classics, Kevin Chase, Moab Adventure Outfitters, 1995.

APPENDIX B
RATING SYSTEM COMPARISON CHART

YDS	British	French	Australian
5.3	VD 3b	2	11
5.4	HVD 3c	3	12
5.5	MS/S/HS 4a	4a	12/13
5.6	HS/S 4a	4b	13
5.7	HS/VS 4b/4c	4c	14/15
5.8	HVS 4c/5a	5a	16
5.9	HVS 5a	5b	17/18
5.10a	E1 5a/5b	5c	18/19
5.10b	E1/E2 5b/5c	6a	19/20
5.10c	E2/E3 5b/5c	6a+	20/21
5.10d	E3 5c/6a	6b	21/22
5.11a	E3/E4 5c/6a	6b+	22/23
5.11b	E4/E5 6a/6b	6c	23/24
5.11c	E4/E5 6a/6b	6c+	24
5.11d	E4/E5 6a/6b	7a	25
5.12a	E5 6b/6c	7a+	25/26
5.12b	E5/E6 6b/6c	7b	26
5.12c	E5/E6 6b/6c/7a	7b+	26/27
5.12d	E6/E7 6c/7a	7c	27
5.13a	E6/E7 6c/7a	7c+	28
5.13b	E7 7a	8a	29
5.13c	E7 7a	8a+	30/31
5.13d	E8 7a	8b	31/32
5.14a	E8 7a	8b+	32/33
5.14b	E9 7a	8c	33
5.14c	E9 7b	8c+	33

Sources: Mountaineering: The Freedom of the Hills, 6th Edition; Climbing Magazine, No. 150, February/March 1995.

APPENDIX C

MOUNTAIN SHOPS, CLIMBING GYMS, AND GUIDE SERVICES

Cedar City
Cedar Mountain Sports
921 South Main Street
Cedar City, UT
801-586-4949

Ephraim
Maple Leaf
480 South 50 East
Ephraim, UT
801-283-4400.

Logan
Adventure Sports
51 S. Main
Logan, UT 84321
801-753-4044

The Trailhead
117 N. Main
Logan, UT 84321
801-753-1541

Moab
Moab Adventure Outfitters
 (shop & guide service)
550 N. Main, Suite B
Moab, UT 84532
801-259-2725

Rim Cyclery
94 W. 100 North
Moab, UT 84532
801-259-5333

Tower Guides (guiding)
P.O. Box 24
Devils Tower, WY 82714
307-467-5589
www.TowerGuides.com

Ogden
Ogden Mountaineering
3701 Washington
Ogden, UT 84403
801-399-9365

Provo/Orem
Hansen Mountaineering, Inc.
757 North State St.
Orem, UT 84057
801-226-7498

Mountainworks
32 South Freedom Blvd.
Provo, UT 84601
801-371-0223

The Rock Garden (gym)
22 South Freedom Blvd
Provo, UT 84601
801-376-2388

St. George
Outdoor Outlet
1062 East Tabernacle
St. George, UT 84770
801-628-3611 or 800-
 726-8106

Salt Lake City
Black Diamond Equipment,
 Ltd.
2084 E. 3900 S.
Salt Lake City, UT 84124
801-278-5533

IME
3264 E. 3300 S.
Salt Lake City, UT
801-484-8073

Kirkham's Outdoor Products
3125 South State Street
Salt Lake City, UT 84115
801-486-4161 or 1-800-
 453-7756

Mastodon Mountaineering
 (guide service)
4867 Floribunda Drive
Salt Lake City, UT 84117
801-272-4679

REI
3285 E. 3300 S.
Salt Lake City, UT
801-486-2100

Rockreation (gym)
2074 E. 3900 S.
Salt Lake City, UT
801-278-7473

Wasatch Body Shop (gym)
1305 E. Gunn Ave.
Salt Lake City, UT 84106
801 484-8073

Wasatch Front Rock Gym
427 West 9160 South
Salt Lake City, UT
801-565-3657

Wasatch Touring (guide
 service)
702 E. 100 S.
Salt Lake City, UT
801-359-9361

INDEX

SYMBOLS

524

527

Y

Z

ABOUT THE AUTHOR

Stewart M. Green is a freelance writer and photographer living in Colorado Springs. He has written eight other books for Falcon Publishing, including *Rock Climbing Colorado*, *Scenic Driving California*, *Scenic Driving Arizona*, and *Scenic Driving New England*. Stewart has more than 30 years experience as a climber and is also a leading climbing photographer with many photographs appearing in catalogues, advertisements, and national publications, including *Climbing*, *Rock & Ice*, *Sports Illustrated for Kids*, and *Outside*. He is currently writing *Rock Climbing Arizona* for Falcon.

DEDICATION

This book is dedicated to Eric Bjørnstad. Eric is one of Utah's unique, historical climbing figures. A long-time Moab local, Eric earned the title of "Desert Rat" because of his early pioneering climbs in the canyon country and numerous desert sojourns and explorations. In the 1980s Eric undertook the daunting task of writing a guide to rock climbs in the canyon country. The result was the classic *Desert Rock*. After it went out-of-print, he divided the book into five comprehensive volumes that will ultimately detail most of the desert's known routes. I've had the privilege of knowing Eric since 1972 when he hauled four of us in his van back to Moses for its second ascent. One of my fondest memories from that year was belaying Jim Dunn on *Anasazi Wall* while Eric, owner of Moab's Tillerman Tea House, whipped up a selection of gourmet coffees and teas on a couple of stoves at the cliff base. All climbers owe Eric a debt of gratitude for his untiring efforts to document desert climbing as well as his sensitive and informative writing about the rock wonders of Utah's canyon country.

ACKNOWLEDGMENTS

Utah's vast and varied rock climbing adventures fascinated me from my first forays into the Utah canyon country in 1970. These trips led to my early ascents of many of the slender spires and perfect cracks in this state. Those extensive climbing trips, long rambles through the desert backcountry, and slickrock camping trips in the back of beyond helped me quickly develop a love and respect for this fragile landscape. The 1970s were a great time to be a desert climber and adventurer. The area was unknown except to a select and intrepid few. All of canyonlands was a vast and uncharted arena for our personal adventures and experiences. Those were the golden, silent days before the pedalhead masses and the foreign invasion discovered the lonely land. This climbing guidebook is a chance to begin to instill some of the love and respect we had for the landscape in the crowds that now head for Utah's sandstone bluffs and towers as well as to its granite domes, quartzite crags, and limestone cliffs.

Writing a climbing guide is an immense research project. This one took 18 months and over 20,000 miles of driving. Every crag, cliff, and tower was visited and documented. I spent hours scoping crags and routes, talking with local climbers about their areas and routes, and then actually getting out the shoes, harness, and rope and sampling some of the rock.

My sincere thanks goes out to everyone who participated in the creation of this comprehensive climbing guide. My first thanks goes to all my desert climbing partners from the old days—Jim Dunn, Earl Wiggins, Doug Snively, Bill

Westbay, Ed Webster, Bryan Becker, Leonard Coyne, Dennis Jackson, and the rest. It was climbing with those guys and photographing them that ultimately led to this book.

Thanks goes to all those Utah and Colorado climbers who happily divulged area information and beta, proofed manuscripts, and checked topos. Special thanks and handshakes go to Ken Sims (Doctor of Geology and climber of towers); Boone Speed (freelance gear designer and hardman); John Barstow (High Exposure Calendar photog and long-time SLC climber); Bret Ruckman (desert crackmaster); Jason Stevens (Maple Canyon pioneer and guidebook author); Todd Goss (St. George guidebook author and prolific first ascensionist); John Middendorf (the Man, the Myth, the Legend of Zion climbing); Fred Knapp (fellow author and adventurer); Jim Dunn (friend and desert rock rat); Kevin Chase (Moab guide and shop owner); Lisa Hathaway (tall blonde crackmistress and Eddie McStiff's bartender); Steve "Crusher" Bartlett (Monument Basin's English connection); Ed Webster (old friend, mountaineer, and desert pioneer); Ben Folsom (SLC climber and guide); Earl Wiggins (friend, author, and the original Indian Creek crackmaster); Jeff Achey (*Climbing* magazine editor and desert pioneer); Dougald MacDonald (*Rock & Ice* editor and soft rock connoisseur); Bob Van Belle (ranger and boulderer at Capitol Reef); Dennis Jackson (climbing partner and guidebook author); Steve Petro (DMM distributor and Indian Creek crackman) and, of course, Eric Bjørnstad (friend, Moab local, guide, and old-time rock jock) who freely gave information from his reservoir of climbing lore and stacks of topos and maps.

Thanks to Falcon Publishing and its able staff who created this stunning guidebook. Thanks to publisher Bill Schneider, guidebook editor Randall Green, and the book's designers and copy editors. Special thanks goes to Martha Morris, a great climbing partner and old friend, who used her artistic sense and ability to create gorgeous topos, maps, and photo-overlays as well as proofreading the manuscript and handling other sordid details. Thanks also to those who shared my Utah trips—Ian Spencer-Green, Brett Spencer-Green, Martha Morris, Rane Morris-Dunn, Dennis Jump, Yvonne Bolton, Joel Ballasy, Fred Knapp, Heidi Benton, the Dangerous Brothers (John and Dave), Nancy Spencer-Green, and Bob D'Antonio. Also a special thanks to Nancy Spencer-Green for maintaining the homefront with good-humored aplomb, proofreading manuscripts from a lay viewpoint, and supporting these long projects.

More Climbing Guides from
Falcon® Publishing and Chockstone Press

ACCESS: It's every climber's concern

The Access Fund, a national, non-profit climbers organization, works to keep climbing areas open and to conserve the climbing environment. Need help with closures? land acquisition? legal or land management issues? funding for trails and other projects? starting a local climbers' group? CALL US!

Climbers can help preserve access by being committed to Leave No Trace (minimum-impact) practices. Here are some simple guidelines:

• **ASPIRE TO "LEAVE NO TRACE"** especially in environmentally sensitive areas like caves. Chalk can be a significant impact on dark and porous rock – don't use it around historic rock art. Pick up litter, and leave trees and plants intact.

• **DISPOSE OF HUMAN WASTE PROPERLY** Use toilets whenever possible. If toilets are not available, dig a "cat hole" at least six inches deep and 200 feet from any water, trails, campsites, or the base of climbs. *Always pack out toilet paper.* On big wall routes, use a "poop tube" and carry waste up and off with you (the old "bag toss" is now illegal in many areas).

• **USE EXISTING TRAILS** Cutting switchbacks causes erosion. When walking off-trail, tread lightly, especially in the desert where cryptogamic soils (usually a dark crust) take thousands of years to form and are easily damaged. Be aware that "rim ecologies" (the clifftop) are often highly sensitive to disturbance.

• **BE DISCRETE WITH FIXED ANCHORS** *Bolts are controversial and are not a convenience* – don't place 'em unless they are *really* necessary. Camouflage all anchors. Remove unsightly slings from rappel stations (better to use steel chain or welded cold shuts). Bolts sometimes can be used proactively to protect fragile resources – consult with your local land manager.

• **RESPECT THE RULES** and speak up when other climbers don't. Expect restrictions in designated wilderness areas, rock art sites, caves, and to protect wildlife, especially nesting birds of prey. *Power drills are illegal in wilderness and all national parks.*

• **PARK AND CAMP IN DESIGNATED AREAS** Some climbing areas require a permit for overnight camping.

• **MAINTAIN A LOW PROFILE** Leave the boom box and day-glo clothing at home – the less climbers are heard and seen, the better.

• **RESPECT PRIVATE PROPERTY** Be courteous to land owners. Don't climb where you're not wanted.

• **JOIN THE ACCESS FUND** To become a member, make a tax-deductible donation of $25.

The Access Fund
Preserving America's Diverse Climbing Resources
PO Box 17010
Boulder, CO 80308
303.545.6772 • www.accessfund.org